i-Net+™
Certification
Study Guide

**Meets CompTIA's
Certification Objectives
for Exam IK0-002**

WestNet Learning Technologies

www.westnetinc.com

CREDITS

Author and Development Editor: Kenneth D. Reed

Editorial and Production Manager: Marilee E. Aust

Book Design and Composition:
D. Kari Luraas, Clairvoyance Design

Proofreader: Larry Beckett

Technical Writer and Editor: Kathy Russell

Indexer: Amy Casey

Illustrator: Lynn Siefken

Cover Design: David Jones

Printer: Johnson Printing

Reed, Kenneth D.
i-Net+ Certification Study Guide
896 pp., includes illustrations and index

1. Review of Network Fundamentals 2. E-Commerce 3. Internet Connectivity Technologies 4. TCP/IP Protocols 5. TCP/IP Applications and Services 6. Internet Clients and Servers 7. Building Web Pages 8. Dynamic Site Technologies 9. Security 10. Troubleshooting

WB-IK0-002

For instructor-led training, self-paced courses,
turn-key curricula solutions, or more information contact:

WestNet Learning Technologies (dba: WestNet Inc.)
5420 Ward Road, Suite 150, Arvada, CO 80002 USA
E-mail: Info@westnetinc.com

To access the WestNet student resource site, go to
http://www.westnetinc.com/student

Contents

Lesson 3
Cash Flow on the Internet 115

Lesson 4
E-Commerce Development Options 125

Lesson 5
Intellectual Property 133

Lesson 6
Crime, Privacy, and Other Legal Issues

Unit 3
Internet Connectivity Technologies

Lesson 1
Overview of the Internet

Unit 4
TCP/IP Protocols 249

Lesson 1
The TCP/IP Protocol Suite 256

Lesson 2
IP 265

INTRODUCTION

**Who Should
Study this Course**

This course introduces the technologies that comprise the Internet, and some of the technical and business practices that are needed to create a successful World Wide Web site. It is a broad-based course that will prepare you to pass either the CompTIA i-Net+ 2002 certification examination, or the Certified Internet Webmaster (CIW) Foundations examination. You should study this course if you want to become an i-Net+ Certified Professional or a CIW Associate, or if you simply want to understand the fundamental principles of Internet communication.

Prerequisites

There are no prerequisites for this course, other than basic experience using a personal computer. Occasional Internet access will help you explore links to information beyond this text, but this is not required.

IMPORTANT NOTES ABOUT CERTIFICATION

This course has been developed to meet the objectives of either of the following certification examinations:

- CompTIA i-Net+ (exam IK0-002, released April 12, 2002)

- CIW Foundations (exam 1D0-410, released June 1, 2001)

Certification is a worthwhile goal, and is probably the reason that you bought this book. However, this is not an "exam cram" study guide that guarantees that you'll pass the test with a minimum of effort.

Our goal is to prepare you to be a successful member of an Internet staff or Web site team. Therefore, this course teaches the technical concepts and principles that you will use every day for the rest of your networking or computing career. If you study this material diligently, you will gain the knowledge that you need to be successful in the Internet industry. That same knowledge will also help you to pass the certification test.

Exam Objectives

The following tables list the exam objectives that were published at the time of this writing (for the latest details, see **www.comptia.org** or **CIWcertified.com**). The table lists the lessons that meet each objective. In the book itself, each lesson also includes the CompTIA objectives that it meets.

When an exam objective includes a broad range of topics, that objective is covered by more than one lesson. Each lesson may explain one part of the objective, or all of the lessons may discuss the same topics in different ways.

How to Study

This course introduces networking concepts in a series of lessons, so that each new concept logically builds on earlier learning. However, this order does not correspond to the way the exam objectives are organized. Thus, you should not study this book by working on the objectives in the order they appear in the table. Instead, we recommend that you study this book from start to finish, and complete each lesson in order.

To pass these certification examinations, you must not only remember facts, but also apply them in combinations to solve common problems. To give you this general understanding, this book presents additional information that is not tested by the certification exam. However, this material is essential to help you understand the material that is tested.

Objectives for 2002 i-Net+ Certification Exam (IK0-002) Objectives copyright © CompTIA. Used by permission. See www.comptia.org for current information on the i-Net+ certification.	**To meet this objective, study ALL of:** Lessons highlighted in bold can also be found in WestNet's Network+ Study Guide.
Domain 1.0 – Internet Basics and Clients	
1.1 Identify the issues that affect Internet site functionality. Content may include the following: Performance, including: • Bandwidth (both client and server) • Internet connection types (both client and server) • Pages taking too long to load • Resolution and size of graphics Security, including: • Authentication • Permissions • Data encryption	Unit 1, Lesson 4 **Unit 3, Lesson 2** **Unit 3, Lesson 3** Unit 7, Lesson 8 Unit 9, Lesson 1
1.2 Understand and be able to describe the concept of caching and its implications. Content may include the following: • Web caching • File caching • Proxy caching • Client side caching versus server side caching	Unit 9, Lesson 3
1.3 Use different types of search indexes - static index/site map, keyword index, full text index. Content may include the following: • Index your site for a search • Use Internet and Intranet search engines • Differences between search engines and directories • Meta search engines • Spider search engines	Unit 2, Lesson 1

Objectives for 2002 i-Net+ Certification Exam (IK0-002) Objectives copyright © CompTIA. Used by permission. See www.comptia.org for current information on the i-Net+ certification.	**To meet this objective, study ALL of:** Lessons highlighted in bold can also be found in WestNet's Network+ Study Guide.
1.4 Understand and be able to describe the infrastructure needed to support an Internet client. Content may include the following: • Knowledge of client operating systems • Knowledge of web server platforms • Operating system TCP/IP stack configuration • Network connection • Web browser • E-mail client • Hardware platform • DHCP • Client software configuration	**Unit 1, Lessons 1-2** **Unit 3, Lesson 4** **Unit 4, all lessons** Unit 5, Lesson 1 **Unit 5, Lesson 5** Unit 6, Lessons 1-2 **Unit 10, Lesson 4** **Unit 10, Lesson 6**
1.5 Use/configure Web browsers and other Internet/intranet clients, and be able to describe their use to others. Content may include the following: • Web browsers • FTP clients • Telnet clients • E-mail clients • All-in-one/universal clients • When to use each type of client • The basic commands (e.g., get and put) for each type of client (e.g., FTP, Telnet. POP3)	**Unit 5, Lessons 2-4** Unit 6, Lesson 1
1.6 Update client software. Content may include the following: • Performing routine maintenance on client applications (e.g. updating virus data files) • Applying service packs and maintenance patches • Upgrading to newer versions of client software, or replacing existing client software with versions from a different software vendor.	Unit 6, Lesson 1
1.7 Assist in the administration of Internet/intranet sites. Content may include the following: • Reset passwords • Configure permissions • Post content to server	Unit 9, Lesson 2

Objectives for 2002 i-Net+ Certification Exam (IK0-002) Objectives copyright © CompTIA. Used by permission. See www.comptia.org for current information on the i-Net+ certification.	**To meet this objective, study ALL of:** Lessons highlighted in bold can also be found in WestNet's Network+ Study Guide.
Domain 2.0 – Development	
2.1 Understand and be able to describe programming-related terms. Content may include the following: • API • CGI script • SQL • Client -side scripting • Server-side scripting • Server-side includes	Unit 8, Lesson 1 Unit 8, Lesson 3
2.2 Understand and be able to describe differences between popular client-side and server-side programming languages. Content may include the following: • When to use the languages • When they are executed Examples may include the following: • Java • JavaScript • XML • ASP • Extensible Stylesheet Language-XSL • Document Type definitions-DTD • JSP • CGI script • Perl • Java Servlets • VBScript • PHP	Unit 8, Lessons 2-4

Objectives for 2002 i-Net+ Certification Exam (IK0-002) Objectives copyright © CompTIA. Used by permission. See www.comptia.org for current information on the i-Net+ certification.	**To meet this objective, study ALL of:** Lessons highlighted in bold can also be found in WestNet's Network+ Study Guide.
2.3 Create HTML pages. Content may include the following: • Cascading Style Sheets - CSS • Extensible Stylesheet Language - XSL • DHTML • XHTML • HTML document structure • Understand and use MetaTags properly • Use page layout principles • Coding simple tables, headings, forms • Compatibility between different browsers • Importance of creating cross-browser coding in HTML • 3 tier models	Unit 7, Lessons 1-7
2.4 Identify when to use various multimedia extensions or plug-ins. Content may include the following: • QTVR (quick time) • Flash • Shockwave • RealPlayer • Windows Media Player	Unit 7, Lesson 9
2.5 Identify when to use various image and multimedia file formats. Content may include the following: • GIF • GIF89a • JPEG • PNG • PDF • TIFF • BMP • MOV • MPEG • AVI	Unit 7, Lessons 8-9
2.6 Identify the common formats used to deliver content to wireless devices. Content may include the following: • XML • WML	Unit 8, Lesson 4

Objectives for 2002 i-Net+ Certification Exam (IK0-002) Objectives copyright © CompTIA. Used by permission. See www.comptia.org for current information on the i-Net+ certification.	To meet this objective, study ALL of: Lessons highlighted in bold can also be found in WestNet's Network+ Study Guide.
2.7 Understand when to use popular tools to connect a Web server to a database. Content may include the following: • PHP • PERL • ASP • ODBC • JDBC	Unit 8, Lesson 1
2.8 Test preproduction Web and e-commerce servers. Content may include the following: • View web content in various browsers and at various screen resolutions • Stress test a server • Stress test the servers' Internet connection • Create sample transactions with an e-commerce server	**Unit 10, Lesson 1**
Domain 3.0 – Networking	
3.1 Understand and be able to describe the core components of the Internet infrastructure. Content may include the following: • Network access points • Backbone • Hardware/software infrastructure knowledge • Internetworking devices such as routers, switches and bridges	Unit 1, Lesson 6 Unit 3, Lesson 1 **Unit 4, Lesson 6**
3.2 Identify problems with Internet connectivity from source to destination for various types of servers. Content may include the following: • E-mail server • Web server • FTP server • News server • Proxy server • Caching server • Media server • DNS server • Certificate server • Directory (LDAP) server • Connecting through a firewall	**Unit 10, Lesson 3** **Unit 10, Lesson 4** **Unit 10, Lesson 5**

Objectives for 2002 i-Net+ Certification Exam (IK0-002) Objectives copyright © CompTIA. Used by permission. See www.comptia.org for current information on the i-Net+ certification.	To meet this objective, study ALL of: Lessons highlighted in bold can also be found in WestNet's Network+ Study Guide.
3.3 Understand and be able to describe the use of Internet domain names and DNS. Content may include the following: • DNS entry types • Hierarchical structure • Role of root domain servers • Top level or original domains • NSlookup	Unit 5, Lesson 6 **Unit 10, Lesson 2**
3.4 Understand and be able to describe the capabilities of popular remote access protocols. Content may include the following: • SLIP • PPP • PPTP • L2TP • PPPOE • Point-to-point multipoint	Unit 3, Lesson 2 **Unit 3, Lesson 4**
3.5 Understand how various protocols or services apply to the function of their corresponding server, such as a mail server, a web server, or a file transfer server. Content may include the following: • POP3 • SMTP • HTTP • FTP • NNTP • LDAP • Telnet	**Unit 5, Lessons 1-4** Unit 6, Lesson 3 **Unit 10, Lesson 3**
3.6 Identify when to use various diagnostic tools for resolving Internet problems. Content may include the following: • Ping • WinIPcfg • IPconfig • ifconfig • ARP • TraceRT • Network Analyzer	**Unit 4, Lesson 2** **Unit 10, Lesson 2** **Unit 10, Lesson 4** **Unit 10, Lesson 6**

Objectives for 2002 i-Net+ Certification Exam (IK0-002) Objectives copyright © CompTIA. Used by permission. See www.comptia.org for current information on the i-Net+ certification.	To meet this objective, study ALL of: Lessons highlighted in bold can also be found in WestNet's Network+ Study Guide.
3.7 Create a logic diagram of Internet components from the client to the server. Content may include the following: • Bridge • Brouter • Router • Switch • Hub • Repeater • Network Adapter • Cable Modem • xDSL Modem • Modem • WAN Link • CSU/DSU • Firewall • Network Address Translation (NAT) server • Proxy Server	**Unit 1, Lesson 1** Unit 1, Lesson 6 **Unit 3, Lesson 2** **Unit 5, Lesson 5** **Unit 10, Lesson 6**
3.8 Describe various hardware and software connection devices and when to use them. Content may include the following: • Network adapter • Bridge • Brouter • Router • Switch • Repeater • Hub • Network Adapter • Cable Modem • xDSL Modem • Modem • CSU/DSU • Firewall • Network Address Translation (NAT) server • Proxy Server	**Unit 1, Lesson 1** Unit 1, Lesson 6 **Unit 3, Lesson 2** **Unit 5, Lesson 5** Unit 9, Lesson 3

Objectives for 2002 i-Net+ Certification Exam (IK0-002) Objectives copyright © CompTIA. Used by permission. See www.comptia.org for current information on the i-Net+ certification.	**To meet this objective, study ALL of:** Lessons highlighted in bold can also be found in WestNet's Network+ Study Guide.
3.9 Understand when to use various site monitoring procedures. Content may include the following: • Viewing server log files • Monitoring network traffic • Monitoring server utilization • Monitoring server network bandwidth utilization	Unit 1, Lesson 4
3.10 Understand and be able to describe how common networking topologies are used. Content may include the following: • Star • Bus • Mesh • Ring	**Unit 1, Lesson 3**
3.11 Understand and be able to describe the capabilities of application server providers. Content may include the following: • Providing Internet based services on an as needed basis, such as: • Custom Web Hosting • Providing e-mail services • Providing Fax services • Providing access to an application over the Web • Providing shared access to expensive hardware, such as a mainframe computer	Unit 2, Lesson 4
Domain 4.0 – Security	
4.1 Understand and be able to describe various Internet security concepts. Content may include the following: • Access control • Authentication • Encryption-PKI • Secure socket layers (SSL) • Access security tools • Auditing • Secure Electronic Transactions (SET)	Unit 2, Lesson 3 Unit 6, Lesson 3 Unit 9, Lessons 1-2

Objectives for 2002 i-Net+ Certification Exam (IK0-002) Objectives copyright © CompTIA. Used by permission. See www.comptia.org for current information on the i-Net+ certification.	To meet this objective, study ALL of: Lessons highlighted in bold can also be found in WestNet's Network+ Study Guide.
4.2 Identify suspicious network activities. Content may include the following: • Multiple log-in failures • Ping floods • Denial of service attacks • Mail flooding • Syn floods • Spoofing • Repudiation	Unit 9, Lesson 2
4.3 Identify various methods for performing intrusion detection. Content may include the following: • Configure auditing on servers and firewalls • Review audit logs • Configure network monitoring software to alert you when suspicious types of traffic occur • Configure servers to notify you when unauthorized accesses are attempted.	Unit 9, Lesson 1
4.4 Identify appropriate access-control security features for an Internet server. Content may include the following: • E-mail server • Web server • APACHE • NES • IIS	Unit 9, Lesson 1 Unit 9, Lesson 3
4.5 Be able to describe the uses and proper instances to use anti-virus software. Content may include the following: • Server anti-virus protection • Client computer anti-virus protection • Network anti-virus protection, such as on a firewall	Unit 9, Lesson 1
4.6 Be able to describe the uses and proper instances to use various client security add-ons. Content may include the following: • Encryption software • Personal digital identification, such as a digital certificate • Personal firewall software	Unit 9, Lesson 1 Unit 3, Lesson 2

Objectives for 2002 i-Net+ Certification Exam (IK0-002) Objectives copyright © CompTIA. Used by permission. See www.comptia.org for current information on the i-Net+ certification.	To meet this objective, study ALL of: Lessons highlighted in bold can also be found in WestNet's Network+ Study Guide.
4.7 Describe how firewalls are used to protect private networks. Content may include the following: • Port filtering • Packet filtering • Application filtering • Intrusion detection filtering	Unit 9, Lesson 3 **Unit 10, Lesson 5**
4.8 Identify when to use various DMZ configurations. Content may include the following: • Bastion Host • Three-homed firewall • Back-to-back firewalls	Unit 9, Lesson 3
4.9 Understand and be able to describe various authentication/encryption technologies. Content may include the following: • Username/password authentication • Smart Card authentication • SSL • Authentication versus encryption • PKI • Asymmetric encryption, including blowfish, RC2, RC4, and RC5 • Symmetric encryption, including DES, triple DES, and Skip Jack • One Way encryption, including MD5 and SHA	Unit 6, Lesson 3 Unit 9, Lesson 1
Domain 4.0 – Business Concepts	
5.1 Understand and be able to describe e-commerce terms and concepts. Content may include the following: • Information Service Providers • Portals • SET (Secure Electronic Transactions) • EFT (Electronic Funds Transfer) • EBT (Electronic Benefits Transfer) • EDI (Electronic Data Interchange) • OBI (Open Buying on the Internet) • OTP (Open Trading Protocol)	Unit 2, Lesson 1 Unit 2, Lesson 1

Objectives for 2002 i-Net+ Certification Exam (IK0-002) Objectives copyright © CompTIA. Used by permission. See www.comptia.org for current information on the i-Net+ certification.	**To meet this objective, study ALL of:** Lessons highlighted in bold can also be found in WestNet's Network+ Study Guide.
5.2 Understand and be able to describe the differences between the following from a business standpoint: Content may include the following: • Private Network • Intranet • Extranet • Internet	**Unit 3, Lesson 3**
5.3 Recognize and explain the current types of e-business models being applied today. Content may include the following: • Business-to-business models • Business-to-consumer models • Business-to-employee models • Business to government • Consumer-to-business • Consumer-to-consumer • Storefront (bricks & mortar) vs. e-business • New and changing customer expectations • e-business and the Internet • Aggregator	Unit 2, Lesson 1
5.4 Identify key factors relating to strategic marketing considerations as they relate to launching an e-business initiative. Content may include the following: • Geographic/Localization considerations (local customs/criteria, etc.) • Public relations; impact/risks of site failure	Unit 2, Lesson 1 Unit 2, Lesson 2
5.5 Identify key factors relating to legal and regulatory considerations when planning e-business solutions. Content may include the following: • Knowledge ownership / Intellectual property rights • Privacy • Jurisdiction	Unit 2, Lesson 5 Unit 2, Lesson 6

Objectives for <u>CIW Foundations Exam</u> (1D0-410) Objectives copyright © ProsoftTraining. Used by permission. Visit www.CIWcertified.com for current information on the CIW Associate certification.	**To meet this objective, study ALL of:**
Describe infrastructure required to support an Internet connection, including hardware and software components.	Unit 3, Lesson 4
Explain important Internet communications protocols and their roles in delivering basic Internet services.	Unit 4, all lessons Unit 5, all lessons
Explain the basic principles of the Domain Name System (DNS).	Unit 5, Lesson 6
Describe how Web browsers can be used to access the World Wide Web and other computer resources.	Unit 6, Lesson 1
Explain how e-mail clients can be used to send simple messages and files to other Internet users.	Unit 6, Lesson 1
Describe Internet services, including but not limited to news, FTP, Gopher, Telnet, and network performance utilities such as ping and traceroute.	Unit 6, Lesson 3 Unit 10, Lesson 2
Explain user customization features in Web browsers, including preferences, caching, and cookies.	Unit 6, Lesson 1
Describe security issues related to Web browsing and e-mail, including certificates and viruses.	Unit 9, Lessons 1-2
Explain how to use different types of Web search engines effectively.	Unit 2, Lesson 1
Describe how to use the Web to obtain legal and international business information.	Unit 2, Lesson 1
Describe issues in developing a corporate Web site, including but not limited to project management, testing, and legal issues.	Unit 3, all lessons Unit 10, Lesson 1
Explain how HTML files are formatted to maintain compatibility with older Web browsers.	Unit 7, Lesson 1 Unit 8, Lesson 3
Explain how to include images and graphical formatting in HTML files.	Unit 7, Lesson 2 Unit 7, Lesson 8
Describe how to create a basic HTML form that accepts user input.	Unit 7, Lesson 7 Unit 8, Lesson 2
Describe how to test and analyze Web site performance issues.	Unit 1, Lesson 4 Unit 10, Lessons 1-2
Explain the features and appropriate use of XML.	Unit 8, Lesson 4
Describe networking and its role in the Internet, including protocols, packets, and the OSI reference model.	Unit 1, Lesson 5

Objectives for <u>CIW Foundations Exam</u> (1D0-410) Objectives copyright © ProsoftTraining. Used by permission. Visit www.CIWcertified.com for current information on the CIW Associate certification.	**To meet this objective, study ALL of:**
Explain the role of networking hardware, and configure common PC hardware for operation.	Unit 1, Lesson 1 Unit 1, Lesson 6 Unit 3, Lesson 4
Discuss the relationship between IP addresses and domain names, including assignment of IP addresses within a subnet.	Unit 4, Lesson 2 Unit 4, Lessons 4-6 Unit 5, Lesson 6
Describe the function and components of the Web server.	Unit 6, Lessons 2-3
Discuss common Internet security issues, including user-level and enterprise-level concerns.	Unit 9, all lessons
Describe common performance issues affecting Internet servers and resources, including analysis and diagnosis.	Unit 1, Lesson 4 Unit 10, Lessons 1-2
Describe how to transmit text and binary files using popular Internet services, including the Web and e-mail.	Unit 5, Lessons 3-4

FEATURES

Several pedagogical features are included in this text to enhance your understanding of the materials and ability to apply concepts. Throughout the course, emphasis is placed on applying concepts to real-world scenarios through end-of-lesson activities, extended activities, and other exercises and examples.

LEARNING OBJECTIVES, UNIT SUMMARIES, DISCUSSION QUESTIONS, AND ACTIVITIES/EXERCISES

Learning objectives, unit summaries, discussion questions, and activities/exercises are designed to function as integrated study tools. Learning objectives reflect what you should be able to accomplish after completing each unit. If you are studying for CompTIA's i-Net+ Certification exam, you can reference the CompTIA objectives listed at the start of each lesson and abbreviated within the textbook's margin, providing you with specific areas where you can glean information appropriate for your certification studies. Unit summaries highlight the key concepts you should master. The discussion questions help guide critical thinking about those key concepts, and the activities/exercises provide you with opportunities to practice important techniques.

KEY TERMS

The information technology field includes many unique terms that are critical to creating a workable language when combined with the world of business. Definitions of key terms are provided in alphabetical order at the beginning of each unit of the textbook and in a glossary at the end of the book.

RESOURCES AVAILABLE IN INSTRUCTOR-LED SETTINGS

An Instructor's Resource Tool Kit accompanies this course when it is used in an academic or instructor-led setting. The online-based kit includes an Instructor's Guide with the answers to the textbook's activities/exercises, unit quizzes, and the end-of-course exam. It also includes PowerPoint presentations organized by lesson, unit, and course. WestNet Learning Technologies' cutting edge course management tools offer a unique online Windows® -based exam software. The Instructor's Resource Web site also includes sample syllabi, discussion topics, puzzles, cryptograms, and up-to-the-minute supplements to the textbooks and course materials. The online course exam engine includes hundreds of lesson, unit, and course questions. These exams can be accessed by individual students and are presented in random order, ensuring that a student never get the same question in the same order. This feature allows instructors to create printed and online pre-tests, practice tests, and actual examinations.

WHY CHOOSE WESTNET?

WestNet Learning Technologies offers comprehensive information technologies (IT) educational and certification programs and curricula to secondary schools, colleges and universities, as well as corporations, resellers, and individual participants around the globe. These programs provide participants with the skills necessary to further their technical knowledge and obtain hands-on experience. This unique program, which is vendor neutral, helps prepare participants to pursue IT careers, earn secondary and post-secondary educational degrees, and/or obtain industry certification.

WestNet Learning Technologies' programs are currently provided to more than 1,000 institutions around the world. Its programs are also offered internationally in more than a dozen countries and in five languages.

COMPTIA AUTHORIZED QUALITY CURRICULUM (CAQC)

CompTIA Authorized Quality Curriculum (CAQC) training products meet strict quality standards and are reviewed by experts to ensure they meet exacting requirements.

Using CAQC training materials assures that candidates will have a number of important study advantages. CAQC study materials cover all exam objectives, were produced using important instructional design principles, and contain reviews that help to judge your learning comprehension and readiness for the certification exam.

What's the best way to study for CompTIA certifications?

CompTIA Technical Certifications are known throughout the worldwide IT community as the best way to build a solid foundation for a career in technology. But when you prepare for the exams, how can you make sure you choose the right curriculum or training program out of the hundreds of options available to you?

CompTIA eases the process of selecting the most appropriate training and study aids with the CAQC program. Through independent third-party experts, CompTIA reviews and analyzes available training programs and content to ensure that they contain what you need to prepare for your certification exam.

What types of programs does CompTIA evaluate?

These programs evaluate materials and programs of all types, including books, self-study guides, classroom training programs, videos, computer-based training and other written and instructor-led programs.

How can I tell if a training material is CompTIA Authorized Quality Curriculum?

Qualifying curriculums and training programs carry the Authorized CompTIA Curriculum and Authorized Training logo on the training or marketing materials. Additionally, all available study aids and training programs are included on CompTIA's searchable online database, where candidates can find the best program—authorized or not—to help you prepare for your certification exam.

How does CompTIA authorize these programs?

When a training material or program provider such as WestNet wants to have its materials evaluated, the company must first complete an initial application with CompTIA. Then, they can select one of several authorized reviewers, who will analyze the material and determine if it maps closely enough with the CompTIA examinations to be considered authorized. Once the material was authorized, WestNet received the appropriate CAQC logos to be used on its authorized training or marketing materials, such as this textbook and advertising materials. You can see the CAQC logo on the cover of this textbook.

Why did CompTIA develop the Authorization program?

CompTIA technical certifications are required for many IT positions, and are an important foundation for several vendor-specific certifications. Many enterprising companies leverage this fact to sell training materials and programs that range in quality from exceptional to poor. CompTIA believes that candidates should have the best study materials available that will help them prepare for and successfully complete a certification exam. The CompTIA Content Authorized Curriculum and Authorized Training Programs will help certificate candidates make better decisions about which training materials to use.

What if the CompTIA logo is used? Does the CompTIA logo signify CAQC?

While any study aid or training program can use the CompTIA corporate logo, only authorized programs can use the CompTIA CAQC logos. WestNet has permission to use both logos with its authorized i-Net+ certification program.

<table>
<tr><td>

How can I learn more about CompTIA CAQC program?

</td><td>

Certificate candidates can learn more about the CAQC programs at **www.comptia.org/certification/caqc**.

</td></tr>
</table>

CAQC

The logo of the CompTIA Authorized Quality Curriculum Program and the status of this or other training material as "Authorized" under the CompTIA Authorized Curriculum Program signifies that, in CompTIA's opinion, such training material covers the content of the CompTIA's related certification exam. CompTIA has not reviewed or approved the accuracy of the contents of this training material and specifically disclaims any warranties of merchantability or fitness for a particular purpose. CompTIA makes no guarantee concerning the success of persons using any such "Authorized" or other training material in order to prepare for any CompTIA certification exam.

The contents of this courseware were created for the CompTIA i-Net+ exam covering CompTIA certification exam objectives that were current as of October 2002.

HOW TO BECOME COMPTIA CERTIFIED

This training material can help you prepare for and pass a related CompTIA certification exam or exams. In order to achieve CompTIA certification, you must register for and pass a CompTIA certification exam or exams.

In order to become CompTIA certified, you must:

1. Select a certification exam provider. For more information please visit **http://www.comptia.org/certification/test_locations.htm**.

2. Register for and schedule a time to take the CompTIA certification exam(s) at a convenient location.

3. Read and sign the Candidate Agreement, which will be presented at the time of the exam(s). The text of the Candidate Agreement can be found at www.comptia.org/certification

4. Take and pass the CompTIA certification exam(s).

For more information about CompTIA's certifications, such as their industry acceptance, benefits, or program news, please visit www.comptia.org/certification

CompTIA is a non-profit information technology (IT) trade association. CompTIA's certifications are designed by subject matter experts from across the IT industry. Each CompTIA certification is vendor-neutral, covers multiple technologies, and requires demonstration of skills and knowledge widely sought after by the IT industry.

To contact CompTIA with any questions or comments:

Please call + 1 (630) 268 1818

questions@comptia.org

Unit 1
Review of Network Fundamentals

This unit reviews the most important networking principles that were presented in the *Introduction to Networking* and *Network+* courses. A solid understanding of these concepts is necessary before you move on to more detailed study of Internet implementation.

We begin by taking a look at the elements that make up a network, starting with the devices that use the network to communicate. The most common type of network endpoint is the computer. All computers, from small desktop computers to powerful mainframes, use the same basic structure and contain the same types of components. We briefly explain the basic concepts of how computers work, introduce the main components and features of computer systems, and explain how different types of devices may either enhance or degrade network performance.

This unit also reviews the Open Systems Interconnection (OSI) Reference Model, which provides an important conceptual framework for discussing and comparing network devices and functions.

Using the OSI Model as a guide, we also explore the various physical layouts or topologies of data networks, and show how the pattern of signal flow depends on the topology of the network. We introduce the main types of internetworking devices that link computers into different topologies, and explain the strengths and weaknesses of each type.

Lessons

1. Internal Computer Components: CPU, I/O, Memory, and NICs
2. Software
3. Network Topologies
4. Network Performance Concepts
5. Review of the OSI Model
6. Review of Internetworking Devices

Terms

active loop—An active loop consists of two or more paths between a pair of devices on a bridged network. This type of loop is formed when one node is inadvertently connected to more than one bridge. See spanning tree algorithm (STA).

American Standard Code for Information Interchange (ASCII)—An ASCII file is a simple text file, or a file that has been converted into ASCII format. The ASCII format is a coding standard for the representation of alphanumeric characters for storage on a computer. Most files available for FTP are ASCII files.

application specific integrated circuit (ASIC)—ASIC is an electronics technology that hard-wires a device to switch a specific Layer 2 protocol, such as Ethernet, or a Layer 3 protocol, such as IP. Switches that use ASIC hardware are much faster than switches that rely on slower software.

Asynchronous Transfer Mode (ATM)—ATM is a connection-oriented cell relay technology based on small (53-byte) cells. An ATM network consists of ATM switches that form multiple virtual circuits to carry groups of cells from source to destination. ATM can provide high-speed transport services for audio, data, and video.

backbone—A backbone is the portion of a network that carries the most significant traffic. It is also the part of the network that connects many smaller networks to form a larger network.

bandwidth—Bandwidth is a measure of the information-carrying capacity of a channel. In analog networks, bandwidth is the difference between the highest and lowest frequencies that can be transmitted across a communication link. Analog networks measure bandwidth in cycles per second (Hz). Digital networks measure bandwidth in Kbps (bits per second), Mbps, and Gbps.

binary—Binary refers to the base 2 numbering system used by computers to represent information. Binary numbers consist of only two values: 1 and 0. In a binary number, each position is two times greater than the position to its right.

bit—A bit, also referred to as a binary digit, is a single value that makes up a binary number. A bit can be either 1 or 0. See binary.

bits per second (bps)—The number of binary bits transmitted per second is measured in bps. For example, common modem speeds are 28,800 bps and 56,000 bps. Another way of writing 28,800 bps is 28.8 Kbps, because "kilo" means 1,000.

bridge—A bridge is a device that operates at the Data Link Layer of the OSI model. A bridge can connect several LANs or LAN segments. It can connect LANs of the same media access type, such as two Token Ring segments, or different LANs, such as Ethernet and Token Ring.

broadcast domain—A broadcast domain is the area of a network through which broadcast packets are forwarded. Routers, Layer 3 switches, and VLANs create network segments that are separate broadcast domains, because they do not forward broadcast packets from one segment to another.

broadcast storm—Due to differences between nodes and bridges in different parts of the network, a broadcast frame can sometimes be misinterpreted. This leads to another broadcast frame by the bridge which misinterprets it. The second broadcast frame is again misinterpreted, and so on. The result is a "storm" of broadcast frames that can severely impact network performance. Sometimes storms can persist and eventually bring down the entire network.

brouter—A brouter is an internetworking device that combines the functions of both a bridge and a router.

channel—A portion of the total bandwidth of a physical transmission path, used to carry a single signal is referred to as a channel. Channels are also called links, lines, circuits, or paths. A physical connection, such as a cable, may support more than one channel.

coaxial—Coaxial cable is a type of copper wiring typically used for cable television transmission and high-speed Internet connectivity. Coaxial cable typically consists of a central copper or copper-coated conductor surrounded by flexible insulation, a shield of wire mesh, and an outer plastic jacket. Older installations of Ethernet LANs also used coax cable.

collision—A collision occurs in an Ethernet network when two frames are put onto the physical medium at the same time and overlap fully or partially. When a collision occurs, the data on the physical segment is no longer valid.

collision domain—A collision domain is the portion of a network where all nodes receive every frame transmitted. It is a part of a network in which nodes compete for access to the same physical medium.

delay—Delay is the amount of time needed for a device, such as a switch or router, to process information (such as a frame or packet). It is the duration from the time a device reads the first byte of a frame or packet, until the time it forwards that byte. In this sense, delay is another word for latency. Delay is also associated with the length of time it takes to get information across a physical link.

Ethernet—The Ethernet protocol, originally developed in the 1970s by Xerox Corporation, in conjunction with Intel and DEC, is now the primary protocol for local area networking. The original Ethernet provides 10-Mbps throughput. Fast Ethernet (100 Mbps) and Gigabit Ethernet (1,000 Mbps) use the same basic technology, but at higher speeds.

Extended Binary Coded Decimal Interchange Code (EBCDIC)—EBCDIC is a character encoding scheme developed by IBM. A character encoding scheme is a way to represent alphanumeric characters on a computer system in binary format.

Fiber Distributed Data Interface (FDDI)—FDDI is a token-passing network architecture that uses two ring channels. FDDI provides 100 Mbps over optical fiber.

frame—A frame is a unit of information transmitted across a data link. Ethernet frames, for example, are frames generated by an Ethernet NIC. Frames typically carry packets across a single physical link. In a LAN, the address found in a frame designates the NIC card that the frame is intended for.

Gbps (Gigabits per second)—A term that identifies the rate at which information travels down a physical medium or through space (wireless). Gbps is equivalent to 1 billion bits per second; 2.488 Gbps is equivalent to 2,488,000,000 bits per second.

hertz (Hz)—Radio signals are measured in cycles per second, or Hz. One Hz is 1 cycle per second; 1,000 cycles per second is 1 kHz; 1 million cycles per second is 1 MHz and 1 billion cycles per second is 1 GHz.

hub—Also called a wiring concentrator, a simple hub is a repeater with multiple ports. A signal coming into one port is repeated out the other ports.

Kbps (Kilobits per second)—A term that identifies the rate at which information travels down a physical medium or through space (wireless). Kbps is equivalent to 1,000 bits per second. 56 Kbps is equivalent to 56,000 bits per second.

latency—Latency is the transmission delay created as a device processes a frame or packet. It is the duration from the time a device reads the first byte of a frame or packet, until the time it forwards that byte.

Mbps (Megabits per second)—A term that identifies the rate at which information travels down a physical medium or through space (wireless). Mbps is equivalent to 1,000,000 bits per second; 1.544 Mbps is equivalent to 1,544,000 bits per second.

modem—The term "modem" is a contraction for modulator/demodulator. Modems are used to convert binary data into analog signals suitable for transmission across a telephone network.

multiplexing—Multiplexing is a technology that allows multiple signals to travel over the same physical medium. Multiple signals are fed into a multiplexer and combined to form one output stream.

multistation access unit (MAU)—A MAU is a device used in Token Ring networks to provide connectivity between individual workstations. It is also called a Token Ring hub.

network interface card (NIC)—A NIC is an expansion board inserted into a computer to enable the computer to be connected to a network.

operating system (OS)—An OS is the basic system software of a computer that provides low-level services to applications.

packet—A packet is a unit of information processed by the Network Layer of the OSI reference model. The packet header contains the logical (network) address of the destination node. Intermediate nodes forward a packet until it reaches its destination. A packet can contain an entire message generated by higher OSI layers, or a segment of a much larger message. IP packets are also referred to as datagrams.

Peripheral Component Interconnect (PCI) bus—PCI bus is a newer 64-bit local bus technology for PCs. A bus connects the central processor of a PC with the video controller, disk controller, hard drives, and memory.

protocol—A protocol is a defined method of communication between computers or computer applications.

random access memory (RAM)—A computer's main working memory is referred to as its RAM. Applications use RAM to hold instructions and data during processing. This type of memory is both changeable and volatile. Applications can repeatedly write new data to the same RAM; however, all data is erased from RAM when a computer loses power or shuts down.

read-only memory (ROM)—ROM is nonvolatile memory in which data, under normal conditions, can only be read and not written to or manipulated.

repeater—A device that regenerates and boosts electrical or radio signals is referred to as a repeater. It can be used to lengthen a wire or a wireless transmission path.

router—A router is a Layer 3 device with several ports that can each connect to a network or another router. The router examines the logical network address of each packet, then uses its internal routing table to forward the packet to the routing port associated with the best path to the packet's destination. If the packet is addressed to a network not connected to the router, the router will forward the packet to another router closer to the final destination. Each router, in turn, evaluates each packet, and then either delivers the packet or forwards it to another router.

signal reflection—Signal reflection refers to the situation where part, or all, of an electrical signal bounces back from an improperly made cable connection. This effect creates signal noise that can be misinterpreted as frame collisions.

spanning tree algorithm (STA)—STA is a bridging algorithm that avoids active loops (multiple paths between nodes that could create infinite loop transmission patterns). If multiple paths exist between a bridge and a destination, the algorithm requires the bridge to use only one path. If the best path fails, the algorithm finds the next best route. See active loop.

switch—A switch is a device that operates at the Data Link Layer of the OSI reference model. A switch can connect LANs or segments of the same media access type. A switch dedicates its entire bandwidth to each frame it switches. Switches are also found in Wide Area Networks (WANs), as devices such as Frame Relay switches and ATM switches are used to move information from one network to another.

T1—T1 is one of the T-carrier telecommunication standards for multiplexing digitized voice signals. A T1 channel operates at 1.544 Mbps. Each T1 channel (64 Kbps) carries a digitized representation of an analog signal that has a bandwidth of 4,000 Hz. Originally, 64 Kbps was required to digitize a 4,000-Hz voice signal. Current digitization technology has reduced that requirement to 32 Kbps or less; however, a T-carrier channel is still 64 Kbps.

terminator—A terminator is an electrical resistor that absorbs an electrical pulse when it reaches the end of a coaxial bus cable segment. If a terminator is not installed, a signal will reflect back down the bus cable, increasing the number of signal collisions.

Thinnet—Thinnet is another name for RG58A coaxial cable, specified in the 10Base2 standard for Ethernet bus networks. Because it is thinner and less expensive than the "Thicknet" used in 10Base5 Ethernets, Thinnet is also known as "Cheapernet."

throughput—Throughput describes the overall capacity of a network to perform useful work. While bandwidth measurements focus on the raw number of bits a network can carry, throughput measurements express the actual or effective data rates of a network. Throughput is most often used to describe the overall performance of a network. It is measured in PPS or bps.

Token Ring—Token Ring is a LAN protocol for ring topologies that operates at 4 and 16 Mbps.

unroutable protocol—An unroutable protocol is a network protocol that does not support routing at OSI Layer 3, such as NetBIOS or DEC-LAT. This type of protocol does not create packets; thus, Layer 3 devices, such as routers, cannot be used.

unshielded twisted pair (UTP)—UTP is the most common type of network cabling, and is used extensively in telephone networks and many data communication applications. UTP can carry a 100-Mbps digital signal 100 meters using twisted pairs of cable without requiring that the signal be repeated.

Lesson 1—Internal Computer Components: CPU, I/O, Memory, and NICs

Before we can learn how computers exchange data over a network, we must first understand how data moves within the computer itself. Users often blame a network for some type of poor performance, when one of the computer's internal systems is actually at fault. This lesson introduces the main components found in most computer systems and outlines the basic principles of the way they work.

Objectives

At the end of this lesson you will be able to:

- Explain what a CPU is and what it does

- Describe the purpose of an I/O bus

- Name the various types of memory and explain the best use of each one

- Describe what a NIC is and explain why it is necessary

Key Point

All internal computer components have various levels of speed and capacity.

CPU

Objective 1.4
Understand and be able to describe the infrastructure needed to support an Internet client. ... Hardware platform

A central processing unit (CPU) is the brain of a computer. It executes the instructions contained in a computer program and directs the flow of information within the computer. At the heart of a CPU is a microprocessor (a highly complex integrated circuit chip), thus the terms "microprocessor" and "CPU" are often used interchangeably. There are two basic characteristics that differentiate microprocessors:

- Data bus size—The size of the bus refers to the number of data bits a CPU can work on in a single instruction.

- Clock speed—The clock speed indicates how many instructions per second the processor can execute. Each "tick" of the clock is called a cycle; thus, clock speed is measured in thousands of cycles per second. A single cycle per second is called 1 hertz (Hz), 1,000 Hz is 1 kilohertz (kHz), 1 million Hz is 1 megahertz (MHz), and 1 billion Hz is 1 gigahertz (GHz). Thus, a CPU that runs at 400,000,000 cycles per second is a 400-MHz processor.

In both cases, the higher the value, the more powerful the CPU. If two processors have the same bus size, the one with the higher clock speed will perform more work in the same time. If two CPUs have the same clock speed, the one with the larger data bus can process more data during each cycle.

The vast majority of all IBM-type PCs incorporate a single Intel architecture processor, such as Pentium. Apple PCs are based on a different processor from Motorola. The difference in these processor architectures is why these two types of computers have fundamentally different characteristics. Although Intel is the world's largest microprocessor manufacturer, it does not have the entire PC processor market. For example, Advanced Micro Devices (AMD) manufactures processors comparable to the Intel Pentium processor.

I/O

Input refers to data that enters a computer from the outside, such as keystrokes from a keyboard, mouse movements, or incoming data from another device on a network. Output is data a computer sends to the outside world, such as print jobs, alert beeps, images on the monitor screen, or outgoing data to be sent to another part of the network.

The I/O of a computer is controlled by a program called the Basic Input/Output System (BIOS). This program contains the most basic instructions in the computer and is permanently written to an area of read-only memory (ROM).

I/O data travels over its own bus, which is a collection of wires that connects all internal computer components to the CPU, main memory, and each other. The I/O bus transmits incoming and outgoing data from one part of a computer to another. The term "local bus" usually refers to a fast internal bus that connects devices directly to a CPU. An "expansion bus" connects expansion boards to the CPU and memory, as illustrated on the Computer I/O Bus Diagram.

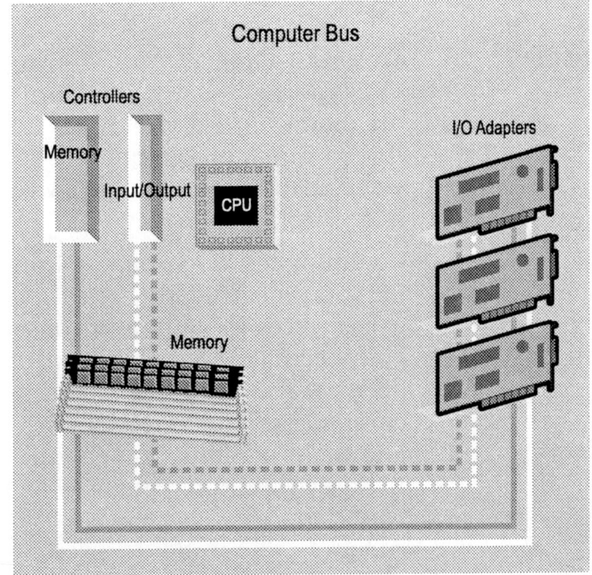

Computer I/O Bus

All buses consist of two parts: an address bus and a data bus. The data bus transfers actual data, and the address bus transfers information about where the data should go. There are two basic types of I/O bus:

- A serial bus streams data 1 bit at a time, like cars on a one-lane road.

- A parallel bus is like a multilane highway that transmits many bits simultaneously, using multiple transmission channels or wires. The size of a parallel bus, known as its width, is important because it determines how much data can be transmitted at one time. For example, a 16-bit bus simultaneously transmits 16 bits of data simultaneously, and a 32-bit bus simultaneously transmits 32 bits of data.

Every bus has a clock speed measured in MHz. A fast bus allows data to be transferred faster, making applications run faster. On PCs, the older 16-bit Industry Standard Architecture (ISA) expansion bus is being replaced by faster buses, such as the 32-bit Peripheral Component Interconnect (PCI) bus. Newer PCs also include a local bus for data that requires especially fast transfer speeds, such as video data.

The width of a bus describes the number of bits the bus can carry at one time. The term "bandwidth" describes the overall data-carrying capacity of a bus.

Video Display

The most familiar type of computer output is its video display. The type and quality of a monitor's image is determined both by the monitor itself, and by a circuit board called a "video adapter," "video card," or "graphics adapter." The monitor plugs into the video adapter, or video port, which generates the signals that produce the visible images.

A computer's video output usually does not affect the network, but may degrade the performance of an individual device by using excessive amounts of memory. This problem is compounded by the fact that many users who need high-quality color displays also need high-speed graphics rendering that burdens a computer's CPU. To remove this burden from the computer's CPU and main memory, some video adapter cards are equipped with their own dedicated memory and video coprocessor chip.

Memory

A computer's memory holds data currently being worked on by the CPU; it is the computer's short-term storage. The term "memory" generally refers to random access memory (RAM), which comes in the form of integrated circuit chips that plug into the main circuit board (motherboard) of the computer. When we say "memory," we are often referring to the chips themselves. RAM is typically volatile, which means it needs a constant supply of electricity to hold data. If the power goes off, all data in RAM is lost.

The term "storage" is used to describe media that hold data for longer periods, even when the power goes off. Typically, computers use magnetic tapes or disks for long-term storage. However, in some cases, the concepts of memory and storage overlap. Some computers can use hard disk storage to supplement RAM in a system called "virtual memory." PDAs, and other small devices without a disk drive, often store data in programmable memory.

When you run a program, it is read from storage, such as a hard drive or compact disk read-only memory (CD-ROM) drive, and put into memory for execution. After the program has completed or is no longer needed, it is typically removed from memory.

NICs

Objective 1.4
Understand and be able to describe the infrastructure needed to support an Internet client ... Hardware platform

Objective 3.7
Create a logic diagram of Internet components from the client to the server ... Network Adapter

Objective 3.8
Describe various hardware and software connection devices and when to use them. ... Network Adapter

There are many types of plug-in expansion cards that add features to a computer. The one we are most concerned about in this course is the NIC. A NIC, also called a network adapter, is an expansion board that physically connects a computer to a network. A NIC fits into an expansion slot on a motherboard's I/O bus. A network cable attaches to the NIC, allowing the computer to both transmit and receive the signals that represent data as illustrated on the Connecting a NIC to the Network Diagram.

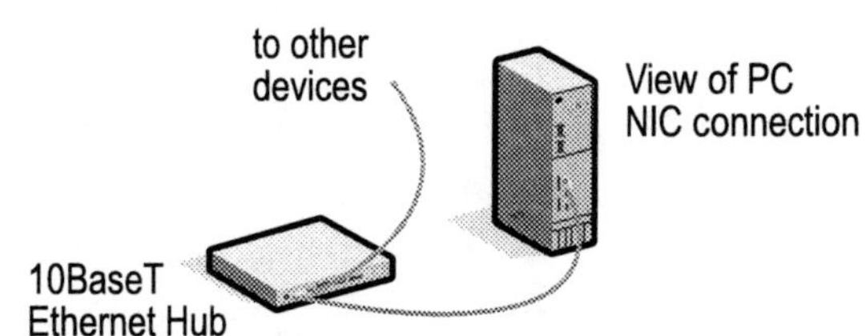

Connecting a NIC to the Network

The speed at which data may be transferred to and from a NIC is determined by many factors: the computer's I/O bus bandwidth and processor speed, design, and quality of the NIC itself, computer's OS software, and type of network in use.

Different Networks, Different NICs

Each type of NIC is defined by three main factors:

- Network transmission protocol, such as Ethernet, Token Ring, or AppleTalk

- Type of transmission medium, such as wire, radio signals, or optical fiber

- Data transmission speed

Thus, a computer would need one type of NIC to send electrical signals over a copper-wired network, and a different NIC to send light pulses over a fiber optic system. If a computer has an Ethernet NIC that only transmits at 10 Mbps, it cannot communicate with other Ethernet NICs that only operate at 100 Mbps.

13

On a copper-wired network, a NIC varies the voltage level on the line in a precise pattern that represents data bits. On a fiber optic network, a NIC converts outgoing bits to flashes of light. On a wireless network, a NIC transmits bits by changing the pattern of a radio wave. In each case, the NIC also receives incoming signals as changing voltages, light flashes, or radio waves, and converts those signals into electrical bit patterns a computer can use.

Regardless of what physical medium a network uses, a NIC's job is to both generate and receive the signals that represent binary 1s and 0s. These signals must be precisely timed; thus, the timing circuitry in sending and receiving NICs must be coordinated. The resulting sequence of bits is called a bit stream.

Each NIC is Unique

Each NIC contains a unique ID number that is built in at the factory. A central organization of computer manufacturers coordinates the assignment of these numbers to ensure that each ID is used by only one NIC anywhere in the world. Thus, in addition to physically transmitting and receiving signals, a NIC also uniquely identifies the device that contains it.

Each network node (computer, printer, or other device) must have a NIC to directly communicate with other nodes. However, if a resource, such as a printer, does not have a NIC, it can be indirectly connected to the network through a computer that does have a NIC. That computer can then be set to "share" its resource with other network nodes. All traffic to that printer would then pass through the computer, and not go to the printer directly.

In this way, a NIC is like a telephone. To "talk" directly with other nodes, a device must have its own communication equipment. However, if a device lacks that equipment, it can sometimes borrow it from another device, just as a person with a telephone may share it with a friend who does not have one.

NIC Connectivity in a PC

The NIC fits into a slot on the motherboard that is connected to the computer bus (also referred to as the input/output [I/O] or expansion bus). This bus connects adapter cards, such as NICs, to the central processing unit (CPU) and random access memory (RAM). The speed at which data is transferred to and from the NIC is a key factor in NIC performance. The wider the bus, the more data that can be transferred simultaneously.

Summary of NIC Characteristics

The NIC Options Table shows some of the main characteristics that distinguish different NICs.

NIC Options

LAN protocol	Ethernet, FDDI, Fast Ethernet, ATM, Token Ring, AppleTalk, etc.
Computer bus supported	MCA, ISA, EISA, PCI, NuBus, VME
RAM buffer size	8 KB, 16 KB, 32 KB, etc.
I/O bus width	8 bit, 16 bit, 32 bit, 64 bit, etc.
Data rate	4 Mbps, 10 Mbps, 16 Mbps, 100 Mbps
Media type supported	Coaxial, UTP, STP, Fiber, Wireless
O/S supported	NetWare, Windows NT/2000, UNIX/Linux, Mac OS, etc.
Processor capability	486, Pentium, Pentium II, Pentium III, etc.

Review of Network
Fundamentals

Activities

1. The function of a CPU is to store programs. True or False?

2. The amount of RAM determines the speed at which a CPU executes instructions. True or False?

3. What is a NIC, and what is it used for?

   ____

   ____

   ____

4. Which device is associated with short-term storage: hard disk or RAM? (Circle one.)

5. What determines the size of a bus: length or width? (Circle one.)

6. Why is the speed of a bus important?

   ____

   ____

   ____

   ____

Extended Activities

1. Acquire the following computer components and use them for a "show-and-tell" session: motherboards, CPU chips, RAM chips, NICs and other expansion cards, network cabling, and anything else you might find interesting.

2. Look through a recent computer catalog or vendor Web site and list the three fastest CPU speeds you find.

   ____

   ____

   ____

3. Go to any computer vendor's Web site or catalog and find prices for RAM. Pay particular attention to the various sizes offered, such as 8 MB, 16 MB, 32 MB, and 128 MB. Calculate the price per MB for the different sizes. Visit other Web sites for price comparisons.

    ____

    ____

    ____

4. Check vendors' catalogs or Web sites for memory terms such as SIMM, DIMM, EDO, SDRAM, SGRAM, then research the meaning of those terms. If you find any others, list those as well.

    ____

    ____

    ____

5. Look up information on "plug-and-play" devices. Can any type of expansion card be used in a plug-and-play environment?

    ____

    ____

    ____

6. Go to a Web site such as **http://www.webopedia.com** and find information on the accelerated graphics port (AGP) interface. Discuss how this is being used.

    ____

    ____

    ____

Lesson 2—Software

In general, software describes the changeable instructions carried out by the computing hardware. A software program does not work alone, but must cooperate with one or more other types of programs. This lesson introduces each of these types of software and explains how they work together.

Objectives

At the end of this lesson you will be able to:

- Give several examples of what an OS does

- Explain what a device driver is and why it is necessary

- Explain the difference between peer-to-peer communication and client/server communication

 **Key Point**

To communicate over a network, a computer must use networking software.

Programs and Processes

The term "program" or "application" tends to mean a complete set of routines that provides a high-level function of some sort. For example, a word processing application performs the general task of creating documents.

However, that broad task is composed of many subprocesses, such as opening files, saving files, copying and pasting text, and deleting data. Therefore, in the literature of data communications, and at some points in this course, the term "process" will be used instead of "program," usually when we refer to some subset of functions (still possibly quite complex) that fits into a larger program or is part of a large system.

This distinction is important because some processes within a program are designed to communicate and cooperate with other processes over a network. Processes generally cooperate using three types of communication architectures: master/slave, peer-to-peer, and client/server.

Master/Slave

Master/slave communication occurs when one node has much greater computing capacity than another. For example, in some networks a mainframe computer runs all the applications, stores all the data, and does all the processing. This powerful central computer is connected to a group of simple "dumb" terminals, which can only send data to the mainframe and receive responses in return. Each dumb slave client terminal has no data storage or real processing capability, but waits for the master mainframe to command it to send information.

Peer-to-Peer

When two processes have roughly the same power and can perform approximately the same services for each other, we call them "peer" processes. A peer-to-peer computer network is created when we interconnect a group of computers of roughly equal power and function. This typically happens when a small office links the desktop computers of its employees. Each person's computer has a different set of applications and data, but the network connection allows various combinations of workers to share files, folders, applications, and printers. No single computer sets the rules for these interactions. However, each computer's user can decide what resources to make available to other peer users.

Client/Server

Objective 1.4
Understand and be able to describe the infrastructure needed to support an Internet client.

Another way that processes can cooperate is for one process to take the role of client and the other that of server. Servers can provide resources that clients need, such as processing power, or access to peripheral devices or special applications. The client process initiates an interaction by issuing a request to the server. The server process responds with a reply satisfying the request.

For example, most World Wide Web interactions use client/server communication. A user's Web browser (the client) requests a Web page from a Web server. The server transmits the page, then waits for another request.

Both client and server processes are dedicated to their respective tasks, and those roles never reverse. However, the same computing machine can run multiple processes. Some of those processes can be servers of some functions, and some can be clients of other servers. Thus, it is important to remember that "server" refers to a process, not necessarily a particular machine. Also, peer-to-peer communication can still occur on a client/server network. If servers have been established for shared functions, such as file sharing or printing, this does not prevent two computers from exchanging data as peers.

Client/Server Advantages

Client/server architecture has two primary advantages:

- Distributed applications—Applications can be distributed on the network based on their requirements for resources. For example, an application that provides computing-intensive services can be installed on a computer with very high processing capacity, while the user's client application runs on a workstation that provides high-end graphic display capabilities.

- Resource sharing—A server process typically can serve many clients; thus, client/server architecture is a good way to share many types of resources across an organization, or share files across the Internet.

Independent Computing Architecture

A variation on client/server communication is a proprietary remote access protocol, from Citrix®, called the Independent Computing Architecture® (ICA). Just as in a regular client/server system, ICA client computers may initiate requests to servers. However, in an ICA network, all processing occurs on the server. Client computers only process interface actions, such as transmitting keystrokes or mouse clicks to the server. Instead of returning live data, the server simply refreshes the user's screen. In essence, the user works with a picture of the data, and not the data itself. This approach sharply reduces the volume of network traffic, which increases the performance of a network across slow and costly wide-area connections.

Hosts

When a computer provides a resource to other computers, that computer is often called a "host." A host can be either a user's PC on a peer-to-peer network or a server in a client/server network. The term is often used to describe any computer capable of two-way communication over the Internet. However, in general, "host" refers to a computer that provides files, applications, or other resources.

Application Software

Objective 1.4
Understand and be able to describe the infrastructure needed to support an Internet client. … Knowledge of web server platforms …Web browser … E-mail client

Applications are software programs used to perform work. Some applications are designed to be directly used by a person, while others interact only with other applications. In either case, each application is a tool made to do a specific job.

Applications can be divided into two basic categories: single-user applications and networked or multiuser applications. Some applications run primarily as single-user applications, and others run almost exclusively as networked applications designed to support multiuser access. Some applications can run in both modes.

There is also a category of "pure" networked applications, or client/server applications, that assume they will always be used by multiple users. These applications—such as database servers, print servers, or Web servers—usually include two complementary applications: one for installation on the server, and one for installation on multiple client desktops.

Operating Systems

Objective 1.4
Understand and be able to describe the infrastructure needed to support an Internet client. … Knowledge of client operating systems

An operating system (OS) is a suite of software programs that provide the basic functions of a computer, such as reading and writing files, running applications, and managing I/O. When an application needs to perform one of these jobs, it makes a request to the OS.

OS software is categorized according to the type of network communication it can enable:

- Peer-to-peer networking software is included with most popular desktop OSs. Each individual user configures software settings to allow or disallow the sharing of that computer's resources by other users. There is no central authority that decides what users may have access to what resources.

- A network OS (NOS), also called a client/server OS, provides centralized control of all network resources. A network administrator can decide what each user may see and do on the network. By far, the most common NOS packages are Novel NetWare and Microsoft Windows NT/2000.

Device Drivers

A computer can be equipped with a nearly endless number of peripheral devices, and it is impossible for an OS to know how to communicate with all of them. Thus, each hardware device usually comes with a small software application (device driver), which contains all of the specialized instructions that allow the OS to control the device.

Each device manufacturer provides drivers for its own equipment. The major OSs often include device drivers for the most popular peripheral devices; however, those drivers were originally provided by the manufacturers. Manufacturers typically make their drivers available for download from their Web sites.

Network Management Software

Network management and utility software is typically used by network administrators and information systems personnel. Communication and management software includes:

- **Security utilities** are designed to prevent unauthorized network access, or prevent damage to an organization's information assets.

- **Management tools** are used to organize the network's structure, troubleshoot problems, and forecast the effects of design changes.

- **Remote access services** allow authorized off-site users to securely connect to the corporate LAN.

- **Backup and recovery utilities** allow an administrator to automatically run a complete system backup when the network is unused or lightly used, often in the middle of the night.

Activities

1. List at least three tasks performed by an OS.

    ____

    ____

    ____

2. A ______________ ______________ controls an item of add-on hardware.

3. How would you go about getting the latest version of a device driver for a 3Com 3C905 NIC?

    ____

    ____

4. For each task below, indicate whether computers are using peer-to-peer communication, master/slave communication, or client/server communication:

    a. Mary saves a file to Joe's hard disk.

        ____

    b. Frank retrieves information from the company's central database.

        ____

    c. A data entry clerk uses a dumb terminal to update records.

        ____

    d. You use a Web browser to visit your favorite Web site.

        ____

    e. In a small office, three users share the same printer.

        ____

    f. In a large office, the shared printer is attached to a computer on the network. Print jobs from all users are sent to that computer, which controls the printing.

        ____

Extended Activities

1. Go to **http://www.netcraft.com** and list the usage rates for the various Web server software programs.

   ____

   ____

2. On the Web, find information about Web clients (browsers) other than Microsoft's *Internet Explorer.* Summarize the features offered by each. If possible, download some of these competing products and try them.

   ____

   ____

Lesson 3—Network Topologies

The physical structure of a network, or its "topology," describes the physical arrangement of wires, connectors, and other devices that connect a group of communicating nodes. A network's topology has a powerful effect on its operation and efficiency.

A network topology is like a system of roads and highways. Over time, different types of road systems have been developed to meet various types of transportation needs. For example, the winding, interconnected streets of a suburban neighborhood are designed for low-speed travel between individual homes. In contrast, straight, wide superhighways provide high-speed travel between cities.

In a similar way, different network topologies have been developed to meet various communication needs. This lesson introduces the main topologies used in data networks. A single network may be based on only one of these topologies or combine several of them.

Objectives

At the end of this lesson you will be able to:

- Draw the following topologies: bus, star, ring, and mesh

- Describe how a signal travels in a bus topology

- Explain the difference between physical and logical topologies

Key Point

The Internet is a mesh topology.

Types of Networks

Before we discuss topologies, let us first introduce the terms that describe networks with regard to their size. The size of a network is measured by the number of devices or nodes that need to communicate, and where these nodes are in relation to each other. There are several different types of networks:

- LANs can range from a few nodes in a home office, to several hundred nodes in a corporation. However, a LAN is typically confined to a single building.

- Campus networks consist of LANs connected across multiple buildings, using transmission links owned by the company that owns the network.

- Metropolitan area networks (MANs) are formed by connecting LANs in several locations across a city or small region. The links between LANs are typically leased from companies that provide telephone and data services.

- Wide area networks (WANs) are essentially the same as MANs, but span longer distances. A WAN may include sites in the same country or multiple countries.

Bus Topology

Objective 3.10
Understand and be able to describe how common networking topologies are used: Bus

A bus topology is one of the simplest network designs and was the first topology used in LANs. A bus is a single electrical cable to which all devices in the network are connected (although the bus might be made up of many individual pieces of wire). This type of network structure is illustrated on the Bus Topology Diagram. The point where a device connects to the bus is called a "tap." Taps are made using different hardware and methods, depending on the type of cable used for the bus.

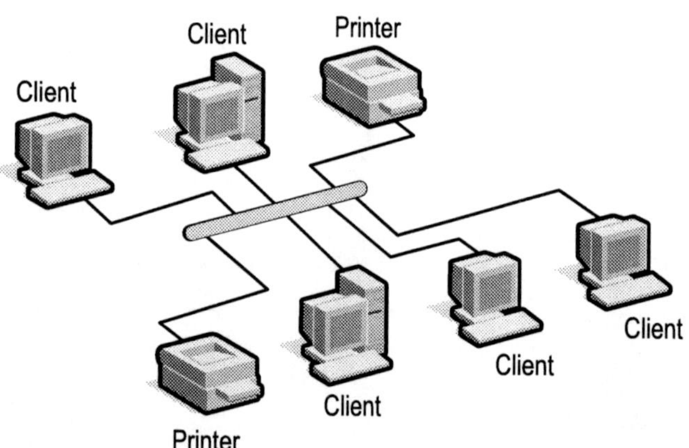

Bus Topology

When a node transmits data, the signal travels down the bus in both directions. Each node connected to the bus will receive the signal as it passes that connection point. However, a node will ignore any signal not specifically addressed to it. Because every node on the bus "hears" every message transmitted by any other node, a bus topology is considered a broadcast network.

When the signal reaches the end of the bus cable, a device called a "terminator" prevents the signal from reflecting back from the end of the wire. A terminator is an electrical resistor that essentially absorbs the signal energy. If a bus network is not terminated, or the terminator has the wrong level of resistance, each signal may travel across the bus several times instead of just once. This problem reduces network performance, because other nodes cannot transmit until the first signal dies down.

A bus topology is simple and easy to understand. However, if the bus cable breaks, the entire network may be disabled. In addition, it can be difficult to change the number and position of nodes on a bus network.

Star Topology

Objective 3.10
Understand and be able to describe how common network-ing topologies are used: Star

A star topology network is the most common type of LAN topology in use today. A star topology consists of multiple computers attached to a central signal-distributing device called a "hub." Each computer or other device is attached to the hub by a separate cable, as illustrated on the Star Topology Diagram.

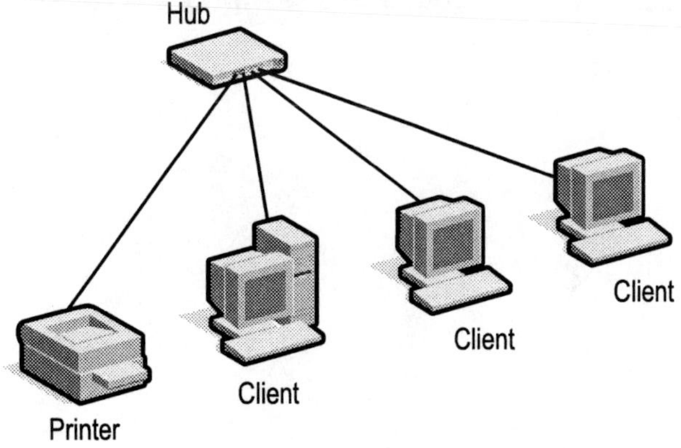

Star Topology

Like bus topology, a star topology is considered a broadcast network. When one computer transmits information to another computer, the signal first travels to the central hub device. The hub then copies the signal to all other computers attached to it. Thus, the hub performs the same function as the bus cable we just discussed. And, like a bus, the entire network may go down if the central hub fails.

However, star networks provide the following advantages over bus topologies:

- Some hubs have features that can detect defective cables and devices.

- Nodes are easily added and removed from a network.

- Network problems are easier to troubleshoot because suspect nodes can easily be disconnected from the hub.

Ring Topologies

Objective 3.10
Understand and be able to describe how common networking topologies are used: Ring

A ring topology is another commonly used topology in computer networks. There are two common ring topologies used in networks: ring and star ring.

Ring

A "pure" ring topology consists of nodes connected in a series of point-to-point links, just as people join hands in a circle. Each node attached to the ring has one input and one output connection, so that each node is connected to two links.

In many rings, when a node receives a signal on its input connection, it immediately passes it to the output connection. Thus, data flows only in one direction, as illustrated on the Ring Topology Diagram. Like nodes on a star or bus network, a ring node only copies signals addressed to it. Each node can send messages by putting new bits onto the ring.

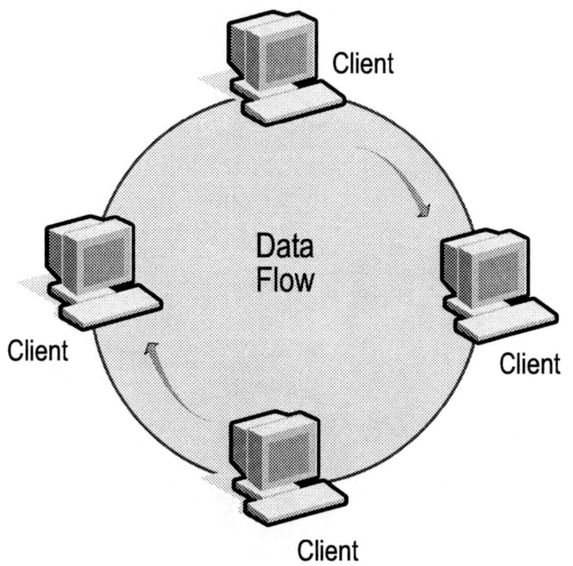

Ring Topology

If a ring node malfunctions or is shut down, it cannot repeat the signals it receives. In that case, the ring is broken, and data transfer stops until the failed node is restored or removed from the ring. The ring can also be broken if any cable between nodes is damaged or broken. To solve the problem of failed cables, some ring topologies incorporate a dual-ring structure. If one cable link fails, the other can immediately take over.

Star Ring

Objective 3.10
Understand and be able to describe how common networking topologies are used: Star, Ring

A star ring topology is built by combining ring and star topologies to obtain a reliable and serviceable configuration. A wire runs from each node to a central ring wiring hub, also called a multi-station access unit (MAU).

A star ring is a physical star configuration; however, information travels from node to node in a logical ring as the MAU copies each signal to each of its nodes in turn.

A star ring topology requires more wire than a pure ring or bus. However, the problems of a pure ring are solved because the MAU performs two important functions:

- It automatically detects when a node is not responding and bypasses it so that the ring can continue to operate, as shown on the MAU Bypassing a Node Diagram.

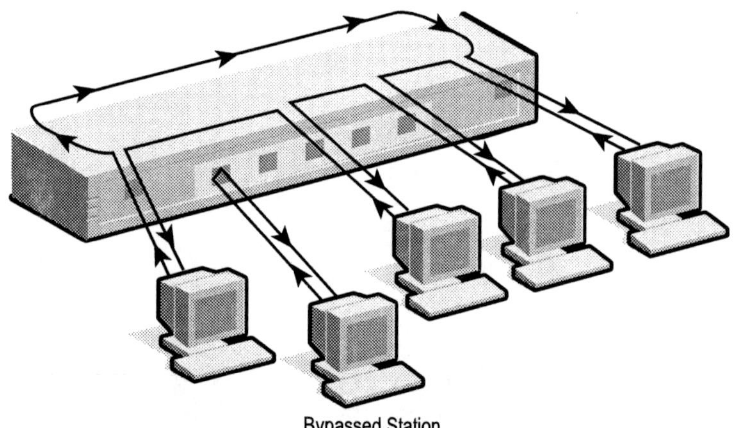

MAU Bypassing a Node

- It provides a "bridge" to other rings, sending information addressed to nodes on other rings across circuits to those rings, and accepting messages from other rings for its nodes. Rings joined in this manner effectively become a single ring. By connecting MAUs to each other, ring size is effectively unlimited, as shown on the Multiple MAUs in a Single Ring Diagram.

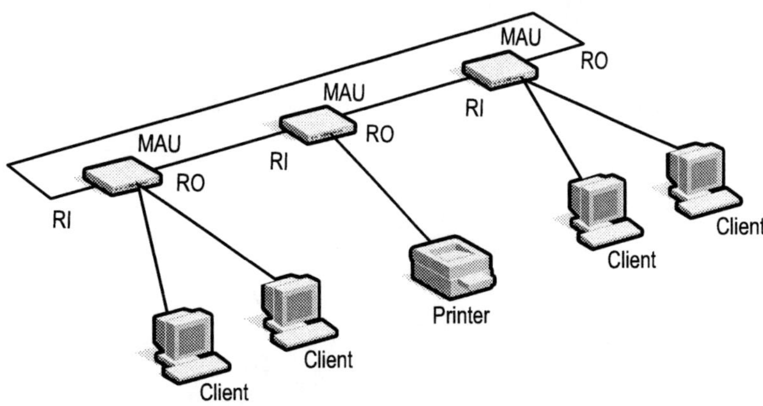

Multiple MAUs in a Single Ring

Each MAU receives a signal on its Ring In (RI) port. The MAU copies the signal to each of its nodes in turn, then sends the signal to its Ring Out (RO) port. The RO port of that MAU is attached to the RI port of the next MAU; thus, the signal continues around the ring.

Wide Area Topologies

As the number of interconnected LANs increases, some networks develop a wide area star topology, in which all branch offices connect to one central headquarters location. However, some organizations need each of their locations to be able to communicate directly with any other, without routing all communications through a central point. Two kinds of wide area topologies have been developed to meet this need: mesh and network cloud.

Mesh

In a mesh topology, point-to-point links directly connect every site to every other site. Mesh networks are usually built over time as new sites are added to the overall network. The Mesh Network Topology Diagram provides an example of a mesh configuration.

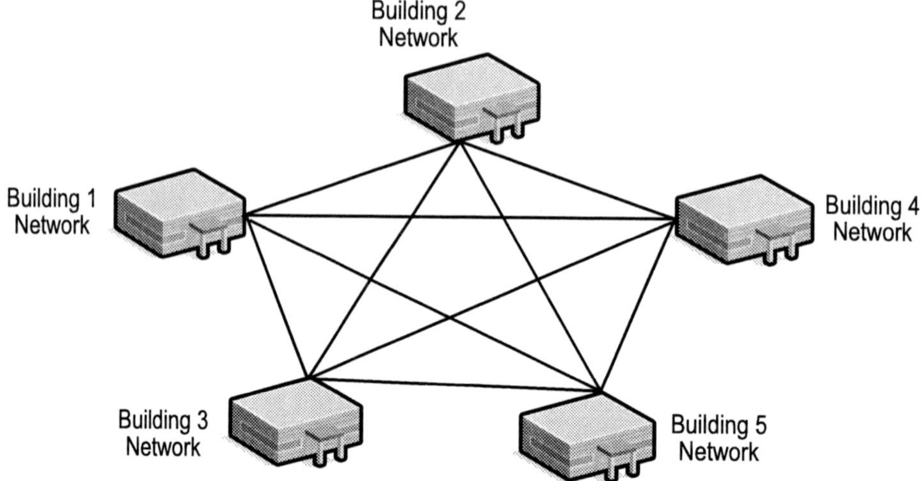

Mesh Network Topology

Mesh networks are fairly simple to understand. However, the number of point-to-point links increases sharply with the number of locations. For example, a three-site mesh network needs 3 links; however, four locations require 6 links, and five locations require 10 links. At that rate, it does not take long before the cost of a mesh network becomes too high.

Network Cloud

A network cloud, shown on the Network Cloud Diagram, is not really a topology. It is a representation of an unknown network structure, typically a transmission service offered by a networking service provider, such as a telephone company.

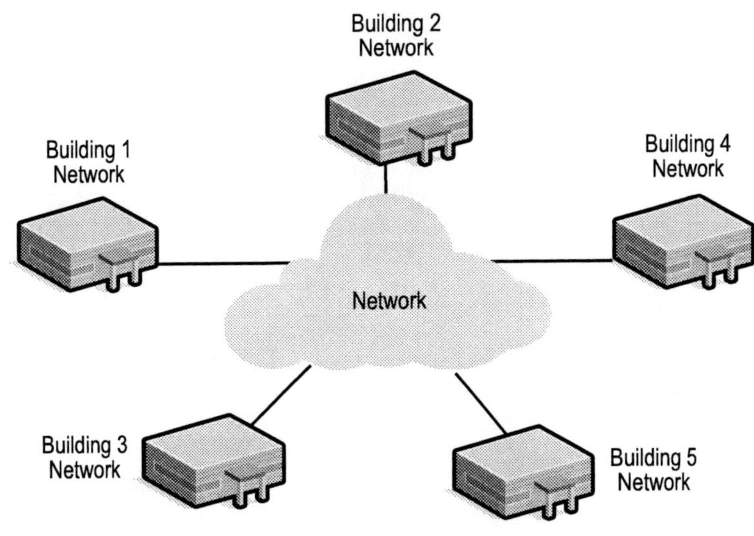

Network Cloud

The cloud symbol represents a private mesh network of switching devices that may span a city, region, or nation. The network is drawn as a cloud because users of the service do not have any knowledge about the internal workings of that network. The public telephone system and the Internet are two well-known examples of cloud networks.

To use the services of a cloud network, a company subscribes to the service, connects its locations to the edge of the cloud, and trusts the network to handle the details of moving each message across the network to its destination.

Advantages of Cloud Networks

Cloud networks offer several key advantages over mesh networks:

- Lower cost—A cloud network can connect many locations with fewer point-to-point links (each location links to the cloud, not to each other). Furthermore, a company must pay for a point-to-point connection even when it is not being used. Most cloud networks charge fees based on the amount of traffic they carry.

- Simplified network management—The cloud service provider, not the subscriber, is responsible for maintaining and upgrading the network's physical switching systems.

- Greater flexibility—With only a few telephone calls and a few slight adjustments to each site's network, a network manager can increase the network bandwidth or number of access points to the cloud.

Hybrid Topologies

A network that mixes two or more topologies is often called a "hybrid" topology. For example, several star LANs can be linked by a ring backbone or the Internet cloud.

Logical and Physical Topologies

There are two ways in which data networking professionals refer to topologies:

- Logical topologies show where signals go. They eliminate some details to make the important relationships easier to see.

- Physical topologies show details about a network's connectors, cabling, and wide area links.

Physical Star, Logical Bus

To understand this difference, think of bus and star topologies. Signals travel exactly the same way in both of these. But, though new broadcast networks almost always use the more flexible star topology, a broadcast network is usually diagrammed as a bus topology. Therefore, a physical star topology is logically the same as a bus, because the drawing of the bus makes it easy to see that all of the devices directly share signals among themselves. Thus, when you see a bus diagram in this book or any other network text, remember that you are probably looking at a hub-centered star network.

Physical Star, Logical Ring

Ring topologies provide another good example of the difference between physical and logical diagrams. Stations on a local area ring network are usually not connected directly to each other. Instead, they are all plugged in to a central MAU. Since the physical diagram of a ring network looks almost identical to that of a star broadcast network, it could be very easy to confuse these two networks. However, if we use logical diagrams, the difference between them is clear: Thus, when you see a LAN represented as a ring, remember that the devices are probably all connected to a central MAU.

Activities

1. On a bus network, each node relays the signal to the node next in line. The recipient node removes the signal from the bus. True or False?

2. On a ring network, a signal is relayed to each node in the ring in turn. True or False?

3. What topology does the Internet use?

____

____

____

____

4. For each of the following situations, what network topology is the most appropriate? Choose from star, ring, mesh, and cloud, and consider how the price of links may affect your decision. You may choose more than one option, if appropriate:

   a. In a small real estate office, four computers need to share a printer.

   b. The builder of a five-building office campus wants to link each building to the others, using a minimum of underground cable. The buildings will be leased to various tenants, thus no one building can be assumed to be the central headquarters.

   c. A fast food chain has 150 restaurants in a three-state area and wants to connect all of them to the headquarters office.

   d. A bank has three branch locations in one city. All three must link to each other and to a central interbank clearing house.

5. Represent a bus by drawing a horizontal line across the page. Draw four nodes connected to the line (bus), and label the Nodes A, B, C, and D.

   If Node B is transmitting data to Node C, circle the nodes that will receive the transmitted data.

6. What topology requires the least cable to connect 10 nodes?

   ____

   ____

7. What topology is more vulnerable to a cable break?

   ____

   ____

Extended Activities

1. In this lesson, we explained that the number of connections in a mesh network increases dramatically as the number of points in the network increases. For the following number of individual networks, determine the number of circuits for a point-to-point solution versus a switched solution in the Number of Circuits Comparison Table shown below. Each node is connected to all other nodes; however, with bidirectional links, each link should be counted only once (not twice).

   The formula for calculating the number of links is $N(N-1)/2$, where N is the number of linked sites.

   For example, 5 links would be $5(5-1)/2$ or 10; 10 links would be $10(10-1)/2$ or 45.

Number of Circuits Comparison

Number of Individual Networks	Point-to-Point Solution	Switched Solution
5	10	5
6		
7		
8		
9		
10		

2. Would a pure ring or star ring topology be easier to maintain and troubleshoot? Explain.

Lesson 4—Network Performance Concepts

When designing or reconfiguring a network, we take precise measurements of network performance and load. However, before we can start measuring, we must have some idea of what to look for. This lesson introduces and explains the major concepts and terms used to understand network performance.

The overriding concept of network analysis is the idea of a "bottleneck": a point, or combination of points, that restricts or reduces the flow of data.

The total performance of an Internet connection depends on the performance of all of its separate components: the server computer, the client computer, the leased lines or dial-up links that connect the server or client to the Internet cloud, or intermediate devices such as ISP routers. If any of these components becomes a bottleneck, then the performance of the connection will suffer. This lesson describes the factors that can cause a network component to become a bottleneck, and shows you what to look for when hunting for bottlenecks.

Objectives

At the end of this lesson you will be able to:

- Explain the difference between bandwidth and throughput

- Explain the relationship between device latency and network response time

- Describe various types of common network bottlenecks

**Key
Point**

An Internet connection is only as fast as its slowest component.

Response Time, Delay, and Latency

Response time, delay, and latency are interrelated terms. Each attribute has an impact on the performance of a network, and each is based on time. Instead of simply defining each term, it is helpful to also illustrate each concept with some examples.

Response time is the total time it takes to receive a response after a request for a service has been initiated. It is often used in reference to interactive terminals requesting information from a host computer. For example, response time is the time that passes between the moment a user presses the ENTER key and the moment a full screen of data is returned to that terminal. It is the time necessary for the user's request to travel through the network to a host, and for the host's response to travel back.

Response Time in a Master/Slave Configuration

The Response Time Components (Traditional IBM Network) Diagram illustrates typical response time components in a traditional IBM network. As you can see in the diagram, response time is the sum of the time necessary for data to pass through each component of a network. Each device, communication link, and process adds its own delay to the overall response time. Some of the most common factors in response time are described in the following subsections.

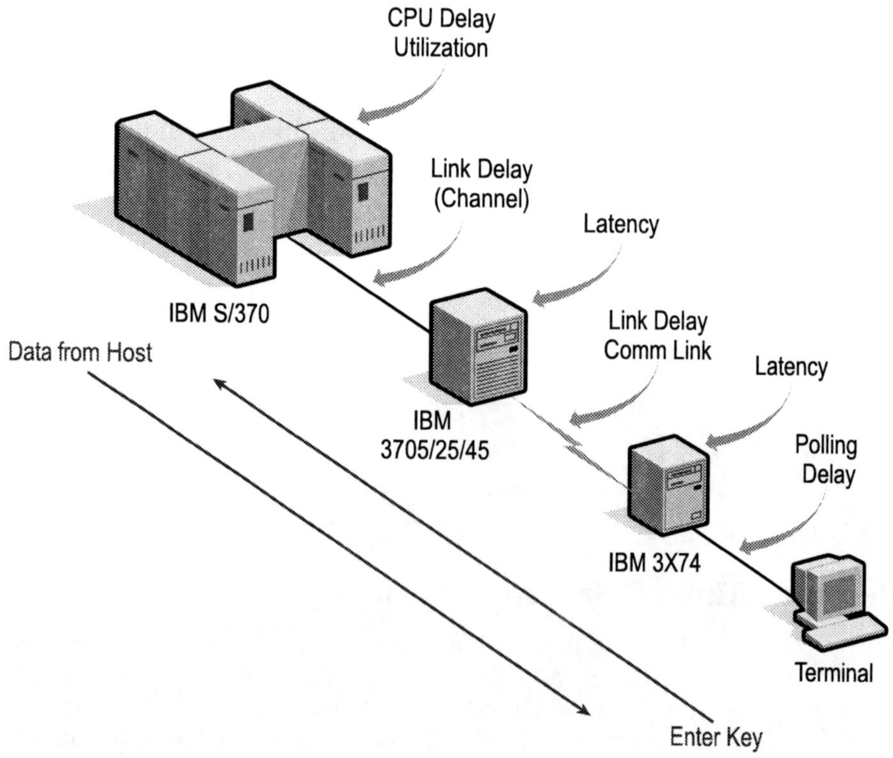

Response Time Components (Traditional IBM Network)

Polling Delay

Polling is a method used to control communication between a master and slave node in an unbalanced data communication configuration. If a slave device (dumb terminal) has data to send, it must wait until it is polled by the master device (upstream controller or host) before it can send data.

Link Delay

Link delay describes the speed at which data can be transferred across a communications link. The higher the link speed, the faster data can travel, and the lower the delay. Common link speeds in this traditional IBM network configuration are 9.6 to 64 Kbps.

Component Latency

Latency is the amount of time it takes a network device, such as a bridge or router, to analyze and retransmit a received packet. Devices that make simple forwarding decisions, such as switches or bridges, have lower latency than devices that perform complex processing, such as routers or gateways.

CPU Delay

Central processing unit (CPU) delay describes the time it takes the server CPU to process a request from the network. In general, the busier the CPU is, the longer it will take to process the request.

Response Time in a Client/Server Configuration

Objective 1.1
Identify the issues that affect Internet site functionality ... Bandwidth (both client and server) ... Internet connection types (both client and server)

Objective 3.9
Understand when to use various site monitoring procedures. ... Monitoring network traffic. ...Monitoring server utilization. ...Monitoring server network bandwidth utilization

In a client/server network, response time is the amount of time it takes for a server to respond to a request from a client workstation. As you can see in the Client/Server Response Time Diagram, there are several factors that impact response time in this configuration, as presented in the following subsections.

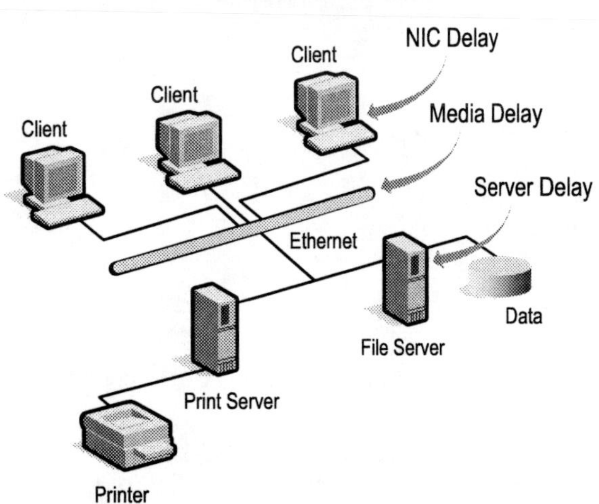

Client/Server Response Time

NIC Delay

Different types of NICs introduce various delays. After a client application requests network access, there is a delay while the client NIC processes the request and transmits the data over the physical medium.

Physical Media Delay

Response time also depends on the transmission speed of the particular LAN architecture. It will take longer for data to traverse a 4-Mbps Token Ring network than a 100-Mbps FDDI network. It will also take longer to transfer a file using small frame sizes versus larger frame sizes because of the amount of overhead (header and trailer) required for each frame.

Server Delay

Depending on the processor speed of the server and the average number of requests the server has to process, server response time may vary widely. Other factors in server delay are queue delays and disk access delays.

Public Network Delay

When request/response traffic travels over a public WAN, response times can vary drastically. For example, wide response time variations can occur when using the Internet, even to the point of losing connections because intermediate links "time out" and no longer stay in session. Network delays of this type are very hard to predict, and often vary according to the time of day (as overall Internet traffic increases or decreases). The Public Network Delay Diagram illustrates this concept.

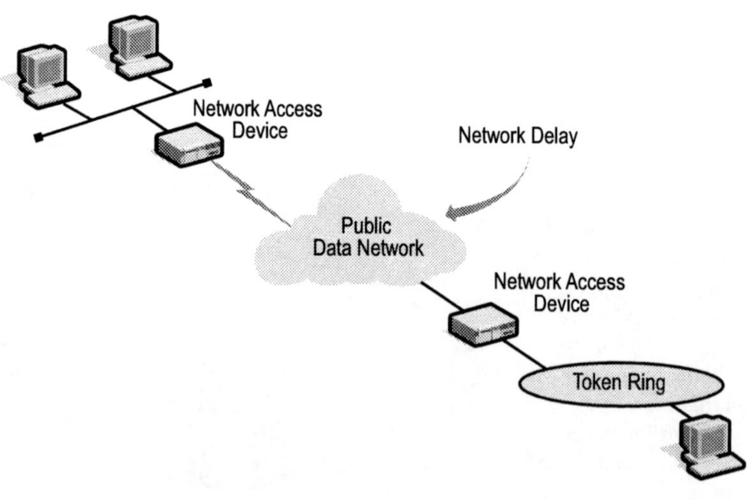

Public Network Delay

When analyzing response time, evaluate all network components to see how much delay or latency each one contributes. Long response times can be caused by one poorly performing component that is acting as a bottleneck in the network. Poor component performance, in turn, often occurs when a component is overutilized. Therefore, the next major traffic analysis concept to consider is utilization.

CPU Utilization

Objective 1.1
Identify the issues that affect Internet site functionality ... Bandwidth (both client and server)

Objective 3.9
Understand when to use various site monitoring procedures ... Monitoring network traffic ... Monitoring server utilization ... Monitoring server network bandwidth utilization

CPU utilization describes how busy a processor is as it processes requests and responses to and from a network. The processing capacity of a CPU, measured in thousands of cycles per second, is constant. If the incoming work requires a greater number of cycles than the CPU has available, some of the work must wait.

A networking component, such as a router, uses a certain number of CPU cycles to process each packet. If the number of packets consistently exceeds the router's CPU capacity, in other words, if the router's CPU utilization approaches 100 percent, the router is a network bottleneck.

In the Network Bottleneck Diagram, the router is being analyzed. Note the performance curve that shows the relationship between router CPU utilization and network performance. The curve clearly shows that as router CPU utilization increases past a certain point, the overall performance of the network degrades because the router is unable to process the incoming flow of packets in a timely fashion.

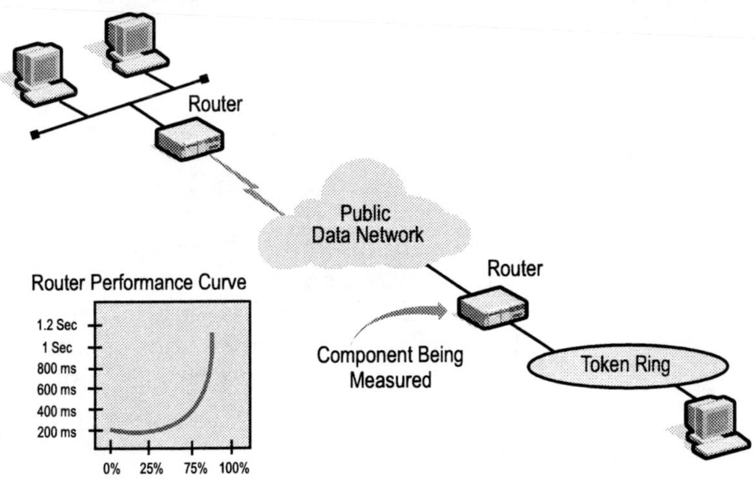

Network Bottleneck

The diagram shows that the router's effective maximum utilization is less than 100 percent. This is because the device must perform other work besides processing frames and packets. For example, routers exchange information to maintain their routing tables, and many routers maintain network management information and respond to network management commands. As routers become more complex and operate higher in the protocol stack, they must spend more of their CPU cycles on these "overhead" tasks. For example, a switch (operating at Layer 2) devotes fewer CPU cycles forwarding traffic than a protocol converter. This is due to the fact that a protocol converter operates at more layers than a switch and more CPU cycles are required to perform basic functions.

Link Utilization

Objective 1.1
Identify the issues that affect Internet site functionality ... Internet connection types (both client and server)

Objective 3.9
Understand when to use various site monitoring procedures
... Monitoring network traffic
... Monitoring server utilization
... Monitoring server network bandwidth utilization

Link utilization is the percentage of the link's total bandwidth that is used effectively. For example, a T1 line has 24 channels, with a maximum bandwidth of 64 Kbps per channel (64 Kbps x 24 = 1.536 Mbps, not including the overhead for signaling). If we only effectively utilize six channels of the 24 T1 channels available, the T1 line's utilization is 384 Kbps, or 25 percent of maximum bandwidth.

Capacity

Capacity typically describes the maximum data-carrying capability of a communications channel or link. For example, the capacity of a T1 channel is 64 Kbps. This does not mean the channel will always contain 64 Kbps of data; it is capable of carrying 64 Kbps of data, but no more. Capacity and bandwidth are often used interchangeably.

Bandwidth

Bandwidth is a measure of the information-carrying capacity of a channel or link. In analog networks, bandwidth is the difference between the highest and lowest frequencies that can be transmitted across a communication link. Analog networks measure bandwidth in cycles per second (Hz). Digital networks measure bandwidth in kilobits per second (Kbps), megabits per second (Mbps), and gigabits per second (Gbps).

A link becomes a network bottleneck when its utilization approaches 100 percent, when traffic volume approaches its capacity. This principle is clearly demonstrated twice each weekday on the highways of any fair-sized city (rush hour).

Throughput

Throughput describes the overall capacity of a network to perform useful work. While bandwidth measurements focus on the raw number of bits a network can carry, throughput measurements express the actual or effective data rates of a network.

Throughput is most often used to describe the overall performance of a network, as illustrated on the Throughput Example Diagram. One measure of effective throughput is throughput rate in information bits (TRIB), typically measured in packets per second (PPS), characters per second (CPS), transactions per second (TPS), or transactions per hour (TPH).

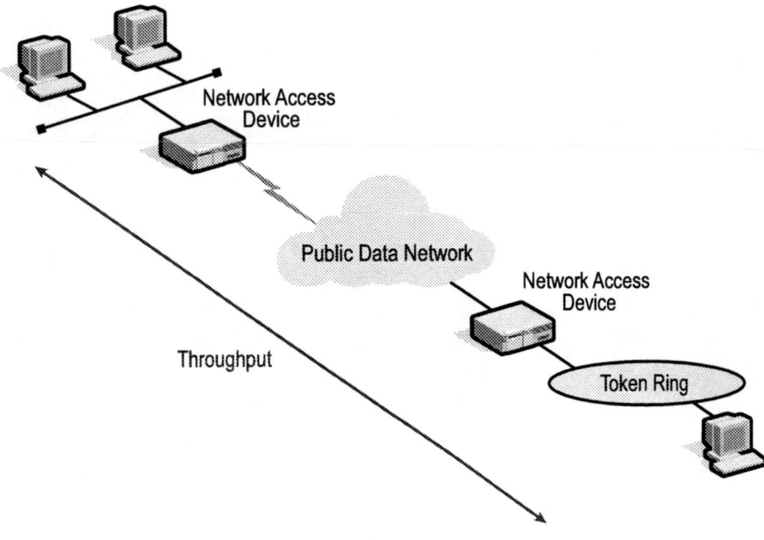

Throughput Example

Of these, TPS and TPH are the most widely used measures of throughput. For example, the same throughput measurement can be expressed as 2 TPS or 7,200 TPH (2 TPS * 600 seconds/hour). PPS is also widely used to express router throughput.

Knowing the TPH is not enough to get a good handle on overall performance; you must also know the average size of each transaction and the TPH relative to the time of day. The Throughput Analysis Diagram shows different measurements of throughput for a given network, and the relationship between packet size and throughput.

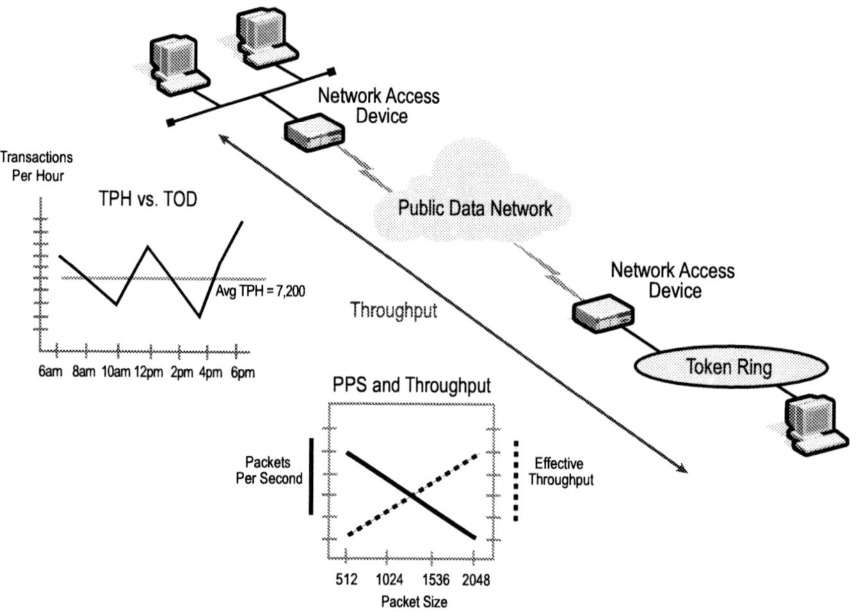

Throughput Analysis

Throughput is affected by all of the delay, latency, and utilization factors we discussed earlier. In addition to those, protocol efficiency influences throughput because some protocols transmit information more efficiently than others. Therefore, effective throughput and response time are directly related, and the terms are often used interchangeably. The higher the effective throughput, the better the response time.

Activities

1. _______________________ describes how busy a processor is.

2. The transmission speed across a cable is characterized by the term _______________________.

3. Describe component latency.

   ____

   ____

4. How are the terms CPU delay and CPU utilization related?

   ____

   ____

5. Describe response time.

   ____

   ____

6. If the capacity of each channel of a T1 line is 64 Kbps, what is the total bandwidth of the line?

   ____

   ____

Extended Activity

Break into focus groups of no more than three to five people, depending on class size. A designated group member will take a piece of 8 1/2" by 11" paper and tear/cut it into approximately 12 pieces. Write a different term from this lesson, such as "CPU delay," on each piece of paper. Fold each piece so that the word or phrase cannot be seen. Put all the pieces in a pile on a table or other convenient place and have each group member draw a piece of paper and describe the term to the other group members.

Lesson 5—Review of the OSI Model

The OSI reference model describes a theoretical protocol stack that consists of seven layers of services and protocols. At the bottom, the concrete Physical Layer contains protocols that transmit bits over physical media. At the top, the abstract Application Layer contains programs such as electronic mail (e-mail).

The OSI model is not a protocol, but an abstract structure that describes the functions and interactions of various data communication protocols. It provides a conceptual framework that helps us discuss and compare network functions and components.

Objectives

At the end of this lesson you will be able to:

- Describe the primary function of each layer of the OSI model

- Name some of the key protocols that operate at each layer

- Explain the difference between addresses used by the Data Link Layer and the Network Layer

 **Key Point**

Each layer of the OSI model uses the services of the layer below it and provides services to the layer above.

Programs, Processes, and Protocols

The term "program," or "application," means a complete set of routines that provide a high-level function of some sort. For example, a word processing application performs the general task of creating documents. However, that broad task is composed of many subprocesses, such as opening files, saving files, copying and pasting text, or deleting data. Therefore, we use the term "process" instead of "program" to refer to some subset of functions (still possibly quite complex) that fits into a larger program or is part of a large system.

This distinction is important because some processes within a program are designed to communicate and cooperate with other processes over a network. The term process is used especially when talking about a program when it is executing (in operating systems [OSs], an executing program is a process).

Protocols

A protocol is a set of communication rules that give meaning to the signals exchanged by two nodes. Two devices or processes can exchange information when they both use the same protocol. Each type of process may use a different protocol, even when multiple processes are running on the same computing device.

A communication protocol typically adds "administrative" data to the beginning of a message. That nonmessage data is called a protocol header. A protocol header functions like an envelope or a packing label to describe the content of a message, its length, the identity of its sender or recipient, the time of day it was sent, and any other information that the communicating processes need to know about the message itself.

Layers of Protocols and Services

Each program or process provides a service to the end user or to another program or process. For example, a World Wide Web (Web) browser provides a service to the user by retrieving Web pages from a Web server, then displaying them on the user's monitor.

Many different protocols may need to cooperate to provide a single service to a user. For example, when a Web server sends data to a Web browser, it uses Hypertext Transfer Protocol (HTTP) in conjunction with Transmission Control Protocol (TCP) and Internet Protocol (IP). Each of these protocols is a separate entity with its own specific functions. They provide services to each other, not directly to the end user. IP provides a service to TCP, TCP provides a service to HTTP, and so forth. The service relationships are often described as the underlying services, as presented on the Layers and Services Diagram.

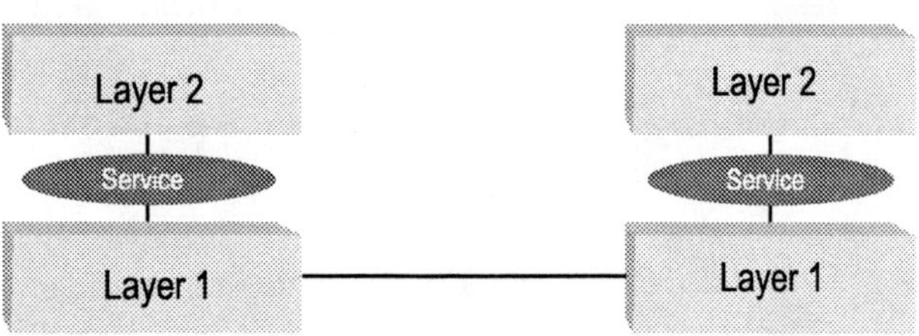

Layers and Services

Review of Network
Fundamentals

These interactions between processes and protocols form a layered hierarchy or protocol stack. In a protocol stack, each process uses the service of the process in the layer below it, and provides a service to a process in the layer above it.

Benefits of Layering

Because a program provides services only to the layer above it and uses services only of the layer below it, a change to any given layer affects only the layer above it. Layering breaks a single large program into parts isolated from one another according to function, making the program easier to write and change. Layering does, however, extract a performance penalty. There is some overhead associated with moving data through multiple layers of protocols; however, the benefit is generally worth the performance price.

Peer Protocols

Layering applies to protocols as well as services. In a system that has a layered architecture, each process communicates only with its peer process. Otherwise, as with services, a change to one process would affect many other processes.

Each pair of peers communicates with a common protocol that is appropriate to the services they provide. Therefore, each layer of processes uses a corresponding layer of protocols.

For example, in a Web interaction, Transmission Control Protocol (TCP) on the client communicates with TCP on the server. Hypertext Transfer Protocol (HTTP) on the client communicates with HTTP on the server, and so forth.

Basic Protocol Operations

When different layers of protocols work together, they use the following basic techniques:

- Encapsulation—On the sending node, each protocol adds its own header to a message as it moves downward through the stack. Each header contains information that is useful to the receiving process. Thus, peer processes communicate through their respective protocol headers.

- Segmentation—If a layer receives a message that is too long, it divides the message into manageable fragments.

- Decapsulation—On the receiving node, each protocol removes its own protocol header before passing the encapsulated message up to the layer above.

- Reassembly—If a message was segmented, one of the processes on the receiving end reassembles the segments into their correct order, then passes the restored message up to the layer above.

Primary Functions of OSI Model Layers

Each layer of the OSI model describes the services that a protocol provides, but it does not specify exactly how a protocol must do that. For example, several different protocols provide the functions of OSI Layer 3 (the Network Layer), and a developer can create a new one at any time.

The OSI Model Layers Table provides an overview of the primary functions of each layer of the OSI model. It also presents the unit of information and address type where appropriate.

OSI Model Layers

OSI Model Layer	Layer Function	Unit of Information	Address Type
Application	User functionality	Program	
Presentation	Character representation Data compression Security	Characters and words	
Session	Establishing, conducting, and ending sessions		
Transport	Transmitting messages from sending computer process to receiving computer process	Message	Process to process between applications
Network	Transmitting individual packets across a network	Packet	Packet address identifying receiver's network and host location
Data Link	Transmitting frames containing packets across a link en route to final destination	Frame	NIC (next node in network)
Physical	Transmitting bits in the form of signals across physical media	Bit	

Physical Layer

The Physical Layer provides the service of transmitting a signal, across a physical communication medium, that represents binary bits. That medium can be a copper cable (coaxial or twisted pair), a fiber optic cable, or a radio channel. Thus, the Physical Layer includes the following types of hardware devices that send and receive signals over each type of physical medium:

- NICs
- Fiber optic transceivers
- Radio transceivers
- Modems

Physical Layer processes are concerned only with the physical signals that represent data bits. Thus, they are only "aware" of signals over the medium, and are not concerned with any device that may be at the other end of the wire or channel. This also means that Layer 1 processes cannot detect errors in data transmission. Most error detection, and all error correction, are the responsibility of higher layers.

Data Link Layer

The Data Link Layer addresses groups of bits to a device located across a single physical transmission path, called a link. Each group of bits that the Data Link Layer transmits is called a frame.

To form a frame, a network interface card (NIC) encapsulates a Network Layer packet within a header and trailer. The NIC then transmits the frame onto the network medium. The header contains the destination node's hardware address, also called its NIC address, physical address, or Data Link address. This address is unique, and built into each NIC by its manufacturer.

The trailer contains a Frame Check Sequence (FCS) value that the receiving node uses for error detection. The Data Link Layer is the only OSI layer that adds a trailer to the data it transmits.

Each frame carries a packet of data across a single physical link. The encapsulated packet does not change, but a new frame is built around the packet for the trip across each link. Thus, we often say that the Data Link Layer is concerned with transmitting data to the next node in the network.

Popular Data Link protocols include:

- LAN protocols such as Ethernet, Token Ring, and FDDI

- WAN protocols such as frame relay, ATM, and ISDN

- High-Level Data Link Control (HDLC)

- Synchronous Data Link Control (SDLC)

- Link Access Procedure for D channel (LAPD), used in ISDN

Network Layer

The Network Layer is responsible for transmitting data packets between source and destination nodes that may not be connected by the same physical link. The Network Layer addresses a data packet to the logical description of a computer that may be located several links away from the source. If the source and destination nodes are not directly connected, then the Network Layer must use intermediate nodes, when necessary, to get a packet to its destination.

Unlike a Data Link address (NIC address), which is globally unique, a Network Layer address is a logical identifier that is only unique within a single network. If a packet's source and destination are in different networks, the Network Layer may have to resolve different addressing conventions and duplicated node addresses used in different types and versions of networks.

The Network Layer also moves packets to and from node types that may use different Data Link protocols. For example, when a router forwards a packet from an Ethernet LAN to a frame relay network, it removes the Ethernet header and trailer and builds a new frame formatted for the frame relay network.

Common Network Layer protocols include:

- X.25—X.25 is an older packet switching protocol that has been largely replaced by faster protocols based on the same basic approach.

- Internet Protocol (IP)—IP is the primary Layer 3 protocol used across the Internet and in many LANs.

- Internetwork Packet Exchange (IPX)—IPX is Novell NetWare's proprietary Network Layer protocol.

Transport Layer

The Transport Layer, or Layer 4, addresses data to a particular process running on a destination computer. Peer software processes at either end of a connection use the Transport Layer to carry on a conversation. Processes in the Transport Layer act as if their nodes are adjacent. They rely on lower layers to handle the details of passing data through intermediate nodes across the network. Thus, Layer 4 insulates the higher levels from all concerns about the transportation of data.

Basic services provided by the Transport Layer include:

- Addressing

- Connection management

- Flow control and buffering

- Multiplexing and parallelization

- Reliable and sequenced delivery

- Service quality management

The most common Transport Layer protocols are:

- Transmission Control Protocol (TCP)—TCP works in conjunction with IP, in the widely used TCP/IP protocol stack.

- Sequenced Packet Exchange (SPX)—SPX is Novell NetWare's Transport Layer protocol. It works in conjunction with IPX.

Upper Layers: Session, Presentation, and Application

The job of the upper layers, taken collectively, is to provide user-oriented services through a set of widely available standard applications, and through specialized applications written for the users by programmers. The Session Layer, and the Presentation Layer above it, provide reusable services for the applications that reside in the Application Layer.

The Session Layer facilitates a step-by-step interaction between two entities. It establishes the session, manages the dialog to prevent simultaneous transmission, and ends the session gracefully. A single session may continue across one or more connections. Similarly, a single connection may support one or more sessions.

The Presentation Layer deals with the format, or representation, of computer information. It resolves differences between different types of character encoding systems, such as Extended Binary Coded Decimal Interchange Code (EBCDIC) and the American Standard Code for Information Interchange (ASCII) character code. It provides security by encrypting and decrypting data. It also compresses data before transmitting it, to use the communication channel more efficiently.

The Application Layer contains programs that invoke the underlying services of the network. Some of these applications are written specifically for one network, while others are widely used standard applications. When these applications need to communicate with peers over the network, they can use their own protocols, plus the services of the lower layers.

Application Layer programs include:

- User applications, such as e-mail or file transfer, provide standard services directly to the user. Each of these applications has its own standard protocol at the Application Layer level.

- Application services, such as virtual filestores, provide services to other applications, but not directly to the user. These facilities simplify application development by allowing programmers to use a common service rather than duplicating the same features in every application.

Logical and Physical Addresses

Each protocol may use a different type of address to direct a message to the correct process on the intended destination device. These addresses fall into two general categories:

- Physical address
- Logical address

Physical Addresses

A physical address is a unique identifier hard-coded into the NIC of each node. Its other common names are:

- Hardware address
- NIC (or adapter) address
- Medium Access Control (MAC) address
- Data Link address

Each NIC comes with a 48-bit hardware address preconfigured from the factory. NIC manufacturers register hardware addresses with a worldwide central authority to guarantee the numbers they assign do not conflict with those of any other manufacturer. This hardware address is the address ultimately required for frames to be delivered to a destination network node.

Logical Addresses

Logical addresses are symbolic identifiers. These are assigned by software and are used by processes operating at OSI Layer 3 and above. There are two primary types of logical addresses:

- Network addresses, such as an IP address (144.25.54.8)

- Port or process addresses, such as a port number (Port 23)

Data often starts out (at the higher layers) addressed to some symbolic name, such as the host name in the command Telnet Serverhost. The name "serverhost" is the logical address of the destination the user is attempting to contact using the telnet (TCP/IP) application and protocol. But if the message is actually to be delivered to this host, the sending computer must somehow discover the destination's physical address. In this case, an intermediate logical address (the IP address) will first be derived from the symbolic name using some sort of a name service process, such as Domain Name System (DNS). Then a protocol such as Address Resolution Protocol (ARP) can find the hardware address that corresponds to that IP address. When the sending node knows all of these addresses, it can finally transmit the data to its destination.

Activities

1. Name the OSI layers, and describe the purpose of each layer.

   ____

   ____

   ____

   ____

   ____

   ____

2. Name a Data Link Layer protocol.

   ____

   ____

3. Name a Network Layer protocol.

   ____

   ____

4. Name a Transport Layer protocol.

   ____

   ____

5. On a sending computer, each layer of protocols adds its own header to a message. This process is called:

   ____

6. Is an IP address a physical or a logical address?

   ____

Extended Activities

1. On a Windows PC that is part of a LAN, open the Control Panel. Select Network (on Windows 98) or Network and Dial-Up Connections (on Windows 2000). Select your LAN connection, then choose Properties.

   View the properties of each of your installed network components, and write down as much information as you can find about the network configuration of this computer (do not make any changes). Arrange these notes according to the OSI model.

2. The terms processes, programs, layers, and protocols can be challenging to keep separate and distinct. Break into focus groups of no more than three people and discuss with each other what these terms mean.

Lesson 6—Review of Internetworking Devices

Before we discuss the process of analyzing a network, it is helpful to briefly review the internetworking devices that control the way data travels through a network. This lesson summarizes the most important features, advantages, and disadvantages of repeaters, hubs, bridges, switches, routers, and gateways (protocol converters).

Objectives

At the end of this lesson you will be able to:

- Draw a diagram of the Open Systems Interconnection (OSI) model, and show where each device fits into the model

- Summarize the functions of repeaters, hubs, bridges, switches, routers, and gateways

Key Point

A few types of devices can be combined to create a nearly endless variety of internetworking solutions.

Repeaters

Objective 3.7
Create a logic diagram of Internet components from the client to the server. ... Repeater

Repeaters, working at the Physical Layer, are the simplest type of internetworking device. Repeaters receive a signal (bits) on a local area network (LAN) segment and regenerate the bit pattern to boost the signal and extend the physical length of the segment.

Because a repeater operates at the Physical Layer of the OSI model, as illustrated on the Repeater and OSI Model Diagram, the job of a repeater is to repeat bits. If a "1" bit is received on the input port of a repeater, a "1" bit is regenerated, with a stronger signal, at the output of the repeater. If a "0" bit is received on the input port of a repeater, a "0" bit is regenerated at the output of the repeater. A repeater is considered a "nondiscriminating" device, because all incoming signals are passed on to each connected segment. These devices are also transparent to the sending and receiving (end) devices.

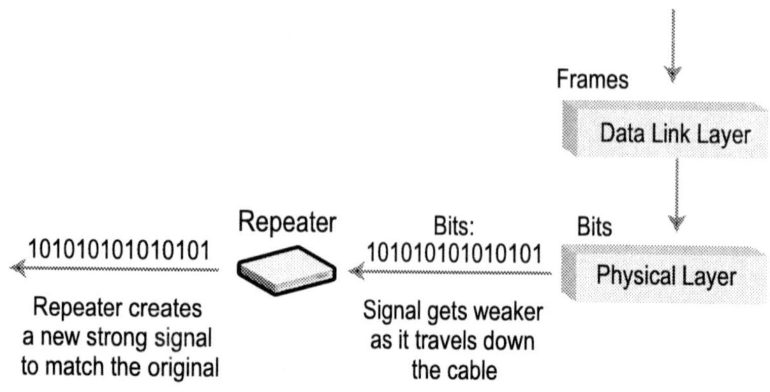

Repeater and OSI Model

Because a repeater reproduces exactly what it receives, bit by bit, it can reproduce errors. However, repeaters are very fast and cause very little delay.

Repeater Advantages

There are several advantages to using repeaters as follows:

- A repeater can connect one segment of a LAN to another, possibly connecting different types of media. For example, a repeater can connect Thinnet Ethernet cables to unshielded twisted pair (UTP) Ethernet cables.

- Repeaters are fast, simple to use, and inexpensive.

- Repeaters can be used to attach "link segments" to extend the overall distance of a network, subject to the Ethernet "5/4/3 rule." This rule states that there can be a maximum of five segments connected by four repeaters with a maximum of three segments containing network nodes.

Repeater Disadvantages

Disadvantages to using repeaters are listed below:

- Because it is only a signal-boosting device, working at the Physical Layer, a repeater cannot connect two different Data Link protocols such as Token Ring and Ethernet. It cannot recognize the contents or format of a frame, or convert one type of Data Link header to another.

- As internetworking devices for Ethernet LANs, repeaters are feasible only for relatively small LANs (less than 100 nodes), confined to a small geographical area such as one or two floors of an office building. A repeater should not be used to connect heavily used LANs, because it cannot isolate traffic between LAN segments. Because each bit is copied to the attached segments, all data passes through a repeater in both directions. Therefore, if we connect multiple LAN segments using a repeater, we may experience performance problems, because total network traffic will increase.

- The Ethernet specification allows no more than four repeater regenerations of a signal. This may constrain large topologies.

When to Use Repeaters

Objective 3.8
Describe various hardware and software connection devices and when to use them.
...Repeater

The main function of a repeater is to extend the physical distance of a LAN segment. Repeaters are not normally used to add more devices to a network, only to extend the distance a workstation or group of workstations can be located from other parts of a network.

Hubs

Objective 3.7
Create a logic diagram of Internet components from the client to the server. ... Hub

Hubs are Physical Layer devices that logically function as a shared bus, or a multiport repeater. All devices connected to a hub belong to the same collision domain, because every device connected to a hub receives frames transmitted by any other device on that hub. They are mainly a convenient way to implement multiple repeaters on twisted pair cable.

Hub Advantages

Using hubs offers several advantages as follows:

- Hubs are inexpensive, and can be used very widely to connect individual devices. Hubs create a simple star topology in which all cables run into the hub. Problems can be solved in the wiring closet, which saves time chasing after cabling problems or changing wiring patterns.

- A network can be designed so that all traffic flows through one or more hubs. This makes it easier to manage traffic flow, avoid bottlenecks, and provide security.

- The technologies that can be included in a high-performance hub seem almost limitless, and most hubs support multiple LAN and wide area network (WAN) protocols. Although this might seem to complicate matters, most network administrators prefer to manage multiple technologies in a single box, rather than in a nonintegrated network.

- As a network grows and more hub ports are needed to connect additional nodes or a server, it is simple to add additional hubs. Many hubs allow one of the hub ports to be used to connect a device or another hub. A switch is normally mounted under this uplink port, to enable either device connectivity or hub connectivity. The Ethernet Hub-to-Hub Connectivity Diagram illustrates this principle.

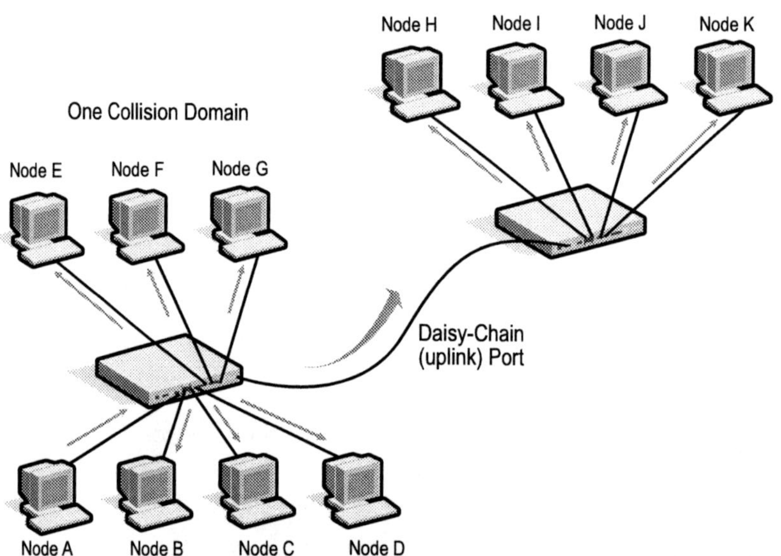

Ethernet Hub-to-Hub Connectivity

In this diagram, the hub port that was attached to Node H is now attached to the new hub. Node H now resides on the second Ethernet hub. This new configuration still represents a single collision domain. If a frame is generated from Node A to the hub, the hub will repeat the frame out each port. This includes the uplink port that attaches the first hub to the second hub. The second hub will then take this frame and repeat it out each of its ports as well. This is the basic operation of a broadcast network.

Hub Disadvantages

Some disadvantage of hubs are listed below:

- As the center of a star topology, a faulty central hub can cause the entire LAN to fail, or break the network into isolated sections. This failure can also happen if power to the hub is lost.

- The Ethernet specification allows no more than four repeater regenerations of a signal. A hub is a multiple-port repeater, so it automatically counts as the first regeneration. This may constrain large topologies.

- A network connected by simple hubs is one large collision domain. As more users share the same collision domain, performance gradually decreases until it is unacceptable. In other words, the bandwidth shared by all devices in the broadcast network will no longer be adequate. When this happens, Ethernet switches are often used to increase performance.

When to Use Hubs

Objective 3.8
Describe various hardware and software connection devices and when to use them. … Hub

Hubs can be implemented in a variety of situations. Floor-level deployment is when a simple wiring concentrator hub is used to link LAN devices scattered around a single office floor. A stackable hub may provide the most cost-effective solution while still allowing for growth.

Building-level deployment incorporates hubs that can connect workgroup LANs across multiple floors, and interconnect those LANs to a high-speed fiber backbone. These hubs should offer bridge and fiber plug-in modules, as well as areas for expansion.

Bridges

Objective 3.1
Understand and be able to describe the core components of the Internet infrastructure … Bridges

Objective 3.7
Create a logic diagram of Internet components from the client to the server. … Bridge

Bridges operate at the OSI Data Link Layer. They listen to all traffic on their connected network segments, examine each destination network interface card (NIC) address, and use an internal table of addresses to decide whether to forward a frame to the rest of the network.

Bridge Advantages

There are several advantages to using bridges:

- One of the primary benefits of a bridge is to isolate traffic between LAN segments that have nodes that only occasionally send traffic across the bridge. Bridges divide a network into separate collision domains, because they use NIC addresses to filter or forward traffic between different network segments. This segmentation provides a larger share of the available bandwidth to each end station in each smaller collision domain. For example, a bridge could isolate the traffic of diverse departments such as engineering and accounting, giving each department more effective bandwidth.

- Bridges are simple to install. To use advanced bridging features, such as custom filters, a minimal amount of configuration is required. The presence of a bridge is transparent to users from the instant it is installed, and bridges adapt automatically to network changes. Bridge-based internetworks can be modified and reconfigured very easily.

- Bridges can connect networks running different high-level protocols, without requiring additional software. They operate at the Data Link Layer of the OSI model; network managers do not need to know in advance which high-level protocols will be used.

- Some protocols are simply unroutable, such as Digital Equipment Corporation's (DEC's) Local Area Transport (DEC-LAT) terminal communications protocol, IBM's Systems Network Architecture (SNA), and network basic input/output system (NetBIOS)/NetBios Enhanced User Interface (NetBEUI). Unroutable protocols must be bridged.

- Bridges form logically single networks. All interconnected network segments have the same network identifier; we can move end stations without configuring new network addresses for them.

- When traffic on a LAN starts to cause performance problems, bridges allow us to reduce the load by segmenting the network, reducing the number of nodes in each collision domain. Bridges can also control traffic between segments and the network backbone.

- Bridges can connect two different LAN technologies, such as Ethernet and Token Ring. These translating bridges convert frames from one format to another.

Bridge Disadvantages

Several disadvantages of using bridges are presented below:

- There is a limit to the size of bridge-based networks. Each time a frame traverses a bridge it is delayed as the bridge software reads the source and destination addresses, checks its address database, and determines whether to forward the frame to each port. If the frame crosses many bridges, this frame latency may cause the destination station to time out and request retransmission. This would result in an unnecessary duplication of frame transmissions. As the network grows, so must the bridge's address table. This would also increase the delay of frames traversing the bridge.

- While network segments attached to a bridge belong to different collision domains, they all belong to the same broadcast domain. This is because bridges allow broadcast frames to flood the network. Bridges themselves also create broadcast traffic that congests the network, as they attempt to resolve unknown destination NIC addresses.

- Bridges cannot prevent broadcast storms that may occur when certain broadcast protocols cause frames to be flooded to every port. If there is a malfunction or an incorrectly configured parameter, these traffic spikes can be severe enough to disable the entire network.

- Bridges cannot take simultaneous advantage of redundant paths in a network. They cannot load-split over network segments.

- Bridges do not provide significant support for fault isolation or other distributed network management capabilities. Networks become harder to manage and maintain as their size and complexity increase. Because bridges form a single logical network, fault isolation in very large bridged networks may become extremely difficult. Bridge-based internetworks may require extra attention from network administrators to track what is running on the network and where.

- Bridges cannot convert protocols above the Data Link Layer.

When to Use Bridges

Objective 3.8
Describe various hardware and software connection devices and when to use them. ... Bridge

Bridges should be used to control segment or workgroup access to the backbone, because an overloaded backbone puts all organizational communications in danger. If we connect only internetworking devices and a few large servers directly to the backbone, we will reduce the number of application, hardware, and other errors that affect the backbone.

Another important use of bridges is to connect LANs across wide area links. A pair of WAN bridges (also called half-bridges) cooperate to route frames across a point-to-point link, using a protocol such as Synchronous Data Link Control (SDLC) or High-Level Data Link Control (HDLC), or across the public network using X.25. However, if the line speed of the wide area link is too slow (for example, a 56 kilobits per second [Kbps] link), applications on the end stations may time out, causing unnecessary retransmission of frames. In addition, the bridge's spanning tree algorithm (STA) will disable one or more wide area links if it detects active loops in the WAN.

Switches

Objective 3.1
Understand and be able to describe the core components of the Internet infrastructure ... Switches

Objective 3.7
Create a logic diagram of Internet components from the client to the server. ... Switch

A switch is a device that consists of many high-speed ports connecting either LAN segments or individual devices on a port-by-port basis. Many types of switches exist, each supporting different speeds and LAN types such as Ethernet, Token Ring, Fiber Distributed Data Interface (FDDI), and Asynchronous Transfer Mode (ATM). Unlike a bridge, which shares the LAN bandwidth among all of its ports, a switch dedicates the entire LAN media bandwidth (such as 10-Mbps Ethernet) to each port-to-port frame transmission. In this way, a switch multiplies the amount of effective network bandwidth.

When a switch connects several LAN segments as shown on the Ethernet Switch Diagram, it is considered a segment-switching device. When a frame sent by Node A is destined for Node E, the switch routes the frame between Port 1 and Port 3. In this case, Port 2 and Port 4 will still be free to send frames at a full 10 Mbps rate. If Node A sends a frame to Node B, the switch restricts the frame to the individual segment that contains both Node A and Node B. Switches therefore maximize overall network bandwidth by creating virtual circuits on a per frame basis.

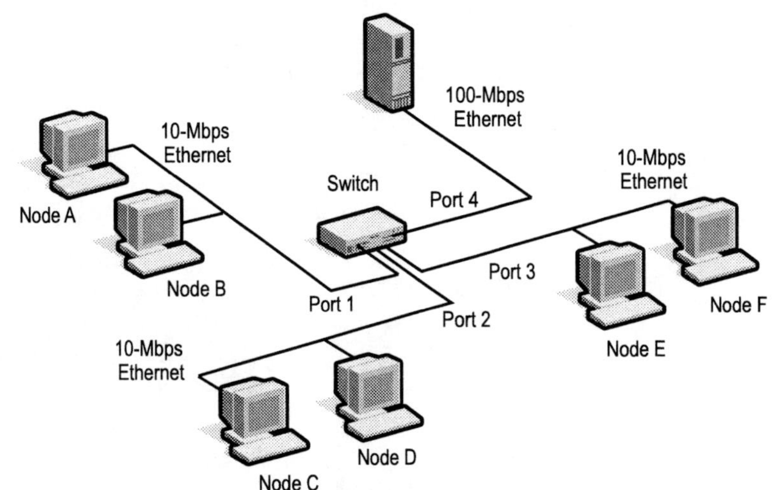

Ethernet Switch

Like a bridge, a switch makes a relatively simple forwarding decision based on the destination MAC address contained in each frame. The forwarding decision does not consider other information encapsulated in the frame. Unlike a bridge, a switch does more of its job in high-speed hardware, providing performance closer to single-LAN performance than bridged-LAN performance.

Switch Advantages

Switches offer several advantages as described below:

- Switches segment a network into smaller collision domains, providing a larger share of the available bandwidth to each end station. Their protocol transparency allows them to be installed in networks running multiple protocols with little or no software configuration.

- Switches also form logically single networks. Administrative overhead is very low for switches, simplifying adds, moves, and changes.

- Switches are totally transparent to end stations. They use existing cabling, repeaters/hubs, and end station adapters without expensive hardware upgrades.

- The use of Application-Specific Integrated Circuit (ASIC) technology allows a switch to provide greater performance at a lower cost per port than a traditional bridge. A switch can simultaneously forward frames at wire speed across multiple port pairs.

- Switching technology allows bandwidth to be scaled in both shared and dedicated LAN segments, and can alleviate traffic bottlenecks between LANs. Switching products are available for Ethernet, Fast Ethernet, FDDI, Token Ring, and ATM technologies.

- A switch provides a high level of performance for a significantly lower cost per port than a router. Router prices can be as high as 10 times the cost per port as an Ethernet switch. A switch is easier to configure, manage, and troubleshoot than a router, because more of a switch's functionality is built into hardware.

Switch Disadvantages

Switch disadvantages are described below:

- Network segments attached to a switch belong to different collision domains; however, they all belong to the same broadcast domain because switches allow broadcast frames to flood the network.

- Switches also create broadcast traffic that congests the network, as they attempt to discover unknown destination NIC addresses.

When to Use Switches

Objective 3.8

Describe various hardware and software connection devices and when to use them. ...Switch

A switch is a special-purpose device specifically designed to address LAN performance problems resulting from bandwidth shortages and network bottlenecks. A switch economically segments a network into smaller collision domains (in the case of Ethernet), providing a higher percentage of bandwidth to each end station.

Switches are not designed with the principal goal of providing control over a network. Switches should be viewed as bandwidth providers, not as sources of security, redundancy, control, or network management, although newer switching products can provide these functions.

Routers

Objective 3.1

Understand and be able to describe the core components of the Internet infrastructure ...Routers

Objective 3.7

Create a logic diagram of Internet components from the client to the server. ...Router

A router operates at the Network Layer of the OSI reference model, distinguishing between Network Layer protocols and making intelligent packet-forwarding decisions based on each packet's network address.

As Network Layer devices, routers are protocol dependent. They can interconnect networks that have the same communications architecture, but possibly different lower level architectures.

Routers are general-purpose devices that can segment a network into separate broadcast domains, and provide security, control, and redundancy between individual broadcast domains.

Routers use specialized routing protocols to maintain and exchange network path information in their internal routing tables. Depending on the protocol in use, these tables can allow routers to flexibly choose routing paths based on distance, speed, quality of service, or other factors.

A router can also provide firewall service and economical WAN access. Routers are essentially software devices. They process complex protocol suites, sometimes many suites, using powerful processors and memory. High-end routers are expensive, and it is too expensive to connect individual devices to them. Thus, high-end routers are used as backbone devices and interconnectivity devices.

Routers Rebuild Frames

As a packet traverses a network, it stays intact. However, routers remove and add frame headers and trailers as the data moves from one type of Data Link Layer protocol to another. For example, consider the network shown on the Routers and Data Links Diagram. Two Ethernet LANs are connected to a FDDI backbone with routers.

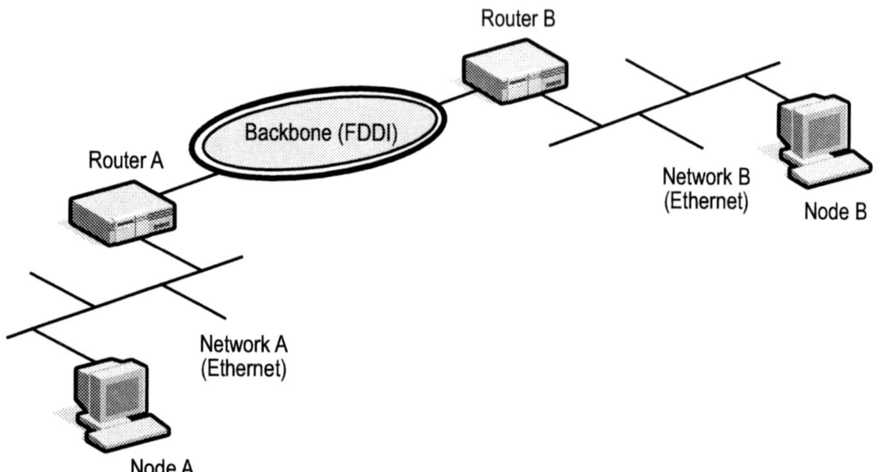

Routers and Data Links

If Node A sends data to Node B, the Node A IP process recognizes that the data is addressed to a distant network and must be forwarded by a router. Thus Node A encapsulates the IP packet (addressed to Node B) within an Ethernet frame addressed to its default router, Router A. Node A then transmits that frame, over the Ethernet network, to Router A.

Router A processes the frame because it is addressed to it. When it inspects the packet header, it sees that the packet is addressed to Network B. Thus Router A encapsulates the packet in a FDDI frame addressed to Router B, then transmits that frame over the FDDI ring.

Router B processes the frame because it is addressed to it. When it inspects the packet header, it sees that the packet is addressed to Node B. Thus Router B encapsulates the packet in an Ethernet frame addressed to Node B, then transmits the frame over the Ethernet network.

By the time Node B receives the data packet sent from Node A, the packet has been encapsulated within three different frames, using two different Data Link Layer protocols. However, during all the changes of frame format, from Ethernet to FDDI and back again, the IP packet was never changed.

Internet Routers

The Internet, as its name implies, is a network of networks. Individual networks, such as those of Internet service providers (ISPs) and telephone carriers, are linked by routers and point-to-point links.

A packet moves across the Internet by being relayed from one network to the next until it reaches its destination. The routers that link those networks handle all the packet forwarding themselves. Individual users do not have to tell their messages what path to travel across the Internet, and could not even if they wanted to.

A router examines the IP network address of each packet, then uses its internal routing table to forward the packet to the routing port associated with the best path to the packet's destination. If the packet is addressed to a network that is not connected to the router, the router will forward the packet to another router that is closer to the final destination. Each router, in turn, evaluates each packet, then either delivers the packet or forwards it to another router.

Router Advantages

Routers offer several advantages as presented below:

- Like a switch, a router provides users with seamless communication between individual LAN segments. Unlike a switch, a router determines the logical boundaries between groups of network segments. A router provides a firewall service, because it forwards only traffic specifically addressed to go across the router. This eliminates the possibility of broadcast storm propagation, the transmission of frames from unsupported protocols, and the transmission of frames destined for unknown networks across the router. Routers keep potentially disastrous events local to the area in which they occur, preventing them from spreading across the corporate network.

- The enhanced intelligence of a router allows it to support redundant network paths, and select the best forwarding path based on several factors in addition to the destination network address. This increased intelligence can also result in enhanced data security, improved bandwidth utilization, and more control over network operations.

- Routers are the only internetworking devices that can provide efficient WAN access. Because routers do not forward broadcast traffic, they help control the traffic load on small, expensive WAN pipes. Routers offer access to a wide variety of WAN technologies, allowing network managers to select the best economic value for their networking needs. Router-based techniques such as data compression, traffic prioritization, and packet spoofing also help make efficient use of WAN bandwidth.

- Routers can flexibly integrate disparate Data Link Layer technologies, such as Ethernet, Fast Ethernet, Token Ring, FDDI, and ATM. They can also consolidate legacy IBM mainframe networks with personal computer (PC)-based networks through the use of Data Link Switching (DLSw).

Router Disadvantages

Routers also have several disadvantages as follows:

- The additional software processing performed by a router can increase packet latency, reducing the router's performance when compared to simpler switch architecture.

- To be "routable," an architecture must have a Network Layer. Not all do; those protocols must be bridged. "Unroutable" protocols include DEC-LAT terminal communications protocol, IBM's SNA, and NetBIOS/NetBEUI.

When to Use Routers

Objective 3.8
Describe various hardware and software connection devices and when to use them. ...Router

Routers are needed when network applications require limiting broadcast traffic, support for redundant paths, intelligent packet forwarding, or WAN access. If the application requires only increased bandwidth to ease a traffic bottleneck, a switch is likely the better choice. The technology choices appropriate for a specific workgroup, department, or building backbone depend upon the organization's business and technical requirements.

One of the functions of a router is to provide traffic isolation to help diagnose problems. Because each port of a router is a separate subnetwork, broadcast traffic is not forwarded across the router. The definition of network boundaries makes it easier for a network manager to provide redundancy and isolate problems resulting from broadcast storms, misconfigurations, chatty hosts, and equipment failures.

Another important benefit of routers is their ability to support mesh network topologies that provide active redundant paths. Unlike switches and bridges, which require a loop-free topology, routing protocols impose few constraints on network topologies, even on those that contain redundant paths and active loops. In addition, routers can perform load balancing over parallel equal-cost paths to make the best use of available bandwidth.

Routers allow the creation of hierarchical network designs that, through delegation of authority, can foster local management of separate regions of the Internet. Routers are necessary to connect a private network to the Internet.

Brouters

Objective 3.7
Create a logic diagram of Internet components from the client to the server. ...Brouter

Objective 3.8
Describe various hardware and software connection devices and when to use them. ...Brouter

A brouter is a device that functions both as a router and a bridge, though a brouter usually does not offer as many features as you would get by using a separate bridge and router. Like a router, the brouter can be configured to support one or more network protocols. If it receives a packet from one of its supported protocols, the brouter will route that packet. If the packet was generated by some protocol that the brouter does not recognize, it will then attempt to bridge the frame that encapsulates that packet.

Brouters are useful when some nodes use unroutable protocols, such as NetBEUI. When transmissions arrive from those nodes, the brouter bridges them based on their frame addresses. But Layer 3 packets, such as IP or IPX, are routed based on their packet addresses.

Gateways

A gateway, also called a protocol converter, converts data between two distinct types of protocol architectures. A gateway operates at all protocol levels above the Data Link Layer, and is transparent to both ends of the connection.

The term "gateway" is also used to describe a router, typically an Internet router that serves as a "remote gateway" between a private network and the public Internet. These router gateways provide access to remote networks; however, they do not convert stacks of protocols. In this section, we discuss gateways that serve as protocol converters.

Gateway Advantages

A gateway is the only internetworking device that can change the form of a network transmission from that of one communications architecture to that of another. For example, a gateway can connect a Transmission Control Protocol/Internet Protocol (TCP/IP) network to an SNA network, as shown on the Gateway Diagram. Another example of a gateway is a node that converts OSI Message-Oriented Text Interchange System (MOTIS) mail to Simple Mail Transfer Protocol (SMTP) for TCP/IP delivery.

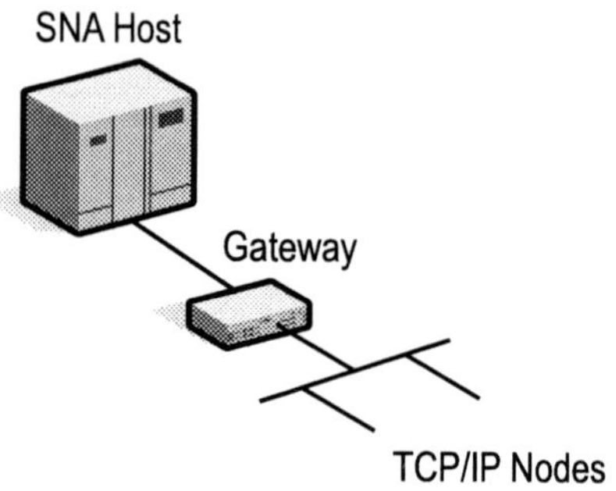

Gateway

Gateway Disadvantages

The key disadvantage of gateways is that protocol conversion is a software-intensive (slow) process, different for each specific pair of protocol stacks. A gateway receives frames from one communications architecture, and must convert them to another architecture by building new headers for every layer of the protocol stack.

When to Use Gateways

Gateways are necessary to connect any two networks that use different communications architectures. For example, we must use a gateway to convert electronic mail (e-mail) as it moves between SNA and TCP/IP environments.

Activities

1. Match the function or characteristic with the device in the lettered list below. Choose more than one letter if applicable.

   Router _______________

   Hub _______________

   Switch _______________

   Repeater _______________

   Bridge _______________

   Gateway _______________

   a. Extends physical LAN segments

   b. Connects NetBEUI networks over a WAN

   c. Can connect different types of media

   d. Has higher latency than a switch

   e. Isolates traffic between LAN segments

   f. Can be used to manage collision domains

   g. Forwards broadcast traffic

   h. Acts as a protocol converter for architectures

   i. Connects devices in a single collision domain

   j. Does not forward broadcast traffic

   k. Supports redundant network paths

   l. Is a protocol-dependent device

2. List one advantage and disadvantage of each type of internetworking device beginning with Layer 1 devices and working your way up the OSI model.

Extended Activity

1. Using your favorite Internet search engine, locate information on Layer 3 switches and briefly describe their operation. (Hint: try 3Com and Cisco).

Summary

In Unit 1, we introduced the computing devices and components that make up a network, and the software and signaling that makes communication possible.

Internal computer components have a varying amount of capacity and power. However, all computers generally include the same basic components. A CPU processes information; the amount of work it can do depends on its clock speed and bandwidth. The I/O bus transfers data between input components, output devices, the CPU, memory, and other internal computer components. Like the CPU, there are a variety of I/O bus types, each with its own performance characteristics.

To physically connect to a network, a computer must be equipped with a NIC. Each type of network cable connection and Data Link protocol requires a different type of NIC. The performance of a NIC depends on the performance of the computer's other components.

The computer hardware is controlled by the OS software and device drivers. An OS is a suite of software that manages applications, user interfaces, storage, and internal and external components. The OS provides many low-level services, such as reading and writing to disks, handling I/O, and assigning memory and processing time to multiple applications. Device drivers are like small OS modules that control internal and external accessories, such as disk drives, network connections, and printers.

Application software is what a user sees and works with. The application software uses the underlying OS to perform low-level functions, such as file access and management. Some applications are designed for one user at a time, while others are made to support multiple simultaneous users on a network.

Network management and utility software is considered a distinct category of software, separate from user applications. This software is used by network and system administrators for managing and accessing network or computer OSs. Network management tools help keep a network healthy by monitoring data traffic flow, managing storage backup and recovery, providing remote network access, and preventing or eliminating viruses.

The physical layouts, or topologies, of networks can vary widely. The topology of a network determines the direction and pattern of signal flow. When network professionals discuss a network design, they usually mean its logical topology, which shows how signals flow in the network. In contrast, a physical topology shows how individual devices are connected to each other.

The bus topology, using coaxial cable, was one of the first small network designs. All nodes attach to a single cable and communicate by sending information along that "bus" cable. The bus topology has been largely replaced by the more flexible star configuration.

The star topology is currently the most popular way to wire a network. A signal-sharing device, called a hub, forms the physical and logical center of the network. Each network node is connected to the hub by a separate twisted pair cable. Because each node is isolated on its own cable, a problem with one node does not necessarily affect the other computers attached to that hub.

The bus and star topologies are both broadcast networks. A hub serves the same logical function as a coaxial bus. All nodes connected to the hub (or bus) receive every signal transmitted; however, a node ignores any transmission not addressed to it.

In a ring network, the logical topology requires each node to receive each signal from its neighbor on one side, then relay the signal to its neighbor on the other side. Ring networks can use one of two physical topologies. In a "pure" ring, point-to-point connections link the nodes in a circle, like beads on a necklace. A break in one of the links, or a malfunction of one of the nodes, can take the entire network down.

In a star ring topology, all nodes are connected to a central MAU that distributes signals to each station in turn. If one node fails, the MAU can simply bypass it and maintain communication with the other nodes.

A mesh topology is a system of point-to-point links that connect each node to every other node. This topology is most often used to link separate locations in MANs or WANs. When the number of nodes in a mesh network grows, most network designers abandon the mesh topology in favor of a subscription to a switched "cloud" network owned by a telecommunications service provider (telephone company).

To arrange nodes into various topologies, we use internetworking devices such as hubs, bridges, switches, and routers. Each of these devices operates at a different layer of the OSI Model, and each is suited for particular tasks. Hubs connect groups of computers into workgroups, so that every node receives every frame transmitted by any other node on that same hub. Bridges and switches isolate traffic within workgroups, by forwarding each frame only to the port that is connected to the destination node. Routers subdivide a network at OSI Layer 3, by forwarding each packet only to the port that is connected to the destination node. By providing communication between different networks, routers are the essential components of the Internet.

Unit 1 Quiz

1. A sound card is what general type of computer component?

   a. Processor

   b. Memory

   c. Input/Output

   d. Storage

2. A NIC is a device used for:

   a. Storage

   b. Processing

   c. Signaling

   d. Memory

3. Which of the following is managed by the OS?

   a. Keyboard input

   b. Screen display

   c. File I/O

   d. Peripheral control

   e. All of the above

4. What type of communication is most common on the World Wide Web?

   a. Client/server

   b. Master/slave

   c. Peer-to-peer

   d. ICA

5. Who creates a device driver?

   a. OS vendor

   b. Device manufacturer

   c. Application publisher

   d. Open-source programming community

6. What is the main advantage of a star topology?

    a. Redundancy

    b. Ease of management

    c. Minimize cable requirements

    d. Speed

7. Which of the following network topologies forms a closed loop?

    a. Bus topology

    b. Broadcast topology

    c. Loop topology

    d. Ring topology

8. Which of the following network topologies connects devices to a shared straight-line cable?

    a. Bus topology

    b. Ring topology

    c. Loop topology

    d. Star ring topology

9. Which of the following is the most widely used LAN topology?

    a. Mesh

    b. Bus

    c. Star

    d. Ring and star ring

10. When the specific topology of a network is unknown, it is commonly called which of the following?

    a. Switch

    b. Cloud

    c. Mesh

    d. Web

11. When a series of point-to-point circuits connect every node to every other, the network is called which of the following?

    a. Bus

    b. Cloud

    c. Mesh

    d. Ring

12. Which of the following hardware devices builds a frame?

    a. Media adapter unit

    b. Node port

    c. Light emitting diode (LED)

    d. NIC

13. Which of the following is the primary purpose of a Physical Layer protocol?

    a. Transmit bits across a physical link

    b. Transmit frames across a physical link

    c. Detect duplicate packets

    d. Transmit packets across a network

14. The Network Layer is to packets as the Data Link Layer is to:

    a. Frames

    b. Signals

    c. Bits

    d. Protocol suites

15. Which activities occur at the Application Layer?

    a. File transfer and access

    b. E-mail

    c. Web browser

    d. All of the above

16. Hubs and repeaters operate at which layer of the OSI model?

    a. Physical Layer

    b. Network Layer

    c. Transport Layer

17. Which of the following is a function of hubs and repeaters?

    a. Provide for cable extension

    b. Repeat digital signals

    c. Interconnect different cable types

    d. All of the above

18. Why shouldn't hubs and repeaters be used to interconnect entire LANs?

    a. They are too expensive.

    b. They are too powerful.

    c. They do not manage traffic efficiently enough.

    d. They cannot connect different physical media.

19. At which OSI layer do switches reside?

    a. Data Link Layer

    b. Physical Layer

    c. Transport Layer

    d. Network Layer

20. Switches can transmit two frames simultaneously. True or False?

21. Which of the following devices can isolate traffic within workgroups?

    a. Bridge

    b. Switch

    c. Router

    d. All of the above

22. Performance will likely increase in an Ethernet network when which of the following occurs?

    a. Switches are replaced by hubs.

    b. Routers are replaced by hubs.

    c. Switches are replaced by bridges.

    d. Hubs are replaced by switches.

23. At which OSI layer do bridges operate?

    a. Data Link Layer

    b. Transport Layer

    c. Physical Layer

    d. Network Layer

24. At which OSI layer do routers operate?

    a. Data Link Layer

    b. Network Layer

    c. Transport Layer

    d. Physical Layer

25. What distinguishes routers from bridges?

    a. Routers operate on packets.

    b. Routers are for the Internet only.

    c. Routers are faster.

    d. Routers are always more expensive.

26. Which of the following scenarios requires a gateway?

    a. Connecting an IP network to an AppleTalk network

    b. Connecting an IP network to an IP network

    c. Connecting three IP networks

    d. Connecting a twisted pair network to a fiber optic network

27. The term "gateway" also means which of the following?

    a. A router that subdivides a network

    b. A bridge that connects a LAN to a wide area link

    c. A router that connects a LAN to the Internet

    d. A Web server

28. The lapsed time between a request and response is referred to as:

    a. Response time

    b. Latency

    c. Delay

    d. Network latency

29. Utilization normally refers to what two areas of networking?

    a. CPU and processor

    b. Processor and router

    c. CPU and network access device

    d. CPU and link

30. As the CPU utilization of a network component increases, what happens to the overall network response time and component latency?

    a. The component latency goes up and the response time goes down.

    b. Both the component latency and response time go down.

    c. Both the component latency and response time increase.

    d. The component latency increases and the response time decreases.

Unit 2
E-Commerce

In the early years of the World Wide Web, both new and existing businesses raced into e-commerce like miners to a gold rush. But, like any gold rush, the Web has seen more failures than successes. Many ill-conceived, hastily-organized e-businesses looked healthy only as long as their venture capital funds held out. But they quickly folded when investors insisted on profits that their weak business models could not deliver. In contrast, many of the companies that survived and thrived on the Web were those that obeyed "conventional" business principles.

Thus, a successful e-commerce professional must both look back to time-tested business practices, and look forward to the cutting-edge technologies that are necessary to implement those business practices on the Web.

This unit begins by introducing the business principles that every e-commerce Web site must consider. We then move on to explore the extensive, invisible "back-end" systems that make online business possible: credit cards and electronic cash, encryption for secure transactions, search engines that bring customers to online storefronts, and integrated systems of specialized servers that handle complex transactions at a distance. Finally, we introduce some of the most important legal concepts and developments that affect the Web professional.

Note: This unit is *not* intended to substitute for personalized legal advice from a knowledgeable attorney. If you think you may need legal assistance, you should talk to a lawyer licensed to practice law in your state—preferably one who understands the Internet and the unique legal situations it can create.

Lessons

1. E-Commerce Business Considerations
2. Globalization and Localization
3. Cash Flow on the Internet
4. Intellectual Property
5. Crime, Privacy, and Other Legal Issues

Terms

business to business (B2B)—A B2B is a business that sells to other businesses, not to consumers.

business to consumer (B2C)—A B2C is a retail business that sells directly to consumers.

business to employee (B2E)—A B2E is a company intranet that provides employees access to company information, forms, and so forth.

business to government (B2G)—A B2G is a business that conducts commerce with the U.S. and foreign governments.

Child Online Protection Act (COPA)—COPA is a federal law passed in response to the Supreme Court's rejection of a portion of the CDA. COPA restricts material that is "harmful to minors," and applies to communications that are made for commercial purposes and that might be accessed by minors.

Child Pornography Prevention Act (CPPA)—A federal law that, among other things, prohibits images that depict or appear to depict minors engaged in sexually explicit conduct. Unlike previous child pornography laws, CPPA restricted images created without the involvement of any actual children. In 2002 the Supreme Court ruled that the CPPA was unconstitutional.

Children's Internet Protection Act (CIPA)—CIPA is a law that makes federal funding for Internet access at public libraries dependent upon the implementation of policies and technologies for blocking obscenity, child pornography, and material deemed harmful to minors.

Children's Online Privacy Protection Act (COPPA)—COPPA is a federal law regulating the collection and use of personal information from children less than 13 years of age.

Communications Decency Act (CDA)—CDA is part of the Telecommunications Act of 1996, which, among other things, prohibited the posting of "indecent" or "patently offensive" materials on publicly accessible Web sites and other Internet forums that might be accessed by minors. The U.S. Supreme Court ruled the CDA portion of the Telecommunications Act of 1996 unconstitutional.

Computer Crime and Intellectual Property Section (CCIPS)—The CCIPS was created by the Criminal Division of the United States Department of Justice to focus on criminal activity related to computers, the Internet, and intellectual property.

Computer Fraud and Abuse Act—The Computer Fraud and Abuse Act is a federal law that addresses crimes such as unauthorized computer access, damage or threats relating to computers, and trafficking in illicit computer passwords.

consumer to consumer (C2C)—Also called marketplace, a C2C is an environment where multiple sellers transact with multiple buyers.

copyright—Copyright is the legal protection of original human expression, such as writings, musical compositions, video productions, and software programs. United States copyright law is specifically authorized by the Constitution, and is implemented through federal laws and regulations. The Library of Congress administers registration of copyrights in the United States.

deep linking—Deep linking is the practice of linking to another site not through its home page, but to a page—or smaller element, such as an image or sound file—located elsewhere within the site.

Digital Millennium Copyright Act (DMCA)—The DMCA is a controversial federal law concerning the protection of copyrighted material in digital formats. Among other things, the DMCA includes provisions to protect ISPs from liability for copyright infringement by users. It also restricts the creation, distribution, and use of devices for circumventing copy protection and access control technologies.

Electronic Benefit Transfer (EBT)—The EBT system is intended to replace food stamps and public assistance checks with a debit type credit card.

Electronic Funds Transfer (EFT)—EFT is the process of transferring funds between accounts, banks, even countries.

fair use—Fair use is the right to reproduce a portion of a copyrighted work for certain kinds of purposes, without needing the permission of the copyright owner. This effectively carves out a small limitation from the copyright holder's rights for the benefit of educators, critics, and others.

framing—Similar to deep linking, framing is the practice of presenting material from another Web site on your own site, surrounded by your own material. This can lead to confusion among users about where "framed" material originates, and who is responsible for it.

globalization—Globalization refers to the process of making a Web site accessible and useful to users in a variety of countries and regions around the world.

intellectual property—Intellectual property is property whose value lies not in any physical object, but in its creative or expressive content. Examples include literature, music, computer software, and the ideas behind practical inventions. Intellectual property is also used to refer to the body of law, including copyright, patent, and trademark law, which governs the protection and use of such property.

Internet service provider—ISPs are companies that provide Internet access to individuals and businesses. ISPs typically provide a range of services necessary to provide corporate networks and other users with dedicated or dial-up access to the Internet.

localization—Localization is the process of adapting a Web site or other software for use in a specific country or region. Usually the Web site or software is adapted to a place other than that for which it was originally developed. Localization requirements can include translation of text into another language, changes to region-specific formats for addresses and telephone numbers, and even the creation of entirely new content for a foreign audience.

marketplace—Also called C2C, marketplace is an application/network infrastructure that brings multiple buyers and multiple sellers together to transact business.

patent—Patent law is the field of intellectual property that protects and encourages original inventions. The holder of a patent has a legally enforceable right to exclusive use of his or her invention for a limited amount of time. In exchange, the patent process requires the inventor to make public the workings of the invention, so that after the patent expires, anyone knowledgeable in the same field will be able to make use of the invention. In the

United States, patent law is specifically authorized by the Constitution, and is administered by the United States Patent and Trademark Office. See United States Patent and Trademark Office.

personal jurisdiction—Personal jurisdiction refers to the power of a court to hear a case and issue a judgment or order that is binding on a particular person (or a corporation). In the United States, a state court generally has personal jurisdiction over persons within the state's borders. A state court can also assume jurisdiction over a person outside the state who has established sufficient contacts within the state (for example, by actively selling or marketing products to residents in the state).

portal—A portal is a Web site that pulls needed information from many different sites.

public-key (asymmetric) encryption—Public-key encryption is a cryptographic system that uses two mathematically related keys: one key is used to encrypt a message, and the other to decrypt it. People who need to receive encrypted messages distribute their public keys, but keep their private keys secret.

registration—Copyrights and trademarks may be registered with the federal government, through the Library of Congress and the USPTO, respectively. Registration is not required for protection of copyrights or trademarks, but it brings definite advantages for the legal enforcement of an owner's rights.

Secure Sockets Layer (SSL)—SSL is an application of both public-key and single-key encryption, which secures an Internet connection between browser and server. Web pages that use SSL carry the URL "https://."

single-key (symmetric) encryption—Single-key encryption is a cryptographic system that uses the same key to both encrypt and decrypt a message. Single-key encryption systems require both the sender and receiver of a message to share the same key before using it to communicate.

slashdot effect—Named for the popular technology news site, **www.slashdot.org**, the slashdot effect is what happens when a large and popular site links to a much smaller site, bringing an overload of traffic and possibly overwhelming the smaller site's server and bandwidth capabilities.

trade dress—Trade dress is a concept related to trademarks. It refers to the distinctive overall appearance of a product or a service provider in the marketplace.

E-Commerce

trademark—A trademark is a name, word, image, or other device with which a business identifies itself and its products in the marketplace. The term can also refer to the field of intellectual property law that provides legal protection for such marks. Ownership of trademark rights to a name, term, or image includes the right to prevent others from using that mark or confusingly similar marks. In the United States, federal and state laws govern trademarks. The United States Patent and Trademark Office administers Federal trademarks.

trade secret—A trade secret is a proprietary business process or method that is kept secret. Although it is generally an owner's responsibility to keep trade secrets secret, the law offers some protection if a competitor obtains a trade secret through improper means despite the owner's best efforts.

trespass—Trespass is entering onto or remaining on someone else's property without permission. It is possible that the law of trespass could be used against someone who accesses computers on the Internet without authorization.

United States Patent and Trademark Office (USPTO)—The USPTO is the office of the federal government responsible for administering patents and Federal trademark registrations.

Lesson 1—E-Commerce Business Considerations

A Web site can deliver information, provide customer service, or provide other support for a traditional brick-and-mortar business. This lesson describes the major types of e-commerce sites currently in use by businesses today, and explores the most common barriers to business success on the Internet.

Objectives

At the end of this lesson you will be able to:

- Name the various types of e-commerce sites

- List some of the common barriers to e-commerce

- Explain why online commerce is not right for every type of business

 **Key Point**

First build a good business, and then build the technology that will help you grow your business.

Types of E-Commerce

Objective 5.3
Recognize and explain the current types of e-business models being applied today.

The various types of e-commerce Web sites are as follows:

- **Business to Consumer (B2C)**—Direct retail sales of consumer goods or services.

- **Business to Business (B2B)**—Sales of goods or services needed by businesses, such as office supplies, raw materials, information, or consulting.

- **Consumer to Consumer (C2C) or Marketplace**—An environment where multiple sellers transact with multiple buyers.

- **Consumer to Business (C2B)**—Customers tell businesses what goods and services they want, and what prices they are willing to pay.

- **Business to Employee (B2E)**—A company Intranet that provides employees access to company information, forms, and so forth.

- **Business to Government (B2G)**—Businesses conducting commerce with the U.S. and foreign governments.

E-Commerce

- **Aggregator**—Web sites that provide many services to their customers. A kind of one-stop-shop.

- **Portals**—A Web site that pulls needed information from many different sites.

B2C

The first e-commerce enterprises were Business to Consumer (B2C) sites. Trailblazer sites such as Amazon.com and CDNow.com quickly led to other high profile, money making retail sites, such as Dell Computers (**http://www.dell.com**).

Growing Share of the Retail Market

Most retail transactions still take place in the brick-and-mortar world. However, this is already beginning to change dramatically. The statistics show that sales on the Internet are continuing to grow. The buying public is choosing to stay at home more, be with family, and use this growing technology to enhance these lifestyle choices. To follow the trends in e-business go to the following Web sites: **www.forrester.com** and **www.marketingpower.com**.

Lands' End, a clothing retailer, provides a good example of how the e-business world is changing. After Lands' End added a Web site to its traditional catalog marketing, online sales have steadily grown. The marketing department wants the site to become Lands' End's primary source of revenue, not just part of its business.

Some traditional "brick-and-mortar" retailers are also using the Web to complement, not replace, their traditional storefronts. Their "bricks-and-clicks" or "clicks-and-mortar" Web sites provide online shopping and ordering, in cooperation with store locations that provide order pickup, customer service, product returns, and other personal services.

B2B

Objective 5.1
Understand and be able to describe e-commerce terms and concepts.

Although Web retailing generally gets more attention, industry experts agree that the real impact of Web-based commerce will be in the Businesses to Businesses (B2B) sector. In 1999, online sales of goods and services to other businesses were five times greater than the volume of online retail sales, and the trend is for B2B sales to continue to expand. More significantly, B2B sales have historically been more profitable than consumer retailing; it is realistic to anticipate this trend carrying over into the online market.

The earliest businesses to use e-commerce were financial institutions. They began with Electronic Funds Transfer (EFT). EFT is the process of transferring funds between accounts, banks, even countries. The process seems simple now compared to the complex transactions taking place today, but when it began, EFT was on the cutting edge of B2B e-commerce.

As the number of online transactions grew, the industry developed a standardized communications protocol called Electronic Data Interchange (EDI). This protocol standardized forms such as purchase orders and invoices to enable businesses to more easily exchange information. EDI brought us one step closer to the Internet we all know today.

Businesses also began using Web sites to find other business services, such as human resources, procurement, shipping, legal, marketing, payroll, training, and customer service.

Today's fastest-growing online markets link buyers with specialized business services. For example, financial services, corporate travel, professional services, administrative support, and telecommunications are top sellers in the B2B market.

Open Buying on the Internet (OBI) is a framework for conducting these business-to-business transactions. It includes detailed technical specifications, compliance, and implementation. Anyone can get a copy of the OBI standard from **www.openbuy.org** and use it to create a product or solution. Several well-known organizations, including American Express, Ford Motor Company, General Electric, Home Depot, and United Technologies have already adopted the OBI standard.

C2C or Marketplace

An online marketplace or Consumer to Consumer (C2C) Web site is an application/network infrastructure that brings multiple buyers and multiple sellers together to transact business. Auction sites such as eBay (**http://www.ebay.com**), Buy.com (**http://www.buy.com**), serve as brokers to thousands of small transactions every day.

C2B

A Consumer to Consumer (C2B) site reverses the usual retail interaction by allowing consumers to specify the prices they are willing to pay for particular goods and services. Businesses then decide whether to sell on those terms. Priceline (**http://www.priceline.com**) was the first site to successfully use this model.

B2E

A Business to Employee (B2E) Web site could also be called an intranet. With more and more people becoming accustomed to using the Web for business, it is only natural that businesses would leverage the technology to communicate with employees. An intranet often provides forms to users, communication on personnel policies, training manuals, internal reporting functions, group calendars, and so forth.

B2G

The Business to Government (B2G) model has many of the same characteristics as the Business to Business (B2B) model. As is usually the case, the government does not fully accept new technologies as quickly as the business sector. Therefore, the government has not fully implemented e-commerce with businesses. Sites are developing, however, that facilitate businesses doing business with the government.

The government is already implementing a benefits system called electronic benefit transfer (EBT). The EBT system is intended to replace food stamps and public assistance checks with smart cards. EBT users can use the cards when they shop for food and withdraw benefits from an automatic teller machine (ATM). The system was developed to cut public assistance costs and help the government track cases of fraud. There are drawbacks. Until a set of standards has been defined and adopted, each state is writing its own rules. EBT users are usually confined to one area of the country and tend to lose benefits because of surcharges or ignorance of the rules.

Another government process that could be conducted on the Internet is the procurement, or purchasing process. The U.S. government has a multi-billion dollar procurement budget that will lend itself to the B2G model. Software is now available that will make use of current technologies to send out notices to bidders, submit bids, conduct auctions, negotiate contracts, make payments, and manage workflow.

B2G will also incorporate the marketplace concept as it applies to bringing approved government buyers and sellers together to do business. Also, the "e-Bay" concept of auctioning products on the Internet will prove useful for selling excess government supplies and materials.

With the government's highly structured procurement process, using a B2G Internet model will allow more vendors to participate and provide increased efficiency for the government and expanded opportunities for business.

Aggregator Model

A Web site based on the aggregator model brings all of a customer's accounts together into a single, personalized site; users can access all information from an institution without having to navigate through the entire site and login repeatedly. Banks that allow customers to conduct all their financial transactions online have enacted the aggregator model of e-commerce. In fact, financial institutions have led the way in developing this type of e-commerce.

The popularity of aggregator sites is growing exponentially. A survey conducted by Booz-Allen and Hamilton and e-Rewards of 1,000 aggregation-service users and 1,900 general Internet users showed that consumer acceptance of account aggregation is growing rapidly. The number of users grew in 2000 from 10,000 in January to 700,000 in December. (Altman, 2001)

Portal Model

Objective 1.3
Use different types of search indexes - static index/site map, keyword index, full text index.

A natural extension to the aggregator model is the portal model. A portal Web site offers the ability to aggregate data from multiple sources and package it in a way that is meaningful to users. You may have visited Web sites that gather price quotes from several different vendors for a product you want to buy. These sites take advantage of Web search engines to provide an even easier and faster way to shop the Web.

Portal sites are not limited to retail sites. Many libraries now provide a Web site that consolidates all materials, either on hand or available through interlibrary loan, for easy searching. Also, the Web sites of many interest groups gather information from various sources to support their view of an issue.

Each portal site is different, designed to attract a different audience. However, most successful portal sites include two essential features: directories and search engines.

Directories

Directories are usually organized in a tree structure, with main topics at the top and subtopics below. The "all of the Internet" directories—such as Yahoo!, Excite, Lycos, and Microsoft Network (MSN)—try to classify everything on the Internet. Specialized directories or indexes focus on specific topics.

Search Engines

Search engines continually scan the Internet by indexing sites and their contents; they then store the location information and provide tools for fast retrieval. There are three general categories of search site interfaces:

- **Crawler-based search engines** create their listings by automatically traversing the Web, looking for appropriate data in each page's <TITLE>, <BODY> text, and <META> tags (We explain HTML tags in "Building Web Pages."). Changing the content of a Web page may increase the number of hits.

- **Human-based directories** use short descriptive listings submitted by Webmasters or marketing personnel to human editors. The search engine looks for matches only in the descriptions submitted. Changing the content of the Web pages has no effect on the order of the listing.

- **Hybrid search engines** use crawlers and also maintain a directory that lists appealing sites chosen by reviewers.

Search engine sites may include some, or all, of the following technical elements, depending on the technology of each site:

- **Spider, crawler, or robot software**—This application visits a Web page, reads it, then follows links to other pages within the site. The crawler returns to the site on a regular basis to look for changes.

- **Index or catalog**—This enormous database lists every Web page a spider finds. If the spider finds that a Web page has changed, the index is updated with the new information. When a user submits a search, the search engine software searches this index database. Therefore, a site must appear in the index to be included in a search. The same query produces different results on different search sites, because some engines index more pages, and some engines index the pages more often.

- **Search engine software**—When a user submits a search, this application searches through millions of index database records to find matches to the search and rank them in what it perceives to be a relevant order. This order is determined by following a set of rules, such as the number of keywords and their location in the Web page.

To avoid getting thousands of matches, a search string must be as specific and unambiguous as possible. To create these precise searches, the user interfaces of most search engines support common command syntaxes or syntax rules, such as:

- Quotes—Use quotes to have a string treated like a keyword. For example: **"sending a fax"**

- Capitalize—Capitalize only if you want the match to be case sensitive. For example: **President Ford**

- Wildcards—Use an asterisk (*) for wildcards. For example: **fax*** will match **fax**, **faxes**, and other words starting with fax.

- Inclusion and exclusion—For simple queries, if you want all keywords to match, prefix the words with a plus sign: **+fax +paper**. To exclude a word from the query, use the minus sign: **+fax –machines**.

- Boolean connectors—For advanced queries, use the Boolean connectors AND, OR, and NOT. AND means both or all keywords are to be present. NOT means that a keyword must not be present. For example, **fax AND paper**, or **fax AND paper NOT machines**. OR is the default. For example: **fax paper** is the same as **fax OR paper**. Use parentheses to make complex expressions: **("vitamin C" OR "vitamin B12") AND (colds OR flu OR influenza)**. There are more syntax additions and variations to help you fine tune your search; most search portals offer online help that explains these options.

Necessary Features of E-Commerce Sites

The following characteristics are present in a successful e-commerce site:

- The system runs well on all browsers and slow Internet connections. Many consumers still operate with very slow modem speeds.

- The interface is easy to navigate. No training is required to find products, place an order, pay the merchant, find information, etc.

- The site integrates current business practices with new Web-based inventory controls.

- The site offers both sales and content (information or entertainment) components.

- The content is updated daily, if not hourly, to keep customers and users returning.

- The site is the central point of procurement for an entire company. Centralized purchasing can help businesses reduce and track all purchasing costs.

- All transactions and account information are secure.

Is E-Commerce Worthwhile for Every Business?

Objective 5.4
Identify key factors relating to strategic marketing consider- ations as they relate to launching an e- business initiative. … Public relations; impact/risks of site failure

An e-commerce site is only worthwhile if it improves relationships with customers and business associates, and increases an organization's revenue. For the revenue to outweigh development and maintenance costs, a business must carefully articulate goals that will define the site's success, and devise strategies for achieving these goals. For every well-known success on the Web, thousands of e-commerce sites are marginally successful or outright failures.

For example, without carefully defining goals and anticipating obstacles, clothing manufacturer Levi Strauss & Co. (**http:// www.levi.com**) launched high-profile sites, hoping to both sell its Levi's and Docker's brands and use direct interaction to learn more about its customers. However, the move damaged relations with the company's established retail network, which was barred from selling those products on the Web. And, for various reasons, consumers stayed away from the sites. In the face of dismal sales and high costs, Levi Strauss & Co. withdrew from e-commerce. It redesigned its sites to offer product information and support to its retailers, who are now allowed to sell Levi products on their own sites.

> If you start with the technology, you're likely going to buy a solution in search of a problem. And you may not get what your business really needs. Start with the business in a pure sense and ask yourself what you want to happen and how you'll measure it. Then ask how the technology will help you achieve your goals.

> www.smalloffice.com
> February 2000

Barriers to Entering the E-Commerce Arena

While many businesses know that a Web presence can comple- ment their traditional activities, fewer are confident about begin- ning to conduct actual business on the Web. Many factors, both psychological and practical, cause some businesses to hesitate to implement e-commerce sites.

Incompatible Business Models

The current structure of some businesses does not fit the e-commerce model. For example, a business that relies on hands-on customer contact, such as a tailor shop, will need to find creative ways to succeed in cyberspace.

Also, the underlying processes of some businesses were not designed with online commerce in mind. For example, a firm with multiple inventory databases will find it harder to move to e-commerce than one with a single database already integrated with its accounting system.

Lack of Leadership and Experience

Many businesses hesitate to enter e-commerce because they simply do not understand it. Management often lacks the necessary vision, or does not understand how the Internet may benefit the business. Furthermore, a business may feel that online commerce is unnecessary or risky if its partners, vendors, customers, or competitors have not set an example by going online first.

Successful e-commerce also requires its own set of technical and business management skills, which many firms lack. A company without practical expertise in Web technology and e-business must either rely on consultants or stay out of the Web.

Cost of Entry

It is a common misconception that it is easy to enter the e-commerce arena. In reality, the initial and ongoing costs of implementing an e-commerce site may be too high for many companies to justify.

The interface that the customer sees is merely the tip of the iceberg; most of the back-end details of a merchant's Web site are hidden from the consumer. Beyond that, the technical issues of Web site development pale in comparison with the integration of the site to the fundamental practices of a business.

Another common misconception is that traffic effortlessly flows to e-commerce sites from search engines. Although search engines are critical to site marketing, e-commerce sites must build a brand identity in the old-guard media: television, print, and radio. With a few exceptions, the busiest e-commerce sites are tightly connected to their offline brands.

Only companies that are willing to make the necessary financial commitment can choose to plant their flag on the Internet today.

E-Commerce

Activities

1. For each of the Web sites below, name its business model:

    a. Retail clothing sales _______________________________

    b. Online computer magazine, with reviews, price comparisons, and advertising _______________________________

    c. A company's human resources site _______________________

    d. An auction site _______________________

    e. Wholesale manufacturing materials sales _______________

    f. The home page of a major ISP, showing news headlines and stock quotes _______________________

2. Explain the relationship between a crawler, a catalog, and a search engine.

    ____

    ____

    ____

    ____

Extended Activities

1. Visit the Open Buying on the Internet Consortium (**www.openbuy.org**) and research the progress of the OBI standard. Summarize OBI in a short report to your class.

2. In a short report, outline the current status of Electronic Benefits Transfer (EBT). What problems is it designed to solve? What drawbacks are standing in the way of its adoption? Are any agencies or local areas successfully using it?

Lesson 2—Globalization and Localization

The reach of the Internet is global. As of 2001, nearly two thirds of all Internet users resided outside the United States, and by 2005 that number is expected to grow to 75 percent. In some nations the Internet is accessible to only the political or economic elite, but in more and more places it is becoming a part of daily life for millions of ordinary citizens.

For businesses, and other organizations, this is one of the Web's great promises. By setting up a Web site, you can make your message accessible to an audience of millions. The Internet makes it easier for even a small business to go global.

But "easier" does not mean "simple." Using the international reach of the Web to its greatest potential raises a variety of questions. Many of the potential answers reveal the obstacles to accessing the Internet. Although your site is available to anyone in the world who can type in the URL, not everyone will discover that your site exists. When end users find it, can they read it? Can they access your U.S-based server with reasonable response times? If you are selling goods and services, can your potential customers easily order, pay for, and receive them? Can you be sure of compliance with local laws in many different nations?

These questions raise a fundamental problem of using the Web for globalization: globalization also requires *localization*. It is not enough to reach hundreds of nations via the Web. In order to do business, or to make any kind of difference, you must be able to connect with the people in those nations in a way that causes them to make your Web site a part of their lives. To do this, you must consider the barriers posed by language, law, money, and other aspects of society.

Objectives

At the end of this lesson you will be able to:

- Identify the aspects of your Web site that may need modification in order to reach foreign audiences

- Choose the level of globalization and localization that is appropriate for your Web site

- Plan a strategy for globalizing and localizing your Web site, either at launch or gradually

- Prepare for the potential legal or cultural challenges of a global Internet presence

 **Key Point**

Serving an international user base on the Web usually requires meeting the general needs of a global audience, as well as the specific needs of a local audience.

Speaking the Language

Objective 5.4
Identify key factors relating to strategic marketing consider-ations as they relate to launching an e-business initiative. … Geographic/ Localization consid-erations (local cus-toms/criteria, etc.)

At its heart, the Web is still a very text-oriented medium. Unfortu-nately, this means that most information we send and receive by means of the Web is set down in a particular language—often English. People cannot use your Web site if they cannot read it; therefore, if you want your Web site to be appealing and useful in the wider world, you may need to consider making your content available in more than one language.

English is more prevalent than any other single language on the Web, but fewer than 50 percent of the people on the Web are native English speakers. This means that by providing an English-only Web site you might be excluding many potential readers or customers.

Many Web users who do not speak English as their first language have a good command of English as a second language and can interact adequately with an English-only site. But there are rea-sons to consider using multiple languages other than basic acces-sibility. As a matter of marketing and public image, you may encourage more readership and e-commerce business if you present yourself to users in their native tongue. Also, local and national laws may impose a requirement to include a non-English version of your Web site.

For example, Quebec and France have both applied their French language laws to the Web sites of businesses and institutions that have a presence in those jurisdictions. Thus, if your business has a branch in Quebec, you may be required to include a French ver-sion of your company Web site.

It is best to consider possible multi-language aspects of your Web-site from the very beginning, when you are developing a site's requirements and architecture. This should allow you to construct the site, and your development and maintenance procedures, in a way that will make it easier to translate and otherwise adapt the site as needed for different versions. For example, you may choose to create and store your large text components as separate files, rather than embedding all of your text in the page's main HTML source. The separate files can then be dealt with by translators as necessary, and can be swapped in and out of the site architecture to create multiple versions in different languages.

In general, the more globalized (some would say internationalized) your site is from the beginning, the easier it should be to "localize" it for any specific part of the world. Even if you have no plans for a non-English version of your site, thinking about these issues up front may prevent headaches if your needs change—and may enhance ease of maintenance even if you stick to an English-only site.

Recently, significant efforts and innovations, such as the Unicode character encoding system, have attempted to ease the use of the Web in the world's many languages. But converting a site to a different language may require more than simply translating the visible text and ensuring the characters can be displayed. Linguistic differences may impact your overall site design. For example, some languages scan from right-to-left rather than left-to-right. While the common up-and-down scrolling structure of most Web sites works well with both left-to-right and right-to-left languages, differences in reading direction may affect the proper placement of menus, graphics, or other elements.

Also, some shortcuts we take for granted in English, such as acronyms, do not exist in all languages, and therefore may affect the design of your menus or other navigation tools. Other changes that may affect your design include the size and format of names, addresses, and telephone numbers.

Localized Content

Depending upon the nature of your site, localization may call for more than just translating the text or even adjusting the design. Your site may also benefit from localized content. If, for example, you are running a news site covering a particular industry, does your German site include coverage of German corporations in the field, or is it just a German translation of an America-centered news report?

The High-End Approach: Region-Specific Sites

Some major Web site operators take the ultimate step in globalization and localization: they spin off entirely separate versions of their operation in different countries. Yahoo!, for example, has over twenty different regional and national editions, each in the appropriate language and featuring different content targeted toward each local audience.

The Low-End Approach: Translation Links

If you do not have the strong need or the resources to translate and localize your site for different countries or regions, but you want to at least acknowledge the needs of users with limited English abilities, you might consider including a link to one of the automatic translation services that exist on the Web. The most popular of these is the Babel Fish (**http://babelfish.altavista.com/**), but others are also available. These services are most appropriate for small self-contained pages or text items. Also, be aware that the computer translations produced by such systems are far from perfect. They should not be relied upon for anything important, or as a way to present your best face to non-English readers. But they do offer a way to make a document generally comprehensible in another language.

Search Engine Hooks

When developing a plan to connect with an international audience, remember to include search engine hooks, such things as page titles and meta tags. Many search engines rely upon these elements to locate and index Web pages. Including search engine hooks in multiple languages can help overseas users find your site.

If localization of your Web site is critical, consider engaging an expert or consultant to assist in the process. Many translation and localization companies specialize in Web sites, and a Web search on "Web localization" or similar terms should connect you to a number of them. Even if you do not choose to use the services of a localization consultant, browsing some of their Web sites may give you more ideas to consider in developing your Web site.

Laws and Regulations

Objective 5.5
Identify key factors relating to legal and regulatory considerations when planning e-business solutions.
... Knowledge ownership/Intellectual property rights
... Jurisdiction

The global reach of the Web vastly increases the benefits and difficulties of deploying and maintaining a site. When you consider the global reach of the Web, both the promises and risks are vastly multiplied. Your Web site might bring you—theoretically, at least—within the legal jurisdiction of many different countries. Furthermore, these different legal frameworks arise from many cultures, which can be very unlike those to which we are accustomed. Each of these cultures may have its own set of values, with its own ideas about what the law can and should regulate.

The policy of the United States on global electronic commerce is that "the private sector should lead," and that laws and regulations should be minimal and should not interfere with the Internet's basic strengths. Some nations join the U.S. in this view, but many nations have differing positions as to how much regulation is necessary and appropriate.

If you expect your Web site to have a significant audience or customer base outside the United States, you should consider at least three areas in terms of other countries' laws:

- Your products

- Your expression

- Your business methods

Your Products

These are the goods or services your Web site provides or promotes. Practically every country in the world has laws that control how, and whether, certain physical items may be bought, sold, and used within their domains. If your Web site is a commercial site that sells a product, you should consider whether this product might be illegal, or otherwise regulated, in other countries. Some products that merit close consideration include firearms and other weapons (including toy and replica weapons), foods and beverages (including alcohol products), books, videos, and other media (that could unexpectedly violate other countries' decency, state secret, religion, privacy, "hate speech," and other laws).

Unless you actually do business with customers in another country, or actively market your Web site to that country, it is unlikely that the country's laws will affect you. However, some countries have attempted to impose their laws on U.S. Web sites on rather thin grounds. In August 2000, Yahoo! lost a case in a French court that left the Web site subject to thousands of dollars worth of fines. A user of Yahoo!'s auction service offered for sale various items of World War II Nazi memorabilia, which are illegal to sell in France. Even though Yahoo's servers were located in California, the French court ordered Yahoo! to pay substantial fines for each day that the auctions were accessible to Web users located in France. A U.S. court in California subsequently found in favor of Yahoo!, ruling that the French law could not be enforced against a U.S. company operating in the U.S. Even so, this case shows how far some governments may go in their efforts to impose local or national laws upon the Web.

United States Law

If you conduct business overseas, also keep in mind that U.S. law includes numerous restrictions on imports, exports, and other aspects of international commerce. This includes restrictions on some types of information technology, both hardware and software. Thus, U.S. law can affect your business even if you ship no physical goods, and provide only services or downloadable software via the Web. If you are involved in international e-commerce, you should investigate what U.S. laws might apply to your products and services, and if necessary, take steps to avoid doing business with users in certain countries.

Your Expression

This refers to the actual words, images, and sounds presented on your Web site—the way in which you present information and ideas. Even when it is being used to sell a product, the Web is primarily a means of expression and communication. United States law includes extensive protections for free expression, but not all countries do. In some places, expression may be subject to strict laws and regulations.

As we have already discussed, some nations and provinces have laws requiring the use of certain languages, and may seek to impose these laws upon Web sites based within their jurisdictions. Other nations have strict laws regarding "indecency." Text and images that do not raise any concern in the United States may be violations of law in such places. Also, many European nations have different, often stronger laws regarding privacy and defamation than the U.S.

As the California decision in the Yahoo! case indicates, it is unlikely that another country will be able to enforce their laws against a U.S.-based site simply because the site is accessible from that country. However, if you are actually doing business in another country, and especially if you or other employees of your company plan to travel to another country, it is wise to investigate whether your Web site's content violates any of that country's laws.

Your Business Methods

This topic deals less with a Web site itself, and more with the business practices behind it. Other countries' laws may affect the way you operate your business, now that its "storefront" exists in many different countries at once. Depending upon your level of involvement with a foreign country, that country may seek to enforce laws requiring, for example, certain accounting and reporting requirements. Another country's privacy laws may dictate the way you collect, store, and use customer data. If you are selling a product, your business may be subject to another country's consumer protection laws. You might be required to register to do business in a country, and may have to appoint a local agent for such things as acceptance of legal service.

Once again, it is unlikely that this will apply to you if your contact with a country is limited to a Web site accessible to anyone on the Internet. However, if your contact with a particular country or region becomes stronger, do not let the ease of Internet globalization trick you into ignoring these important points. Consider the potential risks; it may be wise to hire a knowledgeable attorney to help you comply with another country's legal requirements.

Privacy

Objective 5.5
Identify key factors relating to legal and regulatory considerations when planning e-business solutions.
... Privacy

Privacy is emerging as a key area in which your business practices may need to satisfy the laws of other countries. In general, European countries have greater legal protection for personal privacy online than the United States. A directive of the European Union (E.U.) requires all member countries to enact laws establishing certain data privacy rights. These include a person's right to access personal information collected about him or her, the right to correct such information, the right to know how that data might be used or transferred, and the right to stop further use of the data. The European privacy standards also restrict the transfer of personal data to non-E.U. nations whose laws do not establish a level of protection comparable to the E.U. requirements. Therefore, if you do business with European companies, you may find yourself unable to receive customer data, or you may be required to agree to and honor privacy protection standards approved by a foreign government's privacy office.

Practical Concerns

Objective 5.4
Identify key factors relating to strategic marketing considerations as they relate to launching an e-business initiative.
... Geographic/ Localization considerations (local customs/criteria, etc.)

In addition to legal considerations, serving a global market by means of your Web site will pose a number of practical challenges, from both business and system administration standpoints.

Currency

One common, and usually effective way of dealing with multiple currencies is simply to ignore them. If you are running an e-commerce site expecting limited overseas sales, you can probably state that all sales shall be for U.S. dollars, and expect your customers to convert from their home currency to dollars. As much of the world has become accustomed to doing international business in English, many have also become accustomed to using American dollars for international transactions.

109

Such international transactions are facilitated by the fact that most e-commerce payments are made by credit card, and most major credit card companies can handle currency conversions easily. Card companies are able to credit a U.S. business's account in dollars, and charge users' accounts in their home currencies, at the appropriate exchange rate. Because these currency conversions may require you or your customers to pay extra fees, look into the policies of the credit cards you accept.

For your users' convenience, you might consider including a currency converter on your site. Either a piece of CGI software or a link to a converter on another site will allow a users to see what your prices equate to in their home currency. If you are using any kind of currency conversion system on your site, remember that currency exchange rates can change very rapidly, and you have to be diligent to always provide the most current data.

If you want to create a more advanced site that targets an international audience, consider taking further steps to handle multiple currencies. To serve a specific foreign market, you could include specialized pages that give prices in that country's currency. To deal with multiple currencies, you might ask users up front for their location, and use CGI programming to present a shopping cart total in a specific currency. You could also use dynamic Web pages to present all prices in specific currencies.

In general, unless you are creating separate sites to serve different countries, like Yahoo!, it is safer and simpler to use U.S. Dollars for your transactions. If your e-commerce site grows large enough, it may be worthwhile to spin off separate sites for different countries or regions, each dealing in the appropriate currency.

Time Zones and Calendars

The world never sleeps, and neither does the World Wide Web. Serving a global audience by means of the Web involves being available at any time of every day, across 24 time zones.

Normally this is not a problem on the Web. As long as your server is running and online, visitors can access your Web site. However, global time can be a factor in scheduling the upkeep of a popular site. You may be accustomed to scheduling system backups or other routine maintenance late at night or in the very early morning, during off-peak hours. Remember that it is always "peak time" somewhere on Earth. Of course regular backups and maintenance are necessary, but rather than make assumptions about the best times for these tasks, you should analyze your site's traffic patterns and select a time when your maintenance will have the least performance impact and affect the smallest number of users worldwide.

If your Web site relates to a business that requires customer service, competing globally may mean expanding your service hours to accommodate overseas users. Depending upon the extent of your overseas customer base, you might also consider providing customer service in languages other than English.

Beyond the 24-hour clock of the global Internet, also be aware that your overseas customers may follow a different workweek than in the United States, and will certainly celebrate different legal holidays. Such facts are important not only for predicting periods of peak and off-peak usage, but also for planning shipment of physical products overseas, and for scheduling and selecting content of interest to your foreign readers.

Social Values and Customs

Finally, it is important to recognize that in dealing with audiences from different nations and cultures, your Web site will host people with a wide variety of social customs and values. Many of these values are reflected in the laws of different nations, and we have already seen how some countries attempt to enforce such laws against Web sites that come into their communities by means of the Internet. However, the vast majority of a culture's values and customs are not codified in any law—but they will still affect the way in which your Web site is perceived.

As with language and currency, if you are targeting a specific country or region you should study its culture and try to accommodate it in your Web site, preferably with the help of writers and developers knowledgeable about the location's values and customs. However, it is impossible for your site to accommodate the cultures of every place with Web accessibility. No one can know and understand, let alone follow, the customs and values of every place where your users might reside. Moreover, the customs of one culture might be severe social blunders in another. For example, an e-commerce site might use cookies to determine that James Smith is a repeat shopper, so that when he accesses the site he will be greeted with "Welcome back, James!" In America this may seem like simple friendliness, but in some other cultures it might be considered rude for a merchant's site to address a customer by his first name.

For a media or information site, the best approach to dealing with multiple cultures is to "be yourself." Providing content from a point of view unique to your own country or region is probably one of the most valuable contributions your Web site can make, and it may be a reason for overseas users to come to your site, rather than only visiting sites from their home countries.

111

For business and e-commerce sites, there is probably no better approach than to be polite and businesslike. While these may have different definitions in different places, most customers will respond positively to a straightforward approach—more so than to an approach that seems like a superficial and patronizing attempt to adopt a culture that is clearly not yours.

Furthermore, as the Web's global community grows, it is in the process of developing its own customs and expectations—influenced largely by the United States, but also influenced by many other cultures. It is important for a successful Web site to be a part of and contribute to this growing global culture.

Activities

1. Many of the world's governments provide substantial information by means of Web sites. Search the Web for the government Web sites of three countries, and research the following topics: international business development, investment, tourism, or related topics. For each country, try to find answers to the following:

   a. What is the country's population?

   b. What language or languages are used?

   c. What currency is used? What is its current rate of exchange with the U.S. dollar?

   d. What other nations are the country's main trading partners?

   e. What formalities are required to do business in the country?

   f. Does the country have any stated policies regarding international e-commerce?

2. Visit the Babel Fish (**http://babelfish.altavista.com/**) translation site. Translate at least five common phrases from English to any other language, then back to English again. Summarize your findings, and your opinion about the best uses of automated translation on the Web.

____

____

____

____

____

____

Extended Activities

1. Browse the Web site at **www.amazon.de**. (If you are fluent in German, try **www.amazon.fr**, or another site in a language you do not know well.) Discuss the experience, and consider it in terms of non-English readers who come to your site.

2. If you can read a language other than English, browse some Web sites in that language and take note of any differences in design from most English-language sites. Which differences are due to language? Which are cultural? Do any differences seem based upon different legal systems?

3. Search for, and browse, some Web sites in the .jp, .cn, jo, .kr and .ru top-level domains. How much English do you find? Can your browser display the non-English languages without installing additional fonts? What differences in Web site design do you notice in sites that use non-Western writing systems?

Lesson 3—Cash Flow on the Internet

How do financial information and funds flow between online buyers and sellers? To answer that question we will begin with an overview of the credit card transaction process, which is the dominant form of online funds transfer today. Then we shift the focus to the future by introducing several emerging technologies for online cash transactions.

On the Internet, both credit and cash transactions require additional steps to verify the identities of one, and sometimes both parties involved in a transaction. In a face-to-face transaction, the consumer is already sure of the identity of the merchant, and the merchant can easily verify the identity of the customer. However, over the anonymous Internet, merchants and consumers must rely on technology to validate who they are, confirm what services or products are being exchanged, and ensure that money or credit is available.

Objectives

At the end of this lesson you will be able to:

- Explain the process of a typical online credit card transaction

- Describe the most common forms of electronic cash

- Discuss some of the technical challenges of anonymous electronic cash

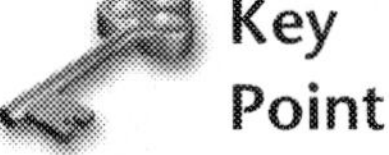

Key Point

Online transactions must verify the identities of one or both of the parties.

Online Credit Card Transactions

Objective 4.1
Understand and be able to describe various Internet security concepts.
... Authentication
... Secure Socket Layers (SSL)

Objective 5.1
Understand and be able to describe e-commerce terms and concepts.
... EDI (Electronic Data Interchange)

Just as a Web business must be based on offline business principles, credit card transactions are basically the same whether the transaction is taking place on the Internet or in a brick-and-mortar store. However, an online transaction adds one additional step that is not necessary at a store: the merchant site authenticates its identity to the user's browser.

Most secure online transactions use Secure Sockets Layer (SSL) to encrypt communications between a buyer and seller. (We discuss SSL in more detail in "Security," Lesson 1.) Therefore, before a secure online transaction can occur, both buyer and merchant must be set up to use SSL.

Players in an E-Commerce Transaction

There are several players in an e-commerce transaction, as described below:

- Consumer, with a browser that supports SSL (such as Netscape Communicator or Microsoft Internet Explorer).

- Consumer's bank (the "issuing" bank).

- Merchant's secure Web server. The server must be configured to support SSL, and have a digital certificate that identifies the merchant and provides the merchant's public encryption key. Most online stores include a separate back-end database server to maintain the online "catalog" and process customer orders.

- Merchant's transaction server, that processes credit card authorizations and other financial transactions with the merchant's bank. Shipping and billing may also be handled by the transaction server, or by both the database and transaction servers.

- Merchant's bank (the "acquiring" bank).

- The Private Inter-Bank Financial Network, using Electronic Data Interchange (EDI) connections.

Step-by-Step Online Credit Card Transaction

The E-Commerce Transaction Flow Diagram illustrates the process of a typical online purchase using a credit card. As you read the following steps, refer to the corresponding numbers in the diagram.

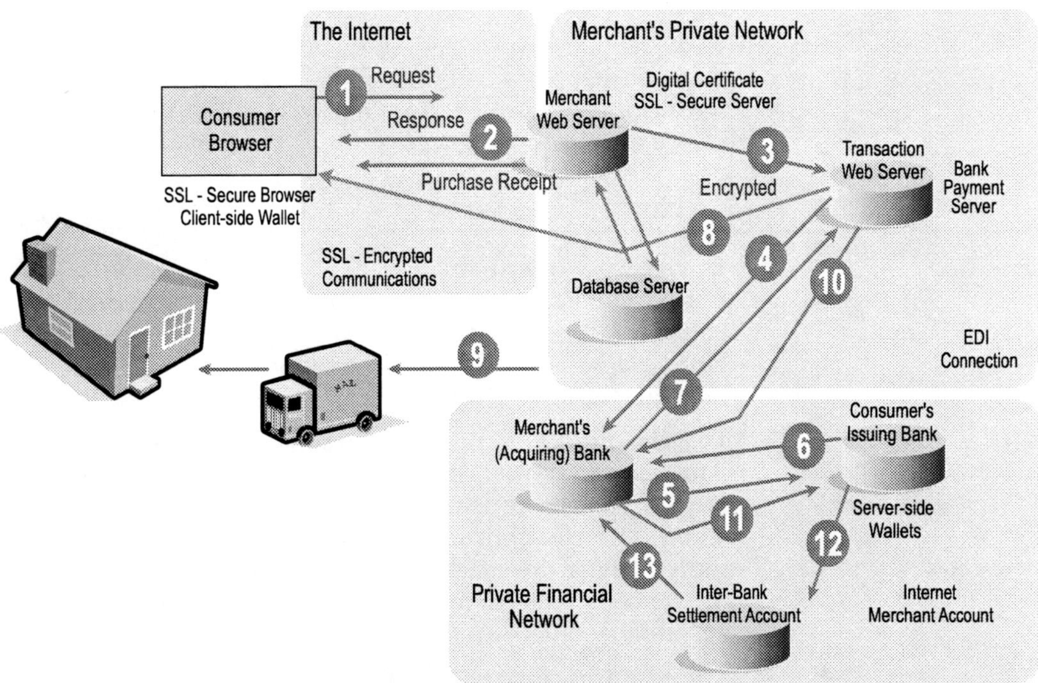

E-Commerce Transaction Flow

E-Commerce Transaction Flow

1. The consumer connects to the Internet and shops at a merchant's Web site. The merchant's Web server displays current product data (catalogs) dynamically created by querying the merchant's database server. When the consumer initiates a transaction, usually by clicking a "checkout" link, the browser and server begin the handshake protocol that establishes an SSL session.

2. During the SSL handshake, the merchant's secure Web server authenticates the merchant's identity by providing its digital certificate to the browser.

3. When the secure connection is established, the consumer provides a charge card number to the merchant. This number is either typed into a Common Gateway Interface (CGI) form page or stored in a client-side or server-side digital wallet. The transaction information and credit card number are encrypted by the browser and sent to the merchant's Web server, which passes them to the transaction server. The information remains secure as long as it remains in the SSL pipeline. Upon entering the merchant's network, security is the merchant's responsibility.

4. The merchant asks its bank (the acquiring bank) for a credit card authorization.

5. The Private Inter-Bank Financial Network sends a message from the merchant's acquiring bank to the consumer's issuing bank, asking for credit card authorization. The Inter-Bank Financial Network uses EDI technology and is separate from public Internet networks.

6. The consumer's issuing bank responds, via the Private Inter-Bank Financial Network, to the merchant's acquiring bank. At this time, the consumer's bank may also place a certain amount of the consumer's credit line on hold, pending the settlement of the transaction. This prevents multiple charges, by the consumer or the banks, against the same funds in the consumer's line of credit or current bank balance.

7. The acquiring (merchant's) bank notifies the merchant that the charge has been approved.

8. The merchant notifies the customer that the order has been processed.

9. The merchant fills the consumer's order by shipping the merchandise.

10. At regular intervals, the merchant sends a batch of credit card settlement requests to the acquiring bank.

11. The acquiring bank sends each settlement request, via the Inter-Bank Financial Network, to the appropriate issuing bank.

12. The consumer's bank debits the consumer's account and places the money (with a possible service charge) into a separate temporary holding location called an Inter-Bank settlement account.

13. The acquiring bank credits the merchant's account and withdraws a similar sum of money from the Inter-Bank settlement account.

14. The actual money then makes its way through numerous banks and intermediaries into the merchant's account. That process is beyond the scope of this lesson; however, be aware that the modern financial system is a truly global, highly integrated network of institutions.

Electronic Cash

The credit system works well for online transactions, but it has two main drawbacks. First, a consumer must have a credit card. This shuts out children, adults with poor credit, and adults who simply prefer to not use credit. Second, a credit card leaves a clear record trail back to a purchaser. A consumer may have many legitimate reasons for preferring to make some transactions anonymously.

Therefore, before Internet commerce can reach the potential sales figure quoted above, it must support secure, provable financial transactions that are as simple and anonymous as dropping a coin into a vending machine. The following financial institutions have sprung up to provide secure, reliable forms of electronic cash.

eCash

eCash (**http://www.ecash.com**) is a third-party transaction service. eCash accepts limited international sales, with offices in the Netherlands, Australia, and United States.

The eCash system essentially works like a check. Before using eCash, both merchants and consumers must open eCash accounts at supporting banks. Consumers download some eCash to their home computers, available to spend at online stores that accept eCash. When a consumer pays a merchant with eCash (similar to writing a check), the consumer's bank transfers the actual funds from the consumer's eCash account to the merchant's account at the merchant's eCash bank.

This system limits the buyer to eCash merchants, but simplifies some aspects of business, such as collections. eCash can also be verified as authentic (noncounterfeit) at any time, through a simple online request.

eCash systems offer two levels of consumer privacy. In an unconditionally anonymous transaction, eCash provides no financial information about a customer; all a merchant ever knows is a customer's shipping address. Conditionally anonymous transactions offer fraud protection by allowing the merchant to learn the identity of a consumer who attempts to spend the same eCash twice.

E-Commerce

CyberCash

CyberCash (**http://www.cybercash.com**) uses 56-bit DES single-key encryption and 1,024-bit RSA public-key encryption to allow secure transmission of conventional credit card information between online merchants and their customers. (In contrast, most SSL sessions use only 40-bit encryption keys. We discuss encryption in "Security.") CyberCash is not a method of payment; it is a third-party transaction service that enables secure Internet payments.

To support CyberCash transactions, a merchant opens a credit card transaction account at a bank, and then installs CyberCash's Cash Register software on the secure Web server.

Meanwhile, consumers must install the free CyberCash Wallet application. This software maintains a local database of each consume's credit cards and other payment instruments. When a consumer first runs the Wallet software, it creates a public/private key combination and passphrase. The passphrase ensures that only the authorized user may place orders, while the key combination is used to encrypt the consumer's financial data on the local hard drive. A backup copy of this data, also encrypted, is stored on a floppy disk.

Once this preparation is complete, the Wallet software contains an electronic version of the consumer's credit card. The consumer can place an order electronically, and have a credit card approved in real-time by the merchant's credit card processor. The process follows the same general steps, and takes about the same amount of time, as if the consumer were standing at the checkout counter in a local mall.

Mondex

Mondex (**http://www.mondex.com**) is a general-purpose digital payment system that uses a proprietary encoding scheme on a smart card with an embedded microcomputer chip. This microprocessor has been programmed to function as a "stored value" electronic wallet that the user can pre-load with digital cash. Using a personal identification number (PIN) code, a smart card can be locked so that only the card owner can access its contents. The digital cash can be used as payment for goods or services, or transferred to another Mondex card, by means of a card reader. After the digital cash has been transferred to a merchant, the actual funds flow to the merchant's account by means of the same electronic banking systems described above.

Mondex is still primarily used in face-to-face transactions, in businesses such as hotels and retail stores. However, a consumer may use a Mondex card for online shopping by first buying a Mondex phone that contains a card reader.

Mondex is still more popular in Europe than the United States. However, the system could potentially simplify Internet trade in low-value goods and services, such as short published articles, images, or music selections. It could also extend the benefits of e-commerce to children and anyone else who cannot use a credit card.

The first development specifications for the Mondex card were issued in 1994. Currently, more than 450 companies in over 40 countries are working on or with the Mondex card. Mondex was introduced in Swindon, England, and is now a subsidiary of MasterCard International (**http://www.mastercard.com**).

First Virtual PIN

The First Virtual Personal Identification Number (PIN), from First Virtual, is an indirect method of using a credit card over the Internet. The credit card information is never sent across the Internet. Instead, a customer authorizes payments by sending the merchant a PIN that represents the consumer's credit card information recorded at First Virtual.

Before using this system, both consumers and merchants open accounts with First Virtual. Each consumer provides information about a credit card to be used for transactions, and is issued a Virtual PIN.

The five steps in a First Virtual PIN transaction are as follows:

1. The customer transmits a First Virtual PIN to the merchant by means of e-mail or a Hypertext Markup Language (HTML) form.

2. The merchant transmits the customer's PIN and transaction amount to First Virtual to be authorized.

3. First Virtual sends an e-mail to the customer, asking for verification of the merchant's charge.

4. The customer replies to First Virtual's e-mail with the word "Yes," "No," or "Fraud."

5. If, and only if, the e-mail reply is "Yes" does First Virtual inform the merchant that the transaction and charges will be processed.

No encryption is used when sending purchasing information or a PIN from consumer to merchant because the verification process makes it very difficult for a thief to use a stolen PIN. Because a PIN cannot lead a thief to a consumer's actual credit information, it is only good for making fraudulent purchases from merchants that use the First Virtual system. Even so, to use a stolen PIN in a

121

fraudulent transaction, a bandit would have to perform two diffi-cult steps:

1. Intercept the e-mail from First Virtual to the actual owner of the PIN, asking for confirmation of the purchase.

2. Falsify the customer's reply e-mail that contains the "Yes" message that authorizes First Virtual to proceed with the transaction.

Finally, even if a thief manages to complete the above two steps, funds are not actually transferred to the merchant's account until 60 days after the transaction. Therefore, a consumer has time to detect any potential fraud in a credit card billing statement.

Electronic Wallets

An electronic wallet is a software application that locally stores financial data to speed transactions and avoid typing errors.

When you shop with an electronic wallet, you only have to enter your billing and shipping information once. Your wallet will then instantly fill out compatible online order forms with just a click of the mouse. To make gift giving easier, the wallet can also store the shipping addresses of friends and family.

Smart Cards

Smart cards are plastic bankcards that contain embedded inte-grated circuit (IC) microprocessors and a standard magnetic strip. In locations without a chip-reading terminal, transactions may still be completed using the card's magnetic strip. Financial insti-tutions are adopting smart cards to allow customers to make pur-chases from a credit account, debit account, or stored value on the card.

The microprocessor can process different kinds of information and applications; thus, various industries can use the same smart card in different ways. For example, frequent flyer program infor-mation could be stored on a travel card, along with hotel prefer-ences, airline seating preferences, bank account balances, pre-paid cell phone credits, and (in the future) an individual's medical his-tory and drug allergies. Visa Cash, a stored value application, allows a customer to pre-load money into the smart card to pay for small-value transactions such as tolls, parking fees, Internet purchases, and laundry services.

Smart cards are currently used in over 30 countries, including Russia, Australia, Brazil, Singapore, Spain, Hong Kong, Japan, Canada, the United States, Taiwan, the United Kingdom, and Argentina. In some cities, financial institutions have formed partnerships with local mass transit systems to allow smart cards to buy public transportation. Smart cards can also be used at some fast food outlets, public telephones, video rental stores, newsstands, gas stations, and convenience stores.

Because smart cards can store information about multiple financial applications, a single smart card can replace a wallet full of bank, credit, mass transit, medical, and insurance cards. Of course, with great convenience also comes great risk; a lost or stolen smart card could mean financial catastrophe.

Activity

1. Match each method of passing funds online between a customer and a merchant with its description.

   Works basically the same whether used online or in person
   ____

   Verifies transactions through the use of multiple, unencrypted e-mail messages _______________________

   Plastic bank cards with embedded ICs designed to allow multiple purchases from one device _______________________

   Program that locally stores financial data _______________________

   Works similarly to writing a check, such that funds are transferred from the consumer's bank to the merchant
   ____

   Uses 56-bit DES and 1,024-bit RSA public-key encryption to secure transactions _______________________

   a. Cybercash

   b. Smart card

   c. First Virtual PIN

   d. Credit card transaction

   e. Electronic Wallet

   f. eCash

Extended Activities

1. Common credit card transactions require that consumers provide their name, address, credit card number, and so forth. Which of the online transaction methods discussed would protect the anonymity of the consumer? How?

2. Journalists and law enforcement investigators who want to uncover illegal activity have long been taught to "follow the money." However, some forms of electronic cash are designed to be untraceable. Discuss whether a free society should be allowed to prohibit electronic cash technology in the interests of law enforcement or public safety. Consider whether it is even possible to forbid this technology.

Lesson 4—E-Commerce Development Options

Most of the complexity of an e-commerce site is contained in its back-end systems: the applications that control inventory and customer databases, order and payment processing, shipping, billing, and other vital business processes. Creating these systems from the ground up requires skills and budgets far beyond the reach of most companies.

However, several viable options exist for businesses that do not need unique back-end systems. The simplest of these development options can make e-commerce a reality for even the smallest merchant.

Objectives

At the end of this lesson you will be able to:

- Name some technical considerations for e-commerce applications

- Describe the various e-commerce development options available to a merchant organization

- Discuss the technical and business trade-offs of each development option

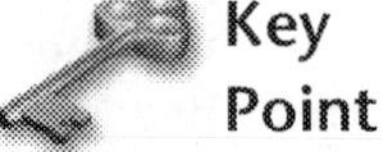 **Key Point**

When developing an e-commerce application, the biggest question is: buy, build, or outsource?

Technical Considerations for E-Commerce Applications

A full-featured e-commerce site is a technically complex enterprise. The following lists include some of the most important factors to consider when implementing an online business.

Web Server and Database Issues

An e-business must be built on a solid infrastructure of reliable servers, network components, and software. The following list describes technical considerations an organization should explore when developing an e-commerce Web site:

- Load balancing technology distributes incoming user requests across multiple identical servers, so that no single machine is overwhelmed.

- Scalability means that a system has been designed to accept later additions of machines, bandwidth, hard drive space, or other hardware as required. The ability to expand, based on ongoing growth requirements, prevents future technical and business bottlenecks.

- Failover reliability ensures that a system contains no single point of failure. For example, if a network interface card (NIC), communications path, or entire computer fails, a backup piece of equipment is in place to automatically take over.

- Database connection pooling saves processing time by pre-opening multiple database connections that wait for user requests.

- Administration of the Web site applications is critical. Is the site staffed by trained personnel who know how to deal with the entire Web site and its applications, and not merely the separate pages?

- Database administration is a full-time job that includes input/output of data, designing and building tables and tablespaces, ensuring data integrity, making backups, restoring data, and upgrading the software and hardware of the database server.

- Database integrity, or the reliability and accuracy of database contents, is vital to dynamic Web sites. For example, if one data entry is updated, are all related entries also updated? If data is partially entered and the connection fails, will that partial order be backed out of the system?

Application Business Logic

Although the technology of a site is important, it must always serve the interests of the overall business. Adapt the technology to the needs of the business, not the other way around:

- Catalog functions must accurately and quickly indicate what items are for sale and in stock, and what nonstock items are available on back order. Furthermore, catalog systems must make it simple to picture and describe items, associate them with other items, or retire them from the catalog.

- Shopping cart functions determine how the site keeps track of customers' choices. Beyond that, shopping cart logic must be able to decide how long to maintain a record of "abandoned" items (if the user leaves the site before completing a transaction), in hopes of a later sale.

- Inventory, shipping, and handling systems are vital to a buyer's perception of good customer service. An e-commerce system must smoothly handle order tracking; reflect the true state of the warehouse inventory; correctly calculate merchandise costs, discounts, and handling fees; arrange shipping and estimate delivery times; and provide a simple way for customers to check the status of their orders.

- Taxation is currently not an issue on the Internet; however, this will probably change. In the not-too-distant future, e-commerce sites will be required to track the origin and destination of each purchase, so that each government entity can get its "fair share" of sales tax revenue. Tax logic will need to account for multiple layers of governmental taxation (city, county, state, and so forth) for each transaction.

- Tracking functions handle the physical packing and shipping of merchandise, track the shipment as it travels from the merchant to the customer, and confirm the customer's receipt of the order. In addition, tracking systems provide mechanisms for accepting customer returns, updating inventory, and managing defective merchandise. They may even automatically contact customers to ask whether they are pleased with their purchases.

- Payment processing systems handle the transfer of funds from customer to merchant. These systems bill the customer; pay the suppliers; accept checks, credit cards or electronic cash; and facilitate the movement of money to and from banks (both electronically and physically).

Buy, Build, or Outsource?

Objective 3.11
Understand and be able to describe the capabilities of application server providers.

The long list of technical considerations for an e-commerce Web site translates to a fairly long list of specialized skills. Large organizations may already have the right business and technical experts on staff. However, the smaller the organization, the less likely it is to employ people with the skills necessary to build an e-commerce site.

As a result, several options are available for e-commerce development, depending on an organization's level of expertise and technical requirements.

Buy a Turn-Key Development Package

A turnkey package is right for a smaller organization that lacks both site development skills and a large budget. A turnkey package is a standardized e-commerce application that a merchant customizes with company and product information. A single service provider hosts and administers multiple turnkey merchant sites. The merchant organization needs no specialized knowledge, and need not install any software. Each organization uses a wizard-style interface to select commonly needed e-commerce features, chooses a visual design theme, configures a few required settings, and types in its product information.

The turnkey approach is fairly inexpensive, and offers fewer special features and less flexibility than a custom-designed site. Examples of turnkey package providers include:

- Yahoo's Stores

    (**http://www.store.yahoo.com**)

- Intershop enfinity

    (**http://www.intershop.com/index.htm**)

- Netscape SellerXpert

    (**http://www.netscape.com/sellerxpert/index.html**)

- Ariba B2B

    (**http://www.ariba.com/corp/home/**)

- Marketplace B2B

    (**http://www.techsmart.com**)

Build with a Template-Based Development Package

These packages offer modifiable templates that provide more options than a turnkey site, but still get the merchant up and running more quickly than a fully custom site. In complexity, cost, and features, this approach falls somewhere between turnkey and custom methods. However, a particular package may not offer all e-commerce features.

Examples of template-based development packages include:

- Intershop 4

    (**http://www.intershop.com/index.htm**)

- HP Bluestone Total-e-Business

  http://www.openview.hp.com/products/smartplugins/spis/ documents/product_html-345.asp.

Build with a Fully Custom Application Toolkit

This approach brings us full circle back to a fully custom Web site. However, in this case, the merchant organization is responsible for designing and developing all of the site components from scratch, as well as integrating them with current business practices. This includes creating custom back-end applications to handle databases, tax management, shipping, payment processing, and any other business function necessary to the merchant's industry.

An e-commerce application toolkit provides development tools for professional programmers. Some of the major development toolkit vendors include:

- Microsoft Site Server Commerce Edition, which uses Active Server Pages (ASP)

  (http://www.microsoft.com/technet/commerce/deploy.asp)

- Macromedia ColdFusion Application Engine, which uses ColdFusion Markup Language

  (http://www.macromedia.com/software/coldfusion)

- IBM WebSphere Commerce Suite

  (http://www-4.ibm.com/software/webservers/commerce/)

Outsource to an Application Service Provider

An Application Service Provider uses the Internet to offer customers temporary use of complex, expensive systems. For example, an ASP might set up and administer a sophisticated financial analysis program. Customers that need occasional financial analysis can then pay to use the ASP's system. Large ASPs make powerful hardware or software tools available to small companies that cannot afford them. Small ASPs serve even smaller customers by providing customized e-mail services, Internet fax services, or any other specialized service that a customer may only need occasionally. ASPs of all sizes offer a wide range of Web development and hosting services.

An Application Service Provider is the right choice for an organization that has enough money to custom-build an e-commerce site, but has no e-commerce expertise, artistic talent, technical ability, or desire to acquire these skills. The Application Service Provider can custom-build a site to the customer's specifications, and administer it afterward.

After the site is launched, the merchant organization stays in constant contact with the ASP. In addition to the application development cost, the outsource firm charges an ongoing monthly service fee for Web hosting, customer support, management, modification, and enhancement.

Examples of Application Service Providers for Web sites include:

- Broadvision One to One Web Applications
  (**http://www.broadvision.com**)

- Oracle Applications
  (**http://www.oracle.com/events/thinkcustomers/
  index.html?content.html?src=263685&Act=11**)

Activities

1. Match the e-commerce application/technical consideration with its description.

    The ability of a system to be readily expanded to avoid performance bottlenecks ___________________

    The technology that allows multiple servers to share the request load ___________________

    A full-time job that includes table design, data input and output, data backup and restores, and system maintenance ___________________

    Using redundant devices to ensure a system has no single point of failure ___________________

    Pre-opening databases to save time ___________________

    a. Database administration

    b. Failover reliability

    c. Database connection pooling

    d. Load balancing

    e. Scalability

2. The e-commerce solution that allows full customized solutions is a ___________________

3. The e-commerce solutions best suited to companies with small budgets and no development skills is a ___________________ ___________________.

4. The e-commerce solution that allows some customizing while still bringing the site online quickly is a ___________________ ___________________.

Extended Activities

1. A friend of yours makes high-quality custom fishing flies in his garage. He wants to try selling his flies on the Web, accepting credit cards as payment. He has limited computer experience, and does not want to invest a huge amount of money in this project. Using the Web, find at least three turn-key development companies that your friend can use to economically launch his online storefront. For each option, detail the start-up and continuing costs, and describe what your friend will need to learn to maintain and administer his site.

2. Would use of an Application Service Provider reduce the amount of control a merchant has over its site? Would a merchant be able to change site content as quickly with an Application Service Provider as he or she would if hosting and maintaining his or her own site?

3. If use of an Application Service Provider increased the time to turn around site changes, could this delay adversely affect sales? Would such a site be capable of staying competitive with other merchants maintaining and hosting their own sites?

Lesson 5—Intellectual Property

Intellectual property refers to human creations that have value not directly connected with their physical form. For example, when you purchase a CD, you are not spending your money in order to get a plastic disk. Rather, you are paying for the music that is encoded on that disk. On the Web it is especially important to understand intellectual property, because in a very real sense that is the only kind of property that exists on the Web. The true value of a Web site lies not in the servers and routers it runs on, but in the words, images, and sounds created by the developers and transmitted to the users.

Property rights in physical objects are fairly easy to understand. If you own a laptop computer, you have the right to possess and use that physical object. If someone steals your laptop, you no longer have it, and the thief has violated your property rights. The intangible nature of intellectual property makes for more complex situations, and special bodies of law have been developed to recognize and protect various types of intellectual property rights.

Objectives

At the end of this lesson you will be able to:

- Identify the principal types of intellectual property

- Determine the type or types of intellectual property most relevant to each aspect of a Web site

- Recognize when your Web site might infringe on the intellectual property of another site

- Recognize your own intellectual property and how it might be protected

 **Key Point**

Several forms of intellectual property rights protect a person or company's creations, inventions, and identity.

Four Types of Intellectual Property

Objective 5.5
Identify key factors relating to legal and regulatory consider- ations when plan- ning e-business solutions.
...Knowledge owner- ship / Intellectual property rights

Four basic types of intellectual property are recognized and pro- tected under United States laws, the laws of most countries, and under certain international agreements. The four types of intellec- tual property are as follows:

- **Copyright**—Protects original works of authorship, such as original text, graphics, and computer programs

- **Trademark**—Protects logos, names, and other items that relate to commercial identity and public perception

- **Patent**—Protects original inventions

- **Trade Secret**—Can protect certain business practices, meth- ods, and information

We will look at copyrights and trademarks in some detail because these forms of intellectual property most relate to the Web. We will also look at patents and trade secrets, but in less detail because they are less likely to impact your work as a Webmaster or Web developer.

During this lesson keep in mind that although our discussion focuses on the law of the United States of America, the global reach of the Web may require you to consider the laws of other nations.

Copyright

Objective 5.5
Identify key factors relating to legal and regulatory consider- ations when plan- ning e-business solutions.
... Knowledge own- ership/Intellectual property rights

Copyright is by far the most critical form of intellectual property right for most Web sites, because it has the potential to affect everything that appears on a site: text, graphics, audio, and video. It may also affect the HTML and other source code that lies behind your site. Because Federal law controls copyright, it does not change from one state to another.

What Is Protected?

According to United States law, copyright protects "original works of authorship," which are "fixed in any tangible medium of expression."

At its simplest, "original works of authorship" means any creative expression that is new and not copied from some other source. To qualify as a "work of authorship," the work must also include some element of human creativity or intelligence. No precise rules govern what qualifies as an "original work of authorship";

the Copyright law intentionally leaves these terms undefined. However, generally, if a human being creates some new textual, graphical, musical, or other form of expression, it can be protected by copyright.

In order to be protected by copyright, works must be "fixed in any tangible medium of expression, now known or later developed, from which they can be perceived, reproduced, or otherwise communicated, either directly or with the aid of a machine or device." This means that the work must be written or recorded in some physical object, such as a book, videotape, or computer disk. A Web site satisfies this requirement by, for example, being written to the host machine's hard drive. Remember, however, that the property protected by copyright is not the physical object, but the intangible expression that is recorded on the object.

The Federal copyright statute includes a list of some, but not all of the kinds of works that can be protected by copyright law. The multimedia nature of today's Web means that practically all of these types of work might exist on a Web site. The Examples of the U.S. Copyright Statute Table lists some of these, along with the elements of a Web site that they might protect.

Examples of the U.S. Copyright Statute

Categories from the U.S. Copyright Statute	Examples Found in Web Sites
"Literary works"	Any original text on your site and computer programs, including HTML source.
"Musical works, including any accompanying words"	Musical compositions presented on a site in any form, such as musical notation or guitar tablatures. (Note that this refers to copyright in the musical composition itself, which is separate from the copyright in a particular sound recording of a performance of the music.)
"Sound recordings"	Downloadable MP3 files, MIDI background music, and spoken word or musical recordings in streaming audio.
"Pictorial, graphic, and sculptural works"	Any original images on your site.
"Motion pictures and other audiovisual works"	Downloadable or streaming video such as MPEG, QuickTime, or RealPlayer files.

U.S. copyright law defines "Literary works"' as "works, other than audiovisual works, expressed in words, numbers, or other verbal or numerical symbols or indicia, regardless of the nature of the material objects, such as books, periodicals, manuscripts, phone records, film, tapes, disks, or cards, in which they are embodied." Because computer programs are expressed in words, numbers, and symbols; they fit this definition. This includes the HTML from which your Web site is built, the Perl or Java code you may write for its interactive features, and even executable binary files.

Copyright protection can also extend to compilations of information, even if no copyright can be claimed in the individual elements of the compilation. For example, if your Web site includes a list of your Top Ten Web Shopping Sites, you can claim copyright in the list as a whole, even if you have no copyright over the site names and URLs that make up the list.

What is Not Protected?

One thing that copyright explicitly does not protect is ideas. If you create a Web site that features biographies of famous composers, you cannot stop others from creating their own Web sites featuring original biographies of composers. All copyright can do is prevent others from copying your biographies onto their Web sites, or copying other elements such as original artwork or HTML source code that you created for your site. (You may also be able to use a trademark law to prevent people from confusing other sites about composers with yours.)

How a Work Gains Protection

Any original creative work covered by copyright law is protected by copyright from the moment it is "fixed in any tangible medium of expression," as discussed above. Therefore, if you write an original page of HTML and save it to your hard disk, that page is automatically protected by copyright. However, to get the most protection afforded by copyright law you should affix a copyright notice when you publish the work, and register your copyright with the U.S. Copyright Office.

Copyright Notice

It is not strictly necessary to include a copyright notice on a work in order to have copyright protection. However, including a copyright notice provides certain benefits, especially if you need to enforce your rights in court. Therefore, it is a wise idea to include a copyright notice on original Web pages that you present to the public. It is also a good idea to include a copyright notice as a comment line at the top of your original HTML and other computer source code, so that anyone who views the source will see that you have a claim of copyright in the work.

A copyright notice must include: (1) The word "Copyright," the abbreviation "Copr.," and/or the C-in-a-circle copyright symbol; (2) The year of first publication of the work; and (3) The name of the copyright owner. Examples of valid copyright notices are as follows:

Copyright 2002 John Q. Smith

Copr. 2002 John Q. Smith

© 2002 John Q. Smith

Copyright © 2002 by John Q. Smith

Note: Although people often use a "c" in parentheses in place of the copyright symbol ©, (c) has no official standing as a notice of copyright. If for some reason you cannot use the © symbol (in an ASCII text file, for example) be sure to use the word "Copyright" or "Copr." On the Web, most browsers render the code "©"; as the © symbol, but it is also a good idea to include the word "Copyright."

Your copyright notice need not appear in any specific place, as long as it gives reasonable notice of your claim of copyright. On a Web page, a copyright notice on the bottom of the home page—or better yet, on the bottom of each page as part of a standard footer—is adequate. If your Web site requires complicated or multiple copyright notices, you may consider including a prominent link labeled "Copyright Notice" that brings users to a page showing all the copyright notices for the site.

Registration

Copyrights can be registered with the United States Copyright Office, which is a part of the Library of Congress. Like the copyright notice, registration is not technically required in order to have copyright protection, but there are benefits to registering your copyrights, especially in works that have significant commercial value. For a work created in the United States, registration is required before you can file a lawsuit against an infringer. Timely registration can also help prove the validity of your copyright claim, and can allow you to recover additional damages and attorney's fees if you win a lawsuit for infringement.

The basic requirements for registration of a copyright are submission to the Copyright office of (1) the appropriate registration application, (2) one or more copies of the work to be registered, and (3) a registration fee. Exact requirements, including copies of registration forms and information about registering online and other digital works, can be found online at **http://www.loc.gov/copyright**.

Copyrights last only for a limited time. For a new work by an individual author, copyright generally lasts for the life of the author plus 70 years. For work made for hire, such as a Web site created in the course of one's employment, when the copyright is owned by the employer, the copyright lasts for 95 years after publication or 120 years after creation, whichever is shorter.

Infringement

Copyright confers several rights upon its owner. Foremost is the right to prohibit other people from making copies of your work. Copyright also confers the right to prohibit or control the production of "derivative works," or works closely based upon the copyrighted work, such as a film adaptation of a novel. Reproducing a copyrighted work without permission, producing a derivative work without permission, or violating another of a copyright owner's rights is copyright infringement, and can bring civil and sometimes criminal penalties.

The wide-open, massively interconnected landscape of the Web encourages sharing and copying. Indeed, frequent copying and reuse of source code, text, and graphics helped fuel the explosion of the Web in its infancy. Most Web browsers make it easy to copy text and images, and to view and copy HTML source code. But ease of copying does not mean it is always legal. As more people and businesses have migrated to the Web, copyright has become a more valuable and more jealously guarded form of property.

To be safe, you should assume that any text, graphics, sound, video, or source code you find on the Web is protected by copyright, unless you have a very good reason to know otherwise. If you want to copy something, ask the owner.

Fair Use

Fair use is a term from copyright law that is often used but little understood. This doctrine allows some copyrighted material to be copied without the copyright owner's permission. However, fair use is a very narrow right. Whether or not copying constitutes fair use depends upon several factors, including the reason for the copying (such as classroom use, review and criticism, news reporting, or parody), the amount of the material you copy (the smaller the excerpt compared to the size of the original work as a whole, the more acceptable), and the effect of the copying upon the value of the original work. Whether the copying is for commercial or nonprofit educational use is a factor to be considered, but copying is not necessarily fair use just because you are not doing it for money.

Trademarks

Objective 5.5
Identify key factors relating to legal and regulatory considerations when planning e-business solutions.
... Knowledge ownership/Intellectual property rights

Trademarks are an important means of establishing and maintaining your identity in the marketplace. They are the words and images by which you can identify your products, ensure that the public knows that you are the source of those products, and prevent the public from confusing someone else's products with yours. Trademark law prevents one business from using another's trademark in a way that could be confusing to the public, or in a way that could harm the value of the trademark.

Note: "Service marks" are similar to trademarks, except that they identify services instead of goods. For example, you might use a service mark to identify a Web design company, a financial consulting firm, or a cleaning service. Because service marks and trademarks are otherwise treated very similarly, the rest of this lesson will refer simply to "trademarks."

Trademarks are important to Web professionals because they can set one site apart from another and help bring users back for repeat visits. After all, once users have visited your site, the main thing that will bring them back is the knowledge that your site—not some other site—gave them the information, entertainment, or service they wanted. Trademarks can help make sure your users remember your site.

Trademark law is governed not only by Federal law, but also by each state's trademark or unfair competition law. Addressing the variations among the different states' laws is beyond the scope of this lesson, so we will concentrate on Federal law and the basic concepts of trademark.

What is Protected?

Trademarks can include names, graphical logos, or other identifying marks. Almost anything that the public might use to uniquely identify your products or services could become a trademark. For a Web site, potential trademarks are most likely to include the site's name, its identifying graphics, and even the site's URL.

Closely related to trademarks, and capable of similar protection, is "trade dress." Rather than a specific word, mark, or logo, "trade dress" refers to the overall appearance of a product in the marketplace. This can include the distinctive shape or design of packaging or the distinctive decor of a retail store. How far trade dress will go in the online world is still unclear. For a Web site, a distinctive page layout or color scheme might be considered trade dress, and therefore might be given some level of protection.

E-Commerce

Limits to Trademark Protection

Trademark and trade dress protection cannot protect the functional aspects of any product or service. If you produce a product and package it in a cardboard box, you can almost certainly have trademark protection for your company's unique name and logo printed on the box. Because of trade dress protection, you may also be able to prevent others from copying the distinctive shape or design of your box. But you cannot keep competitors from packaging their own products in cardboard boxes, because they are functional items.

On the Web, it may be difficult to draw the line between images, identifiers, and aspects of appearance that can be protected and functional items that cannot. That is because the appearance of a Web site is often closely related to its function. For example, your Web site may include a discussion forum. You might claim that the distinctive layout of the forum Web page is your trade dress and should be protected. However, another might argue that this layout—the placement of the user name, subject line, text entry area and navigation tools—is a functional part of the site, facilitating users' contributions to the discussion, and therefore cannot be protected by trademark or trade dress law.

How a Trademark is Claimed and Protected

While copyright rights arise from authorship, trademark rights come from use. Your use of a mark to identify your company and your products is the basis for trademark protection. The longer and more extensive your use, and the more the public grows to associate the mark with your products, the stronger your trademark claim.

The nature of the mark itself is also a factor in how strong your trademark claim can be. The more distinctive your trademark is, the stronger the claim. Made-up words and unique, original graphic symbols can make the strongest trademarks, while purely descriptive terms cannot be easily claimed as trademarks. But the bottom line with trademarks is almost always public perception. The more the public associates or is likely to associate a word or image exclusively with your products, the stronger your claim on that word or image as a trademark.

If you plan to claim trademark rights in words or images, it is a good idea to let the world know. The simplest way to do this is by adding a ^{TM} (or ^{SM} for a service mark) next to the mark. Federal law imposes no regulations on the use of the ^{TM} or ^{SM} notices, and the use of such notice is not required for trademark protection.

Federal law, and some state laws, also provide for registration of trademarks. Registration is not required to protect a trademark, but registration does offer advantages, such as an easier time in court if you have to enforce your trademark rights. Federal registration involves submitting a detailed application, examples of the use of your trademark, and a registration fee paid to the U.S. Patent and Trademark Office (USPTO). You can register trademarks that are already in use or ones that you intend to use in the future.

Once a mark is registered, it should always have the R-in-a-circle registration symbol—®—affixed to it whenever the mark is used. This symbol may be used only on federally registered trademarks. By failing to use it, you may risk some of the benefits of registration. Many trademark owners use the *TM* symbol while their federal registration is pending.

Naturally, the USPTO will not register a trademark if someone else has a claim on that mark, or on a mark that is similar to yours in a way that could cause confusion. Therefore, it is usually advisable to do a trademark search before going to the effort and expense of trying to register your mark. The Trademark Electronic Search System (TESS) is a searchable online version of the USPTO's database of pending and registered trademarks. A link to TESS can be found on the USPTO's main trademark site: **http://www.uspto.gov/main/trademarks.htm.**

TESS is very useful; however, when a mark does not appear in a TESS search, you are not automatically guaranteed permission to register and use that trademark. The USPTO will still do its own detailed search when you apply for registration, and TESS does not include marks that may be in use, but are not registered with USPTO. Many companies exist to perform trademark searches for a fee, and a number of these companies can be found on the Web.

Because trademark law is intended to prevent confusion about the identity and source of competing products, it is possible for business in different industries to use the same or similar trademarks without being in conflict with one another. The USPTO recognizes 42 distinct classes of goods and services, from chemical products to education and entertainment services, and your application for registration must indicate all of the classes in which you wish to have your trademark registered. Therefore, when considering trademark registration, it is important to think about the ways in which you might use the trademark, now and in the future. For example, your Web site might be primarily an "education and entertainment" business, but you may also sell coffee mugs and T-shirts using your trademark.

Unlike copyrights and patents, trademarks are not subject to any time limitation. Ownership of a trademark can continue for as long as it is used in commerce. However, trademark rights can be lost if they are neglected. To keep its trademark rights strong, a company must work to keep others from misusing its trademarks. This fact leads to many of the infamous "nasty lawyer letters" from trademark owners' attorneys to competitors, publishers, and others who are thought to have misused a trademark.

Infringement

If one company misuses the trademark of a competitor, or uses a confusingly similar mark, the trademark owner may bring a lawsuit for trademark infringement. In general, the plaintiff in such a lawsuit must prove that there is a "likelihood of confusion" due to the defendant's infringement. This relies on a number of factors including the strength of the plaintiff's trademark, the similarity of the impression created by the plaintiff's and defendant's marks, the intent of the defendant in adopting the similar mark, and evidence of actual confusion of the public.

Federal law also allows a trademark owner to sue for "dilution" of his or her trademark if someone's misuse of the trademark weakens the public's association of the trademark with its owner, or tarnishes the public's perception of the mark.

Domain Names and Trademarks

Internet domain names and Universal Resource Locators (URLs) have led to a whole new set of trademark issues. Because URLs have become an important way for people to find and identify businesses (both dotcoms and brick-and-mortar companies), they have become an important, new kind of trademark. This has led to new trademark disputes. As we discussed above, two companies can have similar trademarks if they are in different kinds of business. But what happens when both companies want to get on the Web? They may be in different lines of work, but only one "companyname.com" may exist on the Internet. As with most trademark disputes, such domain name conflicts are usually resolved on the basis of public perception, which often means that the biggest company wins.

Patents

Patents protect inventions in the form of machines, processes, manufactured items, compositions of matter, or improvement on any of these. Patents are intended to encourage invention, and public disclosure and use of inventions, by giving inventors exclusive rights to use their inventions for a limited amount of time. In exchange, inventors—in their patent application—must disclose a detailed description of the invention into the public record.

Note: U.S. patent law actually recognizes three different types of patents: Utility patents, which are for most useful inventions, Plant patents, which are for new varieties of plants, and Design patents, which are for ornamental design of manufactured items. In this lesson we will concern ourselves only with Utility patents.

To be patented, an invention must also be novel and nonobvious. This means there cannot be "prior art," which either duplicates some or all of the alleged invention, or which points toward the alleged invention as an obvious next step. The invention must also be useful. In addition, the invention must be described adequately so that someone else skilled in the same field could make use of it, and the inventor's patent application must claim in clear and definite terms the aspects of the invention for which patent protection is sought. It is tempting to think of a patent as protection for an idea; however, to obtain a patent, the idea must be set forth and described in some real-world implementation.

Patents granted on or after June 8, 1995 for useful inventions expire 20 years from the date of the initial patent application, provided the required maintenance fees are paid to the USPTO during that time.

Patents and the Web

Why should a Web professional care about patents? Patent issues do not often arise with regard to Web sites; copyright or trademark law more commonly protects most of the intellectual property in a Web site.

However, the ability to patent a process—a way of doing something, rather than a physical invention, such as a machine—has had an impact on the Web. Any interactive Web site can be viewed as a series of processes. So can any business. Occasionally, one of these processes is sufficiently useful and novel to be patented—or at least close enough to fight over. For example, Amazon.com was granted a patent on "one-click purchasing" technology, which uses browser cookies to enable Amazon customers to make purchases without having to reenter their identity and credit card information each time. Amazon later sued Barnes & Noble for violating this patent on their Web site, and obtained a preliminary injunction ordering Barnes & Noble to stop using its similar Express Lane checkout feature. Barnes & Noble has continued to challenge Amazon's case, and an appeals court later lifted the injunction, saying that while the Express Lane feature probably infringed upon Amazon's patent, Barnes & Noble has presented a strong case that the patent was invalid because the use of cookies for one-click buying was probably obvious to anyone in the e-commerce field.

A great deal of controversy still surrounds software and business-process patents. Many are of the opinion that the USPTO too easily issues patents for processes that are in fact obvious and non-novel. Even Jeff Bezos of Amazon.com has called for a reform of patent law with the aim of fewer software and business process patents and shorter duration for those that are issued.

Ironically, Amazon.com has also been granted a patent for its affiliate sales program—which some have likened to patenting the age-old idea of paying commissions to salespeople. Software and business process patent is definitely an area that will see a great deal of development in the next few years.

Trade Secrets

Trade secret law is unlikely to have a significant impact on your creation and management of Web sites. Briefly, trade secret law provides some help to those who wish to protect their ideas and methods by keeping them secret. This situation is not likely to arise in a medium used mainly for public communication. For example, if you had a special manufacturing process which you diligently tried to keep secret, but which a competitor learned through some improper means, despite your best efforts, you might be able to use trade secret law to prevent the competitor from using your process.

Activity

1. Identify whether the following Web site components would be most likely protected by copyright, trademark, or patent.

   a. Site name _______________

   b. HTML source _______________

   c. Java Script program _______________

   d. Entirely new process for taking and tracking orders _______________

   e. Feature news article _______________

   f. Photograph accompanying trade-show report _______________

   g. Company logo _______________

   h. Book review _______________

   i. Product description from catalog_______________

   j. CGI Perl script _______________

Extended Activities

1. Look at a Web site you have created or your favorite Web site. Identify three aspects of the site that might be protected by copyright and three aspects that might be protected by trademark.

   ____

   ____

   ____

   ____

   ____

   ____

2. Visit **http://www.uspto.gov/main/trademarks.htm** and find the link for the TESS trademark database. Search for the term "yahoo," and browse through the results. List the many different classes for which the mark is registered and the ownership of the mark in each class.

____

____

____

____

3. Search TESS for the name of your favorite Web site or the name of a site you created.

4. Visit the Stanford University site at: **http://www.stanford. edu/**. Browse for more information about copyright and fair use law. Summarize your findings.

____

____

____

____

____

5. Search the USPTO's patent database at **http://www.uspto. gov/patft/index.html** for patents mentioning the term "internet." Note the number of results, and browse through some of them. Try searching for other terms that interest you. Summarize your findings.

____

____

____

____

____

Lesson 6—Crime, Privacy, and Other Legal Issues

Criminal, civil, privacy, consumer protection, and many other laws have become important topics as they relate to the Web. Intellectual property is probably the area of law with the greatest impact on the day-to-day work of a Web professional. But with more and more of society's activities taking place on the Internet, many other laws and regulations have been adapted and created for this new arena.

It would be impossible for this lesson to address every aspect of the law as it applies to the Web. For one thing, the field of relevant law is simply too large to cover here. For another, government and society is still sorting out many aspects of Internet law; thus, this field is developing rapidly. This lesson is intended to give you an overview of the kinds of legal issues you may need to consider in working with the Web, and how they might affect you. In general, however, you should bear in mind that if laws govern an activity in the "real world," then similar laws probably govern similar activity on the Web.

Objectives

At the end of this lesson you will be able to:

- Recognize several key legal provisions governing the Web and the Internet in general

- Identify several types of Web activity that are likely to be subject to laws and regulations

- Explain how the Web may result in expanded legal risks, and identify ways that you might protect yourself from those risks

Key Point

As in the offline world, activity on the Web is subject to several existing and developing types of law.

Crime and the Internet

For well over a decade, state and federal governments have been working to bring their criminal laws and procedures in step with the age of computers and the Internet. The United States Department of Justice has created the Computer Crime and Intellectual Property Section (CCIPS) of the department's Criminal Division to focus on criminal activity related to computers, the Internet, and intellectual property. Other sections of the Department of Justice's Criminal Division, such as the Fraud Section and the Child Exploitation and Obscenity Section, have begun paying special attention to the online aspects of their charter.

This diversity indicates that computer- and Internet-related crime (called "cybercrime" in some Government reports) is not a single field of criminal law. The versatility of computers means that they can play several different roles in criminal activity. A March 2000 report by the President's Working Group on Unlawful Conduct on the Internet identified three basic types of computer-related crime:

- Crimes where computers are the target

- Crimes where computers are used as storage devices

- Crimes where computers are used for communications

In these respects, the Internet is just another tool that criminals have found useful for committing crimes.

New Frontier, Old Crimes

The reach and relative anonymity of the Internet can make some kinds of crimes easier, or at least more tempting, to commit. However, much of the government's approach to cybercrime is fundamentally similar to its approach to more "traditional" forms of crime. The President's Working Group called for a "technology-neutral approach" to criminal law, and found that pre-existing laws are often sufficient to prosecute crimes committed by means of the Internet. Types of Internet crime to which existing laws could be applied include securities fraud and other types of fraud, child pornography and related activities, sales of controlled substances, sales of firearms, and illegal gambling.

New Laws,
New Crimes

Objective 5.5
Identify key factors relating to legal and regulatory considerations when planning e-business solutions.
… Privacy

Although many online crimes are subject to existing laws, lawmakers have also found occasion to create new laws, or to change pre-existing laws, to address either new types of crime or new methods of committing crime on the Internet. The following subsections show some examples of laws that have been passed for the purpose of dealing with Internet crime, or to newly restrict some behavior on the Internet. Some of these laws provide for civil as well as criminal penalties, and many relate to the protection of children, or privacy, or both. As these new laws have been enacted, many of them have been met with constitutional challenges in the courts.

Computer Fraud and Abuse Act

This law added a provision to the Federal fraud statutes to address such crimes as unauthorized computer access, damage or threats relating to computers, and trafficking in illicit computer passwords. This law been amended and strengthened several times since it was first enacted in 1984.

CDA

Part of the Telecommunications Act of 1996, the Communications Decency Act (CDA) included provisions prohibiting the posting of "indecent" or "patently offensive" materials on publicly accessible Web sites and other Internet forums that might be accessed by minors. In June 1997, the United States Supreme Court struck down this provision of the CDA on the grounds that it violated the First Amendment's protection of free speech and freedom of the press, and that the law was too vague and therefore violated the Fifth Amendment. This Supreme Court decision was an important precedent for Internet law because it established that expression on the Internet is entitled to full First Amendment protection, much like the printed word.

COPA

In 1998 President Clinton signed into law the Child Online Protection Act (COPA) which is essentially a more narrowly written version of the CDA. The COPA (called "CDA II" by some) restricts material "harmful to minors," and applies only to communications that are made for commercial purposes, that might be accessed by minors. As soon as the COPA became law, courts challenged it. Federal trial and appellate courts have blocked enforcement of this law on constitutional grounds, and a decision from the Supreme Court is pending.

COPPA

Not to be confused with COPA, this act also became law in 1998. The Children's Online Privacy Protection Act (COPPA) regulates Web sites' collection and use of personal identifying information from children under the age of 13. The act, and the rule which implements the act, require verifiable parental consent before such information is collected, and also sets forth requirements for giving the public notice of a Web site's information collection, disclosure, and privacy policies. The COPPA applies to U.S.-based Web sites and online services that are "directed to children," or which knowingly collect personal information from children under 13.

Unlike some parts of the CDA and COPA, the COPPA has shown itself to have real power. On the first anniversary of the Act's effective date, the Federal Trade Commission (the agency responsible for enforcing the COPPA) announced a settlement with three Web sites for violations of this act. The operators of the three sites, **www.girlslife.com**, **www.bigmailbox.com**, and **www.insidetheweb.com** (no longer operating), agreed to pay a total of $100,000 in civil penalties. The FTC has also used the COPPA—in conjunction with laws against deceptive trade practices—to gain a settlement restricting the sale of customer information by bankrupt online retailer Toysmart.com.

While some have pressed for legislation to protect online privacy for teens and adults, the chairman of the Federal Trade Commission last year urged more enforcement of existing laws, rather than the passage of new laws.

The COPPA also includes a "safe harbor" provision that allows the industry to develop self-policing guidelines which, when approved by the FTC and followed by Web site operators, are deemed to satisfy the requirements of the act. Privacy programs developed by the Children's Advertising Review Unit of the Council of Better Business Bureaus (CARU), the Entertainment Software Rating Board (ESRB), and the TRUSTe organization have all been approved as "safe harbors."

As a result, many Web sites have crafted privacy policies designed to respect the privacy of their customers without waiting for additional laws or industry standards. According to TRUSTe, a privacy policy should be written in clear, simple language, and should answer these typical consumer questions:

- What kind of information does the merchant collect about individual customers?

- How does the merchant use this information?

- Specifically, how does the merchant not use this information?

- How does the customer benefit if the merchant has this information?

- How can the customer remove information from the merchant's records?

- How can the customer update or change incorrect information?

- What is the name of the person who creates and enforces the merchant's privacy policy?

- What is the company's liability if customer information is misused?

CPPA

Another law enacted in 1996, the Child Pornography Prevention Act (CPPA) among other things, criminalizes the possession or distribution of images that depict, or appear to depict, minors engaged in sexually explicit conduct. Although few people argue against criminalizing child pornography, the constitutionality of the CPPA was challenged. One of the principal reasons for criminalizing child pornography has been that the production of such material necessarily harms children. However, the CPPA extended beyond this argument by prohibiting, for example, computer-generated images created without the involvement of any actual children. In 2002, the Supreme Court ruled that the CPPA was unconstitutional because this aspect of the law violated the First Amendment.

CIPA

The Children's Internet Protection Act (CIPA), enacted in 2000 and administered by the FCC, requires libraries that accept certain federal funds for Internet access to employ policies and technologies (such as Web filtering or blocking software) to block Internet images that are obscene or contain child pornography, and to prevent children from accessing material harmful to minors. This law is currently facing legal challenges from the American Library Association and the American Civil Liberties Union on the grounds that the mandatory use of filtering software would hinder access to constitutionally protected speech.

State Computer Crime Laws

The laws discussed so far are Federal laws, usually enacted pursuant to the Federal government's constitutional power to regulate interstate commerce. However, state governments have not remained idle on the subject of Internet law. Many states have enacted computer intrusion, damage, and fraud laws to cover crimes similar to

E-Commerce

those in the Computer Fraud and Abuse Act of 1986, and many have also enacted laws covering other areas such as consumer protection, protection of children online, and "cyberstalking."

Geography, Crime, and the Web

Objective 5.5
*Identify key factors relating to legal and regulatory considerations when planning e-business solutions.
… Jurisdiction*

One of the Internet's biggest impacts on criminal law is the way in which it obliterates traditional notions of geography. The Web makes it relatively easy for anyone to communicate with, do business with, and potentially to harm large numbers of people, including people hundreds or thousands of miles away in other cities, states, and countries. In addition, the Web allows for transactions and interactions that do not occur in any easily identifiable place. If a person in New York uses a Web server in Norway to defraud someone in Idaho, where has the crime occurred?

One reason why it is important to ask where a possible crime has taken place is that this may determine what laws apply. This important initial question may determine whether or not any crime has taken place. An action that is a major felony in one jurisdiction could conceivably be a minor offense in another, and completely legal in a third. In the offline world, it is readily understood that a state or country's laws govern activity within that political entity's geographic borders. But things are not so easy when it comes to online activities. In the fraud example above, New York, Idaho, Norway, and the U.S. federal government might each claim criminal jurisdiction over some aspect of the fraudulent activity.

Police agencies and district attorneys face another difficulty raised by Internet crime: investigating and prosecuting crimes committed in a "place" that is actually distributed across state and national boundaries. This aspect of Internet crime has led to federal initiatives to address the challenges of online law enforcement and to promote cooperation and coordination among governments and law enforcement agencies across state and national boundaries. Among other activities, the previously mentioned CCIPS leads efforts to coordinate training between federal and state law enforcement agencies. In addition, the Department of Justice has established the position of Computer and Telecommunications Coordinator in each United States' Attorney's office, and has established a number of Computer Hacking and Intellectual Property (CHIP) units around the country.

Obscenity and Community Standards

One specific area in which the geography-warping effect of the Web has had startling impact is online obscenity. While "indecent" and "pornographic" material in general are protected by the First Amendment and therefore are not illegal in the United States, the U.S. Supreme Court has ruled that material found to be "obscene" does not receive First Amendment protection. Because of this ruling, many laws in the United States criminalize the production, distribution, and/or possession of obscene material.

However, the definition of what is "obscene" depends in part upon the application of "contemporary community standards." This recognizes that what is considered acceptable in New York City might be considered obscene in small-town Alabama.

When a Web site can be accessed from every city, village, and farm in the country, what "community standards" apply to define obscenity? The answer may be just about any that a prosecutor wants to apply. In 1995, a couple that operated an adult computer bulletin board based in California were prosecuted and convicted under federal law on obscenity charges (among others). The couple was tried and convicted by a federal court in Memphis, Tennessee that applied Memphis community standards. The basis of the conviction was that the couple's service was accessed by people located in Memphis, and therefore transmitted the images in question to Memphis.

It has yet to be seen just how much effect this case will have on the future of the Web. Many observers have criticized the case, and its principle is under attack in other lawsuits. Also, this case dealt with a dial-up bulletin board system, not a Web site. However, as the law stands now, a Web site operator must deal with at least the possibility of being held to the community standards of a distant jurisdiction.

Contracts and Civil Law

Many of the issues raised here with regard to criminal law on the Internet are mirrored in the civil law. The migration of personal and business activity to the Web has led to new applications of old laws and to some entirely new laws.

As with the criminal law, it is a good idea to assume that online activities are subject to the same basic laws as offline activities. Laws and rules such as those against fraud, false advertising, libel and slander, and other wrongful activities apply to the Web as

153

much as they do elsewhere. In addition, the Web may greatly expand your susceptibility to lawsuits by expanding the geographic range in which your actions have effect or "take place."

Lawsuits and Jurisdiction

In order for any particular court in the United States to hear and issue a binding judgment on a case, certain conditions must be met. One of these conditions is that the court has personal jurisdiction over all of the necessary parties to the suit. Ordinarily, the courts of a given state, or the federal courts within that state, have jurisdiction over people who reside in that state, or who can be found in the state and served with a subpoena. In addition, it is sometimes possible for a court to exercise personal jurisdiction over persons outside the state. Under U.S. constitutional law, the courts within any state may assume jurisdiction over a person outside the state only if the person has certain "minimum contacts" with the state. For example, a person who regularly conducts business with customers in another state, or who actively markets his or her products there, would likely have the required minimum contacts to be sued in that state.

What does this mean for the operators of Web sites? Once a site is up on the Web, it can be accessed from any state in the Union. This probably does not mean that every Web site owner faces the possibility of being sued in fifty different state courts. Although this is still a developing area of the law, the rule seems to be that merely operating a "passive" Web site that might be accessed from another state does not create sufficient contact with that state to give its courts personal jurisdiction. However, if your Web site has stronger connections with another state, such as numerous registered users or e-commerce customers residing in that state, you may well be subject to the jurisdiction of that state's courts. Also, if you commit wrongful acts directed toward someone in another state, that state's courts would likely have jurisdiction for the purpose of a lawsuit regarding those acts.

It may be possible to limit your risk by carefully drafting and clearly linking to a set of terms and conditions for users of your Web site. Some useful terms would include specifying your state's laws as controlling for any disputes about the site, and specifying that any such suits must be brought in your home state's courts or the federal courts operating in your state.

Framing and Deep Linking

The very essence of the Web is about linking, which is the process of providing users with links that take them from one page to another, either on the same Web site or on completely different sites. But this wide-open architecture is not always compatible with copyright, trademark, and other laws.

Deep linking refers to the practice of providing a link not to the home page of another Web site, but to a page or image "deep" within the other site. Deep linking bypasses the other site's home page, and sometimes bypasses such things as traffic monitoring software and lucrative banner ads. In the similar practice of framing, a site provides a link that results in the display of content from another site, while simultaneously displaying identifying material from the first site. Framing can suggest that the linked material belongs to or is otherwise associated with the first site.

The basic architecture of the Web permits and may even encourage such practices. But does the law? Several courts have addressed questions related to deep linking and framing, but the matter is not yet settled.

In the case of *Ticketmaster v. Tickets.com*, a federal district court in California stated that deep linking is not a violation of copyright, because "hyperlinking does not itself involve a violation of the Copyright Act ... since no copying is involved. The customer is automatically transferred to the particular genuine Web page of the original author. There is no deception in what is happening. This is analogous to using a library's card index to get reference to particular items, albeit faster and more efficiently."

However, a February 2002 decision by another California federal court came to a somewhat different conclusion. The case of Kelly v. Arriba Soft Corp. addressed issues of framing and deep linking with regard to an image search engine and its display of copyrighted artwork. The court held that the search engine's display of thumbnails derived from the original images was allowable as fair use, but deep linking and framing of the full-sized images was copyright infringement and was not fair use.

Apart from the intellectual property issues involved, practices such as deep linking and framing may also bring about other kinds of legal liability. For example, it may be considered trespass to access a Web site's servers and content in a manner inconsistent with terms and conditions specified on the site or in a "robots.txt" spidering policy file.

DMCA

In 1998, the U.S. Congress passed the Digital Millennium Copyright Act (DMCA), dealing with online and other technological copyright issues. The DMCA has been the subject of much criticism and controversy, and because it is still a relatively new law, it is uncertain just how the provisions of this law will be applied. Some of the DMCA provisions may be of particular interest to Web professionals.

Limitation of Liability for Online Service Providers

The DMCA provides "Online Services Providers," such as ISPs, with a way to minimize their liability for unauthorized copies of copyrighted material that are transmitted by means of their networks and equipment. Online Service Providers (OSPs) can avoid monetary liability for such copyright infringement by doing the following:

- Properly establishing an agent to receive notices regarding potential copyright infringement

- Properly complying with "take down" notices from copyright owners and "put back" counter-notices from the alleged infringers

- Developing and posting a policy for terminating the service of repeat offenders accommodating industry standard copyright protection technologies

This provision can provide protection for libraries, which provide computers for access to the Internet, and can protect ISPs from liability for information transmitted by means of their networks or posted by subscribers to their personal Web space. However, it is not clear how much protection this law would provide to an open discussion Web site, such as Slashdot (**http://www.slashdot.org**), where users can post information. This information includes, in theory, material that violates another's copyright, and those posts are displayed as part of Slashdot's own Web pages.

"Trafficking" in Copy- and Access-Control Devices

Another provision of the DMCA imposes civil and criminal penalties for making or distributing any device or service designed to circumvent access control or copy control technologies. This is important to Webmasters because linking to the wrong software or information could be a violation of this law. For example, the magazine *2600* was found liable for violating the DMCA because it provided a link from its Web site to the code for DeCSS, a program that circumvents the content control system on DVDs (thereby allowing, for example, DVDs to be played using software that is not officially supported by the DVD manufacturers).

Under Construction

The law of the Web continues to develop through legislation and court decisions, and continues to be a subject of controversy. For example, the USA-PATRIOT Act, passed in response to the events of September 11, 2001, gives the federal government expanded powers for online surveillance, making it easier for law enforcement agents to intercept information such as e-mail and Web traffic. Some praise this law as an important aid to homeland security, but others to raise concerns about violations of privacy and due process. Court challenges to this law are likely. As the Internet is pulled between its traditions as a uniquely anarchic space and its growing role in our wider society, this kind of debate will certainly continue.

E-Commerce

Activities

1. Browse **http://www.cybercrime.gov** to view some of the federal government's policies and initiatives regarding computer-related crime.

2. Browse **http://www.eff.org**, **http://www.cdt.org**, and **http://www.aclu.org/issues/cyber/hmcl.html** to view reactions of some civil libertarians to various laws and governmental initiatives.

3. Search the Web for "Terms and Conditions," and you will find "T&C" pages for many Web sites. Read through some of these, paying particular attention to the sections about whose laws apply, where lawsuits may be brought, and limitations on acceptable use, such as prohibitions of deep linking and spidering.

Extended Activities

1. Imagine that your new e-commerce Web site offers a product or service that is legal in 48 states, but strictly illegal in the other two.

   a. Explain how you might avoid criminal or civil liability in those two states.

   ____

   ____

   ____

   ____

   b. Does it make a difference if you are selling a physical product that needs to be shipped, or offering a service delivered entirely over the Web?

   ____

   ____

   ____

   ____

c. How might your solution be different if instead of being legal in most places, your product or service were legal only in your home state and illegal everywhere else?

____

____

____

____

2. Some commentators have suggested that the Internet should be considered a separate "place" with its own "community standards" for some legal purposes, such as the definition of obscenity. Does this make sense to you? Explain your answer.

____

____

____

____

E-Commerce

Summary

The Web has quickly evolved from a hobbyist's toy into a vital component of worldwide commerce. This business evolution has kept pace with, and was made possible by continual improvements in Web technology. Many of the same fundamental principles are necessary for success in both conventional businesses and e-businesses.

E-commerce business models describe the players that a Web site brings together. For example, consumer-to-consumer sites facilitate transactions between individuals, while business-to-government sites help businesses sell goods and services to government agencies.

Most e-commerce sites face two main challenges. First, they must guarantee—or authenticate—the identities of both participants in any transaction. Second, they need methods to securely and privately transfer funds from a buyer to a seller. A variety of technologies solve these problems in various ways, usually through a combination of encryption and password techniques. However, digital payments and authentication are relatively simple requirements compared to the challenges of global commerce. The Internet has made it simple for a buyer in Europe to deal with a merchant in Africa, transferring funds through a bank in the United States. To complete that "simple" transaction, however, a global e-commerce site may need to deal with many different layers of legal jurisdiction, language translations, cultural adaptations, and currency conversions. This unit covered the concept of balancing a global enterprise while meeting the needs of local markets.

The largest businesses keep up with these details by hiring technical, legal, and business professionals with experience in all of these areas. However, even small businesses can establish a global e-commerce presence by working with an application service provider or turn-key Web development service that is experienced in international commerce. We presented ways to protect intellectual property—the only kind of property that exists on the Web—as it applies to words, images, and sounds on the Internet.

We concluded this unit with a discussion of the major Internet concerns of crime and privacy. We presented some of the legislation that has been applied to these issues.

Unit 2 Quiz

1. Which of the following businesses would most likely not benefit from an e-commerce site?

    a. One that provides both online and offline support

    b. One whose business depends on person-to-person contact to complete a transaction

    c. One whose sales personnel have ready online access to sales literature, prices, and current inventory information

    d. One whose products and services can be provided exclusively online

2. Which of the following are barriers to entering e-commerce? (Choose two.)

    a. Age of the company

    b. Incompatible business models

    c. Cost of integration

    d. Size of the company

    e. Type of product or service

3. Portal sites use a _________ to find and index site content.

    a. Spider application

    b. Boolean operator

    c. <META> tag

    d. Wildcard

4. As soon as you have a clear idea of a new design or artistic creation, that concept is protected by copyright. True or false?

5. Which of the following is required before a creative work is protected by copyright?

    a. Place a copyright notice in or on the work

    b. Register the work with the U.S. Copyright Office

    c. Fix the work in some tangible medium of expression

    d. All of the above

6. While surfing the Web, you find a site that uses a mouse roll-over technique that you would like to add to your own site. The JavaScript code for the effect is built into each HTML page, so it is easy to view and copy. Legally and ethically, what is your best choice?

    a. Use it. The code was probably copied from some other site.

    b. Search the Web site of the U.S. Patent and Trademark Office to see if the JavaScript is patented.

    c. Search the Web site of the U.S. Copyright Office to see if the site is copyrighted.

    d. Ask the site owner's permission to use the code.

7. What must you do before you can add the TM symbol to your Web site's logo?

    a. Register the logo with the U.S. Patent and Trademark Office

    b. Register the logo with the Library of Congress

    c. Nothing

    d. Register the logo with the Federal Trade Commission

8. Copyright infringement is most similar to:

    a. Vandalism

    b. Theft

    c. Fraud

    d. Eavesdropping

9. Which of the following allows customers to make purchases without first having a credit card?

    a. EBT

    b. Mondex

    c. First Virtual PIN

    d. EDI

10. Which of the following is NOT a type of electronic cash?

    a. First Virtual PIN

    b. eCash

    c. CyberCash

    d. Mondex

11. __________________ can combine multiple types of information and applications on one card.

    a.   Credit cards

    b.   Mondex

    c.   First Virtual PIN

    d.   Smart cards

12. Which of the following payment methods can a buyer use to make an anonymous transaction?

    a.   Electronic cash

    b.   Credit card

    c.   EFT

    d.   EDI

13. Which of the following e-commerce technical considerations eliminates single points of failure?

    a.   Scalability

    b.   Failover

    c.   Database administration

    d.   Database connection pooling

14. By using an ASP, an organization__________________.

    a.   Builds its own custom application

    b.   Builds its site with a template-based package

    c.   Outsources site administration

    d.   Cannot deploy a customized site

15. For an organization with little site development skills and a small budget, a(n) _____________ development package is the right solution.

    a.   Turn-key

    b.   Template-based

    c.   Fully custom

    d.   ASP

16. Which of the following approaches would an organization choose to have the most control over its e-commerce site?

    a. Turn-key

    b. Template-based

    c. Fully custom

    d. ASP

17. Which of the following is NOT generally used in business-to-business interactions?

    a. EDI

    b. EFT

    c. OBI

    d. EBT

18. You want your Web site to be included in The World's Biggest Directory, which lists sites according to categories. What should you do?

    a. Wait for the crawler to find your site

    b. Submit your site information to the directory's managers

    c. Encourage your site visitors to nominate your site

    d. All of the above

19. Translating an English Web site to another language may also affect:

    a. Position of graphics

    b. Arrangement of menu selections

    c. Formatting of text and numbers

    d. All of the above

20. Your e-commerce site is hosted on a server in California. The site does a significant amount of business with customers in Italy. What laws and regulations should your site strive to comply with?

    a. U.S. Federal laws

    b. California laws

    c. Italian laws

    d. All of the above

21. What method of payment, using multiple currencies, is simplest for both a Web site and its international customers?

    a. Require buyers to use credit cards

    b. Require buyers to use U.S. dollars

    c. Require buyers to use electronic cash

    d. Add a currency calculator to the Web site

22. If you are unsure about the specific social customs of your intended audience, what communication style should your Web site use?

    a. Keep text and graphics friendly and informal

    b. Text and graphics inspired by movies about that region

    c. Ensure that all text and graphics are businesslike and polite

    d. None of the above

23. Law enforcement is difficult on the Internet because cybercrime is totally unlike any "traditional" criminal acts. True or false?

24. Your site provides online gaming for children, and sells CD-ROM versions of those games. According to U.S. law, are you allowed to collect the names and mailing addresses of kids who play on your site?

    a. Yes, if you get verifiable permission from their parents

    b. No, not under any circumstances

    c. Yes, if you get permission from the children

    d. Yes, if the kids say it's OK with their parents

E-Commerce

Unit 3
Internet Connectivity Technologies

This unit introduces the technologies used to connect individuals and organizations to an Internet Service Provider (ISP), or to connect two or more local area networks (LANs) over an extended distance to form a wide area network (WAN). Two main classes of technologies are used for this connectivity: point-to-point/point-to-multipoint services and switched services.

The lessons of this unit will introduce the most popular transmission services, explain how each works, and note their strengths and drawbacks. We will also describe the devices needed to implement each type of service, because each type of transmission service requires specific hardware.

As you will see, there is no single right way to establish an Internet connection or a WAN. When choosing a connection technology, or combination of technologies, a network professional must consider the cost and performance of each service, plus many other factors.

Lessons

1. Overview of the Internet
2. Point-to-Point and Point-to-Multipoint Services
3. Switched WAN Services
4. Options for Internet Connectivity and Remote User Access

Terms

Asynchronous Transfer Mode (ATM)—ATM is a connection-oriented cell relay technology based on small (53-byte) cells. An ATM network consists of ATM switches that form multiple virtual circuits to carry groups of cells from source to destination. ATM can provide high-speed transport services for audio, data, and video.

bridge—A bridge is a device that operates at the Data Link Layer of the OSI model. A bridge can connect several LANs or LAN segments. It can connect LANs of the same media access type, such as two Token Ring segments, or different LANs, such as Ethernet and Token Ring.

broadcast domain—A broadcast domain is the area of a network through which broadcast packets are forwarded. Routers, Layer 3 switches, and VLANs create network segments that are separate broadcast domains, because they do not forward broadcast packets from one segment to another.

Carrier Sense Multiple Access with Collision Detection (CSMA/CD)—CSMA/CD is the technique Ethernet uses for controlling access to the shared transmission medium (the bus). In CSMA/CD, a node may not transmit unless the medium is idle. If the transmitting node detects that another station has begun to transmit at the same time, both nodes stop, then wait a random time interval before attempting to retransmit.

cell—A cell is a unit of data similar to a frame. It is very small (53 bytes for ATM) and fixed in length. Cells are typically associated with ATM technology.

central office (CO)—A CO is a telephone company facility where local loops are terminated. The function of a CO is to connect individual telephones through a series of switches. COs are tied together in a hierarchy for efficiency in switching. Other terms for a CO are "local exchange," "wiring center," and "end office."

channel service unit (CSU)—A CSU is a device that connects to the end of a T1 or T3 line, between the line and a DSU. The CSU maintains an electrical connection on the line and functions as a repeater, regenerating and amplifying both incoming and outgoing signals. A CSU is usually combined with a DSU in a device called a "CSU/DSU."

coaxial—Coaxial cable is a type of copper wiring typically used for cable television transmission and high-speed Internet connectivity. Coaxial cable typically consists of a central copper or copper-coated conductor surrounded by flexible insulation, a shield of wire mesh, and an outer plastic jacket. Older installations of Ethernet LANs also used coax cable.

connectionless—Connectionless transmission treats each packet or datagram as a separate entity that contains the source and destination addresses. Connectionless services can drop or deliver packets out of sequence.

connection-oriented—A connection-oriented data communication mode is one in which the sending and receiving computers stay in contact for the duration of a session, while packets or frames are being sent back and forth.

Data Encryption Standard (DES)—DES is a popular single-key encryption system that uses a 56-bit key. 3DES uses the DES algorithm to encrypt a message three times, using three 56-bit keys. It is considered a hardware solution to encryption because of the time necessary to encrypt and decrypt a message.

data service unit (DSU)—A DSU is a device that converts a binary signal from the format used on a LAN to that used by a T1 line. It resolves differences in the way each system represents binary numbers. It sits between a CSU and a T1 MUX, and is usually combined with a CSU in a device called a "CSU/DSU."

digital access cross-connect switch (DACS)—A DACS is a connection system that establishes semipermanent (not switched) paths for voice or data signals. All physical wires are attached to the DACS once, and then electronic connections between them are made by entering instructions.

Digital Subscriber Line (DSL)—DSL is a modem technology that converts existing twisted pair telephone lines into high-speed data lines that can also carry separate telephone communications. Variants of DSL include ADSL, RADSL, ADSL Lite, IDSL, and VDSL.

domain name—A human-friendly name that identifies a Web site.

Dynamic Host Configuration Protocol (DHCP)—DHCP is a server process that simplifies IP network management by dynamically or statically assigning IP addresses to logical end stations for fixed periods of time.

encryption—Encryption is the process of scrambling data so it cannot be read by anyone except the intended recipient.

facilities—The term "facilities" refers to the physical media that are necessary to provide a telecommunication service. For example, twisted pairs of copper wire, or fiber optic cables, are facilities. Private facilities are owned and used by a private organization. Public facilities are leased from a telecommunication carrier, such as a local telephone company or long-distance service provider.

fractional T1 (FT1)—FT1 is a telephone company service that provides data rates from 64 Kbps to 1.544 Mbps, by allowing a user to purchase one or more channels of a T1 link. If the customer needs less bandwidth than 1.544 Mbps, FT1 is a low-cost alternative to purchasing a full T1.

frame relay—Frame relay is a packet-forwarding WAN protocol that normally operates at speeds of 56 Kbps to 1.5 Mbps.

hertz (Hz)—One hertz is one cycle of an electromagnetic wave in one second. One million hertz (megahertz) (1 MHz) is one million cycles per second.

Integrated Services Digital Network (ISDN)—ISDN is a WAN technology used to move voice and data over the telecommunication network. ISDN operates at speeds of 144 Kbps to 1.5 Mbps.

interexchange carrier (IXC)—An IXC is a long-distance company that provides telephone and data services between LATAs.

Internet Protocol (IP)—IP is a Network Layer protocol responsible for getting a packet (datagram) through a network from source to destination. It is the "IP" in "TCP/IP." IP provides connectionless, best-effort packet delivery service.

Internet service provider (ISP)—ISPs are companies that provide Internet access to individuals and businesses. ISPs typically supply a range of services necessary to provide corporate networks and other users with dedicated or dial-up access to the Internet.

local access and transport area (LATA)—LATAs are the geographic calling areas within which an RBOC may provide local and long-distance services. LATA boundaries, for the most part, fall within states and do not cross state lines, although, one state may have several LATAs.

local exchange carrier (LEC)—A LEC is a company that makes telephone connections to subscribers' homes and businesses, provides telephone services, and collects fees for those services. The terms LEC, ILEC, and RBOC are equivalent.

local loop—A local loop is the pair of copper wires that connects a customer's telephone to the LEC's CO switching system.

modem—The term "modem" is a contraction for modulator/demodulator. Modems are used to convert binary data into analog signals suitable for transmission across a telephone network.

modulation—Modulation is the process of modifying the form of a carrier wave (electrical signal) so that it can carry intelligent information on a communications medium.

multiplexer (MUX)—A MUX is a device that transmits multiple signals over the same physical medium. Multiple signals are fed into a MUX and combined to form one output stream.

port—There are two primary ways the term "port" is used in networking. Port can refer to a physical connection point in a device, such as a port on a switch or multiplexer. Port can also refer to a number that identifies a software process within a computer. "Well-known" ports in TCP architecture are examples of the second type of port.

quality of service (QoS)—QoS defines the type of service a communications link can provide. QoS often specifies factors such as delay, throughput, and error rate.

router—A router is a Layer 3 device with several ports that can each connect to a network or another router. The router examines the logical network address of each packet, then uses its internal routing table to forward the packet to the routing port associated with the best path to the packet's destination. If the packet is addressed to a network not connected to the router, the router will forward the packet to another router closer to the final destination. Each router, in turn, evaluates each packet, and then either delivers the packet or forwards it to another router.

RS-232—RS-232 cables are used for connecting a computer to a modem. The RS-232 specification details the electrical and mechanical interface between the computer and modem.

Synchronous Optical Network (SONET)—SONET is an optical transmission standard that defines a signal hierarchy. The basic building block is the STS-1 51.84-Mbps signal, chosen to accommodate a T3 signal. The STS designation refers to the interface for electrical signals. The optical signal standards are correspondingly designated OC-1, OC-2, and so on.

T1—T1 is one of the T-carrier telecommunication standards for multiplexing digitized voice signals. A T1 channel operates at 1.544 Mbps. Each T1 channel (64 Kbps) was designed to carry a digitized representation of an analog signal (a telephone call) that has a bandwidth of 4,000 Hz. Originally, 64 Kbps was required to digitize a 4,000-Hz voice signal. Current technology has reduced that requirement to 32 Kbps or less; however, a T-carrier channel is still 64 Kbps.

T1 multiplexer (MUX)—A T1 MUX is a device that breaks an outgoing bit stream into T1 time slices, and reassembles incoming time slices into a continuous bit stream. It sits between a LAN and a DSU (or DSU side of a CSU/DSU).

time-division multiplexing (TDM)—TDM is a technology that allows multiple signals to travel over the same physical medium by guaranteeing each signal a fixed amount of bandwidth on a rotating basis.

twisted pair—Twisted pair is a type of copper wiring typically used for telephone and computer network transmission. A twisted pair consists of two thin copper wires, twisted around each other to cancel EMI and RFI.

Universal Serial Bus (USB)—USB is an external bus that can transfer up to 12 Mbps. Up to 127 peripheral devices can be connected to a single USB port.

virtual circuit—A virtual circuit is a communication path that appears to be a single circuit to the sending and receiving devices, even though the data may take varying routes between the source and destination nodes.

virtual private network (VPN)—VPNs use end-to-end network encryption to establish a secure connection from machine to machine. Each VPN is an encrypted data stream that travels over a public network, such as the Internet.

X.25—X.25 is a connection-oriented packet-switching network, public or private, typically built upon leased lines from public telephone networks. In the United States, X.25 is offered by most carriers. The X.25 interface lies at OSI Layer 3, rather than Layer 1. X.25 defines its own three-layer protocol stack and provides data rates only up to 56 Kbps.

Lesson 1—Overview of the Internet

The Internet is a global network of computer networks. Although the idea is simple, its implications are enormous. One of the main features of the Internet is its ability to allow dissimilar computer systems, and even networks of dissimilar systems, to communicate with each other by means of two common protocols: Transmission Control Protocol (TCP) and Internet Protocol (IP). These two protocols function as a common language that personal computers (PCs), mainframes, and minicomputers can all use to talk to each other over the Internet.

For large segments of our population, Internet access has become an essential utility, like water or electricity. And, because the Internet operates over the physical transmission network of the public telephone system, all telephone companies are aligning their services to support the growth of Internet access services.

Objectives

At the end of this lesson you will be able to:

- Describe the early development of the Internet

- Explain briefly how information travels across the Internet

- Describe the relationship of the Internet to the public telephone network

 **Key Point**

The Internet is a worldwide network of networks.

Early History of the Internet

The Internet began in 1969, as a research project to maintain military communications in the event of major disruption (nuclear war) in telephone service. The U.S. Department of Defense Advanced Research Projects Agency (DARPA) created its experimental network (ARPANET) by linking a handful of universities and military contractors by leased telephone lines. Each computer site followed agreed-upon guidelines created by standards committees, and the network soon became indispensable for e-mail, file exchange, and group discussions among the participating sites.

By 1983, the ARPANET system had converted to the TCP/IP protocol. Other TCP/IP networks quickly connected to the ARPANET "backbone," forming the fledgling Internet.

The U.S. government funded the Internet for several years, and allowed only nonprofit, educational, and government use. In 1991, the National Science Foundation (NSF), which paid for approximately 10 percent of the leased lines, loosened the guidelines for Internet use. The NSF started allowing many commercial uses, such as "announcements of new products or services for use in research or instruction, but not advertising of any kind." This change flooded the Internet and has caused enormous growth from the inundation of commercial messages on non-NSF lines.

Enter the World Wide Web

The early Internet was not a user-friendly system. Users first had to know what information a host computer provided, and in what form, then select the appropriate utility (File Transfer Protocol [FTP], Telnet, Gopher, and so forth) to access the form of information.

In 1990, Hypertext Markup Language (HTML) was introduced, a plain-text tagging system that added font formatting, color, and graphics to documents. The Web began to grow exponentially when the first Web browser, NCSA Mosaic, was released in the early 1990s.

Web browsers, designed to display HTML documents, now handle the "dirty work" of Internet document access and file transfer. These easy-to-use programs allow users to access Internet documents without having to remember the particular services or protocols. This simplified interface, along with enhanced HTML features, has added enormously to the Internet's popularity. The Web is now as much an entertainment medium as an information resource.

Who Owns the Internet?

Objective 3.1
Understand and be able to describe the core components of the Internet infrastructure.
… Hardware/software infrastructure
… Internetworking devices such as routers, switches and bridges

The Internet is like a game that anyone is allowed to play. No organization, company, or government actually owns the Internet. Like Olympic sports, the Internet is controlled by independent governing bodies, each with its specific charter.

However, like players in any sport, Internet players must follow certain rules and procedures, and bring certain types of equipment to the playing field.

Internet Standards

Because the Internet is nothing more than a loose collection of computers communicating with one another, the protocols that define communications are extremely important. Therefore, all computers connected to the Internet communicate by using the same family of protocols: TCP and IP at the Transport and Network Layers respectively, and many Application Layer protocols such as FTP for file transfer, Telnet for remote login, or Simple Mail Transfer Protocol (SMTP) for e-mail.

Standards-Making Organizations

The Internet could not function without additional standards that specify other details of the Internet, from the structure of an e-mail message to rules for building Web pages. The following independent organizations govern the Internet by creating and updating these standards and protocols:

- **The Internet Engineering Task Force (IETF)** (http://www.ietf.org) is a loosely self-organized group of people who make technical and other contributions to the engineering and evolution of the Internet and its technologies. The IETF is the principal body engaged in the development of new Internet Standard specifications.

- **The Internet Society (ISOC)** (http://www.isoc.org) is the closest thing to an ultimate Internet authority. ISOC is a non-profit organization with permanent headquarters in Reston, Virginia. In existence since 1992, ISOC was initially proposed by members of IETF who felt that an institution to oversee the Internet Standards process was needed. Today, ISOC fills the crucial role of maintaining Internet Standards.

- **The Internet Architecture Board (IAB)** (http://www. iab.org), formerly the Internet Activities Board, oversees changes and additions to the architectural protocols upon which the Internet operates. It also manages and publishes the series of Request for Comment (RFC) documents that specify all Internet standards and proposed standards.

- **The Internet Research Task Force (IRTF)** (http://www. irtf.org) is composed of a number of small, focused, long-term research groups that work on topics related to Internet protocols, applications, architecture, and technology. In contrast, its parallel organization, IETF, focuses on shorter-term issues of engineering and Standards making.

- **The Internet Corporation for Assigned Names and Numbers (ICANN)** (http://www.icann.org) coordinates the assignment of the following identifiers that must be globally unique for the Internet to function:

  – Internet domain names

  – IP address numbers

  – Protocol parameter and port numbers

Under management of Network Solutions, ICANN handles registration of all domain names that fall under the top-level domains (TLDs). We discuss the domain name system in detail in the lesson entitled "TCP/IP Applications and Services."

The Standards Process

In general, an Internet Standard is a technical specification that is:

- Stable and well understood

- Technically competent

- Has multiple, independent, and interoperable implementations with substantial operational experience

- Enjoys significant public support and is recognizably useful in some or all parts of the Internet

In general, the process of creating an Internet Standard is straightforward:

1. A proposed specification undergoes a period of development and several iterations of review and revision by the Internet community.

2. The specification is adopted as a Standard by the appropriate body, and is published.

In practice, the process is more complicated, due to:

- The difficulty of creating specifications of high technical quality

- The need to consider the interests of all affected parties

- The importance of establishing widespread community consensus

- The difficulty of evaluating the utility of a particular specification for the Internet community

RFC

Each distinct version of an Internet Standards specification is published as part of the Request for Comment (RFC) document series. This archival series is the official publication channel for Internet Standards documents and other publications of the IESG, IAB, and Internet community. RFCs can be obtained from a number of Internet hosts using anonymous FTP, Gopher, Web, and other Internet document-retrieval systems.

The RFC series of documents on networking began in 1969 as part of the original ARPANET. RFCs cover a wide range of topics in addition to Internet Standards, from early discussion of new research concepts to status memos about the Internet. RFC publication is the direct responsibility of the RFC Editor, under the general direction of IAB.

Rules for formatting and submitting an RFC are defined in *RFC 1543, Instructions to RFC Authors*. Every RFC is available in ASCII text, while some RFCs are also available in other formats. Some versions of an RFC may contain material, such as diagrams and figures, not present in the ASCII versions, as they may be formatted differently.

A stricter requirement applies to specifications that are proposed Standards. For these specifications, the ASCII text version is the definitive reference. Therefore, it must be a complete and accurate specification of the standard, including all necessary diagrams and illustrations.

The status of Internet protocol and service specifications is summarized periodically in an RFC titled *Internet Official Protocol Standards* (STD 1). This RFC shows the level of maturity and other helpful information for each Internet protocol or service specification.

Some RFCs document Internet Standards. These RFCs form the STD subseries of the RFC series (*RFC 1311, Introduction to the STD Notes*). When a specification has been adopted as an Internet

Standard, it is given the additional label "STDxxx"; however, it keeps its RFC number and place in the RFC series.

Some RFCs standardize the results of community deliberations on statements of principle or conclusions about the best way to perform some operations or IETF process function. The specification is given the additional label "BCPxxx" (Best Current Practices); however, it keeps its RFC number and place in the RFC series.

Not all specifications of protocols or services for the Internet should or will become Internet Standards or BCPs. Such non-Standards-track specifications are not subject to the rules for Internet standardization. Non-Standards-track specifications may be published directly as "experimental" or "informational" RFCs at the discretion of the RFC Editor, in consultation with IESG.

It is important to remember that not all RFCs are Standards-track documents, and not all Standards-track documents reach the level of Internet Standard. Similarly, not all RFCs describing current practices have been reviewed and approved to become BCPs. *RFC 1796, Not All RFCs are Standards,* presents further information on this topic.

Internet Drafts

During development of a specification, draft versions of a document are made available for *informal* review and comment by placing them in IETF's Internet Drafts directory, which is replicated on a number of Internet hosts. This makes an evolving working document readily available to a wide audience, facilitating the process of review and revision.

An Internet Draft published as an RFC, or one that has remained unchanged in the Internet Drafts directory for more than six months without being recommended (by IESG) for publication as an RFC, is simply removed from the Internet Drafts directory. At any time, an Internet Draft may be replaced by a more recent version of the same specification, restarting the six-month time-out period.

An Internet Draft is not a means of "publishing" a specification; specifications are published through the RFC mechanism described in the previous section. Internet Drafts have no formal status and are subject to change or removal at any time.

Under no circumstances should an Internet Draft be referenced by any paper, report, or Request for Proposal, nor should a vendor claim compliance with an Internet Draft.

Note: It is acceptable to reference a Standards-track specification that may reasonably be expected to be published as an RFC using the phrase "Work in Progress" without referencing an Internet Draft. This may also be done in a Standards-track document itself, as long as the specification in which the reference is made would stand as a complete and understandable document with or without reference to the "Work in Progress."

Equipment

As discussed earlier, any computer can connect to the Internet provided it uses TCP/IP protocols. However, other specialized network devices, such as routers and high-speed telecommunication switches, are necessary to allow large ISPs and telephone companies to serve as the main transfer points for Internet messages and documents. This equipment, and the software that works with it, must also conform to the standards that define Internet operation.

The Internet Hierarchy

Objective 3.1
Understand and be able to describe the core components of the Internet infrastructure.
... Network access points
... Backbone

Although the Internet is often described as a democratic system, all of its players are not equal. Competition and rapid change are creating both diversification and stratification in Internet infrastructure; therefore, it is difficult to create neat categories. However, the entities that compose the Internet tend to fall into a rough three-level hierarchy: Tier 1, Tier 2, or Autonomous Systems.

Tier 1

Tier 1 Internet providers directly peer (exchange traffic with) all other networks on the Internet. These major optical backbone systems, such as MCI's very high-speed Backbone Network Service (vBNS) (**http://www.vbns.net/**), are usually owned by the major interexchange carriers (IXCs). They provide very large-scale connections to Tier 2 providers and large autonomous systems (described next). Global connectivity occurs at the Tier 1 level, and depends on a complex set of relationships between the major telecommunications providers in each country.

Tier 2

Tier 2 providers, which can be regional telecommunications companies, large cable television providers, or ISPs, get their Internet access from Tier 1 providers. In turn, Tier 2 provides regional Internet connectivity ranging from dedicated corporate connections to single-user dial-up services. If you are connected through a Tier 2 provider, your data must traverse that ISP's network before it can get out onto one of the main Internet backbones. Most individual and business customers get their connectivity from a Tier 2 provider.

Autonomous Systems

Autonomous systems are private networks, each administered by a single organization such as a large corporation. Autonomous systems do not provide Internet access to customers, but to their own organizations and employees. These networks can be quite large, and may get their service from Tier 2 ISPs or directly from Tier 1 providers.

NAPs

In the United States, a Network Access Point (NAP) is one of several major Internet interconnection points that link the backbones of the Internet access providers. These common connection points make it possible for an AT&T user in Portland, Oregon, to reach the Web site of a BellSouth customer in Miami, Florida.

Originally, four NAPs—New York; Washington, D.C.; Chicago; and San Francisco—were created and supported by the National Science Foundation (NSF), as part of the transition from the original U.S. government-financed Internet to a commercially operated Internet. Since then, several new NAPs have been created, such as MCI Worldcom's "MAE West" site in San Jose, California, and ICS Network Systems' "Big East."

The NAPs provide major switching facilities that serve the general public. Using companies pay fees to use the NAP facilities, and make their own intercompany data exchange arrangements. However, a significant amount of Internet traffic is handled without involving NAPs, using private intercompany interconnection arrangements within geographic regions.

ISPs

Internet Service Provider (ISPs) are companies that provide Internet access, e-mail services, and Web site hosting to individuals, businesses, and other organizations. They do this over high-speed dedicated lines or through dial-up connections. ISPs typically supply a range of services necessary to provide corporate networks and other users with full access to the Internet. The first ISPs specialized in Internet access. Today, local exchange carriers (LECs), competitive local exchange carriers (CLECs), cable television companies, and other telecommunications firms are providing Internet access along with other communication services.

Because an ISP transfers traffic between individual customers and the Tier 1 backbone, an ISP must have access to the backbone. Thus, it must have its own point of presence (POP) on Tier 1, or a telecommunications connection to another network that has a POP on Tier 1.

An ISP must also connect to its individual and business customers, by means of dial-up connections or dedicated leased lines.

How the Hierarchy Works

When you use the Internet, say to send an e-mail message, your data generally follows this (rather simplified) path:

1. From your computer to your ISP's server

2. From your ISP to the regional network that provides backbone access to your ISP

3. If necessary, through one of the major NAPs in the United States

4. From the NAP across the Tier 1 backbone

5. From the backbone, back down through the NAP, regional network, and destination ISP

Internet, intranet, and Extranet

As a result of the dynamic growth of the Internet, new terminology is emerging almost daily. One source of confusion is the use of the terms Internet (capitalized), internet (noncapitalized), intranet, and extranet.

- "Internet" (capitalized) is generally considered the global TCP/IP network. In other words, the Internet that connects the world.

- "internet" (not capitalized) refers to any interconnection of two or more networks, when the connection uses TCP/IP technology and protocols. This "internet" does not mean a network is connected to the global Internet.

- "Intranet" refers to a "private Internet." It is a private, internal network that uses Internet applications, tools, and protocols; however, it is designed for private use by company personnel. For example, many companies store commonly used information as Web pages, and their employees use Web browsers to retrieve and view the documents.

- "Extranet" includes both Internet and intranet capabilities. An extranet is a private intranet shared between closely aligned organizations. While it is external to each organization, it is not available to the general public. For example, a manufacturing company might work closely with a parts supplier for a specific product. Information about parts inventories could be stored in an extranet accessible to both companies.

Activities

1. The Internet began as a __________.

    a. Graphically oriented medium for sharing information between millions of users worldwide

    b. Private project designed by a major corporation so that the company's private data could move quickly from office to office

    c. Conglomerate of telephone carriers tying their lines together for the good of all mankind

    d. US DOD-funded network designed to allow survivable communications in the event of a nuclear war

2. The public telephone network provides the connections and circuits that allow the Internet to work. True or False?

3. An __________ is a network that provides the capabilities of both the Internet and an intranet.

    a. Internet

    b. Extranet

    c. internet

    d. Intranet

4. Domain name registration is ultimately overseen by __________.

    a. ICANN

    b. IETF

    c. ISOC

    d. NSA

Extended Activity

To get an idea of how large the Internet is, visit **http://www.internettrafficreport.com** and look at the statistics of some of the routers listed. Note that you may look at statistics worldwide. Which countries show the greatest usage, as reflected by the usage index?

Lesson 2—Point-to-Point and Point-to-Multipoint Services

A point-to-point link is a physical connection between two separated LANs or stations. An organization can create a point-to-point link by simply installing its own physical link (cable, fiber, or radio) between its sites. This approach is commonly used to connect buildings within an office park or campus; however, it is prohibitively expensive over a metropolitan area or wider region. Thus, when companies need to connect two or more sites over a wide area, they typically use point-to-point links established over the previously installed facilities of the public-switched telephone network (PSTN). These links come in a variety of data rates, at costs that correspond to their speed and capability.

A point-to-multipoint link is a physical connection between a central site and multiple endpoints. These services, such as Digital Subscriber Line (DSL) and cable modem, are most often used to provide high-speed Internet access to homes and small businesses.

This lesson introduces the most common point-to-point and point-to-multipoint options used to create WANs and connect customer sites to Internet Service Providers (ISPs).

Objectives

At the end of this lesson you will be able to:

- Name and describe the most common WAN point-to-point technologies

- Explain the structure of the Digital Signal Hierarchy

- Describe the main differences between T1 and fractional T1 (FT1) service

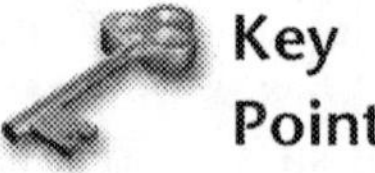

Key Point

A point-to-point link directly connects any two sites. A point-to-multipoint link connects one service provider to multiple subscribers.

Common Point-to-Point Services

Objective 3.4
Understand and be able to describe the capabilities of popular remote access protocols
… Point-to-point

Point-to-point links come in a wide variety of data rates and costs, as summarized in the Point-to-Point Link Options Table.

Point-to-Point Link Options

Service	Link Speed	Equipment Needs
Analog (Dial-Up or Leased)	300 bps to 56 Kbps	Modem
ISDN	128 Kbps to 1.544 Mbps	Terminal Adapter
FT1 (DS0)	64 Kbps to 1.544 Mbps	DSU and CSU
T1 (US)	1.544 Mbps	DSU, CSU, and MUX
E1 (EU)	2.048 Mbps	DSU, CSU, and MUX
T3 (US)	44.736 Mbps	DSU, CSU, and MUX
E3 (EU)	34.368 Mbps	DSU, CSU, and MUX
SONET	51 Mbps to 13.21 Gbps	MUX

POTS Analog Connections

Plain Old Telephone Service (POTS) was originally designed for analog voice transmission, not binary data. Although most of the U.S. telephone network is now digital, most of its local loops, that is, the wires that connect homes to the telephone company, are still analog.

Modems

We can transmit computer data over analog local loops, by using a modem to convert (modulate) data signals to analog signals. The term "modem" is a contraction of modulator/demodulator.

Objective 3.7
Create a logic diagram of Internet components from the client to the server.

Objective 3.8
Describe various hardware and software connection devices and when to use them.
... Modem
... WAN Link

Modems are used in pairs, one at each end of a telephone line, as shown on the Modems and Dial-Up Networking Diagram. Each modem attaches to a computer or terminal by means of an RS-232 cable, the input/output (I/O) bus, or Universal Serial Bus (USB).

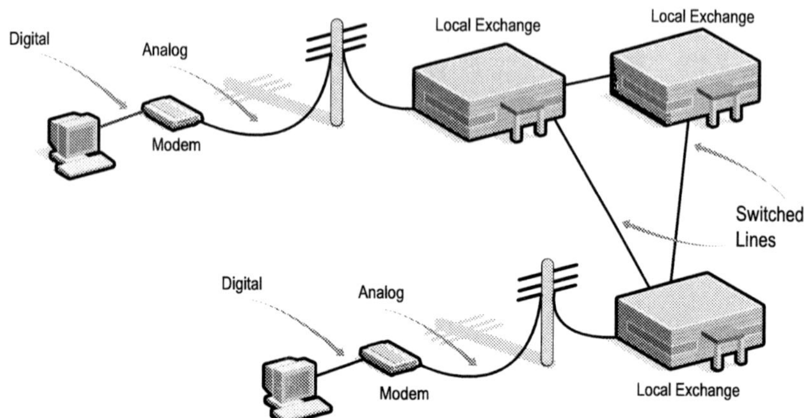

Modems and Dial-Up Networking

To transmit a message, the modem accepts digital data from the computer or terminal on the RS-232 interface. It modulates the telephone line by generating a signal with an audible frequency. The receiving modem demodulates the signal, generating digital data that is transmitted to the terminal or computer. Because the signal falls within the range of 300 to 3,400 Hertz (Hz), it can be transmitted across a telephone network as if it were a voice conversation.

Modems at either end of a connection must use the same modulation/demodulation protocol. A variety of standards have been published by the International Telecommunication Union - Telecommunications Standardization Sector (ITU-T) and International Standards Organization (ISO), so that modems from different manufacturers can be used together.

The simplest modem protocol represents 0s and 1s by switching the audible tone off and on, respectively. This technique can transmit data at a maximum of 1,200 bits per second (bps). More complex protocols can increase the effective data rate to 56 kilobits per second (Kbps). However, that speed is only possible if the local loop is in very good condition. Because that is not usually the case, it is rare for an analog modem to actually deliver 56 Kbps.

Dial-Up Lines

A dial-up line is a temporary point-to-point circuit between two nodes, set up across the switched telephone network. For example, remote workers who need access to a corporate LAN often use a dial-up connection to the company's modem. The Modems Dial-Up Networking Diagram illustrates dial-up connections.

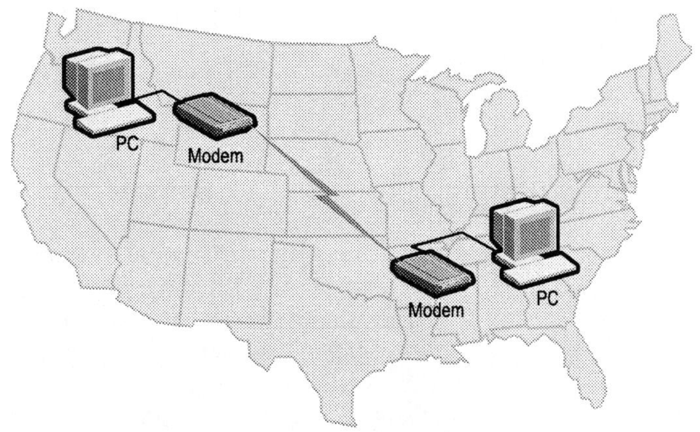

Modems Dial-Up Networking

Dial-up lines have the following characteristics:

- 2.4- to 56-Kbps transfer rates

- Any-to-any connectivity (one circuit at a time)

- Compatible modems at each end

- Transmission only after call initialization occurs

- Inexpensive

Leased Lines

Leased lines are also set up through the telephone network; however, these circuits are set up on a permanent basis. Leased lines are most appropriately used when traffic requirements are steady and uninterrupted service is important.

Advantages of leased lines over private lines include:

- Security of information

- Constant quality of service (QoS)

- Control of circuit

Disadvantages of leased lines are:

- Expense

- Increased equipment needs and costs associated with increased connections

Objective 1.1
*Identify the issues that affect Internet site functionality.
... Bandwidth (both client and server)
... Internet connection types (both client and server)*

Modems and analog lines are used by most home users and many small businesses. However, the top speed of a modem is limited to approximately 56 Kbps, which is barely adequate for most Internet access, painfully slow for large file transfers, and totally inadequate for video services.

T-Carriers and E-Carriers

The T1 line (E1 in Europe) is a purely digital service. It is the basic unit of the U.S. digital telephone transmission system, and is the most popular type of dedicated leased line. T1 was originally designed for digital voice communications between telephone company COs (local exchanges). However, it has become a data transmission workhorse as well, because T1 is a Physical Layer technology. Several higher layer WAN protocols can use the basic transmission services of a T1 line.

Businesses with multiple locations now use T1 lines to connect their separate computer networks into single integrated systems. Companies with high volumes of Internet traffic often use T1 to connect their office networks to their Internet service providers (ISPs).

T1 Bandwidth

Objective 1.1
*Identify the issues that affect Internet site functionality.
... Bandwidth (both client and server)
... Internet connection types (both client and server)*

T1 was originally developed to carry 24 digitized telephone calls over four copper wires, using time-division multiplexing (TDM). TDM transmits multiple signals over the same transmission link, by guaranteeing each signal a fixed time slot to use the transmission medium. A T1 line essentially allows up to 24 different signals to take turns using the transmission line.

To digitize one voice conversation, 64 Kbps is needed, thus 1,536 Kbps of bandwidth is needed to accommodate 24 conversations. To keep the multiplexed signals separated, and help sort them out on each end, approximately 8 Kbps of bandwidth is added to carry control information, just as a train sets aside a seat for the conductor to keep everything organized.

Thus, a "full" T1 line provides a total bandwidth of 1.544 Mbps (although only 1.536 Mbps is usable by customers). That 1.544 Mbps is divided into 24 channels of 64 Kbps each (56 Kbps is usable). An E1 line works the same way; however, it carries 32 channels of 64 Kbps each, for a total bandwidth of 2.048 Mbps.

The T1 level of bandwidth was originally called "Digital Signal Level 1," or DS1. Thus, T1 and DS1 are equivalent terms. Each 64-Kbps channel is called DS0. The multiple channels of a T1 or E1 line provide flexible communication options. For example, a company can order a full T1, then use some of its channels for telephone calls and some for data.

DS Hierarchy

Just as 24 channels are multiplexed to form a single T1 line, multiple T1 lines are multiplexed to form higher capacity digital transmission lines. This method forms a complete Digital Signal (DS) hierarchy, as shown in the DS Hierarchy Table.

DS Hierarchy

DS Level	T-Carrier Level	Bandwidth	Number of Voice Channels
DS0	One channel	64 Kbps	1
N/A	FT1	n x 64 Kbps	1 to 24
DS1	T1	1.544 Mbps	24
DS2*	T2	6 Mbps	96
DS3	T3	45 Mbps	672
DS4*	T4	274 Mbps	4,032

*Rarely used.

T-carriers, such as T1 and T3, are used to connect LANs over extended distances. The Sample T1 Configuration Diagram shows how a T1 or T3 circuit could be used to connect two sites that each include a telephone system and data network. The same physical circuit can serve both types of systems, because each channel of a T1 or T3 line can carry either voice traffic or data traffic.

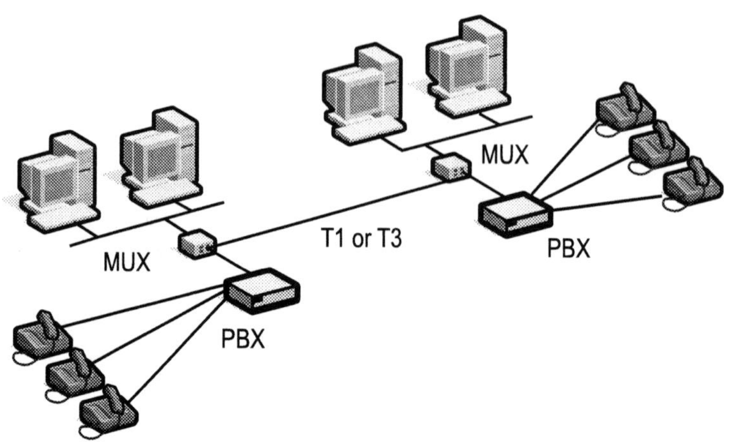

Sample T1 Configuration

FT1

Objective 1.1
Identify the issues that affect Internet site functionality ... Bandwidth (both client and server) ... Internet connection types (both client and server)

Leasing a T1 line means paying for the entire 1.544-Mbps bandwidth 24 hours a day, whether it is used or not. FT1 lets you lease one or more 64-Kbps DS0 channels. You might, for example, lease only 6 of the 24 circuits to obtain an aggregate bandwidth of 384 Kbps.

FT1 is useful whenever the cost of a dedicated T1 is prohibitive. FT1 is not as efficient or flexible as switched services, however, because you are still paying to have the fraction of bandwidth you have leased available on a 24-hour basis.

Other than bandwidth, the main difference between T1 and FT1 service is control over the physical endpoints. Because we are not leasing an entire T1 circuit, we are sharing the T1 with other customers. Therefore, we cannot dictate the location of the other end of the circuit.

To understand this difference, think of the difference between chartering a bus and buying a single ticket. Buying a T1 is like hiring the whole bus. When you rent the whole vehicle, the bus will pick you up at your door and take you all the way to your destination. In contrast, buying an FT1 is like buying a ticket on a bus.

Many others will share the ride with you, thus, everyone must get on and off the bus at a bus station.

In the case of an FT1, the "bus station" is a telephone company CO. There, the remote end of each FT1 circuit terminates in a device called a "digital access cross-connect switch (DACS)." In the DACS, the telephone company has a network of T1 interconnects, where FT1 channels get on and off the T1.

Due to the one-end nature of FT1, a separate FT1 circuit must be leased between each network site and its nearest CO. In contrast, we need only lease one T1 circuit between each pair of nodes. For this reason, as the size of the fraction increases, FT1 eventually becomes more expensive than a full T1.

T1 and FT1 circuits are useful WAN options because they offer adaptable bandwidth at essentially fixed costs within a metropolitan area. T1-capable routers and bridges typically support one or more T1 circuits, and automatically make connections with other routers or bridges in the network.

Customer Premise Equipment for T-Carriers

As we have seen, each type of physical transmission medium requires a particular type of equipment to generate and receive signals. For example, on a LAN, each computer needs a network interface card (NIC). To transmit digital data over an analog telephone line, a computer needs a modem. And, to connect a network to a T1 line, three devices are needed:

Objective 3.7
Create a logic diagram of Internet components from the client to the server.

Objective 3.8
Describe various hardware and software connection devices and when to use them.
… WAN Link
… CSU/DSU

- A T1 Multiplexer (MUX) breaks the outgoing digital bit stream into T1 time slices. (Each time slice represents one DS0 channel.) It also converts an incoming multiplexed signal back into a continuous bit stream.

- A Data Service Unit (DSU) converts the outgoing multiplexed signal into the signaling format used by the T1 line. It also converts incoming signals to the signaling format used by the customer's network. The DSU essentially reconciles differences in the way each transmission system represents a binary 1 or 0.

- A Channel Service Unit (CSU) maintains the electrical circuit between the customer and telecommunication company, and detects basic transmission errors, including loss of signal. The CSU essentially functions as a repeater, regenerating and boosting both incoming and outgoing signals. When the telecommunication company sends special testing signals over the T1, the CSU also repeats those signals back to the telecommunication company CO, in a process called "loopback."

The T1 Connecting Equipment Diagram shows each of these functions as a separate device, and they can be purchased that way. However, the CSU and DSU are usually combined into a single device called a "CSU/DSU," or a T1 Service Unit (TSU). Both of these may also be included as part of a T1 MUX, or all three may be built into another WAN device such as a router. If you look back at the Sample T1 Configuration Diagram, the component marked "MUX" would represent all three of these functions combined in one box.

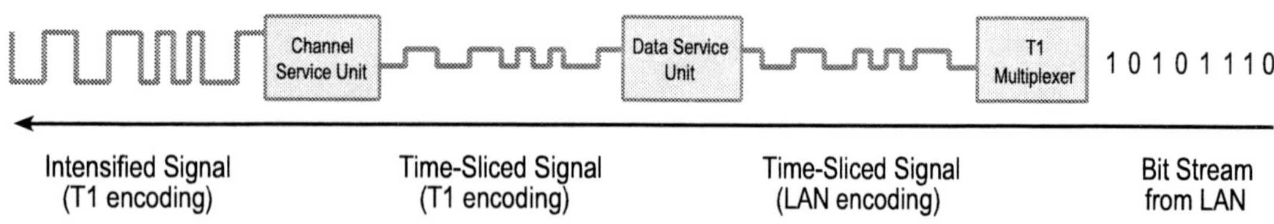

T1 Connecting Equipment

ISDN

ISDN is a circuit-switched digital service that offers all the capabilities of a voice telephone line, as well as data features. Although ISDN has been around for a while, it is finally taking off as customers increase their demand for fast access to the Internet, desktop video, home office connections, and links between LANs.

Another key to ISDN's popularity is that it is an international standard. Therefore, digital telephone calls and data transmissions can be made to more countries across the globe when using ISDN.

How ISDN Works

An ISDN line uses two kinds of channels:

- B (bearer) channels do the real work of carrying signals. Each B channel carries 64 Kbps, and an ISDN line may have either 2 or 23 B channels.

- The D channel carries control information that organizes the B channels. Each ISDN line has one D channel.

BRI

ISDN-Basic Rate Interface (BRI) is a circuit-switched digital service that can be carried over a single pair of copper wires, which makes it attractive to home users and small businesses. ISDN-BRI consists of two B channels of 64 Kbps each, plus one D channel of 16 Kbps, as illustrated on the ISDN-BRI Channels Diagram. Thus, this service is often called "2B+D."

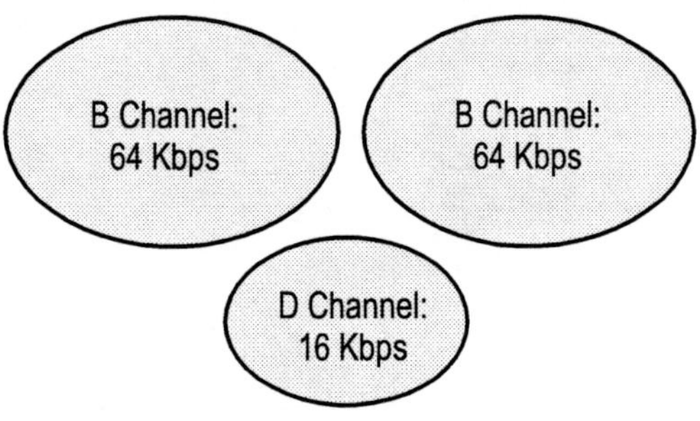

ISDN-BRI Channels

Each of the two B channels can carry digital voice, data, or video. Therefore, we can talk on one channel while sending computer data on the other, or use one channel for voice and the other for video. These two channels can also be combined or "bonded" into a single 128-Kbps channel.

The single D channel is used for control signaling. The D channel can also be used as a separate data channel for fax or packet data applications, such as Internet access. In addition, in many cases, you can now order just a D channel for low-speed, point-of-sale applications, such as communication links for credit card verification and cash register connections.

ISDN-BRI is often used for basic dial-up connectivity for home and small business connectivity, typically connecting individual computers or small LANs over the public switched network. This is shown on the ISDN Basic Connectivity Diagram.

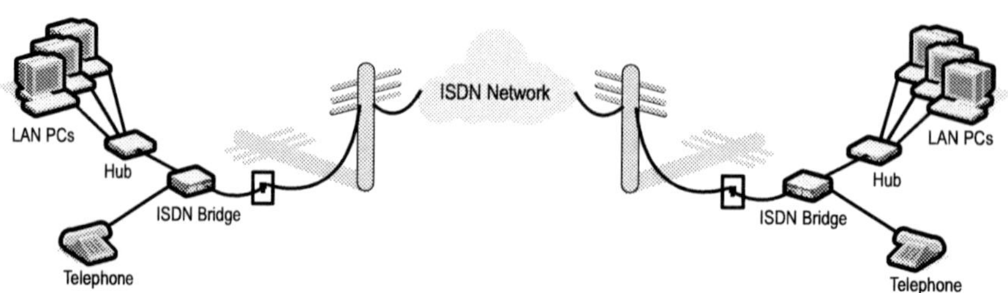

ISDN Basic Connectivity

A device called a "terminal adapter (TA)" is required to attach a non-ISDN device to an ISDN network. The Home ISDN Connectivity Diagram shows how a TA is used to connect a telephone and personal computer (PC) to an ISDN-BRI line. If a voice conversation is not active, the PC can transmit information at the full 128-Kbps bandwidth. After a telephone call is initiated, the 128- Kbps bandwidth is shared between the telephone call and data transfer.

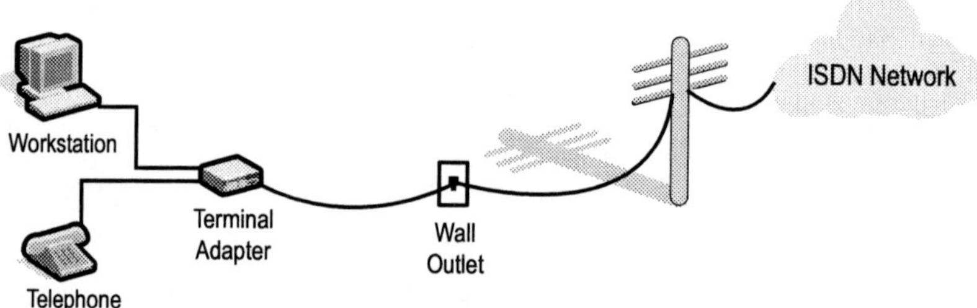

Home ISDN Connectivity

PRI

ISDN-Primary Rate Interface (PRI) is the industrial-strength version of ISDN, often used as a point-to-point connection between LANs, business telephone systems, or both. ISDN-PRI is a Data Link Layer technology that uses the Physical Layer services of a T-carrier. Thus, ISDN-PRI provides the same bandwidth as T1 service.

ISDN-PRI consists of 23 B channels of 64 Kbps each, plus one D channel of 64 Kbps. This "23B+D" setup is illustrated on the ISDN-PRI Channels Diagram.

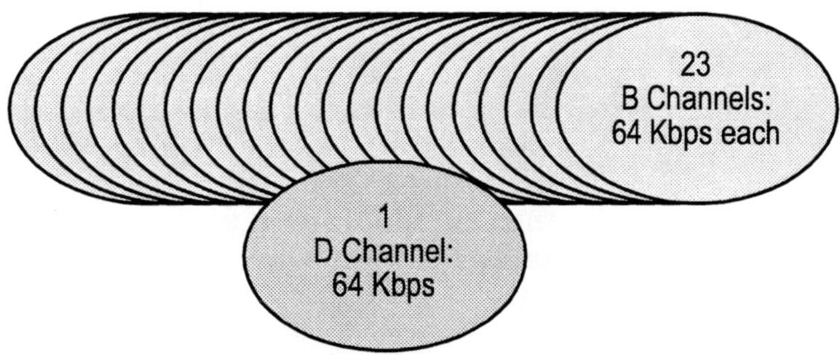

ISDN-PRI Channels

ISDN-PRI operates the same way as ISDN-BRI. Each B channel can carry voice, data, or video. The D channel is used for control signaling and can also be used as another channel for packet data applications.

Channel Bonding

Like T1 channels, 64-Kbps ISDN channels can be bonded, or combined to form a single large channel. ISDN channel bonding is performed by the D channel as part of its control signaling function. The technical term used for ISDN channel bonding is "non-facility-associated signaling (NFAS)." When channels are not bonded, the ISDN line is using facility-associated signaling (FAS).

Objective 1.1

Identify the issues that affect Internet site functionality. ... Bandwidth (both client and server) ... Internet connection types (both client and server)

NFAS offers many practical advantages to ISDN-PRI customers, because each D channel can control up to 20,000 B channels. A customer with 10 ISDN-PRI lines can designate one D channel to control all other B channels, and assign a second D channel as a backup to the first. The eight unused D channels can then be converted to additional B channels, providing even more transmission bandwidth.

This principle is even more powerful when combined with channel bonding. A customer with multiple ISDN-PRI lines can convert unused D channels to B channels, then bond the B channels to support high-bandwidth applications such as video conferencing, high-capacity data transfers, or high-speed Internet access.

Internet Connectivity Technologies

SONET

Synchronous Optical Network (SONET) is a Physical Layer standard that provides rules for converting electrical signals to pulses of light, moving the light signals over fiber optic cable, and converting the signals back to electrical form at their destination.

Like the T-carrier system, SONET defines a method of multiplexing, as well as the bandwidth required to accomplish the multiplexing. Also, like the T-carrier system, each SONET signal can be multiplexed into a larger signal. Put it all together and we have the Optical Carrier (OC) hierarchy (or Synchronous Digital Hierarchy [SDH]) shown in the OC Hierarchy Table.

OC Hierarchy

SONET (OC) Level	Bandwidth	Number of T1 Lines	Number of 64-Kbps Channels
OC-1	52 Mbps	28	672
OC-3	155.5 Mbps	84	2,016
OC-9	466.5 Mbps	252	6,048
OC-12	622 Mbps	336	8,064
OC-18	933 Mbps	504	12,096
OC-24	1.2 Gbps	672	16,128
OC-36	2 Gbps	1,008	24,192
OC-48	2.5 Gbps	1,344	32,256
OC-96	5 Gbps	2,688	64,512
OC-192	10 Gbps	5,376	129,024

Notice that OC-1 is designed to carry the same number (672) of 64-Kbps channels as a T3 circuit. However, the bandwidth requirement is different for T3 (45 Mbps) and OC-1 (52 Mbps). The difference is because SONET uses more bandwidth for the control information necessary to keep its multiplexed signals in synch.

Notice also that, beginning with OC-24, we are no longer talking about bandwidth in Mbps. At OC-24 and above, SONET carrier lines handle gigabits per second (Gbps), or billions of bits.

SONET Rings

SONET is a ring network technology. It can be built as a true ring, using two parallel rings that carry signals in opposite directions. The same signal is sent simultaneously over both rings. This redundancy ensures that if one ring fails, a signal will still get through. A SONET network can also use a point-to-point physical topology. However, signals still flow in a logical ring.

SONET was originally developed to provide high-speed connections between telephone company CO switches across entire regions. However, the SONET standard also extends down to the office desktop. Today, telephone companies offer SONET connections to their large customers that need high-speed optical transmission in their business networks.

However, how can an individual business network connect to a public network that operates at Gbps data rates? The SONET architecture provides what are called "virtual tributaries" of channels, just as a large river is fed by smaller tributaries, and sometimes divides into smaller side streams. A SONET network uses MUXs to add and remove smaller signals from the main data flow. A MUX also cross-connects communication channels, so that one customer location can be connected to a communication channel at another customer location.

Common Point-to-Multipoint Services

Objective 3.4
Understand and be able to describe the capabilities of popular remote access protocols
… Point-to-multipoint

Point-to-multipoint links are usually provided by DSL or cable modem networks, as summarized in the Point-to-Multipoint Link Options Table.

Point-to-Multipoint Link Options

Service	Link Speed	Equipment Needs
DSL	Varies, up to 1.544 Mbps	DSL Modem
Cable Modem	Varies, up to 3 Mbps downstream	Cable Modem

Internet Connectivity
Technologies

DSL

Objective 3.7
Create a logic diagram of Internet components from the client to the server

Objective 3.8
Describe various hardware and software connection devices and when to use them
... xDSL Modem
... WAN Link

Digital Subscriber Line (DSL) is a Physical Layer technology that provides high-speed service over the local loop. Telephone companies are using DSL to provide high-speed Internet access to homes and businesses, in competition with cable television operators.

A DSL line is an analog connection with a special DSL modem on each end of a twisted pair telephone line: one DSL modem at the subscriber's end, and one at the telephone company central office (CO). The DSL Connectivity Diagram illustrates this type of setup. A DSL connection creates three information channels:

- Downstream digital channel (carrying data from the CO to the customer).

- Upstream digital channel (carrying data from the customer to the CO).

- Analog POTS channel, separate from the two digital channels. Analog telephone service is uninterrupted even if DSL fails.

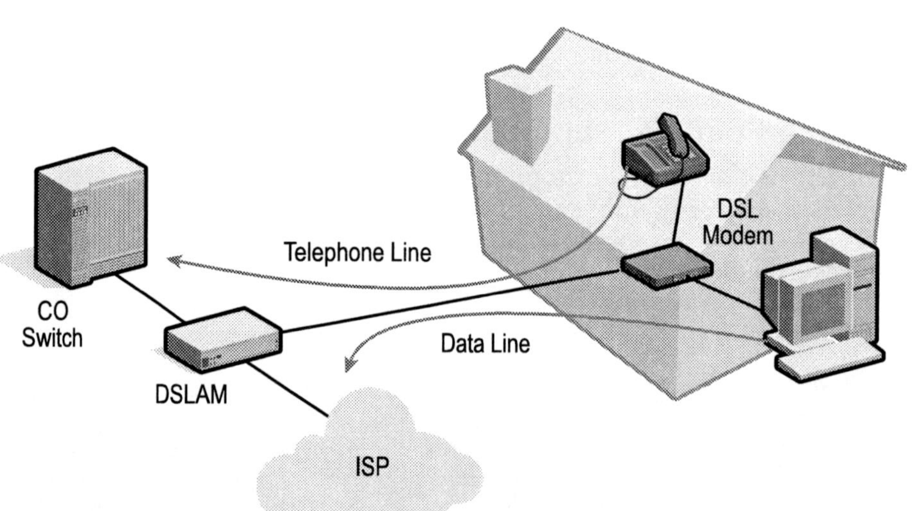

DSL Connectivity

Types of DSL Service

Objective 1.1
Identify the issues that affect Internet site functionality ... Bandwidth (both client and server) ... Internet connection types (both client and server)

The various types of DSL include the following:

- Asymmetric DSL (ADSL)—ADSL provides downstream transmission rates of 1.544 megabits per second (Mbps) across up to 18,000 feet of twisted copper pair wire. ADSL is "asymmetric" because its downstream data rates are much faster than its upstream data rates. Asymmetric solutions are attractive because they match Internet user patterns. For example, to send a 100-kilobyte (KB) graphic image downstream, a World Wide Web (Web) user sends as few as 10 keystrokes upstream.

- ADSL Lite—This is a slightly slower version of ADSL that requires simpler equipment.

- Rate Adaptive DSL (RADSL)—RADSL overcomes the varying conditions and lengths of copper cable. RADSL has the same maximum data rates as ADSL; however, both downstream and upstream rates are adjusted to the physical wire conditions at the time of transmission. Therefore, RADSL can be very fast under good conditions; however, less fast under poor conditions.

- High Bit Rate DSL (HDSL)—HDSL offers both upstream and downstream speeds up to 1.544 Mbps, without the POTS line, over two wire pairs.

- Symmetrical DSL, or Single Line DSL (SDSL)—SDSL offers both upstream and downstream speeds of 384 to 784 Kbps, over one wire pair, including a POTS line.

- Integrated Services Digital Network (ISDN) DSL (IDSL)—This new hybrid technology uses ISDN technology to deliver 128 Kbps. Unlike ISDN, which supports both voice and data, IDSL is a dedicated data communication service only.

- Very High Bit Rate DSL (VDSL)—Although currently not commercially available, VDSL promises downstream rates of approximately 13 Mbps across up to 4,500 feet of wire, and higher rates across shorter distances. To achieve these data rates, VDSL will require fiber optic connections instead of copper pairs.

DSL Bandwidth

DSL has the potential to deliver data at 160 times the speed of the 56-Kbps modems currently used for Internet access over POTS lines.

The ADSL Bandwidth Diagram shows how ADSL provides nearly 10,000 kilohertz (kHz) of bandwidth, compared to the 3 kHz of an analog POTS channel. DSL achieves these high connection speeds by using the additional bandwidth that a copper pair can support.

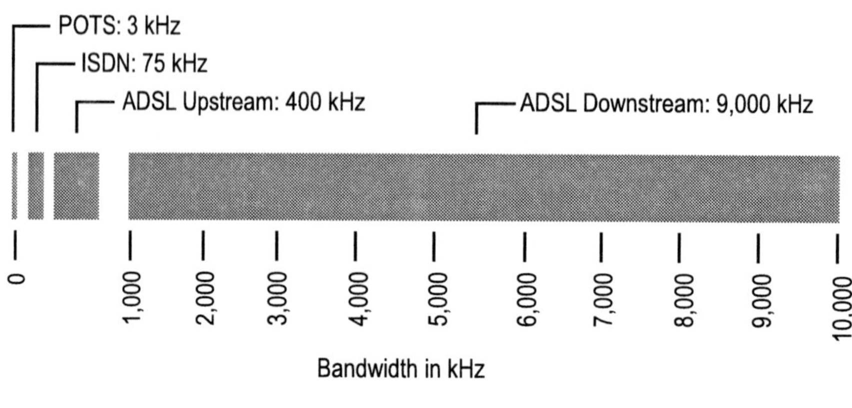

ADSL Bandwidth

DSL Physical Requirements

The speed of a particular DSL installation depends on the type of DSL in use, the thickness and condition of the copper wire, and the user's distance from the telephone company's CO:

- Reach (loop length)—Each xDSL service has a maximum reach, or distance the service can be offered from the CO. Typically, the range of DSL is between 12,000 and 26,000 feet. Customers located beyond the reach of a service cannot receive the service. Generally speaking, higher speeds are possible at shorter distances; however, performance is lower as the distance between the user and CO increases.

- No devices—The copper wires between CO and customer must be free of electronic devices such as repeaters. This is a problem because most copper that extends more than 6,000 feet from the CO contains some kind of electronic repeater to boost the analog signal. It is also essential that the line does not contain loading coils. These were typically installed on analog lines to filter out high-frequency noise by cutting off all frequencies above 4 kHz. However, if we look back at the ADSL Bandwidth Diagram, we will see that such a device would block the wide range of frequencies used by xDSL.

Thus, a telephone company must first remove these devices before it can provide DSL service to many of its customers. This increases the time and cost of many xDSL installations.

- Good wiring—The copper loop must also be in good physical condition, well-installed, with no mismatched wire gauges. The age of the average copper wire plant makes this unlikely. Bellcore estimates the typical U.S. telephone line crosses 22 splices, which allows line noise and crosstalk to reduce effective data rates. In addition, effective data rates are reduced by other problems throughout the telephone system, such as overlong loops that attenuate signals, nonterminated wire pairs, and crosstalk between wires.

DSL Network Configuration

DSL was originally designed to link a single user's computer to an ISP. Thus, the simplest DSL network looks like the Single User DSL Network Diagram.

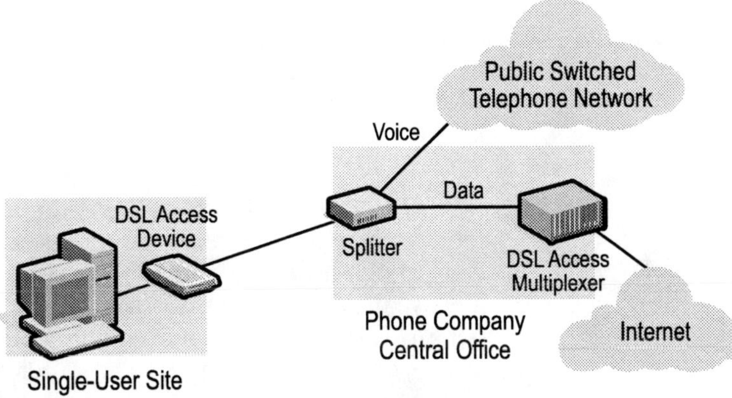

Single User DSL Network

The key elements of this DSL architecture are:

- **A DSL access device** on the customer's end of the copper loop

- **A DSL Access Multiplexer (DSLAM)** in a telephone company's central office (CO)

DSL Access Device

This device is commonly called a DSL modem, but that description is inaccurate because it is actually a Layer 2 (usually Ethernet) bridge. But, like a modem, a DSL access device may be a card installed within a computer, or an external unit connected via the computer's Ethernet NIC or USB port.

DSLAM

The DSL Access Multiplexer (DSLAM) serves as the central connection point for all DSL subscribers served by a single CO. It multiplexes traffic from individual homes, and forwards it to the ISP that provides those DSL connections. From the perspective of DSL subscribers, the DSLAM also functions as an Ethernet bridge. For this reason, this lesson considers DSL to be a point-to-multipoint technology. However, DSL is often marketed as a point-to-point link because only one subscriber typically uses each local loop between a customer site and a DSLAM.

DSL Protocol Architecture

DSL is a Physical Layer technology that transmits digital data over an existing local loop. DSL Internet access service typically uses Ethernet at Layer 2, and TCP/IP at Layers 3 and 4.

Always On?

Once a DSL connection has been set up, the local loop functions as a dedicated point-to-point line between a subscriber and the nearest DSLAM. This eliminates the need to dial up a connection, and provides the "always on" service so often described in DSL advertising.

However, DSL is usually "always on" only at Layers 1 and 2. To reduce costs and conserve IP addresses, ISPs use DHCP to dynamically assign an IP address to each subscriber. Those address leases are usually set to time out in a few hours. So when a subscriber begins using the Internet after being offline all night, there will be a few seconds' delay as the computer contacts the ISP for a new address lease. However, that is much less than the time needed to establish a dial-up connection, and subsequent access will be nearly instantaneous (until the IP address times out again).

DSL Security Concerns

A DSLAM functions as a bridge, isolating most DSL traffic to each local loop. However, all DSL subscribers on the same DSLAM belong to a single broadcast domain in the ISP's network. Windows peer-to-peer networking features, such as Network Neighborhood, use broadcast messages to discover nearby computers, printers, and other resources. If DSL users do not take their own security precautions, their private data will be exposed to their fellow DSL users.

This security hole becomes larger when multiple computers share a connection by using an insecure method such as Internet Connection Sharing (discussed in Lesson 4 of this unit), or by connecting a DSL access device directly to a network hub.

Routers for Improved Security

Security can be improved by running personal firewall software on the computer that is connected to the DSL line. Another simple (though more expensive) solution is to install an Ethernet router between the DSL access device and the LAN. In that case, the ISP assigns a single dynamic IP address to the router's outside interface. The router can use Network Address Translation to securely share that address among multiple internal hosts, and can provide other firewall services.

A network can also improve its DSL security by replacing its DSL bridge with a DSL router. Like an Ethernet router, a DSL router can share a single IP address among multiple hosts. It can also be configured with firewall features such as packet filtering. These advantages prompt most businesses to choose DSL routers as their access devices.

Cable Modems

Objective 3.7
Create a logic diagram of Internet components from the client to the server.

Objective 3.8
Describe various hardware and software connection devices and when to use them.
... Cable Modem
... WAN Link

Cable modems offer much more than basic video services, providing Internet connectivity and other home and small business applications. The Internet Access via Cable Modem Diagram provides an overview of cable modem access over a hybrid fiber-coaxial (HFC) network. HFC networks are composed of fiber feeder from a cable head end to a neighborhood optical node that serves several hundred homes. A signal then travels from the head end to each node, then from each node over a coaxial cable bus that is tapped to serve each home. A network interface unit (NIU) inside the home includes a cable modem and other electronics, and perhaps a power supply.

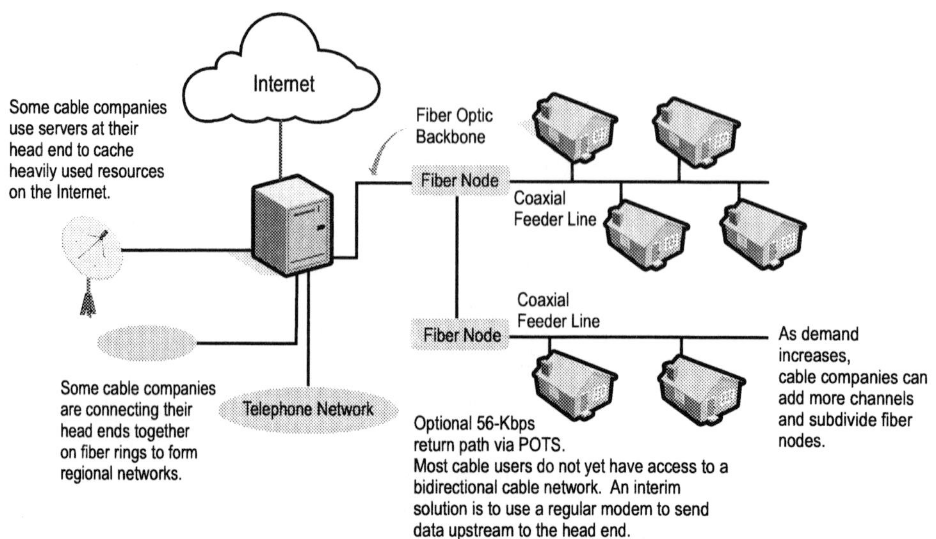

Internet Access via Cable Modem

Cable Modem Configuration

A cable modem is a complex device that incorporates three components: a tuner, which separates data signals from broadcast streams (video) from telephony parts from network adapters, bridges, and routers; network management software agents, which enable a cable company to monitor operations; and encryption devices. Each cable modem has an Ethernet port. As a result of this configuration, up to three cable wires can be provided from the NIU: a coaxial wire delivering broadcast video to a television, a twisted-pair Ethernet wire connecting to a PC, and a twisted-pair wire connecting to a telephone. TCP/IP software is required in a computer.

The current HFC cable network uses a 750-MHz spectrum, equivalent to 110 downstream television channels of 6 MHz each (an FCC limit). The most common cable modems create a downstream data stream out of one of the 6-MHz television channels that occupy the spectrum between 50 and 750 MHz. Downstream transmission can occur at rates as high as 30 Mbps.

Spectrum bandwidth from 5 to 42 MHz is reserved for upstream signaling and telephony. Common cable modems create an upstream channel out of this currently unused band.

The downstream channel is continuous; however, it is divided into time slots that carry IP packets, with each packet addressed to a particular subscriber. The downstream portion of the spectrum supports a mix of analog video, digital broadcast, interactive video, telephone, and data services. Downstream transmission does not disturb transmission of television signals to the television set. Upstream transmission rates vary by modem vendor.

There are two types of cable modems: two-way cable modems and telephone return cable modems. Telephone return cable modems allow subscribers of cable networks that have not been upgraded for two-way communication to obtain the benefits of high speed on the downstream link.

Cable Modem MAC

Cable modem data transmission uses 802.3 Ethernet frame format and addressing. However, because of their larger physical size, these bus networks need a different method of medium access control (MAC) than the CSMA/CD used on an Ethernet LAN.

To control access to the shared bus medium, two-way cable systems use time division multiplexing controlled by the head end controller, a device called a Cable Modem Termination System (CMTS). When each cable modem needs to communicate, the CMTS assigns it an exclusive time slot. Certain time slots are also reserved for the initial messages that cable modems use to request a reserved time slot, and for messages used to synchronize all cable modem clocks to that of the CMTS.

Shared Bandwidth

Objective 1.1
Identify the issues that affect Internet site functionality … Bandwidth (both client and server) … Internet connection types (both client and server)

Cable modem technology can provide very fast data rates, but it requires users to share bandwidth in a traditional Ethernet broadcast network. If many cable modem users are online, downstream speeds can fall substantially below the high advertised data rate. Also, some cable modem providers limit the maximum bandwidth that may be used by a single subscriber, even if no other users are online. As with any other connection service, a customer considering cable modem access should carefully question the service provider about its performance under a typical load.

Security

Objective 4.6
Be able to describe the uses and proper instances to use various client security add-ons ... Encryption software

Because a cable modem network is a broadcast network, every node receives all transmissions from every other node on the same bus. Unless cable systems implement extra security features, a marginally skilled hacker could dig his way into a neighbor's computer files.

Thus, most cable modem networks now offer security features specified in the Data Over Cable Service Interface Specification (DOCSIS). DOCSIS was originally developed by the cable industry to define standard interoperable components, and create safeguards against theft of cable service. However, its Baseline Privacy Interface (BPI) has become one of its most important components because it requires strong encryption to protect communication between the CMTS and each cable modem. Most DOCSIS-compliant systems currently use the proven DES encryption algorithm, but DOCSIS version 1.1 provides flexibility by allowing other algorithms to be used instead of DES.

DOCSIS security only provides privacy within the cable modem network itself, not across the entire Internet. DOCSIS ensures that two cable subscribers on the same bus cannot see each other's data, but it provides no security for that data once it enters the Internet cloud. Thus, cable modem users, like all Internet users, should implement basic security precautions such as personal firewalls.

Activities

1. If you need 30 FT1 channels between Los Angeles and San Diego, it is easiest to order an E1 line. True or False?

2. Leased lines offer less flexibility than dial-up services. True or False?

3. A router can connect two remote LANs; however, a bridge is used to connect LANs located in a metropolitan area. True or False?

4. LANs can be connected using both point-to-point networks and switched networks. True or False?

5. All dial-up lines are point-to-point connections. True or False?

6. What is the top speed of a modem used for dial-up?

   ____

7. If a receiving modem demodulates an analog signal, what did the sending modem do to the original digital information?

   ____

   ____

   ____

   ____

8. List three advantages of leased-line services over dial-up services.

   ____

   ____

   ____

9. How many 64-Kbps circuits are available on a T1 line?

   ____

10. If you lease FT1 service at a 10-channel capacity, how much aggregate bandwidth will you have?

    ____

Internet Connectivity Technologies

11. If DSL service is provided from phone company central offices, why can't everyone get it?

____

12. What three components are required to connect a LAN to a T-carrier line?

____

Extended Activities

1. Identify all of the high-speed Internet access technologies that are available to your home. For each type of connection, list the setup cost, monthly subscription cost, and equipment cost. Also list the best-case and worst-case estimated data rates, and note any special security concerns.

2. Find and discuss information on the V.90 modem standard. What problems does this standard solve?

____

____

3. What is the effective top speed of a 56-Kbps modem? Why this limitation?

____

____

____

Lesson 3—Switched WAN Services

As we learned earlier in this course, the number of point-to-point lines in a full mesh network increases sharply with the number of nodes. Switched services provide more flexibility in connecting WAN nodes. Dial-up or dedicated connections are still necessary to reach the switched network; however, after the switched network is accessed, you have any-to-any connectivity.

In addition, private lines are engineered to meet peak traffic rates. In other words, a network designer must buy enough point-to-point bandwidth to carry the network's highest expected level of traffic. During nonpeak times, however, unused transmission capacity goes to waste. Switched services can provide variable capacity, at rates that vary according to the bandwidth actually used.

Thus, the emphasis in wide area networking is shifting from dedicated private networks to switched alternatives. Public switched networks, such as frame relay and asynchronous transfer mode (ATM), are highly reliable, fast, and efficient. This lesson introduces these services, which are the most popular switched WAN technologies used to connect multiple customer sites to each other and to ISPs.

Objectives

At the end of this lesson you will be able to:

- Explain the advantages a switched service offers over a point-to-point service

- Describe the basic features of frame relay and ATM

- Name the types of traffic and applications that are best carried by each of these services

- Explain what a virtual private network (VPN) does

 **Key Point**

Switched service provides greater connectivity options.

Types of Switched Services

Objective 2.11
Identify the basic characteristics (e.g., speed, capacity, media) of ...
WAN technologies

Packet-switched services fall into two broad categories: connection-oriented networks and connectionless networks. The Packet-Switched Network Options Table provides a summary of the most common switched services offered in networks today.

Packet-Switched Network Options

Service	Link Speed	Type of Service
X.25	300 bps to 56 Kbps	Connection-oriented
Frame relay	56 Kbps to 1.544 Mbps	Connection-oriented
ATM	155 Mbps to 2.48 Gbps	Connection-oriented
The Internet	Varies widely	Connectionless

X.25

X.25 was the first switched network service. An X.25 network, whether public or private, is typically built largely upon the leased-line facilities of the public telephone network. It uses a Network Layer address (telephone number) so that switches can route packet traffic over multiple paths.

X.25 only provides data rates up to a maximum of 56 Kbps. It is still used to switch packet traffic over a wide area. However, it is quickly being replaced by faster technologies, such as frame relay and ISDN, which were built upon the foundation of X.25.

X.25 is connection-oriented, and offers two types of service:

- Permanent Virtual Circuits (PVCs)—This is the X.25 equivalent of a leased line, statically defined and always available as long as a network is up. Unlike leased lines, however, more than one virtual circuit can share a physical link.

- Virtual Connections—This is the X.25 equivalent of a dial-up connection. A network establishes a connection on a virtual circuit, transfers packets until the application is finished, and then releases the connection.

The X.25 standard predates the Open Systems Interconnection (OSI) model. (The first version of X.25 was issued in 1976.) X.25 is now considered a connection-oriented Network Layer protocol because it provides error-free service to the Transport Layer. However, the overhead associated with the necessary error checking is proving to be unacceptable in today's highly reliable digital networks.

Frame Relay

Objective 2.11
Identify the basic characteristics (e.g., speed, capacity, media) of … frame relay

Frame relay is a connection-oriented packet-switched network service that works at the Data Link Layer. A frame relay network carries traffic over virtual circuits.

The term "frame" is used because frame relay builds data frames and can asynchronously multiplex these frames from multiple virtual circuits (endpoints) into a single high-speed data stream. The term "relay" is used because each frame relay device forwards the frames as they move through the network without examining the frame's payload or demultiplexing the data stream.

Logically, a frame relay is an electronic switch or switches running frame relay software. Physically, it is a box that connects to three or more high-speed links, and routes data traffic between them. The Frame Relay Diagram illustrates the operation.

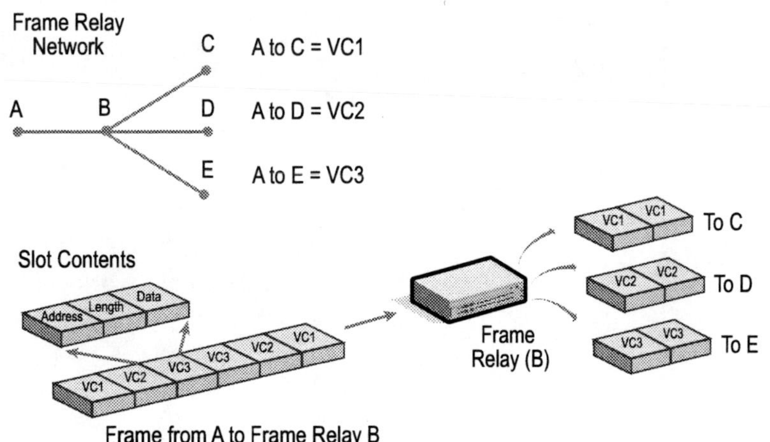

Frame Relay

Assume that virtual circuits have been established as shown on the diagram: VC 1 from MUX A to MUX C, VC 2 from MUX A to MUX D, and VC 3 from MUX A to MUX E. All three circuits flow through Frame Relay B.

Next, assume data for all three circuits flows into MUX A. The MUX places them into the frame, storing an address and length with the data. (This diagram was simplified by showing all data the same length.) The frame is transmitted from MUX A to MUX B. MUX B must demultiplex the frame and then create frames to be sent to MUXs C, D, and E.

Another view of a similar network is shown on the Frame Relay Network Diagram. Here routers feed a frame relay network. VC1 could be a path from Router 1 to Router C. VC 2 could be a path from Router 1 to Router D, and VC3 could be a path from Router 2 to Router E.

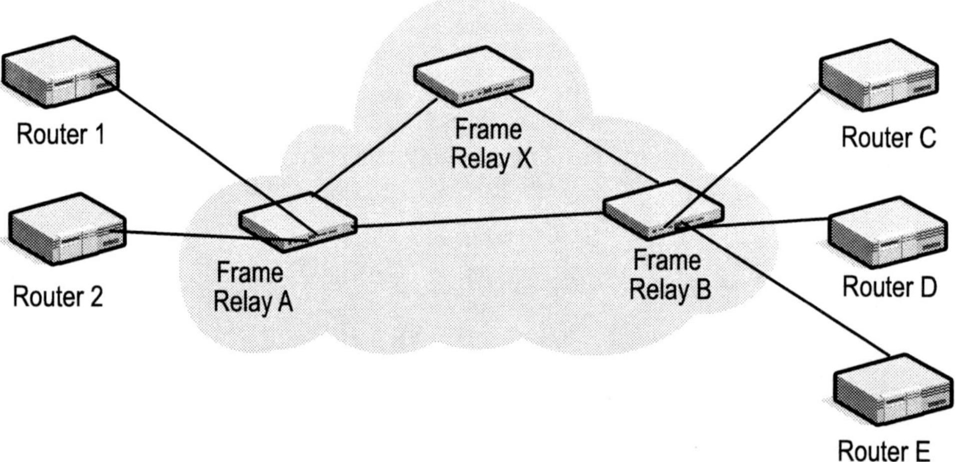

Frame Relay Network

The device that attaches a LAN to a frame relay network encapsulates each LAN data frame or packet inside a frame relay frame before sending it over the frame relay network. This is shown on the Frame Relay Encapsulation Diagram.

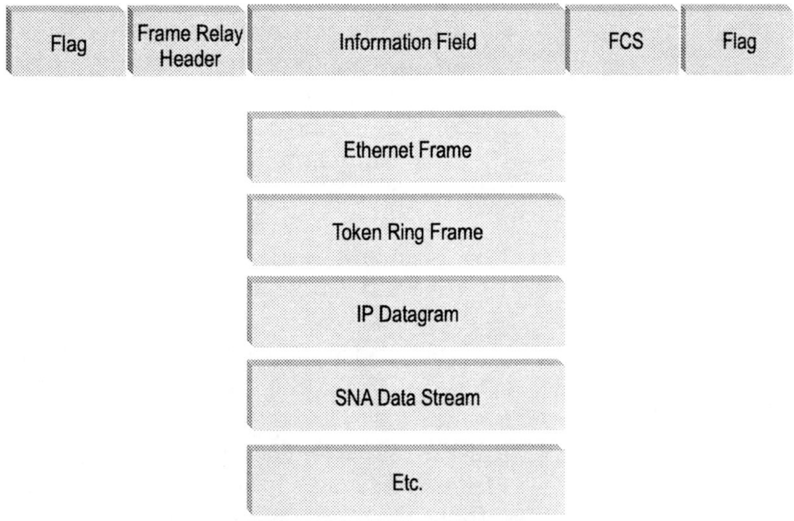

Frame Relay Encapsulation

At the other end of the network, the receiving device decapsulates the frame relay frame and sends the data toward its destination.

Frame Relay Characteristics

The significant frame relay characteristics are as follows:

- Bandwidth up to T1—Frame relay typically uses T1 as the Physical Layer service. (The switches are connected by T1 lines.) Therefore, a frame relay virtual circuit can provide bandwidth up to approximately 1.5 Mbps.

- Fault tolerance—Frame relay switches can monitor network status and take corrective action when necessary, such as rerouting traffic into new virtual circuits. Typical private lines do not have this capability.

- Connection-oriented service—All data in the same virtual circuit travels over the same physical path for the duration of a transmission (unless one of the switches fails or some other network problem occurs).

- No end-to-end error detection or correction—A frame either makes it across the network or it does not. A frame relay switch discards damaged frames without notifying the sender or receiver. It assumes the physical links are reliable, and leaves error recovery to higher layer protocols such as Transmission Control Protocol/Internet Protocol (TCP/IP).

- Bandwidth on demand—Frame relay does not require that a link be up and dedicated at all times. Rather, it uses bandwidth only when there is data to be sent. Other, more traditional WAN transports, such as T1, use TDM, which requires dedicated bandwidth. Thus, a TDM service must be up and running even during times when the network is passing no data.

Most local and long-distance carriers offer frame relay, which was designed to handle various types of LAN traffic. It is ideal for sending data over a wide area because of its speed and flexibility. However, its variable-length frames are not well suited for voice or video, which require a steady data stream.

Frame Relay Implementation

To set up a private frame relay network, a corporation must install a frame relay switch at each site, then connect pairs of switches with point-to-point connections, such as T1 lines. The end of each T1 terminates at a customer's CSU/DSU. The DSU connects directly to the frame relay switch, which connects to the customer's network at each site.

Many corporations prefer to simply access a public frame relay network. To do this, an organization purchases a frame relay access device (FRAD), or installs a software upgrade to a router or bridge to allow that device to generate frame relay frames. The company then sets up a dedicated line (often a T1) between its CSU/DSU and the telecommunication carrier's nearest frame relay switch. The corporation can then subscribe to the frame relay service, usually from a telecommunication carrier.

ATM

Objective 2.11
Identify the basic characteristics (e.g., speed, capacity, media) of ... ATM

Asynchronous Transfer Mode (ATM) is an international standard for a high-speed, connection-oriented, cell-switching technology. ATM operates at both the Physical and Data Link Layers of the OSI model to transmit voice, video, and data across LANs, MANs, and WANs.

ATM transmits data in units called "cells." A cell is essentially the same as a packet, because it consists of data plus a protocol header. However, a cell is always the same size (53 bytes for ATM), while the size of a packet can vary.

The ATM Network Diagram illustrates an ATM "cloud" network. Similar to frame relay, an ATM network consists of switches that provide virtual circuits between multiple inputs. ATM switches forward data very quickly, and the fiber optic links that usually connect ATM switches operate at 155 Mbps.

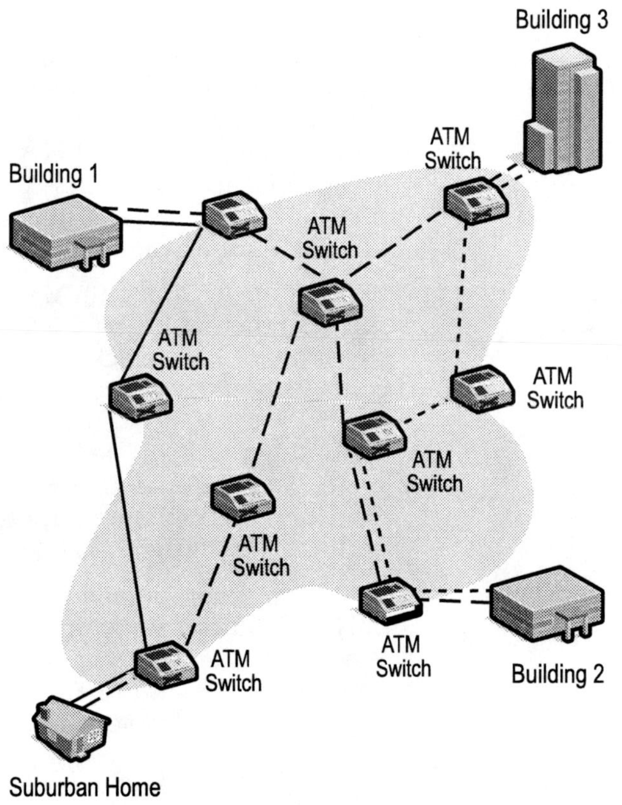

ATM Network

Fiber optic transmission is not the only Physical Layer technology that ATM runs over. ATM is media-independent, because it is not tied to any particular Physical Layer. However, most implementations of ATM use high-speed optical transmission to get the full benefits of this technology.

Transfer Modes

A transfer mode specifies a method of transmitting, multiplexing, and switching data in a network. A network typically uses one of the following three transfer modes:

- Synchronous Transfer Mode (STM)—"Synchronous" means that data communication is organized by a microprocessor clock; a receiving node can detect the beginning and end of a signal because signals start and stop at particular times. Services that use STM, such as T1/E1, divide each transmission frame into a series of time slots, and then allocate particular time slots to each user.

  STM is ideal for transmission of voice and video, because it provides a constant-bit-rate service. In contrast, data transmissions are typically bursty, because a user is idle for relatively long periods of time between short periods of intense data-transfer activity. STM is inefficient for data communications because the same time slot in each frame is reserved for a particular user, regardless of whether the user has data to transmit. When a user is idle, the time slot is wasted, because STM does not reassign unused time slots to other users.

- Packet Transfer Mode (PTM)—In a PTM network technology, such as Ethernet or frame relay, data is broken into variable-size units of data (packets, datagrams, or frames). Each unit contains both user data and a header that provides information for routing, flow control, and error correction. Instead of establishing a dedicated physical connection between the source and destination station, the network relays packets from one node to another, often in multiple parallel paths, until they reach their final destination.

  PTM is excellent for bursty data applications because a station only consumes bandwidth when it needs to transmit data. When a station is idle, its share of network bandwidth can be used by other stations. However, PTM does not provide the guaranteed network access required by constant-bit-rate applications such as voice or video.

- ATM—ATM combines the strengths of STM (constant transmission delay and guaranteed capacity) and PTM (flexibility and ability to handle intermittent traffic) in a single high-speed transfer mode that allows voice, video, and data applications to run across a single integrated network.

ATM Characteristics

There are several important characteristics of ATM as follows:

- Connection-oriented transmission—In an ATM network, a pair of source and destination nodes establishes a virtual connection before the source begins transmitting data. All cells transmitted between a pair of source and destination nodes follow the same virtual path. A later transmission between the same source and destination may follow a different path; however, the path will not change for the duration of the transmission. This approach improves overall transfer speed, and reduces delay, by making it simpler and faster to switch cells through intermediate nodes.

- Fixed-length cells—ATM organizes transmission by formatting data into fixed-size units called "cells." Each cell contains 53 bytes that are divided into a 48-byte payload (data) field and a 5-byte header. The use of fixed-length cells provides the steady data flow that multimedia applications require. It also allows switch hardware to be faster and simpler, by allowing the switch logic to be implemented in firmware instead of software.

- Efficient use of bandwidth—ATM's cell-switching approach allocates cells to applications only as needed. Thus, an ATM station only consumes bandwidth when it has data to transmit.

In computing, the term "asynchronous" usually means that data transmission is coordinated through start and stop signals, without the use of a common clock. However, ATM networks use "asynchronous" to describe how network bandwidth is assigned to user applications. ATM assigns network access to users based on demand, which means that locations in the synchronous data stream are assigned to users in a random or asynchronous pattern.

- No error correction—ATM does not support error correction or flow control on a link-by-link basis. This means that if a physical link introduces a bit error or is temporarily over-loaded resulting in the loss of a cell, no corrective action is taken. An ATM network does not support a facility that allows the node at one end of a point-to-point physical link to request the retransmission of lost or corrupted cells from the node at the other end of the physical link. However, ATM typically runs over fiber optic facilities, which offer very low error rates. And upper layer protocols, such as TCP, can handle error correction and retransmission. Because an ATM network can concentrate on just switching cells and not worry about error correction, cell throughput at each switching node is substantially increased.

- SONET-level bandwidth—Fiber optic transmission is not the only Physical Layer technology that ATM runs over. ATM is media-independent, because it is not tied to any particular Physical Layer. However, most wide-area ATM networks operate over SONET to get the full benefits of this technology. Thus, the bandwidth of a large ATM network typically starts at 52 Mbps (OC-1), is often 155.5 Mbps (OC-3), and may go to 622 Mbps (OC-12) or higher.

Activities

1. WANs are shifting away from switched services and increasingly using dedicated network services. True or False?

2. Frame relay networks use ATM as the Physical Layer service. True or False?

3. In a WAN with many nodes, a frame relay network is more cost effective because it uses fewer lines than a T1 mesh. True or False?

4. ATM is a connectionless service. True or False?

5. A common ATM link speed is _________ Mbps.

6. Describe the difference between a point-to-point network and a switched network.

   ____

   ____

   ____

   ____

7. How is frame relay similar to an ATM network? How do they differ?

   ____

   ____

   ____

8. Draw a T1 mesh network that connects seven geographically dispersed offices. There are LANs on the other side of the routers at all locations. Remember, a mesh network connects the networks to all the other networks in a point-to-point topology. How many T1 lines are being used?

9. If those seven offices were connected by a frame relay network, how many T1 lines would be necessary?

10. Point-to-point services are used when you require more flexibility in connecting WAN nodes. True or False?

11. A frame relay network can operate at OC-48 speeds. True or False?

Extended Activities

1. Visit the Frame Relay Forum site at **http://www.frforum.com**. What is the latest news about this technology?

   ____

   ____

   ____

2. Visit the ATM Forum site at **http://www.atmforum.com**. What is the latest news at this site?

   ____

   ____

   ____

Lesson 4—Options for Internet Connectivity and Remote User Access

Reliable Internet connectivity has become as necessary to business as electricity and telephone service; for some businesses, it is more important than telephones. However, providing smooth Internet service is more complex than arranging for traditional utilities, because there are more factors to consider.

In the early Internet, each organization was completely responsible for learning the rules and procedures, and installing the equipment necessary to connect to the worldwide network. However, today's telecommunications companies and independent Internet service providers (ISPs) simplify this process for their customers, by handling many technical details of Internet access, hosting World Wide Web (Web) sites, providing electronic mail (e-mail) services, and selling the necessary hardware.

This trend has continued down to the home user's desktop. The newest desktop operating systems, such as Windows 2000, include features that simplify the process of setting up and sharing an Internet connection.

In this lesson, we explain the basic steps needed to connect home users and businesses to the Internet. We also introduce Remote Access Server, included with Windows NT Server, which can allow a company to set up remote dial-in access for its traveling or home-office workers.

Objectives

At the end of this lesson you will be able to:

- Explain the difference between a dial-up and dedicated connection to an ISP

- Describe some of the digital facilities commonly used for dedicated connections to an ISP

- Describe the major features and functions of Microsoft's RAS

- Explain how to set up Internet Connection Sharing on a small network

Internet Connectivity Technologies

Key Point

RAS provides network services to remote users by means of dial-up modem connections.

Home Dial-Up Internet Access

An individual user normally accesses the Internet by means of a modem with a dial-up connection over an analog local loop. That connection links the user to an online information service, such as America Online, or a local ISP, as illustrated on the Individual Internet Access Diagram.

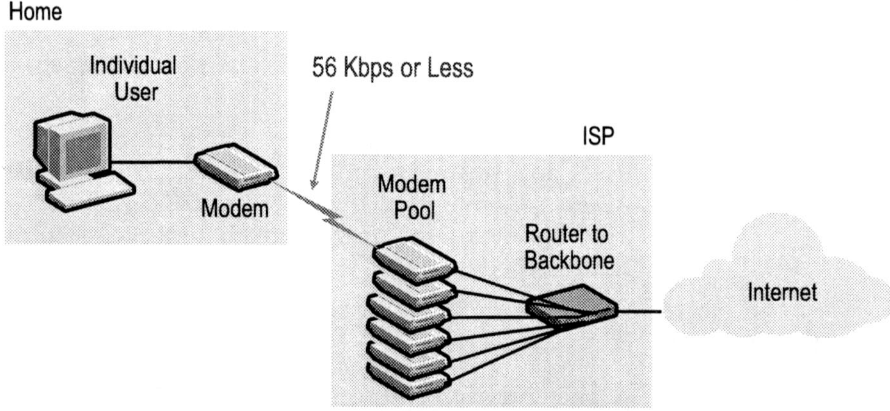

Individual Internet Access

Objective 1.4
Understand and be able to describe the infrastructure needed to support an Internet client.
… Network connection
… Web browser
… E-mail client
… Hardware platform
… DHCP
… Client software configuration

Home Internet connections generally have the following basic components:

- Local loop connection (telephone line).

- Modem.

- ISP account provides Internet access for a monthly fee, and basic services such as e-mail boxes.

- ISP connection software is normally provided by the ISP. The software provides an interface for Internet access and the software that uses the modem to access the Internet. Normally, the dial-up software calls the ISP's access number, the ISP uses DHCP to assign a temporary IP address to the remote user, and the ISP then provides access to the backbone of the Internet.

- Web browser application displays Web pages and handles file downloads.

- Specialized software, either a freestanding application or a browser plug-in, provides support for special multimedia functions. For example, with an audio coder/decoder (codec) and microphone, a user may use the Internet to make telephone calls.

Data Link Protocols for Dial-Up Access

Two special protocols, Serial Line Internet Protocol (SLIP) and Point-to-Point Protocol (PPP), are used to transfer IP packets across a serial link. These two protocols are widely used by ISPs to provide dial-up Internet connections for home or small business users.

SLIP

Objective 3.4
Understand and be able to describe the capabilities of popular remote access protocols.
… SLIP

Serial Line Internet Protocol (SLIP) is a simple encapsulation of an IP datagram asynchronously transmitted over serial lines using an RS-232 interface. SLIP is simple and efficient, but has several drawbacks:

- There is no protocol header that can contain information about the type of data being transported, thus, a SLIP connection can only support one network protocol at a time.

- Each end must know the other end's IP address, because there is no way to exchange this information in the protocol.

- There is no checksum to allow for error detection on noisy telephone lines, which means the higher layers are responsible for error detection and recovery.

PPP

Objective 3.4
Understand and be able to describe the capabilities of popular remote access protocols
... PPP

Point-to-Point Protocol (PPP) is a more robust and flexible serial protocol that has largely replaced SLIP. This Internet standard protocol offers support for multiple network protocols, data compression, host configuration, and link setup. PPP is used by higher layer protocols, such as TCP/IP, to provide simple WAN connectivity between users. PPP supports either asynchronous (character-oriented) or synchronous (bit-oriented) transmission links.

PPP is based on the High-Level Data Link Control (HDLC) standard, which operates at the Data Link Layer of the OSI model. PPP starts with the HDLC frame format, then adds a protocol field to identify the Network Layer protocol carried by each frame.

Microsoft ICS

Objective 1.4
Understand and be able to describe the infrastructure needed to support an Internet client
... Network connection
... Client software configuration

Internet Connection Sharing (ICS) is a Windows 2000 feature that allows multiple hosts to simultaneously transmit and receive Internet traffic over a single dial-up connection. A typical ICS setup is shown in the Internet Connection Sharing Diagram.

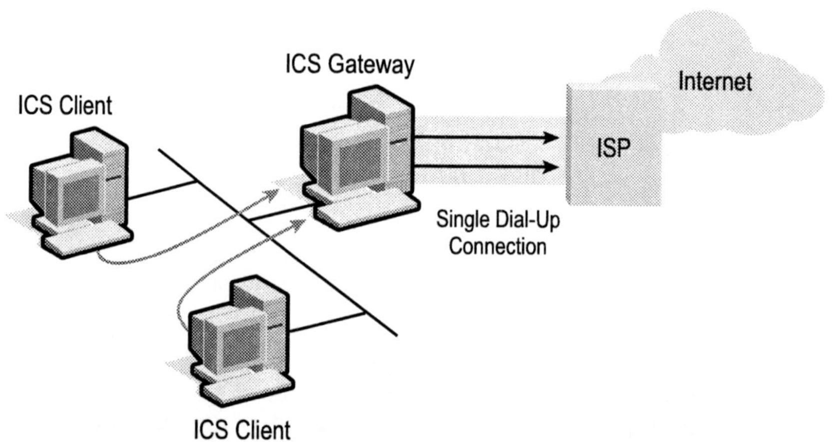

Internet Connection Sharing

In a network that uses ICS, one computer (which may be a workstation) is set up as the ICS gateway. It has an external dial-up connection to an ISP, and an internal connection to the LAN. The other computers are set up as ICS clients. They use the LAN to share the modem connection on the ICS gateway, so they do not need modems of their own. Multiple clients may share the same Internet connection, though its bandwidth will be divided among them.

Setting Up the ICS Gateway

As the gateway between the LAN and the ISP, the ICS gateway must have two physical interfaces. The internal physical interface is usually an Ethernet NIC on the office LAN. The external physical interface depends on the type of telecommunication line (POTS, DSL, ISDN, etc.) that serves the office, and whether the server is using an internal or an external modem.

Internet connection sharing can be enabled while setting up a new Internet connection, or it can be enabled for an existing connection. These steps describe how to share an existing connection:

1. In the Windows 2000 Control Panel, choose **Network and Dial-up Connections**.

2. Right-click the icon for the ISP connection, then select **Properties**.

3. In the Properties dialog box, select the **Sharing** tab.

4. In the Sharing tab, mark the options **Enable Internet Connection Sharing for this connection** and **Enable on-demand dialing**.

Setting Up ICS Clients

Once the ICS gateway is set up to share its connection, the client computers must be set up to use that connection. On each client workstation, use the Network Connection Wizard to create a new Internet connection:

1. In the Windows 2000 Control Panel, select **Network and Dial-up Connections.** Select **Make New Connection** to start the Network Connection Wizard.

2. In the Network Connection Type page, select the option **Dial-up to the Internet** to launch the Internet Connection Wizard.

3. In the Internet Connection Wizard, select the option **I want to set up my Internet connection manually, or I want to connect through a local area network (LAN).**

4. In the Setting up your Internet Connection page, select the option **I connect through a local area network (LAN).**

5. In the Local Area Network Internet Configuration page, select the option **Automatic discovery of proxy server.** (The ICS gateway acts as a proxy.)

All ICS computers, both server and clients, must also be set up for automatic assignment of IP addresses. Once each Internet connection has been created, the administrator configures each computer's TCP/IP properties to obtain an IP address automatically:

1. In the Windows 2000 Control Panel, select **Network and Dial-up Connections**.

2. Right-click the icon for the Internet connection, then select **Properties**.

3. In the Properties dialog box, highlight **Internet Protocol (IP)**, then select **Properties**.

4. In the Internet Protocol (TCP/IP) Properties page, select the options **Obtain an IP address automatically**, and **Obtain DNS server address automatically**.

ICS Security Precautions

ICS does not provide any security features. Therefore, small networks that use ICS should install firewall software on the ICS gateway. Many inexpensive firewall applications can provide reasonable security for small or home networks.

DSL for Home Internet Connectivity

Digital Subscriber Line (DSL) has become extremely popular for home Internet access, because it delivers high data rates over existing copper telephone lines (provided the line is in good condition, and the subscriber is not too far from the telephone company's central office).

Sharing a DSL Connection

As soon as home computers became more popular, DSL users wanted two or more computers to be able to share a single DSL connection. Unfortunately, DSL is a point-to-point technology that assumes there is only one computer at the end of each local loop, and that all traffic coming from the same loop is also coming from the same dynamically-assigned IP address. In spite of this, there are several ways to share a DSL connection as the following sections show.

Pay for Fixed IP Addresses

Sharing a DSL connection is simple if each user's computer has its own static IP address. Many small businesses order this type of service, because a fixed IP address is necessary for a company's Web server or e-mail server. However, this option costs considerably more than most home DSL users are willing to pay.

Internet Connection Sharing

You can also share DSL by connecting one Windows 2000 computer to the DSL line, and configuring that machine as an ICS gateway. The DSL network still "sees" a single endpoint. The gateway computer is responsible for assigning internal private IP addresses, and forwarding IP traffic to and from multiple internal hosts.

PPPoE

Objective 3.4
Understand and be able to describe the capabilities of popular remote access protocols
...PPPoE

Point-to-point protocol over Ethernet (PPPoE) is a new protocol (RFC 2516) that is a variation of PPP designed to operate over a shared medium (unlike PPP, which assumes a point-to-point link). It allows each individual customer host to establish its own independent session with an ISP. Each session is uniquely identified by the Ethernet addresses of both endpoints, and a unique session identifier number.

With PPPoE in place, an ISP can assign a dynamic IP address to each PPPoE session. This allows multiple sessions to operate over the same DSL or cable modem connection.

PPPoE packets are encapsulated within Ethernet frames, essentially creating a double Data Link Layer. To implement PPPoE, a DSL vendor provides special application software to its DSL subscribers.

Connecting a Business to an ISP

There are two ways to connect a business customer to the Internet:

- Dedicated access—A leased line connection is made to the ISP, solely for the purpose of providing Internet connectivity.

- Nondedicated access—A line or circuit is used for intermittent access to the Internet, as well as other uses.

Some technologies, such as dial-up lines and Integrated Services Digital Network (ISDN), can be used for both dedicated and non-dedicated installations. The difference between the two is the type of equipment used to make the connection. For example, the Nondedicated vs. Dedicated Access Diagram illustrates how an ISDN line might be used for either a dedicated or nondedicated application.

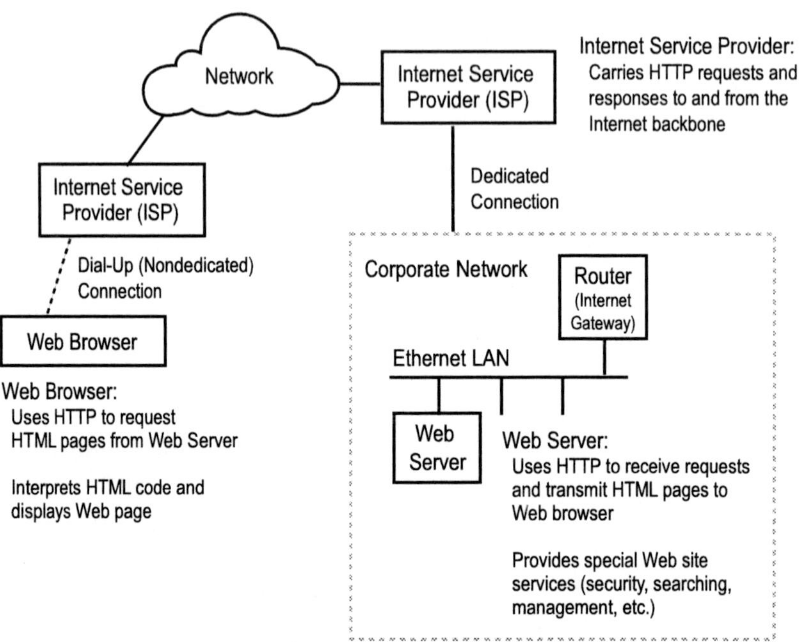

Nondedicated vs. Dedicated Access

Nondedicated Access

Nondedicated access is any connection that is not continuous. The connection is established at the time it is desired and released when no longer needed. The connection is usually made through a switched network, typically the telephone system. The most common method to access the Internet is to use an existing telephone line, although ISDN provides much better performance if it is available.

Dedicated Access

Objective 1.4
Understand and be able to describe the infrastructure needed to support an Internet client … Network connection … Hardware platform

The minimum dedicated connection is a dedicated dial-up modem connection. This type of connection is similar to a non-dedicated access connection, but requires a permanent analog telephone number for the modem connection. The connection speed is primarily controlled by the modem connection speed, which can be poor. Thus, businesses that require dedicated access usually opt for digital services, such as T1, fractional T1 (FT1 [DS0]), DSL, or ISDN.

When a business uses a dedicated line to connect to an ISP, the permanent connection makes it possible for the business to use a domain name and dedicated IP address. This is typically necessary if the corporation wants to establish a Web site.

Components of a Dedicated Connection

Private line Internet connections generally have the following basic components, as shown on the Dedicated Connection to ISP Diagram.

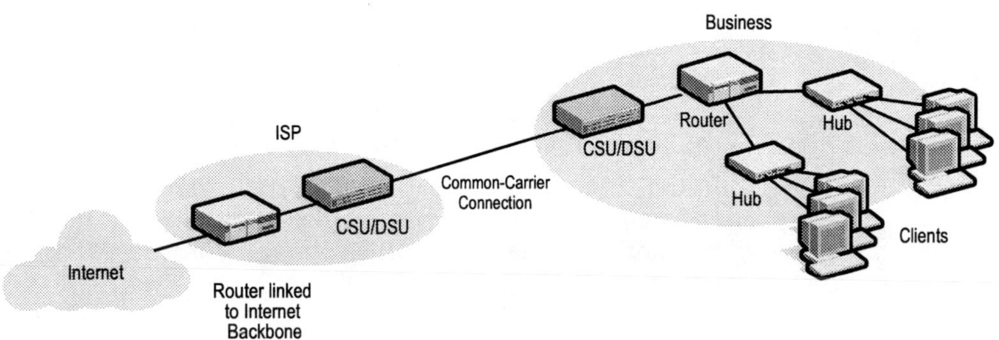

Dedicated Connection to ISP

Common Carrier Connection

There are several choices for dedicated connectivity to the Internet. Frame relay is one of the most common ways to dedicate a connection for Internet connectivity, because it is a cost-effective way to handle the bursty, irregular patterns of typical Internet traffic. Frame relay service is typically available at speeds of 56 kilobits per second (Kbps), 64 Kbps, and increments of 64 Kbps up to 1.544 megabits per second (Mbps).

FT1 private lines are available in multiples of a DS0 connection (64 Kbps per DS0), up to 1.544 Mbps (DS1/T1). However, the cost of a full T1 line usually becomes more attractive long before a business has leased all 24 fractional channels.

The ISP you choose will often suggest a connection technology to use. For example, some ISPs do not support ISDN, or charge as much or more for basic rate ISDN (128 Kbps) than full T1 (1.5 Mbps). In some instances, companies that provide Internet access also provide dedicated circuits. For example, telephone companies have discovered the business advantages of providing package deals that include private lines, networking hardware, and Internet service. However, customers must often deal with multiple vendors, first choosing an ISP, then going to a phone company to get a leased line to the ISP.

DSU/CSU

A Data Service Unit/Channel Service Unit (DSU/CSU) is required to terminate a multiplexed common carrier connection such as a T1 line. It splits out the various digital channels and feeds them to various network devices, such as a router.

Router

A router is necessary to connect a local area network (LAN) to a DSU/CSU. Anyone who needs to directly connect to the Internet must have a router, from backbone service providers to small companies that host their own Web servers.

In the strictest terms, a router is a networking device that forms an interface between two networks. In the simplest terms, a router is a traffic cop that speaks the language of Internet Protocol (IP). A router is a highly intelligent device that forwards IP packets to and from other networks, and gathers up those addressed to its own network.

Routers employed on the Internet are capable of accommodating multiple speeds, channels, protocols, and transmission paths. Some routers have a built-in DSU/CSU. In many cases, ISPs will also suggest the type of router to use, if the equipment has not yet been purchased.

Internet Domain Name

As soon as a business decides to connect to the Internet, its managers should choose the domain name it will use if they decide to add a Web site. Even though the business may not plan to create a Web site any time soon, it is best to reserve a domain name to prevent someone else from registering it.

Remote Access Services

A remote access service allows mobile employees to access the corporate LAN from an outside location. If users have valid user accounts that allow remote access, they can use a modem to dial directly to a telephone line assigned to a remote access server, or reach that server via an Internet connection. Once connected, users have access to the same resources as if they were directly connected to the network as a node. RAS applications include remote file, application, and e-mail access. Network support personnel often use RAS connections to remotely troubleshoot network outages.

Microsoft's Remote Access Service (RAS) supports up to 256 dial-up users accessing Windows NT networks by means of modem pools, X.25, or ISDN lines. RAS acts as a NetBIOS gateway between the network and remote client system. Windows NT supports TCP/IP and IPX routing capabilities between other nodes on the network, as well as NetBEUI connections, Serial Line Internet Protocol (SLIP), and Microsoft RAS protocol. At the Network Layer, RAS supports IP, IPX for NetWare servers and printers, NetBIOS applications, RPC, and LAN Manager application programming interfaces (APIs).

RAS features include:

- Advanced modem support

- LAN topology and protocol independence

- Extensive WAN and routing support

- Support for the Windows NT Server security model

- Support for standard network interfaces

- Ability for servers to receive calls and use callback security techniques

- Asynchronous dial-up access

Internet Connectivity
Technologies

231

A typical RAS setup is presented on the Remote Access Service Setup Diagram.

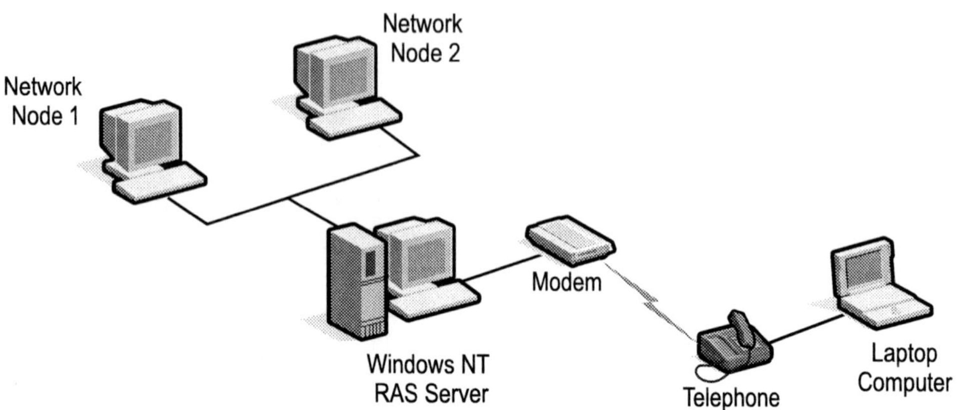

Remote Access Service Setup

RAS Installation and Configuration

RAS requires either serial port hardware and modems, or intelligent serial port cards and appropriate drivers. Before installing RAS, make sure the following hardware requirements are in place:

- Network adapter card with NDIS driver

- Compatible modem(s)

- Multiport adapter card for multiple remote connections

- X.25 smart card for X.25 networks

- ISDN card for ISDN lines

You can install RAS during or after installation of Windows NT. If you install RAS at the same time you install Windows NT, use Custom Setup. If you install RAS after you finish installing Windows NT, use the Network utility in Control Panel. When installing RAS, check that the appropriate protocol is installed and operational. Only members of the Administrators group can install and manage RAS.

Analog Dial-Up Modem Access

Network users can connect through a RAS server in a number of ways. The Modem RAS Service Diagram illustrates one method of connecting multiple remote clients to a RAS server, through a bank of analog modems.

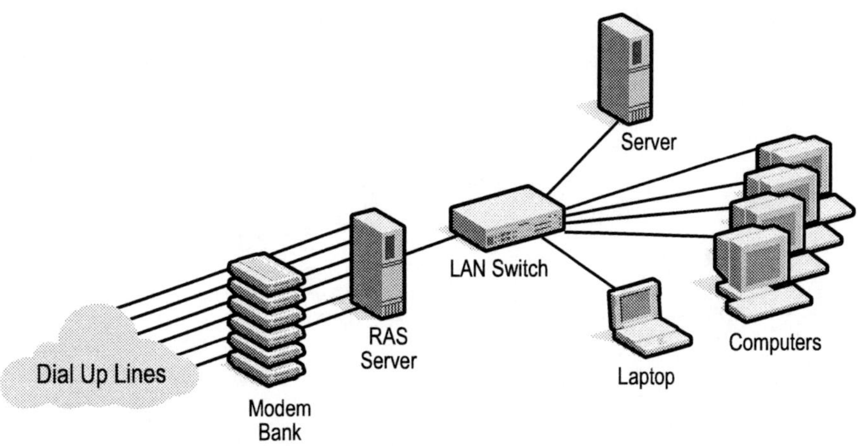

Modem RAS Service

In this configuration, each remote client uses a modem to communicate over a standard analog telephone line. On the LAN side, the telephone service carrier has configured a bank of telephone lines with a feature called "hunting," which automatically connects an inbound call to the next line when the first is busy. This requires callers to remember only one RAS access number, and allows a single access number to support multiple connections.

Each modem in the modem bank is connected to the RAS server over an RS-232 serial connection. The server is equipped with a 12-port serial adapter, with each port connected to one modem.

The RAS server essentially operates as a gatekeeper. It uses passwords or other authentication methods to verify the identity of inbound callers and ensure that they have permission to access the LAN. Once the server authorizes the inbound connection, the server connects a RAS user to the LAN via the LAN switch. Once connected, RAS users can access network resources just as if they were directly connected to the LAN.

However, a dial-up connection is the slowest of the RAS connection options. Interactive response is very sluggish, and users cannot transfer large files across the dial-up link.

ISDN Access

ISDN can provide dial-up access at much faster rates than a standard analog telephone line. The ISDN RAS Service Diagram illustrates a typical setup.

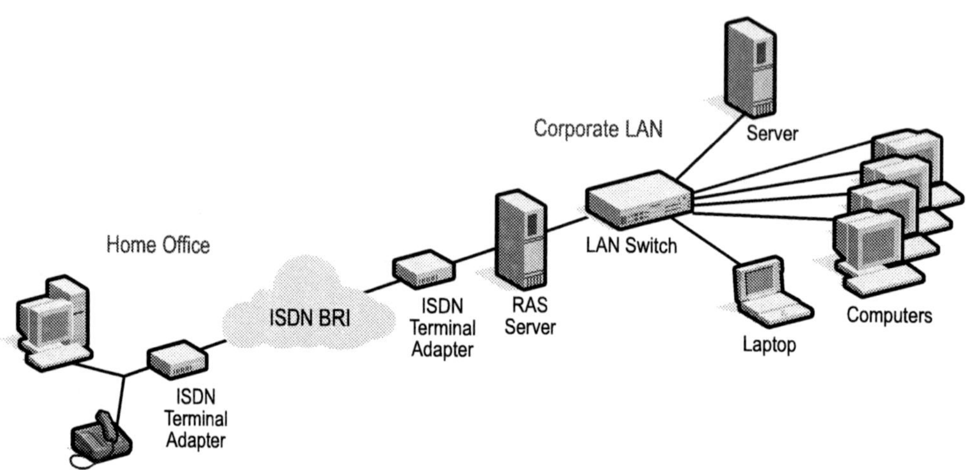

ISDN RAS Service

Here, the remote client and the RAS server both have ISDN-BRI service to their locations. At the remote location, such as a consultant's home office, an ISDN terminal adapter connects a computer to one B channel and a phone to the other. At the corporate LAN, the ISDN terminal adapter connects the ISDN BRI to the RAS server over an RS-232 serial connection. The RAS server acts as a router.

The RAS client configures the RAS server's telephone number in its ISDN terminal configuration. When activated, this connects the remote client to the LAN's ISDN adapter for remote access. Once the call is connected, the RAS server authenticates the caller, and sets up the connection through the LAN switch.

Again, this RAS connection can be used for remote application, file, and e-mail access. Because of the increased bandwidth provided by ISDN connections (128 Kbps per B channel), users will not experience the slow response that dial-up users do.

However, an ISDN-BRI can only support two inbound callers (one for each B channel). If the RAS server must also support outbound connections to the company's ISP, a separate ISDN-BRI and terminal adapter should be installed so that outbound calls don't prevent inbound connections. If a large number of remote users need access, then other connection options should be considered, such as X.25, fractional or full T1, or a frame relay-based virtual private network (VPN).

Virtual Private Networks

Data packets move across the Internet by being forwarded from one network's router to another until they reach their destinations. Because Internet traffic can be intercepted by any router that forwards it, basic Internet transmission is inherently insecure. To ensure privacy, companies that use the Internet as a WAN backbone often set up a virtual private network (VPN).

A VPN is a connection, implemented over a shared network, that simulates a dedicated point-to-point connection. Data packets are securely transmitted across a public routed network, such as the Internet or other commercially available network, in a private "tunnel" created by data encryption. This approach enables network traffic from many sources to travel via separate tunnels across the same infrastructure. An example VPN is illustrated on the Virtual Private Network Diagram.

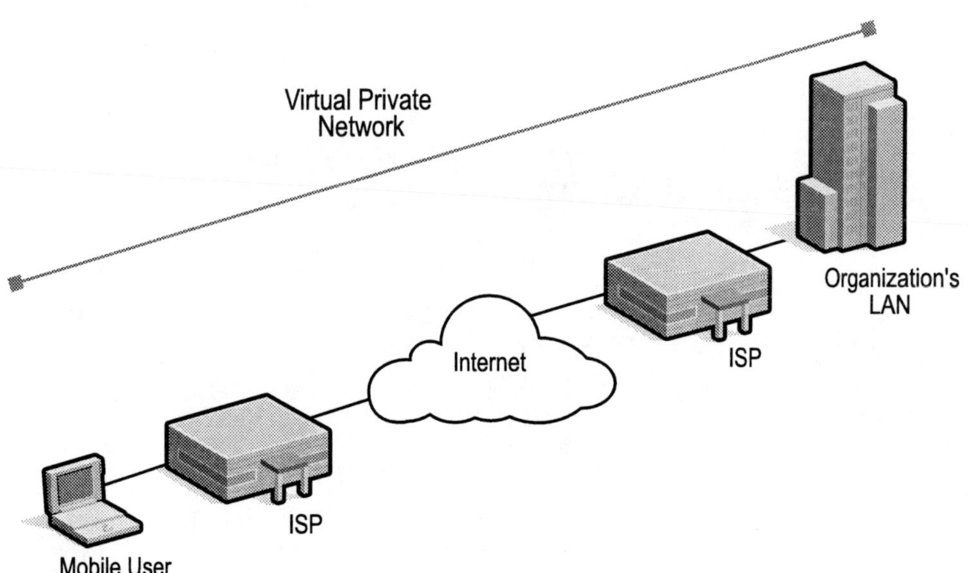

Virtual Private Network

The Internet is still not well suited to the time-sensitive traffic that ATM handles so well. However, a company can enjoy a great deal of flexibility with a VPN, because traveling workers and home-officed employees can use their normal Internet connections to access the corporate network.

The remote user's computer runs a VPN client compatible with the VPN application running on the server. The user first connects to the Internet using a protocol such as PPP. The VPN client then locates and connects to the VPN server, which authorizes the client request for a LAN connection.

Once the client and server have established the tunnel parameters (protocol, encryption, type of service, quality of service, etc.), the client can exchange encrypted data packets with the server.

Tunneling Protocols

A tunneling protocol encrypts the data packet and encapsulates it in a header that enables the encrypted payload to securely traverse the network.

PPTP

Objective 3.4
Understand and be able to describe the capabilities of popular remote access protocols.
... PPTP

Point-to-Point Tunneling Protocol (PPTP) is a Layer 2 (Data Link Layer) protocol that creates a secure virtual tunnel from a remote node, through an ISP, to a corporate network. To do this, PPTP uses both encryption and a special protocol for data encapsulation.

To create a PPTP connection, three elements are necessary:

- A client with PPP and PPTP installed.

- An ISP that provides dial-up connectivity to the client. (If the client does not support PPTP, then PPTP must be installed on a server at the ISP.)

- A Remote Access Service (RAS) server at the destination network, with PPTP installed.

How a PPTP Session Works

The following steps assume the client computer has PPTP installed. We also assume that all nodes use IP; however, PPTP also supports IPX and NetBIOS Extended User Interface (NetBEUI):

1. The client establishes a PPP dial-up connection to the ISP, then uses PPTP to request a secure session with the company's PPTP-enabled RAS server.

2. The RAS server authenticates the client by asking for a user name and password. The user's password then becomes a "shared secret" which both client and server use to generate the same unique key to use for single-key encryption during this session. For additional security, the client may use the server's public encryption key (separate from the session key just created) to encrypt the password before transmitting it to the server.

3. On the client, each outgoing IP packet is addressed to the destination node. Once the PPTP session is established, the PPTP process on the client encapsulates each IP packet within a PPP frame, just as if this were a normal ISP transmission. The client's PPTP then encrypts the entire PPP frame and its contents, using the encryption key just negotiated with the distant PPTP server.

4. The client's PPTP then encapsulates the encrypted frame by adding a header of the Internet Generic Routing Encapsulation (GRE) protocol. This special protocol functions like an inner container, allowing one Layer 3 protocol to ride within another Layer 3 protocol. For example, one IP packet may be encapsulated within another IP packet, as long as a GRE header separates the "inner" IP packet from the "outer" packet.

5. After adding the GRE header to contain the encrypted frame, the client PPTP then adds an IP header addressed to the destination RAS/PPTP server, and a PPP header and trailer to form the frame that is then transmitted to the ISP.

6. The ISP server strips the PPP header and trailer, then forwards the IP packet to the PPTP server. As usual, the ISP and all intermediate nodes disregard the contents of the IP packet.

7. When the PPTP server decapsulates the packet, it finds the encrypted packet from the distant client. By using its session key, it decrypts the data and re-creates the original PPP frame. After decapsulating this frame, the server forwards the original data packet to the destination node on the private network.

L2F Protocol

This transmission protocol, proposed by Cisco Systems, allows a server to frame dial-up traffic using PPP and transmits it over WAN links to a Layer 2 Forwarding (L2F) server (such as a router), which then unwraps the packets before releasing them to the network.

L2TP

Developed by IETF to combine the best features of PPTP and L2F, Layer 2 Tunneling Protocol (L2TP) is a network protocol that encapsulates PPP frames to be sent over IP, X.25, frame relay, or ATM networks. L2TP can either be configured to use IP as its transport mechanism or used directly over a WAN technology such as frame relay.

IPSec

Internet Protocol Security (IPSec) is a Layer 3 protocol that allows IP payloads to be encrypted and then encapsulated in an IP header for secure transfer across a corporate IP internetwork or public IP internetwork such as the Internet. IPSec was designed by IETF as an end-to-end mechanism for ensuring data security in IP-based communications, and is primarily focused on providing Network Layer security for IP. Firewall devices, individual computers, or servers can implement IPSec.

Developed over a period of several years by some of the best experts in network security, IPSec is generally recognized as highly secure. IPSec uses a scheme that authenticates and encrypts IP packets on an individual basis. By enabling server-to-server tunneling, such as between routers, rather than client-server tunneling, IPSec complements the functionality of PPTP and L2TP. It makes for a powerful combination: the flexibility of Layer 2 VPN protocols (PPTP/L2TP) along with the security of IPSec.

ICA Terminal Services

A downside to using RAS and VPNs to remotely access a LAN is that large files and bandwidth-intensive applications can slow the connection to a crawl. On a dial-up connection running at 53 Kbps, a 1 Megabyte (MB) file can take over three minutes to download under ideal conditions. Since some LAN applications download entire database or application files to the client, RAS connections can become agonizingly slow.

Fortunately, there is a solution. Developed by Citrix Systems, Inc., Independent Computing Architecture (ICA) is the technology used in their WinFrame and MetaFrame products to make Windows NT and 2000 multiuser operating systems.

ICA allows multiple remote network users to connect to a single server, or server farm of WinFrame or MetaFrame terminal servers, and run applications on the server as individual application sessions, rather than as shared files (as occurs in a file server environment). Rather that downloading the application executable and associated Dynamic Link Libraries (DLLs) to the local client, the application runs on the server. The only information the client downloads are screen images, mouse movements, and keystrokes.

By running the applications on the server, network bandwidth utilization is kept to a minimum. ICA is compatible with all but the slowest dial-up connections (WinFrame is optimized to support dial-up connections as slow as 14.4 Kbps). Resource intensive processes remain on the server, rather than traversing the network and running on the client.

The ICA Remote Access Diagram is an example of how a remote user might benefit from terminal services running on a network terminal server. Suppose the PDA remotely accesses the LAN over a cellular connection. Cellular connections typically cannot supply bandwidths exceeding 14.4 Kbps in the US, though higher bandwidth solutions are in development both in the US and abroad. Downloading a 1 MB file at 14.4 Kbps would take over 10 minutes. However, when downloading only compressed video, keyboard, and mouse signals, the download time drops to less than one minute over the same cellular connection.

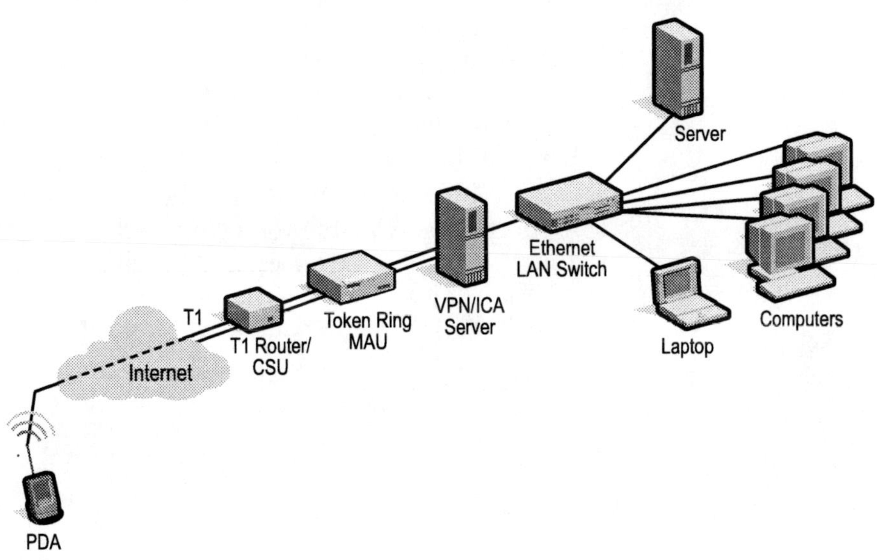

ICA Remote Access

The PDA runs the ICA client, which allows the remote user to run the appropriate applications on the server. The server manipulates the files locally, rather than passing them to and from the PDA over the slow connection. Application response improves tremendously, and the remote user is able to work with little delay.

However, because multiple applications or application instances run simultaneously on the server, ICA server hardware requirements are substantial. Though Citrix Systems suggests running the server in a test environment and sizing the number of CPUs, memory amount, and disk space accordingly, other sources recommend the following hardware to support up to 40 concurrent users on a WinFrame server:

- 4-Pentium 200 MHz or greater processors

- 1 Gigabyte (GB) of RAM (approximately 25 MB per connection)

- 4 GB hard disk space on a RAID 1 or 5 array. (Of course, the more disk space, the better)

Microsoft has licensed Citrix's MultiWin (multiple simultaneous connections to a normally single-use application) for use in Windows NT Server 4.0 Terminal Server Edition. This allows an NT 4.0 server to support multiple client connections just as does Citrix WinFrame, a stand-alone product based on Windows NT Server 3.51. Citrix MetaFrame adds ICA support to NT Server 4.0 Terminal Server Edition, adding remote printing, sound, and other capabilities the Windows technology does not support.

ICA clients are available for 16-bit and 32-bit Window PC environments, handheld devices, DOS, Web clients, Macintosh, OS/2, and UNIX/Linux. This means that with no more than the ICA client loaded, a UNIX host can access and run Windows services.

Activities

1. Explain the functions of a RAS server and client components.

   ____

   ____

   ____

   ____

   ____

2. How does ICA improve client-server interaction via remote access?

   ____

   ____

   ____

   ____

   ____

3. How does RAS connectivity differ from VPN connectivity?

   ____

   ____

   ____

   ____

4. What systems support Internet Connection Sharing?

   a. Windows 98, Windows NT/2000

   b. Any network that uses TCP/IP

   c. Windows 2000 only

   d. Windows 98 only

5. What is a VPN and why is it necessary?

____

____

____

____

6. What best describes the operation of L2TP?

   a. An IP packet is encrypted, then placed within an L2TP frame. The L2TP frame is transmitted over any WAN that supports L2TP.

   b. A PPP frame is encrypted. The encrypted frame is placed within an IP packet or a WAN frame, depending on the WAN technology in use.

   c. A WAN frame is built first, then encrypted.

   d. Instead of placing IP packets within PPP frames, they are placed within PPPoE frames.

7. When is PPPoE necessary?

   a. When two or more hosts on the same LAN need to share a DSL connection.

   b. When two or more hosts need to share a POTS modem.

   c. When a DSL modem and DSLAM use Ethernet to communicate.

   d. When two hosts on the same Ethernet LAN need to set up a PPP connection between them.

Extended Activity

Home users typically get high-speed Internet access through DSL or cable modems. DSL supporters claim that cable modems, as a shared medium, suffer from poor security and unpredictable bandwidth. Cable modem supporters claim that DSL is difficult to set up, especially when using PPPoE. Research both technologies, and summarize their pros and cons.

Summary

This unit introduced the various types of transmission technologies used to connect distant LANs to each other or an ISP. These technologies fall into two main categories: switched services, and point-to-point or point-to-multipoint connections.

Point-to-point services include many Physical Layer services and protocols such as dial-up networking, ISDN-PRI, FT1, and T1. These point-to-point links connect networks in a secure fashion; however, they offer limited options for connectivity. If a WAN needs any-to-any communication among nodes, the number of point-to-point links increases sharply with the number of endpoints.

Point-to-multipoint services include cable modem networks and DSL (though DSL also has some point-to-point characteristics). These networks connect multiple subscribers to a central communications point that is, in turn, connected to an ISP. Because some or all of the transmission medium is shared by multiple users, service providers often implement security features such as encryption. However, these safeguards only affect the service provider's network, and do not protect a user's traffic across the rest of the Internet.

Switched services provide more flexibility than point-to-point services, and are used to connect many networks in a large WAN. Two of the most common WAN switching protocols are frame relay and ATM. These public switching networks can set up permanent or temporary virtual circuits between any combination of endpoints. Many companies are also using the Internet as a WAN backbone. While the Internet is inherently insecure, corporations can use encryption to create VPNs across the public network.

The type of hardware a site requires depends on the type of service used to provide connectivity. Dial-up analog connections require a modem at each end of the line. A T1 or FT1 line requires a CSU/DSU to convert signals from the format used by the telephone system to that used by a LAN. In addition, a router is usually placed between a LAN and its WAN link, to increase security and keep unnecessary traffic off the expensive wide area connection.

WAN services are significantly more expensive than LANs, and the cost of a WAN link is directly related to its bandwidth and quality. A WAN designer always tries to get the highest bandwidth at the lowest cost; however, one must also consider other factors that may be more important than price. Thus, many organizations use more costly services that provide greater security, or better support for time-sensitive traffic.

Internet Connectivity
Technologies

Unit 3 Quiz

1. Which of the following is not a WAN connection type?

   a. Leased

   b. Public data

   c. Dial-up

   d. Ethernet

2. Which of the following is the unit of data transferred by an ATM network?

   a. Frame

   b. Packet

   c. Cell

   d. Message

3. Which of the following is another name for a CO?

   a. Local exchange

   b. PBX

   c. Local loop

   d. MUX

4. Which of the following is the primary difference between a public and private network?

   a. Who owns and maintains the network

   b. The distance between communicating devices

   c. The cost of the equipment

   d. The number of nodes in the network

5. Which of the following devices are not used to connect a LAN to a WAN?

   a. Bridges

   b. Routers

   c. Modems

   d. Hubs

6. Which of the following WAN services usually provides the highest bandwidth?

    a. T1

    b. T3

    c. DSL

    d. SONET

7. Which of the following is a disadvantage to using a dial-up modem?

    a. Cost

    b. Any-to-any connectivity

    c. Transfer rate

    d. Availability of equipment

8. FT1 might be used instead of T1 because of which of the following? (Choose two)

    a. Cost

    b. Speed requirements

    c. Ease of use

    d. Equipment availability

9. ATM is better for multimedia because of which of the following?

    a. All cells are the same size.

    b. Cells are small.

    c. ATM runs over fast fiber optics.

    d. All of the above.

10. Normally, what portion of a WAN is analog?

    a. Trunk lines between COs

    b. Cable between computer and modem

    c. Local loop between CO and customer site

    d. LAN

11. WANs are shifting away from switched services and increasingly using dedicated network services. True or False?

12. Frame relay networks use ATM as the Physical Layer service. True or False?

13. A frame relay network uses fewer lines to connect 10 locations than a T1 mesh, and is therefore more cost effective. True or False?

14. Frame relay, unlike ATM, uses fixed-length frames. True or False?

15. Frame relay outperforms X.25. True or False?

16. It is usually more economical to run two 12-circuit FT1 lines than one full T1 line. True or False?

17. ATM requires fiber media to run. True or False?

18. What is the total raw speed of each of the following link services?

    a. ISDN-BRI _____

    b. T1 _____

    c. One FT1 fraction (one DS0) _____

19. In a cable network, each individual home is connected to what type of topology?

    a. Bus

    b. Star

    c. Ring

    d. Mesh

20. What do cable network providers use to provide data privacy for their subscribers?

    a. Time Division Multiplexing

    b. Encryption

    c. Channel Bonding

    d. Synchronization

21. To provide DSL service, a telecommunications provider must install what device at a central office?

    a. CSU/DSU

    b. CMTS

    c. DSLAM

    d. DSL Modem

22. Your company has three sites that need connectivity to each other and to an ISP. Which of the following factors would lead you to choose a frame relay network for this connectivity, instead of a mesh network of T carrier lines?

    a. The company may add one new site

    b. You may subscribe to a second ISP as a backup

    c. The company may close one site

    d. Both A and B

    e. None of the above

Unit 4
TCP/IP Protocols

The acronym TCP/IP represents the common working combination of the Transmission Control Protocol and Internet Protocol. However, the term is often used to denote much more than just the protocols themselves. The TCP/IP "world" can be considered to include other components, such as the entire suite of protocols, software, and applications that are standard parts of most UNIX-based and PC-based OSs.

TCP/IP is normally used as the protocol stack in UNIX networking implementations. However, those protocols are also supported by all major NOSs. Now that the Internet has become an essential business tool, many corporate networks find it convenient to use TCP/IP as their Transport and Network Layer protocols. Thus, while various networks may use NetWare, Windows NT, or AppleTalk as their network operating system (NOS), it is likely each of those NOSs is also configured to use TCP and IP. This unit introduces the major TCP/IP protocols.

Lessons

1. The TCP/IP Protocol Suite
2. IP
3. UDP and TCP
4. Internet Addressing
5. Subnetting Fundamentals
6. IP Routing

Terms

Address Resolution Protocol (ARP)—ARP is a TCP/IP protocol used to match an IP address with a related physical address, such as an Ethernet address. A host wishing to obtain a physical address broadcasts an ARP request onto the TCP/IP network. The host on the network that has the IP address in the request then replies with its physical hardware address.

Bootstrap Protocol (BOOTP)—BOOTP is an Internet protocol for enabling a diskless workstation to boot and determine its configuration information, such as its IP address, from information available on a BOOTP server.

checksum—A checksum is a simple error detection strategy that computes a running total based on a packet's transmitted byte values and then applies a simple operation to compute the checksum value. The receiver compares the checksums computed by the sender and the receiver, and, if they match, assumes error-free transmission.

Classless Interdomain Routing (CIDR)—CIDR replaces the older IP network addressing system based on classes A, B, and C. With CIDR, a single IP address can be used to designate many unique IP addresses. A CIDR IP address looks like a normal IP address except that it ends with a slash followed by a number, called the IP prefix. The IP prefix specifies how many addresses are covered by the CIDR address, with lower prefix values covering more addresses. For example, an IP prefix of /16, can be used to address 256 former Class C addresses.

connectionless—Connectionless service is a characteristic of the packet delivery service offered by most hardware and the IP. Connectionless service treats each packet or datagram as a separate entity that contains the source and destination addresses. Connectionless services can drop or deliver packets out of sequence.

connection-oriented—A connection-oriented data communication mode is one in which the sending and receiving computers stay in contact for the duration of a session, while packets or frames are being sent back and forth.

cyclic redundancy check (CRC)—CRC is the mathematical process used to check the accuracy of the data being transmitted across a network. Before transmitting a block of data, the sending station performs a calculation on the data block and appends the resulting value to the end of the block. The receiving station takes the data and the CRC value, and performs the same calculation to check the accuracy of the data.

datagram—A datagram is another name for a packet. See packet.

default gateway—A default gateway is a router that provides access to all hosts on remote networks. Typically, the network administrator configures a default gateway for each host on the network.

distance vector algorithm (DVA)—DVA is a routing protocol used to express the route a packet will take as it moves between computer networks. DVA expresses this route in "hops." The entity that is hopped over is any other network which must be traversed on the way to the target network. The hop count is actually the number of routers a packet encounters on the way to its destination. DV routers use hop counts to choose the shortest route for each packet. The Routing Information Protocol (RIP) is an example of a DVA protocol.

Domain Name System (DNS)—DNS is the online distributed database system used to map human-readable computer names into IP addresses. DNS servers throughout the connected Internet implement a hierarchical namespace that allows sites freedom in assigning computer names and addresses. In addition, DNS supports separate mappings between mail destinations and IP addresses.

dotted decimal notation—Dotted decimal notation is the syntactic representation for a 32-bit integer that consists of four 8-bit numbers with periods (dots) separating them. Many TCP/IP application programs accept dotted decimal notation in place of destination computer names (for example, 205.169.85.200).

Dynamic Host Configuration Protocol (DHCP)—DHCP provides configuration parameters to Internet hosts. DHCP consists of two components: a protocol for delivering host-specific configuration parameters from a DHCP server to a host and a mechanism for allocation of network addresses to hosts. DHCP is built on a client/server model, where designated DHCP server hosts allocate network addresses and deliver configuration parameters to dynamically configured hosts.

File Transfer Protocol (FTP)—FTP is a Transmission Control Protocol/Internet Protocol (TCP/IP) Application Layer protocol used to transfer files between two computers.

flow control—Flow control refers to control of the rate at which hosts or gateways inject packets into a network or internet. Flow control is used to avoid congestion and can be implemented at various protocol levels. Simplistic schemes, like ICMP source quench, instruct the sender to cease transmission until congestion ends. More complex schemes vary the transmission rate continuously.

fragmentation—Fragmentation is the IP process of dividing a datagram into smaller pieces that will better suit the transporting network's MTU.

hop count—Hop count is the number of intermediate routers that a packet must traverse to travel from source to destination in a multirouter environment.

Hypertext Transfer Protocol (HTTP)—HTTP is the Application Layer protocol used to request and transmit HTML documents. HTTP is the underlying protocol of the Web.

Internet Control Message Protocol (ICMP)—ICMP is a Network Layer protocol that handles error and control messages about IP communication. Gateways and hosts use ICMP to report problems about packets back to their source. ICMP also includes an echo request/reply used to test whether a destination is reachable and responding.

Internet Corporation of Assigned Names and Numbers (ICANN)—ICANN is a private, nonprofit organization responsible for overseeing the domain name registration process, assigning IP addresses, assigning protocol parameters, and managing the DNS root servers. Learn more about ICANN at **http://www.icann.org**.

Internet Gateway Routing Protocol (IGRP)—IGRP is a DVA protocol developed by Cisco Systems for use in large, heterogeneous networks. It uses metrics, such as bandwidth, delay, MTU, and hop count, to compute the best path to a destination network.

Internet Group Management Protocol (IGMP)—IGMP is the Internet standard by which hosts can communicate their multicast group membership status to multicast routers. This protocol is used to keep up-to-date information on which host is in which multicast group.

IP Version 6 (IPv6)—IPv6, also known as IP next generation, is a new version of the IP currently being reviewed in the IETF standards committees. IPv6 adds features over the current IPv4, including longer addresses (128 bits) and better QoS support.

Maximum Transmission Unit (MTU)—MTU is the maximum amount of information that can be carried by a datagram or frame. For example, the MTU of Ethernet is 1,500 bytes of information.

Network Address Translator (NAT)—NAT is a system that allows an administrator to use one set of IP addresses within a LAN, and another set for external traffic. NAT can shield internal addresses from public networks, and make more efficient use of a few globally unique IP addresses.

Network File System (NFS)—A file management system used with TCP/IP and UNIX systems originally developed by SUN Microsystems. NFS can be found on various systems and platforms, especially PC-based platforms that utilize the TCP/IP protocol.

Network News Transport Protocol (NNTP)—NNTP is the TCP/IP protocol used to distribute news article collections, or news feeds, over the Internet.

Open Shortest Path First (OSPF)—OSPF is an intraautonomous system routing protocol. OSPF is based on link-state technology and scales well with large networks. Its features include least-cost routing, multipath routing, and load balancing. OSPF provides more advantages than the older RIP.

packet—A packet is a unit of information processed by the Network Layer of the OSI reference model. The packet header contains the logical (network) address of the destination node. Intermediate nodes forward a packet until it reaches its destination. A packet can contain an entire message generated by higher OSI layers, or a segment of a much larger message. IP packets are also referred to as datagrams.

Post Office Protocol (POP3)—POP is an e-mail service implemented on TCP Port 110 that provides clients access to a mail drop or post office in which their messages are stored. POP3 is the latest iteration of the protocol.

Proxy ARP—Proxy ARP is a variation of the ARP protocol, where an intermediate device, such as a router, sends an ARP response to the requesting host on behalf of the end node.

quality of service (QoS)—QoS defines the type of service a communications link can provide. QoS often specifies factors such as delay, throughput, and error rate.

Request for Comment (RFC)—RFCs are the working documents of the Internet research and development community. A document in this series may be on any topic related to computer communication and may be anything from a meeting report to the specification of a standard.

Reverse Address Resolution Protocol (RARP)—RARP is the protocol a diskless computer uses at startup to find its IP address. The computer broadcasts a request that contains its physical hardware address, and a server responds by sending the computer its IP address. RARP takes its name and message format from the IP ARP.

Routing Information Protocol (RIP)—RIP is a distance-vector routing protocol supported by TCP/IP and Novell networks, designed for use within small autonomous systems.

Simple Mail Transfer Protocol (SMTP)—SMTP is an Application Layer protocol used to send e-mail from a client to a mail server, and transfer e-mail between mail servers, across a TCP/IP network.

Simple Network Management Protocol (SNMP)—SNMP is a TCP/IP Application Layer protocol used to send and receive information about the status of network resources on a TCP/IP network. Network management, by means of SNMP, consists of several elements that work together, including the managed elements and manager, and means by which they communicate.

socket—A socket is a software object that connects an application to a network protocol. In UNIX, for example, a program can send and receive TCP/IP messages by opening a socket and reading and writing data to and from the socket. A TCP process creates a socket from the host's IP address combined with a port number, and each TCP connection includes two sockets, one for each connected host.

source quench—Source quench is a congestion control technique in which a congested computer sends a message back to the source causing the congestion, requesting that the source stop transmitting. In a TCP/IP internet, gateways use ICMP source quench to stop or reduce the transmission of IP datagrams.

subnet address—Subnet address is an extension of the IP addressing scheme that allows a site to use a single IP network address for multiple physical networks. Gateways and hosts using subnet addressing interpret the local portion of the address by dividing it into a physical network portion and host portion.

subnetwork—A subnetwork is a smaller network created by borrowing host bits (subnetting) from a larger Class A, B, or C network.

Telnet—Telnet is a TCP/IP Application Layer protocol that provides remote login capability to another computer on a network.

Time to Live (TTL)—TTL is a technique used in best-effort delivery systems to avoid packet loops. Each IP datagram is assigned an integer TTL when it is created. IP gateways decrement the TTL field when they process a datagram and discard it if the TTL value reaches zero.

Trivial File Transfer Protocol (TFTP)—TFTP is the TCP/IP protocol for file transfer with minimal capability and overhead. TFTP depends on the unreliable, connectionless, datagram delivery service, UDP. TFTP is designed for use on diskless workstations that keep such software in Rom.

UNIX to UNIX Copy Program (UUCP)—UUCP is a standard UNIX utility that copies files between UNIX systems. It can be used for e-mail transfer.

User Datagram Protocol (UDP)—UDP is a Transport Layer protocol that provides a simple, connectionless datagram delivery service, without error checking, for certain specialized application services that do not require the full services of TCP.

Lesson 1—The TCP/IP Protocol Suite

The TCP/IP protocol suite is the combination of protocols that make up TCP/IP software. This lesson covers the basic operation of a TCP/IP system, and introduces its most important protocols.

Objectives

At the end of this lesson you will be able to:

- Describe the Internet protocol suite
- List the protocols at the Application, Transport, and Network Layers

Key Point

Each TCP/IP architecture layer has a specific purpose.

TCP/IP Protocol Layers and the OSI Model

Objective 1.4
Understand and be able to describe the infrastructure needed to support an Internet client ... Operating system TCP/IP stack configuration

The TCP/IP Protocols Diagram shows a detailed picture of the TCP/IP layers; the corresponding OSI layers are also presented.

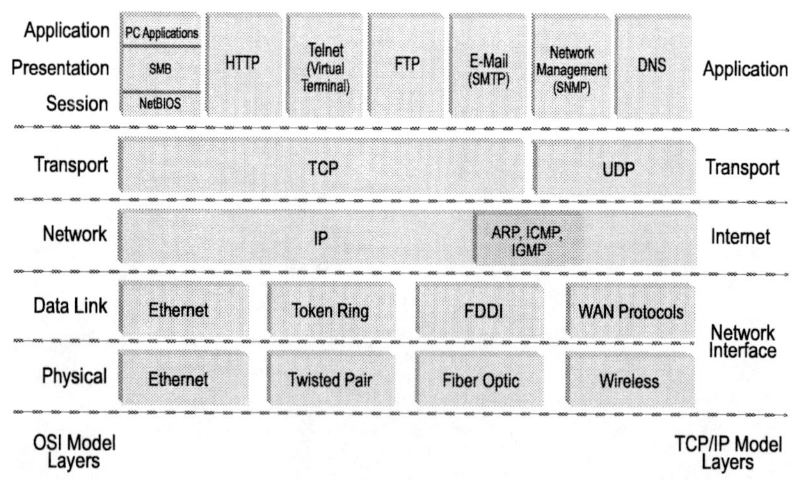

TCP/IP Protocols

As shown, the TCP/IP protocols map to specific OSI model layers; TCP/IP also provides its own layered model. The TCP/IP Protocols Diagram also shows the TCP/IP model layers.

The TCP/IP model layers function as follows:

- Network Interface Layer—Encompasses the functions of the OSI model Physical and Data Link Layers, providing bit and frame transmission services, depending on the network type.

- Internetwork Layer—Delivers packets to their destination across multiple networks, as does the OSI model Network Layer.

- Transport Layer—Provides reliability and flow control similar to the OSI model Transport Layer.

- Application Layer—Provides the high-level protocols users and application programs use for communicating over the network.

Network Interface Layer Protocols

Although messaging services are primarily provided by Application Layer protocols, the lower layer TCP/IP protocols are required for carrying the messages from end to end.

The Network Interface Layer protocols define rules that determine how a host accesses a LAN. These low-level protocols define how a host connects to the network. The physical network's operation is left up to the physical network topology's specific Layer 1 and 2 protocols.

Internetwork Layer Protocols

The Internetwork Layer protocols define the basic unit of transfer across a network and provide support for a global addressing scheme and routing. IP is the Network Layer protocol responsible for routing a packet, transporting it to its final destination. IP, in its current version 4, provides the following functions:

- A global addressing structure

- Service type requests—IP provides, within the packet header, quality of service (QoS) information, such as packet priority and throughput requirements

- Packet fragmentation

- Packet reassembly

Other protocols at the Internetwork Layer include:

- Address Resolution Protocol (ARP)/Reverse ARP (RARP)—Maps an IP host address to a physical address (ARP) or a physical address to an IP address (RARP). RARP is often used in master/slave network environments where a terminal must download an IP address before it can communicate with the host server.

- Internet Control Message Protocol (ICMP)—Provides trouble-shooting utilities, such as ping and traceroute, for testing and verifying network connectivity between devices through error and status messages intended for use by the TCP/IP software rather than for users.

- Internet Group Management Protocol (IGMP)—Used to allow hosts to participate in IP multicast (group) addressing schemes.

A new version of the IP protocol, version 6, is now in development. It expands the IP Address fields from 32 to 128 bits.

Transport Layer Protocols

The Transport Layer's primary function is to provide communication from one application program to another.

A Network Layer protocol only provides a packet delivery service, allowing a host to inject packets into the Internet with some degree of confidence that they will be delivered to the correct destination. User applications, however, typically require a specific service level. This may involve specific levels of reliability, error rate, delay, or some combination of these characteristics. A Transport Layer protocol provides the Application Layer's required level of service.

TCP/IP provides applications two different levels of service:

- TCP—Provides an end-to-end data stream service containing mechanisms to ensure reliable data transmission. These mechanisms include checksums, sequence numbers, timers, acknowledgments, and retransmission procedures. TCP, a connection-oriented protocol, provides reliable, sequenced data delivery for the Application Layer.

- User Datagram Protocol (UDP)—Provides an end-to-end, transaction-oriented, best-effort, connectionless service for those applications that do not require a reliable data delivery service. An application uses UDP when it depends more on speed than reliability, or when the application itself provides reliability.

Application Layer Protocols

An application passes data to the Transport Layer protocols, which sequence the data into messages, or byte streams, for transport across the network. The TCP/IP protocol suite includes the following Application Layer protocols, which we discuss in detail in the next unit:

- Telnet—Telnet is a remote terminal access protocol that uses TCP's connection-oriented services. Telnet allows a local host terminal to communicate with a remote host program as if the local terminal were directly connected to the remote.

- File Transfer Protocol (FTP)—FTP enables a facility to send files from one host to another. Like Telnet, FTP uses the reliable service provided by TCP to ensure the file segments are not lost.

- Simple Mail Transfer Protocol (SMTP)—SMTP contains the electronic mail (e-mail) mechanisms. SMTP also uses TCP for reliable mail message transfers. Though not commonly used explicitly (most frequently implemented by a server or client service), SMTP provides a simple protocol for sending e-mail between a client or a server and another server.

- Simple Network Management Protocol (SNMP)—SNMP provides a standardized network management protocol that allows management of TCP/IP hosts and routers. At the Transport Layer, SNMP uses UDP.

- DNS—DNS provides a name-to-address look-up service. DNS allows us to enter a Uniform Resource Locator (URL) instead of an IP address and still access the remote server. DNS may use either UDP or TCP, first attempting a TCP connection.

- Post Office Protocol 3 (POP3)—POP3 is the protocol that allows us to retrieve our e-mail from the mail server on which it is stored. POP3 uses TCP at the Transport Layer.

- Hypertext Transfer Protocol (HTTP)—HTTP allows web clients and servers to negotiate and interact with each other. HTTP is a stateless protocol; that means that when the transaction is completed, the logical connection is dropped. HTTP uses TCP at the Transport Layer.

- Network News Transfer Protocol (NNTP)—NNTP is the TCP/IP protocol used to distribute news article collections, or news feeds, over the Internet. NNTP allows companies to publicly post information that users may readily download to a news reader client. NNTP uses TCP at the Transport Layer. Many e-mail systems provide NNTP services.

- UNIX-to-UNIX Copy Program (UUCP) protocol—UUCP allows us to transfer files between UNIX systems. It is commonly used as an Internet low-end access protocol.

Communication Using TCP/IP

Objective 1.4
Understand and be able to describe the infrastructure needed to support an Internet client.
… Operating system TCP/IP stack configuration
… E-mail client

Consider an example in which you wish to send an e-mail message to another host on the network. The following sections describe this process.

Application Layer

Simple Mail Transfer Protocol (SMTP) is an Application Layer protocol for e-mail. SMTP defines a set of commands that one mail server sends to another. These commands are used to specify both the sender and recipient of the message, as well as the message text.

The data stream shown on the Your Mail E-Mail Message 1 Diagram makes up the e-mail message.

YourMailMessage

Your Mail E-Mail Message 1

This stream of data is sent to the TCP module that is responsible for ensuring that the e-mail message gets through to the other end. Think of TCP as a library of routines that applications use for reliable network communication with other computers.

Transport Layer

TCP breaks a large e-mail message into manageable pieces, as shown on the Your Mail E-Mail Message 2 Diagram. Each piece (or segment) will eventually be placed in its own packet. It is the responsibility of the destination station's TCP process to reassemble the individual segments into the complete e-mail message.

Your Mail E-Mail Message 2

After it breaks up the message into segments, TCP keeps track of the pieces by placing a header on the front of each segment. The TCP header includes a source port, destination port, and sequence number. If we, for the sake of illustration, abbreviate the TCP header as "T," the entire e-mail file now looks like Your Mail E-Mail Message 3 Diagram.

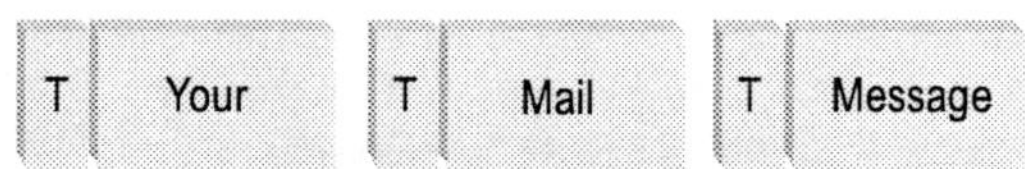

Your Mail E-Mail Message 3

The packet (or datagram) is now passed down to the Network Layer for processing and eventual transmission by IP. TCP tracks what it sends, and retransmits anything that does not get through.

Network Layer

The interface between TCP and IP is relatively simple. TCP simply hands a datagram with a destination to IP. IP has no knowledge of how this datagram relates to any other datagram before or after it; IP merely exists to deliver the packet to the end node.

IP's job is to find a route for the datagram and get it to its final destination. IP places a header on each segment to send the encapsulated datagram on to its final destination, as shown on the Your Mail E-Mail Message 4 Diagram. The IP header includes the source and destination IP addresses, a protocol number indicating the Transport Layer protocol (in this example, TCP), and a checksum. If we abbreviate the IP header as "I," the e-mail message now looks like the Your Mail E-Mail Message 4 Diagram.

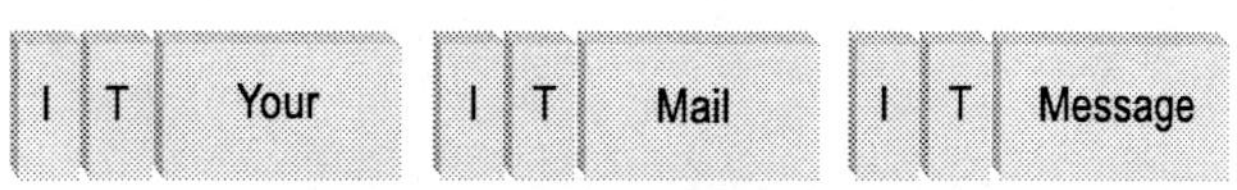

Your Mail E-Mail Message 4

Each datagram is now passed down to the Network Interface Layer for injection into the physical network as a sequence of bits.

Network Interface Layer

The physical network places its own header on each datagram. Assume we are trying to access an Ethernet network. If we represent the Ethernet header with an "E," and the Ethernet checksum with a "C," the e-mail message is now composed of the following three datagrams, as shown on the Your Mail E-Mail Message 5 Diagram.

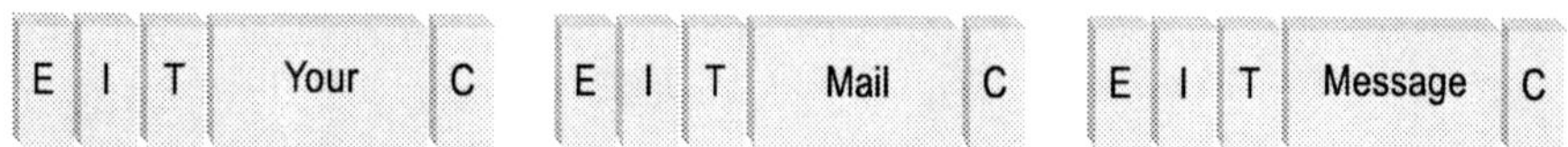

Your Mail E-Mail Message 5

Destination Station

When the destination station receives the packets, the datagrams are processed, in reverse, by the various protocol stack layers. The Ethernet interface looks at the Ethernet Type field and passes the datagram up to IP.

IP looks at the Protocol field and passes the datagram up to TCP. TCP looks at the sequence numbers and other information to recombine the segments into the original e-mail message. The Transport Layer then passes the message up to the e-mail application on the destination computer.

Activities

1. The TCP/IP model Network Interface Layer maps to which OSI model layer(s)? (Choose all that apply.)

   a. Physical

   b. Network

   c. Transport

   d. Data Link

2. Which three of the following are functions of the TCP/IP Internetwork Layer protocols? (Choose three.)

   a. A global addressing structure

   b. Packet fragmentation

   c. End-to-end data stream service

   d. Service type requests

3. Which three of the following are TCP/IP Internetwork Layer protocols? (Choose three.)

   a. IGMP

   b. IP

   c. UDP

   d. ARP

4. Which TCP/IP Application Layer protocol allows companies to publicly post information over the Internet?

   a. FTP

   b. SMTP

   c. UUCP

   d. NNTP

5. Which TCP/IP Transport Layer protocol provides an end-to-end, transaction-oriented, best-effort, connectionless service?

   a. TCP

   b. UDP

   c. RTP

   d. RSVP

Extended Activity

A Token Ring LAN is using the TCP/IP suite. Draw a diagram that shows how an SMTP message is encapsulated by the time a frame is transmitted onto the network.

Lesson 2—IP

IP is responsible for transmitting blocks of data (datagrams or packets) through an interconnected set of networks. IP receives these blocks from higher level protocols such as TCP or UDP.

Objectives

At the end of this lesson you will be able to:

- Describe the basic functions provided by IP

- Discuss IP frame encapsulation

- List the network monitoring features provided by IP options

- Discuss the functions of ICMP

- Describe the various ICMP message types

Key Point

IP provides connectionless delivery of datagrams across a TCP/IP network.

Overview of IP

Objective 1.4
Understand and be able to describe the infrastructure needed to support an Internet client. … Operating system TCP/IP stack configuration

IP provides a connectionless (datagram) delivery service between end-stations. Each datagram carries a full destination IP address, and is routed through the system independent of all other datagrams. No connections or logical circuits are established.

An IP software module resides in all hosts and routers running the TCP/IP protocol stack. These modules share common rules for internet datagram address field interpretation and fragmenting and reassembling. Additionally, these modules provide procedures for making routing decisions and other help functions, such as Address Resolution Protocol (ARP) and Internet Control Message Protocol (ICMP) messages.

IP provides internetwork communication by passing a datagram from one host's IP module to the IP module on another host, until the datagram reaches its final destination. The datagram can traverse several hosts on its way to its destination; each host through which the datagram passes is called a hop. The network routes the datagram from host to host, based on the destination IP address carried in the IP header. The datagram may travel through several networks before reaching its final destination, as shown in the Routed Network Diagram.

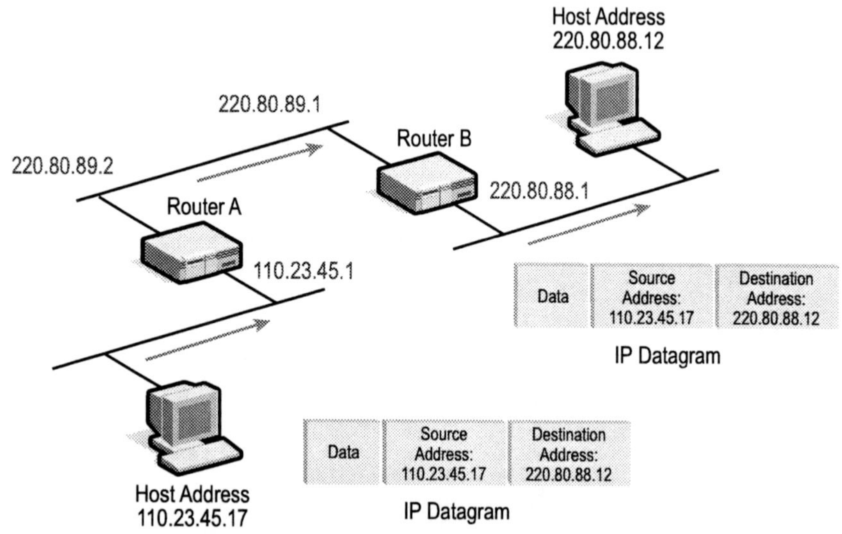

Routed Network

Best-Effort Service

IP is known as a "best-effort" service because of the following characteristics:

- There is little data error control. Receiving nodes use a 16-bit header checksum to validate packets, and discard packets with invalid checksums.

- There are no end-to-end or hop-by-hop receipt acknowledgments.

- There are no provisions for the retransmission of lost or corrupted data.

- There are no packet sequencing or flow control mechanisms.

Multiplexing Protocols

IP can carry more than one Transport Layer protocol in a given data stream. For example, two communicating hosts might be sharing HTTP and DNS information simultaneously. HTTP uses TCP as its Transport Layer protocol, and DNS can use UDP. Both TCP and UDP can use the services of IP.

Multiplexing is a process that sends out multiple types of communication signals over a single communication channel. Demultiplexing, on the other hand, refers to the practice of separating a single input into several outputs, as illustrated on the Demultiplexing Transport Protocols Diagram.

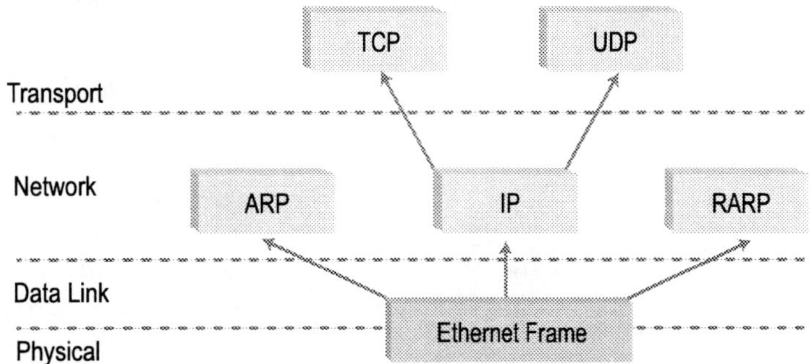

Demultiplexing Transport Protocols

IP identifies each upper-layer protocol with a number in the Protocol field of the IP packet header. The original source of an IP datagram places a value in the Protocol field to indicate whether the source Transport Layer protocol was TCP or UDP.

The receiving computer uses this Protocol value to forward the incoming datagram to the correct Transport Layer process. If the receiving device sees a Protocol field set to 6, it knows to send the datagram's data to the TCP protocol. If it sees 17 in the Protocol field, it knows to send the data to the UDP protocol.

IP Packet Encapsulation

The Ethernet Packet Diagram shows an IP datagram encapsulated as the data portion of an Ethernet frame.

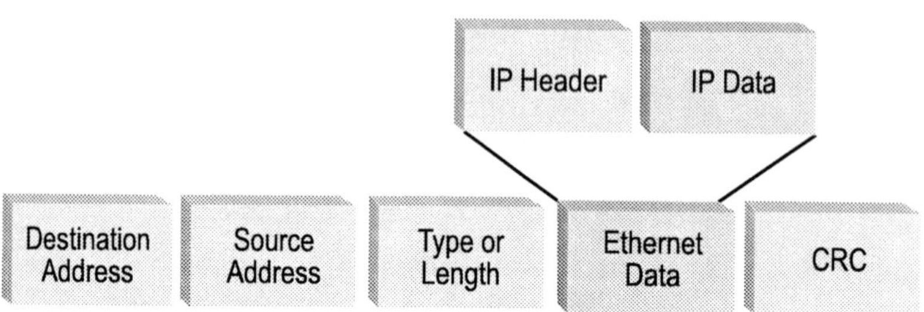

Ethernet Packet

An IP packet encapsulates data sent to it from the Transport Layer. The Data Link Layer protocol (in this example Ethernet, but it could be any LAN or WAN Layer 2 protocol) in turn encapsulates the IP packet as its own data. Physical addresses help the frame find its way across the wire, and when the packet must move to another network, the Data Link Layer frame is stripped away. The next hop device forwards the packet on toward its destination by using the destination IP address.

Each time the IP packet must travel across a physical link, it is encapsulated in a new Layer 2 frame. No matter how many hops the packet traverses, the source and destination IP addresses and Layer 4 data remain intact.

IP Version 6

Objective 1.4
Understand and be able to describe the infrastructure needed to support an Internet client. … Operating system TCP/IP stack configuration

IP version 6 (IPv6) was designed as an upgrade to IPv4, the current version in use worldwide. During the 1980s, when the U.S. government was first privatizing the Internet, IPv4 was more than sufficient to handle the total of 213 Internet hosts. But rapid Internet growth gave rise to a number of problems, the most prevalent being the limited number of IP addresses available. IPv6 solves the following problems, plus many others:

- Expanded addresses—IPv6 expands IP addresses from the current 32 bits to 128 bits. This greatly expanded address range (2^{128}) ensures that the Internet will not exhaust its address supply in the near future.

- Non-IP addressing formats—The long address space provides adequate room for translations of Internetwork Packet Exchange (IPX), network service-access point (NSAP), Ethernet, and other non-IP addresses into IPv6 addresses. This allows existing networks to connect to the Internet with a minimum of address reconfiguration.

- Multimedia ready—IPv6 makes it possible to use the Internet to deliver real-time data requiring guaranteed bandwidth and latency, and to ensure that packets arrive at a steady, predictable pace.

- Plug and Play address discovery—Currently, users or network managers must manually configure each host with an IP address. IPv6 allows hosts to discover their own addresses from a router during startup.

- Automated address changes—Because a router distributes network addresses, network addresses can be changed by updating only the router. In addition, all addresses include lifetimes, enabling the router to specify a time to switch addresses.

IPv6 Address Format

Dotted decimal notation is a simple way to represent 4-byte IPv4 addresses. However, the 16-byte addresses of IPv6 make dotted decimal difficult to use. For example, consider the following IPv6 address:

128.111.0.56.0.0.0.0.0.0.2.10.231.0.255.255

Colon hexadecimal ("colon hex") notation uses several methods to simplify long addresses. First, the address is organized in groups of 16 bits instead of 8 bits. Each 16-bit value is represented in hexadecimal, separated by colons. The dotted decimal address above is much shorter in colon hexadecimal:

806F:038:0:0:0:020A:E70:FFFF

As you can see, 0s are represented more compactly. If a 1- or 2-byte value equals zero, it is represented by a single 0, instead of the typical hexadecimal notation of a 0 for each byte. A repetitive sequence of 0s can also be represented by a double colon:

806F:038::020A:E70:FFFF

| **IPv4 Compatibility** | Because of the huge installed base of IPv4 hosts and routers, specifications for IPv6 include mechanisms designed to ensure a smooth, gradual transition from IPv4 to IPv6: |

- IPv4 Address Translation—IPv4 addresses are easily translated into IPv6 addresses by adding an IPv6 address prefix of leading 0s.

- Dual Protocol Stacks—For the foreseeable future, all implementations of IPv6 will also include an IPv4 stack.

- IPv6 Tunneled Over IPv4—IPv6 hosts will be able to communicate with each other through IPv4 routers by encapsulating IPv6 packets within IPv4 packets.

ICMP

Internet Control Message Protocol (ICMP) allows a router or destination host to report an error in datagram processing to the packet's original source. ICMP is a required companion of IP. This means that all hosts and routers that implement IP must also implement ICMP.

ICMP's Purpose and Limits

As we know, IP was not designed to provide a reliable delivery service. The main function of an ICMP message is to provide feedback about various problems that may occur in the communications environment. ICMP was not designed as a quick fix to make IP reliable; higher level protocols that operate as IP clients must implement their own reliability procedures if reliable communication is required.

ICMP messages are encapsulated as the data portion of an IP datagram. As a result, they are routed like any other IP datagram. Because ICMP messages are transmitted in IP datagrams, the ICMP message sender is not guaranteed that the message will be delivered to its ultimate destination.

Because the use of ICMP messages cannot be considered reliable, there is no guarantee they will not be lost or discarded. To avoid complex problems caused by ICMP attempting to track messages about messages, ICMP sends no messages about lost or discarded ICMP messages. Also, ICMP messages are only sent when errors occur in the processing of an unfragmented datagram or in the first fragment of a fragmented datagram.

Encapsulation

ICMP is a member of the TCP/IP protocol architecture's Internet Layer. Despite this position in the TCP/IP stack, ICMP is actually an IP user (client). An IP datagram carries the ICMP header and data, appending to the ICMP message an IP header to carry the message to its destination.

The client constructs an ICMP message and then passes it to the local IP process, as illustrated on the ICMP Encapsulation Diagram. IP appends to the message an IP header and then transmits the resulting datagram over the physical network to the destination host or router.

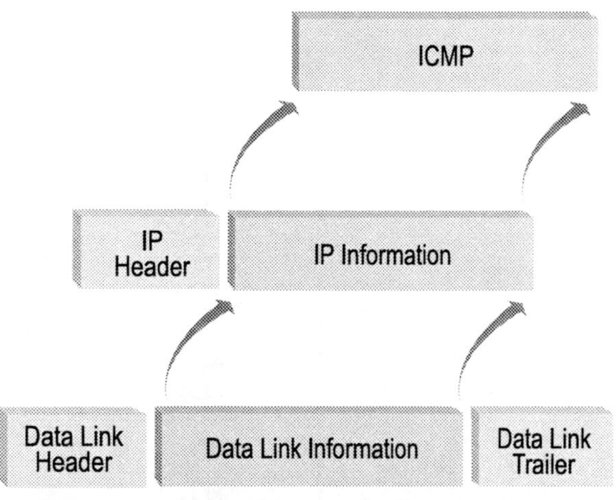

ICMP Encapsulation

The reason that IP was selected to deliver ICMP messages is that the messages may need to traverse several routers and networks to reach their final destination. A simple Data Link Layer protocol encapsulation is not sufficient to deliver a message across a router.

Message Types

The header of an ICMP message includes a Type field. The number in this field specifies the meaning of the message and the format of the rest of the packet. Thirteen types of ICMP messages have been defined as presented in the ICMP Header—Type Field Table.

ICMP Header—Type Field

Type Field	Message Type
0	Echo Reply
3	Destination Unreachable
4	Source Quench
5	Redirect
8	Echo Request
11	Time Exceeded
12	Parameter Problem
13	Timestamp Request
14	Timestamp Reply
15	Information Request
16	Information Reply
17	Address Mask Request
18	Address Mask Reply

Some types of ICMP messages have different header structures, appropriate to the type of information they contain. For example, the Code field is used in an ICMP Destination Unreachable message to explain why a destination is unreachable, such as "5" (source route failed).

The IP header is included in an ICMP message so the source host can match the ICMP message with its own data stream. The first 64 bits of data are included because they contain the Transport Layer header (TCP or UDP).

The ICMP message types presented in the ICMP Header—Type Field Table are described in the following sections.

Destination Unreachable (3)

This message includes a number of contingencies:

- A router will return this message if it does not know how to reach the destination network.

- If the datagram specifies a source route that is unstable, a Destination Unreachable message is returned.

The destination host may send a Destination Unreachable message to the source host if the IP module in the destination host cannot deliver the datagram because the indicated protocol module or process port is not active. A router will return a message and discard the datagram; if the router must fragment the datagram, but the "don't fragment" flag is set, a message is returned and the datagram is discarded.

Time Exceeded (11)

A router will return a Time Exceeded message if it is forced to discard a datagram because the TTL field has been reduced to zero. A host will also transmit a Time Exceeded message if it cannot complete the reassembly of a fragmented datagram because of missing fragments.

Parameter Problem (12)

A router or host must discard a datagram if the router or host processing the datagram finds a problem with the header parameters and cannot completely process the datagram. The router or host may also use the Parameter Problem message to notify the source host. This Parameter field contains a pointer to the byte in the original header where the error was detected.

Source Quench (4)

This message type provides a basic form of flow control. When datagrams arrive too quickly for a router or host to process, they must be discarded. The computer discarding the datagrams sends an ICMP Source Quench message to request that the original source slow down its rate of sending datagrams. The recipient of a Source Quench message should lower the rate at which it sends datagrams to the specified destination until it no longer receives Source Quench messages. The source host can then gradually increase its transmission rate until it again receives Source Quench messages.

Redirect (5)

Routers send ICMP Redirect messages to hosts on directly connected networks. These messages inform the host that a better route exists for the destination network. ICMP Redirect messages are not sent to other routers. Therefore, Redirect messages are not used to propagate and update routing information among routers.

Echo Request (8) and Echo Reply (0)

Objective 3.6.
Identify when to use various diagnostic tools for resolving Internet problems.
... Ping

The ICMP Echo Request/Reply message is better known as the Packet Internet Groper (Ping) command. These messages provide a mechanism to determine whether communication is possible between two computers. The Ping command uses an Echo Request message to send data to a destination (using the domain name or IP address). If the destination node is active, the destination node will echo the data back to the sender in an Echo Reply message.

Timestamp Request (13) and Timestamp Reply (14)

These ICMP messages provide a mechanism for sampling the delay characteristics of a network. The sender of a Timestamp Request message includes an identifier in the Parameters field, and places the time that the message was sent in the Information field. The receiver appends a receive timestamp along with a transmit timestamp, and returns the message as a Timestamp Reply message.

Information Request (15) and Information Reply (16)

A host uses an ICMP Information Request message to discover the address of the network to which it is attached. The requesting host sends the message with the network portion of both the source and destination IP Address fields set to 0. Recall that an IP address with a network portion of 0 means "this network." The reply arrives with the address fully specified.

Address Mask Request (17) and Address Mask Reply (18)

A host may use the Address Mask Request message to discover the subnet mask for the network to which it is attached. The host broadcasts the request on the network and waits for a router to respond with an Address Mask Reply message that contains the subnet mask.

Activities

1. List the features of IP that make it a "best effort" protocol.

   ____

   ____

   ____

   ____

   ____

   ____

2. An IP packet travels from a source node, across an Ethernet LAN, across the Internet, across a Token Ring LAN, to a destination node. What happens to the IP packet during this process?

   ____

   ____

   ____

3. Can IP serve only one Transport Layer connection at a time? Explain why or why not.

   ____

   ____

   ____

4. How many unique addresses are possible with IPv6?

   ____

5. Why are we running out of IP addresses?

   ____

   ____

6. Using ICMP Type field values, indicate what you expect given the following situations:

   a. The reply to an ICMP Type 8.

   ____

   b. The ICMP response when a network cannot be located.

   ____

   c. The ICMP type when an IP address does not reply to an echo request after a given amount of time.

   ____

7. Match the ICMP message type to its description.

   a. Information request (15) and Reply (16)

   b. Source quench (4)

   c. Timestamp Request (13) and Reply (14)

   d. Parameter problem (12)

   e. Redirect (5)

   A router does not have the buffering capacity to forward a datagram.

   A host or router discovers an IP header syntax error.

   A router asks a source host to use another router that provides a shorter path.

   A router wants to sample a network's delay characteristics.

   A host wishes to discover the address of the network to which it is attached.

Extended Activities

1. For each of the following ICMP Message types, describe what situation might cause the message to occur:

   a. Time exceeded

   ____

   b. Source quench

   ____

2. Go to the following Web sites to learn more about IPv6:

   http://www.ietf.org/html.charters/ipngwg-charter.html

   http://playground.sun.com/pub/ipng/html/ipng-main.html

   http://www.cis.ohio-state.edu/htbin/rfc/rfc1752.html

   http://www.ipv6.org/

Lesson 3—UDP and TCP

User Datagram Protocol (UDP) and Transmission Control Protocol (TCP) are the two major Transport Layer protocols that reside on top of IP. This lesson compares and contrasts the operation of these two important protocols.

Objectives

At the end of this lesson you will be able to:

- Compare the services and operation of UDP and TCP

- Describe port-number-based demultiplexing

- Name the most common well-known listener ports for TCP and UDP

- Describe TCP's use of ports, sockets, and sequence numbers

- Describe TCP and UDP frame encapsulation

 **Key Point**

TCP is a reliable, byte-stream-oriented, virtual circuit protocol. UDP is a connectionless, unreliable counterpart to TCP.

Features Common to Both UDP and TCP

Objective 1.4
Understand and be able to describe the infrastructure needed to support an Internet client ... Operating system TCP/IP stack configuration

As Transport Layer protocols, both UDP and TCP use the services of IP. Thus, a TCP or UDP message is encapsulated in an IP datagram as it travels across the internetwork. The Frame Encapsulation Diagram illustrates this.

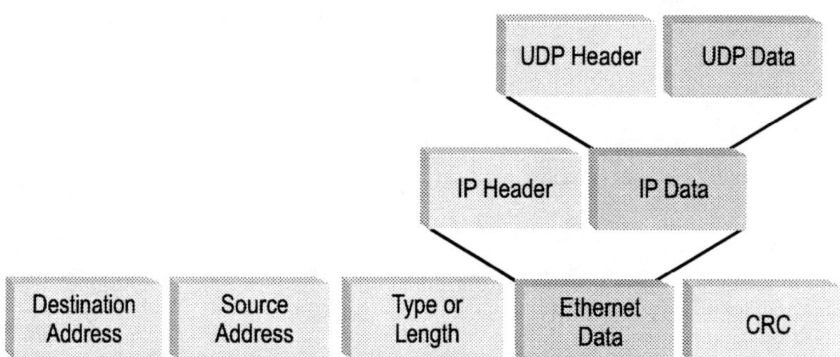

Frame Encapsulation

The main IP services used by TCP and UDP include:

- Addressing of source and destination stations on different networks

- Ability to route datagrams across different networks

- Ability to fragment and later reassemble datagrams for transmission across networks that support smaller packet sizes

- Ability to demultiplex Transport Layer protocols based on IP-defined protocol numbers

Demultiplexing Based on Port Number

One of the additional features that TCP and UDP provide is the ability to demultiplex data to an application process based on a destination port number. While IP supports the routing function that allows communication between two hosts across an internetwork, UDP and TCP can distinguish among multiple application destinations within a given host. This mechanism allows multiple, simultaneously executing application programs on a given host to send and receive datagrams independently. The Demultiplexing Diagram illustrates this feature.

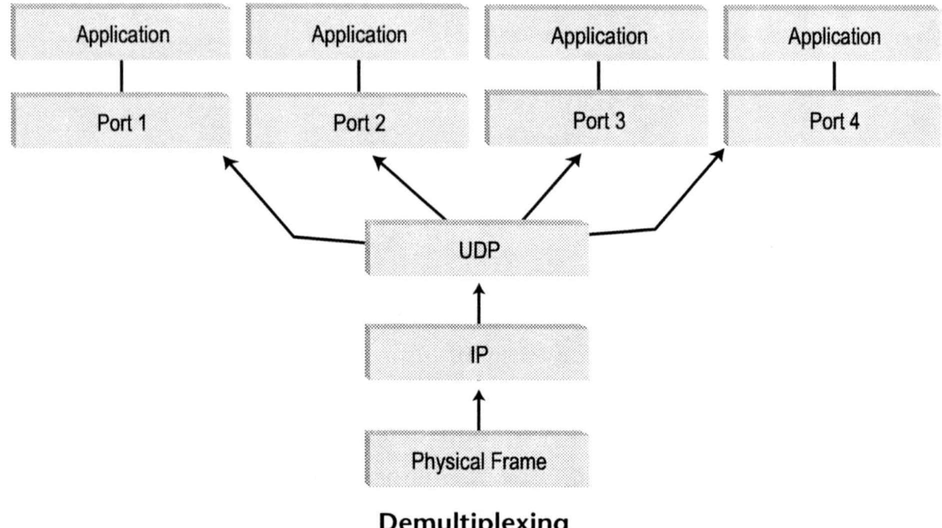

Demultiplexing

UDP and TCP each provide an interface for separate transactions between client and server processes. The client process is an active UDP or TCP client, while the server process runs passively on a server hosting the target application. The passive server application maintains a listening socket on a port number dedicated to the given service.

For example, a Web server application listens on Port 80, the port dedicated to HTTP. A browser transmits HTTP requests to Port 80, and the server responds on the same port.

Specific port numbers have been reserved for special server processes that simply wait for client requests. These ports are called the well-known ports.

The active client requests a service from the remote passive server by sending a packet to the remote server's IP address. The packet carries a UDP or TCP segment, part of which specifies the well-known port on which the target application resides.

The passive server listens patiently on this port, waiting for any active client requests. When the server receives a packet sent to its IP address, it reads the packet and decapsulates the IP header, exposing the UDP or TCP segment within. It recognizes that the segment specifies one of its available, well-known ports, and passes the data to the associated application. Contained within the UDP or TCP segment is the port over which the client wishes the server to answer, and thus, the server targets this client port in its reply.

The Connecting to a Device via Well-Known Ports Diagram illustrates the concept of connecting by means of ports.

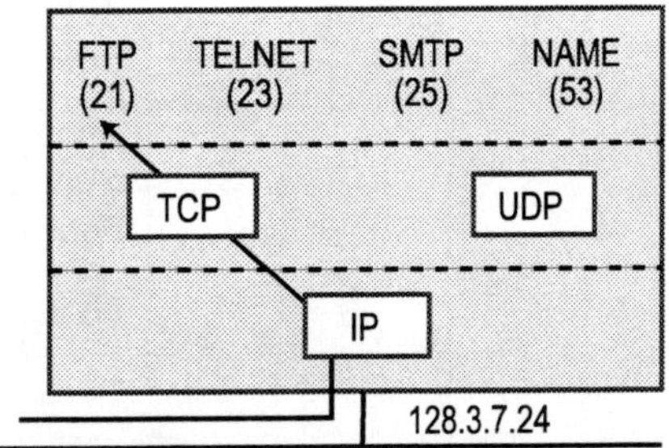

Connecting to a Device via Well-Known Ports

The client can specify any port it wants; this does not have to be a well-known port. However, if the server does not know to listen on this alternate port, the transaction will fail.

Ports and Addressing

When establishing a connection, the client TCP or UDP must specify not only the IP address of the target host, but also the application process port number to access. Many network professionals follow this principle by specifying a port number as part of the IP address of a destination process. For example, the diagram above shows a connection to the FTP process (port 21) on the host with IP address 128.3.7.24 (we will explain IP addressing in detail soon). Thus, it is common to refer to the address of that FTP process as 128.3.7.24.21.

Well-Known Port Numbers

In most cases, UDP and TCP use the same well-known port numbers. The most common of these are presented in the Selected Well-Known Port Numbers Table.

Selected Well-Known Port Numbers

Port Number	Description
20	File Transfer Protocol (FTP), data
21	File Transfer Protocol (FTP), control
23	Telnet
25	Simple Mail Transfer Protocol (SMTP)
39	Resource Location Protocol
42	Host Name Server
43	Who Is
53	Domain Name Server (DNS)
67	Bootstrap Protocol (BOOTP) Server
68	Bootstrap Protocol (BOOTP) Client
69	Trivial File Transfer Protocol (TFTP)
70	Gopher
79	Finger
80	HyperText Transfer Protocol (HTTP)
110	Post Office Protocol 3 (POP3)
119	Network News Transfer Protocol (NNTP)
161	Simple Network Management Protocol (SNMP)
443	Secure HyperText Transfer Protocol (HTTPS)

UDP

Objective 1.4

Understand and be able to describe the infrastructure needed to support an Internet client … Operating system TCP/IP stack configuration

UDP provides a transaction-oriented, best-effort delivery service for applications that do not require a reliable data stream service. The major Application Layer protocol clients of UDP are:

- Network File System (NFS)

- Domain Name System (DNS)

- Trivial File Transfer Protocol (TFTP)

- Simple Network Management Protocol (SNMP)

Because UDP uses IP's services, it provides the same connectionless delivery service and lack of reliability as IP. However, UDP does implement flow control to manage the information exchange rate between hosts. UDP does not send or receive acknowledgments to guarantee the successful transmission of data. Neither does UDP provide a method to sequence packets so they can be placed in their proper order by the destination station. Applications requiring reliable and sequenced delivery should use the services of TCP, or should provide reliability on the application itself when using UDP.

Why use UDP? UDP provides a simple transaction service with minimal protocol overhead (unlike TCP). UDP is suitable for carrying protocols that either provide their own error detection and recovery systems or have no need for these services. UDP supports two additional features above those already provided by IP:

- UDP provides the ability to demultiplex data for an application process based on a destination port number.

- The UDP header includes a checksum that detects errors that occur when data is transmitted from a source host to a destination host.

TCP

Objective 1.4

Understand and be able to describe the infrastructure needed to support an Internet client … Operating system TCP/IP stack configuration

TCP provides applications with a reliable, connection-oriented service, in the form of a virtual point-to-point connection between the client and server applications. The major TCP clients are the following Application Layer protocols:

- Telnet

- FTP

- SMTP

TCP causes a connectionless IP end-to-end service to appear as a continuous, uninterrupted data stream carried over a dedicated data channel. The main TCP features include:

- Basic data transfer

- Reliable and sequenced packet delivery

- Flow control to protect hosts from data overflow

- Multiplexing and demultiplexing among multiple applications

- Connection establishment and termination

Basic Data Transfer

A segment is the basic TCP transfer unit between communicating hosts. TCP views a data stream as a sequence of bytes, broken into segments for transmission. An IP datagram transmits each segment across the internetwork as a single IP data field, unless an intervening small-packet network requires packet fragmentation.

After a connection is established, the size of each segment may vary based on network and host conditions. Therefore, all segments do not necessarily contain the same number of bytes. The local TCP process determines the number of bytes to include in a particular segment. The many complex issues that affect this decision are beyond the scope of this course.

Reliable and Sequenced Packet Delivery

TCP must be able to recover from data that is damaged, lost, duplicated, or delivered out of sequence. Thus, TCP assigns a sequence number to each byte transmitted, and requires that the destination TCP return a positive acknowledgment (ACK). If the sender does not receive an ACK within a specified time period, it retransmits the unacknowledged segment(s). The destination station uses the sequence numbers to correctly reorder segments that may have been received out of sequence, and to eliminate duplicate segments.

A checksum included with each segment handles damaged data as it is transferred. The receiving host examines the checksum and discards any damaged segments. Discarded segments are not acknowledged and, therefore, are retransmitted by the source station.

Flow Control

TCP provides a mechanism for the destination station to control the amount of data sent by the source station. A receiving host sets a receive window with each ACK it sends, indicating how many additional bytes it is willing to accept from the source. As the receive buffer fills, the advertised receive window size shrinks. As the receive buffer empties, the receive window's advertised size increases.

Multiplexing and Demultiplexing

Like UDP, TCP uses ports to identify the destination application, so multiple processes within a single host can use TCP communication services simultaneously.

Each host independently handles binding ports to processes. For frequently used processes, it may be useful to assign a well-known port number and make that number known to the public. Other devices can then access services assigned to the port through the well-known port addresses.

Connection Establishment

TCP's reliability and flow control services require that it initialize and maintain important status information for each data stream; a connection is a combination of this status information. A connection includes socket numbers, sequence numbers, and a great deal of window management information. A pair of sockets uniquely identifies each side of a virtual circuit connection.

When two processes wish to communicate, the TCP on each host must first establish an application connection. The connection initializes the status information for each side of the virtual circuit. After the hosts complete their data exchange, the TCP processes terminate the connection to free up the resources for other users.

During data transfer, the TCP on each host communicate to verify reliable data transfer. If the established connection fails because of network problems, both computers will detect the failure and report it to the appropriate application program.

Sockets

A socket identifies the ultimate destination of TCP's traffic. A pair of sockets (one for each host) uniquely identifies each connection. Moreover, a socket may be used simultaneously in more than one connection.

A TCP socket connection is defined by a set of four numbers:

- IP address at each end (two numbers)

- TCP port number at each end (two numbers)

Every datagram contains these four numbers. IP addresses are placed in the IP header, and port numbers are included in the TCP header. To keep things straight, no two connections can have the same set of numbers; however, each connection can share one number as long as the other ends are unique.

285

Activities

1. Name the application associated with each well-known port number.

   a. Port 53

   ____

   b. Port 68

   ____

   c. Port 69

   ____

   d. Port 123

   ____

   e. Port 161

   ____

   f. Port 67

   ____

   g. Port 20

   ____

   h. Port 21

   ____

   i. Port 23

   ____

   j. Port 25

   ____

   k. Port 80

   ____

   l. Port 443

   ____

2. List three main differences between TCP and UDP.

____

____

____

____

____

____

3. How does TCP or UDP support multiple application destinations on the same host?

   a. It supports multiple paths between the source and destination applications.

   b. It carries port numbers in its header, used to logically address a destination application.

   c. It maintains a listening socket for each sending application, which waits for the destination server application server to poll them.

   d. It multiplexes IP packets so they can share the same physical link between the source and destination nodes.

4. Which is a true statement concerning UDP?

   a. UDP is a connection-oriented protocol, used to establish virtual circuits between network applications.

   b. UDP provides error detection and recovery features for reliable communications across an IP network.

   c. UDP clients must listen on well-known ports when awaiting server replies to their service requests.

   d. UDP servers must listen for service requests on well-known ports, or else the transactions may fail.

Extended Activities

1. Draw a diagram illustrating the UDP or TCP demultiplexing process.

2. Draw a diagram illustrating an Ethernet frame encapsulation of an IP datagram, in turn encapsulating a TCP segment.

3. On the Web, find a complete list of well-known port numbers for UDP and TCP. Who assigns these numbers? How many well-known ports are available?

Lesson 4—Internet Addressing

Any global communications system requires a universally accepted method to identify individual computers. Computing devices, or hosts (also called nodes), on a TCP/IP-based network, are assigned unique addresses called IP addresses. These hosts may be personal computers (PCs), terminal servers, ports on a terminal server, routers, network management stations, UNIX hosts, and so forth. This lesson presents the structure of IP addresses.

Objectives

At the end of this lesson you will be able to:

- Describe IP addressing fundamentals

- Explain IP address routing and bridging

Key Point

Unique addressing is critical in networking.

IP Addresses

Objective 1.4
Understand and be able to describe the infrastructure needed to support an Internet client ...Operating system TCP/IP stack configuration ... Network connection ... Client software configuration

There is one thing that all computers running the TCP/IP suite have in common: each is assigned its own IP address. The Internet Corporation of Assigned Names and Numbers (ICANN), a private, nongovernment organization, issues all globally-unique publics IP addresses. Some devices, such as routers, which have physical connections to more than one network, must be assigned a unique IP address for each network connection, or port.

IP addressing uses a 32-bit Address field; the bits in the Address field are numbered 0 to 31. This field is then divided into two parts: the right part identifies the host (the host portion), and the left part identifies the network on which the host resides (the network portion). Hosts attached to the same network must share a common prefix designating their network number.

IP addresses take the form of four numeric fields, separated by periods:

field1.field2.field3.field4

There are five IP address classes: Classes A-E. We can easily determine the address class from its leading (highest-order) bits.

Note: The IP software residing on network hosts uses a unique bit pattern to identify the address class. After the IP software has identified the address class, it can determine which bits represent the network number and which bits identify the host portion of the address.

Class A Address

A Class A network address has the leading bit set to 0, a 7-bit network number, and a 24-bit local host address. The first octet ranges from 0–127, although 0 and 127 are reserved and cannot be assigned to networks and hosts, as shown on the Class A Network Address Diagram. We can define a total of 126 Class A networks, with up to 16,777,214 hosts per network.

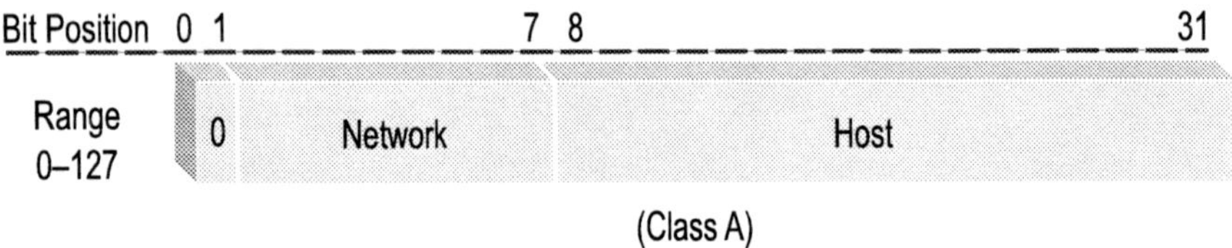

Class A Network Address

Additionally, network addresses 0.x.y.z and 127.x.y.z are reserved for special functions that we will learn about later. Therefore, we can only assign the Class A ranges 1.x.y.z through 126.x.y.z to network hosts.

Although 2^{24} equates to 16,777,216, we can only assign 16,777,214 host addresses per Class A network. Recall that we cannot assign a host address of all 0s or all 1s. Consequently, we then have to subtract these two unassignable addresses from the total number of available host addresses. We will revisit this addressing restriction again when we discuss subnetting.

Class B Address

A Class B network address has the two highest-order bits set to 1-0, a 14-bit network number, and a 16-bit local host address. The first octet ranges from 128–191, as shown on the Class B Network Address Diagram. A total of 16,382 Class B networks can be defined with up to 65,534 usable hosts per network.

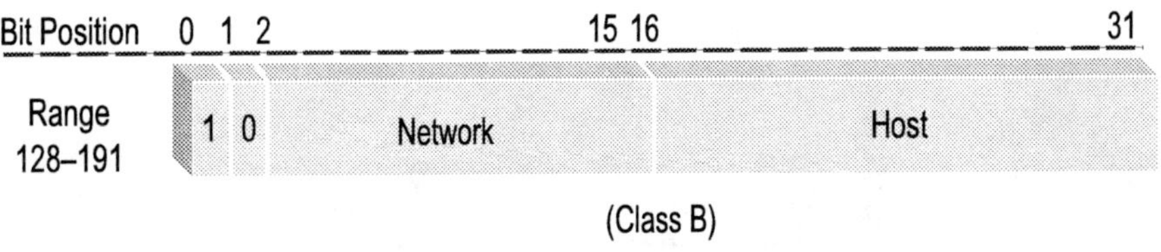

Class B Network Address

Class C Address

A Class C network address has the three leading bits set to 1-1-0, a 21-bit network number, and an 8-bit local host address. The first octet ranges from 192–223, as shown on the Class C Network Address Diagram. A total of 2,097,152 Class C networks may be defined with up to 254 usable hosts per network.

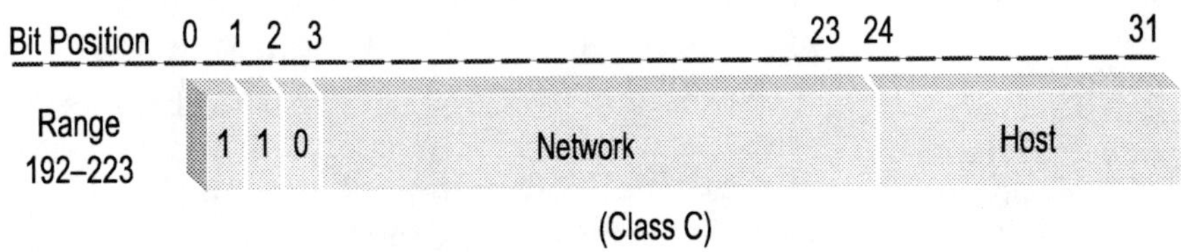

Class C Network Address

Class D Address

The fourth address type, Class D, is used as a multicast address. The four highest order bits are set to 1-1-1-0, and the remaining 28 bits specify a multicast group ID. The first octet ranges from 224–239. This concept is illustrated on the Class D Network Address Diagram.

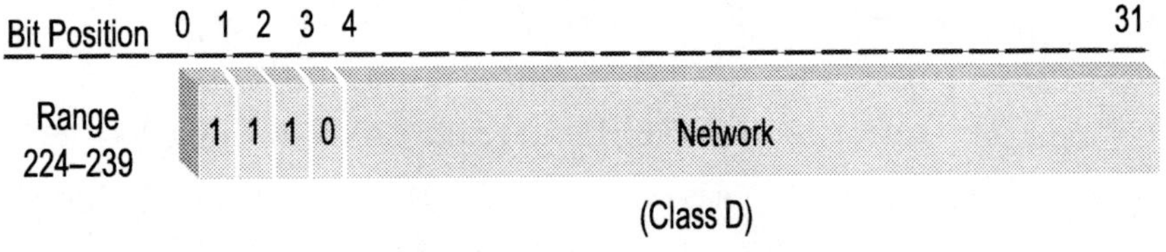

Class D Network Address

Class E Address

The final IP address type is the Class E address; it is reserved for future use. The five highest order bits are set to 1-1-1-1-0, and the first octet ranges from 240–247, as illustrated on the Class E Network Address Diagram.

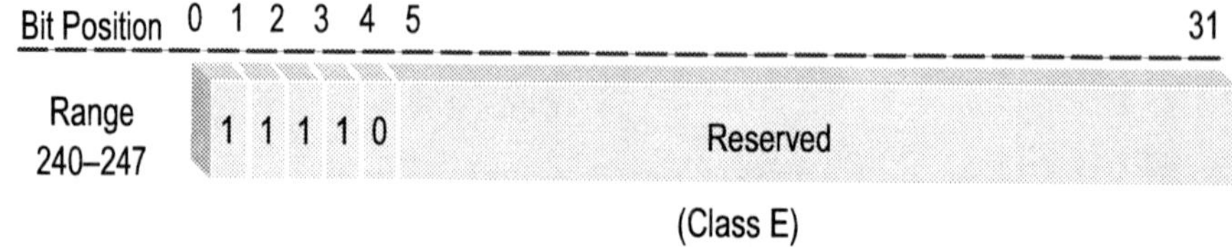

Class E Network Address

Dotted Decimal Notation

Objective 1.4
Understand and be able to describe the infrastructure needed to support an Internet client.
… Operating system TCP/IP stack configuration
… Client software configuration

To make it easier for people to read and understand IP addresses, the addresses are often written as four decimal numbers, each separated by a dot. This format is called dotted decimal notation.

This notation divides the 32-bit address into four 8-bit (byte) fields, or octets, and independently specifies the value of each field as a decimal number. For example, if given the Class B IP address specified by the bit pattern:

10000001 00001111 00010001 00000011

The value of each byte, specified in a string of four decimal numbers, is:

129 15 17 3

The complete IP address, shown in dotted decimal notation, is:

129.15.17.3

The valid network numbers for each address class are provided below. The "hhh" represents the host portion of the address assigned by the network administrator:

Class A: 001.hhh.hhh.hhh through 127.hhh.hhh.hhh

Class B: 128.001.hhh.hhh through 191.254.hhh.hhh

Class C: 192.000.001.hhh through 223.255.254.hhh

Class D: 224.000.000.000 through 239.255.255.255

Class E: 240.xxx.yyy.zzz through 247.xxx.yyy.zzz

Addressing Rules

Objective 1.4

Understand and be able to describe the infrastructure needed to support an Internet client. … Operating system TCP/IP stack configuration … Client software configuration

The following rules pertain to assigning IP addresses:

- The bits that define the host portion of an IP address should not be all 1s. According to the RFCs, any IP address with the host portion consisting of all 1s is interpreted as meaning "all," as in "all hosts." For example, the address 128.1.255.255 is interpreted as meaning all hosts on Network 128.1.0.0.

- The bits used to define the network portion of an IP address should not be all 0s. According to the RFCs, a host portion address of all 0s is interpreted as meaning "this," as in "this network." For example, the address 0.0.0.63 is interpreted as meaning Host 63 on this network.

- The Class A network number 127 is assigned the loopback function. This means that a datagram sent by a higher level protocol to a Network 127 address should be processed within the same host.

  In a UNIX environment, network sockets are used not only for communication with other computers, but also used for interprocess communication. If Program A wishes to communicate with Program B running on the same computer, it would do so using IP network number 127. No datagram should ever appear on any network with a source or destination network address of 127.

Sample Network Using Class A Address Format

Segments connected by switches share the same network fields, while having different host fields. Segments interconnected by routers must have different network fields, as illustrated on the Sample Class A Network Diagram.

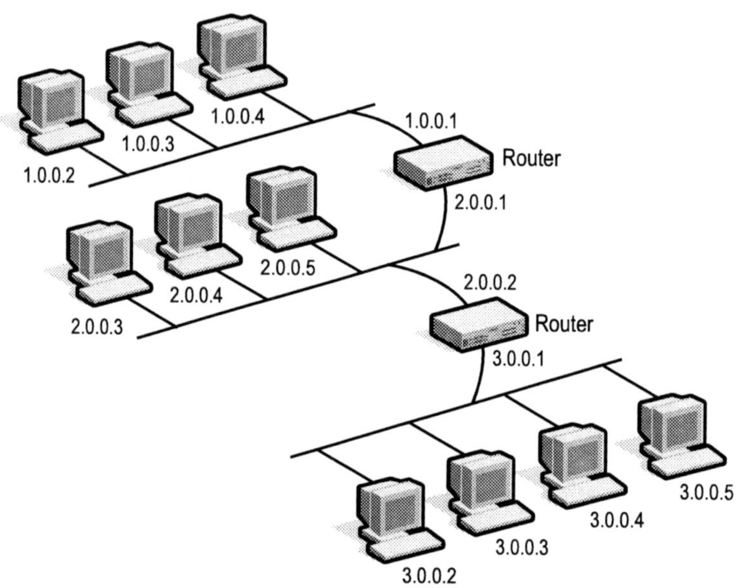

Sample Class A Network

In this example, we have three separate Class A networks, each using a different first octet number. We must connect these separate networks through routers for them to communicate. Routers, which are Layer 3 devices, route IP packets across networks based on source and destination addresses, such as IP logical addresses.

Whenever a host on the 2.0.0.0 network wishes to communicate with a host on the 1.0.0.0 network, it must first send its message to its local router port. The local router then determines the appropriate path to use to forward the packet along to the destination network.

The destination network router receives the packet sent from the originating router, and determines if the destination host is on its local network. If so, the destination router forwards the packet out its local network port to the destination host. If not, the router forwards the packet on to the next hop router in the packet's path.

Getting an IP Network Address

The process of assigning a network's IP address ranges from fairly simple to fairly complex, depending on how much Internet access is required.

Public Networks

Objective 1.4
Understand and be able to describe the infrastructure needed to support an Internet client.
… Operating system TCP/IP stack configuration
… Network connection
… Client software configuration

A public network consists of hosts that directly communicate with the rest of the global Internet. Thus, public network hosts must have globally unique IP addresses. To guarantee that each Internet host address is unique, all public IP addresses and World Wide Web domain names are administered by a central authority, the Internet Network Information Center (InterNIC), (**http:// www.networksolutions.com**).

When an ISP or big corporation wants to connect directly to the Internet, InterNIC assigns the organization the network portion of a numbered IP address. The ISP's network administrators then assign individual host addresses to their Internet devices (servers, routers, and any hosts that need direct access).

For security reasons, an organization will choose to not assign public IP addresses to many of its internal hosts. In that case, it may request a smaller range of unique IP addresses, enough for the routers and servers that relay traffic between the private network and the public Internet.

Private Networks

To the Internet community, a private network consists of nodes that have no direct access to the Internet. Private networks may use any IP addressing scheme that is convenient, because there is no chance of conflicting with other nodes in the Internet.

A small office with dial-up Internet access through an ISP is still a private network. That's because the ISP temporarily assigns one of its IP addresses to each new dial-up connection. When the ISP's router forwards traffic from a dial-up connection, it places that temporary address into those packets. So when a real estate broker dials in to surf the Web, the rest of the Internet sees the ISP's address, not the internal IP address of the broker's office PC.

For network administrators who prefer to be cautious, the following IP address ranges have been designated as private or reserved addresses. Internet routers do not route these address ranges, so they will not travel beyond the private network:

- 10.0.0.0 through 10.255.255.255

- 172.16.0.0 through 172.31.255.255

- 192.168.0.0 through 192.168.255.255

Organizations should use these private address ranges when:

- Network hosts do not require access to other enterprises or the Internet.

- Mediating gateways, such as Application Layer gateways, routers, or firewalls, can act on the network hosts' behalf. Hosts may only require limited Internet services, or the mediating gateway can translate private addresses to Internet routable public addresses. Each gateway must have a unique IP address, however.

Organizations benefit from using these private addresses by:

- Conserving globally unique IP addresses when this uniqueness is not required

- Gaining more network design flexibility, because a large address range is available

- Preventing address clashes when obtaining Internet access without obtaining a full range of assigned public addresses

Private IP addressing has its drawbacks, as well:

- To provide hosts future Internet access, you will have to renumber some hosts, or perform address translation at the Internet access point.

- In the case of a corporate merger, if all hosts on both networks use private IP addresses, you will likely have to reassign at least some of the host addresses.

Activities

1. Which are considered private IP addresses?
   (Choose all that apply.)

   a. 10.0.0.0

   b. 172.31.255.255

   c. 192.168.0.0

   d. 172.32.0.0

2. What does the Class network number 127.x.y.z designate?

   a. A private IP address

   b. A multicast address

   c. A loopback address

   d. An experimental address

3. Which two statements are true concerning IP addressing?
   (Choose two.)

   a. The host portion should not be all 1s.

   b. The network portion bits should usually be all 0s.

   c. The IP address range 172.16.0.0–172.31.255.255 is a public IP address range.

   d. The network portion bits should not be all 0s.

4. In which three ways do organizations benefit from using private IP addresses? (Choose three.)

   a. They conserve private IP addresses when uniqueness is required.

   b. They gain more network design flexibility with a large address range.

   c. They prevent Internet address clashes when obtaining only a small range of ICANN assigned addresses.

   d. They conserve public IP addresses when uniqueness is not required.

5. Which two of the following are considered reserved IP addresses? (Choose two.)

   a. 0.x.y.z

   b. 172.16.y.z

   c. 127.x.y.z

   d. 126.x.y.z

6. Fill in the blanks to the right of each address range with its IP Class.

   Class A

   Class B

   Class C

   Class D

   Class E

   a. 240.xxx.yyy.zzz through 247.xxx.yyy.zzz ________

   b. 128.001.hhh.hhh through 191.254.hhh.hhh ________

   c. 001.hhh.hhh.hhh through 127.hhh.hhh.hhh ________

   d. 224.000.000.000 through 239.255.255.255 ________

   e. 192.000.001.hhh through 223.255.254.hhh ________

Extended Activity

Visit the Internet Network Information Center (**http://www.net worksolutions.com**) to learn more about the process of assigning Internet IP addresses.

Lesson 5—Subnetting Fundamentals

Subnets are logical subdivisions of a single Internet network number. For technical or administrative reasons, many organizations divide their TCP/IP networks into several smaller network segments. We use networking devices, such as routers, to connect these smaller networks. The main advantage of subnetting is to provide IP addressing flexibility.

Objectives

At the end of this lesson you will be able to:

- Explain why subnet addressing is necessary

- Explain basic subnetting principles

- Describe IP broadcast addresses

 **Key Point**

A subnet is a network subdivision, and a single broadcast domain.

The Value of Subnetting

*Objective 1.4
Understand and be able to describe the infrastructure needed to support an Internet client
...Operating system TCP/IP stack configuration
... Network connection
... Client software configuration*

The Network Layer is responsible for moving data through internetworks. Remember that for devices to communicate over a routed network, their network protocols must supply them a Layer 3 address. Through the Layer 3 protocols, organizations build a hierarchical addressing scheme. This hierarchical addressing allows networks to easily scale from few to many hosts, and to span across geographical locations. Network Layer protocols provide a means of routing data between networks, and work with Layer 3 devices to control broadcast traffic.

When an organization does not need Internet access, they can build their TCP/IP network with the three private IP address ranges. However, when an organization wishes to connect to the Internet, they must lease or purchase a routable Class A, B, or C network number from their ISP, carrier, or the Internet Corporation for Assigned Names and Numbers (ICANN).

The IP Address Crisis

The world is running short of IPv4 addresses. In fact, if each organization needing Internet access used an entire Class A, B, or C network address, fewer than 17 million network segments could be uniquely addressed before all the IPv4 network addresses were depleted. Additionally, many host addresses would be wasted in the process. For example, if a small organization of 256 hosts owned an entire Class B address, they would leave over 65,000 host addresses unused. Subnetting, along with Classless Interdomain Routing (CIDR) and Network Address Translation (NAT) has helped mitigate this problem by allowing organizations to segment their TCP/IP networks and more efficiently utilize their available host addresses.

Why Multiple Network Segments?

There are good reasons why an organization would need multiple network segments. If they grow significantly, their local network segment traffic can increase to the point where it becomes unmanageable. Many businesses run networks consisting of several hundred segments, all assigned their own network addresses. These addresses usually come from a larger single network address, such as a Class A or B address. Global enterprises need some method of communicating between remote sites. If they wish to communicate over the public Internet, they must somehow break up their assigned network addresses. Subnetting allows network administrators to break up a single network address into smaller network addresses, creating router-connected network segments, all with their own unique network address space.

Interconnection of TCP/IP Networks

Objective 1.4
Understand and be able to describe the infrastructure needed to support an Internet client.
… Operating system TCP/IP stack configuration
… Network connection
… Client software configuration

To interconnect multiple TCP/IP networks across routers, we must assign each network a different network address. We may create subnets from any of the Class A, B, or C network addresses.

For example, in the Subnet Addressing Diagram, the network's administrator has created two subnetworks from a single Class B network address, 135.15.0.0, by using the network address's third byte (135.15.x.0). The router receives all inbound traffic for Network 135.15.0.0 and selects the correct outbound interface based on this subnetted third byte (the subnet identifier, or subnet portion, of the network address).

If the network had not been broken into subnets, it would have required each network segment to have a separate Class B network address. Depending on the number of hosts on each segment, many host addresses could have remained unused.

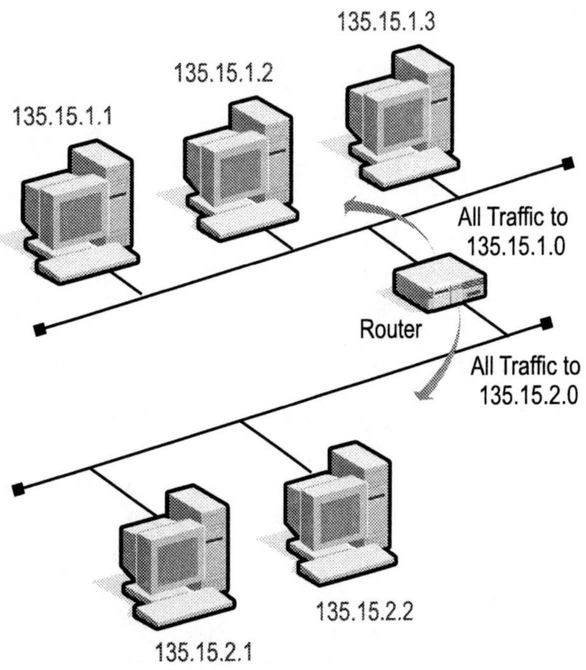

Subnet Addressing

When we subnet, we divide an IP network address's host portion into two parts, as shown on the Subnetted Address Diagram:

- One left part is used to identify the subnet address portion.

- One right part is used to identify the host address portion.

Original Network Address

Network Portion	Host Portion

Subnetted Network Address

Network Portion	Subnet Portion	Host Portion

Subnetted Address

We subnet by borrowing bits from the host address portion to create the subnet address portion. Recall that a router uses the network portion to determine the network on which a host resides:

- Class A network portion—the first octet

- Class B network portion—the first and second octets

- Class C network portion—the first, second, and third octets

The remaining octet(s) are the host portion, which identifies the destination node. Network devices determine these portions using the network mask.

The Network Mask

Objective 1.4
Understand and be able to describe the infrastructure needed to support an Internet client.
...Operating system TCP/IP stack configuration
... Network connection
... Client software configuration

A network mask (net mask) is a 32-bit binary number network device used to isolate an IP address's network portion from its host portion. Each IP address class is assigned a default net mask, as shown in the Default Network Masks Table.

Default Network Masks

Class	Dotted Decimal	Binary
A	255.0.0.0	11111111.00000000.00000000.00000000
B	255.255.0.0	11111111.11111111.00000000.00000000
C	255.255.255.0	11111111.11111111.11111111.00000000

Note the octets in each class where the net mask reads 255 (all binary 1s) and where it reads 0 (all binary 0s). In Class A addresses, the first octet reads "255," while the last three octets read "0.0.0." The binary 1s in the mask designate the network portion, and the binary 0s designate the host portion.

Creating Subnets

A subnet mask is a modified net mask that extends into a network address's host portion. Just as we use the default net mask to determine the network address portion of an IP address, we can use extended net masks to create subnet masks. We use the subnet mask to determine which bits from an address's host portion define the subnet portion. This subnet portion then becomes part of the subnetted network address's network portion.

What does all that mean? Let us return to the Subnet Addressing Diagram. We have broken up the 135.15.0.0 Class B network into two separate subnetworks. We did this by borrowing 8 bits from the default host portion and assigning them to the network portion. So instead of using the default Class B net mask of 255.255.0.0, our new net mask includes the third octet in the network portion: 255.255.255.0.

The Subnet Addressing Diagram shows that the network is now divided into two subnetworks:

- 135.15.1.x

- 135.15.2.x

The remaining eight host bits are then used to address individual hosts in each resulting subnetwork.

Since we borrowed eight bits from the sixteen host bits originally provided by our Class B address, we could define many more subnetwork numbers. When it's not necessary to create so many subnetworks, the administrator simply borrows fewer bits from the host portion of the address. For example, if we borrow only four host bits from a Class B address, here's how the resulting network mask looks in both binary and dotted-decimal formats:

Default net mask	11111111 11111111 00000000 00000000	255.255.0.0
Subnetted mask	11111111 11111111 11110000 00000000	255.255.240.0

IP Prefixes

We can represent the subnet mask in another manner, as a prefix rather than a dotted decimal value. Rather than writing the above subnet mask in dotted decimal format, we can represent the same mask as "/20." The number /20 represents the total number of the subnet mask bits set to 1. Therefore, if we want to represent address 192.14.16.8, and show that the subnet mask for that address is 255.255.255.240, we can write it as 192.14.16.8/28.

IP Broadcast Addresses

As we learned earlier, the network and/or host IP address portions cannot be set to all 1s. This is because those bit patterns represent broadcast addresses, which are special purpose addresses networks used to pass data to multiple destinations simultaneously.

There are four IP broadcast address types:

- Limited broadcast—The address is set to 255.255.255.255. This address is used for configuring hosts at startup, such as when a host obtains an IP address from a Dynamic Host Configuration Protocol (DHCP) or Bootstrap Protocol (BOOTP) server.

- Nondirected broadcast—This address takes the form *netid*.255.255.255 (for example, *126.255.255.255*). Networks use this address to send packets to all hosts on a specific network segment.

- Subnet-directed broadcast—In a subnetted network, a subnet-directed broadcast is limited to only those hosts on the specified subnet.

- All-subnets-directed broadcasts—On a subnetted internetwork, network devices can send broadcasts to all hosts on all subnets. This is now considered obsolete, and has been replaced by Class D multicast addresses.

Limited Broadcast

A packet sent to IP address 255.255.255.255 is classified as a "limited broadcast" packet. In a broadcast packet destined for the local network, the destination address network and host portions are all 1s (255.255.255.255). Limited broadcasts should never pass through a router, only through repeaters and Medium Access Control (MAC) Layer bridges.

Directed Broadcast

A packet sent to a destination IP address where only the host portion of the IP address is all 1s, such as 180.100.255.255, is classified as a "directed broadcast" packet. Directed broadcasts may pass through a router and are broadcast to all hosts on the target network. A directed broadcast can be a network-directed or sub-network-directed broadcast:

- A network-directed broadcast IP address has the host portion of the IP address as all 1s and a valid network portion. The broadcast reaches all hosts on the network.

- A subnetwork-directed broadcast IP address has the host portion of the IP address as all 1s, a valid network portion, and a valid subnet portion. The broadcast reaches all hosts on the subnet.

CIDR

Objective 1.4
Understand and be able to describe the infrastructure needed to support an Internet client ... Operating system TCP/IP stack configuration ... Network connection ... Client software configuration

The Internet continues to nearly double in size every year. Studies performed in the early 1990s indicated that by mid-1994, Internet router routing tables would have reached their maximum theoretical size of 60,000 entries, effectively shutting down Internet growth. Additionally, too many addresses went unused. The default Class B address ranges supplied more addresses than most single organizations could use, and Class C address ranges supplied too few. Therefore, organizations had no choice but to obtain a Class B range, and hold many unused addresses in reserve.

Classless Interdomain Routing (CIDR) is designed to resolve these two issues. CIDR supports address summarization, or aggregation. Address aggregation assigns a network provider a contiguous Class C address block. The provider then suballocates these blocks to their customers. The provider's Internet routers only advertise routes to the aggregate block's network address, not the individual customer addresses. This reduces the number of routing table entries.

Additionally, CIDR provides more flexible address assignments, allowing organizations to more efficiently cover their host addressing requirements by obtaining consecutive Class C addresses, rather than a single Class B. CIDR treats these consecutive addresses as a single, aggregate supernetwork.

How CIDR Works

CIDR restructures the old, class oriented routing process of assigning Class A, B, and C addresses. Instead of limiting addresses to network portions 8, 16, or 24 bits long, CIDR provides prefixes from 13 to 27 bits in length. Administrators can assign address blocks to as few as 32 hosts, or to over 500,000. These address block assignments can much more closely fit an organization's specific addressing needs.

A CIDR address includes the standard 32-bit-long IP address and information on how many bits compose the network prefix. For example, the CIDR address 207.14.3.48/25 represents the first 25 address bits as the address's network portion, leaving the remaining bits as host bits. The CIDR Prefixes Table lists the CIDR prefixes, the number of Class C addresses each creates, and the number of hosts per network.

CIDR Prefixes

CIDR Prefix	Number of Equivalent Class C Networks	Number of Host Addresses per Network
/27	1/8 of a Class C	32
/26	1/4 of a Class C	64
/25	1/2 of a Class C	128
/24	1	256
/23	2	512
/22	4	1,024
/21	8	2,048
/20	16	4,096
/19	32	8,192
/18	64	16,384
/17	128	32,768
/16	256 (1 Class B)	65,536
/15	512	131,072
/14	1,024	262,144
/13	2,048	524,288

CIDR is based on supernetting, which is essentially subnetting in reverse. Recall that subnetting incorporates bits borrowed from the host portion into an address's network portion. On the other hand, supernetting allows us to move the network portion to the left, giving more bits to the host portion. This classless supernetting technique reduces the number of routing table entries carriers present to the Internet routing domain, aggregating a group of smaller, class oriented networks into one larger, single routing table entry.

Large ISPs obtain address blocks prefixed with 15 or more bits (512 Class Cs, 131,072 hosts). They then suballocate these blocks to their customers with /27 to /19 prefixes; this suballocation process is called nesting. In turn, these customers may suballocate, or nest, their blocks even further.

An important concept concerning CIDR is that the ISP's routers only advertise the ISP's single address block; any Internet traffic destined for the nested customer address blocks routes first to the ISP's router interfaces. The ISP's internal routers route the customer traffic to their individual networks.

Activities

1. Represent the following subnet masks with the appropriate IP prefixes.

    a. 255.224.0.0

    ____

    b. 255.254.0.0

    ____

    c. 255.255.128.0

    ____

    d. 255.255.248.0

    ____

    e. 255.255.254.0

    ____

    f. 255.255.255.192

    ____

2. How does CIDR allocate IP addresses more efficiently?

    ____

    ____

    ____

    ____

3. Explain the difference between a default net mask and a subnet mask.

    ____

    ____

    ____

    ____

4. Explain the difference between a limited and a directed broadcast address.

____

____

____

____

____

____

____

Extended Activities

1. What is the binary equivalent of this subnet mask: 255.255.240.0

2. If the subnet mask above is applied to a Class B address, how many bits does it borrow from the host portion of the address?

3. If the network administrator needs to borrow two additional bits from the host portion (in addition to those bits already borrowed), what would the new network mask look like, in both binary and dotted-decimal?

Lesson 6—IP Routing

The Internet is a large collection of networks and hosts intercon-nected by routers. Routers are specialized computers that connect two or more packet-switching networks.

Routers function as intermediate packet switches that forward traffic from one network to another. Routers are also called gate-ways in Internet literature. The Transmission Control Protocol/Internet Protocol (TCP/IP) protocol suite was designed to provide communication services that allow an individual host to commu-nicate with any other host on any of the networks that make up the Internet or an enterprise internet.

Note: The term "internet," noncapitalized, refers to any TCP/IP internetwork. This term is often used to describe two or more networks interconnected using TCP/IP technology and proto-cols, not necessarily connected to the global Internet.

Objectives

At the end of this lesson you will be able to:

- Describe the Internet architecture
- Compare direct and indirect routing
- Describe the basic model of operation for the Internet
- Explain static, default, and dynamic routes

Key Point

Routers connect two or more packet-switching networks.

Overview of Internet Architecture

Objective 3.1
Understand and be able to describe the core components of the Internet infra-structure
… Hardware/soft-ware infrastructure knowledge
… Internetworking devices such as rout-ers, switches, and bridges.

If a host on one network wishes to communicate with a host on another network, the source host must transmit the packet to a router directly connected to its local network. After receiving a datagram, the router forwards the packet through the intercon-nected system of networks and routers until it eventually reaches a router attached to the same network as the destination host. This final router delivers the packet to the specified host on its local network. The Internet Architecture Overview Diagram illus-trates a routed network.

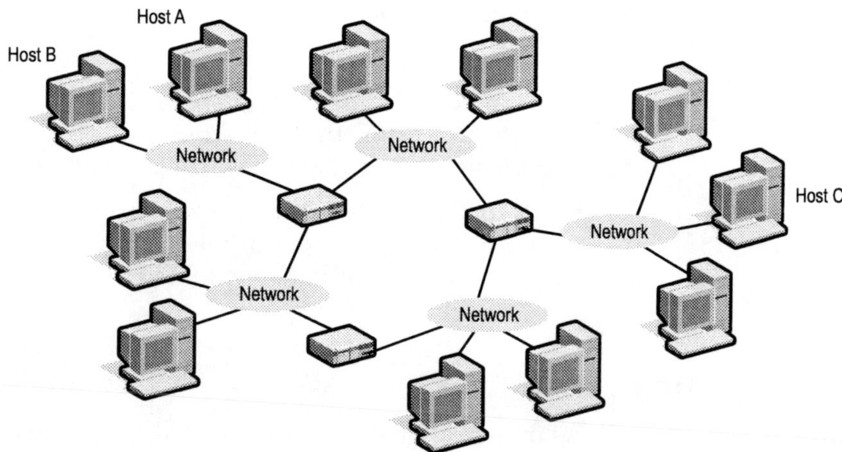

Internet Architecture Overview

Host A can communicate directly with Host B because they are both attached to the same physical network. However, if Host A wishes to communicate with Host C, Host A must transmit the datagram to the nearest exit router, also known as the default gateway, to the outside networks. This gateway router then injects the datagram into the system of routers that connect the internet-work. The datagram is passed from router to router until it even-tually reaches the router attached to the same physical network as Host C. This final router uses the services provided by the local network to deliver the datagram to Host C.

A router makes its forwarding decisions based on the information contained in the router's routing table. This information includes the destination network number, rather than the actual physical address of each destination host. Because the routing table is based on network numbers rather than host addresses, the amount of information a router needs to maintain its routing table is directly proportional to the number of networks that make up the internetwork. This reduces the routing table's size, because a router does not have to maintain information about every single host connected to the internetwork.

Router Characteristics

For many purposes, you can consider "router" and "gateway" synonyms. More specifically, a router is a host that connects subnetworks within a network, while a gateway is a router that links a network to a larger intranet or the Internet.

A router is simply a host that has two specific characteristics:

- A router is "multihomed," because it has at least two network interface cards. In other words, it is a member of more than one network, and can pass packets between them.

- A router is programmed with the IDs of other subnets and networks within the internet. A router uses this information, stored in its routing table, to determine the best path for each packet it must forward.

Direct Routing

A computer on any physical network can transmit a datagram to any other computer on the same network; this type of communication does not require the services of a router. To transmit an IP datagram, the host encapsulates the datagram in a physical frame, uses Address Resolution Protocol (ARP) to map the destination IP address to a media address, and uses the network hardware to deliver the datagram.

To determine whether a host lies on a directly connected network, the source host must examine the network portion of the destination IP address. The source host compares the destination network number to its own network number. If they are the same, the datagram can be sent directly. If they differ, the source host must send the datagram to a router for delivery. The concept of direct routing is illustrated on the Direct Routing Diagram.

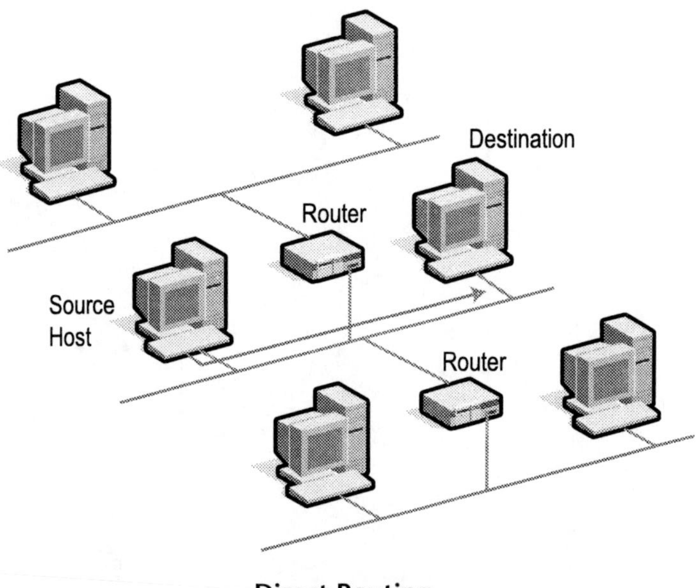

Direct Routing

Indirect Routing

Objective 1.4

*Understand and be able to describe the infrastructure needed to support an Internet client.
… Operating system TCP/IP stack configuration
… Client software configuration*

Objective 3.1

*Understand and be able to describe the core components of the Internet infrastructure.
… Hardware/software infrastructure knowledge
… Internetworking devices such as routers, switches, and bridges.*

Indirect routing occurs when the destination is not on a directly attached network. Indirect routing requires that the source host send the datagram to a router for delivery. This type of routing is more complex because the source host must identify not only the final destination, but also a router through which the datagram can pass. It is then the router's job to forward the datagram toward its destination network. Indirect routing is illustrated on the Indirect Routing Diagram.

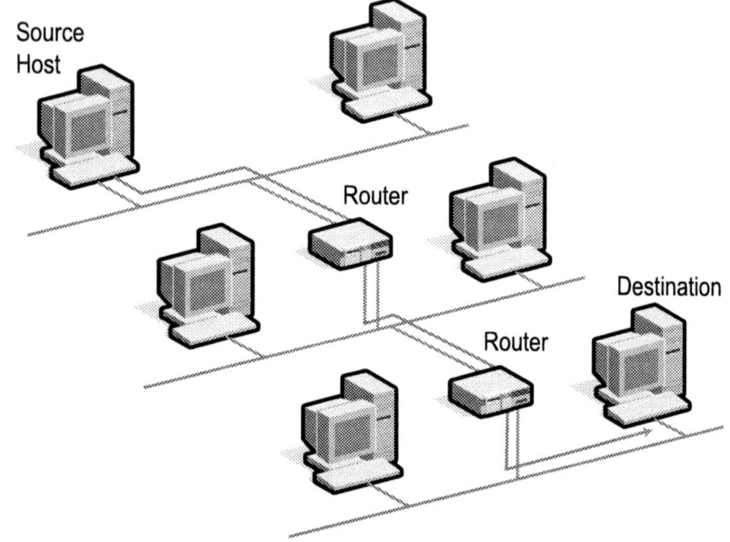

Indirect Routing

There are three different types of indirect routing:

- Static routing—These routes are configured by the network administrator. They have the benefit of reduced router overhead, no bandwidth usage passing updates between routers, and added security. Disadvantages include high administrative overhead updating and maintaining the routing entries and poor scalability on large networks.

- Default routing—These are manually configured routes designed to send any packets without an assigned route to the next hop router by means of a default router port. These can only be used on routers with a single outside interface.

- Dynamic routing—These are routes built by routers sharing routing information. Dynamic routes use routing protocols to exchange routing information updates. Some dynamic routing protocols are Routing Information Protocol (RIP), Interior Gateway Routing Protocol (IGRP), and Open Shortest Path First (OSPF).

Static Routing

In static routing, a network administrator must sit down at a router console or Telnet session and enter each destination network and the associated next hop address. Static routes are best used on stub networks, that is, networks with only one entry and exit point.

By defining static routes, we can ensure that our packets only take one path to their destination. This could be preferential routing behavior if we only wanted our packets to traverse a particular link between networks. Static routes also protect network topology information, providing added network security. As you will see, dynamic routing protocols share network topology information with other routers, exposing information about the internal network we might want to protect. Static routes share no information between routers.

Characteristics of static routing include the following:

- The network administrator keeps a table of networks, and manually updates these tables whenever there is a change within the routing domain.

- Static systems do not operate well in an environment of rapid growth or change. Routing tables cannot be completely responsive in case of failure, because backup routes may need to use the resources of a failed network or device.

- As new networks are added and the physical topology changes, every router in the routing domain must have its tables manually updated. This can require a tremendous amount of time on the part of the network administrator.

Errors in the configuration of static routing tables in large networks may not be easy to find or correct. Static routes require the network administrator to have a good understanding of the network's topology.

Default Routing

If a router cannot find a path for a datagram in its routing table, the router is required to discard the packet. A default route allows the router to pass a packet on to a default gateway instead of discarding it.

The special address 0.0.0.0/0 is used to describe a default route. If a path to a destination network cannot be located and a default route has been defined, the routing routines will forward the datagram to the default router the default route defines.

Default routes are generally used to reduce the size of a routing table. As a result, routing is simplified, because it consists of a few tests for local networks and a default for all other destinations. Another advantage of default routes is that the size of the routing table update messages exchanged between routers can be substantially reduced. Some disadvantages of default routes include the possible creation of multiple paths, creation of routing loops, and misconfigurations.

Dynamic Routing

Dynamic routing protocols allow associated routers to share routing information among themselves. Routers that use dynamic routing protocols respond automatically to changes in the network topology, by informing each other of changes, then adding or deleting entries from their routing tables.

Dynamic routing allows routers to choose the best of a number of possible routes between networks based on metrics such as hop count, bandwidth, delay, and other variables. We can implement load balancing and fault tolerance using dynamic routing. Dynamic routing is much less administration intensive than static or default routes.

However, these advantages come at a price. Dynamic routing updates use router resources, in the form of increased central processing unit (CPU) and memory usage, when building and sharing routing table updates, and increased network bandwidth usage when routers send and receive updates to and from other routers.

Dynamic routing presents network management challenges as well, primarily in the form of routing loops. It takes time for routing updates to propagate among all the internetwork routers. Thus, it is possible for a router or routers to believe they have a good route to a network where, in fact, the link has failed. This routing table update propagation is called convergence, and the faster the protocol can converge, the better. If the routers have not yet converged their routing tables with other routers in the network, a routing loop can occur.

Building the Routing Table

Typically, most routers use a combination of static and dynamic techniques to obtain information needed for their routing tables. Each router first establishes an initial set of routes. This information is usually obtained by reading a basic routing table from disk at startup. The information for this table is supplied by the network administrator and generally includes the attached networks and possibly some static routes to remote networks. Another way a router might learn initial routing information is by broadcasting to other routers requests for their routing table contents.

After the initial routing table has become memory resident, the router must have the ability to respond to new routes or changes in the network topology. In a small network, the routing table may be managed and updated by the network administrator (static routes). For large networks, such as the ever-growing and evolving Internet, manual updating is too slow and labor intensive, and thus a dynamic method must be used.

The Sample Routing Table Entry Diagram illustrates a sample routing table entry. This is a typical entry for a routing protocol such as RIP, which uses hop count as the routing metric.

Sample Routing Table Entry

Each entry in the routing table includes the following information that determines how a packet is routed if the router chooses that particular route:

- Destination Address—IP address of the destination network, subnets, or host.

- Next Router—IP address of a remote router to which the local router must send the packet before the packet can be routed to the destination. This is the IP address of the next hop router.

- Hop Count—Number of hops between the router and destination. Each router a packet must pass through is referred to as a hop.

- Owner—Name of the routing protocol that supplied the entry in the routing table.

- Time—Amount of time since the entry was last updated. The timer is reinitialized each time an update for a given network is received. This information "ages out" old routes.

Fundamental IP routers maintain a routing database containing only one route for each possible destination network. Some implementations, however, may contain more than one route to a destination network. The example in the diagram contains three routes to the destination network.

Sample Network Routing Table

The Sample Small Internet Diagram illustrates a small internetwork composed of four networks and three routers. The hosts attached to each network are not shown, because each router makes its forwarding decision based on a network number, not on each individual host address. Again, a router uses ARP to find the physical address that corresponds to the IP address for any host or router on its directly attached networks.

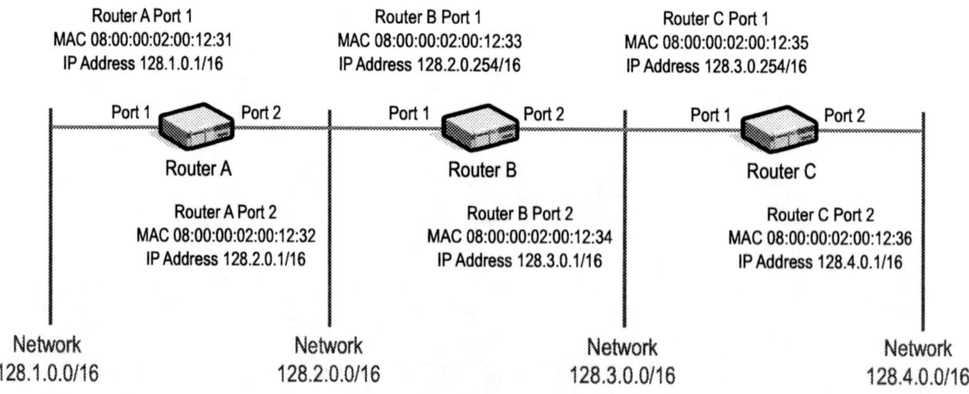

Sample Small Internet

The routing tables for each router shown on the earlier diagram are presented in the Routing Tables for Routers A, B, and C. The routing tables contain one entry (row) for each route. The columns of the tables include the destination IP network number, IP address of the next hop router, and metric (shown in hops, but metrics can take many forms) used to select the least cost by route if more than one route exists for the destination network.

Routing Table for Router A

Destination Network	Next Hop Router	Metric (Hops)
128.1.0.0	Direct Port 1	0
128.2.0.0	Direct Port 2	0
128.3.0.0	128.2.0.3	1
128.4.0.0	128.2.0.3	2

Routing Table for Router B

Destination Network	Next Hop Router	Metric (Hops)
128.1.0.0	128.2.0.2	1
128.2.0.0	Direct Port 1	0
128.3.0.0	Direct Port 2	0
128.4.0.0	128.3.0.3	1

Routing Table for Router C

Destination Network	Next Hop Router	Metric (Hops)
128.1.0.0	128.3.0.2	2
128.2.0.0	128.3.0.2	1
128.3.0.0	Direct Port 1	0
128.4.0.0	Direct Port 2	0

How Routers Move Packets Between Networks

Objective 1.4
Understand and be able to describe the infrastructure needed to support an Internet client ...Operating system TCP/IP stack configuration ... Client software configuration

Objective 3.1
Understand and be able to describe the core components of the Internet infrastructure ... Hardware/software infrastructure knowledge ... Internetworking devices such as routers, switches, and bridges.

The model of operation for transmitting a datagram from one host to another over an internetwork is shown on the Sample Topology of Transmission Over an Internet Diagram. This example involves a source host (Host A), destination host (Host B), three intermediate routers, and four distinct physical networks. The IP and Ethernet addresses for each host and router port are also presented.

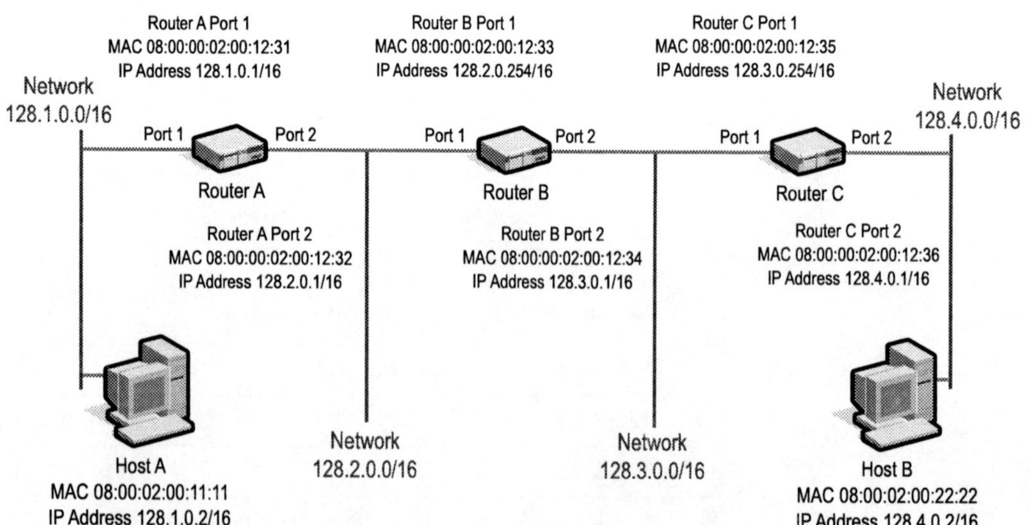

Sample Topology of Transmission Over an Internet

The Internet can be viewed as a large virtual network with the IP datagram taking the place of the network frame. The path a datagram takes is not determined by a central source, but is the result of examining each routing table used in the journey. Each router defines only the next hop in the path and relies on the next hop router to send the IP packet on its way. Intermediate routers pass the datagram up to the IP layer, which routes it back out again onto a different network. Only when the datagram reaches the final destination does the local IP process extract the message and pass it up to the higher protocol layers.

Host A

Host A on Network 128.1.0.0 wishes to make a connection to Host B on Network 128.4.0.0 using the Telnet protocol (illustrated on the next four diagrams). As the packet moves from router to router, the next four diagrams show how the IP header defined by Host A remains constant and does not change. The only addresses that change as the packet moves toward its final destination are the source and destination Ethernet addresses.

Packet on Network 128.1.0.0

Because Host A and Host B are on different networks, Host A must perform indirect routing and use the services of an IP router. Upon initialization, Host A has learned that the IP address of its default gateway is 128.1.0.1. As a result, Host A knows it must use Router A to transmit a packet to any host residing on a different network. If Host A does not have an entry in its ARP cache for device 128.1.0.1, it will issue an ARP request and wait for Router A to respond.

When it has an ARP cache entry for its default router port, Host A transmits an Ethernet frame with a destination Medium Access Control (MAC) address of 08:00:02:00:12:31 (Router A), source MAC address of 08:00:02:00:11:11 (Host A), and Type field of 0800h (IP). The structure of the packet placed on Network 128.1.0.0 is shown on the Packet on Network 128.1.0.0 Diagram.

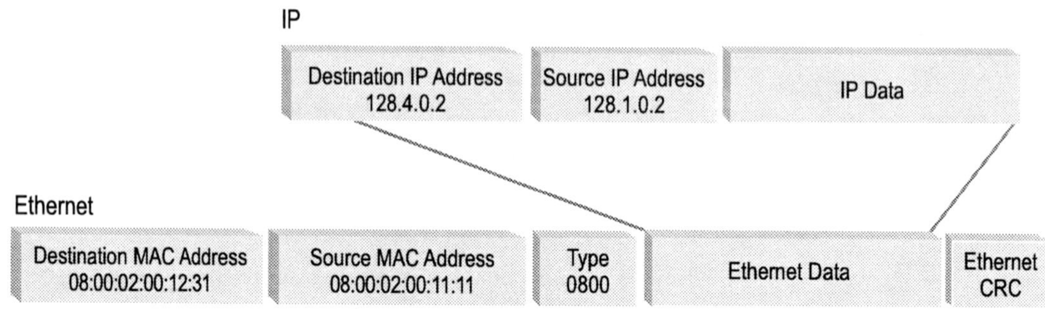

Packet on Network 128.1.0.0

Packet on Network 128.2.0.0

Upon receipt of the packet, Router A removes the Ethernet header and passes the datagram to its IP process. The IP process examines the destination network number contained in the IP header, and locates the route to Network 128.4.0.0 in its routing table (see Routing Table for Router A).

Router A knows that the destination network is two hops away, and that it must forward the datagram to Router B at IP address 128.2.0.254. If Router A does not have the address mapping in its ARP cache, it makes an ARP request and waits for Router B to respond.

Finally, Router A transmits an Ethernet frame on Port 2 with a destination MAC address of 08:00:02:00:12:33 (Router B) and a source MAC address of 08:00:02:00:12:32 (Port 2 of Router A). The structure of the packet placed on Network 128.2.0.0 is shown on the Packet on Network 128.2.0.0 Diagram.

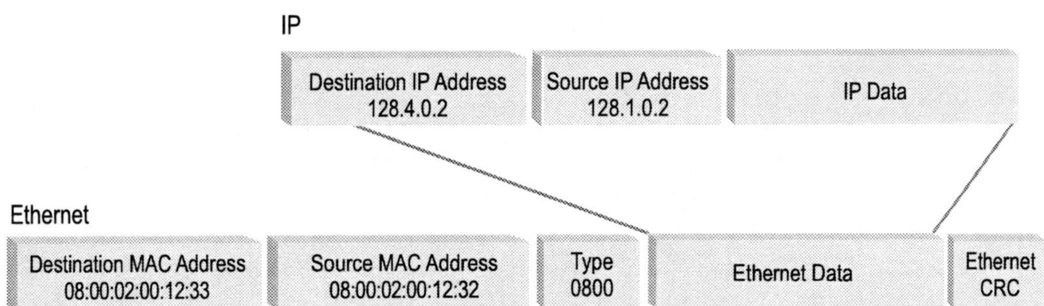

Packet on Network 128.2.0.0

Packet on Network 128.3.0.0

Upon receiving the packet, Router B removes the Ethernet header and passes the datagram to its IP process. The Router B IP process examines the destination network number contained in the IP header and locates the route to Network 128.4.0.0 in its routing table (see Routing Table for Router B). Router B learns that the destination network is one hop away, and that it must forward the datagram to Router C at IP address 128.3.0.254. If Router B does not have the address mapping in its ARP cache, it makes an ARP request, and waits for Router C to respond.

When the mapping is obtained, Router B builds and transmits an Ethernet frame on Port 2 with a destination MAC address of 08:00:02:00:12:35 (Router C) and source MAC address of 08:00:02:00:12:34 (Router B Port 2). The packet's structure for Network 128.3.0.0 is shown on the Packet on Network 128.3.0.0 Diagram.

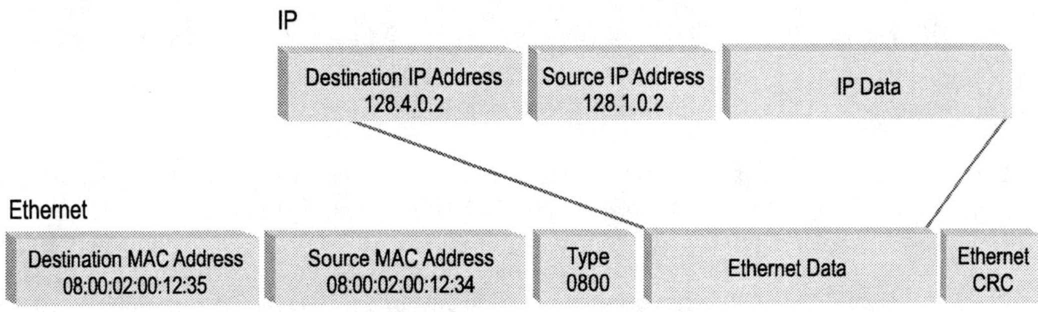

Packet on Network 128.3.0.0

Note: Although the MAC addresses change from hop to hop, the destination and source host IP addresses in the IP datagram never change.

Packet on Network 128.4.0.0

Upon receipt of the packet, Router C removes the Ethernet header and passes the datagram to its IP process. The IP process examines the destination network number in the IP header, and locates the route to network 128.4.0.0 in its routing table (see Routing Table for Router C).

Router C discovers that the destination network is directly connected to its own Port 2, and that it does not need to send the datagram to another router. In other words, Router C can deliver the datagram directly. If Router C does not have the address mapping in its ARP cache, it makes an ARP request and waits for Host B to respond.

When it has the mapping, Router C builds and transmits an Ethernet frame on Port 2 with a destination MAC address of 08:00:02:00:22:22 (Host B) and source MAC address of 08:00:02:00:12:36 (Port 2 of Router C). The structure of the packet placed on Network 128.4.0.0 is shown on the Packet on Network 128.4.0.0 Diagram.

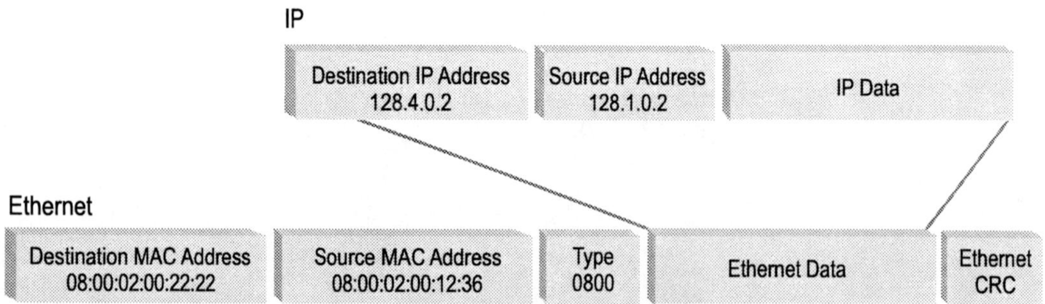

Packet on Network 128.4.0.0

Host B

Host B receives the packet, removes the Ethernet header, and passes the request to the IP module. The IP process determines that the datagram is addressed to the local host, removes the IP header, and passes the datagram to TCP for further processing. TCP examines the port number and passes the datagram to the input queue for the Telnet process.

Activity

This exercise demonstrates how frames, packets, and port addresses are used together in a TCP/IP network. Refer to the diagram below and fill in the table. Note that there will always be one port number associated with the sending and receiving applications. There will always be one IP number; however, there may be multiple local area network (LAN) IDs because frames are built when packets are sent across a network.

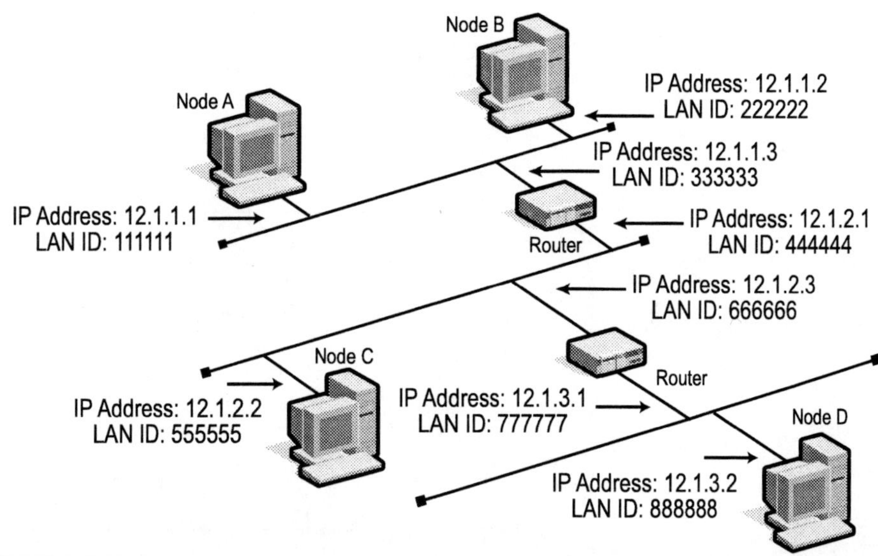

FTP Port = 21 Telnet Port = 23	Direct or Indirect Routing	Source Port	Destination Port	Source IP	Destination IP	Source LAN IDs	Destination LAN IDs
FTP from A to B							
FTP from A to C							
FTP from A to D							
FTP from D to B							
Telnet from D to C							
Telnet from D to A							

Extended Activity

1. Research and summarize the following Requests for Comments (RFCs):

   a. RFC 791

   ____

   ____

   ____

   ____

   b. RFC 793

   ____

   ____

   ____

   ____

   c. RFC 768

   ____

   ____

   ____

   ____

Summary

This unit introduced the key TCP/IP protocols, specifically those used to move application information between source and destination computers across the Internet.

We began by looking at IP, which is a connectionless, Network Layer protocol. The main service of IP is to forward packets across multiple networks. Each IP process that receives a packet must determine whether to process it or forward it to the next network on the way to its destination. While IP makes internetwork communication possible, it is not reliable. As a best-effort protocol, IP simply attempts to deliver packets. If a packet is damaged, IP cannot request a retransmission. If a packet is lost, IP does not know about it.

UDP is a connectionless Transport Layer protocol that uses IP to move information between applications using port numbers. The port numbers identify the applications using the TCP/IP network. Because UDP is connectionless, it relies on Application Layer protocols to handle error processing and sequencing of information. UDP handles packet sequencing, but does not provide reliable transmission.

TCP is the connection-oriented counterpart to UDP. It also uses well-known port numbers to establish connections between nodes, and sequences packets. However, TCP provides reliable transmission by acknowledging every packet.

Other protocols cooperate with these major protocols, or enhance their effectiveness. ARP resolves logical IP addresses to physical (NIC) addresses. ICMP provides feedback that both users and network devices can use to help resolve network problems. Ping is a common IP utility that uses ICMP messages.

IPv6 is an ongoing project designed to resolve many limitations imposed by the commonly used IPv4. IPv6 provides for more addresses and provides better built-in QoS functions. IPv6 can translate IPv4 addresses and tunnel over existing IPv4 router connections.

Unit 4 Quiz

1. An Application Layer utility transmits network administration and control messages between nodes. It must not use any more of the network's bandwidth than absolutely necessary. If messages are corrupted or lost, the utility handles retransmission, so it doesn't need this service from the lower layers. This application should use the services of:

   a. TCP

   b. UDP

   c. ICMP

   d. RARP

2. A Ping command uses which ICMP message types? (Choose two.)

   a. Echo Request

   b. Source quench

   c. Redirect

   d. Echo Reply

3. Which best describes IP's use of the TTL value?

   a. The TTL designates how long the sending host has been online.

   b. The TTL specifies the time a datagram is allowed to remain on the network.

   c. The TTL designates the number of seconds the packet has been on the network segment.

   d. The TTL counts the number of seconds a datagram has been queued at each router.

4. Which three of the following applications use UDP services? (Choose three.)

   a. FTP

   b. TFTP

   c. SNMP

   d. DNS

5. Which best describes the UDP demultiplexing process?

    a. UDP enables the destination host to route received packets across multiple IP addresses.

    b. UDP uses link numbers to allow multiple applications to communicate simultaneously on the same host.

    c. UDP uses port numbers to allow multiple applications to communicate simultaneously on the same host.

    d. UDP allows multiple hosts to communicate across a single, virtual circuit.

6. Which three choices are TCP features? (Choose three.)

    a. Best effort packet delivery

    b. Flow control

    c. Packet error recovery

    d. Demultiplexing multiple applications

7. Which statement best describes TCP's use of sequence numbers?

    a. They identify the next expected sequence number.

    b. They identify the next application the source wishes to contact.

    c. They specify the number of SYN bits the host has received during the current session.

    d. They identify the sequence number of the first data byte in the segment.

8. Which addresses combine to create a TCP socket?

    a. MAC and IP

    b. IP and port

    c. Port and MAC

    d. Port and application

9. The main reason for the creation of IP version 6 is:

    a. IPv4 is too slow

    b. Internet video requires packet prioritization

    c. IPv4 does not provide enough unique addresses

    d. Jumbograms are now standard on most LANs

10. At which two points in a one-way, multiple hop, end-to-end IP communications session will a frame have to be built? (Choose two.)

    a. At the receiving host's LAN port

    b. At each hop's router outbound port

    c. At the sending host's LAN port

    d. At each hop's router inbound port

Unit 5
TCP/IP Applications and Services

"TCP/IP" represents the names of two protocols developed for the original Advanced Research Projects Agency Network (ARPANET). However, the term is often used to denote entire suites of protocols, software, and applications that are standard parts of many operating systems (OSs).

This unit introduces the core TCP/IP applications and services that provide the underlying functionality of many Web sites. These protocols and services, such as Hypertext Transfer Protocol (HTTP), File Transfer Protocol (FTP), and Telnet, logically form the Open Systems Interconnection (OSI) model Application Layer.

Each TCP/IP application uses its own Application Layer protocol. For example, the Telnet application uses the Telnet protocol to allow a user to log in to a remote computer. But the FTP application on the same computer uses the FTP protocol to download files from an FTP server.

Lessons

1. HTTP

2. Telnet

3. File Transfer: FTP

4. Messaging: E-Mail and News

5. IP Address Management: BOOTP, DHCP, and NAT

6. IP Name Resolution: HOSTS, DNS, and WINS

Terms

address translation table—An address translation table is the internal-to-external IP and/or port address mappings maintained by a NAT device. The table's contents will vary depending on the NAT type used.

Advanced Research Projects Agency Network (ARPANET)—ARPANET is a long-haul network funded by the ARPA (later DARPA) and built by Bolt, Beranek, and Newman, Inc. From 1969 through 1990, ARPANET served as the basis for early networking research, as well as a central backbone during development of the Internet.

American Standard Code for Information Interchange (ASCII)—ASCII is one of the most widely used codes for representing text in computers. ASCII codes represent letters, numerals, punctuation, and keyboard characters as numbers. For example, when the character "A" is pressed on the keyboard, the ASCII binary representation of that character is 100 0001 (hexadecimal 41). The basic ASCII character set uses 7 bits to represent the 128 text and keyboard elements.

Base64—Base64 is a standard algorithm for encoding and decoding non-ASCII data for attachment to an e-mail message; it is the foundation for MIME. Base64 uses a 65-character subset of ASCII to represent non-ASCII data in e-mail attachments.

Bootstrap Protocol (BOOTP)—BOOTP is an Internet protocol for enabling a diskless workstation to boot and determine its configuration information, such as its IP address, from information available on a BOOTP server.

cc:Mail—cc:Mail is a Lotus Development Corporation proprietary mail system. cc:Mail does not provide Internet mail access, and thus must use an e-mail gateway to send and receive SMTP mail.

country code top level domain (ccTLD)—Each country in the world is assigned an Internet country code, a two-character code designating the country in which a domain resides. This country code is appended to the end of the FQDN.

cut—A DNS cut divides DNS zone responsibilities between the root domain name server and subdomain nameservers, and in turn between subdomains and further subordinate domains. For example, in the domain westnetinc.com, a subdomain contracts.westnetinc.com could exist. When the DNS administrator cuts the westnetinc.com domain, he or she delegates responsibility for the subdomain contracts.westnetinc.com to the subdomain nameserver.

daemon—A daemon (pronounced "dee-mon") is a UNIX process that runs in the background and performs an operation at a specified time or in response to a certain event. A Microsoft Windows equivalent to a daemon is a service or system agent.

DHCP lease—A DHCP lease is the IP address the DHCP server dynamically issues to DHCP clients. The server maintains the lease for a specific period of time, and as the lease expiration time approaches, the client must renew the lease.

DHCPv6—Short for DHCP version 6, DHCPv6 assigns host IPv6 addresses dynamically. DHCPv6 is specified in Internet Draft form, and adds additional message types and larger Address fields, commensurate with IPv6 addressing, over DHCPv4. DHCPv6 uses UDP Port 546 for the client, and 547 for the server.

digital signature—A digital signature is a digital code that can be embedded into a document to prove its authenticity. Digital signatures are an application of public-key encryption technology; the sender of a document uses a private encryption key to encrypt a text string or the digest of the message. Document recipients use the sender's public-encryption key to decrypt the signature and authenticate the sender.

disk operating system (DOS)—DOS is the low-level software that resides on many PCs and controls the operation of a computer and its peripheral devices. MS-DOS is the operating system that preceded Microsoft Windows and still exists as an extension of the Windows OS.

Domain Name System (DNS)—DNS is the online distributed database system used to map human-readable computer names into IP addresses. DNS servers throughout the connected Internet implement a hierarchical namespace that allows sites freedom in assigning computer names and addresses. In addition, DNS supports separate mappings between mail destinations and IP addresses.

Domain Name System (DNS) zone—The part of the DNS namespace for which a DNS server has complete information is organized into units called zones; zones are the main units of replication in DNS. A zone contains one or more resource records (RRs) for one or more related DNS domains. Each DNS server contains the resource records (RR) relating to those portions of the DNS namespace for which it is authoritative (for which it can answer queries sent by a host). When a DNS server is authoritative for a portion of the DNS name space, those systems' administrators are responsible for ensuring that the information about that DNS name space portion is correct. To increase efficiency, a given DNS server can cache the RRs relating to a domain in any part of the domain tree.

Dynamic Host Configuration Protocol (DHCP)—DHCP provides configuration parameters to Internet hosts. DHCP consists of two components: a protocol for delivering host-specific configuration parameters from a DHCP server to a host and a mechanism for allocation of network addresses to hosts. DHCP is built on a client/server model, where designated DHCP server hosts allocate network addresses and deliver configuration parameters to dynamically configured hosts.

File Transfer Protocol (FTP)—FTP is a Transmission Control Protocol/Internet Protocol (TCP/IP) Application Layer protocol used to transfer files between two computers.

fully qualified domain name (FQDN)—The FQDN is the complete Internet system name. The FQDN includes the hostname and the domain name. An example of a FQDN is ken.westnetinc.com.

graphical user interface (GUI)—A GUI provides easy access to computer programs and often hides details of a program from the user.

graphics interchange format (GIF)—GIF is one of two graphic image formats used in HTML (JPEG is the other type). GIF files, the more popular format for small or simple images, are limited to 256 colors, have a lower resolution than JPEG files, offer lossless compression, and can be made transparent for a popular type of borderless effect.

Hypertext Markup Language (HTML)—HTML is a text-based formatting language used to generically format text for Web pages. It is a simplified derivative of SGML, that tags different parts of a document in terms of their function rather than appearance. A Web browser reads an HTML document and displays it as indicated by the HTML formatting tags and the browser's default settings

Internet Message Access Protocol (IMAP)—IMAP is a protocol used for retrieving e-mail messages from a mail server. IMAP4 is a version of IMAP similar to POP3, but it supports additional features such as allowing keyword searches in e-mail messages while the messages remain on the mail server.

Joint Photographic Experts Group (JPEG)—JPEG is an open standard that defines a method of compressing still images. See JPEG File Interchange Format.

JPEG File Interchange Format (JFIF)—JFIF is a public domain graphic compression format that conforms to the JPEG standard for image compression. It is one of two popular graphic image formats used in HTML pages (GIF is the other). JPEG/JFIF files offer higher resolution, with up to 16.7 million colors, and are generally used in continuous-tone images such as photographs. However, JPEG/JFIF compression is lossy (some image information is lost), even at the highest quality setting.

management information base (MIB)—A MIB is an SNMP database that lists information objects relevant to each managed object. A managed element's MIB includes its own information objects. The management application's MIB is a compilation of all the individual managed element's MIBs.

Motion Picture Experts Group (MPEG)—MPEG is a standard for compressing video to fewer bits for storage and transmission.

Multipurpose Internet Mail Extension (MIME)—MIME is an extension of SMTP that supports the exchange of a wide variety of document files by means of an e-mail system.

Network Address Port Translation (NAPT)—NAPT is also known as "masquerading" because it is a NAT technique that hides all internal devices behind a single public IP address (usually the NAT's outside port IP address). The NAT assigns each internal device connection this address and a new TCP or UDP port number taken from the registered port number range. This IP address/registered port number combination identifies a specific internal host on the Internet.

Network Address Translator (NAT)—NAT is a system that allows an administrator to use one set of IP addresses within a LAN, and another set for external traffic. NAT can shield internal addresses from public networks, and make more efficient use of a few globally unique IP addresses.

Network Basic Input/Output System (NetBIOS)—IBM and Sytek developed NetBIOS to link a NOS to specific hardware, augmenting DOS to provide LAN functions to the operating system. NetBIOS uses SMBs as the message format for sharing Windows files, directories, and devices.

Network File System (NFS)—A file management system used with TCP/IP and UNIX systems originally developed by SUN Microsystems. NFS can be found on various systems and platforms, especially PC-based platforms that utilize the TCP/IP protocol.

Network Management System (NMS)—NMS is a comprehensive equipment system used to monitor, control, and manage a data communications network.

Network News Transport Protocol (NNTP)—NNTP is the TCP/IP protocol used to distribute news article collections, or news feeds, over the Internet.

Post Office Protocol (POP3)—POP is an e-mail service implemented on TCP Port 110 that provides clients access to a mail drop or post office in which their messages are stored. POP3 is the latest iteration of the protocol.

programmable read-only memory (PROM)—A PROM is a memory chip on which you can store a program. After the PROM has been programmed, you cannot wipe it clean and reprogram it.

protocol data unit (PDU)—The concept of a PDU is used in the OSI reference model. From the perspective of a protocol layer, a PDU consists of information from the layer above plus the protocol information appended to the data by that layer. For example, a frame is a PDU of the Data Link Layer, and a packet is a PDU of the Network Layer.

public-key encryption—Public-key encryption is a cryptographic system that uses two mathematically related keys; one key is used to encrypt a message and the other is used to decrypt it. People who need to receive encrypted messages distribute their public keys but keep their private keys secret.

read-only memory (ROM)—Unlike RAM, ROM cannot be written to after it is initially programmed. However, the data contained in ROM is nonvolatile; data is not lost if the power is turned off. Computers almost always contain a small amount of ROM that holds instructions for starting up the computer.

resolver—The DNS resolver is a DNS system component that performs DNS queries against a DNS server (or servers). The resolver is a part of the DNS client and is usually installed when TCP/IP is installed.

resource record (RR)—An RR is a DNS database record containing information relating to a domain that a DNS client can retrieve and use. For example, the host RR for a specific domain holds the IP address of that domain (host); a DNS client uses this RR to obtain the IP address for the domain.

Reverse Address Resolution Protocol (RARP)—RARP is the protocol a diskless computer uses at startup to find its IP address. The computer broadcasts a request that contains its physical hardware address, and a server responds by sending the computer its IP address. RARP takes its name and message format from the IP ARP.

Secure/MIME (S/MIME)—S/MIME is a MIME version that supports message encryption using public-key encryption technology. This ensures that e-mail is sent and received in a manner that is secure from interception or tampering.

Sendmail—Sendmail is a UNIX application that handles electronic mail. Sendmail supports backend message routing and handling for SMTP-based e-mail systems.

Server Message Block (SMB)—SMB is the IBM PC LAN protocol used to communicate with devices located on a LAN. It uses NetBIOS at the Session Layer to communicate across a LAN. Functions requiring LAN support, such as retrieving files from a file server, are translated into SMB commands before they are sent to a remote device.

shell—A shell is another term for a user interface. OSs sometimes provide an alternative shell to make program interaction easier. For example, the shell may provide a menu-driven system that translates user menu choices to OS commands.

Simple Mail Transfer Protocol (SMTP)—SMTP is an Application Layer protocol used to send e-mail from a client to a mail server, and transfer e-mail between mail servers, across a TCP/IP network.

Simple Network Management Protocol (SNMP)—SNMP is a network management protocol based on the manager/agent model, in which a complex central manager directs simple device-based agents to supply information or change configurations.

Standard Generalized Markup Language (SGML)—SGML was developed by the International Organization for Standards (ISO) in 1986. SGML does not specify any particular formatting; rather, it specifies the rules for tagging different parts of a document in terms of their function rather than appearance.

store-and-forward—In a messaging system, a store-and-forward application accepts messages on their way to their final destination and stores them until the destination host requests them. When the destination host requests the messages, the store-and-forward system forwards them on to the requesting host. POP3 is a store-and-forward application protocol.

Telnet—Telnet is a TCP/IP Application Layer protocol that provides remote login capability to another computer on a network.

terminal emulation—A terminal emulation program allows a local computer to connect to a remote computer and appear to be logged on to the remote computer locally. Terminal emulation programs are often used to access mainframe computers.

top level domain (TLD)—TLDs are the groupings of lower level domain types. A TCP/IP network can be segmented into a hierarchy of domains or groupings; the Internet is an example of this segmentation type. For example, the .com TLD groups commercial domains, while the .edu TLD groups educational institutions.

Trivial File Transfer Protocol (TFTP)—TFTP is the TCP/IP protocol for file transfer with minimal capability and overhead. TFTP depends on the unreliable, connectionless, datagram delivery service UDP. TFTP is designed for use on diskless workstations that keep such software in ROM.

Uniform Resource Locator (URL)—A URL is an Internet address used to locate resources from within a Web browser. It can lead you to an Internet-connected computer anywhere in the world.

Usenet—Usenet is a global news distribution service that relies on the Internet for much of its news traffic. News servers agree to share and distribute newsfeeds, which are collections of related news articles. Users post news messages in newsfeeds using a news reader client.

User Datagram Protocol (UDP)—UDP is a Transport Layer protocol that provides a simple, connectionless datagram delivery service, without error checking, for certain specialized application services that do not require the full services of TCP.

Uuencode—Uuencode is a set of algorithms for converting e-mail attachments into a series of 7-bit ASCII characters for transmission over the Internet. Uuencode originally stood for UNIX-to-UNIX encode, but is now considered a universal protocol used to transfer file attachments between different operating system platforms. Nearly all e-mail applications support uuencoding.

Waveform Audio File (WAV)—WAV is one of several formats for storing sound in files developed jointly by Microsoft and IBM. Support for WAV files is built-in to Windows 95, making it the de facto standard for sound on PCs. WAV sound files end with a .WAV extension and can be played by nearly all Windows applications that support sound.

Windows Internet Naming Service (WINS)—WINS is a Microsoft client/server application that resolves network computer host names to IP addresses. WINS works in conjunction with DHCP, where the WINS server maintains a dynamic database of hostname-to-address mappings. Because DHCP clients may not maintain the same address over time, WINS works well for this application. Standard DNS supports only hosts with statically assigned IP addresses.

Windows service—A Windows service is the equivalent of a UNIX daemon. Windows services provide specific functions, such as enabling file sharing or automatic virus protection, and can start automatically on system startup, manually as directed by the user, or when scheduled to run at a particular time of the day.

zone of authority—A DNS zone of authority is the DNS zone namespace for which a DNS nameserver is responsible. When a DNS domain is created, the new domain's root becomes the domain and its subdomains' zone of authority. A DNS server can maintain responsibility for more than one zone of authority.

Lesson 1—HTTP

Hypertext Markup Language (HTML) is the file formatting language used to describe the contents of a Web page. The HTML formatting of a Web page is interpreted and displayed by a Web browser. Hypertext Transfer Protocol (HTTP) is the protocol used between a Web browser and a Web server. HTTP is used to request and receive data, including Web pages formatted in HTML.

Objectives

At the end of this lesson you will be able to:

- Describe the function of HTTP

- Explain the function of request messages

- Explain the function of response messages and response headers

Key Point

HTTP is used to transfer Web information.

HTTP Communications

Web browsers are the front-end client software used to access HTTP servers by means of the Internet. HTTP servers are commonly referred to as Web servers. A typical Web server can handle thousands of client requests in a short period of time. In a typical session, the following actions take place:

1. The Web browser sends a connection request to the HTTP server.

2. The HTTP server accepts the request and notifies the browser of the successful connection.

3. The browser then transmits the document request to the server.

4. The server retrieves the document and transmits it to the browser.

5. The browser receives the incoming document data and displays it for the user.

6. After the server has transmitted the entire document, it breaks the connection with the browser.

One reason HTTP servers can handle thousands, and perhaps millions of requests per hour is the statelessness of the connection. Every time a client browser wants to retrieve a document, a separate request is sent to the server. If a user spends several hours reading a particular Web page, the server has no knowledge of it.

Overview of HTTP

Objective 1.4
Understand and be able to describe the infrastructure needed to support an Internet client.

Objective 3.5
Understand how various protocols or services apply to the function of their corresponding server, such as a mail server, a web server or a file transfer server.

HTTP is defined in a Request for Comment (RFC). Specifically, *RFC 2616* states:

> The Hypertext Transfer Protocol (HTTP) is an application-level protocol for distributed, collaborative, hypermedia information systems. It is a generic, stateless protocol which can be used for many tasks beyond its use for hypertext, such as name servers and distributed object management systems, through extension of its request methods, error codes, and headers. A feature of HTTP is the typing and negotiation of data representation, allowing systems to be built independently of the data being transferred.

In simpler terms, HTTP is a protocol that operates at the Application Layer, usually riding on top of TCP/IP, that allows for the transport of data between heterogeneous systems. HTTP is a message-based protocol; a client sends a request message to the server and the server sends a response message back to the client. A typical HTTP client/server interaction is shown on the HTTP Client/Server Session Diagram.

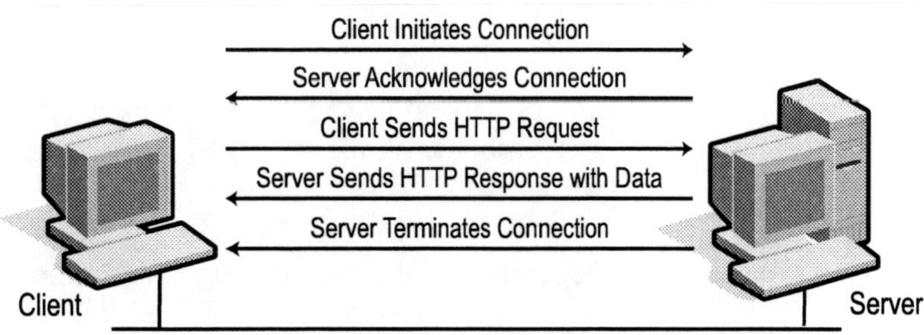

HTTP Client/Server Session

As with other server applications, an HTTP server "listens" for a client request on a "well-known" TCP port, typically port 80. Web browsers or other client applications connect to the HTTP server on this port, then send the HTTP request message to the server. The server processes the request, returns the response message to the client, and then terminates the TCP connection. Because a single connection to the server results in only a single request/response, HTTP is known as a "stateless" protocol. This means that the server retains no knowledge of the connection request or response after each single transaction takes place.

Protocol Definition

While HTML has gone through several revisions to add user-desired functionality, the purpose and functionality of HTTP has changed very little. In function, HTTP is similar to File Transfer Protocol (FTP) in that its primary intent is to transfer files over the Internet. As such, HTTP has gone through very few revisions since its inception. The first version of HTTP was version 0.9, which was an extremely simple protocol. It did little more than transfer raw data over TCP/IP networks. The first revision to this specification, version 1.0 defined in *RFC 1945*, added Multipurpose Internet Mail Extension (MIME)-like features to the message passing semantics, but it added little more. The current specification, version 1.1, "allows an open-ended set of methods that indicate the purpose of a request," allowing for greater functionality, including "hierarchical proxies, caching, the need for persistent connections, and virtual hosts."

Although HTTP was designed to run on TCP/IP networks, nothing in the specification requires TCP/IP as the transport. The only restriction placed on the lower protocol layers is that HTTP "presumes a reliable transport; any protocol that provides such guarantees can be used." Despite this flexibility, the proliferation of the Web has made TCP/IP the protocol stack most commonly used with HTTP. When run on TCP/IP, HTTP defaults to port TCP 80, but any port may be used.

Regardless of the protocol stack and communication medium over which HTTP is deployed, HTTP is a relatively simple protocol. Most HTTP communication is initiated by a user agent and consists of a request to be applied to a resource on some origin server. Although intermediaries, such as proxies, may exist between the client and server, interaction between the intermediaries and other machines follow the same request-response paradigm. Features such as session control, security, error detection and correction, and routing are all handled by the lower-level protocols.

Request Messages

Objective 1.4
Understand and be able to describe the infrastructure needed to support an Internet client.

An HTTP request follows a simple format designed to meet the limited needs of the protocol. The first line of a request message from a client to a server includes:

- The method to be applied to the resource

- The resource identifier

- The protocol version in use

The method is the service that the client is requesting of the server. The method is case sensitive. The identifier is the object upon which the method is to be performed; the identifier is transmitted in Uniform Resource Identifier (URI) form.

An example of a complete and properly formatted request message is:

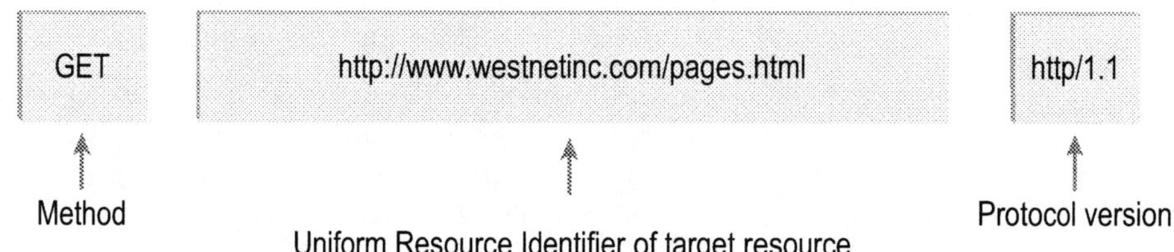

HTTP Methods

HTTP version 1.1 details eight methods (requests), but is extensible. The described methods are OPTIONS, GET, HEAD, POST, PUT, CONNECT, DELETE, and TRACE. According to the specification, all HTTP servers must support the GET and HEAD methods, but all other methods are optional. If the other methods are supported, the support must conform to the specifications listed within the RFC.

The eight methods are described as follows:

- OPTIONS—A request by the client for additional information relating to the communications options available. The purpose of this method is to allow the client to obtain additional information regarding options and requirements without initiating any actions on the part of the server.

- GET—A request for transfer of a resource, such as a Web page, from the server to the client.

- HEAD—A request for transfer of header information without transfer of the entire resource. This method is most frequently used for testing purposes and verifying modification and update information. Search engines also use HEAD to display TITLE and META information.

- POST—A request that the receiving station make the enclosed resource a subordinate of the listed URI. Specific uses for POST include annotation of existing resources; posting a message to a bulletin board, newsgroup, or mailing list; providing a block of data to a data-handling process; and appending to a database.

- PUT—A request that the enclosed resource be stored under the URI specified. If the PUT request references a resource that already resides under the URI, the receiving station "should" (but is not required to) treat it as though it were an update to the previously existing resource.

- DELETE—A request that the receiving station delete the resource specified if it exists on the listed URI. The receiving station is not required to grant a DELETE request.

- TRACE—A request to the receiving station to return a copy of the sender's request message, exactly as it was received (loop-back). A TRACE request is used for testing; it allows the sending station to "see" how a message was received.

- CONNECT—A request to a proxy that can dynamically switch to being a tunnel (for example, SSL tunneling).

Uniform Resource Identifiers

A Request URI is the URI of the document, file, or other resource being requested. URI is the generic term for all types of names and addresses located on the Web. A URL is one kind of URI. A URI may be provided in absolute or relative form. An absolute URI is allowed only when a request is being made to a proxy, and has the following format:

http://www.bighorn.com/

or

http://www.westnetinc.com/

A relative URI, which is the most commonly used, defines a resource in relation to some base URI known to the server, and it takes the following form:

    /dir/subdir/document.html

HTTP-Version

HTTP-Version is the version of HTTP being used, and takes the form:

```
HTTP/[Version #]
```

For example:

```
HTTP/1.0
```

The following example incorporates all elements of a request line:

```
GET /html/document1.html HTTP/1.0
```

or

```
GET /html/document1.html HTTP/1.1
```

The request line is terminated with a carriage return/line feed pair (hexadecimal values 0x0D 0x0A).

Response Messages

Objective 3.5
Understand how various protocols or services apply to the function of their corresponding server, such as a mail server, a web server or a file transfer server.

Upon receiving an HTTP request, an HTTP server must reply with a response message. This response message informs the sending station that the request was received, and provides additional information on how the request will be handled. The status line is the first line of a response message. An example of a complete and properly formatted response message status line is:

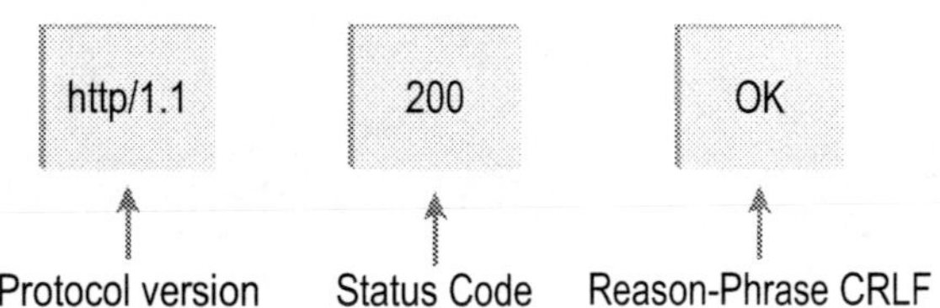

The status code is primarily intended for use by the receiving client computer so it can display a text message to the user, if necessary. The first digit of the three-digit status code defines the class of the error code. Five classes are currently defined:

- Class one messages are informational

- Class two messages indicate success

- Class three messages are redirection responses (responses requiring further action)

- Class four messages represent client error

- Class five messages represent server error

An HTTP client must recognize the class of an error code, but the client is not required to recognize any specific codes within the class. When an unrecognized status code is received, the client is required to respond to the status code as though it were the x00 code of the corresponding class. The only restriction that the HTTP specification places on the response to an unrecognized status code is that the browser is prohibited from caching the status code. Although many HTTP clients display the text phrase associated with an unrecognized status code, the specification does not require this text phrase.

The HTTP RFC lists 40 different status codes and provides recommended text phrases. The list is not exhaustive because the specification is extensible, and vendors may implement additional status codes within their products. Although recommended, the exact wording of the text phrases listed within the RFC is not required, which allows vendors to modify text phrases. The complete list of status codes from *RFC 2616* is provided below:

- **Informational**

    100 : Continue

    101 : Switching Protocols

- **Success**

    200 : OK

    201 : Created

    202 : Accepted

    203 : Non-Authoritative Information

    204 : No Content

    205 : Reset Content

    206 : Partial Content

- **Redirection**

    300 : Multiple Choices

    301 : Moved Permanently

    302 : Found

    303 : See Other

    304 : Not Modified

    305 : Use Proxy

    307 : Temporary Redirect

- **Client Error**

    400 : Bad Request

    401 : Unauthorized

    402 : Payment Required

    403 : Forbidden

    404 : Not Found

    405 : Method Not Allowed

    406 : Not Acceptable

    407 : Proxy Authentication Required

    408 : Request Time-Out

    409 : Conflict

    410 : Gone

    411 : Length Required

    412 : Precondition Failed

    413 : Request Entity Too Large

    414 : Request-URI Too Large

    415 : Unsupported Media Type

    416 : Request Range Not Satisfiable

    417 : Expectation Failed

- **Server Error**

    500 : Internal Server Error

    501 : Not Implemented

    502 : Bad Gateway

    503 : Service Unavailable

    504 : Gateway Time-Out

    505 : HTTP Version Not Supported

HTTP Headers

When data is transferred via HTTP, HTTP adds its own header before passing the data down the stack for transmission across the network. Each layer below, such as TCP and IP, encapsulates the data from above by adding its own header to the data from above. So HTTP headers (and the data to be sent) are encapsulated inside TCP headers, which are then encapsulated inside IP headers. IP packets are encapsulated inside local area network (LAN) or wide area network (WAN) headers used to transport information across a specific link, such as an Ethernet LAN. This is illustrated in the HTTP Encapsulation Diagram.

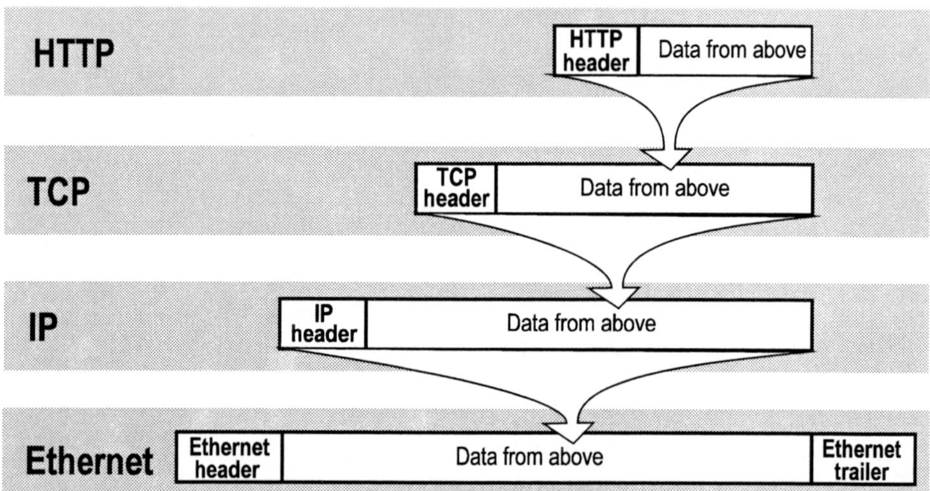

HTTP Encapsulation

HTTP headers fall into four categories:

- **General headers**—Apply to either request or response messages

- **Request headers**—Allow the client to send additional information about itself or the request to the server

- **Response headers**—Allow the server to respond to the client

- **Entity headers**—Identify additional information about the entity body

General Headers

General headers are used in both client requests and server responses. Some examples of general headers are:

- **Cache-Control**—Directives ("directives" are a comma-separated list of modifiers to the Cache-Control general header). An example of a Cache-Control request directive is:

  ```
  max-age = seconds (do not send responses older
  than x seconds)
  ```

- **Date**—Date/time of the request or response.

- **Pragma**—Headers that allow the client to send additional information to a proxy system, such as a proxy server. Pragma headers do not affect the target server, only the proxy system. An example of a Pragma general header is a "no-cache" header to inform the proxy server not to get a response out of its cache, but to send the original browser URL request along to the target server.

Request Headers

Request headers allow a client (browser) to send additional information to the server regarding the request or the client itself. Some examples of request headers are:

- **Accept**—Specifies the media types in which the client prefers to receive data. Two examples are "image/gif" and "application/msword."

- **Authorization**—Allows a client to authenticate itself with a server. This might take the form of an authorization scheme, such as BASIC, followed by an encoded user name and password.

- **From**—Allows the client to send a user's electronic mail (e-mail) address to the server.

- **If-Modified-Since**—Allows the client to conditionally retrieve the requested information based on the last date modified.

- **Referer**—Allows the client to notify the server of the requesting URI source document. This permits the server to log sources, track erroneous links, etc.

- **User-Agent**—Allows the client to send information about itself, primarily to enable the server to tailor responses for limitations of the requesting client application. This could be the name and revision level of the browser and the operating system such as Windows 95.

Response Headers

Response headers allow the server to pass additional information to the client regarding the response. This information cannot be placed in the status line. Some examples of response headers are:

- **Location**—Defines the exact location of the resource.

- **Server**—Contains information about the server software, such as the software name and revision number (Server: Apache 1.3).

- **WWW-Authenticate**—Included with unauthorized (code 401) response messages. This tells the client that the server wants a certain type of authorization scheme to be sent back, such as BASIC.

Entity Headers

Entity headers provide additional information to the client about the information being transmitted. The following is a list of some entity headers:

- **Allow**—Notifies the recipient of valid methods (GET, POST, etc.) available for this resource.

- **Content-Encoding**—Used as a modifier for media type. This header notifies the client of the type of compression used to compress a resource; thus, allowing the recipient to apply the proper decompression application to the resource.

- **Content-Length**—Specifies the length of the entity body being transferred.

- **Content-Type**—Describes the media type and subtype of the entity body.

- **Expires**—Specifies the time when the information becomes invalid.

- **Last-Modified**—Specifies when the resource was last modified.

Sample Request Messages

The following examples illustrate request messages sent by Internet Explorer and Netscape Communicator. Reviewing the request messages sent by the client (browser) is helpful to understand the communication taking place between the client and server components.

```
GET / HTTP/1.0
Accept: image/gif, image/x-xbitmap, image/jpeg,
image/pjpeg, application/vnd.ms-excel,
application/msword, application/vnd.ms-
powerpoint, */*
Accept-Language: en
UA-pixels: 1024x768
UA-color: color8
UA-OS: Windows 95
UA-CPU: x86
User-Agent: Mozilla/2.0 (compatible; MSIE 3.01;
Windows 95)
Host: javatogo.bighorn.com
Connection: Keep-Alive
```

Request Message from Internet Explorer

```
GET / HTTP/1.0
Connection: Keep-Alive
User-Agent: Mozilla/4.0b4 [en] (WinNT; I)
Host: javatogo.bighorn.com
Accept: image/gif, image/x-xbitmap, image/jpeg,
image/pjpeg, */*
Accept-Language: en
```

Request Message from Netscape Communicator

Below is a typical HTTP response header, including the entity body, which is a Web page in this example.

```
HTTP/1.0 200 OK
Server: Microsoft-PWS-95/2.0
Date: Wed, 9 June 1999 21:18:53 GMT
Content-Type: text/html
Accept-Ranges: bytes
Last-Modified: Wed, 9 June 1999 21:11:52 GMT
Content-Length: 160


<!DOCTYPE HTML PUBLIC "-//W3C//DTD HTML 3.2
Final//EN">
<HTML>
<HEAD>
    <TITLE>Test Page</TITLE>
</HEAD>
<BODY>
This is a test page
</BODY>
</HTML>
```

HTTP Response Message

Additional Services

HTTP allows for more advanced services than the eight defined methods. Information relating to these advanced services is communicated within the general, request, response, and/or entity header fields. The current HTTP specification details 9 general headers, 19 request headers, 9 response headers, and 11 entity headers. The specification does allow for extensions to these headers, but warns against this practice. In cases where a header field is not recognized, the header "should be ignored" by the receiving station. However, the unrecognized header may be processed as though it were part of the body, and errors in communication may occur.

Activities

1. Draw a diagram illustrating an HTTP session between a Web client (browser) and a Web server. Use arrows and label each step.

2. Describe what is meant by the term "stateless" as it applies to the connection between the Web browser and Web server.

     ____

     ____

3. HTTP is a protocol that operates at layer four of the OSI model.   True or False?

4. An HTTP server software process normally "listens" for client requests on TCP port 80. True or False?

5. HTTP is a remote procedure call (RPC) protocol. True or False?

6. After the HTTP (Web) server receives a client's (browser's) connection request and processes the request, the HTTP server waits for another request from the client until the client changes the state of the connection. True or False?

7. Does the browser display HTTP or HTML on the screen?

     ____

     ____

8. HTTP can run on any reliable transport and doesn't require TCP. True or False?

9. If the HTTP status code returned by the Web server indicates a "200," the HTTP request was successful. True or False?

10. A "505" error might indicate a browser sent an HTTP 1.1 request to a server that supported HTTP 1.0. True or False?

11. Match the functions with the methods listed below. (Choose a letter.)

    Request a transfer of a resource from the server. __________

    Request information for additional communications options. __________

    Request the return of a sent message by the receiving application. __________

    Request the receiving station remove a resource, if it exists. __________

    Request resources be stored under the URI specified. __________

    Request to store the enclosed resource under an existing resource. __________

    Request for the transfer of header information. __________

    Request to a proxy that can dynamically switch to being a tunnel. __________

    a. OPTIONS

    b. GET

    c. HEAD

    d. POST

    e. PUT

    f. DELETE

    g. TRACE

    h. CONNECT

12. List the four types of HTTP headers.

    ____

    ____

    ____

    ____

13. What is the name of the header that gives the type and version of the Web server?

14. What header would be sent telling a proxy server not to use the cached entry?

15. Describe what the ACCEPT header does.

16. What header tells a Web server what type of browser the client is running?

17. What header is used to tell the server about the type of O/S running on the client?

Extended Activities

1. Research the significance of the following terms, found in the example request messages:

    a. Mozilla/4.ob4

    b. GMT

    c. Keep-Alive

2. Download and review *RFC 2616* (**http://www.w3.org**).

Lesson 2—Telnet

Telnet is an application and protocol that is widely used to provide remote-login capability on a TCP/IP network. With Telnet, you can log on as a regular user with whatever privileges you have been granted to the specific application and data on that computer.

Telnet was one of the first services to take advantage of Internet connectivity. Many years ago, before the widespread distribution of microcomputers, terminals were used to communicate with large mainframes and minicomputers. Telnet is simply a way to offer this same kind of interaction over a TCP/IP network. In today's world of fancy and flashy graphical interfaces, Telnet may seem archaic. However, it still provides useful functionality.

Objectives

At the end of this lesson you will be able to:

- Describe common Telnet uses

- Demonstrate use of Telnet with a browser

- Demonstrate use of Telnet with a command line

Key Point

Telnet is commonly used to run a program on a remote computer.

Common Telnet Uses

Telnet is a protocol that allows a user to remotely connect to another system, with privileges to run specific programs on that system. Implementations of Telnet usually work between different operating systems. For example, a Telnet client may be on a Windows computer, and the server may be running UNIX. The Telnet Session Diagram shows a typical Telnet session. Common Telnet uses include:

- Connecting to a system to use specific programs, such as e-mail and statistics programs

- Remotely configuring or inspecting a networking device

- Connecting to an online database of information

- Connecting to an online forum to interact and communicate with other users

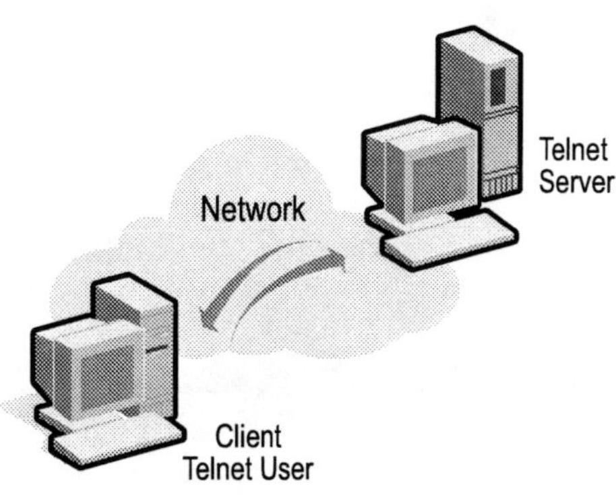

Telnet Session

Telnet Server Software

Objective 3.5
Understand how various protocols or services apply to the function of their corresponding server, such as a mail server, a web server or a file transfer server

Before a user can use Telnet to connect to a remote computer, a Telnet server application must be running on the target computer. This server software is usually called a service on Windows systems, or a daemon ("demon") on UNIX systems. Either way, a Telnet server runs in the background, and waits for client requests to come in on well-known port 23.

A Telnet server essentially acts like a doorway into a computer. Once a user has connected to a computer using Telnet, that user may run applications or access files as if sitting at that machine's keyboard. A server's administrator sets up usernames and passwords to control who may use Telnet on each system. A user's access to a computer's resources depends on the rights and permissions that have been defined in the user's account on that machine.

Using Telnet by Means of a Command Line

Objective 1.5
Use/configure Web browsers and other Internet/intranet clients, and be able to describe their use to others
… Telnet clients
… The basic commands for each type of client

To use Telnet on your Windows client, type **telnet** at the command prompt, and press ENTER. After the Telnet client opens, you can connect to the Telnet host with which you wish to communicate. You can also connect to a port or service other than the standard Telnet port. This particular Telnet feature is useful when a Telnet client is used to access something other than a Telnet process. After your host connects to the remote system, the Telnet window title bar shows the remote system's name. Depending on the OS, there are several ways to run Telnet. A sample session follows.

Using Telnet With Windows

The following steps illustrate how to use Windows Telnet client to initiate a remote login to an Internet host:

1. Start Telnet. This step is different for different OSs. Telnet can normally be started from the PC DOS prompt or from within a browser. The Telnet From Command Prompt Screen Capture shows the initial screen that appears when **telnet** is typed into the Run dialog box using Windows 95 or 98.

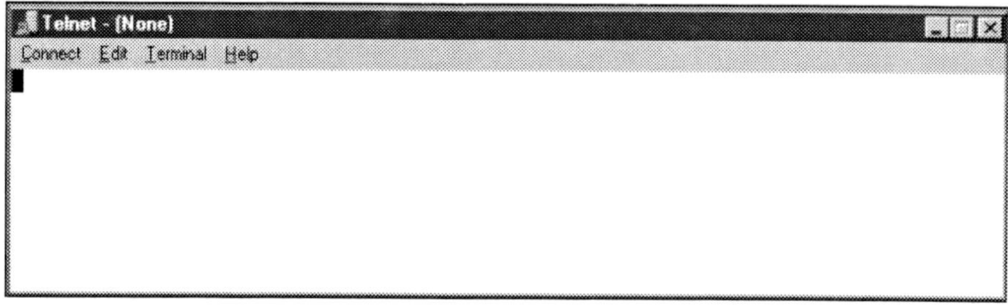

Telnet From Command Prompt

2. Under the Connect menu, select **Remote System.** A dialog box like the one shown in the Telnet Connect Screen Capture will appear.

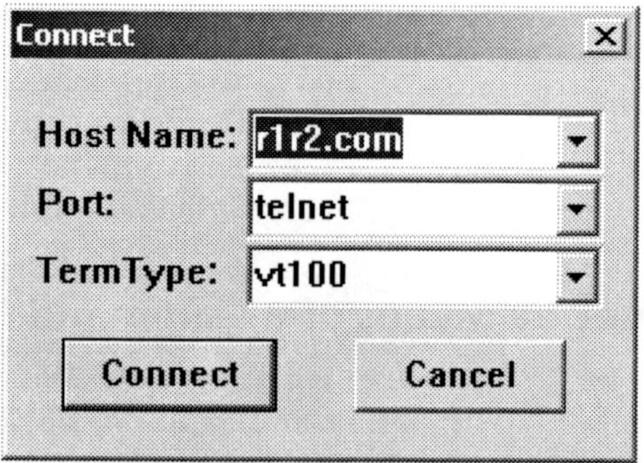

Telnet Connect

3. In the box marked Host Name, enter the Telnet address for your desired location (you can use r1r2.com).

4. Click **Connect**, or press **ENTER**, to initiate the connection. The Telnet Connectivity Screen Capture is displayed.

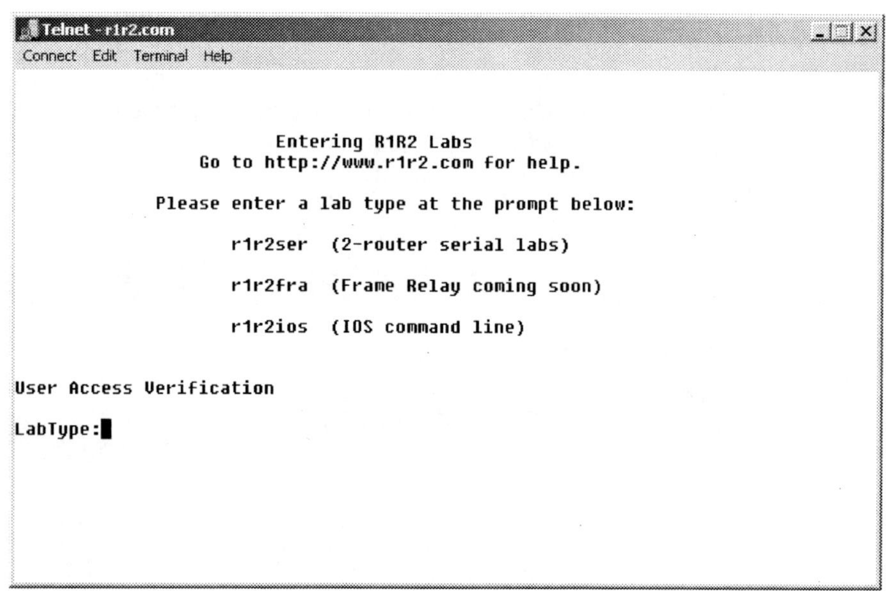

Telnet Connectivity

Note: After you log on to the remote site, pay attention to the instructions that appear on the screen to help you navigate on that particular system. Menu options are usually easy to understand; however, commands vary from system to system. You can usually get help by typing **help** or **?** as you navigate.

Basic Telnet Commands

Basic Telnet commands include:

*   OPEN—Establishes a connection to the specified host.

*   CLOSE—Closes an open connection and leaves you in the Telnet software.

*   QUIT—Closes any open Telnet sessions and exits the Telnet software.

5. To end your session, type **exit** or **logout** at the command line. You may also go to the Connect menu and choose **Disconnect**.

Using Telnet by Means of a Web Browser

Objective 1.5
Use/configure Web browsers and other Internet/intranet clients, and be able to describe their use to others
... Web browsers
... All-in-one/ universal clients

Using Telnet to access a remote computer by means of a Web browser is basically the same as using Telnet directly. The primary difference is that instead of having to find and open the Telnet client and specify the address of the remote computer, the Web browser does this for you when you click on a link to a Telnet-accessible resource. Alternately, you may type the command **telnet:// r1r2.com** in the browser's address line, as shown in the Browser Telnet Screen Capture.

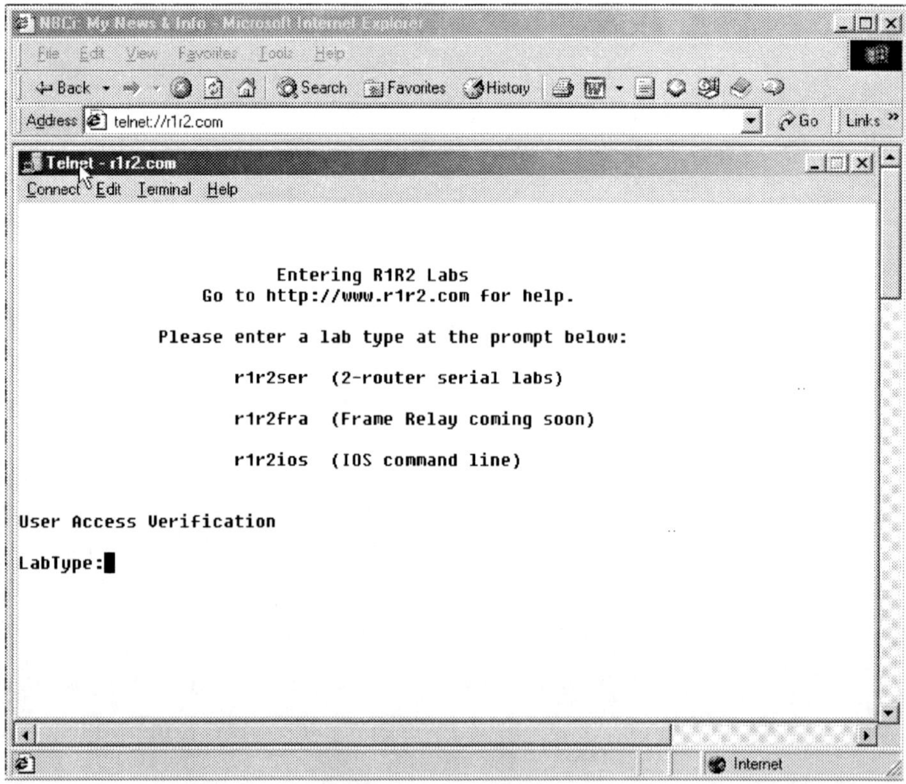

Browser Telnet

Activities

1. Which of the following is NOT a common use of Telnet?

    a.   Connect to an online database

    b.   Run a program on the local computer

    c.   Connect remotely to run a specific application

    d.   Connect to a router for network information

2. Which basic Telnet command opens a session to a specified host?

    a.   Open

    b.   Close

    c.   Hello

    d.   Quit

3. Which Telnet command closes a Telnet session but leaves the Telnet software running?

    a.   Quit

    b.   Close

    c.   Exit

    d.   Logout

Extended Activities

This activity has you Telnet into a publicly available site that provides free access to Cisco routers. You will examine the router configuration and list the commands you might issue from the router privileged EXEC mode.

1. On your PC, start a Telnet session:

    a.   Open a Command prompt window

    b.   Type **telnet**

2. At the Telnet> prompt, type **open r1r2.com**

3. At the LabType: prompt, type **r1r2ser**

4. At the Username: prompt, type **cisco**

5. At the Password: prompt, type **ccna**. A welcome screen appears.

6. Press the Enter key on your keyboard. A Router prompt, similar to Router>, appears.

7. If the prompt reads Router>, type **en**. The prompt changes to Router#. The "#" indicates that you are in the router privileged EXEC mode.

Note: The router may prompt for another password. If it does, disconnect and try later. These are publicly used routers, and others can set passwords at their discretion. The site managers reset the router configurations from time to time; thus, you will be able to access the routers at a later time.

8. At the Router# prompt, type **show running**. This displays the router's current configuration.

9. Press the space bar to scroll the screen pages.

10. At the Router# prompt, type **?**. This lists all the commands that you can issue from the Router# prompt. Scroll the pages with the space bar.

11. At the Router# prompt, type **exit**. This logs you out of the router.

12. Close your Telnet session.

Lesson 3—File Transfer: FTP

File Transfer Protocol (FTP), which is as old and as widely used as Telnet, uses TCP to copy files between computers. The operation and appearance is as if we used Telnet to connect to a remote computer. But instead of connecting via Telnet, then typing commands that are specific to the operating system of the remote computer, FTP provides a short list of standard commands to do tasks such as list files and directories, or move files between the local and remote computer.

Objectives

At the end of this lesson you will be able to:

- Explain basic FTP operation

- Demonstrate the difference between using command line FTP and browser-based FTP

 **Key Point**

FTP is used to move files between two computers.

Why Use FTP?

FTP is used to transfer files between hosts on a TCP/IP network. Although other avenues exist for passing files, FTP is the best choice when we must work with large files, especially over slow connections. For example, many of us are used to sending and receiving files as e-mail attachments. This works fine for smaller files; however, who has not waited for several minutes for their e-mail to download over a dial-up connection because a well-meaning friend or colleague sent a 1 or 2 megabyte (MB) file attachment? Additionally, many ISPs conserve mail server resources by limiting e-mail attachment sizes to 2 MB or less.

FTP is ideal for downloading large file attachments. FTP offloads the burden these large files place on the e-mail server and the network and allows us to better control file downloads. If the e-mail server experiences file-transfer problems, you may not receive it at all. Additionally, the mail server may hold the file in queue for delivery until an administrator deletes it. With FTP, if you experience an error, you simply initiate the transfer again.

FTP Server Software

Objective 3.5
Understand how various protocols or services apply to the function of their corresponding server, such as a mail server, a web server or a file transfer server

Not all computers on the Internet allow for or are capable of FTP. First, to allow connections, the computer must run an FTP server. This server service, or daemon, manages connections from clients requesting file retrieval or transmission. In effect, an FTP server is like a window into the remote computer's hard drive. The user who sets up an FTP server controls what areas of the hard drive are visible, what files can be read or written, and who can access them. If no one configured an FTP server on a computer, an FTP client cannot read that computer's files.

FTP servers are set up for private use, and usernames and passwords control access. This means that an administrator must give a user explicit access to the FTP server, and that user must have been assigned a unique username and password so they may access the server's facilities.

An FTP server logs all traffic. You can consult the server logs to determine the amounts of traffic the server handles, what is accessed, and who is accessing it.

Anonymous FTP

In addition to using FTP for an organization's internal use, there are many public-access documents and software archives, including shareware and public domain archives, that use FTP services. Users access these archives by what is known as anonymous FTP, where the FTP server requires a username, but the username is "anonymous." The associated password is normally an e-mail address.

To protect sensitive resources on the FTP server, administrators first verify that no sensitive information is accessible by anonymous FTP. One reason for using anonymous FTP is security; FTP passes credentials as plain text data. Hackers can intercept these unencrypted usernames and passwords and use them to steal or destroy sensitive data. If an administrator allows anonymous FTP, then users will pass no sensitive credentials across the network.

Is Anonymous FTP Really Anonymous?

When using anonymous FTP, most FTP servers will require that the user supply his or her e-mail address as a password. This means the archive maintainers will have a record of the user's e-mail address, cross-referenced with the files the user transferred. However, most archive maintainers stipulate that the e-mail address will be used only for their own purposes, such as demographic studies and pursuing any abuse of the archive services. A user is unlikely to receive unsolicited e-mail in connection with using an anonymous FTP archive.

Note: Few FTP servers verify that the e-mail address you supply is valid; thus, you do not have to use your own. You can make one up, if you wish.

Using FTP Clients

Objective 1.5
Use/configure Web browsers and other Internet/intranet clients, and be able to describe their use to others.
... FTP clients

There are a large number of client programs available that can be used for FTP, with varying user interfaces. They fall into three main types:

- Command-line applications—The most basic is a program called "ftp." This program offers a command line interface, similar in some ways to a DOS or UNIX shell, which can be used to explore a remote computer's directory tree and transfer files. The program has one main advantage; it is standard and has been written for most computer platforms.

- Graphical applications—There are also numerous programs available that provide a more graphical, point-and-click interface to FTP. These programs, for various platforms, are available on many Web sites that provide downloadable software.

- Browsers—Most Web browsers can also be used to obtain files by means of FTP.

Using Command Line FTP

The following is a demonstration of a command line FTP session and illustrates how some of the basic commands work:

1. At a DOS or Windows command prompt, type **ftp** followed by an FTP site, for example:

    ftp telnet.westnetinc.com

    You may also type **ftp** at the command line to start FTP, then use the OPEN command to open the appropriate FTP site. This is illustrated in the Command Line FTP Screen Capture.

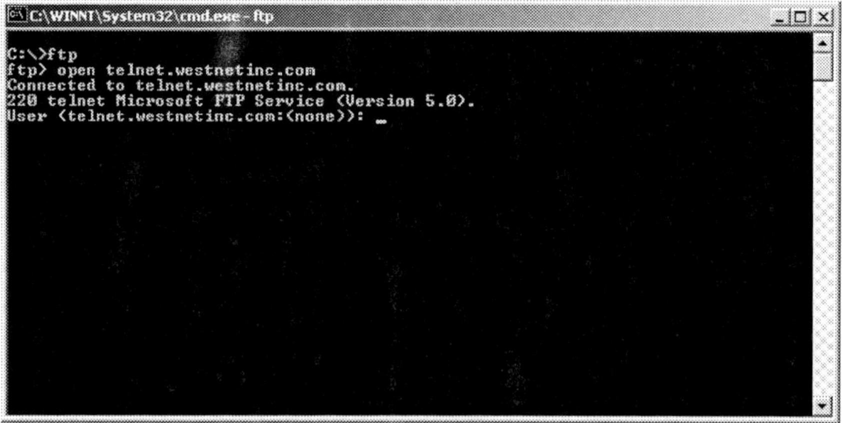

Command Line FTP

Recognize that the FTP site address could have easily been **ftp.westnetinc.com**, but in this case we use the same computer as both a Telnet and an FTP server.

The computer responds with the following message:

User <telnet.westnetinc.com:<none>>:

2. At the prompt, type **anonymous**.

    The server responds with:

    ```
    331 Anonymous access allowed,
    send identity (e-mail name) as password
    ```

3. At the prompt, type in your complete e-mail address.

   If the server accepts your login information, it responds with:

   `ftp>`

4. At the prompt, type the **dir** or **ls** command to see what files are located in this directory. A screen similar to the one in the FTP DIR Command Screen Capture will appear.

```
Command Prompt - ftp telnet.westnetinc.com
Microsoft Windows 2000 [Version 5.00.2195]
(C) Copyright 1985-2000 Microsoft Corp.

C:\>ftp telnet.westnetinc.com
Connected to telnet.westnetinc.com.
220 telnet Microsoft FTP Service (Version 5.0).
User (telnet.westnetinc.com:(none)): anonymous
331 Anonymous access allowed, send identity (e-mail name) as password.
Password:
230-Welcome to the WestNet Learning Technologies FTP site. All documents herein
are copyright WestNet Learning Technologies. All rights reserved.
230 Anonymous user logged in.
ftp> dir
200 PORT command successful.
150 Opening ASCII mode data connection for /bin/ls.
drwxrwxrwx   1 owner      group            0 Aug 13 12:30 ~tmp
-rwxrwxrwx   1 owner      group            0 Aug 12 11:53 file_id.diz
-rwxrwxrwx   1 owner      group            0 Jun 23  8:37 mT200kbOham
drwxrwxrwx   1 owner      group            0 Aug 17  9:20 pub
226 Transfer complete.
ftp: 273 bytes received in 0.01Seconds 27.30Kbytes/sec.
ftp>
```

FTP DIR Command

After issuing the DIR command, the first part of the file listing has a series of letters and dashes. If the first series is a "-" it means the item is a file. If it is a "d" it indicates a directory. The FTP DIR Command Diagram Screen shows all directories.

You can change directories with the CD command. Use CD PUB to change to the pub directory. You can then type **dir**, and the screen illustrated in the Listing of Pub Directory Screen Capture appears.

```
C:\WINNT\System32\cmd.exe - ftp                                    _ □ ×
250 CWD command successful.
ftp> ls
200 PORT command successful.
150 Opening ASCII mode data connection for file list.
AlienSong.mpg
Apple.pdf
CTI-RFP.Doc
DECNet.pdf
dv_all.hlp
FDDI.pdf
Glossary.doc
Integrate.pdf
IP Telephony.pdf
LANs.pdf
NetNeighbor.doc
POP3 Lab.pdf
Protocol Traces.pdf
scs.pdf
sh_histo
SMTP Lab.pdf
SNA.pdf
SNMP.pdf
226 Transfer complete.
ftp: 234 bytes received in 0.01Seconds 23.40Kbytes/sec.
ftp>
```

Listing of Pub Directory

The directory listing shows the files available for manipulation in the designated directory. For example, if we choose to download the file Glossary.doc, we can type the command get Glossary.doc at the ftp> prompt and retrieve the designated file.

Basic FTP Commands

Objective 1.5
Use/configure Web browsers and other Internet/intranet clients, and be able to describe their use to others.
... The basic commands for each type of client

You may use many commands at the ftp> prompt. Some of the most common include:

- DIR—Displays the contents of the working directory on the remote computer. DIR [*directory name*] displays a specified directory. DIR [*local file name*] writes the directory information to a file on the local computer.

- LS—Lists the files contained in the remote working directory. LS [*directory name*] lists files in a specified directory. LS [*local file name*] writes the file list to a file on the local computer.

- CD [*directory name*]—Changes the working directory on the remote computer.

- CD UP—Changes the working directory on the remote computer to the parent of the current working directory.

- DELETE [*remote file name*]—Deletes a file from the remote computer.

- MKDIR [*remote directory name*]—Creates a new directory within the remote working directory.

- RMDIR [*remote directory name*]—Deletes a directory from the remote computer.

- GET [*remote file name*] [*local file name*]—Copies the specified file from the remote computer to a new file name on the local computer. If a local file name is not specified, the file retains its original file name.

- PUT [*local file name*] [*remote file name*] or SEND [*local file name*] [*remote file name*]—Copies the specified file from the local computer to a new file name on the remote computer. If a remote file name is not specified, the file retains its original file name.

- RENAME [*current file name*] [*new file name*]—Renames a file on the remote computer.

- ? or HELP—Displays help documentation.

- CLOSE or DISCONNECT—Ends the file transfer session but does not exit the FTP application.

- QUIT or BYE—Ends the file transfer session and exits the FTP application.

Using FTP With a Browser

Objective 1.5
Use/configure Web browsers and other Internet/intranet clients, and be able to describe their use to others.

You can also connect to an FTP site using a Web browser:

1. Open a browser.

2. Type the FTP site address in the space where Uniform Resource Locators (URLs) are entered. For example, to access the westnetinc.com FTP site, you must type the following in your browser:

ftp://telnet.westnetinc.com/pub

This will allow you to download files using FTP from the **telnet. westnetinc.com/pub** address. Recognize that we have gone directly to the pub directory in this example, as illustrated on the FTP Using a Browser Screen Capture.

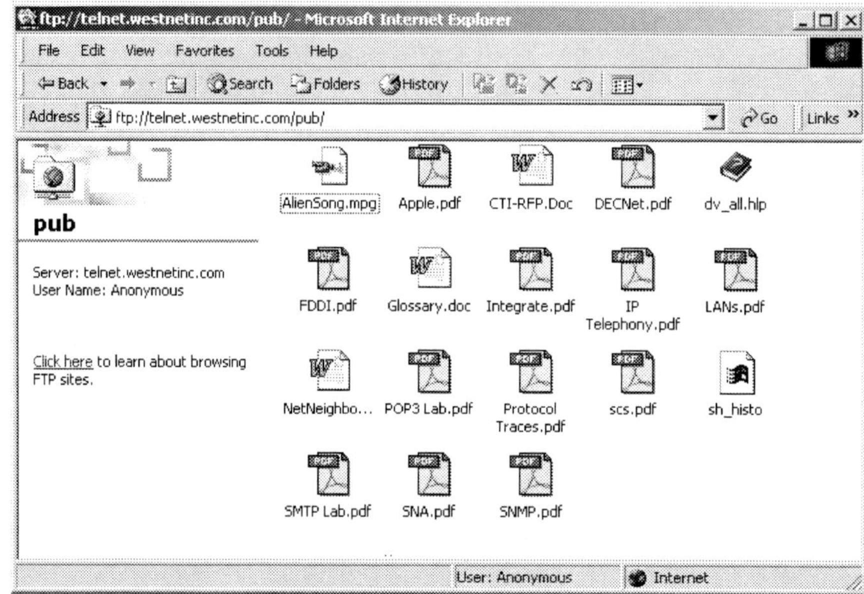

FTP Using a Browser

3. To download a file, click its name in the list.

Same Application, Different Interfaces

FTP is used in both of these hands-on examples. Only the user interface is different in each case.

Activities

1. Which is the best reason to use the FTP application?

    a. When you need to configure a router or switch

    b. When you need to access a Web site

    c. When you need to pass large files over a slow connection

    d. When you need to remotely access a mainframe computer

2. As a result of issuing the FTP DIR command, each file listing entry begins with a "-"; what does the "-" indicate?

    a. The entries are files

    b. The entries are directories

    c. The entries are executable files

    d. The entries are invalid

3. Which FTP command allows you to change directories within a file listing?

    a. CHDIR

    b. CDIR

    c. CD

    d. NEWDIR

4. An FTP server administrator can control server access in which three ways? (Choose three.)

    a. Allow only remote access

    b. Make only portions of the drive visible

    c. Control read and write privileges

    d. Limit file access

Extended Activities

1. Go to the Website **http://www.downloads.com**, and download the latest version of the Ipswitch, Inc. FTP application WS_FTP LE. Scan the download for viruses and install the application.

2. FTP to the **telnet.westnetinc.com** site using both command line FTP and the WS_FTP application. Change to the Pub directory, and locate and download the file Glossary.doc. Which is easier to use, the command line utility or the WS_FTP application?

Lesson 4—Messaging: E-Mail and News

E-mail is the most popular and widely used Internet application. E-mail is a fast and efficient way to communicate with anyone connected to the Internet. We can use e-mail to communicate with one or thousands of people at a time. We can receive and send files and other information with our e-mail messages. We can even subscribe to electronic journals and newsletters. Literally, billions of e-mail messages are sent every day across the Internet.

Network News Transfer Protocol (NNTP) allows Internet sites to exchange USENET news articles, which are organized into topic areas such as programming in C++ or gaming. To access a newsgroup, one opens a news browser client, which connects to a news server. One must be authorized to access the news server to read and post information.

Objectives

At the end of this lesson you will be able to:

- Explain basic e-mail operations

- Describe the parts of an e-mail address

- Identify the key protocols used to send and receive e-mail

- Explain the operation of USENET newsgroups

Key Point

E-mail is the most widely used Internet application.

Reading an E-Mail Address

The source and destination of Internet e-mail are identified by using a two-part name structure. A typical e-mail address consists of a character string that has the following format:

<user>@<domain-name>

The domain name identifies a specific host that has the ability to send and receive e-mail. The user identifies a particular mailbox on a computer identified by the domain name.

E-Mail Protocols

Objective 3.5
Understand how various protocols or services apply to the function of their corresponding server, such as a mail server, a web server or a file transfer server.

TCP/IP networks combine several protocols for implementing an e-mail network, including:

* SMTP

* UNIX-to-UNIX encoding (Uuencode)

* Multipurpose Internet Mail Extensions (MIME)

* POP3

* Internet Message Access Protocol (IMAP) 4

SMTP

SMTP is an Application Layer protocol used to transfer mail across a TCP/IP network. When e-mail is being sent across a TCP/IP network such as the Internet, it is encapsulated in an SMTP header before traversing the network.

The SMTP mail process is composed of two parts:

* Sender SMTP—Concerned with transmission of outgoing e-mail messages

* Receiver SMTP—Involved with reception of incoming e-mail messages from the internet

SMTP is only concerned with the delivery of e-mail from one mail server computer to another. It does not specify how a user edits and presents e-mail to the e-mail system for delivery. SMTP is not concerned with how a user receives notification and retrieves incoming e-mail. SMTP does not specify how e-mail is to be stored or how often messages should be sent. SMTP simply defines the conversation that takes place between the sender SMTP and receiver SMTP. The Model for SMTP Use Diagram illustrates the relationship between sender SMTP and receiver SMTP.

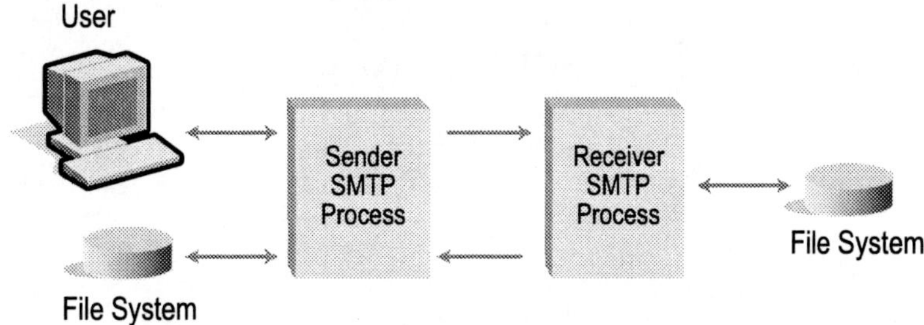

Model for SMTP Use

One of SMTP's limitations is that it limits e-mail messages to 1,000 or less 7-bit ASCII characters. Before sending a message, users are forced to convert any nontextual data (file attachments) into 7-bit bytes represented as printable ASCII characters. One of the first of these encoding methods is Uuencode; another is MIME.

Uuencode

Uuencode takes a binary file such as a Word document and converts it to ASCII for transmission; Uuencode originated on UNIX systems. Though the encoded file is visible in any text editor, it makes no sense until decoded. Some mail systems do not support MIME; thus, file attachments must be encoded with Uuencode.

MIME

MIME is used in conjunction with SMTP for supporting more than just standard ASCII text files. Using MIME, many different types of data can be sent through e-mail. Examples of MIME-supported data types are:

- Binary information—Word processed documents or spreadsheets

- Graphic images—Graphic Interchange Format (GIF) or Joint Photographic Experts Group (JPEG) files

- Video—Moving Pictures Expert Group (MPEG) files

- Audio—Waveform Audio File (WAV) files

MIME is actually an SMTP extension. It enables encoding and transporting within a single message multiple objects that represent body text and character sets, and allows extensions to the original MIME standard. Exceptions include ASCII, images, and audio fragments. RFC 1341 initially described MIME; this has been superseded by RFCs 1521 and 2045.

MIME creates an "envelope" around the attachment consisting of several header fields, indicating the MIME version, the message's content, the type of encoding used, and other extended fields.

S/MIME

Secure/MIME (S/MIME) is a specification for secure electronic messaging. The S/MIME specification was designed to be easily integrated into e-mail and messaging products.

MIME represents e-mail attachment data with a simple Base64 coding technique. Though the attachment is encoded, any device capable of decoding Base64 can intercept and decode the message. S/MIME uses digital signatures and public-key encryption to protect messages from tampering while in transit. S/MIME encrypts the message and encloses it in a digital envelope, which may only be opened by someone holding the sender's public key.

POP3

POP is used to transfer information from a mail server to a user's computer so users can read, delete, or otherwise manage their e-mail; POP3 is the latest version, specified in RFC 1939. A POP mail server stores e-mail until the client requests it. The user uses a desktop e-mail program, such as Lotus Notes, Eudora, or Outlook, to access the mail server and download messages. The POP3 server is responsible for authorizing access in the form of a username and password.

IMAP4

IMAP is another protocol for e-mail message retrieval. The latest version, IMAP4, is similar to POP, but it supports some additional features. POP requires that we first download our messages before we can work with them. With IMAP4, we can search for keywords in our e-mail messages while the messages remain on the mail server. As a result, we can download only those messages we choose. Like POP, IMAP uses SMTP for communication between the e-mail client and server. Refer to **http://www.imap.org/** for more information. RFC 1730 specifies IMAP4.

Mail Server Configuration

Objective 3.5
Understand how various protocols or services apply to the function of their corresponding server, such as a mail server, a web server or a file transfer server.

The E-Mail Communication Diagram illustrates a typical e-mail configuration. The components in this diagram are local mail clients, remote mail clients, and a mail server.

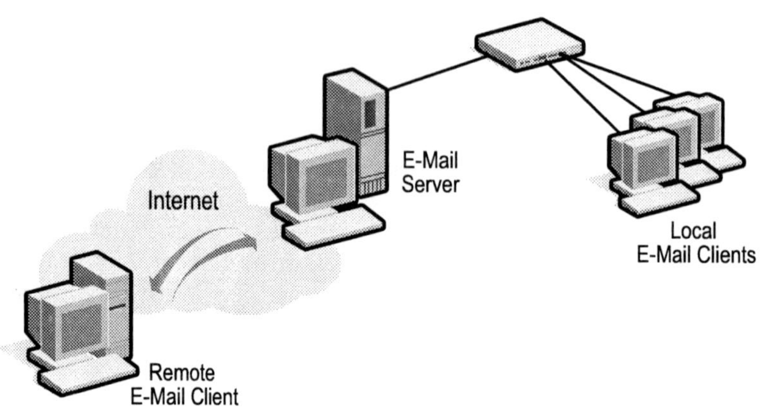

E-Mail Communication

Objective 1.5
Use/configure Web browsers and other Internet/intranet clients, and be able to describe their use to others.

The mail server is the computer that stores and forwards e-mail for all clients that use this particular mail server. Each client must be configured to access the mail server; the clients must know either the server's FQDN or IP address, and present to the server the correct authorization information. Most mail servers today support POP3 or IMAP4; thus, each network client can retrieve information as needed. It is also important that the mail server use MIME for transferring binary information.

Mail gateway software is also used on the mail server to send e-mail messages between different types of e-mail programs. Some e-mail programs use SMTP, while others use proprietary e-mail protocols such as cc:mail. Mail gateways are only needed in systems that do not use SMTP.

Store-and-Forward Mail Systems

SMTP provides delivery of mail from source to destination, that is, end-to-end delivery or direct delivery. Other protocols are referred to as "store-and-forward," meaning the information is sent to a mail server and then to the final destination. The problem with direct delivery of mail is that when the receiving device is turned off, mail cannot be delivered, and the delivery fails. The Direct vs. Store-and-Forward E-Mail Diagram demonstrates the difference between the two types of systems. SMTP is like a mail carrier, responsible for transporting mail. POP3 and IMAP4 are like the post office, responsible for receiving, storing, and forwarding mail.

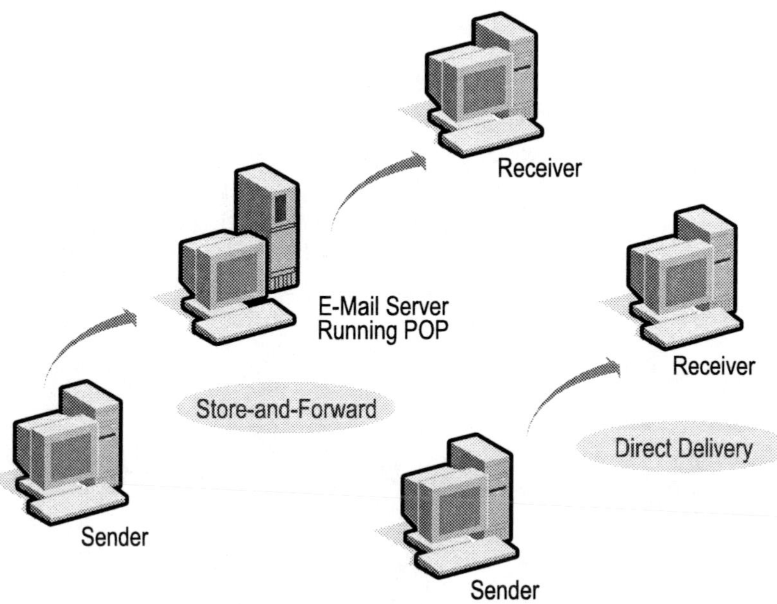

Direct vs. Store-and-Forward E-Mail

Most systems send e-mail to a server first. The information is stored on the server until the host requests the information. The most common method for doing this is to send mail to a server that uses a protocol to move information to the final destination. POP3 or IMAP4 are used for this purpose.

NNTP

Network News Transfer Protocol (NNTP), also called News Transfer Protocol (NTP), is the TCP/IP protocol used to distribute news articles, or newsfeeds, on TCP/IP networks. RFC 977 defines NNTP. Commonly, we find newsfeeds on the Internet; however, we can also place NNTP servers on local internets, intranets, and extranets.

Messages are stored on one or more computers running news server software (NNTP servers). Some news servers replicate their data to others, so traffic for popular newsgroups is not handled by a single server. An NNTP server stores, maintains, and distributes a central database of news articles and newsgroups. NNTP allows a news reader client to post articles to and retrieve articles from a newsgroup, and allows news servers to interact by exchanging newsfeeds.

NNTP is reliable in that it uses TCP as a transport protocol. Because of its interactive capabilities, it provides advantages over other server-to-server or client-to-server copy programs. Rather than transferring an entire database file between communicating nodes, NNTP only transfers the database contents a client or server request. Clients can pick from a list the news articles they wish to read, leaving the remainder on the server.

The NNTP News Reader Screen Capture shows Microsoft Outlook Express used as a news client.

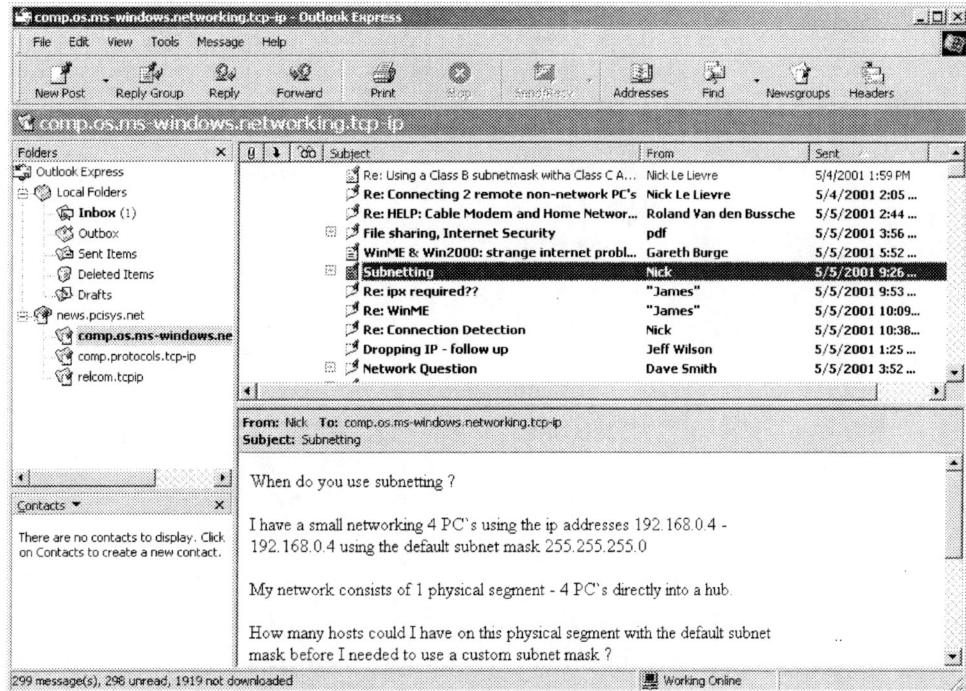

NNTP News Reader

You can download a list of available newsgroups from the news server, and then pick those that pertain to your needs. You can then download the news messages into the reader, and sort them as you would your e-mail messages.

Activities

1. Which is a valid e-mail address?

   a. westnetinc.com@kdr

   b. kdr.westnetinc.com

   c. com westnetinc@.kdr

   d. kdr@westnetinc.com

2. Which two choices are TCP/IP e-mail protocols? (Choose two.)

   a. SMTP

   b. SNMP

   c. LDAP

   d. IMAP

3. Which of the following services does SMTP use?

   a. UDP

   b. TCP

   c. RTP

   d. POP

4. Which of the following statements concerning SMTP is correct?

   a. SMTP notifies users when mail is received.

   b. SMTP defines the message format.

   c. SMTP retrieves mail for the client application.

   d. SMTP delivers mail from one computer to another.

5. Which two protocols deliver e-mail directly to the e-mail client? (Choose two.)

   a. POP3

   b. IMAP4

   c. SMTP

   d. MIME

6. How does S/MIME protect e-mail from forgery and interception?

   a. It only sends messages to the designated recipient.

   b. It encrypts the messages using Base64 encoding.

   c. It hides the sender address from all but the designated recipient.

   d. It uses digital signatures and public-key encryption techniques.

7. Your network Help desk calls and asks you to help troubleshoot an e-mail problem. Several users have complained that when they send e-mail messages with attachments, the recipients reply that the attachments are unreadable. The message body is legible, however. You know that your users encode all attachments using MIME. Which is the best solution to this problem?

   a. Install new e-mail clients for the complaining users, and set the encoding method to MIME.

   b. Tell the users to fax the attachments instead.

   c. Have the users only send text attachments.

   d. Contact the recipients, and have them use MIME to decode attachments.

8. You are a networking consultant for a major telecommunications firm. They ask you to help them resolve a hacked e-mail problem. It seems that someone is intercepting e-mails between district offices and inserting pornographic pictures in place of legitimate e-mail attachments. How might you resolve this problem for them?

   a. Have the users send attachments as Base64 encoded text.

   b. Implement S/MIME encoding on all outbound e-mail attachments.

   c. Implement Uuencoding on all outbound external e-mail attachments.

   d. Switch users from a POP e-mail client to an IMAP client.

Extended Activities

In this activity, you will Telnet into your POP mail server and list the messages waiting for retrieval. You should close your e-mail client before performing this activity. Some e-mail services, such as MSN or AOL, may not allow this.

1. In your e-mail client, look up your ISP's POP e-mail server's FQDN. It will take the form mail.<isp>.net or pop.<isp>.net. Note the FQDN.

2. Open a Telnet session.

3. At the Telnet> prompt, type the FQDN you noted in Step 1. Enter the port number 110.

Note: In the Windows Telnet utility, enter the port number in the Port: line. At the Command prompt, type the FQDN followed by the port number, as in **mail.yahoo.com 110**.

4. After the "+OK POP3 …" line, type **user** followed by your username.

5. After the "+OK Password required for <user> line," type **pass** followed by your password.

6. After the "+OK <user> has x messages line," type **list**. This lists the messages waiting for retrieval from the server.

7. Close the Telnet session.

Lesson 5—IP Address Management: BOOTP, DHCP, and NAT

IP address management generally describes the process of assigning IP addresses to nodes. When both LANs and the Internet were small, administrators used simple, manual methods of address management. But now that the Internet is outgrowing the original IP address space, and enterprise networks may include thousands of nodes, administrators need more sophisticated and efficient tools. This lesson introduces the main protocols and techniques for managing network addresses.

Objectives

At the end of this lesson you will be able to:

- Describe how BOOTP supports dynamic IP addressing

- Explain how Dynamic Host Configuration Protocol (DHCP) dynamically assigns host addresses

- Describe how NAT conserves IP addresses

- Explain how a network can use private addresses and still communicate over the Internet

Key Point

DHCP and NAT conserve scarce IP addresses by temporarily assigning them to nodes.

BOOTP

Bootstrap Protocol (BOOTP) is a TCP/IP Application Layer protocol designed to hand out IP addresses on demand. Though it is not used as frequently as is DHCP, BOOTP provides the basic procedures on which the more capable DHCP is based. Thus, this section serves as the groundwork to our upcoming discussion on DHCP.

RFC 951 defines BOOTP as an IP/UDP bootstrap protocol, designed to allow diskless workstations to discover their own IP addresses. Additionally, BOOTP supplies the workstation's BOOTP server host address and a boot file for the workstation to download and execute. RFC 1542 further clarifies the protocol. BOOTP earned its name from the fact that it is meant to run from within a client workstation's Boot Programmable Read Only Memory (PROM) chip. BOOTP messages are carried within IP datagrams. The BOOTP and OSI Diagram illustrate BOOTP's position in the OSI model.

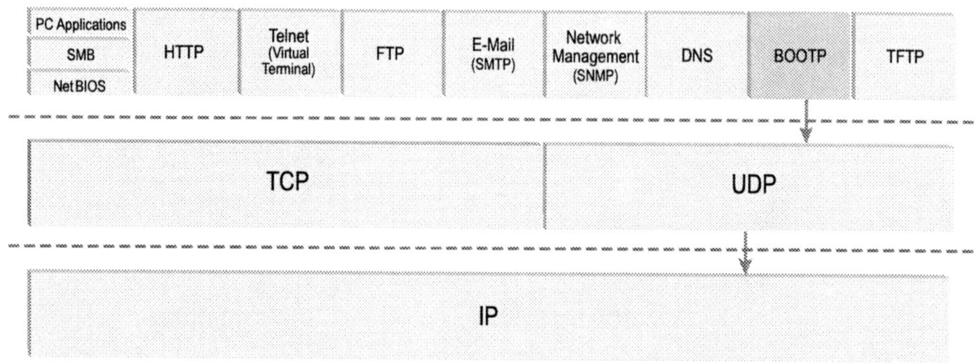

BOOTP and OSI

BOOTP Operation

BOOTP has a client and a server side. A BOOTP client broadcasts a request for configuration information (BOOTREQUEST), and a BOOTP server responds (BOOTREPLY).

Client BOOTREQUEST Message

The client workstation boot PROM must contain enough intelligence to:

- Build the BOOTP message

- Maintain a one entry ARP cache so it can answer ARP requests for its own IP address, if known

The client builds the BOOTREQUEST message on startup. Each of the message header fields captures one item of data that the client must send to the server. Some of the key data fields include the IP addresses of client and server, and the name of the boot file that the client needs, if any.

Server BOOTREPLY Message

When the BOOTP server receives the BOOTP request(s), it verifies and processes it. The server responds to the client's BOOTRE-QUEST message with a BOOTREPLY message that includes information such as the path to the client's boot file and the client's assigned IP address.

After the client processes the server's reply, it knows its own IP address. If necessary, it can then use Trivial File Transfer Protocol (TFTP) to request its boot file (the path was provided by the server).

BOOTP Relay Agents

A BOOTP relay agent allows BOOTP clients to obtain boot information from a server residing on a subnet separate from their own. Although it can operate as a router service, a relay agent performs a function distinct from a router. A router forwards packets from network to network transparently, reading but not altering the packet and its contents. A BOOTP relay agent, on the other hand, accepts BOOTP messages as a final destination, and generates new BOOTP messages as a result. A relay agent can be a router function or a separate device located on the client's subnet.

TFTP

TFTP (RFC 1350) is a very simple file transfer protocol that works with BOOTP and uses the services of UDP. Because TFTP is simple and small, it can be embedded in a device's ROM. Network devices, such as routers and switches, use TFTP for software and firmware upgrades, and for downloading configuration information from a central TFTP server.

TFTP is a connectionless protocol that uses a "lock-step" packet delivery approach. In other words, TFTP requires an acknowledgment for each transmitted packet before it sends the next. TFTP supports only a few packet types:

- Read Request (RRQ)—Sent when the client wishes to download a file.

- Write Request (WRQ)—Sent when the client wishes to upload a file or when the packet begins "mail" mode.

- Data (DATA)—Data fields are typically 512 bytes long, but the last packet may have a shortened Data field.

- Acknowledgment (ACK)—Sent in response to a correctly received packet.

- Error (ERROR)—Sent in response to an error, such as a lost packet or a device input/output (I/O) error.

TFTP transfers files. It does not provide a directory listing and is not particularly reliable. However, it is very easy to implement, uses few network and host resources, and provides built-in rate and error-control in the form of the required ACK packets.

DHCP

DHCP provides a framework for passing configuration information to IP hosts. Though it is based on BOOTP, DHCP adds capabilities to automatically allocate reusable IP addresses for a finite lease period and pass additional IP configuration information. The DHCP to OSI Diagram shows how DHCP maps to the OSI model.

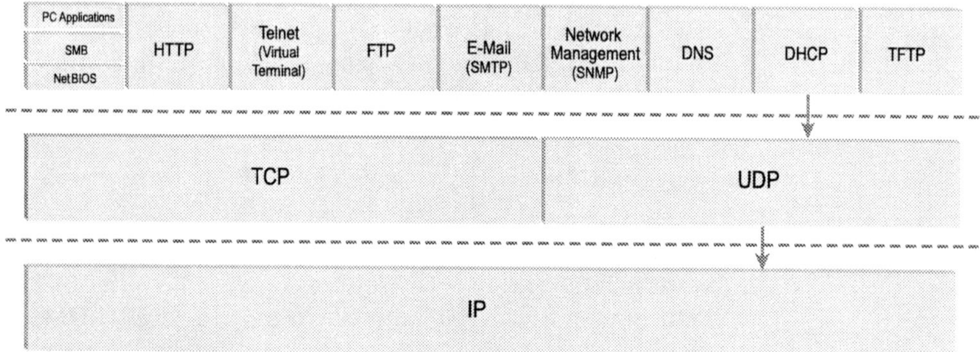

DHCP to OSI

RFC 1531 originally defined the Dynamic Host Configuration Protocol (DHCP) as an Application Layer TCP/IP protocol used to assign reusable IP addresses and configuration information to hosts. DHCP is an extension to BOOTP, adding functionality to the original BOOTP specification. Various RFCs have refined the original; RFC 2131 is the latest revision.

Remember that BOOTP referenced a static, administrator-configured database. Though DHCP does require some initial configuration, it can hand out IP addresses to hosts upon request, without requiring the administrator to manually enter each MAC-to-IP address mapping. Instead, DHCP builds this mapping dynamically and maintains this database as hosts request and release their mapped addresses.

DHCP consists of two components: a protocol for delivering host-specific configuration parameters from a DHCP server, and a mechanism for host network address allocation. DHCP is a client/server application. The host requesting configuration parameters is the client, while the host supplying the configuration parameters is the server.

**DHCP Address
Allocation
Mechanisms**

DHCP provides three address allocation mechanisms:

- Automatic allocation—The DHCP server assigns a client a permanent address. The DHCP server cannot reallocate the address after it is assigned.

- Manual allocation—The administrator sets the IP-to-MAC address mapping, and the DHCP server merely passes on this information to the client.

- Dynamic allocation—The DHCP assigns reusable addresses to the DHCP clients.

Dynamic allocation is the most desirable of these three, for a number of reasons. First, dynamic allocation suits instances where hosts only connect to the network for a short time period or when the server has only a small pool of addresses available. Many ISPs use dynamic IP addressing for their clients, both dial-in and directly connected. This way, when the client disconnects or goes offline, the ISP can reassign the address to another host. Another reason for using dynamic address allocation would be in a case where a new host is added to a network when an old host is retired, and the DHCP address pool is limited. The new host obtains the old host's address, or another address; this way, the address pool maintains the same ratio of hosts to addresses.

One might use manual allocation to avoid the error-prone process of manually configuring hosts. Instead, the DHCP administrator can statically configure the host on the server and allow the client to download its configuration from the server.

ISPs use DHCP to dynamically assign most clients IP addresses when they connect to the ISP's network. This simplifies remote client support by automatically passing such information as the ISP's DNS server and default gateway router addresses, and the client's network address and subnet mask.

DHCP Operation

Where BOOTP defined only two steps (BOOTREQUEST and BOOTREPLY), DHCP RFC 2131 defines four basic address allocation and configuration steps, and additional optional steps. We will concentrate on the four basic steps here: DHCPDISCOVER, DHCPOFFER, DHCPREQUEST, and DHCPACK.

DHCP Services

DHCP provides two services:

- Configuration parameters repository—A DHCP server must provide persistent storage for network client parameters. This is normally in the form of a database, where the client hardware address or hostname references its IP address and other parameters. The DHCP Manager Screen Capture shows a screen snapshot taken from a Microsoft DHCP server.

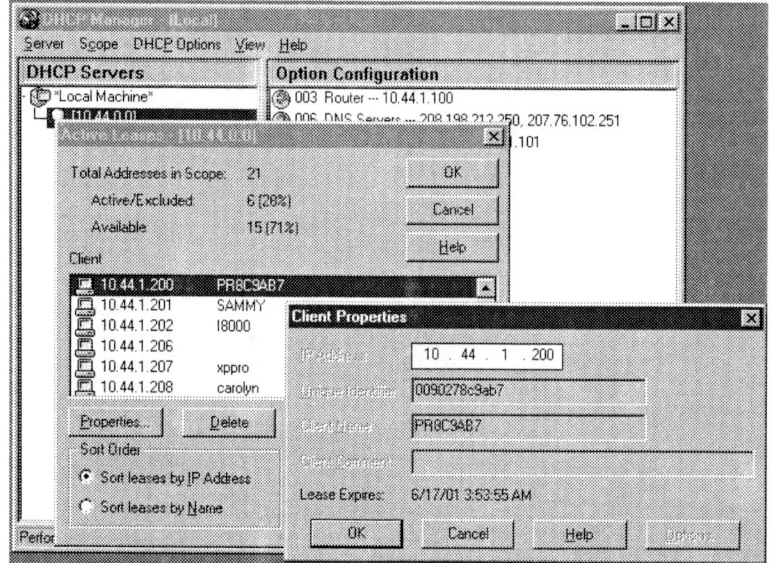

DHCP Manager

The assigned IP address to hostname mappings are shown. You can also see in the background some of the optional parameters passed to the DHCP clients upon their acceptance of the offered lease.

- Dynamic network address allocation—The DHCP server allocates IP addresses to clients, either temporarily or permanently. It does this from the DHCP database, either dynamically or statically.

How DHCP Clients Obtain Configuration Information

As in BOOTP, a DHCP client requests an address, and a server responds. The DHCP Client Initialization Diagram illustrates the DHCP client/server interaction when a client initializes.

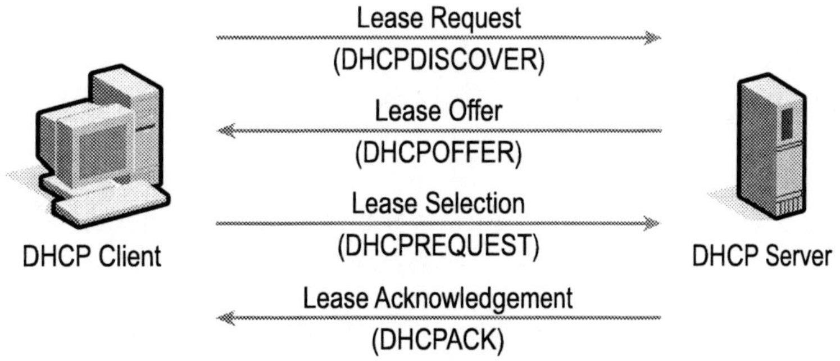

DHCP Client Initialization

When a DHCP client first initializes, it loads a limited version of TCP/IP and enters a number of lease acquisition states in order to obtain an IP address lease from a DHCP server. The process steps are:

1. The client broadcasts a DHCPDISCOVER message to its local subnet. At this point, the client is in the INIT state.

2. A DHCP server responds to the DHCPDISCOVER message with a DHCP offer (DHCPOFFER) message.

3. If no server responds, the client will not initialize TCP/IP. Instead, it continues to resend DHCPDISCOVER messages until it receives a response.

4. When the client receives an offer (or offers), it enters the SELECTING state. It then selects from the received offers a preferred offer, and builds a reply. If more than one server responds to the DHCPREQUEST, the client normally chooses the first offer it receives.

5. The client enters the REQUESTING state by replying to the selected server with a DHCP request (DHCPREQUEST) message.

6. The offering server replies to the DHCPREQUEST with a DHCP acknowledgment (DHCPACK) message.

7. When the client receives the DHCPACK, it configures its TCP/IP properties and joins the network, entering the BOUND state.

In some cases, a DHCP server returns a DHCP negative acknowledgment (DHCPNAK) in response to the client's DHCPREQUEST message. This occurs if a client requests a duplicate or invalid address. The client initialization process fails in this case, and the client must restart from Step 1.

DHCP Client Lease Renewal

All DHCP clients attempt renewal when 50 percent of the lease time has expired; this is the client RENEW state. They do this with a DHCPREQUEST message sent directly to the server that supplied the lease.

If the server is available, it renews the lease with a DHCPACK message, supplying a new lease time and any updated configuration parameters. The client then updates its configuration with this information.

If the server is unavailable, the client can continue to use the lease. At the 87.5-percent lease time point, the client enters the REBIND state. The client broadcasts a DHCPREQUEST to any DHCP server. If the client receives a DHCPACK, it renews the lease and other configuration information. If the client receives a DHCPNAK, it must return to the INIT state.

If the client cannot renew its lease, and the lease expires, client TCP/IP communications stop until the client obtains a new address. Any TCP/IP applications will experience errors until the client obtains a valid IP address.

DHCP Relay Agents

DHCP relay agents are similar to BOOTP relay agents. As a matter of fact, BOOTP routers which are RFC 1542 compliant can support DHCP, as well. The DHCP Relay Agent Diagram illustrates the use of a DHCP relay agent on a subnet remote from the DHCP server.

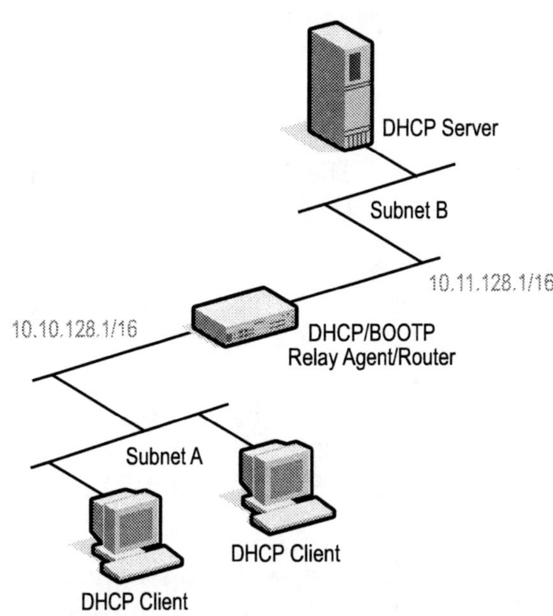

DHCP Relay Agent

A DHCP relay agent works as follows:

1. The relay agent receives a packet containing a DHCPDIS-COVER broadcast message. The packet source address is 0.0.0.0, and the destination address is the limited broadcast address 255.255.255.255. The UDP destination port is 67.

2. The relay agent examines the Giaddr field, and if set to 0.0.0.0, fills the field with the relay agent logical interface address on which the request was received. It then forwards the DHCPDISCOVER message to the DHCP server.

3. When the DHCP server receives the packet containing the DHCPDISCOVER message, it examines the Giaddr field; it then determines from which DHCP scope it must assign the client IP address. A DHCP scope is a range of IP addresses an administrator configures on a DHCP server for assignment to requesting hosts. The scope can cover several subnets; thus, the server must choose for the client an address on the client's home subnet. Otherwise, the client will not be able to communicate using TCP/IP.

4. The DHCP server sends a DHCPOFFER directly to the relay agent identified in the Giaddr field (the original, forwarding relay agent), containing the client IP address lease offer.

5. The router relays the DHCPOFFER to the client by means of broadcast on the requesting client's subnet.

6. The relay agent forwards the subsequent DHCPREQUEST and DHCPACK messages, as well.

IP Address Conflicts

DHCP is a very effective way to manage large scopes of addresses. However, DHCP cannot manage address changes that it is not aware of. IP address conflicts can be caused by simple errors, such as these:

- Two or more DHCP servers have overlapping scopes. This can happen if a new device is misconfigured (by entering the wrong scope during installation), or if a new device installs and runs DHCP by default (without the administrator's knowledge). DHCP servers do not synchronize their databases, so if scopes overlap, two or more servers may assign the same address to different nodes.

- An address is manually configured at a node, and not excluded from the DHCP scope. If a node (such as a Web server) must have a fixed IP address, the administrator can permanently assign it from within DHCP. In that case, DHCP knows to not assign that address to another node.

NAT

Objective 3.7
Create a logic diagram of Internet components from the client to the server
... Router
... NAT

Objective 3.8
Describe various hardware and software connection devices and when to use them
... Router
... NAT

When data, such as a Web page request, is transmitted out of a LAN across the Internet, that packet contains the IP address of the source node. However, there are good reasons why network administrators usually do not want outgoing Internet traffic to identify each source node with a unique IP address.

First, the worldwide Internet community has a short supply of unique IP addresses. This means that each network often uses its own private addressing system that conflicts with the globally unique addresses used across the Internet.

Second, the practice of assigning fixed IP addresses to internal nodes is a potential security risk. A criminal hacker could use that information to penetrate the private network, just as anyone with your phone number can call you in the middle of the night.

RFC 1631, authored in May 1994, describes the Network Address Translator (NAT). NAT allows a private internetwork to use any range of IP addresses it chooses, only presenting to the public Internet a limited public IP address range. Some NAT implementations also provide a modicum of network security, as the internal network can be effectively hidden from the outside world.

A NAT can be a network router or firewall, running network address translator software. It will generally have two physical network interfaces: one on the internal, private network side, and the other on the external, public network side. As we already know, in order for hosts to communicate on the same TCP/IP segment, they must share the same network and subnet IP address portions. Therefore, the administrator assigns the inside NAT port an address on the inside subnet, and the outside port an address on the external network.

The inside, stub domain addresses may be reused anywhere in the world. Private IP address users don't own those address ranges, they are there for all to use. The NAT is installed at the point the private domain needs public access, such as in an Internet gateway router. If a network has more than one public interface, each NAT must use the same address translation table.

NAT Address Spaces

For proper NAT operation, the NAT device must maintain two address spaces: one for the internal, private (local) IP addresses, and one for the external, public (global) IP addresses. Local addresses must not be duplicated, as this will cause the NAT device to lose track of which local device is mapped to which local IP address.

NAT must map private IP addresses to public IP addresses. The NAT device does this in one of two ways:

- Assigns internal devices a unique, global IP address for the extent of the external connection. This is called IP address translation.

- Assigns internal devices the same global IP address and unique TCP or UDP port number. This is called Masquerading or Network Address Port Translation (NAPT).

IP Address Translation

When a NAT uses IP address translation, it assigns global addresses from an address pool. The NAT Address Pool Table is an example of such a pool.

NAT Address Pool

NAT Address Pool: 100.158.0.0—100.158.255.255	
Original Host IP	Translated IP
192.168.2.3	100.158.2.3
192.168.3.4	100.158.3.4
192.168.4.5	100.158.4.5

The NAT device must maintain a table mapping internal addresses to external addresses so it knows which internal device incoming and outgoing packets belong to. NAT devices build these tables in a number of different ways.

Static Address Translation

The above table could represent a simple, static NAT table. The NAT administrator manually configures a set of allowed internal addresses and a NAT netmask of 255.255.0.0. This mask identifies the first two octets as the network portion of each address.

The assigned public address range is 100.158.0.0/16; thus, the NAT maps each internal address's first two octets to the 100.158.0.0/16 network and sets the last two octets as the original host address. Only those devices statically mapped can access the public network.

Thus, as the NAT device processes each outgoing packet, it converts the first two octets to the public address range's first two octets (100.158), and the original last two octets (the host portion) remain as they were in the original address. Likewise, the NAT device converts the first two octets of each incoming packet to the private internal network address (192.168).

Dynamic Address Translation

Dynamic address translation is another type of IP address translation. A static NAT administrator must manually map every internal address that needs external network access. For a large number of hosts, this means maintaining a large map, using a large range of public addresses. A solution to this administrative burden, especially where the public address range is limited and cannot match the number of internal hosts needing external access, is a NAT that provides dynamic address translation.

In dynamic NAT, the NAT device hands out IP addresses on demand, from a preconfigured pool. Normally, the pool's internal-to-external address ratio is something more than one-to-one, meaning that there are more internal addresses needing external access than there are available external addresses. This introduces a potential problem with dynamic address translation: the available external address pool can deplete before all external connection requests are satisfied. When no more external addresses are available, the NAT device must refuse additional connection requests, returning to the requesting host a "host unreachable" message, or something equivalent.

Enhanced Network Security

Dynamic address translation provides a security benefit static address translation cannot. Because static address translation maintains a preconfigured internal to external address mapping, someone wishing to hack into a specific internal host can obtain the host's statically mapped IP address and target that address for attack. As long as that host is online, the hacker can repeatedly attempt to break into the host, until they succeed. However, if a host draws its address from a pool, then a hacker with an intercepted address will likely target different hosts, never having enough time to break into one specific host.

When dynamic address translation is used, externally initiated connections are only possible when a device either has a static mapping assigned, or the NAT device has the dynamic mapping active in the NAT table. Outside connections responding to an internally initiated connection request can progress without problems, as the NAT has the internal host-to-external address mapping still stored in its address translation table. However, when an outsider attempts a connection to one of the internal devices, and no mapping exists for that device, then the outside connection will fail. Additionally, if a connection for an internal device is active at the time the external connection is initiated, it is only active for the duration of the original internal-to-external connection, and thus the externally initiated connection will drop when the original connection drops.

The Dynamic Address Translation Diagram illustrates a sample NAT device configuration using dynamic address translation.

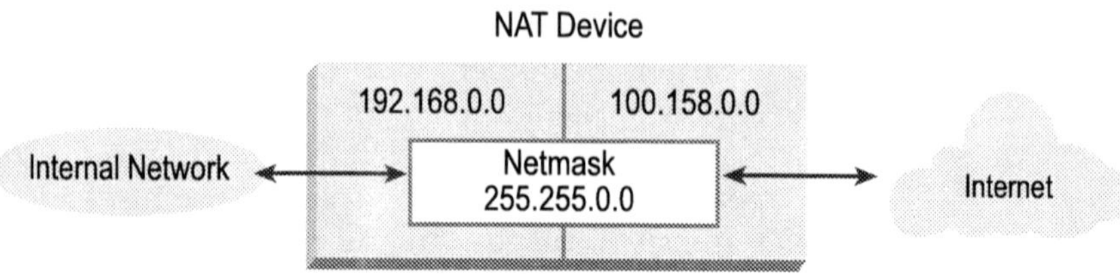

Internal IP	External IP
192.168.1.3	100.158.1.3
192.168.1.4	100.158.1.4
192.168.3.3	100.158.3.3
192.168.2.10	100.158.2.10
192.168.2.1	100.158.2.1
192.168.4.12	100.158.4.12
192.168.0.3	100.158.0.3
192.168.1.6	100.158.1.6

NAT Table

Dynamic Address Translation

The NAT device maintains the address map until the internal device drops the connection and the mapping timeout expires. Note that communication is bidirectional; that is, the NAT device not only allows internal-to-external network connections, but also allows devices to respond to internally initiated connections.

Masquerading/ NAPT

Masquerading is a NAT technique that hides all internal addresses behind one external address. This is also known as Network Address Port Translation (NAPT).

NAPT presents one obvious benefit, and that is that only one public IP address is needed. How can multiple internal hosts use the same address? Instead of the NAT handing each internal host its own external address, NAPT assigns each internal connection a port address associated with a single, shared external IP address. The NAT takes advantage of TCP's ability to multiplex simultaneous connections to the same IP address.

How NAPT Works

NAPT dynamically assigns each internal connection a TCP port associated with the single external address and maintains a mapping of these internal connections to external ports. For example, suppose that a host with address 192.168.4.3 wanted to connect with the Hypertext Transfer Protocol (HTTP) service on the World Wide Web (Web) server with the address 67.89.127.145. This host initiates a connection to the external network server by means of the NAT device, which is configured as the internal host's default gateway. The internal host specifies its own local address as the source address and its locally assigned TCP port as the source port. It specifies the external Web server as the destination IP address and the server's HTTP service well-known TCP port as the destination port. The Internal Host Connection Diagram illustrates this.

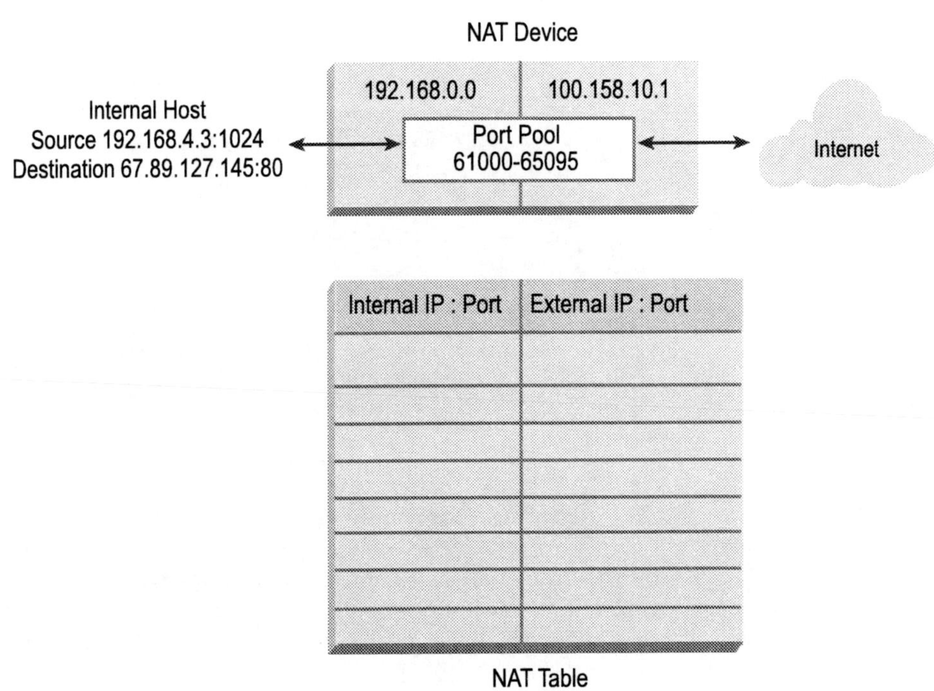

Internal Host Connection

The NAT translates the internal host's IP address to the single, external IP address (in this case, its own external port address), and the source TCP port to one of its available, pooled source ports. It leaves the destination IP and port addresses as the internal host originally specified them. The Assigned External IP and Port Address Diagram illustrates this.

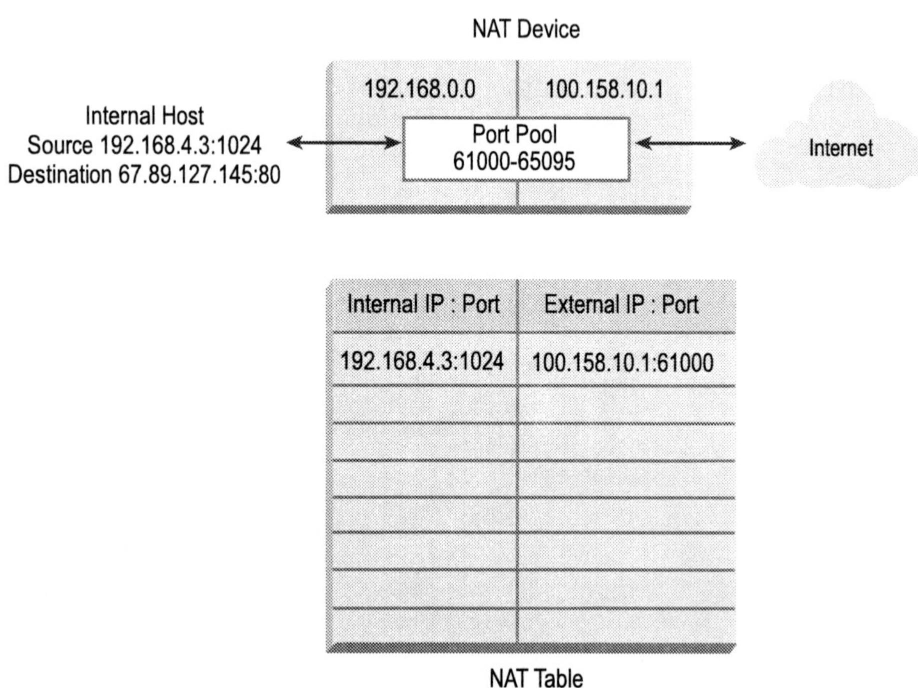

Assigned External IP and Port Address

The internal host can then connect with the external Web server using the NAT-device-assigned shared external address and port. The NAT table reflects this mapping, and the NAT device maintains this mapping for the connection's duration. The Web server can answer the internal host by targeting the NAT assigned public IP address and port, and the NAT will map both connections appropriately.

The NAT can handle additional connections as well, until it exhausts its port pool or its physical resources (central processing unit [CPU], memory, or port throughput). The Multiple NAPT Connections Diagram illustrates a NAPT-capable NAT device with multiple host connections established.

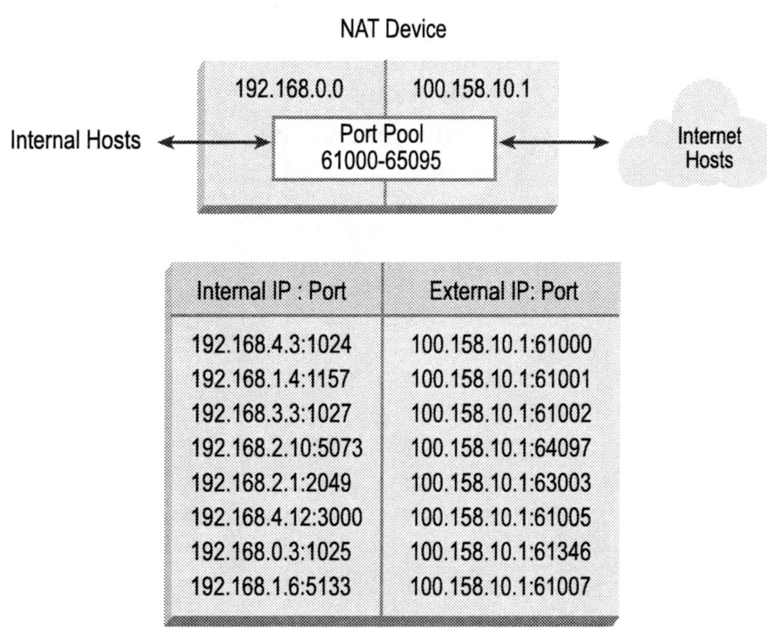

Multiple NAPT Connections

The NAT maps each separate internal host connection to a unique port using the same external IP address, and maintains the mapping for each connection's duration.

NAPT for More Security

When using NAPT, incoming externally initiated connections are virtually impossible. When a host has an entry in the NAT table, this entry is only valid for the active TCP connection. This compares with dynamic IP address translation, where as long as the host is connected to the external network, the NAT maintains a mapped entry. Even ICMP replies reporting connection status (*host/port unreachable*) do not automatically get through the NAT to the internal host, but instead must be filtered and relayed by the NAT device's software.

If for some reason network administrators must allow external connections through the NAT device, they can take additional measures to enable them. For example, they could set up the NAT device so it relays all externally initiated HTTP port connections to a specified internal host. However, because the network has just one externally visible IP address, the NAT device must listen on different ports, one for each service and internal host IP. Because most applications listen on well-known ports that cannot be changed easily (or transparently, to the outside world), this solution is quite inconvenient and often no option at all.

The only solution then is to provide static IP address mappings for whatever internal services that need to listen to the external network on well-known ports. This means maintaining more than one external IP address on the NAT, but in this manner the network can provide some externally accessible services while also protecting the internal network's privacy.

Activities

1. How does NAT help secure a private network from outside attacks?

   a. It allows network administrators to assign private IP addresses to public Internet router ports.

   b. It creates a "sandbox" inside that outside applications run before they execute on a local host.

   c. It encloses all inbound traffic in a secure packet directed at only the target host.

   d. It allows networks to use private IP addresses on the internal network, and still access the Internet.

2. DHCP can pass much more information to a client than just an IP address. True or False?

3. Which NAT address mapping technique maps multiple internal IP addresses to a single, external IP address?

   a. Direct Address Port Translation

   b. Unique Address Translation

   c. IP Address Translation

   d. NAPT

4. Which statement best describes NAT masquerading?

   a. It hides all internal addresses behind one external address.

   b. It hides all internal addresses behind one internal address.

   c. It statically assigns all internal addresses to a single external address.

   d. It hides all internal addresses behind a single port number.

5. If a network has more than one DHCP server, what precaution must the administrator take?

   ____

   ____

   ____

   ____

6. How does NAPT handle an IP packet's source and destination port and IP addresses?

   a. It leaves the source port and address as is, and changes the destination port and IP address to its own external addresses.

   b. It leaves the source and destination ports as is, and changes the source and destination IP addresses to addresses from its address pool.

   c. It leaves the destination port and address as is, and changes the source port and address to addresses from its address pool.

   d. It changes the source port, but leaves the source address, destination port, and address as is.

Extended Activity

You administer a NAPT NAT device, which also serves as your network router.

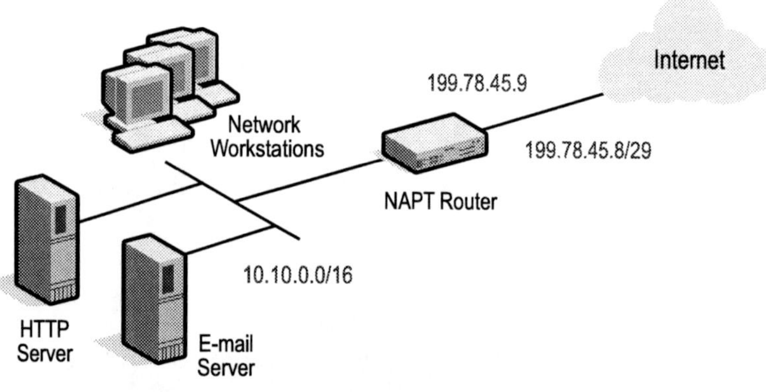

NAPT

Given the following information, and the NAPT Diagram:

- You own the public IP subnetwork 199.78.45.8/29

- You host internal HTTP and SMTP/POP e-mail servers. Their addresses are as follows:

  - HTTP Server: 10.10.0.250, listens on Port 80

  - SMTP/POP E-Mail Server: 10.10.0.251, listens on Ports 25 (SMTP) and 110 (POP3)

- The NAT device's outside interface IP address is 199.78.45.9/29

- The NAT maps internal connections to external addresses using the registered TCP and UDP port numbers 1024–65535

1. Fill out the following table, mapping the HTTP and SMTP/POP e-mail servers and four client connections through the NAT device. The e-mail server only allows internal client connections.

Internal Address	Internal Source Port	External Address	External Source Port
10.10.1.2	1028		
10.10.0.17	4350		
10.10.3.120	1200		
10.10.4.5	1029		
10.10.0.250	80		
10.10.0.251	25		

Lesson 6—IP Name Resolution: HOSTS, DNS, and WINS

Network nodes communicate with one another through numeric hardware or network addresses. However, most users find it difficult to remember numeric addresses, preferring instead to give descriptive names to computer hosts and resources.

The compromise between these needs is called name resolution. Just as you can use a friend's name to look up his telephone number in a phone book, various systems of name resolution allow a computer to use a descriptive computer name to look up the numeric IP address assigned to that node.

This lesson introduces the most common methods of name resolution: the hosts file, the Domain Name System (DNS), and Windows Internet Naming Service (WINS).

Objectives

At the end of this lesson you will be able to:

- Name and describe the key methods of name resolution

- Describe the DNS tree structure

- Explain the structure of a domain name

- Describe how NetBIOS names are mapped to IP addresses

Key Point

Name resolution translates user-friendly computer names to numeric IP addresses.

HOSTS File

A file named HOSTS (with no extension) is most similar to our phone book example. This text file lists descriptive computer names, as well as the IP address assigned to each name. When an application uses "Mail Server" as the destination of a message, lower-layer processes can check the HOSTS file for the IP address of that destination computer.

HOSTS file entries are arranged in columns, separated by spaces, as follows:

IP-address   Official-host-name   aliases

The HOSTS file provides very fast name resolution, because a copy of the file is located on each computer's local drive. However, there are several drawbacks to this method:

- Manual updates—An administrator or user must manually update the HOSTS file to add, delete, or change network addresses. On a network of more than a few nodes, this quickly becomes a burden.

- No synchronization—Since each computer has its own HOSTS file, those individual files quickly become inconsistent.

- Limited scope—If a very small network never needed to connect to the Internet, then a HOSTS file might be sufficient. But it is impossible for a single file to list all IP addresses on the Internet.

For these reasons, and more, the HOSTS file has been largely replaced by the Domain Name System (DNS). However, each PC that uses TCP/IP usually still has a HOSTS file somewhere on its drive. For example, a Microsoft Windows PC places its HOSTS file in the Windows directory. That default file usually contains only one entry for the IP loopback address (used for local testing): 127.0.0.1. The HOSTS File Diagram shows a default HOSTS file from a Windows 2000 workstation.

```
# Copyright (c) 1993-1999 Microsoft Corp.
#
# This is a sample HOSTS file used by Microsoft TCP/IP for Windows.
#
# This file contains the mappings of IP addresses to host names. Each
# entry should be kept on an individual line. The IP address should
# be placed in the first column followed by the corresponding host name.
# The IP address and the host name should be separated by at least one
# space.
#
# Additionally, comments (such as these) may be inserted on individual
# lines or following the machine name denoted by a '#' symbol.
#
# For example:
#
#      102.54.94.97     rhino.acme.com          # source server
#      38.25.63.10      x.acme.com              # x client host

127.0.0.1       localhost
```

HOSTS File

DNS

Sit down at your PC, open your browser, and type in a URL, for example, **http://www.westnetinc.com**. Watch the lower left corner (Internet Explorer) and you will see a line that states "Connecting to site 205.169.85.247." This is DNS in action; you type a URL, and your client resolves the user-friendly URL to a PC friendly IP address. You could type into your browser the server's IP address, **http://205.169.85.247**, and make the same connection, but imagine how difficult it would be to remember your favorite Web sites if you could only connect by IP address.

Hierarchical Structure

Objective 3.3
Understand and be able to describe the use of Internet domain names and DNS
… Hierarchical structure
… Top level or original domains

DNS grew from a need to expand the Internet name database. Until DNS, Stanford Research Institute Network Information Center (SRI-NIC) maintained and updated a central database in the form of a HOSTS table. Network administrators submitted their changes, and the SRI-NIC updated the table. Network administrators then used FTP to download the latest host table and update their local domain name servers. A central database was efficient when there was a small group of users, and database entries seldom changed.

However, as TCP/IP became more widely adopted, it became increasingly difficult to keep the central host table current. Therefore, it was necessary to find a naming system that would allow local name administration and maintenance, while at the same time providing a single, consistent naming scheme.

The DNS protocol extended the Internet name database by devising a system whereby names could be placed into distributed categories that could later be further partitioned. Categories were defined according to domains of authority. So instead of a "flat" list file, DNS establishes rules for a tree-structured hierarchy of names. And instead of storing all names in a single centralized file, individual branches (and subbranches) of the tree can be stored in separate locations and administered by different organizations.

TLDs

The tree-structured DNS namespace starts at the root level. This is where the domain authority distribution begins, and is designated by a "." (period).

Initially, six top-level domains (TLDs) were defined, located immediately below the root, to reflect current users, as well as new groups adopting TCP/IP networks. These original domain names are:

- gov (government)

- edu (education)

- com (commercial)

- mil (military)

- org (organization, usually nonprofits)

- net (network service providers)

Each country is assigned a two-letter TLD code; the United States uses .us (though it is often not shown), and other countries have their own codes. The complete top-level domain country code listing may be found at **http://www.iana.org/cctld/cctld-whois.htm**.

Additionally, on November 16, 2000, the Internet Corporation for Assigned Names and Numbers (ICANN) approved seven new TLDs. These are:

- aero (air transport industry)

- biz (businesses)

- coop (cooperatives)

- info (unrestricted)

- museum (museums)

- name (individual name registration)

- pro (professional occupations)

Distributed Authority

The DNS domain authority is distributed. The ICANN authorizes distributed domain registrars to administer the top-level domains, and these registrars authorize qualified organizations to participate as next-level domains in the hierarchy. The ICANN authorized domain registrars give up some of their authority to second-level domain administrators, who administer their domains and can authorize the addition of subdomains. Adding domains and granting authority over names to new subdomains proceeds in a similar manner down the hierarchy. The Hierarchical Structure for Three Top-Level Domains Diagram shows DNS as a tree structure that starts with top-level domains.

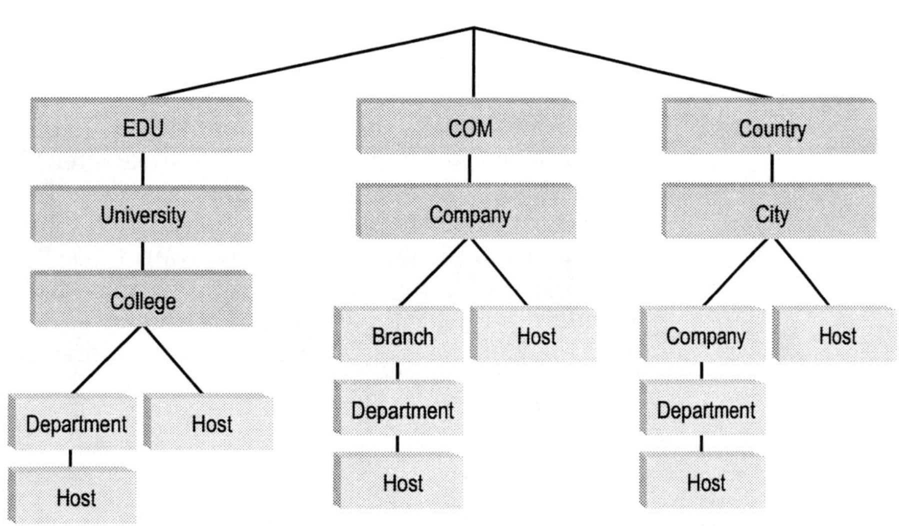

Hierarchical Structure for Three Top-Level Domains

Second-Level Subdomains

Each domain has an administrator who can authorize the formation of a new subdomain. A new subdomain has a specific scope of authority, called zone of authority, usually over the named nodes within a given network system or group of systems.

Second-level domain administrators register their domain names with ICANN-designated domain name registrars (listed on the ICANN Web site). For a fee, these registrars will register your company or private domain name and place the name to address mapping in the global DNS namespace.

Second-level domains can also be categories of top-level domains. For example, the .us TLD is categorized by state, such as Colorado:

.co.us

Second level domain administrators may break down their subdomains into smaller subdomains, such as:

support.instructors.westnetinc.com

Zones

Domain administrators cut their domain space subtrees to form zones based on organizational or protocol family requirements. Zones are domain groupings formed and administered as DNS subtrees.

Each zone consists of at least one domain name, and all nodes within a zone are connected. Each zone is often identified by the name of the node that is closer to the root. That node, which hosts a name server application, is usually responsible for resolving name inquiries for its particular zone. In DNS terminology, we say that the name server is "authoritative" for that zone. For example, on the Sample Domain Names in Two-Zone Tree Structure Diagram, Zone X is Education (.education.stanford.edu), and Zone Y is Physics (.physics.stanford.edu).

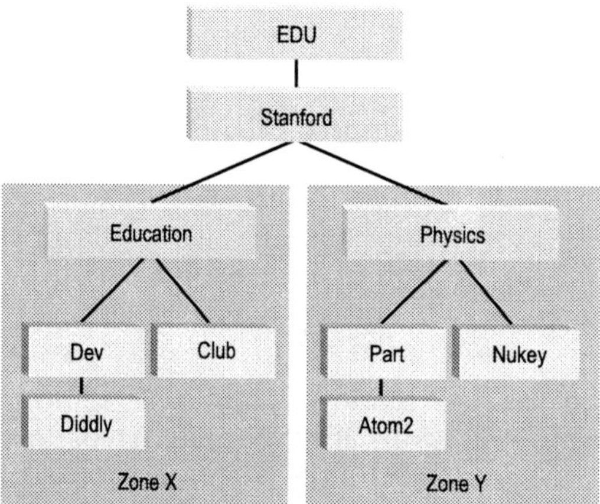

Sample Domain Names in Two-Zone Tree Structure

Domain Names

The DNS hierarchy allows it to use names in the same intuitive way that people do. Each DNS host name is not required to be unique. Unique host addressing is achieved by using as much of the naming hierarchy as is necessary to distinguish one host from another.

For example, a small company called ACME has so few employees that its internal documents can simply say "Refer this to Fred." If Fred were a network host, then his DNS name would be:

> fred.ACME

Since there is only one Fred in the company, the ACME network can be configured to simply use "fred" as a node address.

When the company grows big enough to have multiple departments and locations, it can ensure uniqueness by subdividing its domain. Each domain can then include a different employee named Fred:

> fred.sales.ACME

> fred.accounting.ACME

Now that there is more than one Fred, node names must be more complete, such as "fred.sales." As long as we are still working within the same organization, it is not necessary to include more information. But to ensure uniqueness among multiple organizations, we need to specify all of a DNS name:

> fred.sales.ACME

> fred.sales.Megacorp

Types of Domain Names

There are two types of domain names:

- Relative name—A relative name includes the starting labels of a domain name, usually the minimum ones required for unique identification within a known system. Relative names are used within a subtree or subdomain, where the software can readily resolve the complete name of the host or resource.

- Absolute name, or fully qualified domain name (FQDN)—This name includes all labels in the DNS hierarchy, from the host name to the top-level domain label, and includes a dot after the last label.

Domain Name Syntax

Domain names are expressed as alphanumeric strings separated by dots. Each part of a domain name is referred to as a label; a label is a character or digit string separated from other labels in the domain name by dots. The maximum length of a label is 64 characters, and the maximum length of a domain name is 255 characters. Domain names are case-insensitive.

DNS Client/ Server Operation

DNS is a client/server system. DNS server applications, also called name servers, provide the name resolution service; the DNS client side is known as a resolver.

Name Servers

Objective 3.3
Understand and be able to describe the use of Internet domain names and DNS.
… DNS entry types
… Role of root domain servers

Name servers are designated according to the level of the DNS hierarchy for which they are responsible:

- **A root name server** is authoritative for the worldwide top-level domains. The worldwide DNS database is replicated among a small handful of root servers.

- **A primary name server** is authoritative for a portion of the DNS namespace, such as one corporation's subdomain, or a zone within that subdomain. If a network is connected to the Internet, the primary name server represents that network subdomain to the rest of the Internet. Each primary name server must know the address of at least one root name server.

- **A secondary name server** contains a copy of the DNS information stored on a primary name server, and provides name resolution if the primary name server fails.

Name servers maintain domain name information in a text file. In this file, each node's name and address is listed on a single line, called a resource record (RR). Each name server can serve as a repository for more than one zone. In turn, DNS requires that each zone have its information stored in more than one name server. Thus, a zone commonly has one primary name server and one or more secondary name servers.

A name server's main function is to answer queries regarding names, addresses, and name-to-address or address-to-name mappings. To do this, name servers use the hierarchical structure of DNS. For example, a LAN's name server can resolve internal IP addresses for its own network. But when a user wants to connect to a distant Web site, the LAN's name server may ask for that address from a name server at the company's ISP. If the ISP's name server doesn't know the address, it can query another server, and so on.

To provide quick responses to queries, name servers manage the following two domain name information types:

- Local data for the zone(s) that it supports or over which it has authority. Local data can include pointers to other name servers that might provide additional required information.

- Cached data that contains information gathered from responses resolved, or answered, by other name servers.

Resolvers

A resolver is a client program that uses the services of name servers to resolve names to IP addresses. When a user program needs an IP address, it sends the request to a resolver program that is generally located on the same computer. The resolver passes that request to the name server. When a resolver receives the address from the name server, it returns the information in a form compatible with the local host's data formats. A resolver also keeps a cache of prior queries and uses this cache to answer new queries, when applicable.

In some implementations, the resolution function is moved from the requesting computer to the name server. This might be done to centralize the cache, or because some requesting computer (such as a PC) does not have the resources to maintain a resolver.

Querying the Name Database

A resolver formulates a query, based on the client's request, and directs the query to name servers that can provide the information. The Querying the Name Database Diagram illustrates this function. The resolver starts with a list of name servers to query.

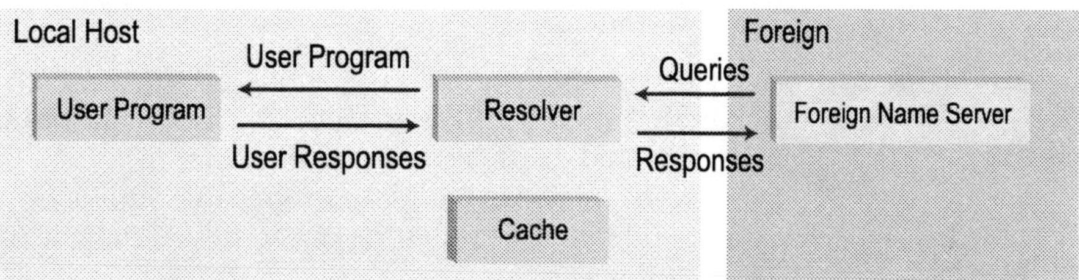

Querying the Name Database

Name servers handle queries iteratively or recursively, as described below:

- Iterative approach—When the requested domain name is not in its database, the name server refers the client to another server and allows the client to pursue the query with that server. A standard query is handled iteratively.

- Recursive approach—The name server takes responsibility for tracking down a response to the client's query. If the domain name requested is not in its database, the name server pursues the query on another server.

NetBIOS Name Resolution

Windows network communication was based on NetBIOS and NetBEUI. Instead of using DNS names to identify hosts, Windows 95/98/NT uses 16-character NetBIOS computer names. When a NetWare client is installed over a Windows desktop OS, that workstation is also identified by a NetBIOS name. Thus, before a Windows or NetWare client can use TCP/IP, it must be able to resolve NetBIOS names to IP addresses. There are three methods of NetBIOS name resolution:

- Broadcasts

- LMHOSTS files

- Windows Internet Naming Service (WINS)

Broadcasts

A node broadcasts a request for the IP address that corresponds to a destination NetBIOS name, and the destination node responds with its address. On small networks, this approach is simple and effective. On large networks, it can create excessive broadcast traffic. Also, since broadcasts are not forwarded by routers, this method cannot resolve addresses on distant subnets.

LMHOSTS file

Each computer has a copy of this text file, which statically maps NetBIOS names to IP addresses. LMHOSTS has the same advantages (speed) and disadvantages (administration) of the HOSTS file. Small networks may use broadcasts to resolve addresses within each subnet, and LMHOSTS files for key addresses outside of a subnet.

WINS

Windows Internet Naming Service (WINS) is a Windows server-based application that provides dynamic mapping of NetBIOS computer names to IP addresses. WINS maintains a central list that maps NetBIOS names to IP addresses.

As each client workstation boots up and connects to the network, it checks in with the WINS server to see if its computer name is valid. If no other computer is using the requested name, the server registers the computer's name and IP address in the WINS database. So even if the client has just received a new IP address from DHCP, that new address will be updated in WINS.

If the requested name is already in use, the server tells the client to choose another name. Thus, WINS ensures that NetBIOS names are unique within each network.

When a client needs to resolve a computer name to an IP address, it sends a query directly to the WINS server. This reduces network traffic by eliminating the broadcast messages used for name resolution.

For fault tolerance, two or more WINS servers on the same network can exchange databases. If a network's only WINS server fails, all clients simply fall back to the broadcast method of name resolution. However, since broadcast traffic is not forwarded across routers, this approach will only ensure communication within each subnet. To continue internetwork communication after the failure of a single WINS server, each client must also have an LMHOSTS file that lists key outside addresses.

Name Resolution Challenges

As you have seen in this lesson, there are two major systems of centralized IP name resolution: DNS and WINS. Depending on the network operating system(s) in use, and the specific technical requirements of the network, an organization may choose to use either one of these, or both:

- UNIX/Linux uses DNS as its native method of name resolution. Those systems do not use NetBIOS names.

- Windows 95/98/NT, and NetWare clients over Windows, use NetBIOS names. Either LMHOSTS or WINS is needed to resolve those names to IP addresses.

- Windows 2000 uses DNS as its name resolution system. But Windows 2000 servers also include WINS to support hosts running Windows 95/98/NT.

Incompatible Systems

Name resolution becomes complex when systems that use Net-BIOS names also need DNS for Internet connectivity. WINS and DNS are completely independent of each other, and each maintains its own mapping file.

Static vs. Dynamic

When DNS was designed, IP addresses were still manually assigned to each device, and static DNS mapping files were built and maintained by human administrators. But like many other aspects of network administration, static DNS systems don't make sense for larger, fast-changing networks that use DHCP to assign IP addresses.

A proposed standard called Dynamic DNS (RFC 2136) promises both the convenience of DHCP and the flexibility of DNS. Dynamic DNS creates a cooperative relationship between a DHCP server and a DNS name server. Each time the DHCP server assigns an IP address, it sends an update message to the name server, which updates the DNS tree. Both NetWare 5.1 and Windows 2000 servers include applications that support this approach.

Activities

1. Which two mechanisms might a host use to resolve FQDNs to IP addresses? (Choose two.)

    a. LMHOSTS

    b. HOSTS table

    c. WINS

    d. DNS

2. A small office has ten Windows 98 hosts on a single peer-to-peer network with no Internet connection. To use TCP/IP for internal communication, what must each computer have?

    a. LMHOSTS

    b. WINS

    c. DNS

    d. DHCP

3. Where does the DNS namespace begin?

    a. The root

    b. Top level domains

    c. Hostnames

    d. Country code domains

4. The maximum DNS domain name length is how many characters?

    a. 64

    b. 128

    c. 200

    d. 255

5. Which two of the following are examples of relative domain names in the westnetinc.com domain? (Choose two.)

    a. telnet.westnetinc.com

    b. telnet

    c. telnet.westnetinc

    d. host1.telnet.westnetinc.com

6. A local area network includes three Windows 2000 servers, 85 Windows 2000 clients, and five UNIX clients. All nodes need to communicate using TCP/IP, and everyone needs Internet connectivity. What method of IP name resolution is best for this network?

   a. WINS

   b. DNS

   c. HOSTS

   d. LMHOSTS

7. Zones maintain domain name information in which record types?

   a. Zone records

   b. Resource records

   c. Domain records

   d. Authority records

Extended Activities

1. Look at your HOSTS file. If you are running Windows 95/98, look for the file in your Windows directory. On a Windows NT/2000 system, HOSTS is located in the **%systemroot%\system32\drivers\etc** folder. To identify your systemroot folder, select Start, Run, and type %systemroot%.

2. Log on to the InterNIC network solutions address at **http://www.networksolutions.com/**. Enter a name you would like to register and see whether it is available. If the name is not available, go to the "whois" selection and type the name to see who registered the domain name.

Summary

This unit provided an overview of some of the more important applications that support the functionality of World Wide Web sites.

Hypertext Transfer Protocol (HTTP) allows communication between Web clients (browsers) and Web servers. A client transmits an HTTP request to a Web server, and the server responds with an HTTP message that may also include an HTML document.

Telnet allows a local computer to run applications on a remote computer. One common Telnet use is to connect to a device, such as a switch or router, in order to configure it. A user calls a Telnet program, either from the command line or through an Internet browser, such as Netscape.

FTP sends and retrieves files across a network. As with Telnet, FTP can be run from a command line or a browser. Many different clients can access an FTP server, as long as they are also running the FTP program. Transferring files is the most common use for FTP.

E-mail is the most frequently used application in computer networking. SMTP is the TCP/IP Application Layer protocol used to move mail between mail servers in a TCP/IP environment. Other important protocols that work with SMTP are POP3, MIME, and IMAP4. POP3 is used to download mail messages from a mail server to a client. MIME is used to attach various file types to an e-mail message. IMAP4 allows clients to manipulate messages directly on the server, allowing them to download only those files they choose.

Several application protocols help an administrator assign and manage IP addresses. BOOTP allows diskless workstations to retrieve IP addresses and startup files from a server. DHCP efficiently uses a pool of addresses by assigning each one for a limited period of time. NAT serves as an IP proxy by mapping multiple internal hosts to a small number of publicly-unique IP addresses.

Other protocols and services resolve human-friendly computer names to IP addresses. DNS, a standard protocol, uses a distributed tree-structured database to identify computers and map computer names to addresses. DNS provides name resolution both across the Internet and within private LANs. WINS, proprietary to Windows NT servers, resolves Windows NetBIOS names to IP addresses. WINS and DNS operate independently of each other, but new applications can synchronize their separate databases.

Other application protocols are also used in TCP/IP networks; however, these protocols are the most widely used. These applications all use underlying TCP/IP protocols to move information across LANs, campus networks, metropolitan area networks (MANs), and WANs, between source and destination computers.

Unit 5 Quiz

1. NNTP allows TCP/IP users to perform which of the following?

   a. Terminal emulation

   b. Download e-mail

   c. Collect network information

   d. Download news articles

2. The underlying Application Layer protocol of the Web is:

   a. IP

   b. TCP

   c. FTP

   d. HTTP

3. A daemon is the equivalent to which Windows component?

   a. Device driver

   b. Kernel

   c. Service

   d. Control

4. For what purpose would you choose to run the Telnet application?

   a. To access a Web site

   b. To configure a router

   c. To download a file

   d. To manage the network

5. FTP is used for what purpose?

   a. To manage remote devices

   b. To download e-mail files

   c. To download HTML files

   d. To download large files

6. Why does SMTP need additional protocols to carry nontext data as attachments?

   a. An SMTP packet is limited to 1,000 bits in size.

   b. SMTP only carries ASCII text characters.

   c. SMTP is incompatible with MIME attachments.

   d. SMTP is too slow on its own to carry large attachments.

7. SMTP is which type of message delivery system?

   a. Store-and-forward

   b. Direct delivery

   c. Unreliable

   d. Best-effort

8. Which two of the following are MIME supported data types? (Choose two.)

   a. Uuencode

   b. MPEG

   c. GIF

   d. POP

9. Which TCP/IP application uses a lock-step packet delivery approach for file transfers?

   a. TFTP

   b. FTP

   c. SMB

   d. HTTP

10. To resolve FQDNs to binary IP addresses, resolvers contact which type of TCP/IP application server?

    a. WINS

    b. NetBIOS

    c. DHCP

    d. DNS

11. Which DHCP network address allocation mechanism assigns a host a temporary IP address?

    a. Automatic

    b. Dynamic

    c. Manual

    d. Static

12. What statement about HTTP is false?

    a. HTTP communication is stateless

    b. HTTP provides the mechanism for moving HTML documents

    c. HTML packets are encapsulated within HTTP frames

    d. HTTP's list of messages and methods is extensible

13. What information will you probably need to provide before you can download a document from an anonymous FTP site?

    a. An e-mail address

    b. Your username and password

    c. Nothing

    d. Your digital certificate

14. From largest to smallest, the DNS namespace is divided into:

    a. Zones, subdomains, and top level domains

    b. Top level domains, subdomains, and zones

    c. Domains, zones, and cuts

    d. Top level domains, zones, and subdomains

15. An HTTP server listens on what well-known port?

    a. 110

    b. 80

    c. 79

    d. 23

16. What HTTP method does a Web browser use to request a page?

    a. SEND

    b. COPY

    c. RETRIEVE

    d. GET

17. What happens when a node's DHCP lease expires?

    a. The node cannot communicate using TCP/IP

    b. The node continues to use its last-assigned IP address

    c. The node assumes the role of the DHCP server, and issues an address to itself and any other node that requests one

    d. The node begins using 0.0.0.0 as its IP address

18. Which statement is NOT true about network address translation?

    a. NAT maps each internal address to a different external address

    b. LAN security is stronger when using NAPT

    c. NAPT maps each internal address to a single external address but a different port number

    d. A public Web server cannot coexist with a NAT

19. If a DHCP client fails to renew its lease at the 50-percent point, what happens next?

    a. It must immediately cease using the lease.

    b. It enters the REBIND state at 75-percent lease time.

    c. It broadcasts a DHCPREQUEST message.

    d. It tries to renew again at 87.5-percent lease time.

20. In a typical DNS query, what happens if the requested domain name is not in a name server's database?

    a. The name server contacts the master ICANN name server, copies the record to its database, then returns the answer to the client

    b. The name server returns a "record not found" message to the client

    c. The name server contacts other name servers until it finds the information, then returns the answer to the client

    d. The name server refers the client to another name server that might have the information

21. A request header is used to:

    a. Allow the client to send additional information to the server

    b. Allow the server to send additional information to the client

    c. Allow the client to redirect requests to a mail server

    d. All of the above

Unit 6
Internet Clients and Servers

The Internet is a worldwide client/server environment, in which the heaviest work is usually done by the servers. In most cases, complex server applications respond to requests from relatively simple client applications such as browsers and e-mail readers.

This unit introduces the server computers and applications that enable various Internet services, such as e-mail, FTP, and the World Wide Web. Traditionally, each type of server was accessed by a different, corresponding client application. But as you will see, multiple types of servers are increasingly being accessed by a few multipurpose clients.

Lessons

1. Client Applications

2. Server Platforms

3. Server Applications

Terms

Active Server Pages (ASP)—ASP is a Microsoft technology for dynamic Web pages. ASP contains blocks of VBScript or Jscript, which a Web server interprets to create a unique HTML page for each browser request.

browser (Web browser)—A Web browser is an Internet client application used to locate and display Web pages. The two most popular browsers are Netscape Navigator and Microsoft Internet Explorer.

cache memory—Disk cache memory is a portion of random access memory (RAM) that holds a copy of most-commonly requested data. Using disk cache speeds up computer operations because accessing data stored in RAM is much faster than accessing data stored on a hard drive.

cache server (proxy server)—A cache server is a hardware device that holds copies of frequently requested Web pages. It reduces traffic on a Web server by intercepting and responding to HTTP requests for pages held in cache.

Certificate Authority (CA)—A CA is an organization that creates digital certificates for individuals and Web servers, after verifying the identity of those persons or sites. A CA signs each digital certificate with its own digital signature; thus, vouching for the identity and trustworthiness of the owners of the certificates.

client—A client is any program that requests a service or resource from another program, either on the same computer or a different one. This term is often used to refer to the computer that hosts the client program; however, a client program may also run on a computer that normally functions as a server. See server.

client-side script—A client-side script is a program that runs on the client side of a client/server process. For example, client-side scripts in Web pages run on Web clients (browsers).

Common Gateway Interface (CGI)—CGI is a standard specification for creating Web server programs that accept data from Web clients, process the data, and return a result. For example, each HTML form needs a corresponding CGI program to process form data sent to its Web site. CGI programs can be written in a variety of languages, including C, Perl, Visual Basic, and Java.

cookies—A cookie is a small file that a Web site places on your computer. The cookie stores information about your preferences or about what you viewed on the site previously. The next time you visit that site, the cookie gets sent back to the site. Cookies can be used to rotate the banner ads that a site sends. They can also be used to customize pages for you based on information you have provided to the Web site. Settings in your browser allow you to control how it handles cookies.

daemon—A daemon is a UNIX process that runs in the background and performs an operation at a specified time or in response to a certain event. A Microsoft Windows equivalent to a daemon is a service or system agent.

digital certificate—A digital certificate is a unique electronic file used to authenticate a user, program, provider, service, or transaction. Usually, the certificate consists of a file containing a copy of the user's or service's public encryption key, along with the signature of a trusted person verifying that the key does, indeed, belong to the user or service claimed. A CA creates a certificate, and the certificate is encrypted in a way that makes it impossible to forge.

Domain Name System (DNS)—DNS is the online distributed database system used to map human-readable computer names into IP addresses. DNS servers throughout the connected Internet implement a hierarchical namespace that allows sites freedom in assigning computer names and addresses. In addition, DNS supports separate mappings between mail destinations and IP addresses.

encryption—Encryption is the process of scrambling data by changing it in a series of logical steps, called an encryption algorithm. To increase security, an encryption algorithm uses a numerical pattern, or "key," to guide the scrambling process. Different algorithms and keys each produce data scrambled, or encrypted, in different patterns.

File Transfer Protocol (FTP)—FTP is a TCP/IP Application Layer protocol used to transfer information between a client and a server attached to a network.

firewall—A firewall is, according to the National Computer Security Association, "a system or combination of systems that enforces a boundary between two or more networks." It is a controlled gateway between one network and another, typically between a private network and the Internet, which blocks messages that do not meet specified security criteria.

FrontPage extensions—Extensions are optional Web server software components that support additional functionality on Web sites created with Microsoft's FrontPage authoring application. For example, if a Web server supports the FrontPage extensions, a site author can use FrontPage to easily add features such as searching and forms support.

hit—Each request for a file on a Web server is recorded as one "hit" in the server's log. One hit is recorded for each HTML page, graphic image, or other file that a server transmits to a client. Thus, several hits may be generated for each page that a client views.

Hypertext Markup Language (HTML)—HTML is a text-based formatting language used to generically format text for Web pages. It is a simplified derivative of Standard Generalized Markup Language (SGML) that tags different parts of a document more in terms of their function than their appearance. A Web browser reads an HTML document and displays it as indicated by the HTML formatting tags and the browser's settings.

Hypertext Transfer Protocol (HTTP)—HTTP is the Transmission Control Protocol/Internet Protocol (TCP/IP) Application Layer protocol used to request and transmit HTML documents. HTTP is the underlying protocol of the World Wide Web (WWW).

Internet Message Access Protocol (IMAP4)—IMAP is a protocol used for retrieving e-mail messages from a mail server. IMAP4 is a version of IMAP similar to POP3; however, it supports additional features, such as searching for keywords in e-mail messages while the messages are still on the mail server.

JScript—As Microsoft's implementation of ECMAScript, JScript is the international standard based on Netscape's JavaScript. JScript is natively supported by Microsoft ASP, and is preferred for writing ASP client-side script blocks.

Lightweight Directory Access Protocol (LDAP)—LDAP is an Internet standard for organizing information in a hierarchical tree structure that conforms to the X.500 directory standard.

load balancer—A load balancer is a device that intercepts incoming HTTP requests and evenly distributes them to multiple identical Web servers. Load balancing improves overall site performance, and it provides fault tolerance by automatically routing traffic around a malfunctioning server.

Multipurpose Internet Mail Extension (MIME)—MIME is an extension of Simple Mail Transfer Protocol (SMTP) that supports the exchange of a wide variety of document files via an e-mail system.

Network News Transfer Protocol (NNTP)—NNTP is the TCP/IP protocol used to distribute news article collections, or news feeds, over the Internet.

network operating system (NOS)—NOS is the software that manages server operations and provides services to clients. The NOS manages the interface between the network's underlying transport capabilities and the applications resident on the server.

operating system—An OS is the basic system software of a computer that provides low-level services to applications.

patch—Patches, also called service packs, apply relatively small changes to a portion of an application's code. Patches are distributed free of charge to correct bugs or security vulnerabilities that cannot wait for the next upgrade release.

Post Office Protocol (POP)—POP is an e-mail service implemented on TCP Port 110 that provides clients access to a mail drop or post office in which their messages are stored. POP3 is the latest iteration of the protocol.

proxy—See cache server.

public key (asymmetric) encryption—Public-key encryption is a cryptographic system that uses two mathematically related keys: one key is used to encrypt a message, and the other to decrypt it. People who need to receive encrypted messages distribute their public keys, but keep their private keys secret.

Secure Sockets Layer (SSL)—SSL is an application of both public-key and single-key encryption that secures an Internet connection between browser and server. Web-page URLs that use SSL begin with "https://."

server—A server is any program that provides a service to a client program. This term is often used to refer to the computer that hosts the server program; however, a server program may also run on a computer that normally functions as a client. See client.

Simple Mail Transfer Protocol (SMTP)—SMTP is an Application Layer protocol used to send e-mail from a client to a mail server, and transfer e-mail between mail servers, across a TCP/IP network.

streaming—Streaming is the ability to begin playing a downloaded audio or video file as it arrives at the user's computer, without waiting for the entire file to be received first.

Telnet—Telnet is a TCP/IP Application Layer protocol that provides remote login capability to another computer on a network.

upgrade—Upgrades are new versions of an application, that implement new features. An upgrade may be installed by replacing an old application with a new one, or by installing a partial code change.

Visual Basic Scripting Edition (VBScript)—Microsoft's VBScript is similar to its Visual Basic, but is simpler to use. VBScript is natively supported by Microsoft ASP, and is preferred for writing ASP server-side script blocks. Microsoft Internet Explorer supports client-side VBScripts, but the lack of VBScript support in Netscape Navigator limits this practice. Many ASP developers follow the mantra "JScript on the client, VBScript on the server."

well-known port—Any preassigned port number for a specific use by a Transport Layer protocol, such as TCP or UDP, is referred to as a well-known port. Examples of well-known ports include ports assigned to remote login (Telnet) servers and FTP servers.

Windows service—A Windows service is the equivalent of a UNIX daemon. Windows services provide specific functions, such as enabling file sharing or automatic virus protection, and can start automatically on system startup, manually as directed by the user, or when scheduled to run at a particular time of the day.

Lesson 1—Client Applications

Each type of Internet service can be accessed by a corresponding client. Some of these clients, such as FTP or Telnet, are very simple applications that use command-line interfaces. However, most of these simple tools have been replaced by full-featured applications that may combine several client functions into a single graphical interface. These sophisticated clients are not absolutely necessary for Internet access, but they can make the user's experience simpler and more productive.

This lesson introduces the two most commonly-used Internet client applications: Web clients (browsers) and e-mail clients. We also explore the trend toward generic, or "universal," clients that can handle multiple communication tasks.

Internet Clients and Servers

Objectives

At the end of this lesson you will be able to:

- Explain the relationship between HTTP and Web browsers

- Describe the main differences between the two major browsers

- Customize several settings in Internet Explorer or Netscape Navigator

- Find and apply software patches

Key Point

Each client application accesses a different type of Internet service.

Web Browsers

Objective 1.4
Understand and be able to describe the infrastructure needed to support an Internet client ... Web browser

A Web browser is a TCP/IP client application that allows a user to retrieve hypertext documents from a remote host computer called a Hypertext Transfer Protocol (HTTP) server. The Web browser reads the document and displays it as indicated by both the HTML formatting code and the user's display preferences stored in the browser. Because the intelligence to format and display HTML documents is built into the browser, the documents are generally fairly small in size.

The Web Browser and Server Diagram illustrates the relationship of these components.

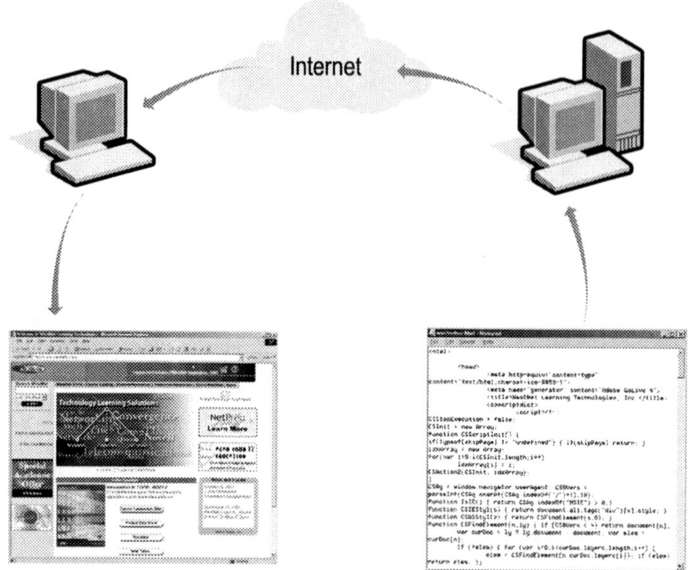

Web Browser and Server

Because the browser controls how a page is displayed, we can customize Web browsers to display pages the way we want to see them. Web developers try to create pages that will display well in at least the two major browsers: Microsoft Internet Explorer and Netscape Navigator. Browser users can override the Web developer's design by setting browsers to display specific fonts and colors. Some users customize their settings to accommodate disabilities like impaired vision or color blindness, while others simply prefer to view only certain fonts or colors. You can even "turn off" viewing images if all you are looking for is text information and want to speed download times.

Viewing Pages Using Internet Explorer and Netscape Navigator

Objective 1.5.
Use/configure Web browsers and other Internet/intranet clients, and be able to describe their use to others.
… Web browsers

The two most popular browsers are Microsoft Internet Explorer and Netscape Navigator. Viewing Web pages in either of the two major browsers is very similar. Some of the terminology is different, and they support different plug-ins and extended HTML capabilities.

The Internet Explorer Window Screen Capture and the Netscape Navigator Window Screen Capture show the same Web page displayed in each browser.

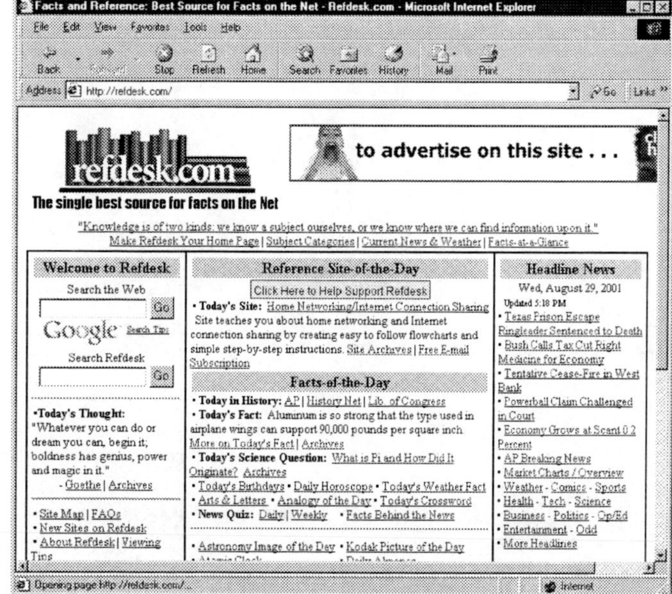

Internet Explorer Window

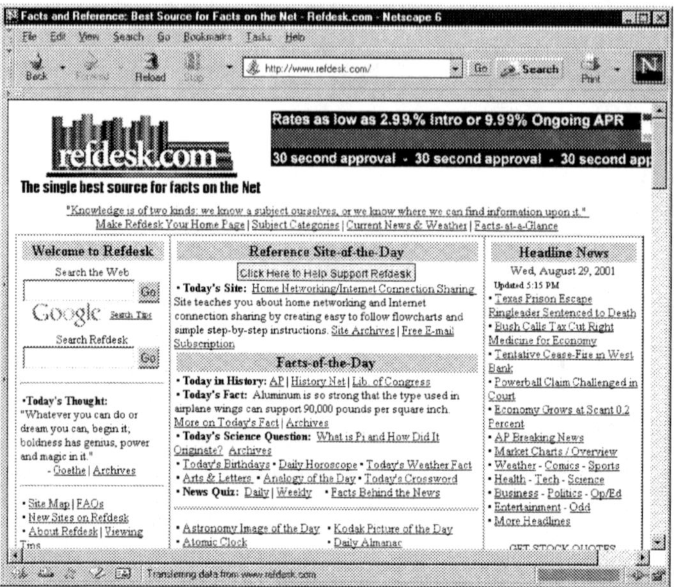

Netscape Navigator Window

You can see that the browsers display the Web page in the same way, but there are differences in the tool bars. The Toolbar Features Table lists both browsers' tool bar buttons and their actions.

Toolbar Features

Internet Explorer	Netscape Navigator	Comment
Back	Back	Returns to the previous Web page. This button is unavailable when you have viewed only one page.
Forward	Forward	Proceeds to the page you viewed before you clicked the Back button. This button is unavailable when you have viewed only one page or when you have not used the Back button.
Stop	Stop	Stops loading the current page.
Refresh	Reload	Sends a new request to the server to display the page.
Home	Home	Displays the home page. You can designate the Web page that you want for your home page. See "Customizing Browsers" on page 436 for more information.

Toolbar Features (Continued)

Internet Explorer	Netscape Navigator	Comment
Search	Search	**Internet Explorer**: Displays the Microsoft search window on the left side of the browser window. It allows you to search for Web sites, people, businesses, previous searches, or maps. **Netscape**: Displays Netscape's search page. It allows you to choose a commercial search engine for your Web search. It contains links to find shopping, resources, news, and to search for people and businesses.
Favorites (Upper tool bar)	Bookmarks (Lower tool bar)	Favorites and Bookmarks allow you to save the addresses of Web sites you want to visit again. You can create and manage folders and organize saved addresses. In Internet Explorer, click on the Favorites menu and select **Organize Favorites**. In Netscape, click on **Bookmarks** and select **File Bookmarks** or **Edit Bookmarks**.
History (Tool bar)	Go (Menu)	The History and Go functions allow you to see and click on the Web page addresses you have recently visited.
Mail	Send Page (File Menu)	Opens your default e-mail client to send the current page.
Print	Print	Opens the Print dialog to print the current page.
	Netscape	Displays the MyNetscape site, which is a portal for Web searching, news, and information.
	Security	Displays the Netscape Security information page that explains how Netscape's security works and how to change security settings.
	Shop	Displays the Shop@Netscape page.
Address	Location	Shows the current Web site address (URL). Allows you to enter an address and press Enter to go to another site.

Customizing Browsers

Objective 1.5.
Use/configure Web browsers and other Internet/intranet clients, and be able to describe their use to others.
... Web browsers

Most browsers allow you to customize the way you want text and images to appear. You can also set the home page, determine how many days to store the Web sites you visit, and organize your bookmarks. This section discusses how to customize Internet Explorer and Netscape Navigator browsers.

Internet Explorer

Internet Explorer provides an interface called Internet Options, where you can customize most of the display features and settings. From the main menu, select **Tools** > **Internet Options**. The Internet Options window opens, as shown on the Internet Options Window Screen Capture.

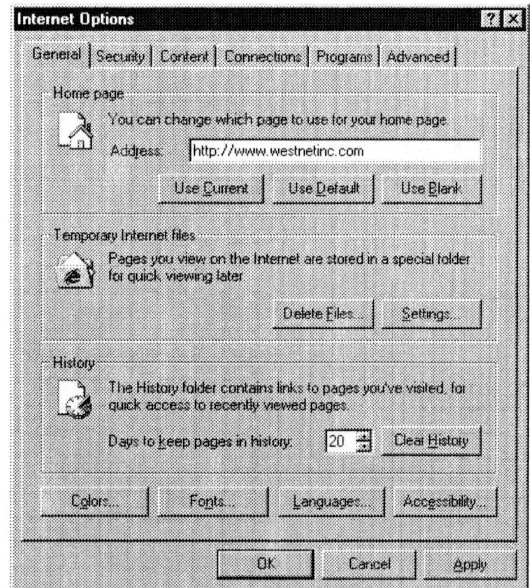

Internet Options Window

In this window, you can customize the way that the browser displays Web pages. The following list describes some of the common settings you may want to customize:

- **Home page**—This setting determines the Web page that displays when you start an Internet Explorer session. To change the home page to the page that is currently displayed, click **Use Current**. You can also type the address of any page and click **OK**.

- **Fonts**—This feature allows you to set how text displays. In the General tab of Internet Options window, click **Fonts**. You will see the Fonts Screen as shown on the Fonts Screen Capture.

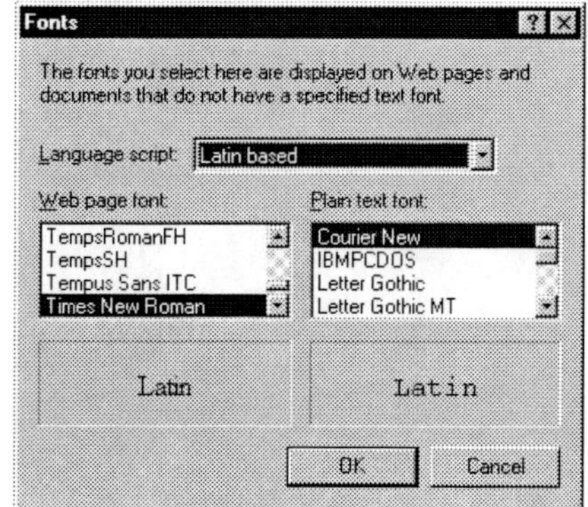

Fonts

You can change the language displayed by using the Language Script drop-down list. Change the Web page font or Plain text font in their respective lists and click **OK**. To change font size, close the Internet Options window. From the main menu, select **View** > **Text Size**. Select the appropriate size, and the new font size displays in the Web page you are viewing.

- **Image Loading**—This setting allows you to turn off image loading while viewing Web pages. Since many sites use images that slow download times, you may want to turn off image loading when you are doing research or just want to speed page loading times. To turn off image loading, from the main menu, select **Tools** > **Internet Options**. In the Internet Options window, click the **Advanced** tab, as shown on the Internet Options–Advanced Tab Screen Capture.

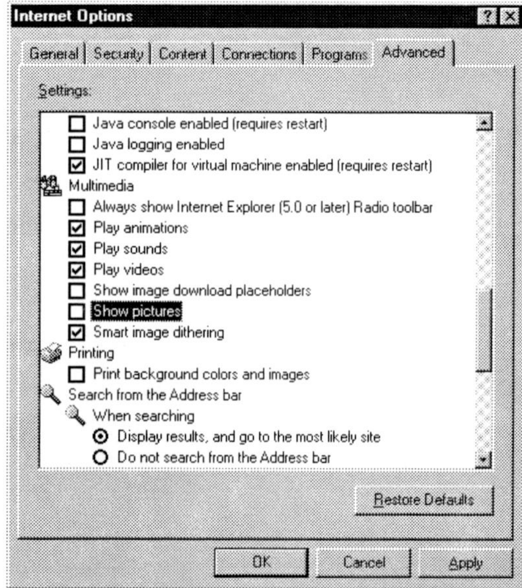

Internet Options–Advanced Tab

Scroll down through the settings until you see the Multimedia section. Under Multimedia, find the **Show Pictures** check box. The default setting is on (checked). Click this check box to turn it off and click **OK**.

- **Temporary Internet files (browser cache)**—This feature determines the amount of disk space used to save copies of the pages you have visited. In the Internet Options window, select the General tab. In the Temporary Internet Files area, click **Settings** to display the Settings Screen, as shown below.

Settings

To change the amount of disk space used to store viewed pages, move the slider to the right or left, or enter a number in the text field and click **OK**.

To delete temporary files from memory, use the **General** tab of the Internet Options window. In the Temporary Files area, click **Delete Files** to display the Delete Files Screen as shown here.

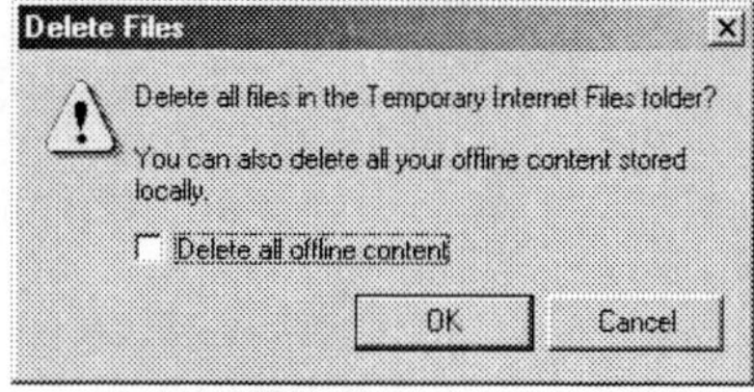

Delete Files

Select the **Delete all offline content** check box to delete files that you have saved to view offline, or just click **OK** to delete temporary files.

- **History**—This setting determines the number of days that the browser stores Web addresses you have visited. In the Internet Options window, select the **General** tab. In the History area, you can change the number of days by using the up or down arrows or by typing another number in the text field. To delete the stored links, click **Clear History**.

- **Favorites**—This feature lets you organize your list of favorite sites. From the main menu, select **Favorites** > **Organize Favorites** to display the Organize Favorites Screen Capture, shown below.

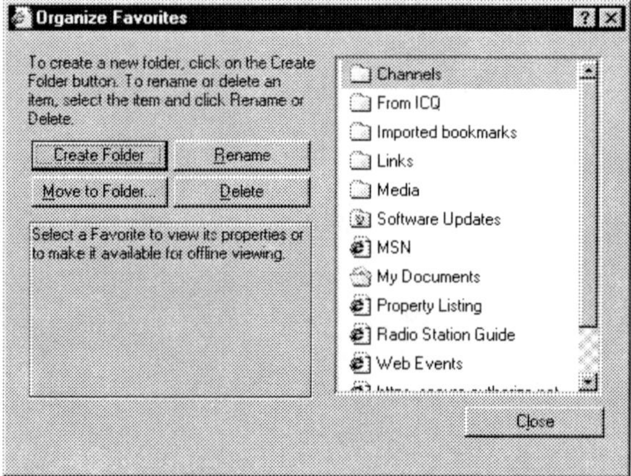

Organize Favorites

In the Organize Favorites window, click **Create Folders** to make a new favorites category. To move favorites into a folder, drag and drop an item or select a favorite from the list, and click **Move to Folder** to select the location.

- **Cookies**—This setting is a part of security options. A cookie is a small file that a Web site places on your computer. The cookie stores information about your preferences or about what you viewed on the site previously. The next time you visit that site, the cookie gets sent back to the site. Cookies can be used to rotate the banner ads that a site sends. They can also be used to customize pages for you based on information you have provided to the Web site. Settings in your browser allow you to control how it handles cookies.

In the Internet Options screen, click the **Security** tab, as shown on the Internet Options Screen Capture.

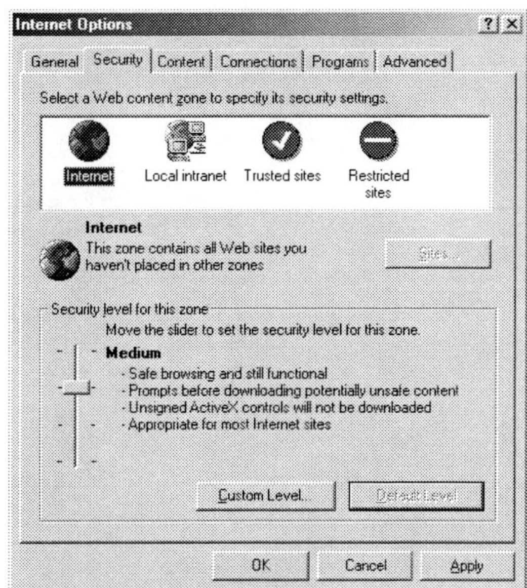

Internet Options

Click on the **Internet** icon. This category covers all the Web sites you visit, unless you enter Web site addresses into other categories. The default setting is Medium. This means that the browser accepts cookies, but prompts you about security information on Web sites. Microsoft recommends this setting, but you can change it to High, which accepts no cookies and disables other features that might be a security problem. For more information on security, view the Internet Explorer Help file.

*Netscape
Navigator*

Netscape Navigator provides an interface called Preferences, where you can customize many display and setting options. The Preferences window allows you to customize the home page, fonts, cache, and image loading. You can organize your bookmarks using another menu option that we will discuss at the end of this section. The examples in this section are taken from Netscape version 6.1.

To access Preferences, from the main menu, select **Edit** > **Preferences**. The Preferences Screen appears, as shown on the Preferences Screen Capture.

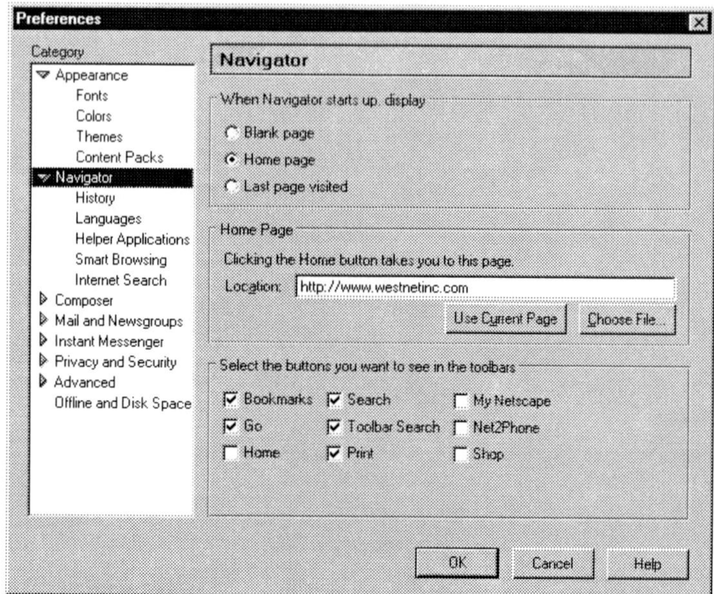

Preferences

- **Home Page**—In the Preferences window, double-click the Navigator Category. To change the home page to the page that is currently displayed, click **Use Current Page**. You can also type the address of the page you want in the Home Page location area and click **OK**.

- **History**—This setting determines the number of days that the browser stores visited Web addresses. You can change the number of days by typing another number in the text field. To delete the stored links, click **Clear History**.

- **Browser Cache**—This feature determines the amount of disk space you want to use to save copies of the pages you have visited. In the Preferences window, double-click the **Advanced** category. Under the Advanced options, click **Cache** to display the Cache Screen, as shown on the Cache Screen Capture.

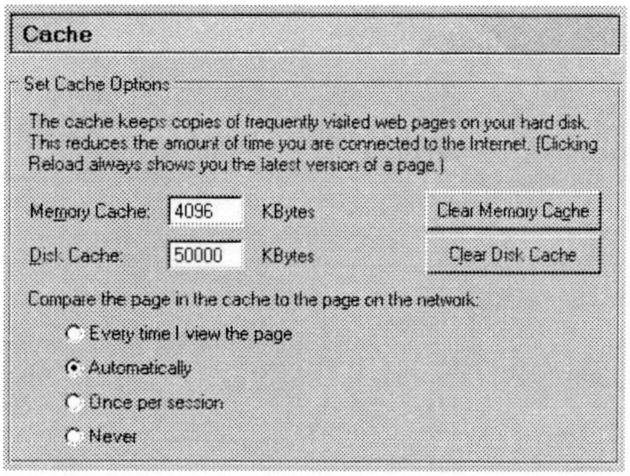

Cache

In the Cache portion of the window, you can change the size of memory and disk caches. You can also delete the items in the caches by clicking **Clear Memory Cache** or **Clear Disk Cache**.

- **Fonts**—This feature allows you to set how text displays. In the Preferences window, double-click the **Appearance** category. Under Appearance, click **Fonts** to display the Fonts Screen, shown on the Fonts Screen Capture.

Fonts

In the Fonts portion of the window, use the pull-down menus to change the font and size settings. The check box in this window allows you to choose to view the fonts designated by Web pages or to always use the fonts you have selected. Keep in mind that if you use your default fonts, Web pages may not appear as their developers intended.

To change font size, close the Preferences window. From the main menu, select **View** > **Increase Font** or **View** > **Decrease Font**. Keep increasing or decreasing the font size until you reach the size you prefer. The new font size will display in the Web page you are viewing.

- **Bookmarks**—This feature allows you to rename, edit, or delete bookmarks. From the menu, select **Bookmarks > Manage Bookmarks**. The Bookmarks Screen appears, as shown on the Bookmarks Screen Capture.

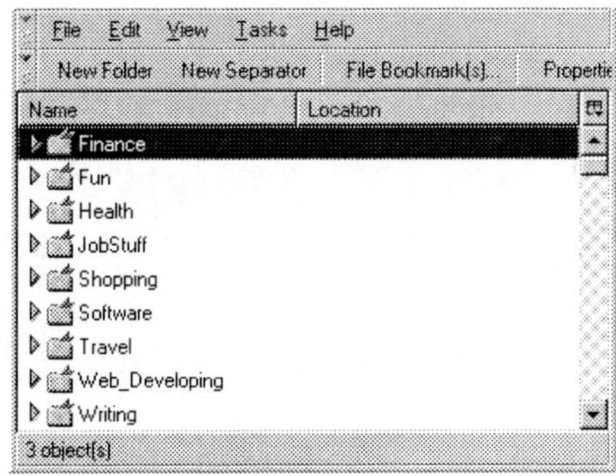

Bookmarks

In the Bookmarks window, you can create a new folder by selecting **File** > **New Folder**. Drag and drop a bookmark to move it into a folder. To delete a bookmark, select the bookmark, then select **Edit** > **Delete**.

- **Cookies**—As explained earlier, Cookies store information about your preferences and can be used to customize pages for you. Settings in your browser allow you to control how it handles cookies.

In the Preferences window, double-click the Privacy and Security Category. Under the Privacy and Security options, click **Cookies** to display the Cookies Screen, as shown on the Cookies Screen Capture.

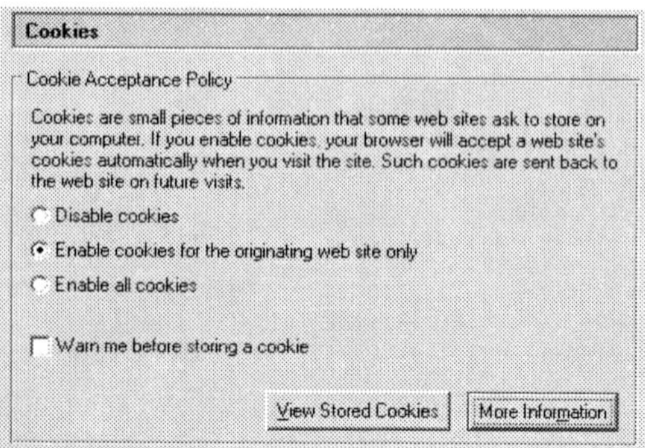

Cookies

In the Cookies portion of the window, you can change the security settings. The available settings are:

- **Enable all cookies**—This is the default setting, which is the lowest level of security. It allows cookies from the site you are visiting, as well as foreign cookies. Foreign cookies are cookies from other sites with a link to the site you are visiting. For example, an advertising banner from another site could place a cookie on your computer.

- **Enable cookies for the originating web site only**—This setting allows cookies from the site you are visiting, but disables foreign cookies.

- **Disable cookies**—This setting allows no cookies.

- **Warn me before storing a cookie**—This check box enables a prompt for each cookie. You can selectively accept cookies when you use this feature.

E-Mail Clients

Objective 1.4
Understand and be able to describe the infrastructure needed to support an Internet client.
… E-mail client

Objective 1.5.
Use/configure Web browsers and other Internet/intranet clients, and be able to describe their use to others.
… E-mail clients

There are many Internet e-mail clients available for use across many different operating systems; space does not allow us to address them all. Instead, we will discuss the procedures necessary to configure Microsoft's Outlook Express and Netscape Messenger to send and receive e-mail from an SMTP/POP mail server.

Configuring Outlook Express

To configure a new account in Outlook Express, from the main menu, select **Tools** > **Accounts**. In the Internet Accounts window, click the **Add** button and select **Mail**. The Outlook Express Client Diagram illustrates the Outlook Express Client Internet Accounts configuration window.

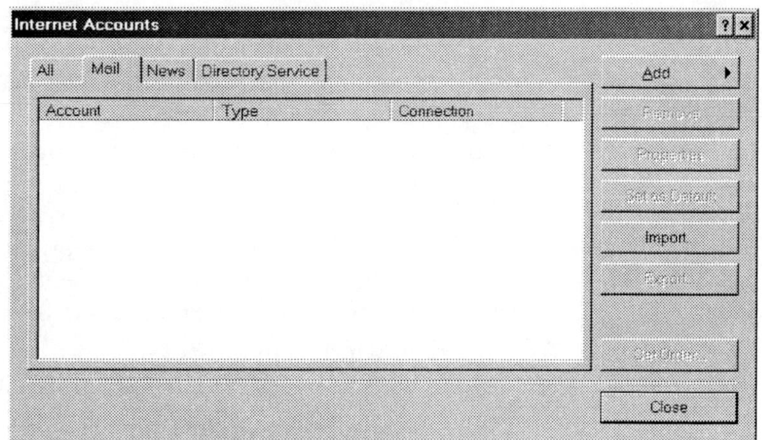

Outlook Express Client

The Internet Connection Wizard appears. Follow the wizard prompts to enter an account Display name, followed by the account's e-mail address. Once these are entered, the Internet Connection Wizard prompts for the incoming and outgoing mail server information. The Internet Connection Wizard Diagram illustrates these options.

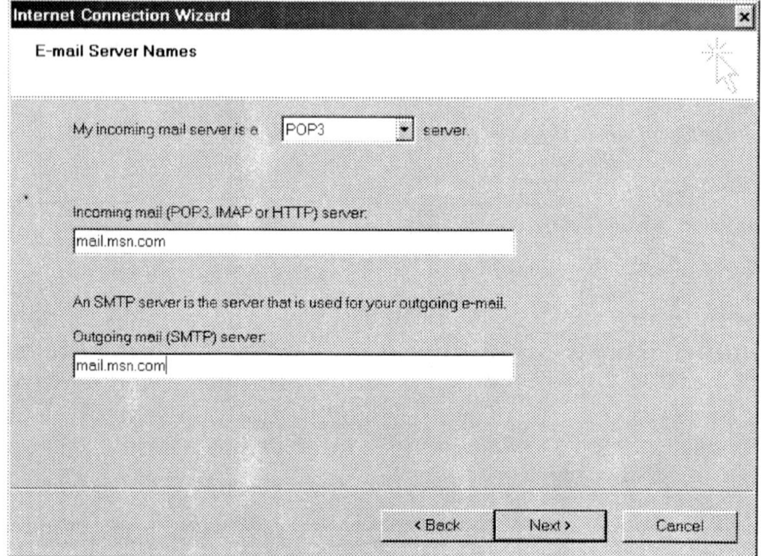

Internet Connection Wizard

The wizard prompts for the incoming mail server protocol type. The options are POP3, Internet Message Access Protocol (IMAP), and HTTP. Choose the POP3 server type from the pull-down menu, then enter the incoming and outgoing mail server IP addresses or names. In this example, we entered the server name mail.msn.com. The outgoing server type is always SMTP.

The next window prompts for your user name and password. The final step is to select **Finish** to complete the client setup.

When you connect to the Internet to download new e-mail messages, the incoming server validates the user name and password. You may configure the client to download e-mail periodically. Each time the client requests new messages, it passes your user name and password to the incoming server. The outgoing mail server does not require a user name or password; it accepts mail on the client's behalf without the need for account credentials.

Configuring Netscape Messenger

The process for configuring Netscape Messenger is similar to the process for Outlook Express. In Netscape Messenger, start from the main menu and select **Edit** > **Mail/News Account Settings**. Click the **New** button to access the Account Wizard. Follow the wizard prompts to set up your e-mail account.

Inboxes and Address Books

E-mail inboxes and address books contain some of the most important data on a user's computer. Like any other vital files, these should be regularly backed up to protect them from damage or accidental deletion.

When users upgrade or change an e-mail application, they often panic when they find that their mail inboxes and address books have mysteriously disappeared. In most cases, this problem is caused by one of two reasons:

- One vendor's application uses a different message or address format than another.

- A new version of the same application stores messages or addresses in a different location, or in a different file.

Changing E-Mail Applications

Some e-mail readers, such as Netscape Communicator, use standard formats for e-mail messages and address book entries. Microsoft applications use proprietary formats for these data.

Fortunately, recent versions of both Microsoft Outlook and Netscape Communicator can import messages and address books from each other. Thus, users can often import their old messages and addresses either during or after the process of installing a competing e-mail application.

However, a new mail reader may not recognize files created by an older version of a competing program. In that case, you may need to export data to an intermediate format before importing it into the new e-mail application. Third-party applications are also available to simplify some conversions.

Upgrading the Same E-Mail Application

To enable new features, new versions of an e-mail application may use different files or locations to store address books. Most installation wizards offer users the opportunity to convert existing inboxes or address books during the upgrade process. If users skip that step, the new application leaves the old files intact without converting them. The data still exists, but is not visible to the new application. This problem is usually corrected by importing the old address book into the new application.

Mail and address conversion procedures vary according to the specific product versions involved, so consult the product documentation before attempting to convert either messages or addresses.

E-Mail Privacy

The need for corporate security has led to increased monitoring of employee communications and computers. It is a fact that one of the largest security risks for companies is intentional or unintentional security breaches by employees. The need to secure computer systems has encouraged the development of many different monitoring and encryption technologies.

As an employee, you should understand that your company has the right to read your e-mail messages, listen to your voice mail, and access the files in your computer, since the devices that produce them are the company's property.

The issue of privacy on the Internet is still ambiguous and will probably be resolved through various court cases in the future. The 1986 Electronic Communications Privacy Act (ECPA) extends the federal wiretapping statute to cover electronic communications. This law hinges on whether employees have a "reasonable expectation of privacy" in the workplace.

This is why most companies have a written policy that details security issues and privacy rights. These policies generally state that the need for security outweighs concerns about personal privacy, and the courts have supported this notion in most cases.

Signature Files

An e-mail signature is usually a text file that you create, and that appears at the end of messages that you send. This eliminates the need for you to "sign off" at the end of every message. Signature files can include any of the following: your name, title, physical or e-mail address, a link to your Web site, or a phrase that describes your philosophy. You can put as much or as little information in a signature file as you want people to know about you.

Configuring Outlook

To create or edit a signature file in Outlook, select **Tools > Options** from the main menu. In the Options window, select the **Mail Format** tab. Within the Mail Format tab, click **Signature Picker** at the bottom right. The Signature Picker Screen appears, as shown on the Signature Picker Screen Capture.

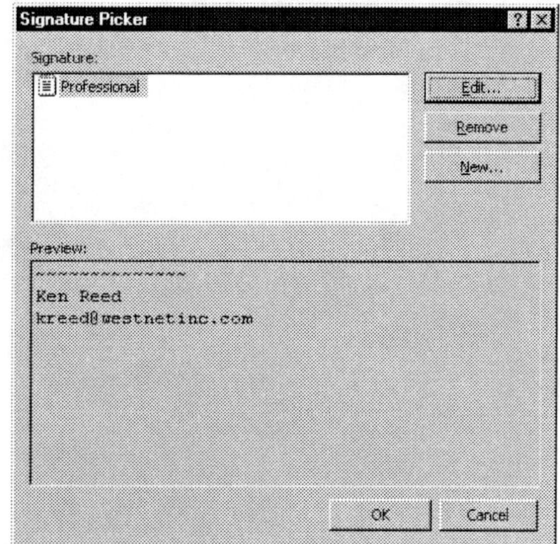

Signature Picker

In the **Signature Picker** window, you can select an existing signature to edit, or you can create a new signature by clicking **New**.

Configuring Netscape Messenger

Netscape Messenger does not allow you to create a signature file, so you create the file in a word processor and save it as a text file. Within Messenger, you navigate to the location of the file.

To attach an existing signature file, select **Edit** > **Preferences** from the main menu. In the Preferences window, double-click the **Mail and Newsgroups** category. Under Mail and Newsgroups, select **Identity**. The Identity information appears in the right side of the window, as shown on the Identity Screen Capture.

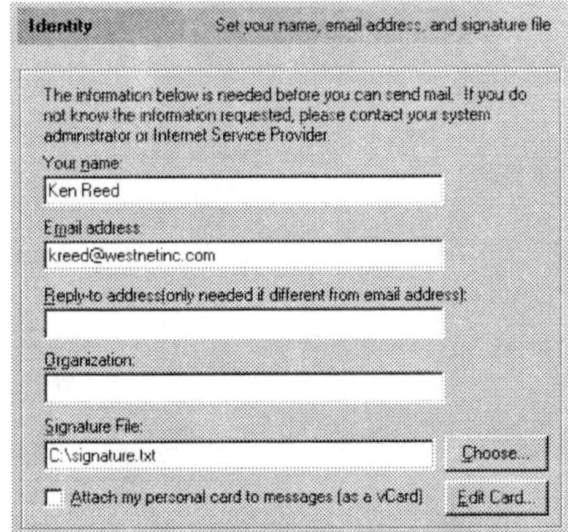

Identity

In the **Identity** portion of the window, select **Choose** to navigate to an existing signature file. You can attach or edit a vCard as your signature.

News Accounts

Objective 1.5.
Use/configure Web browsers and other Internet/intranet clients, and be able to describe their use to others.
... E-mail clients

You can configure your e-mail client to receive newsgroup messages from some newsgroups. At one time, e-mail was the primary method that people used to access newsgroups, but now many of the free newsgroup sites allow you to view the messages only through a browser.

There are several sites that list news servers that you can subscribe to through your e-mail client. One good site is **http://www.new-zbot.com**. When you find a server that interests you, follow the directions in the following sections, depending on which browser you use.

Configuring Outlook

To configure a news server, from the main menu select **Tools** > **Accounts**. In the Internet Accounts window, select the **News** tab. Click on the **Add** button and select **News** to start the Internet Connection Wizard.

The Internet Connection Wizard asks you a series of questions. Follow the directions to enter your user name, e-mail address, and news server IP address or name. Click **Finish** to complete the wizard setup. In the Internet Accounts window, you will see your new account listed in the News accounts, as shown on the Internet Accounts Screen Capture.

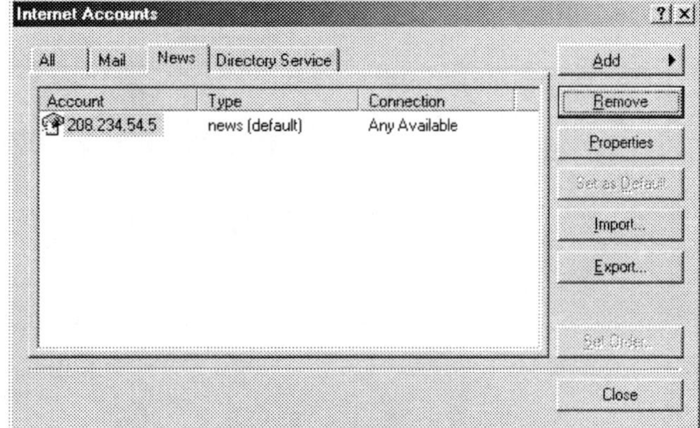

Internet Accounts

Click **Close** and a message will appear, asking if you want to download the available newsgroups from the news server. Click **OK**. It may take a few minutes to download the newsgroups. When the download is complete, click on the group(s) you are interested in, and click **Subscribe**. Click **OK** to exit. You will see that your newsgroup is listed as a folder. Click on the newsgroup folder to list the current messages.

Configuring Netscape Messenger

To configure a news server, from the main menu select **Edit** > **Mail/News Account Settings**. In the Account Settings Window, click **New Account**, which opens the Account Wizard. Follow the wizard instructions to select a newsgroup account, and enter your user name, e-mail address, and news server IP address or name. Click **Finish** to complete the wizard setup. In the Account Settings window, you will see the new account in the list of accounts. Click **OK** to close the Account Settings window. Now you can subscribe to one or more newsgroups on the server account you just added. To subscribe, from the main menu, select **File** > **Subscribe**, which opens the Subscribe window, as shown on the Subscribe Screen. In the Subscribe window, select the Server that you just added. The available newsgroups will download (this may take a few minutes). From the available groups, select one that interests you and click **Subscribe**. A check mark appears next to the selected newsgroup, as shown here on the Subscribe Screen Capture.

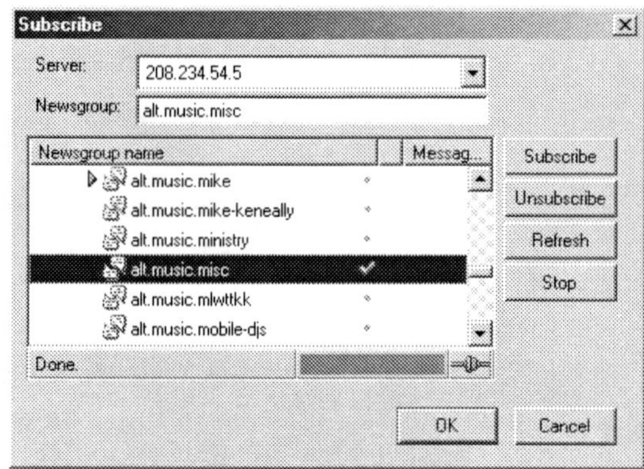

Subscribe

Click **OK** to close the Subscribe window. The newsgroups you subscribed to appear as folders in Netscape Messenger. Click on the newsgroup folder to list the current messages.

Universal Clients

Objective 1.5
Use/configure Web browsers and other Internet/intranet clients, and be able to describe their use to others.
... All-in-one/universal clients

So far, this course has discussed specialized client applications that each access a different type of service: a Web browser to view Web pages, an e-mail client to read mail messages, an FTP client for file transfers, and so on.

But the boundaries between client applications are becoming blurred. For example, as you have just seen, an e-mail client can be set up to retrieve newsgroup messages. Some e-mail providers now allow subscribers to view and manage mail messages through a Web interface that uses HTTP instead of POP3. E-mail messages can also be sent and received as HTML documents, which makes it possible to add text formatting and graphics to e-mail. Some applications, such as Netscape Communicator, offer multiple features, such as Web browsing, e-mail retrieval, and more. While some applications may still be advertised as browsers or e-mail clients, they may be more accurately described as "universal clients" that provide a single consistent user interface for a variety of communication tasks.

Full-featured browsers, or universal clients, also offer significant benefits to Web application developers. In the past, a company that wanted to offer complex services over the Internet may have needed to distribute a dedicated client application to each user. But as browsers have become more powerful, Web applications can provide the necessary client-side interaction through scripts, embedded in Web pages, that supplement the processing and navigation features included in the browser.

Upgrading and Maintaining Client Applications

Objective 1.6
Update client software.

Users must keep Internet client applications up to date so they can take advantage of new Web site functionality that relies on the latest client features. In general, client applications are maintained with two types of changes to their programming code:

- **Upgrades** are new versions of an application, that implement new features. If users must pay for the application, then they also must pay a fee for its upgrades. Upgrades to free software, such as the major Web browsers, are also free. An upgrade may be installed by replacing an old application with a new one, or by installing a partial code change.

- **Patches, or service packs,** apply relatively small changes to a portion of an application's code. Patches are distributed free of charge to correct bugs or security vulnerabilities that cannot wait for the next upgrade release.

Other than price, the most important difference between patches and upgrades is the way a user finds out about them. Software publishers send upgrade offers to all registered users, because the cost of that communication is part of the advertising necessary to sell upgrade software. In contrast, when publishers post free patches on their Web sites, they do not generally spend money to tell users about them.

Therefore, users, LAN administrators, and Web administrators are responsible for finding and installing the patches necessary to keep their applications up to date. Periodically check the software publisher's support site for new patches, then follow each publisher's instructions for installing them. It's also wise to check for patches and current support information before installing new software.

For an individual user, or the administrator of a small LAN, it's simple to install upgrades directly onto each computer. However, large companies use centralized LAN administration tools to automate the installation and maintenance of applications on hundreds of client desktops. By using tools such as Novell's ZENWorks, a LAN administrator can "push" a new Web browser to every computer in the company, typically in the middle of the night. These management tools do not reduce the cost of software, because each desktop must still have a valid license for each application it runs. Rather, these automated applications save many hours of the network staff's time, and ensure that all users run the same version of a client application.

Activities

1. By default, how do both Internet Explorer and Netscape Navigator handle cookies?

   ____

   ____

   ____

   ____

2. Name at least three differences between a patch and an upgrade.

   ____

   ____

   ____

   ____

   ____

3. You and a coworker enjoy tasteless and explicit jokes, but your boss disapproves and has written a company computer use policy that prohibits this material. Could any problems occur if you and your friend trade these jokes over the company's e-mail system? Why or why not?

   ____

   ____

   ____

   ____

   ____

   ____

Extended Activity

Experiment with changing your browser settings to see what changes most affect the appearance of Web pages.

Lesson 2—Server Platforms

When we speak of a server "platform," we generally mean the hardware and operating system that form the foundation on which server software can run. However, this does not mean that the platform and the server applications function independently of each other. In reality, each component of a server— hardware, operating system, and applications—affects the operation of every other. Thus, the process of designing and building an Internet server is a challenging task, because a functioning server is far more complex than the sum of its parts.

Furthermore, each technical decision should consider the business effects of each available choice. In other words, determine the business needs first. Then choose the technologies, both hardware and software, that are best capable of meeting those needs.

This lesson discusses some of the most important points to consider when choosing the hardware and operating system components of an Internet server. In most cases, we will focus on the needs of Web servers (HTTP servers). However, these principles apply equally to other Internet servers, such as e-mail or FTP servers. We will discuss those server applications in the next lesson.

Objectives

At the end of this lesson you will be able to:

- Name the most commonly used Web server operating systems

- Describe the trade-offs to consider when choosing an operating system

- Describe how operating systems interact with server hardware and applications

- Describe the most critical hardware components of a server

- Explain how hardware choices affect Web server performance

Key Point

Server hardware and software must be chosen to meet business needs and support the desired server applications.

Server Components

Objective 1.4
Understand and be able to describe the infrastructure needed to support an Internet client.
... Knowledge of web server platforms

The term "server" is somewhat nebulous from a technical perspective, because it can refer to multiple parts of a whole or the conglomeration of the parts. A server, in its most basic form, is composed of three distinctly different but equally important parts:

- A physical machine connected to the Internet

- A network operating system (NOS) that runs on the machine and manages all basic networking functionality

- Server software that processes incoming client requests for a particular type of service (HTTP, Telnet, FTP, etc.)

For example, a typical Web server includes the three components illustrated on the Web Server Parts Diagram.

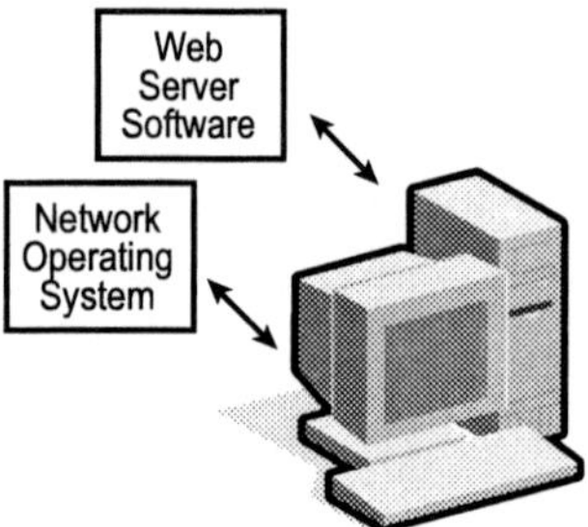

Web Server Parts

In a more complex system, a server computer may also run special additional software such as database engines, transaction processors, or site and server management tools. The server computer may also be connected to specialized hardware, such as a caching server, firewall, or telephony equipment.

On a large site, a Web server may actually consist of several physical machines working together to provide the appearance of a single point of entry. Special load balancing software distributes the total workload evenly among the group of computers, so that no single platform becomes overloaded. This technique ensures high availability for high-traffic Web sites. If one computer fails, or needs maintenance, the remaining platforms automatically take up the slack.

Hardware Considerations

Objective 1.4
Understand and be able to describe the infrastructure needed to support an Internet client. … Hardware platform

Different hardware platforms have different strengths and weaknesses. Thus, the choice of a server's hardware is one of the most critical decisions made during the design process. Upgrading hardware at a later date is an expensive process that generally requires taking the server offline. Additionally, the NOSs available for the platform, and the support software that can be installed, depend on the hardware. Great care must be taken in setting up the physical system, and decisions must be made in the context of the whole system. When designing the hardware platform, it is important to understand which hardware components are the most important in a Web server and design around the requirements.

In general, Internet/intranet servers are unique among servers in that they do not require high speeds from any of their components. Most of the work involved in serving requests for Web pages and associated files is handled by operating system subsystems and hardware components. Most of the work does not require many system resources. Any bottlenecks tend to occur at the interface of the system with the Internet, or at the client's link to the Internet. Even moderate hardware is capable of meeting the needs of the average Web server.

However, high-traffic systems and servers providing processor-intensive services, such as database integration, server-side scripting, and e-commerce, require greater system resources. The level and type of these resources (disk space, processor speed, etc.) depend heavily on the work the server will do. For example, a catalog retailer's site needs fast processing and disk access times as it builds database information into dynamic Web pages. Thus, the choice of a Web server platform, like any computer, must be based on business requirements.

Processor

Web server software is available for every major processor architecture including Intel, Digital Equipment Corporation (DEC) Alpha, Advanced Micro Devices (AMD), and Apple PowerPC. The speed of the processor for most Web servers is immaterial, because the tasks of answering HTTP requests and transferring files is handled primarily by the hard disk drive and networking subsystems.

Any Intel (or compatible) processor of Pentium class or higher, and any Alpha or PowerPC chip, should be sufficient for most Web servers. Web servers that will be running software in addition to the server may require a more powerful processor.

The primary concern in choosing a processor is the availability of software compiled for the platform. Although Alpha and PowerPC processors are generally more powerful than Intel processors, the availability of software for the Intel platform, especially when running Microsoft Windows NT Server, may outweigh the performance issue by a vast margin.

Random Access Memory

The main purposes for random access memory (RAM) on a Web server are running software and providing a cache space for highly accessed pages. In a simple system, the amount of RAM required to run the NOS and Web server software is low. Different software packages and NOSs have different requirements.

Platforms running Microsoft Windows NT Server and IIS require more RAM than systems running Apache and Red Hat Linux. Systems with additional software packages running or that have added functionality, such as embedded databases, also require more RAM. In general, 96 megabytes (MB) is sufficient for most low-use Web servers, and 128 or 256 MB is sufficient for all but the most high-end systems. Specialized hardware that offloads processes and functionality from the main system, such as a cache server, may reduce the RAM requirement.

Disk Drives

Where the average e-mail or file server can never have enough disk space, a Web server generally requires very little. Web pages, most of which are nothing more than ASCII text and small graphic files, are optimized for Internet transfer by being as small as the designer could make them. The result is that most Web sites use very little disk space. ISPs and Web site hosting services that have several Web sites on one server may need a high-volume hard disk drive. In most cases, the amount of disk space necessary is determined by the NOS and installed software. For most Web servers, two or three gigabytes (GB) of drive capacity should be sufficient. Most new servers come equipped with at least 20 GB hard drives.

Regardless of the size of the installed disk drives, one important consideration is disk redundancy. Because the Web server is a mission-critical piece of equipment to most businesses, a down Web server can cause a measurable loss of revenue. Many schemes exist for using multiple physical disks to mirror data and provide fault tolerance; all options should be explored. Because most NOSs support disk mirroring to one level or another, the possibility of using Redundant Array of Inexpensive Disks (RAID) level 5 (a high level of redundancy) should be seriously considered.

Network Connectivity

Objective 1.4
Understand and be able to describe the infrastructure needed to support an Internet client ... Network connection

The most common bottleneck for Web servers occurs at the connection to the Internet. Insufficient bandwidth can bring the efficiency of even the most powerful server to near zero. When designing the Web server, it is critical that the network equipment, both within and supplemental to the server, is capable of meeting the server needs. Because virtually all Web servers use the TCP/IP protocol stack, Ethernet is generally adequate for connecting a Web server to a router. In some cases where high bandwidth is a concern of the server being integrated into an already existing network, Fast Ethernet, Token Ring, or Asynchronous Transfer Mode (ATM) may be used.

The amount of bandwidth necessary for connecting the router, which may be the Web server itself but is usually a separate device, to the Internet is determined by the number of "hits" the Web server receives. In most instances, traditional T-carrier service leased through local telephone companies provides sufficient bandwidth with a high level of scalability.

As with disk drives, fault tolerance in the connection to the Internet is a high-priority concern. Because we must prepare for a failure at the service-provider level, leasing multiple lines through different service providers is almost essential.

Additional Hardware

Depending on the specifics of the installation, a typical Web server may use several other pieces of hardware. One extremely critical piece of equipment that should be added to every Web server, without exception, is a tape drive or other backup storage device. The mission-critical nature of information on the hard disks makes it imperative that the data is backed up reliably and regularly. Key backups should also be stored off-site as part of an overall disaster recovery plan. Using a good disk mirroring scheme reduces to almost zero the possibility of data loss; however, the risk of data loss can never be eliminated. If data is lost from the hard disk, a recent backup may be the only way the data can be recovered. Due to the low cost of backup devices on most Web servers, there is no reason not to install a backup device. The capacity of the backup device is dictated by the capacity of the installed hard disk drives.

Three other specialized hardware devices are commonly used by Web servers:

- **Firewalls**, either hardware, software, or a combination, are often installed between Web servers and the Internet. Firewalls increase the level of security and can help protect sensitive data from outside attack.

- **Cache servers** are hardware devices that store copies of commonly accessed Web pages. By caching the pages on a separate system, the cache server can intercept HTTP requests and provide a response, thereby minimizing the traffic being passed through to the server. Cache servers can greatly increase the performance of a Web server system without making any changes to the server itself.

- **Load balancers** are devices that intercept HTTP requests destined for a Web server and divide the requests between multiple identical Web servers. This process greatly reduces the total amount of traffic handled by each server, while providing a high degree of fault tolerance. If one server fails, the load balancer automatically forwards all requests to the functioning servers.

Web Server Operating System Considerations

Objective 1.4
Understand and be able to describe the infrastructure needed to support an Internet client.
… Operating system

Choosing the correct NOS may be the most important decision in the design of a Web server. Hardware can always be added or replaced on an existing server, and software packages can always be uninstalled in favor of other packages. The NOS, however, is nearly eternal. Changing the NOS is a major task that requires many hours of work and significant expense.

Desktop Operating Systems

Desktop operating systems, such as Microsoft Windows 95/98/ME, or Macintosh operating system (MacOS) can be used for Web servers, but their performance will be limited. These operating systems are not optimized for a multiuser environment, and many advanced security and file handling features are not present. Additionally, the range of Web server products available for these platforms is limited. Subsequently, desktop operating systems should not be used for Web servers at any level outside of home use.

NOSs

Many network operating systems (NOSs) are available from a variety of vendors, and all have different strengths and weaknesses. When choosing a NOS, it is important that it be chosen in the context of available software. Many in the technology industry spend most of their careers working under one NOS, and as experts in that system they become blind to other options.

Prioritizing business needs is a difficult but necessary step in the development process. If the needs analysis is thorough and accurate, the choice of NOS should adequately meet the needs of the system. If the NOS chosen proves to be inadequate, a refined needs analysis should be performed.

Apple Macintosh (Mac OS)

Although Apple Macintosh was primarily considered a workstation for high-end graphics and multimedia work, Apple Computers has been trying for several years to insert itself into the server market. The combination of the Mac OS X Server with Macintosh Server G3 is one of the fastest servers available on the PC level.

Along with the usual file, print, mail, and Web access services, Mac OS X Server includes a scalable Web application server in WebObjects 4. The operating system uses Posix application programming interfaces (APIs), so that developers can port many UNIX applications. In addition to incorporating the full suite of AppleTalk networking products, the Macintosh G3 Server comes equipped with a full suite of TCP/IP tools bundled into a package marketed as AppleShare IP.

The main drawbacks to using a Macintosh G3 Server as a Web server, despite its outstanding performance, are the operating system and lack of available software. Although MacOS has received numerous awards for its usability and stability, it is still primarily a desktop operating system that was not designed as a NOS. The high level of performance obtained is due more to the hardware than to the operating system. Additionally, the server tools available are less abundant and less established than those of many other operating systems. Using a Macintosh G3 Server as a Web server is especially useful for a predominantly Apple solution.

Microsoft Windows 2000

Windows 2000 is Microsoft's next-generation OS, based on the features of Windows NT. Central to Windows 2000 is the built-in Web server: Internet Information Service (IIS) 5.0. This server can host Web sites that use interactive applications. IIS 5.0 supports Internet standards and is one of the most popular Web servers.

IIS 5.0 improvements over previous versions come from advances made to the operating system. IIS 5.0 includes an enhanced version of the Active Server Pages (ASP) server-scripting environment.

Windows 2000 provides integrated application services that work with IIS 5.0 to allow developers to build Web applications and e-commerce sites. Windows 2000 also offers GUI security and database integration features.

Microsoft provides a Small Business Server 2000 package for companies that need only five user licenses. It provides tools to share files and data, connect to the Internet, manage e-mail and faxes, and log in remotely. It bundles Windows 2000 Server, Exchange 2000 Server, Outlook 2000, SQL Server 2000, Internet Security and Acceleration Server (IAS), Shared Modem Service, and Shared Fax Service. Windows 2000 has had problems with security, and Microsoft has provided patches that fix those problems.

Microsoft Windows NT

Windows NT is a 32-bit, fully protected NOS designed to be usable as both a file server and application server. The chief strengths of Windows NT are its GUIs, designed to make administration as easy as possible, and an abundance of off-the-shelf applications. Additionally, Windows NT can be run on virtually every major processor including Intel, Alpha, and PowerPC. Although more software is available for Windows NT when running on an Intel processor, the software selection when running on other processors is still very competitive.

The GUIs that make Windows NT easy to administer also require additional resources, as do the protective features of the operating system. Other criticisms of Windows NT are that its security features are not as robust as some commercial versions of UNIX, and that the ability to fine-tune the operating system performance is limited by the need to use the graphic interfaces to make any changes.

OS/2 Warp Server

OS/2 was originally developed by IBM and Microsoft in a joint venture, but corporate disagreements caused Microsoft and IBM to part ways. Microsoft went on to develop Windows NT, while IBM continued to develop OS/2. OS/2 is a 32-bit operating system that is regarded throughout the industry as a highly stable platform. OS/2 Warp Server, the flagship LAN NOS of IBM, is designed to run on an Intel-based server and support heterogeneous clients over numerous protocols. One of the greatest strengths of OS/2 Warp Server is its interoperability with IBM mainframes, which are currently experiencing a resurgence.

As a Web server, OS/2 Warp Server has much to offer. Its stability as an application server and wealth of features are its primary selling points. The main criticism of OS/2 Warp Server is its extremely proprietary nature. Although there are an abundance of networking and Internet products available for OS/2 Warp Server, most of these are IBM products. Although many feel that the interoperability offered by a one-vendor solution is desirable, many also feel that the lack of choice that exists for OS/2 Warp Server applications is a hindrance to efficiency.

Commercial UNIX

UNIX is the operating system the Internet was built on, and it still maintains a large share of the NOS market, especially in areas involving the Internet. UNIX is an open architecture operating system and several versions (both 32-bit and 64-bit) exist, each produced by a different vendor and compiled for only that vendor's hardware. Some of the most common "flavors" are HP-UX of Hewlett-Packard, Sun Microsystems' SunOS for Solaris systems, IRIX of Silicon Graphics Inc., and OpenServer/UNIXWare of Santa Cruz Operation (SCO).

The main strength of any UNIX platform is the longevity of the operating system. UNIX has been used in academia and industry since the 1970s, and few products in the computer industry can boast such an accomplishment. The stability, functionality, and reliability of UNIX are beyond question.

The two main criticisms of UNIX are that it is difficult to administer and the available software is less than desirable. UNIX has its roots in the days before GUIs, and despite the proliferation of the X Window system, is still primarily a command-line operating system. Making even small changes to the operating system's functionality often requires manual editing of configuration files that are often cryptic (at best) and may be different from one UNIX variation to another. Proponents of UNIX claim that the ability to edit the configuration files directly gives UNIX a performance advantage over every other NOS on the market; however, this performance advantage is often achieved through a greater total cost of ownership.

Linux

Linux is a freeware variation of UNIX initiated as a class project by a Finnish graduate student named Linus Torvalds. By distributing the source code for the kernel over the Internet and actively encouraging any and all to participate in its development, Linux has grown into a widely respected NOS. Linux received a great deal of publicity when the production company that created the special effects for the movie *Titanic* used a server farm of DEC servers with Alpha processors running Red Hat Linux (one of several distributions). The power and stability displayed by Linux on this project, as well as its ability to run all Portable Operating System Interface for UNIX (POSIX)-compliant commercial UNIX applications, has caused many network managers to seriously consider Linux's place in the NOS market.

One of the strengths cited by Linux devotees is that it is based entirely on new technology. While commercial versions of UNIX are all based on source code that may be decades old, Linux has been developed since 1992. Linux regularly outperforms commercial packages on benchmark tests. Another advantage of Linux is cost. Linux is freeware, so distributors can charge only for the distribution media and any proprietary software included with the media. The market has fixed the price of most Linux distributions to a range of $30 to $50, and this one-time purchase provides the capability to outfit an entire enterprise of any size.

A primary and significant criticism of Linux is its lack of vendor support. Vendors of commercial network systems justify the high price, in part, by offering continued support for their products. Because there is no one vendor of Linux, available support is limited, at best. Proponents of Linux believe there is better support than commercial vendors can provide by means of a Linux "community" ready and willing to provide assistance. Network managers must weigh this option of support with the peace-of-mind that comes with having a formal service contract.

Novell NetWare

NetWare 5 is Novell's answer to the Internet. NetWare had previously chosen to use its proprietary Internetwork Packet Exchange/Sequenced Packet Exchange (IPX/SPX) protocol stack instead of supporting TCP. Now NetWare 5 supports both IP and IPX to support local network users as well as Internet/intranet users. NetWare 5 runs applications in protected mode without sacrificing performance. According to serverwatch.com, "This means that NetWare is one of the most stable Internet server platforms available. Only Linux matches NetWare on the PC level in this capability."

NetWare 5 includes Novell Directory Services (NDS). NDS in NetWare 5 includes support for LDAP 3, providing a link between NDS and Internet/intranet mail servers. NDS also provides support for Domain Name Servers (DNS) and Dynamic Host Configuration Protocol (DHCP) utilities with a Java-based management application, making it easier to administer than other server platforms. Benchmarking tests show that Novell does well in comparison to Windows 2000, but it does not scale well to multiple CPUs.

UNIX vs. Windows 2000

Although any NOS can be used as a Web server platform, the two main contenders for market dominance are UNIX and Microsoft Windows 2000. Much of the disagreement between proponents of UNIX and those of Windows 2000 is more philosophical than technical, and this unfortunate propensity among technical professionals shows no signs of changing. What is important to understand is that the business model must take priority over the quasi-religious feelings of the technical staff. The NOS chosen must meet the needs of the business model. When considered from this perspective, both UNIX and Windows 2000 have areas generally regarded to perform well.

Administration

Whenever a NOS is chosen, regardless of the purpose for which the system is designed, administration of the system is one of the principal concerns. Administration, in relation to a network, is the act of ensuring the network is installed correctly and runs smoothly. Administration includes managing user accounts and security, installing and maintaining software applications, configuring user services, managing the file system, and performing many other associated tasks.

The administrative burdens of UNIX and Windows 2000 are vastly different. Despite the development of the X Window system, UNIX is still and will always be primarily command-line driven. Even when a graphical tool has been developed for a specific function, the tool rarely does more than edit configuration files based on input from a window. A UNIX administrator is still capable of making the same changes manually. This offers an unparalleled, high degree of control over the operating system. However, the knowledge level required to properly administer a UNIX server is very high; experienced administrators are in demand and can command high salaries. UNIX administration is so technical that many UNIX administrators have little knowledge of networking outside UNIX.

Windows 2000 and NT, conversely, have been designed for ease of administration, and this trend will continue as Microsoft moves forward with its "Zero Administration" initiative. Every aspect of the operating system is controlled by a graphical tool and rarely, if ever, are the inner workings of these tools accessible to the administrator. Many feel that this lack of access to the operating system internals makes fine tuning nearly impossible, but this issue is debatable. What is certain, however, is that Windows servers can be administered to a moderate level by an administrator with less technical knowledge than required by UNIX, and that

469

the amount of time dedicated to administering a Windows server is generally less than required for a UNIX server.

Stability

UNIX has been running computers for over three decades and many of the bugs that plague new systems have been corrected for years. It is not uncommon for UNIX servers to function reliably for years without ever crashing or requiring a reboot. This level of stability is unmatched by any system short of a mainframe and is one of UNIX's greatest strengths. The key to this level of stability, however, is the knowledge level of the server administrator. Only experienced administrators can be expected to maintain a UNIX system operating in a heavy production environment. For moderate-use servers, however, the administrative demand is less and the stability of UNIX is considerable.

Despite a high degree of protection and fault tolerance in the core operating system, Windows 2000 is prone to crash more frequently than UNIX. Moreover, some product installations require Windows 2000 to be rebooted, causing a loss of service during the process. This has given Windows 2000 a reputation for being less stable than UNIX. One of the weaknesses of Windows 2000 that complicates this issue is the closed nature of the software. The UNIX kernel source code has been available in the public domain for years, and many UNIX administrators are also experienced kernel hackers who have a thorough understanding of how the system works.

Windows 2000 is a much newer operating system modified and updated by Microsoft at an astounding pace. Few Windows administrators can boast the level of knowledge of Windows 2000 that many UNIX administrators can of UNIX. The ease of administration of Windows 2000, however, has led to many of these systems being managed by people who are not full-time administrators or who do not have a high level of experience. This trend helps reduce the total cost of ownership for the Windows 2000 system, but it can lessen the stability of the system. Proper administration by qualified professionals can provide a Windows server stability comparable to that of a UNIX system.

Security

Windows servers have gained bad press because of security flaws in the operating system. What has received much less press is the fact that these security flaws are easily correctable. When a typical installation is performed so that Windows 2000 is configured "out of the box," there are several security issues that must be addressed. For example, the operating system directory is set as a shared folder, as are all MS-DOS partitions. Simply turning off the file sharing on these and other sensitive folders can close many security gaps. The problem with Windows 2000 is that the ease of installation combined with inexperienced administrators can cause Windows 2000 to be installed with unnecessary services and features that result in additional security flaws. If a strong security plan is created and enforced, and Windows 2000 is installed with only the necessary services, a high degree of security can be achieved.

UNIX, under most circumstances, installs with a higher degree of security than Windows 2000. The high level of operating system control that can be achieved over a UNIX system allows for an even greater level of security to be achieved. As with anything else under UNIX, this security requires a higher administrative burden. One problem that plagues UNIX servers more than Windows 2000 servers is the frequency with which UNIX systems are attacked. Because every college freshman studying computer science has some UNIX experience, and many of them have spent time reviewing and modifying kernel source code, the number of low-level attacks on UNIX systems is far greater than on Windows systems. For serious data pirates, the availability of volumes of information on the inner workings of UNIX is as much a boon as it is to the UNIX administrator. Although UNIX is generally considered to be the more secure operating system, a good security model is just as essential on a Windows 2000 system.

Product Availability

The one area where Windows 2000 is generally considered to have a clear advantage over UNIX is in the availability of software. For every UNIX program available there are usually several programs available for Windows 2000. For network administrators looking to deploy off-the-shelf solutions, this can be a tremendous selling point for Windows 2000.

Although fewer applications exist for UNIX (often carrying a higher price than similar applications on Windows 2000), much of the available UNIX software has been in production for years, if not decades. These programs have a reputation for reliability that rivals the operating system itself. One weakness of UNIX, however, is that there are several different vendor-specific variants of UNIX, and an application that runs on one version may not run on another or may not be as reliable.

Activities

1. Describe at least three hardware components to consider when choosing a Web server platform.

   ____

   ____

   ____

   ____

2. Platforms that run Microsoft Windows NT or Windows 2000 require less RAM than LINUX systems. True or False?

3. Disk drive capacity is the most common bottleneck when operating a Web server. True or False?

4. T-carrier service is sufficient bandwidth for most applications. True or False?

5. When choosing a hardware platform that yields the most flexibility in software choices, which platform would you select:

   a. PowerPC

   b. Alpha

   c. Intel (or compatible) processor

6. A load balancer is a device that intercepts an HTTP request and switches to the server with the fastest processor. True or False?

7. Briefly describe the relationship between the Web server hardware, the Web server application, and the Web server NOS.

   ____

   ____

   ____

Extended Activities

1. Using the information in this lesson, rate each of the following items for importance to your organization (in terms of Web server choice).

   a. Administration

   ____

   b. Scalability

   ____

   c. Server management

   ____

   d. Security

   ____

   e. Multiple URL hosting

   ____

   f. Product Integration

   ____

   g. Development tools

   ____

2. Visit the following vendor sites, and research the functionality and cost of their Web server computers.

   a. **http://www.ibm.com**

   ____

   ____

   b. **http://www.dell.com**

   ____

   ____

   c. **http://www.sun.com**

   ____

   ____

3. List four Network Operating Systems (NOSs) that are used as the software platform for Web servers today. Following each NOS, list two strengths and weaknesses.

   ____

   ____

Strengths: _________________________________

Weaknesses: ________________________________

   ____

   ____

Strengths: _________________________________

Weaknesses: ________________________________

Strengths:

Weaknesses:

Strengths:

Weaknesses:

Internet Clients and Servers

4. Make two column headings: one labeled "UNIX/LINUX," and the other "Windows 2000" (do not write the column headings right next to each other). On the left side, make four row headings labeled "Administration," "Stability," "Security," and "Product Availability." Leave plenty of white space to print a few brief items under each heading and in each row. Compare these two network operating systems in the four areas listed by entering a brief statement in each row under both column headings.

Lesson 3—Server Applications

The heart and soul of any server is the server software. While the hardware platform and NOS provide the framework of the system, it is the server software that provides the functionality and feature set that define each type of Internet service, such as FTP or e-mail. Each of these server applications listens for client requests on its own well-known port, and has its own unique set of strengths and weaknesses.

Small organizations often install several server applications on a single platform, making that computer into an all-purpose Internet services platform. Larger organizations prefer to install each server application on a separate platform, to simplify maintenance and enhance security. For example, if a company's FTP and Web servers run on different computers, it's less likely that vandals can use FTP to upload unauthorized content to the Web site.

This lesson introduces some of the most common server applications found on the Internet. As usual, we pay more attention to Web servers. However, other Internet servers provide essential features for most Web sites and corporate intranets.

Objectives

At the end of this lesson you will be able to:

- Name the most popular Web server applications, and compare their advantages and disadvantages

- Explain what features an LDAP directory can provide

- Describe the similarities and differences between e-mail and news

Key Point

Each Internet service is provided by a different server application.

Daemons and Services

When a typical application is launched by a user or another application, it is loaded into memory. It then does its job, shuts down, and is cleared from memory. In contrast, a Windows service or UNIX daemon (pronounced "demon") is a process that continually runs in the background, waiting for a particular type of event, or a protocol message on a well-known port.

Each service or daemon provides a specific type of server-side functionality. For example, the Telnet daemon (telnetd) provides Telnet services. The daemon runs on a server, listens on the well-known TCP port 23, and responds to Telnet requests from remote clients. Other daemons provide HTTP or FTP services, while some daemons coordinate the work of other daemons. For example, the Internet Daemon (inetd) handles requests for several Internet services.

Web Server Software

Objective 3.5
Understand how various protocols or services apply to the function of their corresponding server ... HTTP

Web server software prices range from free to thousands of dollars, and packages are available for nearly every operating system. Functionality ranges from small-footprint embedded personal Web servers to full-blown solutions that combine Internet/intranet Web services, FTP, e-mail, e-commerce features, database access, site-creation tools, and server monitoring. Determining the best Web server for a given situation requires a complete understanding of business needs and peripheral factors such as budget, knowledge level of Information Services (IS) staff, and future growth expectations.

According to an ongoing Web server use survey conducted by Netcraft, which compiled data from millions of Web sites, the leading Web server for public Internet sites is Apache, which commanded more than a 50 percent share. The Web Server Use for Public Web Sites Diagram illustrates the breakdown.

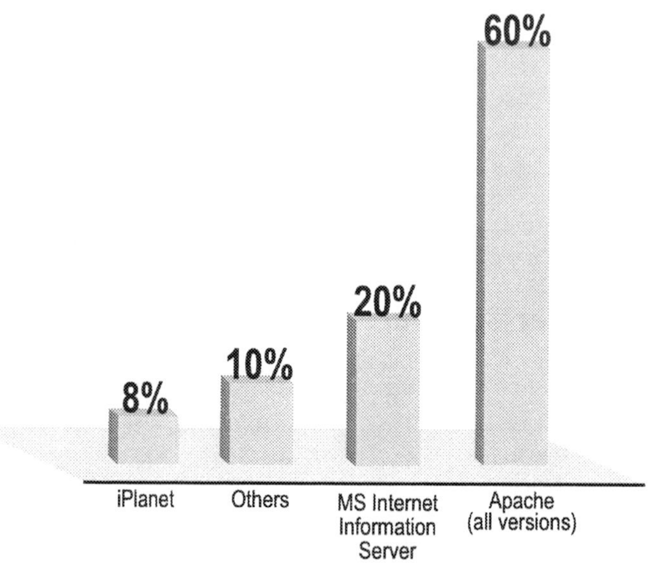

Web Server Use for Public Web Sites

The two most popular Web servers— Apache and Microsoft Internet Information Server (IIS)—represent over 80 percent of the total servers in use. Netscape and Sun Microsystems combined efforts to form iPlanet, which holds less than 10 percent of the market share for Web servers.

Apache HTTP Server

The Apache Web server was originally developed in 1995 by eight independent developers. They founded the Apache Project as "a collaborative software development effort aimed at creating a robust, commercial-grade, featureful, and freely-available source code implementation of an HTTP (Web) server." Using the source code for the NCSA HTTPd server, combined with numerous patches and bug fixes, they created the Apache Web server ("A PAtCHy server").

Today the Apache Group is a jointly-managed group of volunteers located around the world who use the Internet and Web to communicate, plan, and develop the server and its related documentation. Hundreds of users have contributed ideas, code, and documentation to the project.

One of the principal strengths of Apache is that it is free. All executables, the source code, updates, patches, fixes, frequently asked questions (FAQs), and available documentation can be downloaded from the Apache Web site (**http://www.apache.org**). The source code can be modified freely, so custom features can be added as necessary. The strong freeware mentality that exists in the UNIX community (the platform for which Apache was originally developed) has helped drive the development of Apache to a level equal to or surpassing many commercial packages.

The major disadvantage of the Apache Web server is that it is difficult to configure. Unlike products developed by Windows-oriented vendors, Apache does not have a rich graphical environment in which to operate. Changes to the server must be made by modifying the configuration files. This task can be daunting to those without a strong UNIX background, and mistakes, some of which can be devastating, are easy to make.

The dependence on a command-line interface, however, can also be one of Apache's greatest strengths. No other Web server provides the operator with as much control over how the program operates. When performance is of utmost importance, Apache is normally the server of choice.

Another area where Apache tends to lag behind the competition is in content support. Apache comes with only basic Web page-authoring tools, no content management tools, a limited search engine, and no built-in SSL support. The open nature of the product does allow development of add-on modules by third parties much easier than for most other Web servers. These add-on modules, many of which are freely available over the Internet, make Apache the most extensible Web server on the market.

Microsoft IIS

Microsoft Internet Information Server (IIS) is free to all licensed users of Windows NT and the two products are highly integrated. IIS 5.0 is now also included with Windows 2000. This high level of integration makes IIS a good choice for companies that already have a Windows NT network in operation. Companies that have enterprise networks built on UNIX may not find IIS a very good choice because it only runs on Windows NT/2000, and Microsoft has no plans to develop it for other platforms.

One of the biggest selling features of IIS is its integration with a full line of other Microsoft products. All of Microsoft's BackOffice products, as well as FrontPage, SQL Server, Proxy Server, Site Server, Systems Management Server, Certificate Server, Transaction Server, Message Queue Server, Index Server, and Exchange Server, are designed to combine into a full enterprise networking solution.

Another advantage, or possible drawback, to using IIS is the support that it provides to proprietary Microsoft Web services. IIS is one of the few Web servers to support both Active Server Pages and FrontPage extensions. These features allow users of IIS to add dynamic content to their sites, which is not possible when using other Web servers. Using them, however, may ultimately limit growth and choice because an all-Microsoft solution may be necessary to support the Web site.

Netscape/Sun iPlanet Web Server

Netscape and Sun Microsystems have formed an alliance and created the iPlanet Web Server. The iPlanet Web Server replaces Netscape's Enterprise Server, which was very popular. The iPlanet suite includes many different software applications that support different demands. Other products related to the Web Server are the Application Server and the Directory Server.

Sun and Netscape (which is now a part of AOL) combine experience with the Web and e-commerce to provide server solutions for providers. Sun has brought Java enhancements to the server. iPlanet has an advantage over IIS in its ability to program the hooks provided to develop and run applications.

The iPlanet Server version 4.1 runs on Windows NT, multiple UNIX platforms, and Linux. Administration is straightforward, and is able to work with multiple processors, a server farm, or directory services.

Serverwatch (**http://serverwatch.internet.com/**) calls iPlanet Web Server "a serious contender in at least any situation where performance features or Java support are paramount." The database features are improved over Enterprise server, and they include native drivers for common databases (Oracle, Informix, DB2, and Sybase).

The advantages to iPlanet are that it is great if you need Java and database support. It also supports high traffic demands and is relatively easy to administer. Disadvantages include a lack of testing for some of the more complicated Java support and unreliable support and documentation.

Other Web Server Choices

There are literally dozens of Web server choices, other than the most popular ones already discussed. The power and functionality of these other servers varies greatly and many may not be suitable for your business needs. A few, however, provide performance and features that may be suitable to the needs of a given enterprise. Some of these options are discussed in the following subsections.

Zeus Web Server

This Web server is designed for companies providing Web hosting, content, and secure e-commerce. It provides Web-based management and integration capabilities. Zeus Web server runs on: HP-UX, Solaris, Linux, IBM AIX, SGI IRIX, Compaq Tru64, FreeBSD, OpenBSD, SCO Unixware, Mac OS X, and BSDi. For more information, see **http://www.zeus.com**.

Macromedia ColdFusion

ColdFusion MX is a Web application server for developing e-commerce applications. It includes an integrated suite of visual tools, powerful server technology, and an open language environment. ColdFusion runs on: Linux, HP-UX, Digital UNIX, Solaris, Windows 95/98/NT/2000, and IBM AIX. For more information, see **http://www.macromedia.com/desdev/mx/coldfusion/**.

IBM WebSphere Application Server

WebSphere is a Java-based Web application server for a wide range of applications, from simple sites to more complicated business sites. It is available in Standard, Advanced, and Enterprise editions. WebSphere runs on: IBM AIXand OS/400, and Windows NT. For more information, see **http://www.ibm.com**.

Oracle Application Server

This server deploys all Web sites and applications. It includes Java support for the latest J2EE standards, XML and PL/SQL. It integrates with Oracle Internet Developer Suite tools. Oracle Application Server runs on: UNIX and Windows NT. For more information, see **http://www.oracle.com**.

Web Server Software Considerations

Many factors influence the choice of the application software used to develop a Web server. As always, the driving concern is the business model. In other words, why does the organization need a Web server, and what business functions should it perform? A 10,000-employee corporation developing an intranet, onto which it intends to migrate their custom applications, will have vastly different needs than a small, privately owned specialty store developing a Web server that will advertise its presence but offer no additional services. Understanding these concerns is the first step in developing a system.

Administration

The amount of time, training, and technical ability required of the support staff are all factors that contribute to the ease or difficulty of server administration. Large companies with a significant internal technology staff may find administration of one additional server a small burden. A small company with a limited or nonexistent technology staff may not have the capability of handling even the simplest tasks, and it may have to outsource administrative services. To this company, a system that is easy to administer may be the only realistic option.

Scalability

Growth, the goal of every business, will have a significant impact on all components of a Web server. The future Web needs of a business may be significantly different from the needs at the time the Web server is built. As a rule of thumb, networks should never be designed around current needs; they should be designed to grow on the same scale as projected business growth expectations. The added expense for future planning rarely, if ever, outweighs the potential loss of revenue that could occur if a system outgrows its capacity.

The specific circumstances of the organization will determine the projected needs that the Web server design must meet. One factor that will weigh heavily into this decision is the scalability of the systems involved. A system that is highly scalable, meaning that its capabilities can be increased dramatically with minimal effort, will require less future disruption than a less-scalable solution.

Server Management

A Web server is not a static device that can be turned on and ignored. It is a dynamic device that needs constant monitoring and adjustment. Without continual configuration and capability changes, a Web server will not be able to operate at peak efficiency. Many tools are available that will monitor the performance of a Web server and provide analytical data on performance features, such as the number of hits received, efficiency of the cache, and response time.

Two management factors that are sometimes at odds with one another, that must be considered are: the level of control that can be exerted over the Web server and the ease of use of available tools. The Apache Web server running on a UNIX platform is considered by many in the industry the solution that provides the ultimate level of control; however, this control is achieved through the modification of text-based configuration files. The process of "tweaking" server performance can be a daunting task for even the most seasoned professional. Microsoft IIS, at the other end of the spectrum, benefits from Microsoft's "Zero Administration" design, and is considered easy to manage. However, many feel that the graphical nature of IIS gives the administrator less control over server functionality. The business model for which the Web server is being designed will determine what management criteria are priorities.

Security

One of the more serious concerns in designing a Web server is the level of security needed. An intranet server for a small company that has no Internet access will likely not have very stringent security needs. A large corporation planning to provide online transactions or extranet access to sensitive information will have a much greater security concern. Capabilities such as secure transactions (by means of Secure Sockets Layer [SSL] and other security paradigms), data encryption, IP filtering, and proxy authentication may be desired features. All products used as part of the Web solution must support and be compatible with the security plan.

Multiple URL Hosting

If a Web server is being designed to host multiple sites, such as for an Internet Service Provider (ISP) or a Web development and hosting firm, the server must be capable of handling requests for multiple domains. Several mechanisms have been developed for accomplishing this, some open and some proprietary. Many businesses may not require the capability to host multiple domains, but those that do will usually find this feature of their server solution to be mission critical and must plan accordingly.

Product Integration

Because a functional Web server is really a conglomeration of separate products, the level at which these products function together and the ease of managing the overall system will be an important consideration in designing a Web solution. Many tools are designed to work together, such as the Microsoft suite of Internet tools. Independently, these tools may not be the best tools for a given situation, but combined in a more complex system, their high level of integration may generate the most efficient solution. A large company with a correspondingly large support staff may find the task of managing several disparate products on multiple platforms to be relatively minor. A smaller operation may find that the administrative burden of nonintegrated products may be an unacceptable resource burden. Again, the business model will dictate the solution.

When evaluating product integration, there are three classes of products that must be considered as shown in the following subsections.

Server Tools

Server tools are products designed to add functionality to the basic Web server. Electronic commerce (e-commerce) servers, database engines, messaging servers, Common Gateway Interface (CGI) interpreters, run-time libraries, and proxy servers are examples of server tools. When designing a system that uses any of these tools, it is important that their ability to function with one another, as well as their stability on the desired NOS, be fully tested and evaluated. A Web server is only as strong as its weakest link, and a failure of only one of these products can render the entire system inoperable.

Development Tools

Although a simple Web page can be built with any text editor, full-featured Web sites require a number of interoperating tools. HTML editors/generators, scripting tools, site management programs, graphics editors, programming suites, and word processors are only some of the tools in the "virtual" tool belt of a Web designer. Many of these products are part of larger packages that offer a high degree of integration that may be desirable, whereas others may have no integration with the server tools. A complete evaluation of the possible development tools and their integration with the available and necessary tools may help in determining which products to use.

Web Browsers

Objective 1.4
Understand and be able to describe the infrastructure needed to support an Internet client. ... Web browsers

The other set of products whose interoperability with various Web servers should be considered are Web browsers. In many instances, the level of integration between a Web browser and a Web server will be immaterial. Customers accessing a Web site over the Internet are not necessarily using any specific browser. In some situations, however, certain assumptions about the browsers may influence the choice of Web server.

Several newer technologies are not supported by older browsers or browsers produced by certain manufacturers. Visual Basic Script and Microsoft ActiveX, for example, are supported by Microsoft Internet Explorer, but not by Netscape Navigator. If a corporation's designers wish to use these technologies for the corporate intranet, they may do so knowing that all users accessing the intranet will be using Microsoft Internet Explorer. In this example, the level of integration of Microsoft Internet Explorer with Microsoft IIS may become a factor in developing the Web solution. If another corporation plans to host an intranet for an enterprise composed entirely of UNIX workstations and servers, browser integration may not be a concern.

Vendor-Specific Features and Service Contracts

A final concern in designing a Web server is the available vendor-specific features. As competitive as the Internet technology market is today, vendors of Web server products must constantly add new features to compete. The feature sets available may include functionality not offered on other platforms, but may also consist of free upgrades, telephone or on-site support, and product warranties. A corporation whose Web server is mission critical, but that cannot afford to employ a large in-house support staff, may find that the service contract offered by an established vendor such as IBM may be a justified, almost necessary expense. A larger corporation with proprietary needs, such as a Web development and hosting firm, may find that having access to the source code for the Apache Web server may provide a competitive edge that outweighs the lack of vendor support. The vendor features that are desirable and required will, as always, depend on the business model.

Other Internet Servers

Objective 3.5
Understand how various protocols or services apply to the function of their corresponding server. … POP3, SMTP, FTP, NNTP, LDAP

The World Wide Web is only one of many features supported by the Internet. Some of the following Internet services have been around for much longer than the Web, while others provide new technology to enhance the content of Web sites.

Small sites may run several of these server applications on a single computer. Larger sites often dedicate a separate computer to each server, both to improve performance and enhance security.

E-Mail Servers

A mail server application functions like a post office. Like a Web server, a mail server is continually connected to the Internet. It receives SMTP messages, from other servers, that contain incoming mail for local users. It stores those messages until users request them via POP3 or IMAP4. Users' new mail messages go via POP3 or IMAP4 to the local mail server, which uses SMTP to forward them across the Internet to the mail server at the destination network.

To help protect networks and users from viruses, some mail servers can be configured to remove or quarantine potentially damaging e-mail attachments. For example, most corporate mail servers will not deliver a mail message with an executable attachment.

FTP Servers

An FTP server application manages a repository of files that are available for public or private download. This server functions as a simple librarian, acting on client requests to copy or change files, add new files to the repository, or do other file management tasks. A user's access rights can be controlled based on username and password, so that a public document database can prevent most users from deleting or moving files. However, FTP transmits usernames and passwords as unencrypted data ("cleartext") that can be easily intercepted. Thus, many FTP administrators also implement some type of encryption to protect users' authentication information.

News Servers

A news server (NNTP server) stores and maintains a central database of news articles and newsgroup messages. It distributes these messages to clients, and accepts new messages from clients, via NNTP. A news server may function independently, or replicate its database to other servers to improve redundancy and user response time.

News, like e-mail, is distributed as individual messages. However, news messages are sent to the newsgroup, not an individual, and any subscriber of the newsgroup may download them. Unlike e-mail, news readers can display related news messages in "threads," that show the order of postings and replies.

Some organizations set up public newsgroups to serve as online user groups. However, others install news server software on their private news servers to create privately operated newsgroups using NNTP technology.

Media Servers

Media server software distributes streaming audio, video, and other multimedia content to clients across the Internet or on a corporation's intranet. High-performance media servers are essential tools for entertainment sites such as Internet radio stations. Many other corporations use smaller servers to deliver product demonstrations, or remote corporate training.

Multimedia files tend to be large. Thus, in addition to streaming, media servers use compression and IP multicast addressing to make the most efficient use of network bandwidth.

DNS Servers

A DNS server, or name server, maintains a database that resolves human-friendly domain names to numeric IP addresses. Except for the small handful of name servers that form the worldwide root of the hierarchical DNS namespace, each DNS server only resolves domain names for a small subbranch of the DNS system. If a name server cannot answer a query for an IP address, it refers the requesting client to another server, usually on a higher level in the hierarchy.

Certificate Servers

Objective 4.1

Understand and be able to describe various Internet security concepts.
... Authentication
... Encryption-PKI

Public key encryption, or asymmetrical encryption, is an essential tool for providing secure communication across the public Internet. Each person who wants to receive encrypted messages must first have a pair of encryption keys. The public key is distributed to anyone who wants to send a secure message to the recipient. The private key is used, only by the recipient, to decrypt messages. The same encryption technology can also be used to create digital certificates and digital signatures, which can verify the source of messages or securely authenticate the identity of a remote user.

Independent companies, called Certificate Authorities (CAs), issue key pairs and digital certificates for a fee. However, large companies that need many key pairs can save money by installing their own certificate servers. These applications generate and manage key pairs and digital certificates for internal use by employees.

Directory (LDAP) Servers

Objective 4.1

Understand and be able to describe various Internet security concepts.
... Access control
... Authentication
... Encryption-PKI

Objective 4.9

Understand and be able to describe various authentication/ encryption technologies.
... PKI

The Lightweight Directory Access Protocol (LDAP) is an Internet standard for organizing information in a hierarchical tree structure. An LDAP server, or directory server, stores and manages one or more online directories. With an LDAP client application, a user requests information or submits changes (provided that the user has permission to edit the directory). An LDAP client may be a dedicated application that is specific to one company or directory, or LDAP client features can be built into a generic Internet client application such as an e-mail reader.

Directories and databases can store the same types of information. However, directories differ from databases in a few important ways.

- Directories organize data into particular relationships. In contrast, a relational database stores facts in a neutral structure, and lets the user discover relationships among those facts.

- Directories are selective. A good directory helps users by showing only relevant information, such as a list of printers on the same floor of a building, or the names of the employees who handle health insurance questions.

- Directories are set up for more reading than writing. They do not offer transaction features, record locking, and other safeguards that are common in database management systems.

- Directories are not well suited for reporting, or exporting data to other formats. Database management systems are better for those tasks.

Directories are the best choice for data that must be frequently updated, but which is read much more often than it is changed. For example, an online company directory should be frequently updated to reflect personnel changes. An LDAP directory can include detailed information about each person or department, such as links to e-mail addresses and web pages. It also offers the big advantage of allowing users to update their own entries (provided the directory was designed to allow them this access). So basic information such as phone numbers or addresses can be updated immediately by the users themselves, rather than adding to the workload of the intranet staff.

Directory servers are also important tools for maintaining lists of links on portal sites or large intranets. As each new page is added to a site, the directory server can automatically add a new entry to the site directory.

An online directory can also be an important element of a company's public key infrastructure (PKI), which manages users' security tools in a central, publicly-accessible location. A directory can provide each user's public encryption key and digital certificate, along with e-mail addresses, phone numbers, and other contact information. By selecting the public key from the directory, a sender can encrypt the first message to a recipient. This approach makes it simple for noncompany people to securely communicate with company employees, and makes it easier for security administrators to control tools such as digital certificates and key pairs.

Activities

1. List the "big three" Web servers.

   ____

   ____

   ____

2. Why would you choose Apache Web server over Microsoft Internet Information Server?

   ____

   ____

   ____

   ____

3. Why would you choose Microsoft Internet Information Server over Apache Web server?

   ____

   ____

   ____

   ____

4. Match each of the following features with the type of server that can deliver it.

   a. Deliver streaming audio

   b. Maintain a company roster that can be updated by employees themselves

   c. Create keys for public-key encryption

   d. Public online discussion group

   e. Display HTML pages

   f. Transmit messages between individuals or small lists of people

   g. Maintain central file storage for remote employees

News server __________

Media server __________

Web server __________

Certificate server __________

E-mail server __________

FTP server __________

Directory server __________

Extended Activities

1. Use the Web to find the current percentage of market share for the Web server applications discussed in this lesson.

    ____

    ____

2. List five factors that would influence your selection of a Web server. Following each factor, briefly describe how each would affect the selection process. For example, "Server Management" might be one of the considerations, and the desire to minimize administration time and costs may be what drives that part of the decision. In order to make this activity more realistic, assume a given application profile such as noncritical/low hits, E-commerce/mission-critical, database intensive, or multiple site hosting.

    ____

    ____

    ____

    ____

    ____

Summary

Most Internet activity consists of a client's request for services, and a server's response to that request. For example, when you click a link to a Web page, your browser transmits an HTTP request to the server that hosts that HTML document. The server then transmits that page back to your browser, then waits for another request. The specific features of these interaction are often controlled by the way users configure their client applications. Depending on their personal or physical needs, users may accept or decline cookies, decide whether to download Web graphics, or adjust the size or color of on-screen text.

Originally, a different client was needed to interact with each type of server. Gradually, however, vendors of Web browsers have added support for protocols such as Telnet, FTP, or NNTP. Many experts see this trend continuing until users only need a single universal client to handle all of their Internet communication.

Servers handle most of the heavy work of providing Internet-based services. The term "server" generally includes three components: the physical computing machine, the operating system, and the server application software necessary to provide a particular service. When designing any type of Internet server, all three of these issues must be considered in combination. Because there are so many options available in hardware, operating systems, and applications, server design and implementation is a big challenge.

However, a good technical solution is not always the one that meets the business needs of the organization. The smoothest and most stable server is a bad solution if it is too complex or expensive, or if it cannot easily expand to keep up with a growing business. A good Web administrator must always consider business needs first, then develop a technical solution that best meets those needs.

Unit 6 Quiz

1. Which of the following is not an NOS?

   a. NT

   b. Linux

   c. Apache

   d. NetWare

2. Which of the following is proprietary software?

   a. Microsoft NT

   b. Apache

   c. Linux

   d. None of the above (they are all open source)

3. Which of the following is not a server hardware concern?

   a. RAM

   b. CPU

   c. Network connectivity

   d. Internet address

4. Which of the following is not normally needed for Web server connectivity?

   a. IP

   b. TCP

   c. HTTP

   d. All of the above are needed.

5. A Web server is a static device. After it is up and running, it rarely needs human intervention. True or False?

6. A Web server must be specifically designed to service multiple Internet hosts. True or False?

7. When does a Web server application run?

   a. When a client application launches it

   b. When a packet arrives addressed to Port 80

   c. Continuously

   d. None of the above

8. You must install a new e-mail reader on five new computers. Which of the following will most help the installation go smoothly?

    a. The latest vendor support information and patches

    b. A copy of ZENWorks

    c. A virus control program

    d. A digital certificate for each user

9. You must install a new Web browser on five new computers. Which of the following will most help the process go smoothly?

    a. The latest vendor support information and patches

    b. A copy of ZENWorks

    c. A virus control program

    d. A copy of the network IP address assignments

10. Which of the following is Internet Explorer's default security setting for cookies?

    a. The browser verifies the contents of a cookie before accepting it.

    b. The browser accepts all cookies, without notifying you.

    c. The browser does not accept cookies.

    d. The browser accepts cookies, but prompts you about security information on Web sites.

11. Which of the following is NOT generally considered a component of a Web server?

    a. The computing hardware

    b. The operating system

    c. The HTML pages

    d. The HTTP server application or daemon

12. Load balancing means:

    a. Connecting a server to the Internet using several links from different Internet Service Providers.

    b. Distributing incoming client requests among a group of identical servers.

    c. Writing copies of all data to two or three different hard drives.

    d. Conditioning electrical power to remove spikes and sags.

13. A virtual workgroup has members who live in five time zones. They want a simple way to discuss projects online that does not require them to all be logged on at the same time. You don't want to add a recurring task to your workload. You should suggest:

    a. A private newsgroup

    b. An LDAP server

    c. Instant messaging

    d. A Web site

14. All e-mail reader applications use a standard format to store address book entries. True or False?

15. When an e-mail server transmits an SMTP message, that message is going to:

    a. A user

    b. The destination mail server

    c. The mail system administrator

    d. A network management application

16. A media server handles:

    a. News articles

    b. Floppy disks, backup tapes, and CD-ROMs

    c. Streaming audio and video

    d. Downloadable corporate background information for reporters

17. Which of the following Web servers would you be least likely to encounter on the job?

    a. IBM WebSphere

    b. Netscape/Sun iPlanet

    c. Apache

    d. Microsoft IIS

Unit 7
Building Web Pages

In this unit you will learn how to create simple Web pages, which are formally referred to as Hypertext Markup Language (HTML) documents. Most of the following lessons will give you hands-on experience building and enhancing a Web page. After you have become familiar with building HTML pages "by hand," you will be ready to more productively use the powerful applications that simplify the most tedious aspects of Web development.

Lessons

1. Creating Basic Web Pages
2. Adding Graphics
3. Adding Hyperlinks
4. Formatting Text
5. Incorporating Tables
6. Working With Frames
7. Using Forms
8. Graphic Formats
9. Multimedia Formats

Terms

ActiveX control—ActiveX is a broad category of software components that can be downloaded and run by a Web browser, to add extra functionality to a Web page. ActiveX, developed by Microsoft, is an outgrowth of two technologies: Object Linking and Embedding (OLE) and Component Object Model (COM).

coder/decoder (codec)—A codec is a hardware/software device that takes an analog video signal and converts (codes) it to digital format for compression and transmission. On the receiving end, the digital signal is put back (decoded) into the original analog signal.

Common Gateway Interface (CGI)—CGI is a standard specification for creating Web server programs that accept data from Web clients, process the data, and return a result. For example, each HTML form needs a corresponding CGI program to process form data sent to its Web site. CGI programs can be written in a variety of languages, including C, Perl, Visual Basic, or Java.

Extensible Hypertext Markup Language (XHTML)—XHTML is defined by the World Wide Web Consortium (W3C) as "a reformulation of HTML 4.0 as an application of XML." In XHTML, all HTML 4 markup elements and attributes are supported. Unlike HTML, XHTML can be extended by anyone that uses it. Programmers can define and add new elements and attributes to those that already exist.

Extensible Markup Language (XML)—XML is a simplified version of Standard Generalized Markup Language (SGML) that allows Web designers to add functionality beyond HTML by creating their own formatting tags. W3C created the official XML recommendation for XML 1.0.

form—A form is a Web page designed to collect information or input from a user and send it to a Web server for processing. Forms can contain data-entry fields, checkboxes, drop-down lists, buttons, and other interactive controls.

frames—Frames are HTML documents displayed in separate areas of the browser display. Each frame contains its own set of headers, footers, and body of text.

Graphics Interchange Format (GIF)—GIF is one of the popular graphic image formats used in HTML. Other popular types for the Web are JPEG and PNG. GIF files, the more popular format for small or simple images, are limited to 256 colors, have a lower resolution, offer lossless compression, and can be made transparent for a popular type of borderless effect.

heading—A heading in HTML is text that is tagged to appear larger or bolder than plain text. HTML offers six levels of headline size: from largest (<h1>) to smallest (<h6>). The specific type style and size of each heading depends on each user's browser settings.

hyperlink—A hyperlink is a connection to another Web page or location within the current page. When a user clicks the text or graphic that contains the hyperlink, the browser displays the Web page targeted by the link. Hyperlinks are created with the HTML "anchor" (<a> ...</a>) container tags, plus the `href` attribute and a Uniform Resource Locator (URL).

Hypertext Markup Language (HTML)—HTML is a text-based formatting language used to generically format text for Web pages. It is a simplified derivative of Standard Generalized Markup Language (SGML) that tags different parts of a document more in terms of their function than their appearance. A Web browser reads an HTML document and displays it as indicated by the HTML formatting tags and the browser's default settings.

Joint Photographic Experts Group (JPEG)—JPEG is a graphic file format compatible with HTML. JPEG files offer higher resolution, with up to 16.7 million colors, and they are generally used in continuous-tone images such as photographs. However, JPEG compression is lossy; even at the highest quality setting, some image information is lost.

line break—A line break in HTML is a tag that commands the browser to display text on a new line. The <br> tag creates a line break. A line break does not insert extra vertical space between lines.

Motion Picture Experts Group (MPEG)—MPEG is a standard for compressing video to fewer bits for storage and transmission.

MPEG, Audio Layer 3 (MP3)—MP3 is an audio coding technique to reduce the number of bits required to represent audio signals by removing redundant and irrelevant sounds. MP3 files offer high quality sound with compression ratios of approximately 1:12.

ordered list—An ordered list in HTML is a list of numbered items. To create an ordered list, use the container tags `<ol>` and `</ol>`.

paragraph break—A paragraph in HTML is a tag that commands the browser to display text on a new line and add extra empty vertical space between the old and new lines. To create a paragraph break, use the `<p>` and `</p>` tags.

plug-in—A plug-in is a software module that adds a specific function to a browser. For example, plug-ins for the Netscape Navigator browser enable it to play sound files and animations.

Portable Network Graphics (PNG)—PNG is a file format for image compression that may replace the GIF file format. The PNG format was developed by an Internet committee to be patent-free.

push technology—Push technology is the process by which customized Web content is automatically sent to a subscriber, according to predetermined user preferences.

RealAudio, RealVideo—RealAudio and RealVideo are popular formats for playing streaming audio and video files.

Rich Music Format (RMF)—RMF is an audio file format that includes features such as embedded copyright information and custom "mixing" of tracks.

Standard Generalized Markup Language (SGML)—SGML was developed by the International Organization for Standards (ISO) in 1986. SGML does not specify any particular formatting; rather, it specifies the rules for tagging elements. HTML is a text-based formatting language used to generically format text for Web pages. It is a simplified derivative of SGML, that tags different parts of a document in terms of their function rather than appearance.

streaming—Streaming is the ability to begin playing a downloaded audio or video file as it arrives at the user's computer, without waiting for the entire file to be received first.

table—A table is a section of an HTML document that arranges information in rows and columns. Table cells can display numerical or text data, or they can be used to provide an invisible layout framework to control the placement of text and graphics on a Web page.

tag—A tag is an HTML command inserted in a document that specifies how the document, or a portion of the document, should be formatted by a Web browser.

unordered list—An anchored list in HTML is an unnumbered list of items, usually displayed as a bullet list. To create an unordered list, use the container tags `<ul>` and `</ul>`.

Virtual Reality Modeling Language (VRML)—VRML is a specification for displaying three-dimensional images on the Web.

Wireless Markup Language (WML)—A subset of XML that is optimized to display small items of information on handheld wireless devices such as cellular phones.

Building
Web Pages

Lesson 1—Creating Basic Web Pages

HTML was developed by Tim Berners-Lee at CERN, the European Laboratory for Particle Physics, in Geneva, Switzerland. HTML is a simplified derivative of Standard Generalized Markup Language (SGML). Both of these languages use descriptor tags to mark the content of a document in terms of its structure (headings, lists, body text, etc.). With a few exceptions, HTML markup describes what each part of a document is, and lets each user's Web browser decide how to display those parts. In this lesson, you will use Windows Notepad to produce a simple Web page using the most basic HTML tags.

Objectives

At the end of this lesson you will be able to:

- Create a basic Web page

- Explain the format of an HTML document

 **Key Point**

HTML is the underlying language of Web pages.

HTML Overview

HTML is the language used to create documents on the Web. HTML has gone through many changes and updates in its short history. Variations such as Virtual Reality Markup Language (VRML), Extensible HTML (XHTML), Extensible Markup Language (XML), and Wireless Markup Language (WML) are quickly becoming standards in Web design.

There are several tools on the market that make it simpler and faster to create HTML pages. For Microsoft Windows 95, 98, 2000, or NT users, the tools include Hot Dog, Microsoft FrontPage, Dreamweaver, and HTML Assistant Pro. Editing tools such as Claris Home Page, Bbedit, and Dreamweaver are available for Macintosh users.

Some major software packages, such as Microsoft Word, Powerpoint, and Excel, have built-in HTML converters that convert a document to HTML, thus allowing browsers to read the documents.

Even though there are several tools on the market to help write HTML, it is good to learn to build your first pages "by hand" in a text-only editor. Becoming familiar with the language will help you to be more flexible with HTML code.

Basic HTML Elements

Objective 2.3
Create HTML pages ... HTML document structure ... Coding simple tables, headings, forms

There are some basic coding elements you need to know about before creating an HTML document. These elements include angle brackets, tag names, and attributes. Along with these issues, we point out the importance of consistency in your coding.

Basic Tag Types

HTML tags are case-insensitive elements contained within angle brackets. You use tags to format the content of a Web document. The basic tag types are described in the following subsections.

Container Tags

Container tags include both opening and closing tags, so the pair of tags may contain other information. For example, to use bold text, you use the <b> tag at the beginning of the text, and </b> at the end of the text that you want to appear in bold font. Good coding includes start and ending tags, even though some browsers do not require end tags. For example, a paragraph tag should use the <p> tag at the beginning of the paragraph, and end with the </p> tag.

Empty Tags

Empty tags use only opening tags. For example, the image tag for inserting a graphic image in a page is an empty tag. Another example is the break tag (<br>), which indicates a line break within a paragraph.

Tag Names

Some tags indicate formatting for a word, sentence, or part of a Web page. For example, the <p> ... </p> tags surrounds the text of a new paragraph that starts on a new line. The <i> ... </i> tag appear on either side of text that you want to display in italics. Other tags convey information to the browser. For example, the <title> tag tells the browser the title of the page, but this title does not appear in the page text.

Browser Versions and Tags

Recent versions of browsers support a larger set of HTML tags than earlier browsers. For example, older browsers do not support the use of tables or frames, so page layouts based on those features will appear very strangely. To avoid these problems Web designers

501

often use client-side scripts to detect what browser and version that a user has installed. The script can either advise the user to upgrade, or can request an alternate version of a page that is compatible with the simpler browser.

Main Page Sections

Each HTML page consists of four main sections. Each section is marked off, or contained, by its own starting and ending tags:

- `<html>` begins an HTML document. `</html>` ends the document.

- `<head>` begins a section of descriptive information about the document. `</head>` ends the HEAD section. HEAD section elements do not appear in the browser window, but can be very useful in other ways.

- `<title>` begins the title of each Web page, and `</title>` ends the title. The `<title>` tag must be contained by the `<head>` and `</head>` tags. The text of a Web page title appears in the browser window's title bar, but it does not appear in the Web page itself. Search engines and browser History lists display titles, so choose a title for each page that is descriptive and relatively short.

- `<body>` begins the visible content of the page. `</body>` ends that content.

Page Structure

There is a syntax structure to entire pages and to individual paragraphs. Tags define the page type (`<html>`), the formatting of headings, paragraphs, words, and of all the page content. This content can be plain text, graphics, tables, and other elements like animations, video, and audio files.

Tags within an HTML document are "nested." Nested tags are tags within tags. The following example illustrates the tags discussed above, in their proper nesting order:

```
<html>

<head>

    <title>    </title>

</head>

<body>

</body>

</html>
```

You can see that there are several tags nested within the opening and closing HTML tags. The title tags are also nested within the head tags.

The following example illustrates the syntax of a typical HTML tag:

```
<font face="Comic Sans MS" size="+2"
color="red"> Hello world!</font>
```

This example displays the text "Hello world!" in red, Comic Sans font, two point sizes larger than the default font size.

Attributes

Attributes to HTML tags allow you to change the default values for a particular tag, such as a font. You can set font attributes, such as size and color, to values different from the default value. For example, the default paragraph text in most browsers displays in the Times font. You can change the value to display Comic Sans font by specifying:

```
<font face="Comic Sans MS">.
```

It is important to enclose attributes within quotation marks if the text contains spaces. It is good coding practice to get in the habit of enclosing all attributes in quotation marks to avoid problems.

Note: If you must use a word processor to create your test pages, be sure to save each page as plain text (ASCII).

Create a Simple Web Page

Objective 2.3

Create HTML pages … HTML document structure

… Coding simple tables, headings, forms

Use the following steps to create a simple Web page:

1. Launch Windows Notepad and open a new document. Enter the following:

```
<html>

<head>

<title>Simple Web page test</title>

</head>

<body>

</body>

</html>
```


503

2. Save the file as a text document, and name it **mypage1.htm**. Keep the document open in Notepad.

3. Open your browser. From the **File** menu, select **Open**. In the **Open** dialog box, locate **mypage1.htm** and open it.

   What happened?

   Your page is blank because you haven't yet added any visible content to it. The page title appears in the browser window title bar, but you'll have to add a few more elements to make this a real Web page.

4. Switch back to Notepad, and add the following new content to **mypage1.htm**:

```
<html>

<head>

<title>Simple Web page test</title>

</head>

<body>

<h1>Very simple Web page #1</h1>

This is plain text. It does not require a tag.
Plain text appears differently for each user,
depending on individual browser settings.

</body>

</html>
```

5. Save the changes under the same file name.

6. Switch back to your browser and click the **Refresh** button. Your page should now look like Example Screen #1.

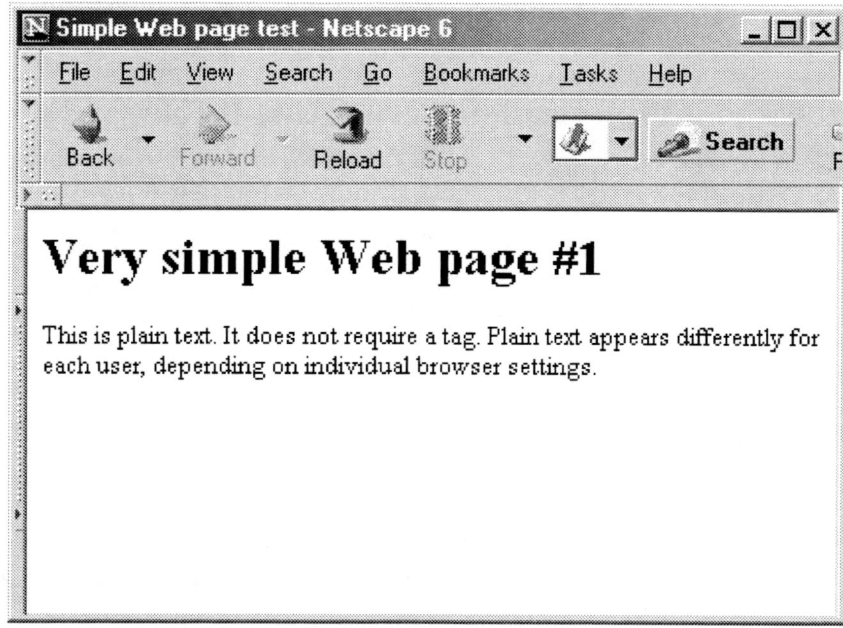

Example Screen #1

Heading Tags

HTML supports six different heading sizes, ranging from `<h1>` (largest) to `<h6>` (smallest). Headings must appear in the body of a page (between `<body>` and `</body>`), but they do not need to appear in any particular order. For example, you may put an `<h3>` heading at the very top of your page, followed by an `<h1>`.

The size and font of each heading will vary from browser to browser, depending on each individual user's browser preferences.

Are End Tags Really Necessary?

End tags tell the browser where the current style of formatting ends and where to expect the next to begin. Missing end tags are one of the most common and annoying bugs in HTML coding.

To see how your browser handles a missing end tag, remove the `</h1>` tag so that part of **mypage1.htm** looks like this:

```
<h1>Very simple Web page #1

This is plain text. It does not require a tag.
Plain text appears differently for each user,
depending on individual browser settings.
```

Save your page, refresh your browser, and see what happens.

Plain Text

No tags are required to insert plain text into a Web page. As with headings, the size and font of plain text will depend on each individual user's browser preferences.

Experiment With Heading Levels, Line Breaks, and Lists

Objective 2.3
*Create HTML pages
… HTML document
structure
… Coding simple
tables, headings,
forms*

Now that you have added plain text to your page, it's time to add headings and arrange text in new ways.

**Testing the
Heading Levels**

1. In **mypage1.htm**, replace this line:

    ```
    <h1>Very simple Web page #1</h1>
    ```

    with these lines:

    ```
    <h1>Heading level 1</h1>

    <h2>Heading level 2</h2>

    <h3>Heading level 3</h3>

    <h4>Heading level 4</h4>

    <h5>Heading level 5</h5>

    <h6>Heading level 6</h6>
    ```

2. Save **mypage1.htm** and refresh your browser to see the six heading levels. Remember that these headings only appear this way on your browser; other users will see different fonts and sizes, though H6 should still be smaller than H1.

3. Switch back to **mypage1.htm** and insert paragraph breaks in the plain text section, so it looks like this:

    ```
    This is plain text.

    It does not require a tag.

    Plain text appears differently for each user,
    depending on individual browser settings.
    ```

4. Save **mypage1.htm** and refresh your browser. Nothing happened? That's because HTML ignores tab characters, extra spaces, and extra empty lines (carriage returns). To control line breaks in text, you must insert specific HTML tags that instruct the browser what to do.

Inserting Line and Paragraph Breaks

1. Switch back to **mypage1.htm** and change the plain text section to look like this:

```
This is plain text. <p>It does not require a
tag. </p><br>Plain text appears differently for
each user, depending on individual browser set-
tings.
```

2. Save **mypage1.htm** and refresh your browser. Your page should now look like Example Screen #2.

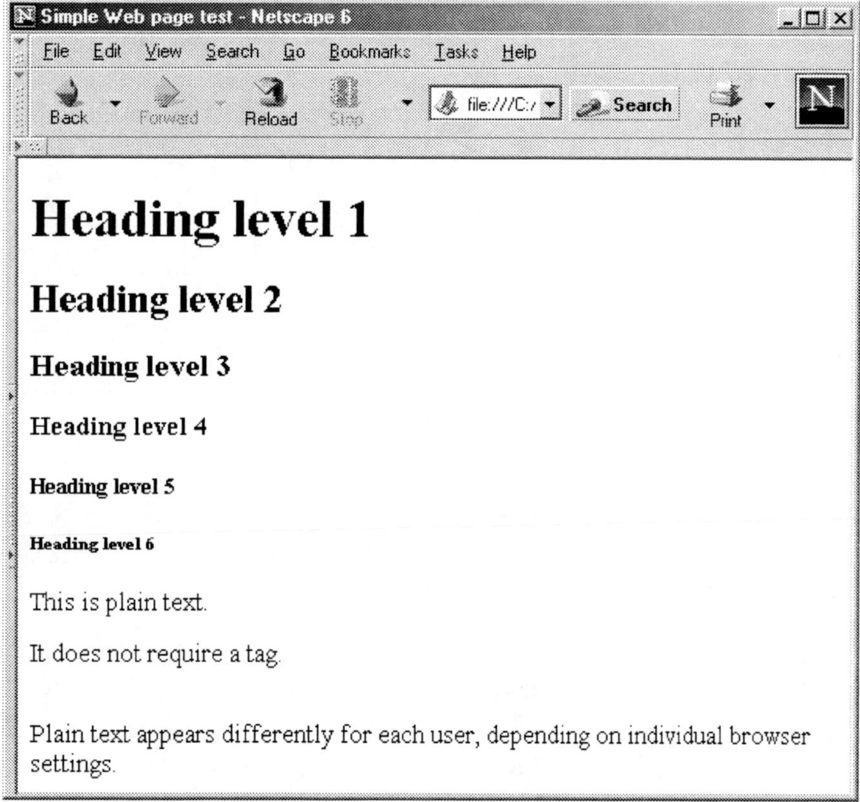

Example Screen #2

The paragraph tags (`<p>` ... `</p>`) are technically container tags, but the HTML specification lists the closing tag as optional. However, leaving the closing `</p>` tag out can cause browser bugs when dealing with more advanced techniques, such as style sheets. Therefore, get into the habit of always using the closing `</p>` tag when developing your HTML pages. The line break tag, `<br>`, on

Building
Web Pages

the other hand, is an empty tag and has no corresponding end tag. Both of these tags insert a line break into any text (even headings) with these differences:

- <p> ... </p> adds vertical space (an empty line) before and after the paragraph. (This is true of all HTML elements that form a "block" of text.)

-
 (line break) breaks a line without adding extra vertical space.

Creating Ordered and Unordered Lists

Inserting line breaks would seem to be a natural way to create lists of short items on your page, but there are two easier ways to create lists:

1. Switch back to **mypage1.htm**, and delete the following lines:

```
<h2>Heading level 2</h2>

<h3>Heading level 3</h3>

<h4>Heading level 4</h4>

<h5>Heading level 5</h5>

<h6>Heading level 6</h6>
```

2. Now add these new lines after the plain text section, so that your complete code looks like this:

```
<html>

<head>

<title>Simple Web page test</title>

</head>

<body>

<h1>Heading level 1</h1>

This is plain text. <p>It does not require a
tag. </p><br>Plain text appears differently for
each user, depending on individual browser
settings.

<h3>These are a few of my favorite things</h3>

<ul>

<li>Raindrops on roses</li>

<li>Whiskers on kittens</li>

<li>Bright copper kettles</li>
```

```
<li>Warm woolen mittens</li>

</ul>

<h3>Things to do today</h3>

<ol>

<li>Create a great new game</li>

<li>See that it becomes the next fad</li>

<li>Go public</li>

<li>Retire</li>

</ol>

</body>

</html>
```

3. Save **mypage1.htm** and refresh your browser. Your page should now look like Example Screen #3.

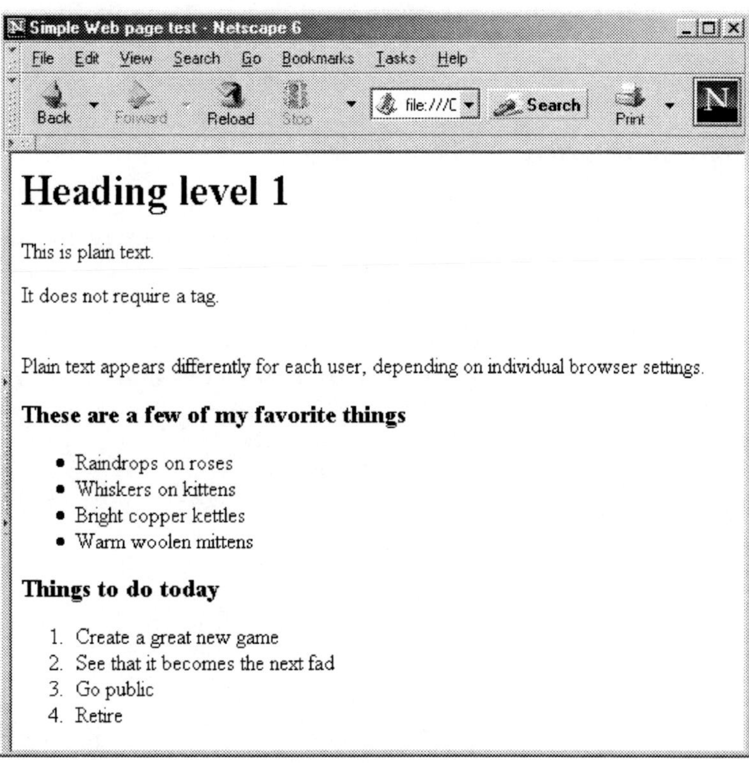

Example Screen #3

Unordered Lists

Use an unordered list to present a list of items that does not need to appear in any particular order. Browsers usually display unordered lists as bulleted lists. To create an unordered list, you'll use two types of tags:

- `<ul>` and `</ul>` are container tags that mark the start and end of the unordered list.

- `<li>` and `</li>` are container tags that mark the start and end of each list item. The list items appear between the `<ul>` and `</ul>` tags.

Ordered Lists

Use an ordered list to present a list of items that must appear in a particular sequence. By default, browsers display ordered lists as lists of numbered steps. You can create "lettered" steps as well, but the default behavior is numbered. To create an ordered list, you'll use two types of tags:

- `<ol>` and `</ol>` are container tags that mark the start and end of the ordered list.

- `<li>` and `</li>` are container tags that mark the start and end of each list item. The list items appear between the `<ol>` and `</ol>` tags.

Organizing Your HTML Code

By this time, the HTML code for your first simple Web page has grown from a few lines to a screen full of text and strange looking tags. By remembering that HTML ignores extra spaces and empty lines, you can make your HTML code test pages easier to understand by using the following techniques:

- **Indenting** tagged elements can make them easier to find, and can show their "nested" relationship to other elements.

```
<body>

    <h1>Neat code enhances your reputation</h1>

</body>
```

- **Extra line breaks** won't show up in the browser, but are extremely helpful for making sure that each element has the right tag, and that start tags have a corresponding end tag. For example, the browser will accurately display this line:

```
<ol><li>snap</li><li>crackle</li><li>pop</li>
</ol>
```

However, most people find this form easier to understand:

```
<ol>

<li>snap</li>

<li>crackle</li>

<li>pop</li>

</ol>
```

- **Comments** are notes to yourself, inserted in the code to help you remember what something is supposed to do. Comments start with `<!--` tag and end with the `-->` tag. Comments do not appear on the Web page.

```
<!--

  Text between these marks will not appear.

-->
```

<META> Tags

Objective 2.3
Create HTML pages ... Understand and use MetaTags properly

Like `<title>`, the `<meta>` tag also appears within the `<head>` section of an HTML page. However, `<meta>` tags are optional. A page designer may choose to use none of them, or many.

Unlike other tags, `<meta>` tags do not affect the appearance of a page. Instead, they contain additional noncontent information about a Web document itself. This "meta data" can be used by client or server applications, such as browsers or search engines.

Basic Metadata

The simplest use of a `<meta>` tag records some item of information that is hidden from a user, but may be accessed by an application that knows what to look for. For example, if this lesson were an HTML document, the following tags could provide its keywords, description, and copyright information to a search engine:

```
<meta NAME="keywords"  CONTENT="HTML, tags, syn-
tax, structure, Web, meta data">

<meta NAME= "description"  CONTENT="A brief
overview of basic HTML page structure and tag-
ging rules.">

<meta NAME= "copyright"  CONTENT="Copyright 2002
WestNet Learning Technologies">
```

The example above illustrates several points about the `<meta>` tag:

- A separate tag is used to define each type of meta data. You may include as many of these tags as you like, so a Web page may include a great deal of meta data if necessary.

- `<meta>` does not require an end tag.

- This basic use of the `<meta>` tag includes two attributes:

  - **NAME** identifies the type of information in the tag. There is no standard list of NAME values, so a Web author may use any word to identify a piece of metadata. However, authors must be careful to use the same NAME values that their intended applications are designed to look for. For example, most search engines look for "keywords," not "subjects."

  - **CONTENT** contains the actual data stored by the tag. So in this case, "CONTENT" represents the actual list of keywords, or the copyright statement, or the description sentence that should appear on a search results page.

Simulating HTTP Response Headers

As you learned earlier, a Web server responds to a browser request by transmitting an HTTP response header. The response header includes instructions to the browser, or additional information about HTML data that may be following behind the response header.

The HTTP-EQUIV attribute allows a `<meta>` tag to simulate a server's response header. In other words, when the browser receives an HTML page with this type of tag, the browser behaves just as it would if it received the same instruction in an HTTP response header from the server.

The following example is one of the most common uses of this tag. It waits 10 seconds, then mimics the HTTP "refresh" header to automatically redirect a user to a new page URL:

```
<meta HTTP-EQUIV= "refresh"  CONTENT="10, http:/
/www.bigsite.com/newpage.html">
```

This tag is also commonly used to embed an expiration date and time into a document, which forces a cache to retrieve a fresh version of a page. For example, if you add the following tag to your home page for June 15, all browsers that access the page on June 16 or later will retrieve a fresh version from the server, and not simply display a copy of the page from their caches:

```
<meta HTTP-EQUIV= "expires"  CONTENT= "Sat, 16
June 2002 00:00:01 GMT"
```

There are many HTTP response headers, and it takes considerable technical knowledge and programming experience to use many of them. A complete discussion of this topic is beyond the scope of this lesson, so the main point to remember is that any HTTP response header can be simulated by the HTTP-EQUIV attribute of the `<meta>` tag.

Activities

1. A ______________ is an HTML command inserted into a document that gives directions to a Web browser for formatting the document.

2. Match the HTML function with the respective tag listed below.

   Marks the beginning of a document. __________

   Marks the end of a section of descriptive information about the document. __________

   Causes text to appear in the browser window's title bar. __________

   Embeds invisible information that can be used by an application. __________

   Marks the beginning of the main content of the Web page. __________

   Marks the beginning of a numbered list. __________

   Marks the end of a bulleted list. __________

   Used to create the largest size of text. __________

   Used to indicate a list item in a numbered or bulleted list. __________

   Used to create a comment statement. __________

   Used to insert an extra space between paragraphs. __________

   a. `<p>`

   b. `<title>`

   c. `<h1>`

   d. `<li>`

   e. `<body>`

   f. `<html>`

   g. `</head>`

   h. `<ol>`

   i. `</ul>`

   j. `<!--`

   k. `</ol>`

   l. `<meta>`

Extended Activities

1. Create a simple home page.

   a. Open **mypage.htm** file in Windows Notepad.

   b. Create a Level 1 heading that says "My name is (fill in your name here). This is my homepage."

   c. Create a bulleted list with the heading "These are my hobbies:" List three of your favorite hobbies.

   d. Create a numbered list with the heading "These are my favorite TV shows:" List your top three favorites.

   e. Save the file in Notepad and open it using your browser.

2. Visit **http://www.doubleclick.com**, and read about banner ads and demographics. Research how much it costs to run one of the banner ads, and how many user responses an ad can be expected to generate.

Lesson 2—Adding Graphics

Web pages need graphics to be more informative and entertaining than plain text. There are many ways to add graphics to Web pages. This lesson will show you the basic methods of adding graphics and backgrounds to Web pages. In Lesson 8 of this unit, we discuss graphic formats in more detail.

Objectives

At the end of this lesson you will be able to:

- Add graphics to Web pages

- Add backgrounds to Web pages

Key Point

Web pages are more interesting when you use graphics.

Inserting Horizontal Rules

Objective 2.3
Create HTML pages ... HTML document structure

A horizontal rule is a simple graphic element that you can add with a single <hr> tag. This tag adds a shaded horizontal line to divide sections of a Web page. The <hr> Tag Attributes Table lists several attributes that you can add to the <hr> tag to control the look of a rule. You may use as many or as few of these attributes as you like.

<hr> **Tag Attributes**

Attribute Tag	Description	Example
Align=left, right, or center	Aligns the rule with the left or right margin, or centers the rule	`<hr align="left">`
Size=number	Specifies the height of the rule, in pixels	`<hr size="5">`
Width=number or percent	Specifies the length of the rule, in pixels or a relative width in percentage of the browser window width	`<hr width="75">` `<hr width="50%">`
Noshade	Creates the rule without a 3-D effect	`<hr noshade>`

Try the following steps to practice using the <hr> tag:

1. Launch Windows Notepad and open **mypage1.htm**. Between the two lists, add this line:

    ```
    <hr>
    ```

2. After the ordered list, add this line:

    ```
    <hr width="50%" size="5" noshade>
    ```

Save **mypage1.htm**, and refresh your browser. Your page should look like Example Screen #4.

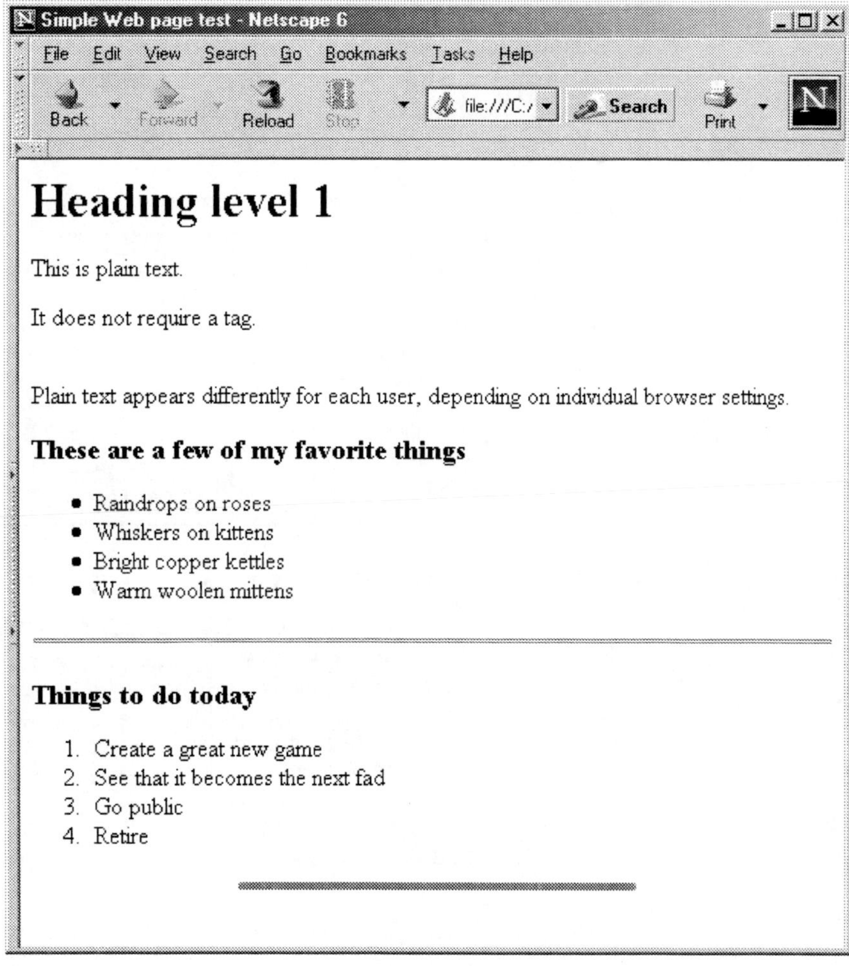

Example Screen #4

Inserting Graphic Files

Objective 2.3
*Create HTML pages
... HTML document
structure*

Two basic types of graphic images used in HTML are Graphics Interchange Format (GIF) and Joint Photographic Experts Group (JPEG) files. JPEG files are higher-resolution images, generally used for photographs. GIF files are composed of a maximum of 256 colors and have a lower resolution, but they can have transparent regions and animation. A third file format, known as Portable Network Graphics (PNG), combines many of the best features of GIF and JPEG and is gaining popularity among Web page developers.

Inserting graphics in HTML is done by using the `<img>` tag with the `src` attribute, which defines the image to be displayed. For example: `<img src="soccer.gif">`. Other attributes to the `<img>` tag allow you to modify the appearance of the image and align the adjacent text relative to the image. These attributes are presented in the `<img>` Tag Attributes Table.

`<img>` **Tag Attributes**

Attribute Tag	Description	Example
src=filename	Specifies the location and name of the image to be displayed	`<img src="soccer.gif">`
alt=text	Specifies alternate text for browsers not loading images	`<img src="soccer.gif" alt="Welcome to My Hobbies">`
width=number, height=number	Specifies the width and height of the image, in pixels	`<img src="soccer.gif" width=50, height=100>`
align=top	Aligns the text with the top of the graphic	`<img src="soccer.gif" align=top>`
align=middle	Aligns the text with the middle of the graphic	`<img src="soccer.gif" align=middle>`
align=bottom	Aligns the text with the bottom of the graphic	`<img src="soccer.gif" align=bottom>`

`<img>` **Tag Attributes (Continued)**

Attribute Tag	Description	Example
align=left	Aligns the left of the text to the left margin	`<img src="soccer.gif" align=left>`
align=right	Aligns the right of the text to the right margin	`<img src="soccer.gif" align=right>`
vspace=number	Designates the amount of white space on the top and bottom of the image, in pixels	`<img src="soccer.gif" vspace=5>`
hspace=number	Designates the amount of white space on the left and right of the image, in pixels	`<img src="soccer.gif" hspace=5>`
border=number	Specifies the width of the border around the image in pixels	`<img src="soccer.gif" border=1>`

Experiment With Inserting Graphic Files

Objective 2.3
Create HTML pages ... HTML document structure

Before you can practice adding graphics to your Web page, you'll need some graphics to add. Fortunately, the Web is a treasure trove of free Web page images. Before you move on in this lesson, use your favorite search engine to find a site that gives away GIF or JPEG images. When you've found a good site, bookmark it and download the following images:

- One small picture or piece of clip art. An image of a soccer player would be nice, but isn't required.

- One small image to use in a tiled (repeating) background. Look for a light-colored image with a subtle pattern.

When you've got your images, move them to the same directory as your test pages. Now you're ready to continue the lesson:

1. In Windows Notepad, close **mypage1.htm** and open a new document. Save it as plain text, name it **graphics.htm**, and enter the code shown below. Enter your name, and the filename of your clip art image, where indicated. Our example uses "Bob" for the name:

```
<html>

<head>

<title>Adding a graphic</title>

</head>

<body>

<h1>My name is [your name here]. <br>This is my
home page.</h1>

<hr>

These are my hobbies<br>

<img src="your graphic file name">

<ul>

<li>Playing soccer</li>

<li>Reading about soccer</li>

<li>Talking about soccer</li>

</ul>

</body>

</html>
```

2. Save **graphics.htm**.

3. In your browser, open **graphics.htm**. Your page should look something like Example Screen #5.

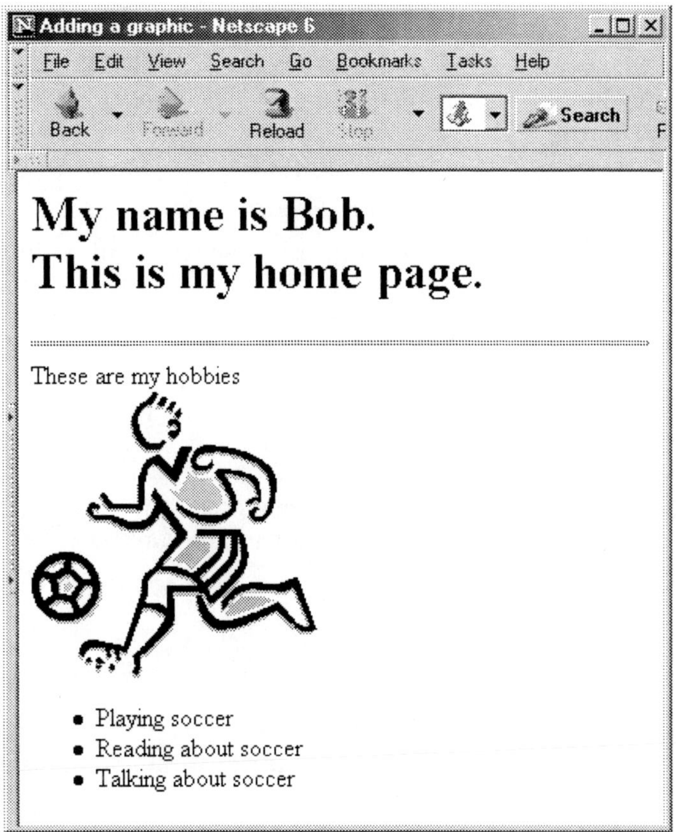

Example Screen #5

4. Experiment on your own. Change the attributes of your graphic, save the file, then refresh the browser to see the effect. Try combinations of attributes to see how they work together.

Adding a Background

Objective 2.3
*Create HTML pages
... HTML document
structure*

There are two ways to add a background to your Web page. First, you can specify a solid background color. Second, you can add a repeating background image.

Solid Color Backgrounds

You can specify page background color with the bgcolor attribute of the <body> tag. The simplest way to specify this color attribute is to use a special color name. For example:

```
<body bgcolor=green>
```

However, color names are often browser-specific (what works for Netscape Navigator might not work for Microsoft Explorer). It's more reliable to specify colors by a hexadecimal "triplet" that represents the color's RGB values, which are the relative intensities of red, green, and blue that comprise the color. In the RGB system, color intensities range from 0 (no color) to 255 (full strength). Therefore, a solid green would be represented in RGB as 0, 255, 0; in hexadecimal form as 00 FF 00. When specifying a hexadecimal value, always precede the value with a "#" character. Here's how to use the hex number in the bgcolor attribute:

```
<body bgcolor=#00FF00>
```

Try the following:

1. Switch back to **graphics.htm**, and change the <body> tag to:

    ```
    <body bgcolor=cyan>
    ```

2. Save **graphics.htm** and refresh your browser.

3. Now change the <body> tag to:

    ```
    <body bgcolor=#8470FF>
    ```

4. Save **graphics.htm** and refresh your browser. Experiment with a few different number combinations.

Repeating Graphic Backgrounds

Graphic image backgrounds are created with a <body> attribute called background. To add a background to your Web page:

1. Switch back to **graphics.htm**, and add the background attribute to the <body> tag. Use the filename of the background graphic you downloaded earlier.

    ```
    <body background="your background graphic">
    ```

2. Save **graphics.htm**.

3. Remember to copy your background graphic image file to the same directory where you have saved **graphics.htm**.

4. Refresh your browser. Your page should look something like Example Screen #6.

Example Screen #6

A Word of Caution About Backgrounds

Objective 2.3
Create HTML pages ... Use page layout principles

Backgrounds composed of dark colors can give your pages a dramatic look, when carefully combined with white, or light-colored, foreground type of an appropriate font, size, and weight. (in Lesson 4 of this unit, we will show you how to format text.) Unfortunately, the wrong combination of colors can make your text difficult or impossible to read. Legibility also suffers when text is placed over backgrounds made from "busy" repeating graphics.

When in doubt, keep your background effects subtle. This will ensure that your pages are always easy to read and understand. The Color Values Table shows some common colors and their hexadecimal values.

Color Values

Color	Hexadecimal Value
Red	#FF0000
Green	#00FF00
Blue	#0000FF
White	#FFFFFF
Black	#000000
Yellow	#FFFF00
Magenta	#FF00FF
Cyan	#00FFFF
Sky Blue	#3299CC
Silver	#E6E8FA
Pink	#BC8F8F
Orange	#FF7F00
Tan	#DB9370
Violet	#AF2FAF
Navy Blue	#23238E
Dark Green	#2F4F2F

Activities

1. Which HTML tag is necessary to create a horizontal rule, aligned with the right margin?

   ____

2. A _______________ is the type of graphic image format used in HTML documents that provides high resolution.

3. Describe how to control the thickness of a horizontal rule:

   ____

   ____

   ____

   ____

4. Which HTML tag is used to insert graphics into a document?

   ____

5. Use the appropriate HTML tag to insert a graphic called "corplogo.gif" into a document and create a 10-pixel border of white space both horizontally and vertically.

   ____

6. Use the appropriate HTML tag to insert a graphic called "mycat.jpg" into a document and line up the base of the image with the text.

   ____

7. Use the appropriate HTML tag to place a border around the image in Activity 5.

   ____

8. Use the appropriate HTML tag to make a blue background for a page.

   ____

9. Use the appropriate HTML tag to insert the file "niceback-grnd.gif" as a background for your Web page.

   ____

Extended Activities

1. Open **mypage.htm** file in Notepad.

   a. Experiment with the horizontal rule tag attributes, changing the way the rule looks.

   b. Add a graphic (or two) to your page. Try to find Web sites on the Internet that have free graphics.

   c. Add different backgrounds to your page, using either a color or background image.

Lesson 3—Adding Hyperlinks

Links to other Web pages are called "hyperlinks." Hyperlinks are the essential ingredient of hypertext systems like the World Wide Web. Typically, we click a hyperlink to jump to a new Web document referenced by the hyperlink. The linked document can be a file on the same server as the Web page containing the link, or it can be a file on a Web server anywhere in the world.

Objectives

At the end of this lesson you will be able to:

- Create a hyperlink

- Explain how relative hyperlinks work

 **Key Point**

Hyperlinks are electronic links to Web documents.

Creating a Text Hyperlink

Objective 2.3
Create HTML pages ... HTML document structure

To create a text hyperlink, you use a set of anchor tags (`<a>`, `</a>`) to contain a section of text that will form the clickable link. The `href` attribute, plus a URL, specifies the page to display when the hyperlink is clicked. In the following example, the word "WestNet" is the hyperlink; clicking on it displays the WestNet home page:

```
<a href="http://www.westnetinc.com">WestNet</a>
created my networking textbook.
```

To create a text hyperlink:

1. In Windows Notepad, open **graphics.htm**. Save it as a new file called **links.htm**.

2. In **links.htm**, change the page title to "Adding hyperlinks."

```
<title>Adding hyperlinks</title>
```

3. Just before the line "These are my hobbies..." insert this new line:

```
I am attending a
<a href="http://www.westnetinc.com">WestNet</a>
course, learning to create Web pages.<br><br>
```

4. Save **links.htm**. In your browser, open **links.htm** to see the new hyperlink.

5. Click the hyperlink to test it. Use the browser's Back button to return to your test page.

Creating a Relative Hyperlink

Objective 2.3
Create HTML pages ... HTML document structure

A relative hyperlink is a link to another page that is stored in the same Web directory or Web site. You use the same <a> tag to form a relative hyperlink, but you do not need to include the "http://" prefix, nor do you need to include the domain name of the Web site. To create a relative hyperlink:

1. Switch back to **links.htm**. After the line you just added, insert one more:

```
So far, I have created <a href="mypage1.htm">one
other page.</a><br><br>
```

2. Save **links.htm**. In your browser, open **links.htm** to see the new hyperlink.

3. Click the hyperlink to test it. Use the browser's **Back** button to return to **links.htm**.

Creating a Link From a Graphic

Objective 2.3
Create HTML pages ... HTML document structure

Graphic images can be very effective Web page hyperlinks. To create a linked graphic image, combine the <a> tag with the <img> tag:

1. Switch back to **links.htm**. Find the line that inserts the graphic and add a hypertext anchor to contain the <img> tag:

```
These are my hobbies
<a href="http://www.dailysoccer.com">
<img src="yourgraphicfilename.jpg" hspace=5
align=top></a>
```

2. Save **links.htm**. In your browser, open **links.htm**. Click the soccer graphic, and you should display the home page of the Daily Soccer Web site.

3. Use the browser's **Back** button to return to **links.htm**.

Creating Links to Other Parts of the Current Page

Objective 2.3
Create HTML pages ... HTML document structure

Links to other parts of the current Web page can help the viewer quickly find other parts of the document. To create a link to the target, you first mark and name the part of the document to which you want the link to go. Next, you create a hyperlink to the named part:

1. Switch back to **links.htm**.

2. Add two lines to your test page, so the code looks like this:

```
<html>

<head>

<title>Adding hyperlinks</title>

</head>

<body>

<h1>My name is Bob. This is my home page.</h1>

<a href="#sites">Click here</a> to see my list
of favorite links.

<hr>

These are my hobbies

<img src="yourgraphicfilename.jpg" hspace=5
align=top>

<ul>

<li>Playing soccer</li>

<li>Reading about soccer</li>

<li>Talking about soccer</li>

</ul>

<a name="sites">My favorite web site</a> is

<a href="http://www.dailysoccer.com">
Dailysoccer.com.</a>

Check it out!

</body>

</html>
```

3. Save **links.htm**. In your browser, open **links.htm**.

4. Reduce the size of your browser window, so that nothing appears below the "**Click here...**" line.

5. Click the "**Click here**" link. The display should scroll up to show the "**My favorite Web site...**" line.

Activities

1. A _____________ can be a connection to another web page or a jump to a location within the current page.

2. Show how to create three separate text hyperlinks to the following Web sites: 3Com, Microsoft, and Cisco.

   ____

   ____

   ____

   ____

3. Describe the difference between a hyperlink and a relative hyperlink.

   ____

   ____

4. Using a file named "newslink.gif," create a graphic hyperlink to the CNN Website (**http://www.cnn.com**).

5. Creating links to other parts of the current page requires two distinct HTML tags. One is the "target" reference and the other is the reference that jumps to the target. Write an HTML fragment (not a complete page) that illustrates a jump to the "top of page."

Extended Activities

1. Create a Web page for your resumé.

2. Add links at the top of your resumé that reference its main sections, such as work experience, education, or goals.

3. In your resumé page, add links to the Web sites of your employers or educational institutions.

Lesson 4—Formatting Text

In this lesson, you will learn how to format the text on your Web pages. You can make your pages more attractive and interesting by controlling the font, size, and color of text.

Objectives

At the end of this lesson you will be able to:

- Format Web page text

- Explain why text appearance may vary across browsers

 **Key Point**

Text formatting can make Web pages more readable.

Setting Default Text Attributes

Objective 2.3
Create HTML pages … HTML document structure … Coding simple tables, headings, forms

HTML offers two levels of text formatting:

- **Default attributes** set the basic text formatting style for an entire Web page. You can set the default font and color of all text on your page, as well as the base font size of plain text.

- **Individual attributes** set the formatting of text that you specifically mark. For example, you can choose to display one word in red and leave the rest of the text black.

Text Color

There are two ways to set the default text color for each Web page, and each way produces the same results. No matter which method you use, specify a color using the same rules as for background colors:

- You can use the `text` attribute of the `<body>` tag. For example:

```
<body text="red">
```

or

```
<body text=#FF0000>
```

- You can also use the `color` attribute of the `<basefont>` tag, which must appear between the `<body>` and `</body>` tags. For example:

```
<basefont color="blue">
```

or

```
<basefont color=#0000FF>
```

Link Text Color

You can control the color of hyperlink text by using three attributes of the `<body>` tag: `link` (color of unclicked links), `alink` (color of link during a click), and `vlink` (color of visited links). Specify color using the same rules as for background colors. For example:

```
<body link="green" alink="blue" vlink="red">
```

or

```
<body link=#00FF00 alink=#0000FF vlink=#FF0000>
```

When you choose a color for your background, you should always check out how your text color and the link colors contrast with the background. Rather than relying on browser defaults, it is better to specify the color for text as well as the three link colors to maintain control over how the page will look in various browsers.

Default Text Font

To set the overall text font for each page, use the `face` attribute of the `<basefont>` tag, which must appear between the `<body>` and `</body>` tags. You may specify more than one font, in order of your preference. The user's browser will then display text in the first font on your list that is installed on the user's computer. For example:

```
<basefont face="verdana, helvetica, arial">
```

You are free to specify any fonts you wish. However, remember that the user's browser won't display a font unless the user has installed the same font.

Default Text Size

The default plain text size, or basefont size, is the starting font size for all relative font size changes in a Web page. Basefont size can range from 1 to 7 (default is 3); each user's browser preferences will determine exactly how large to display text based on the basefont size.

To set the basefont size, use the `size` attribute of the `<basefont>` tag, which must appear between the `<body>` and `</body>` tags. For example:

```
<basefont size=4>
```

Setting Multiple Default Attributes

You can combine as many attributes in a `<basefont>` as you need. For example, to set default text face, color, and size all at once:

```
<basefont face="verdana, helvetica, arial"
color=#0000FF size=2>
```

Note: Be careful about using the `<basefont>` tag, as it has inconsistent browser support. If you want to control the basefont by using this tag, be sure to test your pages in all the browsers your intended audience might be using.

Setting Individual Text Attributes

Objective 2.3
Create HTML pages … HTML document structure … Coding simple tables, headings, forms

You can vary the font, color, or size of any individual piece of text by using the `<font>` container tag with the `face`, `size`, and `color` attributes. The use of these attributes is similar to those described with the `<basefont>` tag. Remember to end each selection with the `</font>` tag. See the `<font>` Tag Attributes Table.

`<font>` Tag Attributes

Attribute	Description	Example

size=relative or specific number	Specifies the font size as a relative change to the basefont, OR as specific value in the range of browser text sizes (1-7)	`<font size=+1>a little bigger</font>`
		 or
		 `<font size=5>pretty big</font>`

color=color or hexadecimal number	Specifies text color, using special color words OR hexadecimal triplet representing RGB value of the color	`<font color="red">red text</font>`
		 or
		 `<font color=#0000FF>blue text</font>`

face=font name	Specifies one or more fonts, in order of the designer's preference	`<font face="Verdana, Times, MS Serif">I'd rather use Verdana</font>`

As with other attributes, you can combine these font attributes. For example:

```
The page basefont is blue Arial, but
<font face="Times" color=#FF0000>this phrase is
set in red Times Roman.</font>
```

To add simple additional formatting, use one or more of the simple text style tags listed in the Text Styles Table.

Text Styles

Style	Description	Example
bold	Makes text bold	`<b>this is bold</b>`
italics	Makes text italic	`<i>this is italic</i>`
underline	Underlines text	`<u>this is under-lined</u>`
strikethrough	Places a line through the text	`<s>strike through this</s>`
bigger	Displays the enclosed text in a larger font	`<big>this is bigger</big>`
smaller	Displays the enclosed text in a smaller font	`<small>this is smaller</small>`
monospaced	Displays the enclosed text in "teletype" (monospaced) font	`<tt>this is mono-spaced</tt>`
strong	Emphasizes the text; usually makes text bold (depends on browser settings)	`<strong>emphasized</strong>`

As with other attributes, you can combine these style tags. For example, to make a selection both bold and italic:

```
I want to <b><i>really, really emphasize</i></b>
this point.
```

Activities

1. Write an HTML <body> statement that makes the text purple.

   ____

2. What's wrong with this HTML tag:

   ```
   <basefont    face="helvetica    garamond    arial"
   color=blue size=4>
   ```

   ____

   ____

3. Describe what this HTML line does:

   ```
   This is <strong><i>very good</i></strong>coffee!
   ```

   ____

   ____

4. What is the difference between the following two HTML lines? (Assume the current font size is the default size before the browser acts upon each tag.)

   ```
   <font size=+2>this is some text</font>
   ```

   ```
   <font size=2>this is some text</font>
   ```

Extended Activities

1. Open **myresume.htm** file in Notepad. Use the different attributes of the <font> tag to make your resumé more distinctive.

Lesson 5—Incorporating Tables

A table is a part of a document where information is arranged in rows and columns. For Web pages, tables provide an orderly arrangement of data. This lesson explains how to create tables within Web pages.

Objectives

At the end of this lesson you will be able to:

- Create a Web page table

- Use attributes to modify the appearance of a table

 **Key Point**

Tables help to organize Web pages.

The Parts of a Table

Objective 2.3
*Create HTML pages
… HTML document
structure
… Coding simple
tables, headings,
forms*

HTML uses different terms and formatting tags to create and format each part of a table:

- The **table** itself is created by inserting the `<table>` and `</table>` tags into the HTML document.

- Each **row** of the table is created by inserting the `<tr>` and `</tr>` tags between the `<table>` and `</table>` tags.

- Each **cell** of a table row is created by inserting the `<td>` ("table data") and `</td>` tags between the `<tr>` and `</tr>` tags of the row where each cell should appear.

Create a Table

This exercise begins by creating the simplest table HTML displays:

1. In Windows Notepad, open a new document, save it as **tables1.htm**, and enter this HTML code:

```
<html>

<head>

<title>Tables #1</title>

</head>

<body>
```

```
<h1>Tables test #1</h1>

<p>This is an HTML table:</p>

<table border=1>

  <tr>

    <td>This is a one-row, one-cell table.</td>

    </tr>

</table>

</body>

</html>
```

2. Save **tables1.htm**, then open **tables1.htm** in your browser. Your page should look like Example Table Screen #1.

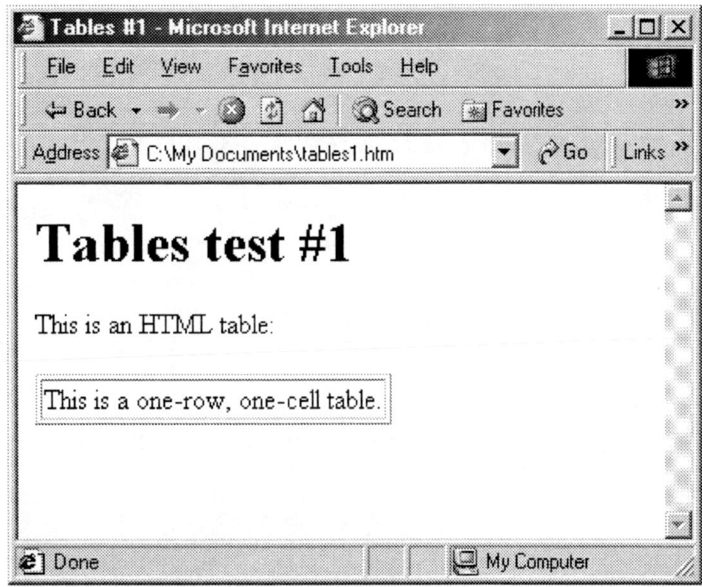

Example Table Screen #1

The `<table>` Tag Attributes Table lists several attributes to the `<table>` tag that you can use to control overall table formatting.

`<table>` **Tag Attributes**

Attribute	Description	Example
Border=number	Specifies the width of the border around the table	`<table border=1>`

Bgcolor=color or hexadecimal number	Specifies the color of the table background	`<table bgcolor="yellow">`
		or
		`<table bgcolor=#FFFF00>`

Cellspacing=number	Specifies thickness of lines between cells in the table	`<table cellspacing=5>`
Cellpadding=number	Specifies amount of space between text and cell borders	`<table cellpadding=5>`

Width=number or percentage	Specifies the width of the table in pixels or a percentage of the browser window	`<table width="150">`
		or
		`<table width=80%>`

Align=left, right, or center	Aligns the table on the page	`<table align=left>`

Add Formatting to Your Table

Use the following steps to add formatting to your table:

1. Switch back to **tables1.htm**, and make this change to the `<table>` tag:

   `<table border=2 width=75% cellspacing=10>`

2. Save **tables1.htm**, refresh your browser, and see your changes.

Add Cells to the Table Row

Use the following steps to add cells to the table row:

1. Switch back to **tables1.htm**, and add these changes to the table:

```
<table border=2 width=75% cellspacing=10>

   <tr>

       <td>Row 1, cell 1.</td>

       <td>Row 1, cell 2.</td>

       <td>Row 1, cell 3.</td>

   </tr>

</table>
```

2. Save **tables1.htm** and refresh your browser. Your page should look like Example Table Screen #2.

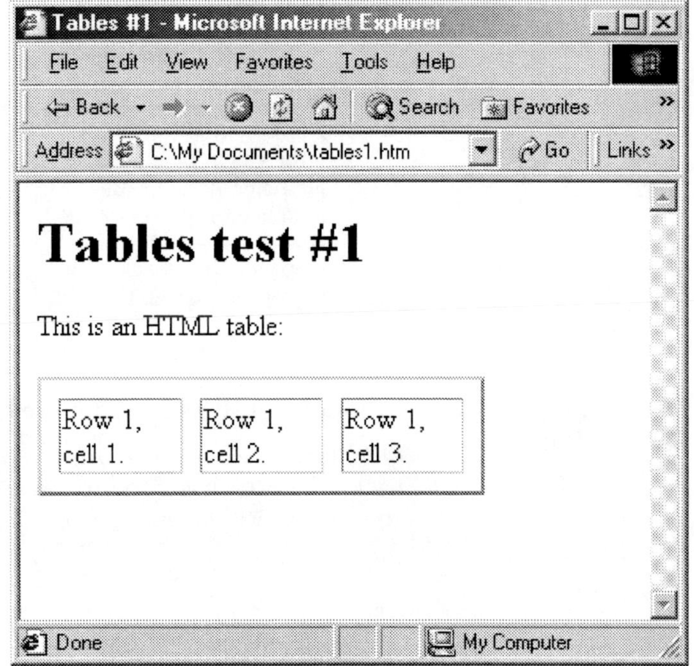

Example Table Screen #2

The Cell Formatting Attributes Table lists several attributes to the `<td>` tag that you can use to control the formatting of each table cell.

Cell Formatting Attributes

Attribute	Description	Example
Align=left, right, center	Aligns images or text in a cell	`<td align="right">`
Valign=top, middle, bottom, baseline	Aligns the contents of the cell vertically	`<td valign="top">`
Nowrap	Instructs the browser not to let the text wrap in the cells	`<td nowrap>`
Colspan	Stretches the cell across multiple columns	`<td colspan="2">`
Rowspan	Stretches the cell across multiple rows	`<td rowspan="3">`
Width	Specifies the width of the cell in pixels or a percentage of the table width	`<td width="75">` or `<td width="50%">`
Bgcolor	Specifies the back-ground color of specific cells	`<td bgcolor="blue">` or `<td bgcolor="#0000FF">`

More Table and Cell Formatting

Use the following steps to add more formatting to your table:

1. Open a new Notepad document, and save it as **tables2.htm**. Enter the following code to see the effect of different format-ting attributes:

```
<html>

<head>

<title>Table formatting</title>

</head>

<body>

<table align=left bgcolor=yellow border=5
```

```
cellpadding=5 cellspacing=5 width=75%>

    <tr>

        <td align=center colspan=3><b>My
Favorite Hobbies:

        </b></td>

    </tr>

    <tr>

        <td align=center>Bowling</td>

        <td align=center>The Internet</td>

        <td align=center>Sewing</td>

    </tr>

</table>

</body>

</html>
```

2. Save **tables2.htm** and open it in your browser. Your page should look like Example Table Screen #3.

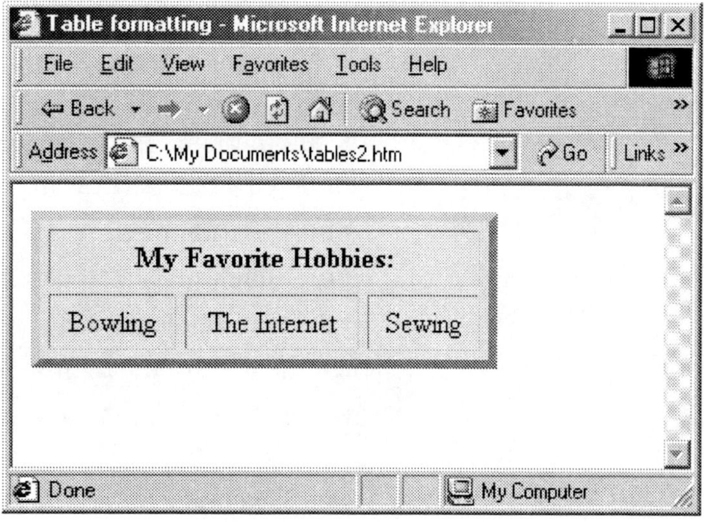

Example Table Screen #3

Activities

1. A ______________ is an HTML mechanism that arranges information in rows and columns.

2. Match the HTML function with the respective tag listed below.

   Marks the beginning of an HTML table. ___________

   Marks the end of a table row. ___________

   Marks the end of a table cell. ___________

   Marks the beginning of a table cell. ___________

   Marks the beginning of a table row. ___________

   a. `</table>`

   b. `</td>`

   c. `<table>`

   d. `<tr>`

   e. `</tr>`

   f. `<td>`

3. Create an HTML document, using default settings, containing a one-row, two-celled table. For the text inside the cells use: `This is R1 C1` and `this is R1 C2`.

4. Add the following items to the HTML document created in Activity # 3:

   a. Add another row.

   b. Set the cell spacing to 15.

   c. Set the cell padding to 7.

   d. Set the table width to 50 percent.

   e. Set the table border to 3.

   f. Align the table to the right side of the page.

5. Remove the border from the document created in Activity # 3.

Extended Activities

1. Create a new test page with new tables. Experiment with changing different table and cell attributes.

2. Many graphically-intensive Web sites use invisible tables to precisely control the placement of text and images on each page. Find one of these complex pages (preferably one with a white or light-colored background) and follow these steps to reveal the table structure:

   a. From your browser's View menu, select **Source...**

   b. The page's HTML code appears in a Notepad window.

   c. From the Notepad File menu, select **Save as...** and save the code as a file in your practice directory.

   d. From the Notepad File menu, select **Open**. Find and open the HTML file you just saved.

   e. In the HTML file, find the <table> tags and check the border attributes. Wherever the border is set to 0, change it to a 1. Save the changed file.

   f. In your browser, find and open the HTML file you just changed and saved. The invisible table borders should now appear.

Lesson 6—Working With Frames

A feature supported by most Web browsers enables a Web author to divide the browser display area into two or more sections (frames). Each frame can display a different Web page. Frames provide great flexibility in designing Web pages, but many designers avoid them because they are supported unevenly by current browsers and often confuse the function of the Back button.

Objectives

At the end of this lesson you will be able to:

- Describe the purpose of a frame

- Create a frame in a Web document

Key Point

Frames provide separate subsections of a Web page.

Creating Frames

Objective 2.3
*Create HTML pages
… HTML document
structure
… Coding simple
tables, headings,
forms*

Frames are subsections of a Web page that can each display an HTML document. Each frame contains its own set of headers, footers, and body of text.

To create a framed document, we start by creating an HTML document that specifies the layout. This frame document uses the `<frameset>` container tag to define the layout. This container tag replaces the `<body>` tag in other HTML documents. Unlike the `<body>` tag, however, the `<frameset>` tag can include other `<frameset>` tags to create a nested set of frames. To create a framed document:

1. In Windows Notepad, open a new document and save it as **frames.htm**. Enter the following code:

```
<html>

<head>

<title>Frames test</title>

</head>

<frameset>
```

```
</frameset>
```

```
</html>
```

The <frameset> tag has two attributes that determine how the browser window is divided:

- **rows** divide the browser window vertically, by absolute numbers of pixels or by percentages of the window depth. The depth value of each frame is separated from the next by a comma. For example, to create two frames, each half of the depth of the window, enter:

```
<frameset rows=50%, 50%>
```

  You can use an asterisk (*) to mean "fill the remaining space." For example, to create three frames, with the first one 50 pixels deep, the second one 100 pixels deep, and the third one taking what-ever space is left:

```
<frameset rows=50, 100, *>
```

- **cols** divide the browser window horizontally, by absolute numbers of pixels, or by percentages of the window width. The width value of each frame is separated from the next by a comma. For example, to create three frames, each 200 pixels wide, enter:

```
<frameset rows=200, 200, 200>
```

2. In **frames.htm**, make the following change to the <frameset> tag:

```
<frameset cols=100,*>
```

```
</frameset>
```

   Now your page has two vertical frames: the first is 100 pixels wide; the second takes up the remaining width.

3. Between the <frameset> tags, add the lines that will create visible content for each frame:

```
<frameset cols=100,*>

<frame src="sidelinks.htm" scrolling="no">

<frame src="mypage1.htm" name="main"
scrolling="yes">

</frameset>
```

The <frame> tag specifies the content of each document frame. The <frame> Tag Attributes Table lists the ways you can control the display of an HTML file within a frame.

<frame> **Tag Attributes**

Attribute	Description	Example
Src=filename	Specifies the URL of the document to load into the frame.	`<frame src= "mypage.htm">`
Name=frame name	Assigns a name to the frame. Works with the `<base target>` tag.	`<frame name="side">`
Marginwidth=number	Specifies a left or right margin size. If omitted, browser uses default value.	`<frame margin-width=5>`
Marginheight=number	Specifies a top or bottom margin size. If omitted, browser uses default value.	`<frame margin-height=5>`
Scrolling=yes or no	Specifies whether the frame will have a scrollbar.	`<frame scroll-ing="yes">`
Noresize=noresize	Keeps users from resizing the frames.	`<frame noresize>`
Frameborder=0, 1	Specifies whether the frame will have a border: 1 = border 0 = no border	`<frame framebor-der=0>`

Now each frame has content assigned to it. The rightmost frame displays **mypage1.htm**, which you created in earlier lessons. The leftmost frame will display a page called **sidelinks.htm**, which you must now create.

4. Save **frames.htm**, and open a new Notepad document. Save it as **sidelinks.htm,** and enter this code:

```
<html>

<head>

    <title>Side links</title>

</head>

<body>
```

```
<base target="main">

<p><a href="mypage1.htm">Home</a></p>

<p><a href="graphics.htm">My graphics page
</a></p>

</body>

</html>
```

Note: If you have saved your test pages under different names, then use those names for the two hypertext links.

5. Save **sidelinks.htm**. In your browser, open **frames.htm**. Your page should look like Example Frame Screen #1.

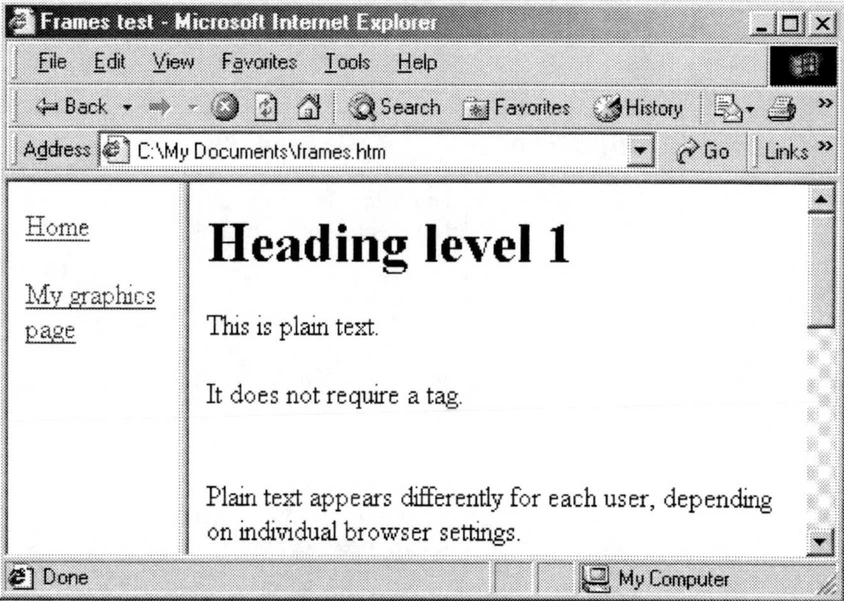

Example Frame Screen #1

Frame Target Names

If one frame contains hyperlinks to display new HTML documents, you can specify the frame in which those documents should appear. For example, **sidelinks.htm** is a small table of contents document that appears in the leftmost frame. **Sidelinks.htm** contains two links to Web pages, but when you click on one of these links, you don't want the new document to appear in the first frame and replace **sidelinks.htm**. Instead, you want it to appear in the larger frame at the right.

To do this, you first specify one frame as a base target for all hyperlinks in the first frame. Look at **sidelinks.htm**. The line `<base target="main">` tells the browser that all documents linked from **sidelinks.htm** should be displayed in the frame named "main."

Now look back at **frames.htm**. The `<frame>` element for the rightmost frame includes the attribute `name="main."` This identifies this frame as "main" to the browser.

Instead of specifying an overall target frame with the `<base>` tag, you can also specify a target frame with each hyperlink by using the `target` attribute. For example:

```
<a href="mypage1.htm" target="main">
```

The Target Name Table contains a list of special, reserved frame target names that you can also use in hyperlinks.

Target Name

Target Name	Description	Example
_self	Loads the new page in the same window as the link	`<a href="mypage.htm" target="_self">`
_top	Loads the new page in a new unframed page within the same window, replacing the frameset contents	`<a href="mypage.htm" target="_top">`
_blank	Loads the new page in a new unnamed window separate from the window containing the frameset contents	`<a href="mypage.htm" target="_blank">`
_parent	Loads the page in the parent frame of the document containing the links	`<a href="mypage.htm" target="_parent">`

Activities

1. List some advantages and disadvantages of using frames.

    ____

    ____

    ____

2. Describe your opinion of Web sites that use frames and if you like navigating Web sites that use frames.

    ____

    ____

    ____

3. What would a `<frameset>` tag look like if a Web page was divided into two equal-sized vertical sections?

    ____

    ____

4. How would you prevent a user from resizing frames?

    ____

    ____

5. What HTML tag does the `<frameset>` tag replace?

    ____

6. What HTML tag is used to specify the content of a frame?

    ____

7. What does the following HTML tag do?

    ```
    <frameset rows=75, 300, *>
    ```

    ____

8. What does the reserved frame target name "_self" allow a Web page designer to do?

    ____

    ____

Extended Activities

1. Create a new framed document called **resframe.htm**, using the following specifications:

   a. Title the document "**Resume Frames**."

   b. Divide the document into two columns, one 20 percent and one 80 percent.

   c. Name the first column frame "**reslinks**," and have it contain the file **reslinks.htm**.

   d. Name the second column "**main**," and have it contain the file **resume.htm** (or the name of your resumé page).

2. Open your resumé page and mark the major headings as named references, so they can serve as the targets of hyperlinks.

3. Create a new HTML document called **reslinks.htm**. In it, create links to the main sections of your resumé page. Add a tag to **reslinks.htm** so that all hyperlinks load into the main frame.

4. Save all HTML files. Open **resframe.htm** and test it. Fix problems and make improvements until you are satisfied with the way your resumé works in a framed window.

Lesson 7—Using Forms

HTML forms allow a user to enter and send information to a Web site. As a designer, you can choose from a wide variety of fields and controls to build your forms.

Objectives

At the end of this lesson you will be able to:

- Create a form

- Describe the use of form attributes

 **Key Point**

Forms provide for user input on a Web page.

Overall Form Attributes

Objective 2.3
*Create HTML pages
... HTML document
structure
... Coding simple
tables, headings,
forms*

A form is created by the `<form>` container tag. The `<form>` tag uses two attributes to specify how to process the data captured by the form. These attributes are listed in the `<form>` Tag Attributes Table.

`<form>` **Tag Attributes**

Attribute Keyword	Description	Example
Action= cgi filename (requires a CGI program on the server)	Specifies the URL of the CGI script on the server that will process the form	`<form action="http://www.west-netinc.com/cgibin/myform.cgi">`
Method=get or post	Indicates which HTTP method to use (GET or POST) to send the information to the server	`<form method="post">`

Form Fields and Controls

Each field or control on the form is specified by an <input> tag, which must appear between the <form> and </form> tags. The <input> Tag Attributes Table presents the many possible attributes of the <input> tag.

<input> Tag Attributes

Attribute	Description
Type=options	Specifies the type of input field or control the form generates. The options are **text, file, hidden, button, password, checkbox, radio, image, reset, and submit.**
Name=field name	Defines the name of the field; required for all types except reset and submit.
Value=5	Defines the default value returned by the field or button.
Size=number of characters	Defines the size of the field in characters for text or password fields.
Maxlength=number	Defines the maximum number of characters allowed in text or password fields.
Checked	A self-contained attribute that automatically checks a radio button or checkbox in the form; can be deselected.

Hidden Form Fields

In the <input> Tag Attributes Table, notice that one of the options for the Type attribute is "hidden." This attribute creates an invisible form field that the user cannot access. This type of field is useless to the user, but it can be a convenient container for data needed by a server-side or client-side script. Web developers often use hidden fields to pass additional information from a form to a Web site.

For example, the following form code creates an invisible field, then stores a value in that field (in this case, the version number of the form). When the form's data is submitted to the Web site, this hidden information will come along with the user-submitted data in the other fields.

```
<input type="hidden" name="version" value="3">
```

The values of hidden fields can also be set or read by client-side scripts, providing even more flexibility.

Drop-Down List Boxes

Each drop-down list box is specified by the `<select>` and `</select>` tags, which must appear between the `<form>` and `</form>` tags. The `<select>` Tag Attributes Table lists the attributes of a drop-down list.

`<select>` **Tag Attributes**

Attribute	Description
Name	Specifies the name of the field; required.
Size	Specifies how many choices to show at a time. If omitted or set to 1, browser displays a drop-down list box. If set to 2 or higher, browser displays a scrollable window.
Multiple	Allows users to select more than one option from the list (browser displays a scrollable window).

Each individual item to appear in the list is created by an `<option>` tag. The values placed between the `<option>` tags are sent to the server unless overriden by using in the optional `value` attribute. For example:

```
<select name="Choose cereal sound">

   <option value="S">Snap</option>

   <option value="C">Crackle</option>

   <option value="P">Pop</option>

</select>
```

Freeform Text Boxes

To create a scrolling text box, use the `<textarea>` and `</textarea>` tags as shown in the `<textarea>` Tag Attributes Table.

`<textarea>` **Tag Attributes**

Attribute	Description
name=text name	The name of the returned text.
cols=number	The width of the box, in monospaced characters.
rows=number	The depth of the box, in rows. (User can scroll down to display more text).

Manipulating the Form's Data

Objective 2.3
Create HTML pages
... HTML document
structure
... Coding simple
tables, headings,
forms

The real work of a form happens when the user clicks a button to order a product, answer a survey, or select a Web site option. At that moment, the form transmits its data to the Web server, to be processed by a script or Common Gateway Interface (CGI) program running on the server. Each form needs a corresponding, custom-written CGI program to process the form's data in whatever way is required for that data and that Web site. For example, CGI programs can append form data to a database, send it to an e-mail box, or pass it to a transaction processing system.

Learning to create server-side programs is beyond the scope of this course; *Mastering the Web* will teach you those skills. There are, however, many free services on the Web that will process forms for you. (See **http://cgi.resourceindex.com/Remotely_Hosted/Form_Processing/**.) For now, you can test your form-building skills on a test CGI program located on the WestNet Web server. This program will accept your form input and return a page that simply echoes that data back to you.

Creating a Test Form

In Windows Notepad, open a new file and save it as **formtest.htm**. Enter the following code:

```html
<html>

<head>

<title>Example Order Form</title>

</head>

<body>

<h1>Herman's Hairpieces</h1>

  <form Method="post"
action="http://www.westnetinc.com/it/
postquery.asp">

  <p><b>Your name: </b><input type="text"
size=32 name="user-name"></p>

  <p><b>What is your head size?</b><br>

  <input type="radio" value="Small"
name="size">Small

  <input type="radio" value="Medium"
name="size">Medium

  <input type="radio" value="Large"
name="size">Large
```

```
<input type="radio" value="Extra Large"
name="size">Extra Large

</p>

<p><b>Choose your hair color(s):</b><br>

<input type="checkbox" value="red"
name="color">red<br>

<input type="checkbox" value="brown"
name="color">brown<br>

<input type="checkbox" value="black"
name="color">black<br>

<input type="checkbox" value="blond"
name="color">blond</p>

<p><b>What style hair would you like?</b><br>

<select name="hairstyle" size=1>

  <option>Patrick Stewart</option>

  <option>Bart Simpson</option>

  <option>Jimi Hendrix</option>

  <option>Gumby</option>

  <option>Don King</option>

  <option>Albert Einstein</option>

  <option>Dilbert</option>

</select>

</p>

<p><b>Your comments?</b><br>

<textarea name="soundoff" rows="3"
cols="30"></textarea>

</p>

<input type=submit value="Send this">

<input type=reset value="Erase it">

</form>

</body>

</html>
```

Save **formtest.htm**. In your browser, open **formtest.htm**, and input some data to test it. Depending on your browser, your form may look slightly different from the Example Form Screen Capture.

Example Form

Click the **Send this** button to send the form data to the post-query test gateway program at the NCSA site. The post-query program should return a page that looks something like Example Form Result Screen Capture.

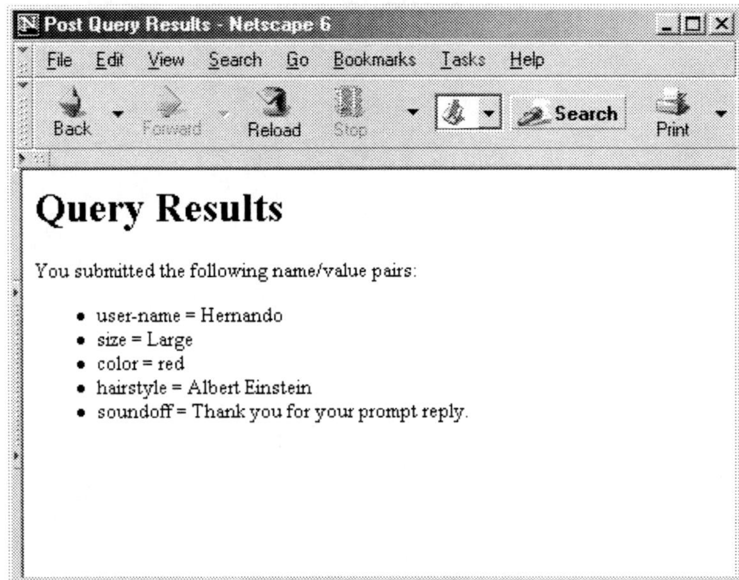

Example Form Results

Activities

1. A _______________ is used in an HTML document to provide a way for a user to input information to a web server's CGI program.

2. What does an HTML <form> container tag allow a Web page designer to do?

   ____

   ____

3. List some applications that might use the functionality provided by the <form> tag.

   ____

   ____

4. Contrast the <form> tag's two attributes, METHOD and ACTION, and describe what each does in a <form> statement.

   ____

   ____

   ____

   ____

5. Consider the <input> tag and the types "radio" and "checkbox." Which type would you use if you wanted to limit a user's choice to only one item?

   ____

6. Which HTML container tag is used to generate a drop-down box?

   ____

7. Generate a small HTML document using the <form> tag to allow a user to select, by checking a box, at least two answers to a multiple-choice question. Use the GET method, and for the ACTION point to a script called "answers.pl". The script is a PERL script located on a Web server with the name of "free!cool scripts!.com" in their "cgi-bin" directory.

8. There are five errors in the following code. The lines (starting with the line after the <body> tag) are marked with a unique line number. Reference the line number and indicate the exact problem with the HTML code.

```
<html>

<head>

<title>YOUR FEEDBACK</title>

</head>

<body>

line 1<hr size="3" width="100%" align=left><p>

line 2

line 3<h3><font color="#9c31ff">Please enter
your feedback!</font></h3>

line 4<hr size="3" width="100%" align=left><p>

line 5

line 6<form method="action"

line7action="http://www.mycompany.com/cgibin/
myform.cgi">

line 8<p><b><font size="+1">Your Name</font>
</b></p><input

line 9type="text" name="name" value=" "
size="40" maxlength="80" align="top">

line 10<p><b><font size="+1">Did you like our
Web site?</font></b></p>

line 11<input type="radio" name="website"
value="yes" checked>yes

line 12<input type="radio" name="website"
VALUE="maybe">no

line 13<p><b><font size="+1">How did you find
out about Our

line 14Company?</font></b></p>

line 15<select name="how">

line 16<option value="Friend">Friend</option>

line 17<option value="University">University
</option>
```

```
line 18<option value="Partner">Partner</option>

line 19<option value=Work>Work</option>

line 20<option value="Advertisement">
Advertisement</option>

line 21

line 22<p><b><font size="+1">Your Phone Number
</font></b></p><input

line 23type="TEXT" name="phone" VALUE=" "
size="40" maxlength="80"

line 24align="top">

line 25<p><b><font size="+1">Your Email
Address</font></b></p><input

line 26type="TEXT" name="address" VALUE=" "
size="40" maxlength="80"

line 27align="top">

line 28<p><b><font size="+1">Your Question Or
Issue</font></b></p>

line 29<textarea name="question" rows="5"
cols="40"

line 30wrap="Physical"></textarea>

line 31<p></p><input type="subscribe"
value="Click This Button To Forward Your

line 32Question"></form>

line 33</center><p>

line 34

line 35<h3><font color="#9C31FF">Thanks for your
feedback!</font></h3>

line 36<p>

</body>

</html>
```

a. Problem 1, Line Number: _________

____

____

____

b. Problem 2, Line Number: _________

____

____

____

c. Problem 3, Line Number: _________

____

____

____

d. Problem 4, Line Number: _________

____

____

____

e. Problem 5, Line Number: _________

____

____

____

Extended Activities

1. A good Web site should always provide a way for a user to contact the site. One of the simplest and easiest contact methods is a hypertext anchor that includes a `mailto` link in the URL. For example, when a user clicks the following hyperlink, it launches the default e-mail application, opens a new message, and addresses the message to the WestNet webmaster:

   ```
   <a href="mailto:webmaster@westnetinc.com">
   ```

   Insert a hypertext anchor into one of your test Web pages, using your own e-mail address in a `mailto` link. Test it to see that it correctly inserts your address into a new message.

2. On the Web, locate a complete HTML tag reference. Explore the many other tags that HTML offers, and use these new tags to expand and improve your test pages. Experiment with the different forms and attributes of each tag. Be sure to bookmark the HTML reference site, because you'll use it often!

   If you prefer to use Microsoft Explorer as your Web browser, download and install a copy of Netscape Navigator. If you prefer to use Navigator, download and install Explorer. Now load one of your most complex test pages into both browsers, side by side, and note the differences. While HTML is theoretically a standardized language, you'll see that each browser has its own style of interpreting the appearance of tags. Experienced HTML designers test all changes in both browsers.

Lesson 8—Graphic Formats

Still, or static, graphics are the primary visual component of most Web sites. Users demand a rich visual experience from a Web site, similar to that of television. Unfortunately, most users connect to the Internet over slow dial-up connections that are inadequate to carry a flood of large graphics. Thus, graphic design for Web sites requires endless compromises between quality and efficiency. This lesson introduces the most popular formats for still graphic images, and compares their technical advantages and disadvantages.

Objectives

At the end of this lesson you will be able to:

- Identify when to use GIF, JPEG, PNG, or PDF files

- Name the technical factors that cause Web sites to appear and perform differently on different computer systems

- Explain why it is important to minimize file sizes on a Web site

Key Point

Graphics and multimedia require larger Internet bandwidths.

Challenges for the Multimedia Web Designer

Objective 1.1
Identify the issues that affect Internet site functionality ... Bandwidth (both client and server) ... Pages taking too long to load ... Resolution and size of graphics

The Web environment offers a new set of limitations on how information can be presented. Be prepared to compromise. Web designers do not have the same kind of control over the user's experience that we have over a printed page. A Web page designed on one system will not necessarily look exactly the same on another, because the appearance and performance of a site varies according to the following factors on each user's desktop:

- Computer hardware limitations

- Internet connection bandwidth

- Color inconsistencies

Computer Hardware Limitations

Most users have simple, low-resolution computers. While better, cheaper home computers are available every day, many systems are still limited to 640x480 pixel resolutions using 256 colors. To reach the widest audience, Web sites must look good on these systems.

Internet Connection Bandwidth

Multimedia files tend to be large. To give a user a visual experience, each one of these bytes must travel to the viewer's screen. Unfortunately, most home users still have 56 Kbps modems, and telephone line problems often reduce actual bandwidth to much less than 56 Kbps. An HTML page, with multiple frames, Java-Scripts, spinning logos, scrolling advertisement banners, audio, and/or video can take seemingly forever to load.

Heavy traffic at peak access times is also a great equalizer of access speeds, much to the chagrin of corporate cubicle dwellers with high-bandwidth connections. A midday browse of a popular Web site from a corporate Internet connection may be as slow or slower than from home on a PC with an average-speed modem.

This problem is made worse by user impatience. A typical Web browsing user will give about two seconds of attention to the home page of a Web site before deciding whether to look around or go elsewhere. Web developers face the constant dilemma of showing enough glitz to make the visitor stay, while keeping the page simple enough that it does not take forever to load.

Thus, a Web designer must carefully include only the graphic and multimedia elements that add value to the users' experience. To users, there is nothing more discouraging than waiting for a media-rich page to download, only to discover that they get little or no value for the time invested.

Color Inconsistencies

Each computer operating system maintains its own palette of pure colors. Each palette contains different colors depending on the operating system. A Macintosh 8-bit color palette is different from the default Microsoft Windows 8-bit color palette.

A "Web safe" palette was developed several years ago to address this problem. This palette is a collection of 216 colors that represent the intersection of the various operating systems' base palettes. Examples of the safe palette are available at many Web design sites. At that time, most users were using eight-bit, 256-color displays, so the palette displayed colors fairly consistently. Now many users have systems that run High Color and True Color displays, which make the Web safe palette less "safe." Some of the colors in the palette display inconsistently across browsers and operating systems.

As with any other development, the key to good Web site design is testing your pages on each of the operating systems and browsers that your users are likely to use.

Graphic File Formats

Objective 2.5
Identify when to use various image and multimedia file formats ... TIFF, BMP

Most Internet applications can display the GIF, JPEG, PNG, or PDF graphic file types. (While TIFF and BMP are popular formats for other computer applications, they are not generally used on the Web.) Each of these graphic formats has its own strengths and weaknesses. The following explains the differences of each format and how these differences may influence a decision of which one to use.

GIF Files

Objective 2.5
Identify when to use various image and multimedia file formats ... GIF, GIF89a

Graphics Interchange Format (GIF) is the most popular still-image format for Web publishing. GIFs are used for most nonphotographic images, such as buttons, diagrams, or logos. A GIF image (.gif) can contain a maximum of 256 colors.

The GIF format is owned by Unisys. Internet users can make, view, and send GIF files freely, but they cannot develop software that builds GIF files without paying royalty fees to Unisys.

File Compression

The format uses Lemple-Ziv & Welch (LZW) compression, a lossless method of reducing file size. Lossless compression is a data compression technique that reduces the size of a file without sacrificing any of the original data. LZW uses a compression method called run-length encoding (RLE), which works by scanning through an image file, pixel by pixel. When it finds a "run" of pixels of the same color, it uses a shorthand notation to describe the number of pixels and their common color. Good RLE software can also recognize and record repetitive patterns, such as stripes or checks. Thus, GIF files that contain large blocks of the same color can achieve very high compression ratios.

GIF87a and GIF89a

There are two types of GIF files: GIF87a and GIF89a. The GIF87a is the standard, more common GIF file format. GIF89a adds the ability to tack on extra information to the file, enabling regions to be selected and masked out to become transparent or invisible.

The GIF89 format also supports animated GIF files, which are a series of images that, when viewed in succession, work like a slide show or give the impression of movement. Do not overuse animated GIF files—one per page is usually enough. Animated GIF files are further described in Lesson 9 of this unit.

Interlaced GIF files can be either GIF87a or GIF89a. Interlaced GIF files appear on a Web screen in chunks, starting at low resolution and resolving after several seconds to their finished form. This lets the graphic display progressively and show up sooner than if it were fully downloaded before displaying.

Custom Palettes and Palette Reduction

The GIF format allows for the definition of alternative color palettes. The number of colors used can be reduced in the default palette, or a custom palette can be created that contains just the colors required by the graphic image. Reducing the number of colors needed and the size of the file results in smaller file sizes that yield faster file delivery. An image that contains 256 colors is nearly four times the file size of the same graphic designed to use 64 unique colors.

Palette reduction also reduces file size by improving the efficiency of the compression algorithm. The fewer colors an image contains, the more likely it is that the RLE compression software will find long runs of the same color or pattern.

Another technique for creating small GIF files is to allow the graphic to dither to a given palette. In dithering the picture elements (pixels) are combined from colors available in the selected palette and placed next to each other to simulate another color. This method provides the least amount of control over what the final delivered image will look like and, depending on the computer system, it may significantly reduce the quality of an image.

JPEG Files

Objective 2.5
Identify when to use various image and multimedia file formats ... JPEG

Joint Photographic Experts Group (JPEG) images are the second most common image format used on the Web and the best file format for true color, continuous tone (photographic type) images.

JPEG files use lossy compression, a data compression technique in which some data is deliberately discarded to achieve massive reductions in the size of the compressed file. When saving a graphic as a JPEG, the designer may choose the quality of the image. The higher the image quality, the larger the file size.

JPEG images (.jpg) can display up to 16.7 million colors. A JPEG is usually small in size. However, because the file must be decompressed after downloading, it tends to take a little longer to display than a GIF file. JPEG files can also transfer in chunks, similar to interlaced GIF files, by using a progressive JPEG format. However, progressive JPEG files may not work on all browsers.

PNG Files

Objective 2.5
Identify when to use various image and multimedia file formats ... PNG

Portable Network Graphics (PNG) is a file format created by the PNG development group, which consists of members from the World Wide Web Consortium (W3C) and Unisys. The idea behind developing the PNG format is to provide a patent-free replacement for the GIF file format. In 1995, Unisys suddenly announced that programs implementing GIF would be required to pay royalties. This was one of the many factors that led to the development of the PNG format.

Like the GIF format, a PNG file is compressed in a lossless fashion. Typically, a PNG file can be 10 to 30% more compressed than the same graphic in the GIF format. PNG files are interlaced, and "develop" faster than do GIF files. PNG also supports gamma correction, which allows adjustment of color brightness. Images in the PNG format can be saved using 24-bit True Color, as well as the color palette and gray-scale formats provided by GIF. Most exciting for designers, PNG supports variable transparency so that a pixel can appear anywhere from fully opaque to fully transparent. In other words, a pixel may be translucent, or faded, to reveal part of another image beneath it.

Unlike the GIF (GIF89a) format, the PNG format does not support animation, because it cannot contain multiple images. However, the PNG format is "extensible." Therefore, software developers will be able to create variations of PNG that contain multiple and scriptable images.

PDF Files

Objective 2.5
Identify when to use various image and multimedia file formats ... PDF

The Portable Document Format (PDF) is a de facto standard for electronic document distribution, developed by Adobe Systems. A PDF file is a multipurpose document that can be used for high-quality print publishing or online distribution. As an electronic document, a PDF file preserves the appearance of a printed piece, including fonts, colors, page layout, and graphics. Using the freely-distributed Adobe Acrobat Reader, a user can navigate, search, or print a PDF file. Document designers can also create PDF documents that include hyperlinks, or interactive multimedia such as audio and video.

PDF is the format of choice for documents that must preserve a particular visual appearance, such as product documentation, sales brochures, electronic books, or technical papers. Optional navigational features, such as a hyperlinked table of contents, make it simple to navigate PDF books that are hundreds of pages long.

Popular desktop publishing and word processing programs include features to export documents to PDF format. For more precise control, document designers typically create PDFs using an Adobe application such as Acrobat Distiller or Acrobat PDFWriter.

Choosing a File Format

The Graphic Format Usage Table provides a guide for using GIF, JPEG, PNG, or PDF files.

Graphic Format Usage

Design Factor	GIF	JPEG	PNG	PDF
Type of image	Nonphoto-graphic images: icons, diagrams, buttons, or logos Flat color areas	Photographic/ continuous tone images	Nonphoto-graphic images: icons, diagrams, buttons, or logos Flat color areas	Reproductions of printed documents, such as brochures or user manuals
Browser Support	Universal	Universal	Recently released	Requires a free reader application
Color Resolution	Up to 256 colors	Up to 16.7 million	Up to millions of colors (with True Color) Flat color areas	Widely variable, resolution depends on whether documents are for print or the Web
Optional Effects	Fully transparent pixels Interlaced display Simple animation	Progressive display Variable quality settings	Variably transparent pixels Brightness (gamma) control	Hyperlinks Table of contents Multimedia files

Scalable Vector Graphics

GIF, JPEG, and PNG files are fixed-size bitmaps, technically known as raster graphics. In contrast, the Scalable Vector Graphic (SVG) format describes an image using mathematical statements rather than a bit-pattern. Thus, the SVG format allows a graphic to be viewed smoothly in any size display. Whether the graphic is displayed on an LCD screen on a cell phone or on a 21-inch monitor, an SVG is easy to reduce or enlarge without damaging the image quality. Additionally, SVG files are typically smaller and arrive quicker over the Internet.

Because of these values in the SVG format, Macromedia has added the ability to create this graphic format in many of its web design applications, such as Freehand 10, Fireworks 4, and Flash 5. In the case of Flash 5, all graphics are eventually converted to SVG when exported as an animation or static SWF format.

Additionally, the SVG format is recognized as an application of Extensible Markup Language (XML). Therefore, any web browser capable of reading XML can also read a standard SVG file.

Because GIF, JPEG, and PNG are extremely versatile and widely used, the SVG file format probably won't take over the Internet graphic world any time soon, despite its significant advantages. However, the SVG format is becoming more popular as sites use Flash 5 for dynamic visual effects. (We discuss Flash in more detail in Lesson 9 of this unit.)

Building
Web Pages

Activities

1. What is the most difficult challenge to overcome when delivering multimedia content on a Web page?

2. Describe a browser-safe palette.

3. What does the acronym GIF stand for?

4. What does the acronym JPEG (or JPG) stand for?

5. What does the acronym SVG stand for?

6. Animated GIFs can be created using the GIF87a format. True or False?

7. An interlaced GIF can be either GIF87a or GIF89a. True or False?

8. Decide which graphic file type—GIF, JPEG, PNG, or PDF—would be best to use in the situations listed below:

   a. Photographic images

   b. Small diagrams

   c. Images with areas of flat color

d.   Exact copy of a printed document

____

e.   Universal browser support

____

f.   Searchable electronic book

____

g.   Continuous tone images

____

h.   Corporate logos

____

i.   Images that need translucent pixels

____

Extended Activities

1.   Use the Web to find sites that contain GIF, JPEG, and PNG files that can be downloaded. Collect several of each type of image, and build a simple Web page to display them.

2.   Use the Web to find sites that offer downloadable examples of the safe color palette. Set several different computers to use True Color for their monitor displays, then see if the safe palette looks different on some of those systems.

3.   Users can create PDFs using an Adobe online service called Create Adobe PDF Online (**http://createpdf.adobe.com**). Visit this site and create a few PDF files.

4.   Go to the following sites to find and download the most popular plug-in applications:

For Netscape: **http://home.netscape.com/plugins/**

For Internet Explorer: **http://www.microsoft.com**

Lesson 9—Multimedia Formats

The term "multimedia" is generally used to refer to moving images and sound, though multimedia sites also include still images. This lesson introduces the most important formats and technologies for delivering sound, animation, and video over the Internet.

Objectives

At the end of this lesson you will be able to:

- Explain how streaming works

- Name the dominant formats and standards for audio, animation, and video

- Identify the multimedia formats that can best meet a given requirement

- Describe the most popular animation techniques

 **Key Point**

Animated GIF files add movement to a Web page.

How Streaming Works

Digital technologies for audio, animation, and video have improved steadily over the past several years. However, multimedia was not really practical over the Internet until the invention of a single technique called "streaming."

Streaming simply means that a file can begin playing before the user's computer has finished downloading the entire file. A browser plug-in or ActiveX control receives data into a buffer on the user's computer; when that buffer has filled, the plug-in begins to play the received data, while continuing to receive the rest of the file. As the playback proceeds, the download continues to fill the buffer.

Before streaming was developed, users had to completely download audio or video files before they could begin to play them. Thus, users were unwilling to download long files. But streaming makes it possible to begin playing a one-hour multimedia file after only a few minutes spent receiving the front of the data stream.

The fastest speed at which data moves is limited to the slowest connection through which the data travels—usually a user's modem (running at 53 Kbps or slower). As you will see, some streaming technologies adjust the quality of the content (and its file size) to the speed of the Internet connection.

Plug-In Technology

Objective 2.4
Identify when to use various multimedia extensions or plug-ins.

A plug-in is a software module that adds a specific feature to a browser. For example, plug-ins for the Netscape Navigator browser enable it to play multimedia files such as sound and animations.

When you view a site that requires one of these modules, the site will send a message that prompts you to install the plug-in. There is usually a link to download a program that installs the plug-in you need. In some cases you will need to shut down the browser to install the program. Once it is installed, you can return to the site and view the feature that requires the plug-in technology.

Some of the most popular plug-ins are:

- Adobe's Acrobat Reader, which displays Portable Document Format (PDF) files

- RealNetworks' RealPlayer, which plays streaming audio and video

- Macromedia's Shockwave, which plays animation or audio files

- Macromedia's Flash, which plays vector-based animations

- Apple's QuickTime, which plays streaming audio and video

- Microsoft's Media Player, which plays streaming audio and video

We discuss most of these formats in this lesson.

Streaming Audio Formats

The ability to deliver audio over the Internet has recently gone through many transformations. Streaming technology has improved the way audio is delivered in real-time. Of course, this is great news for many Internet users who depend on delivering or receiving quality audio files. However, this convenience for Internet users has become a problem for owners of copyrighted materials.

RMF

The Rich Music Format (RMF) was developed by Beatnik, Inc. for playback on the Beatnik player. RMF has some unique features, such as copyright information embedded in the RMF file and custom "mixing" of tracks. Files are played back instantly when triggered and can generate a high-fidelity sound track that's interactive in real-time. Users can manipulate the RMF file to their liking, adjust instruments within different tracks, and associate graphics with sound files. When browsing an HTML file that contains RMF files, the sounds are activated when the mouse passes over the graphic associated with the file—there's no need to click the mouse. The sound is active as long as the mouse is over the graphic, and stops when the mouse is moved away.

There are three types of RMF files. The first file type does not contain any sound files, but rather instructions on how to make the Beatnik Player produce sound. The instructions tell all of the instruments, programmed inside the Beatnik Player, when to play, what notes to hit, how loud or soft to play, and when to stop playing. The second type of RMF file can contain one or more converted .wav, .au, .aiff, or .mp3 file(s). The third type is a combination of the first two RMF types. In this case, the instructions are provided to control the individual files contained in the RMF. For example, one set of instructions can control a .wav file for a guitar, while another set of instructions controls an .mp3 file of drums.

The plug-in for RMF file formats can be found at the Beatnik Web site at **http://www.beatnik.com**.

MPEG, MP3

Objective 2.5
Identify when to use various image and multimedia file formats ... MPEG

MP3, or MPEG-Layer 3, is an audio-coding technique for reducing the bandwidth or number of bits required to represent audio signals. This goal may not mean much, but it can be better understood with the help of a little history.

In the late 1980s, the motion picture industry realized that motion pictures would soon be stored on tape or disc and transmitted to televisions in digital format. Because of this realization, the industry needed a way to compress the information to fewer bits for storage and transmission. Working under the joint direction of the International Standards Organization (ISO) and International Electrotechnical Commission (IEC), the industry formed the Moving Picture Experts Group (MPEG). The group established standards for compression algorithms, first MPEG-1 and then MPEG-2. (MPEG-2 is assumed if someone simply says MPEG.) The standard covers compression of both audio and video information; however, the audio compression format, particularly that from Layer-3 of MPEG-1, has become popular by itself.

The MPEG-1 audio compression format has various implementations; the most powerful is "Layer-3." Layer-3's performance at reducing the bit rate (or bandwidth) ranges from 96:1 for a "telephone quality" sound at 8 Kbps, to 12:1 for "CD stereo quality" sound at approximately 128 Kbps.

These reductions in the required bit rates allow transmission of good-quality audio over lower-speed channels, such as modems, in a reasonable amount of time. In fact, real-time (or continuous) "FM-like" sound can be sent over the Internet using a 56 Kbps modem. "CD quality" sound can be sent in roughly two to three times the length of the recording. For example, a three-minute song can be sent over a 56 Kbps modem in approximately eight minutes. Today's computer systems are fast enough to decode MP3 in stereo at the "near CD quality" level.

There is a lot of activity in the area of music distribution over the Internet, and MP3 is playing a key role. MP3 is also being promoted as an alternative to RealNetwork's encoding format. To obtain the most current information on MP3, visit the Web site at **http://www.MP3.com**.

RealAudio

RealAudio is one of the most well-known formats for streaming audio. RealAudio and RealVideo (discussed later in this lesson) have been combined into RealPlayer, a single plug-in and player, as shown in the RealPlayer Screen Capture.

RealPlayer

Real Networks developed the RealProducer, RealServer, and RealPlayer technologies specifically for the creation, delivery, and consumption of media via the Internet. In addition, RealNetworks has allowed the RealMedia (.rm) format to be an export option in many of the leading media-creation software programs. This combination has contributed to RealPlayer's success as one of the leading downloaded plug-ins.

The RealServer delivering the sound file talks to RealPlayer on the PC, and the two negotiate a transmission speed based on the current bandwidth of the connection. The speed of the connection determines the quality of the file that the server sends to the player. Thus, a higher-speed connection, such as a Digital Subscriber Line (DSL), yields a player file with better sound quality than a slower dial-up connection.

RealPlayer is available at: **http://www.real.com**.

Animation Techniques

Similar to old-fashioned flip pages, animations on the Web are simply a sequence of still graphics displayed in rapid succession, simulating movement. The fluidity of the movement depends on the size and complexity of the images and the speed at which the data for the graphics is transmitted, received, and displayed.

Animated GIF Files

Objective 2.5
Identify when to use various image and multimedia file formats ... GIF89a

We introduced the GIF file format in the previous lesson on static graphics. Animated GIF (GIF89a) is a fairly recent addition to the GIF family of file types. An animated GIF89a is actually a sequence of images, played in succession, resulting in animation. Software compatible with the GIF89a file format will load the image and "play" the animation in a loop sequence, for a predetermined number of iterations. The Animated GIF File Diagram shows four frames from a GIF89a animation that show a butterfly opening its wings. The actual GIF file these images were captured from consisted of 20 frames played in succession.

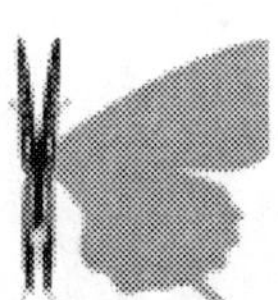

Animated GIF File

Animated GIF files represent the easiest way to add movement to a Web page, because of their relatively small size. They are also loaded, or cached, on the browsing PC, rather than relying on constant communication with the host server and embedded HTML references within the pages on the site.

Flash

Objective 2.4
Identify when to use various multimedia extensions or plug-ins ... Flash

Macromedia developed the Flash program to create animations that are more Internet friendly than the computer-based or CD-ROM applications created by Director and Authorware (the "Lingo" language to be more specific).

Flash animations combine ActionScript, vector-based graphics, and MP3 (since the Flash 4 version) audio to form one of the most file-size friendly formats for Internet delivery. ActionScript, a variation of JavaScript, provides a common, functional, and dynamic scripting language. Vector-based graphics are scalable and can be easily compressed. MP3 is not the only audio option for Flash animations, but it offers the best compression currently available for audio. A "swiff" file (.swf) is the published file format for animations created in Flash.

Streaming and Playback Performance

How well a Flash movie plays when streamed depends on how much data is required for each frame. For a Flash movie to play smoothly from start to finish, the following issues must be considered:

- The size of the data required to display each frame should be as small as possible.

- The size of the data required to display a series of frames should take no longer to download than it takes to play the series of frames.

To play any frame, Flash requires all elements of the frame to be downloaded in their entirety: event sounds, bitmaps, vector shapes, and so on. If the movie reaches a frame that cannot be rendered because all the data has not yet downloaded, playback stops until the needed data has finished downloading.

Therefore, if a movie has complex items or a large number of items in the first frame, it may take a while to download all the items before the first frame can be displayed. If other frames are also large or complex, a movie may play in spurts, slowing down to wait for data, and then speeding up when Flash has enough data to play the frames faster.

Flash players are available for download at the Macromedia site at **http://www.macromedia.com/software/**.

Virtual Reality Modeling Language

So far, most Web images are two dimensional, displayed on flat monitor screens. However, many Web professionals are already working to add another dimension to the Web user's experience.

Virtual Reality Modeling Language (VRML) is a markup language for describing three-dimensional spaces and objects. VRML data is interpreted and displayed by a VRML viewer on a client computer, or Web browser plug-in, so the VRML document itself can be fairly small.

A user does not simply view a VRML document, but interacts with it by rotating or moving the image. Users can also move their virtual point of view through a three-dimensional scene. This added dimension makes exciting styles of interaction possible. For example, a mechanical engineer can show customers a VRML model of a new object, which the customers can view from all angles. Architects can take customers on virtual tours through proposed building designs.

Links to VRML plug-ins and creation tools are available at the Web3D Consortium site at **http://www.vrml.org**.

Streaming Video Formats

Until recently, most video on the Internet was in the form of stored clips that were downloaded entirely before being played from the client's hard drive. But streaming technology and network lines with increased bandwidths have changed everything. Streaming video uses the same streaming technology used for real-time audio. New codec formats also decrease the file size of video clips and make streaming easier.

For example, leased lines, from 128 Kbps ISDN to dedicated T-1 and greater, support real-time videoconferencing, up to full-broadcast quality of 30 frames per second in audio/video. These advances in technology provide streaming video for millions of Internet clients on a variety of connection speeds. However, the quality of the video stream depends on the codec used, the server streaming the video, the type of connection the client has, and the type of media player the client is using.

RealVideo

RealVideo, created by the same company that pioneered RealAudio, employs new-generation codec compression algorithms to squeeze video files to a small size. When a video file is requested by clicking an icon on a Web site, the file begins traveling to the remote PC where it is received into a buffer. Using "SureStream," the server sending the file from the far site senses the transmission speed based on how fast the buffer fills up. The server then makes a determination about what quality and, subsequently, file size to transmit. Again, a lower speed results in a smaller file and poorer quality, while a faster connection yields a smoother, higher-quality video playback.

The RealVideo codec encodes up to eight different stream speeds. However, there are two different RealVideo codecs currently being used: RealVideo G2 and RealVideo 8. The RealVideo G2 codec processes faster, but visual quality is poorer. The RealVideo 8 codec requires more processor power on the client side, but it results in a visual quality superior to that of the G2 codec. The RealVideo G2 is the older of the two and is preferred by some producers, because it does use less processor power on the client side. Either way, RealNetworks has developed a solution capable of delivering media to technically diverse audiences.

Windows Media Player

Objective 2.4
Identify when to use various multimedia extensions or plug-ins ... Windows Media Player

Objective 2.5
Identify when to use various image and multimedia file formats ... AVI

Any PC that uses a newer Windows OS also has Windows Media Player included under normal installations. Originally, the Windows Media Player was developed in 1991 to play CDs and .wav audio files following the release of Creative Labs' first Sound Blaster card. In 1994, Microsoft introduced a new media player in the release of Windows 95. This was the first 32-bit media player; it allowed playback for some of the first video codecs developed for the Audio Video Interleaved (.avi) format. By the time Windows 2000 was released in 1999, the media player introduced in this version unified the player with streaming technology. Finally, in October 2001, Windows Media Player 8.0 was released with the Windows XP OS. Version 8.0 integrates CD burning in the OS, allows DVD playback, and supports MP3.

Windows 2000 Server includes Windows Media Server for streaming .wav or .avi files to machines using the Windows Media Player. This addition is great for everyone using a machine running Windows. Corporations that exclusively run Windows machines can use Windows Media Player to run a simple, cost-effective streaming media solution over an intranet. Windows Media Player, as shown below, is available for download at: **http://windowsmedia.com/** on the Windows Media Player Screen Capture.

Windows Media Player

Complex Multimedia

So far, this lesson has introduced technologies that combine moving images with audio. However, a compelling multimedia experience often must combine many different file formats, such as motion photography, vector animation, sounds, and still images.

QuickTime

Objective 2.5
Identify when to use various image and multimedia file formats ... MOV

QuickTime was developed by Apple Computer, Inc. and was first released in 1992. Originally, QuickTime was only available on the Macintosh (Mac) platform for the delivery of video, audio, graphic, and animation data. However, in a successful attempt to reach a wider audience, QuickTime soon became available for both the Mac and PC.

The technology that drives QuickTime is different for the Mac and PC platforms. On a PC, QuickTime is implemented through a dynamic-link library (DLL). On a Mac, it is implemented as a set of extensions that can be installed with Mac OS 7.1.1 or later. Apple distributes the browser plug-ins in separate versions for the PC and the Mac. Authoring programs, such as Adobe Premiere and Macromedia Flash, include the necessary programming interfaces in the compilation of the Windows or Macintosh code. Though the back end of QuickTime is different for the PC and the Mac, the result and user interface is exactly the same.

Nearly 20 different video codecs are available for creating Quick-Time Movies (.mov). This large quantity is due to the fact that QuickTime is open source. As an open source application, anyone with the know-how can develop a codec for QuickTime movies. Some codecs are eventually adopted by Apple and included as a standard codec.

Besides processing video data, QuickTime handles still images, animated images, vector graphics, multiple sound channels, MIDI music, 3D objects, virtual reality objects, and text. This versatility and the longevity QuickTime has had on the market make it one of the best choices for delivering any of the multimedia assets mentioned above.

QuickTime player, as shown on the Apple QuickTime Screen Capture, is available for download at: **http://www.apple.com/quicktime/**.

Apple QuickTime

QuickTime Virtual Reality

Objective 2.4
Identify when to use various multimedia extensions or plug-ins ... QTVR

QuickTime Virtual Reality (QTVR) takes QuickTime's capabilities a few steps further by making an image into an interactive experience. For example, the Apple Web site provides several demonstration files; the exterior of the Louvre is shown on the Apple QuickTime VR—Louvre Demonstration Screen Capture. When you click on a link to the file, the file downloads and displays in the QuickTime viewer plug-in window. It looks like an ordinary, flat image. But when you click in the image and move the cursor, the image moves to show you a complete panorama of the Louvre courtyard. You can also zoom in on any detail in the image, or zoom out for a wider view.

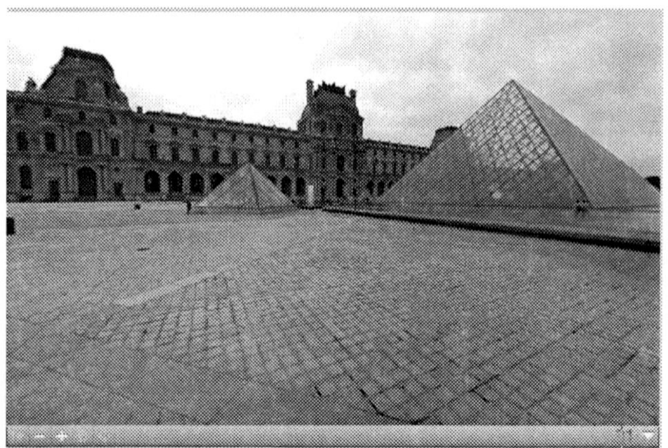

Apple QuickTime VR—Louvre Demonstration

Most applications that can view QuickTime movies can view QuickTime Virtual Reality movies. This means that users need only the free QuickTime viewer plug-in to view these movies, but developers must purchase the QuickTime VR Studio to produce them.

Shockwave

Objective 2.4

Identify when to use various multimedia extensions or plug-ins … Shockwave

One of the most popular and complex multimedia technologies is Macromedia Shockwave. Macromedia is well known among developers for its Director and Authorware multimedia applications. Programmers assemble a wide variety of media elements—music clips, still images, video, and animations—into Director or Authorware, then add Lingo scripting to create "movie" files. These movies can then be exported as "runtime" files that can be distributed and played on computers that have not installed the expensive Director or Authorware programs.

However, the runtime versions of Director movies tend to be too "fat" for the Internet, because they contain application information within the file to allow the computer to play the movie without the main application present. The solution is to "shock" the file with Macromedia's Afterburner utility.

After a movie file is shocked (converted and compressed to a different file format), it is much leaner than the original. A browser plug-in called Shockwave caches and plays the shocked file when it is called on by an HTML tag. Using streaming technology, the Shockwave file begins playing as it is received by the computer. The animation occurs on the PC within the browser page, and sometimes in a separate window that opens when the file is activated. Shockwave closes when the file finishes playing.

Shockwave players are available for download at the Macromedia site at **http://www.macromedia.com/software/**.

Activities

1. Explain how streaming works.

   ____

   ____

2. Explain how RealPlayer adjusts the quality of audio or video according to the connection speed.

   ____

   ____

3. What is the main difference between an animated GIF and a Flash animation?

   ____

   ____

   ____

4. An animated GIF can use either the GIF87a or GIF89a format. True or False?

5. Animated GIFs are the easiest way to add movement to a Web page. True or False?

6. Browsers need a plug-in to play animated GIFs. True or False?

7. Browsers need a plug-in to play Shockwave or Flash files. True or False?

8. Complete the following sentence: A Flash movie plays smoothly only if Flash is able to receive the data over the net connection at the rate that...

   ____

9. Name two techniques that allow Flash to reduce animation files size for Internet delivery?

   ____

Extended Activities

1. Download a free trial of a GIF animation tool and create an animated GIF from **http://www.gif.com**. (Search for "animation freeware".)

2. Find an example of a Flash or Shockwave animation published on the Internet. What characteristics of this animation are improved by the technology behind Flash or Shockwave?

3. Using a multimedia computer, record an audio session and save it as a file. Play it back using a product such as RealPlayer.

4. Compare the RealPlayer, QuickTime, and Windows Media players. Listen to audio and view video files recommended at each of these technologies' Web sites. Which media player do you like the best? If you were able to make one change to each media player or the technology, what would you change?

____

____

____

____

Building
Web Pages

Summary

The process of creating Web pages is both artistic and technical. This unit covered basic technical information on how to build Web pages, as well as information on making Web pages more interesting.

In a series of hands-on lessons, you learned to code an HTML page by hand. Because most professional Web developers use powerful site-building applications, these hands-on exercises may have seemed like wasted effort. However, all good Web developers agree that a thorough understanding of HTML coding is essential for creating reliable sites that look good on many different browsers. Many Web professionals learned HTML in a text editor, and often work both in graphical views of a page and its underlying HTML code.

But a designer's method of building Web pages is less important than the information contained in those pages. Most sites present text information, but graphics have become the workhorse of the Web. Most simple diagrams or icons use the GIF format, though the newer PNG format is quickly gaining ground because of features such as brightness control and variable transparency. Photographic images usually are stored as JPEG files. Each of these formats uses a different method of file compression, to make the most efficient use of scarce Internet bandwidth. A Web designer who understands these compression schemes can create visually rich Web pages that still load quickly.

Today, multimedia applications comprise the primary advances in Web development. Static Web pages are being replaced by Web pages that provide high-end graphics, sound, and video streams. As the bandwidth of the Internet increases, multimedia applications will be used more and more.

Streaming technologies have made multimedia Web sites practical, in spite of the slow connections that still limit the bandwidth of many users. Streaming allows the beginning of an audio or video file to begin playing before the entire file has been downloaded to the client. Plug-ins are freely available to add streaming support to many popular Web browsers.

As you use the Web, take time to look carefully at good Web sites. Note how they are designed and built. Every now and then, view the source HTML of these pages to see exactly how some of the world's best Web designers work.

Unit 7 Quiz

1. HTML documents begin and end with what tag pair?

   a. `#html#...#/html#`

   b. `<html>...</html>`

   c. `//hypertext//...//end hypertext//`

   d. `[webdoc]...[/webdoc]`

2. URL stands for:

   a. Universal Resource Locator

   b. Uniform Repository Link

   c. Uniform Referral Location

   d. Uniform Resource Locator

3. Which HTML tag creates a frameset of two equally sized columns?

   a. `<frameset cols="50%,50%">`

   b. `<frameset cols="50%,*">`

   c. Both a and b

   d. None of the above

4. The Web browser translates what type of Internet protocols?

   a. HTTP and HTML

   b. PPP and SLIP

   c. FTP and SMTP

   d. None of the above.

5. HTML tags are enclosed in which of the following brackets?

   a. `{ }`

   b. `[ ]`

   c. `( )`

   d. `< >`

6. The comment tag is displayed as:

   a. `<!--comment text-->`

   b. `<html>...</html>`

   c. `//hypertext//...//end hypertext//`

   d. `[webdoc]...[/webdoc]`

7. The size, color, and type of text can be formatted by using:

   a. `<!--text-->`

   b. `<font>` tag in HTML

   c. `//hypertext//...//end hypertext//`

   d. `[webdoc]...[/webdoc]`

8. What type of graphic file formats are used on the Web?

   a. GIF

   b. Microsoft bitmaps

   c. JPEG

   d. All of the above.

   e. a and d

9. The HTML tag `<input type=submit value="OK">` displays:

   a. A button with the caption OK.

   b. A button with the caption Submit.

   c. Input submitted by the user.

   d. None of the above.

10. The visible content of a Web page follows which of the following tags?

    a. `<head>`

    b. `<title>`

    c. `<body>`

    d. `<contents>`

11. Which of the following tags creates a line break without adding extra vertical space?

    a. `<break>`

    b. `<p>`

    c. `<head>`

    d. `<br>`

12. A clickable link to another Web page would be contained in which of the following?

    a. `<a></a>`

    b. `<title></title>`

    c. `<href></href>`

    d. `<link></link>`

13. If text is enclosed within `<title>` and `</title>`, where does it appear?

    a. In a search engine's results display

    b. In large type at the top of a page

    c. In the browser's title bar

    d. It is invisible, only used by scripts or the site developer

    e. a and c

    f. None of the above.

14. Text will not appear on a Web page unless it has been tagged. True or False?

15. What tag pair encloses a bulleted list?

    a. `<ol> </ol>`

    b. `<ul> </ul>`

    c. `<bl> </bl>`

    d. `<td> </td>`

16. What color does this tag assign to the background of a Web page?

    `<body bgcolor=#0000FF>`

    a. Red

    b. Blue

    c. Green

    d. Black

17. Which HTML tag creates a table that spans the full width of the browser screen?

    a. `<table width=100%>   </table>`

    b. `<table width="100">   </table>`

    c. `<table width="full"> </table>`

    d. `<table span=100%> </table>`

18. Which statement is true about HTML tables?

    a. A table must contain at least two cells

    b. A cell must contain at least one row

    c. A table must contain at least one row, and that row must contain at least one cell

    d. A cell and a table are equivalent

19. Which of the following is created by the tag: `<option>pepperoni</option>`

    a. A choice in a drop-down list

    b. A radio button

    c. A checkbox

    d. A text field

20. What technology is most important for multimedia delivery?

    a. Compression

    b. Encryption

    c. Hypertext

    d. Hypergraphics

21. What does a software plug-in do?

    a. Increases efficiency

    b. Adds functionality

    c. Increases bandwidth

    d. None of the above.

22. Because of bandwidth problems, video cannot be sent to individual users. True or False?

23. Scalable Vector Graphics represent images as mathematical statements rather than a bit-pattern. True or False?

24. Video information that travels over the Internet is not in digital format. True or False?

25. Your hot-air balloon manufacturing company in Michigan needs to show a proposed design to a customer in Asia. The customer wants to see how the balloon will look from all angles, including above and below. You should use:

    a. Flash

    b. Shockwave

    c. GIF89a

    d. VRML

26. Which of the following does GIF89a offer that PNG currently cannot?

    a. Variable transparency

    b. Animation

    c. Gamma control

    d. Compression

27. Your tech support department wants to make all user manuals available for download. The company's quality control department insists that these online documents be identical to printed documents. What formation should you suggest for the online manuals?

    a. HTML

    b. ASCII

    c. PDF

    d. PNG

Unit 8
Dynamic Site Technologies

Static, unchanging sites aren't very interesting. If your site's viewers see the same content they saw last time, they'll probably never return.

Of course, you could regularly edit the site and add new information. But it takes a lot of time and effort to keep a site fresh and lively with manual updates. The solution, of course, is to automate the site update process.

Each lesson in this unit presents a general overview of a technology that can make dynamic sites possible. Each of these technologies is a complex subject in its own right, so this unit provides only a broad description of what they can do.

Lessons

1. Dynamic Sites and Databases
2. Common Gateway Interface Overview
3. Overview of Web Programming Technologies
4. Structured Content

Terms

Active Server Pages (ASP)—ASP is a Microsoft technology for dynamic Web pages. ASP contains blocks of VBScript or Jscript, which a Web server interprets to create a unique HTML page for each browser request.

ActiveX Data Objects (ADO)—ADO is Microsoft's interface for data objects. ADO is designed to replace Data Access Objects (DAO) and Remote Data Objects (RDO). Unlike RDO and DAO, which are designed only for accessing relational databases, ADO is more general and can be used to access all sorts of different types of data, such as spreadsheets and Web sites.

application programming interface (API)—API is a software interface that formats requests from an application to a network operating system.

client-side script—A client-side script is a program that runs on the client side of a client/server process. For example, client-side scripts in Web pages run on Web clients (browsers).

client/server—Client/server (or client server) is a model in computer networking where individual PCs can access data or services from a common high-performance computer. For example, when a PC needs data from a common database located on a computer on a LAN, the PC is the client and the network computer is the server.

Common Gateway Interface (CGI)—CGI is a standard specification for creating Web server programs that accept data from Web clients, process the data, and return a result. For example, each HTML form needs a corresponding CGI program to process form data sent to its Web site. CGI programs can be written in a variety of languages, including C, Perl, Visual Basic, or Java.

compiler—A compiler is a software program that takes source code from a programming language such as C++, and converts it into machine-readable, executable code to be run on a computer.

database management system (DBMS)—A database management system is a suite of applications for creating, maintaining, and querying database files.

Document Type Definition (DTD)—A DTD is a specification that accompanies an XML document and defines the codes that are used to format a document, such as a code that has been defined to separate paragraphs or identify topic headings and so forth, and how each is to be processed.

ECMA Script—ECMA Script is a standard object-oriented scripting language derived largely from Netscape's Java Script. The European Computer Manufacturers Association (ECMA) supervised the development of ECMA Script to provide a standard, cross-browser language for Web scripting. However, like Java Script, ECMA Script may also be used to create non-Web applications.

Extensible Hypertext Markup Language (XHTML)—XHTML is defined by the World Wide Web Consortium (W3C) as "a reformulation of HTML 4.0 as an application of XML." In XHTML, all HTML 4 markup elements and attributes are supported. Unlike HTML, XHTML can be extended by anyone that uses it. Programmers can define and add new elements and attributes to those that already exist.

Extensible Markup Language (XML)—XML is a simplified version of Standard Generalized Markup Language (SGML) that allows Web designers to add functionality beyond HTML by creating their own formatting tags. W3C created the official XML recommendation for XML 1.0.

form—A form is a Web page designed to collect information or input from a user and send it to a Web server for processing. Forms can contain data-entry fields, checkboxes, drop-down lists, buttons, and other interactive controls.

Hypertext Markup Language (HTML)—HTML is a text-based formatting language used to generically format text for Web pages. It is a simplified derivative of Standard Generalized Markup Language (SGML) that tags different parts of a document more in terms of their function than their appearance. A Web browser reads an HTML document and displays it as indicated by the HTML formatting tags and the browser's default settings.

interpreter—An interpreter is a program that reads and executes programming script written in a high-level language. The interpreter reads a script line by line, and then executes it line by line. See parser.

Java Database Connectivity (JDBC)—JDBC is the Java API for accessing relational databases.

method—Methods are active capabilities of an object. They often represent verbs. For example, one method of an object representing a database command may be Execute.

Open Database Connectivity (ODBC)—ODBC is an API that mediates SQL communication between multiple applications and databases.

parser —A parser is a program that reads and executes programming scripts written in a high-level language.

Personal Home Page (PHP)—PHP is a popular open source, server-side scripting language that is especially suited for creating Web sites featuring dynamic content and complex Web applications.

plug-in—A plug-in is a software module that adds a specific feature to a browser. For example, plug-ins for the Netscape Navigator browser enable it to play sound files and animations.

Practical Extraction and Report Language (Perl)—Perl is an interpreted programming language designed for processing text. Because of its strong text-handling features, Perl has become one of the most popular languages for writing server-side CGI scripts.

Python—Python is an interpreted, object-oriented programming language. Python interpreters are available for most operating systems.

scripts—Scripts are interpreted programs that are both human readable and executable, in contrast to compiled programs, which are converted into machine-readable code that humans cannot understand. Common interpreted scripting languages include Perl, UNIX Shells, JavaScript, and VBScript.

server-side includes—Server-side includes are a type of HTML embedded command that allow Web developers to create customized Web pages, depending on time of day or other factors. These documents usually have an SHTML extension.

server-side script—A server-side script is a program that runs on the server side of a client/server process. For example, server-side Web programs (such as CGI programs and server-side scripts embedded in Web pages) run on Web servers.

Standard Generalized Markup Language (SGML)—SGML was developed by the International Organization for Standards (ISO) in 1986. SGML does not specify any particular formatting; rather, it specifies the rules for tagging elements. HTML is a text-based formatting language used to generically format text for Web pages. It is a simplified derivative of SGML, that tags different parts of a document in terms of their function rather than appearance.

Structured Query Language (SQL)—SQL is a standardized language used to retrieve data from a database.

table—A table is a section of an HTML document that arranges information in rows and columns. Table cells can display numerical or text data, or they can be used to provide an invisible layout framework to control the placement of text and graphics on a Web page.

tag—A tag is an HTML command inserted in a document that specifies how the document or a portion of the document should be formatted by a Web browser.

Web services—Web services is a strategy and set of technologies that enable Internet-based applications to be seamlessly and easily integrated into a broad range of disparate business system platforms. Web-based software applications can be developed as reusable components, called services. Web service components can then be individually used and linked together at the enterprise level, making use of XML as a common data exchange medium and the Internet as the service-delivery network.

Lesson 1—Dynamic Sites and Databases

Dynamic sites present information that constantly changes. They can do this using various technologies, but all dynamic sites separate content from presentation to some degree.

This lesson describes some of the basic business and technical principles shared by all dynamic Web sites. We'll also briefly outline the database fundamentals that will help you understand how databases serve as the "back end" of many dynamic sites.

Objectives

At the end of this lesson you will be able to:

- Name the most important business reasons for dynamic sites

- List the typical kinds of live site data

- Explain the benefit of ODBC

 **Key Point**

Dynamic Web sites display changeable information.

The Need for Live Sites

Web audiences demand a steady supply of fresh, interesting information. But there are other good reasons to create a site that automatically displays live data:

- Dynamic sites provide a better user experience, by creating customized pages based on stored user preferences or browser types.

- The sites are easier to maintain. Content experts can add new material without having to edit HTML pages.

- All information is presented in a consistent format. Since page appearance is defined independently of its content, you can change the look of a site without editing each specific piece of content information.

- Dynamic sites are more accurate. When data comes from a live source, such as a central database, you can be sure that it is correct. For example, if the phone number for a customer service representative comes straight from your human resources database, any change to that information is instantly available to your Web site.

The nature of certain businesses also makes a dynamic site a mission-critical requirement for many organizations:

- Publications and news networks use dynamic techniques to schedule articles and provide a consistent view of their constantly-changing content.

- Commerce sites depend on live content from inventory databases, auction results, user input (reviews and classified ads), or shopping carts. Some sites, such as airline reservations services, provide different "front end" access points to a shared database such as the SABRE system.

- Changing external conditions affect the success of some businesses. For example, the quality of a ski area's product is determined by weather conditions that can change hourly. Many ski resort sites feature live data that describe current conditions to potential ski visitors, such as weather reports and forecasts, snow condition reports, and automatically-updated "web cam" photos.

Types of Dynamic Techniques

Web site designers can create dynamic content with many techniques that range from very simple to highly complex.

Gathering Data From Outside Sources

Your site can read a page from another site (with permission), or download a page via FTP from a service provider. For example, the Accudata weather service provides data to many resorts.

Time-Sensitive Pages

Some server technologies, such as Microsoft FrontPage, can mark HTML files with start and end dates that define the effective lifespan of each file. This "meta data" can be stored in the HTML file itself; the server automatically ignores all files with expired dates.

User-Supplied Data

Dynamic sites can also capture data from users, by recording their preferences, shopping carts, viewing histories, and other specific information. Stored in a cookie file, this data can make a high degree of interactivity possible on a good dynamic site.

Database-Driven Sites

In many sites, the Web pages exist only as templates that define the appearance of data stored in a separate database. This concept is similar to the process of inserting data fields into a mail-merged form letter that provides the overall structure and appearance.

These databases range from very small to very large. However, most databases follow common principles for organizing and accessing their data. The rest of this lesson outlines these fundamental database concepts.

Database Concepts

A database is a collection of categorized data. Each general type of data is collected in a table, which organizes information into records (rows). Each record, or row, consists of a series of fields arranged into columns. For example, the Rockbottom Company organizes its employee data in an Employee Table.

The Employee Table

Employee ID	FirstName	LastName	DeptName	Email	HireDate
000002	Fred	Flintstone	Quarry	fflint@rockbottom.com	11/2/0003
920274	Oliver	Stone	Production	ostone@rockbottom.com	1/3/1993
638592	Rock	Hudson	PR	rhudson@rockbottom.com	1/4/1956

This row and column organization makes it simple to search for one type of information independent of the others. When it is important that each row be unique, each record will include a unique value called a "key" or "primary key." In this table, the EmployeeID field is the primary key; if the company employs two Oliver Stones, their unique ID numbers will prevent confusion.

Most databases, even small ones, further categorize information into multiple tables that contain different types of data. For example, the Rockbottom Company records information about each of its departments and managers in a Department Table.

Department Table

DeptName	Building	AdminID	AdminEmail
PR	A10	485993	ruby@rockbottom.com
Production	A20	374949	crystal@rockbottom.com
Quarry	A3	485939	sandy@rockbottom.com

In a relational database, data in one table can be linked to data in another table if their records share at least one common value. For example, both the Employee and Department tables contain fields that store a department name and an employee ID number (the content of the field is important, not its name). That common information can be used to form temporary links that allow access to information in both tables.

Database Management Systems

The very simplest database can consist of a plain text file structured into rows and columns. Different applications can perform simple tasks by reading data from the file and adding records to the file. However, it is much more difficult to create applications to perform even the simplest data management tasks, such as sorting records or creating relationships between tables. Therefore, most application programmers delegate these jobs to a database management system (DBMS).

A DBMS is a suite of applications that lets a user interact with a database. There are many different kinds of DBMSs, but most of them include the following components:

- The user interface includes tools for creating and modifying the database structure, as well as the data it contains.

- The database engine does the actual work of reading and writing a database file. The engine functions as a layer between the user interface and the actual database files. When users need to add new data to a database, they use the interface to pass the data and instructions to the engine, which writes to the file. When users need to read data, they pass a specially formatted question, or query, to the engine. The engine then searches the data and passes the answer back to the user interface.

603

- An application programming interface (API) allows a separate application to work with an engine directly, without having to go through the database's user interface.

- A query interface simplifies the process of constructing queries, allowing users to retrieve data without understanding the details of SQL.

- A report writer formats and prints the data that a query retrieves. Some report interfaces also create graphical displays and charts.

SQL

Objective 2.1
Understand and be able to describe programming-related terms … SQL

Most applications store data in databases that support Structured Query Language (SQL). SQL, pronounced either as separate letters or as "sequel," is a standardized language for retrieving data from a database. IBM designed the original version in 1974, and Oracle Corporation released the first commercial SQL in 1979. In 1986, the American National Standards Institute (ANSI) adopted a core version of SQL as a standard. In 1991, the standard was updated to include new features; that version is known as SAG SQL.

SQL statements combine actions and modifiers to precisely describe what data to extract from a file. For example, the following statement will return all records in the Customers table that contain the word "Watson" in the LastName field:

SELECT ALL IN CUSTOMERS WHERE LASTNAME = "WATSON"

A query can pull data from several related tables, and select records based on combinations of field values and other conditions. Those SQL statements can be extremely complex, which is why all DBMSs offer some sort of query interface to shield the user from the details of SQL.

UDA
Specification

Objective 2.7
Understand when to use popular tools to connect a Web server to a database … ODBC

Each database engine communicates with other applications using a proprietary language. While all of the engines understand the core of SQL, each SQL statement must be delivered as part of a message written in each engine's proprietary language. In this way, each engine is like a person with one communication channel to the outside world: one person communicates by telegraph, another by letter, and another by telephone. Although they all understand the same language, they communicate that language using a different set of symbols.

When an application needs to interact with a database engine, the application must be programmed to communicate using the database engine's internal language. If an application must interact with several different database engines, each message must be formatted for the engine that controls a particular type of data. Unfortunately, applications that work this way are difficult to program and maintain.

To simplify this situation, Microsoft developed the Universal Data Access (UDA) specification. This set of high-level procedures allows applications to access data regardless of its structure or the engine used to create it. There are three main components of the UDA specification:

- Open Database Connectivity (ODBC) is an API that mediates SQL communication between applications and databases, called "data sources." An application uses ODBC API commands to submit SQL queries. Instead of then directly querying a particular data source, the application passes a query to the Driver Manager that includes an SQL statement and the name of the target data source. The Driver Manager passes the query to the database driver that corresponds to that data source. The driver then translates each communication to and from the proprietary language of the database engine that controls that database. Each database engine has its own database driver. This concept is illustrated on the ODBC Diagram.

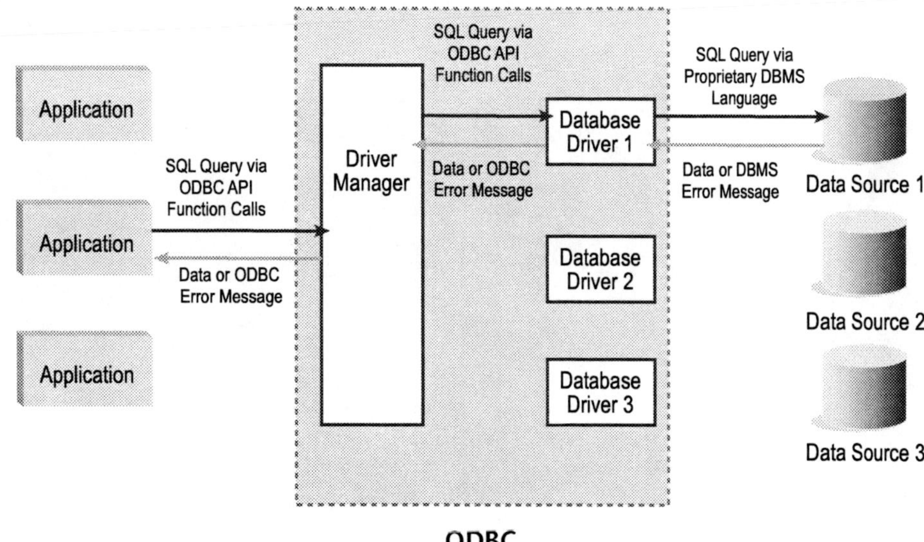

ODBC

- ActiveX Data Objects (ADO) is a high-level interface for exchanging data objects between applications. In addition to databases, ADO can be used to access other forms of data, such as spreadsheets, word processing documents, or Web pages.

- Object Linking and Embedding (OLE) allows a user to create a data object in one application, then link or embed it within a document created by another application. For example, OLE allows a user to embed a spreadsheet within a word processing document. If the user later needs to edit the numbers, the spreadsheet application can be launched from within the word processing application.

Activities

1. Your Customers table and Orders table each have the following fields. If you wanted to retrieve all orders for a particular customer, what field would you add to both tables?

   CustomerOrders

   First NameProduct Name

   Last NameOrder Date

   AddressShipping Date

   Phone NumberTotal Price

   ____

   ____

   ____

   ____

2. What does ODBC mean, and what does it do?

   ____

   ____

   ____

   ____

3. When does a table require a primary, or unique, key field?

   ____

   ____

   ____

Extended Activity

Your software company wants you to develop a simple database to capture data about technical support calls. Upper management wants to be able to extract the following items of information from the database:

- Name of each caller

- Reasons for calls

- How many calls each support technician handles

- How many calls the support center takes per week, month, or year

- All calls from a single customer

Given these requirements, sketch a simple database design for this company. Determine how many tables are needed and how they will be related to each other (what fields they will share in common). List what fields each table should contain, and note why they are necessary. (You do not need to limit yourself only to these requirements.)

Lesson 2—Common Gateway Interface Overview

When Web servers were first being designed, it was clear they needed a protocol to enable them to use Hypertext Transfer Protocol (HTTP) to communicate with other processes (whether on themselves or on other servers), and for those processes to return information to the server for transmission back to the ultimate client. CGI was developed to permit this interaction.

Objective 2.2
Understand and be able to describe differences between popular client-side and server-side programming languages ... CGI script

CGI is not a programming language. It is an interface, protocol, and methodology that defines the rules for communication between Web clients, Web servers, and server-side programs. Any program that follows those rules is called a CGI program.

Because so much of the Internet and Web is deeply rooted in the UNIX world, it is no surprise that a great deal of Web programming is done in C/C++ and various UNIX shell scripting languages. But virtually any language that can read and write to standard I/O can be used to write CGI programs. Some platforms have preferred scripting tools, such as AppleScript for the Macintosh, or Microsoft's Visual Basic Scripting Edition (VBScript) for Active Server Pages (ASP). However, any programming language can be used to create CGI applications, as long as the resulting program meets the CGI requirements.

Objectives

At the end of this lesson you will be able to:

- Explain what CGI is and name some of its common uses

- Explain the difference between the HTTP GET and POST methods

- List the programming and scripting languages commonly used with CGI

- Explain how a CGI program interfaces with HTTP to process data from a Web browser

Key Point

CGI programs can be written in many different programming languages.

A Typical CGI Process

The CGI Process Diagram summarizes the steps that make up a typical CGI process.

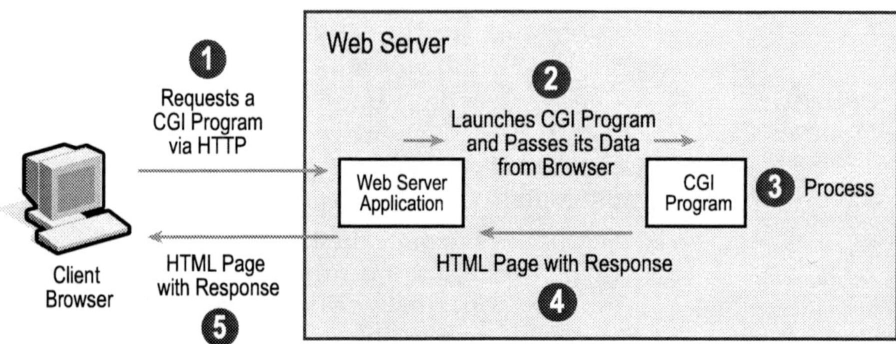

CGI Process

The process begins when a Web browser uses HTTP to request a Hypertext Markup Language (HTML) page that contains a call to a server-side CGI program. Most commonly, this call is part of a form on the page; the Action attribute of the <form> tag specifies the Uniform Resource Locator (URL) of a particular CGI program that will process the form data.

When the Web server receives the browser's request, it launches the CGI program named in the HTTP request, then passes the client's data to the CGI program. If the CGI program is written to return a response to the client (and not all do), it builds an HTML page that includes the response, and passes that page back to the Web server. The server then transmits the response page to the client.

Exchanging Data With CGI

Objective 2.2
Understand and be able to describe differences between popular client-side and server-side programming languages. ... CGI script

The CGI Data Exchange Diagram illustrates the two ways a Web server and CGI program can exchange data.

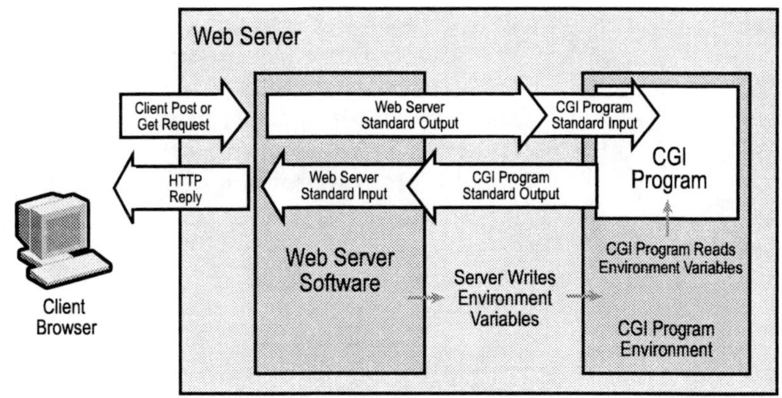

CGI Data Exchange

Standard Input/ Output (I/O)

Every program has a standard input (STDIN) and standard output (STDOUT) that work like a doorway to pass data into a program and return data from it. For example, many programs get keyboard input from STDIN and pass the program output through STDOUT to the display.

Each CGI program is a subprocess of the Web server application (Apache, Internet Information Server [IIS], etc.). STDIN of the Web server becomes STDIN of the CGI process; subsequently, STDOUT of the CGI process becomes STDOUT of the Web server process. Thus, when the Web server receives incoming data by means of its STDIN, the data automatically flows to the STDIN of the CGI routine. When the CGI program returns a response from its STDOUT, it passes through the server's STDOUT.

Different CGI programs do not compete for access to STDIN and STDOUT, because each HTTP request creates another instance of the Web server. Each separate Web server process has its own working environment. In operating systems that support "child" processes, each CGI process inherits the environment of its respective Web server, including STDIN and STDOUT.

Environment Variables

When a server launches a CGI program, it assigns the program a small block of working memory called its "environment." The server uses this area as a sort of notepad where it writes items of data the CGI program needs to do its job. Each item of data is assigned a special name, called an environment variable.

CGI defines a comprehensive list of environment variables that the server uses to communicate with CGI programs. The CGI Environment Variables Table describes these variables (some servers support a longer list of variables). Every time an HTTP server launches a CGI program, it writes some or all of the environment variables to the program's environment space, as necessary.

CGI Environment Variables

CGI Environment Variable	Description
AUTH_TYPE	Authentication method used to authenticate a user; see also REMOTE_USER and REMOTE_IDENT
CONTENT_LENGTH	Length, in bytes, of data passed to the CGI program through standard input
CONTENT_TYPE	Media type of the query data
DOCUMENT_ROOT	Root directory from which Web documents are served
GATEWAY_INTERFACE	Version number of CGI used by the server
HTTP_ACCEPT	List of media types the client can accept
HTTP_FROM	E-mail address of the requesting user
HTTP_REFERER	URL of the document pointed to by the client prior to accessing the CGI program
HTTP_USER_AGENT	Identification of the browser or client issuing the request
PATH_INFO	Extra path information
PATH_TRANSLATED	Translated version of PATH_INFO
QUERY_STRING	Additional information passed to the request by the client; appended to the URL following a question mark (?)
REMOTE_ADDR	Remote IP address of the requesting user

CGI Environment Variables (Continued)

CGI Environment Variable	Description
REMOTE_HOST	Remote host name of the requesting user
REMOTE_IDENT	User making the request
REMOTE_USER	Authenticated name of the user
REQUEST_METHOD	Method (GET, POST, HEAD) with which the request was made
SCRIPT_NAME	Virtual path of the script being executed
SERVER_NAME	Server's host name or IP address
SERVER_PORT	Port number of the host (usually 80)
SERVER_PROTOCOL	Name/version of the protocol the request came in with (typically HTTP/1.0)
SERVER_SOFTWARE	Name and version of the server software answering the client request

Difference Between GET and POST

HTTP includes seven methods that Web clients and servers use to interact with each other. Two of these methods, GET and POST, are commonly used to send data from a Web page form to a server-side CGI program.

GET Uses Environment Space

A Web client normally uses the GET method to request a Web page (identified by a universal resource identifier [URI]) from a server. The GET method appends the form data to the URI of the CGI program (using a "?" character to separate the data from the URI), and then passes it to the Web server. The server places the form data into the CGI environment variable QUERY_STRING. The CGI program running on the server then retrieves the data from the QUERY_STRING variable.

If the form only transmits a few bytes of data, the GET method is probably adequate. However, memory used for holding environment variables is a scarce resource; typically only a few thousand bytes are available for all environment variables. If form data is too big for the environment, the Web server could crash (hackers have used this as a method of attacking Web servers). Well-written CGI programs check for the size of incoming data to ensure this problem does not occur.

POST Uses Standard Input/ Output (I/O)

If a form can possibly transmit a large amount of data, POST is the better method to use. The POST method passes data to a CGI program using its STDIN. In other words, instead of writing form data to the small "notepad" of the environment space, the Web server streams the form data through the "doorway" of standard input/output (I/O).

Therefore, the POST method is a safer, more flexible approach for passing form data to a CGI routine. The POST method sends data to the server as part of the normal HTTP body portion. The server calculates the length of the data it received from the browser, sets the CONTENT_LENGTH environment variable to this value, and then passes the data to the CGI program by means of its STDIN.

The following example shows how a form uses the POST method to send its data to a program called "post-query" located in the "cgi-bin" directory of the National Center for Supercomputing Applications (NCSA) Web site:

<FORM Method="POST" Action="http://hoohoo.ncsa.uiuc. edu/cgi-bin/post-query">

Placing CGI Programs on a Web Server

For security purposes, each Web server administrator usually designates a space where CGI scripts can be stored and called. In most cases, the "cgi-bin" is the only place this can occur.

Security issues also require each administrator to decide how to allow programs to be sent to the server. Before creating pairs of client-side and server-side scripts, ask the Web server administrator to explain the site's security policies and posting practices.

Activities

1. How do HTTP and CGI work together to process data?

   ____

   ____

   ____

2. How do CGI STDIN and STDOUT processes relate to Web server processes?

   ____

   ____

   ____

3. The CGI program's environment is its ________________.

4. Choose the Web server interaction method (GET or POST) that best suits the statement.

   a. Uses the environmental variable QUERY_STRING

   ____

   b. Makes use of a server's STDIN _________

   c. Does not use scarce environmental space _________

   d. Provides an opening for hackers to crash a Web server

   ____

Extended Activities

1. Go to **http://hotwired.lycos.com/webmonkey/programming/perl_cgi/** and review the article "CGI Scripts for Fun and Profit" by Tim Ziegler. Follow the procedures to download the guestbook Perl script, and install this script and the accompanying HTML pages to your server. Finally, perform the recommended security changes and script variable "tweaks" and test your script.

2. Visit **http://www.cgi101.com/class** and explore some of the CGI scripting capabilities listed here, including passing cookies, redirects, and form processing. Try your hand at some of the examples presented.

Lesson 3—Overview of Web Programming Technologies

Whenever you want a computer to do something, you run a program. Your favorite Web sites get their interactive features from programs written especially for that purpose. Depending on the task it will perform, a program can run on a Web client (browser) or Web server. Many tasks, such as form handling, require both a client-side program and a server-side program working together. This lesson briefly introduces the programming languages used to enhance the Web experience.

Objectives

At the end of this lesson you will be able to:

*   Describe the many programming languages used to provide Web functionality

*   Determine when to use which technology in your Web programming

 **Key Point**

Each language provides a different solution for a different situation.

Client-Side vs. Server-Side Scripting

Objective 2.1
Understand and be able to describe programming-related terms.

Before a Web developer writes a program, someone (often the same developer) must decide whether the program must run on the client computer or Web server.

When making the server/client decision, a developer considers the trade-offs. Running an application on a Web server allows the server to control the program execution, and gives the application direct access to server data. However, it may stress the server's processing capacity. Running the application on a client browser causes less stress on the server. However, this approach requires a client who is capable of executing the application on the browser. Furthermore, the client must download the application before it can be run.

Therefore, like all programming questions, the decision to run on a client or server depends on the specific job that needs to be done.

When to Run on the Client

According to the discussion of client/server trade-offs earlier, a program should run on a client if the following conditions are present:

- The program does not require much processing power

- The program is small enough to download quickly

Some client-side scripts (short programs that do not require a compiler) execute as soon as a browser reads them; others do not run until a user of the program performs some action, such as clicking on a button. Client-side programs commonly perform the following tasks:

- **Browser Detection**—Can detect what type of browser (or version of a browser) a client is using, and request pages tailored to the capabilities of that system.

- **Form Validation**—Makes the best use of time by ensuring that a form is complete and correct before sending it to a server for processing.

- **Simple Services**—Client-side scripts can convert units of measurement or perform other simple calculations based on a user's input.

- **Cookies**—Stored on a client, a cookie records client-specific information used in an interactive Web session. Cookies are often necessary for Web interactivity because Hypertext Transfer Protocol (HTTP) is a stateless protocol, which means the server is only "aware" of one HTTP request at a time. Web servers maintain cookie files on client computers to make possible interactive services, such as tracking the progress of a transaction, recording user preferences, or maintaining a shopping cart. Server-side programs write most cookies, but client-side programs can also access them. For example, a site's client-side script can read each user's name from that site's cookie, and use the information contained in the cookie to display a personal greeting.

- **Enhanced Navigation and User Interface**—Commonly used to change the color or image of a hyperlink when the mouse pointer moves over it. These "onMouseOver( )" scripts can also create navigation menus that expand to reveal subtopics.

- **Page "Decoration"**—Used to cycle through page color changes, create flashing elements, or create conspicuous effects.

When to Run on the Server

Following this same reasoning, a program should run on the server to meet these technical needs:

- The program requires a great deal of processing power

- The program is large

- The program requires access to other server-side resources, such as customer account databases, product databases, billing systems, or financial applications

Some server-side scripts are embedded into the HTML code of Web pages. The server executes these instructions when it prepares to serve a page to a client. Other server-side programs are free-standing applications that are stored on the server. These programs are run in response to client instructions, and often use the CGI technology we just discussed. Server-side programs commonly perform tasks such as the following:

- **User Authentication**—Before a site gives users access to confidential information, it must verify their identities using passwords or some other form of authentication information stored on the server.

- **Dynamic Content**—Instructions embedded in HTML pages are replaced with variable data each time a page is served. For example, once a bank's server authenticates John Jones, it can display his current account balance or the date on which his next safe deposit box fee must be paid.

- **Searching**—A server-side application can search an entire site, and display only the pages of interest to the user.

- **Interaction With Other Systems**—An order to an e-commerce site triggers a chain of activity with other electronic systems, such as credit card verification or shipping.

Programming Languages and Tools

Objective 2.2
Understand and be able to describe differences between popular client-side and server-side programming languages.

The first Web servers were developed on the UNIX operating system. As a result, many of the first programs used to activate the Web were UNIX shell scripts. Thus, programs for both Web servers and clients are commonly called "scripts," despite the fact that Web programming has grown far beyond its UNIX roots. As a result, the most popular tools for activating both the client and server sides of the Web are called scripting languages.

The most commonly used scripting languages are what programmers refer to as interpreted languages. This means that a separate application, called an interpreter, translates the script code into low-level machine instructions each time the script is run. In contrast, stand-alone applications are usually written in compiled languages. This means that the program code is translated into machine instructions, or "compiled," when the application is written.

Interpreted languages are often simpler to learn and use than compiled languages. However, an interpreted program can only run on a platform that has installed its interpreter. For example, Netscape does not support ActiveX without a separate plug-in (information at **http://www.its.esker.fr/documents/980602011B.htm**). Therefore, a decision to use client-side ActiveX controls may effectively shut out viewers who use Netscape.

A Web developer's toolbox includes several scripting languages and tools. Each one has its own strengths and weaknesses, and some can be used for both client-side and server-side programming. Thus, the choice of a language or tool depends on the job to be done.

Client-Side Technologies

Client-side programs handle processing that does not require direct access to information on a Web server. Support for some programming languages is built into major browsers. Code written in those languages can be embedded in HTML pages, and automatically run by the browser. Other languages require the installation of plug-ins or other software components.

ActiveX

Microsoft developed the ActiveX language in 1996, for the purpose of client-side scripting. Like a Java applet, an ActiveX control is a small program that is downloaded to the client and executed on the client. ActiveX controls can only be run on browsers that include an Active X interpreter. Therefore, Netscape browsers do not support ActiveX controls.

Java Applets

Even the unprecedented popularity of the Web does not match the astounding growth curve of Java. Java is a full-fledged compiled/interpreted language developed by Sun Microsystems. Designed to write both stand-alone applications, as well as browser-based applets, it provides more functionality than scripting languages.

Advanced programmers can use Java to build dynamic Web sites that interact with the user based on their choices and decisions. One use for Java applets (small programs for specific tasks) might be calculating mortgage rates on a Java-enabled Web page based on user input.

Java applications can be run on virtually any type of computer and operating system that has installed the Java compiler. Java code is meant to be portable from computer platform to computer platform with few to no changes. For this reason, Java is said to be "platform-independent."

Java applets are compiled to a universal byte code that is then interpreted by each Virtual Java Machine (a piece of code built into browsers that supports Java applets).

JavaScript

The most common client-side scripting language is JavaScript, developed by Netscape (now owned by America Online). JavaScript is an interpreted language supported by all major browsers. It also complies with the new standard for Web scripting languages, ECMAScript. For more information visit **http://www.ecma.ch/ ecma1/STAND/ECMA-262.HTM**

Jscript

Microsoft browsers support a JavaScript-like language called JScript. JScript is an interpreted, object-based scripting language. It has fewer capabilities than full programming languages such as C++ and Java; for example, it has no ability to read or write files. However, JScript has more than enough power for most client-side scripting tasks. Like JavaScript, JScript has also been rolled into the new ECMAScript standard.

Server-Side Technologies

A variety of technologies and languages is used to create dynamic Web pages on the server side. Some of these exploit standard features built into Web servers or the HTTP protocol, while others are proprietary approaches that rely on special software installed on the server.

Server-Side Includes

Server-side includes (SSI) are simple commands, embedded into HTML code, that tell the server to replace the include with a short piece of variable data before a page is served to a client. A Web page that includes SSI uses the extension .SHTML, which stands for "server parsed HTML."

All server-side includes are placed within the symbols that indicate an HTML comment. Thus, if the server fails to follow the SSI command, the browser will not display the instruction code. The general form of an include is:

```
<!--#directive  parameter="value" -->
```

The directive is a command to the server. The parameter describes a type of data, such as a CGI environment variable or a text file. The value is the specific name of the parameter. For example, the following include tells the server to display the CGI environment value that contains the current date:

```
<!--#echo var="DATE_LOCAL" -->
```

Most Web servers support the same body of directives, though some also support additional directives. Web developers must therefore write their pages to comply with the SSI supported by the site's server.

Practical Extraction and Report Language Perl (Perl) is an interpreted programming language created during the late 1980s. Because Perl was designed to manipulate text, it excels at many of the mundane text processing tasks required of CGI scripts. Thus, Perl has become one of the most popular scripting languages for CGI programming.

The syntax of Perl reveals its roots in the UNIX world; therefore, UNIX and C programmers usually have an easier time learning Perl. However, the basics of Perl are not difficult to grasp.

Unlike JavaScript, the Perl interpreter is not built into your browser. Fortunately, Perl is easy to install, and is distributed free at several Internet sites. Each distribution contains the Perl interpreter and extensive HTML documentation. You can download a Perl distribution for your platform from **http://www.perl.com**. If you have never installed a copy of Perl, download the binary distribution.

ASP

The release of Microsoft's IIS V3.0 proprietary Web application server software in 1997 marked the introduction of a new Web development technology, Active Server Pages (ASP).

Active Server Pages (ASP) are a Microsoft proprietary server-side scripting environment, that can be used to create interactive Web pages and applications, similar to those created using ColdFusion and PHP Web-application scripting languages. ASP server-side technology supports VBScript (a subset of Microsoft's popular Visual Basic programming language). Microsoft's Internet Information Server (IIS) and Personal Web Server (PWS) software feature ASP technology, and are supported by Microsoft Windows 95, 98, NT, and 2000 operating systems.

Organizations that use Microsoft ASP technology include the NASDAQ Stock Market Inc., Burger King, and Dell Computer Corporation. Because Microsoft is an industry leader, with a strong partner, developer, and user support program, many organizations and development professionals have chosen Microsoft IIS Web application server technology featuring Active Server Pages technology as their enterprise Web application solution.

ColdFusion

Originally developed by Allaire Corporation, Macromedia's Cold-Fusion is a proprietary development environment for database-driven Web sites and applications. When the client-side ColdFusion Studio software is coupled with the server-side ColdFusion Web application server, the resulting application can be used to rapidly develop, deploy, and efficiently maintain dynamic database-driven Web applications.

ColdFusion runs on Microsoft Windows, Linux, Solaris, and HP-UX operating systems. It can connect to Oracle, SQL Server, Informix, DB2, Sybase, and other popular relational database solutions, through native and Open Database Connectivity (ODBC) database drivers.

ColdFusion is used by organizations such as BMW, Half.com (an eBay subsidiary), and the Scripps Institution of Oceanography at the University of California at San Diego. The ColdFusion solution has won favorable industry reviews and awards.

PHP

The "PHP Hypertext Preprocessor," is a popular open source, server-side scripting language that is primarily used on Linux-based Web servers. PHP provides features that are similar to Microsoft's Active Server Pages and Macromedia's ColdFusion solution.

Sections of PHP script are embedded within the HTML code of a Web page. When the server retrieves a page, but before it sends it to the user, it performs the embedded PHP commands and makes any necessary changes to the page. The server then serves the resulting page to the client.

Rasmus Lerdorf began creating PHP in 1994 when he wrote a Perl/CGI script for his Web site, which served to log information on potential employers who visited his site. Because his site used the logging code on its home page, he named the script Personal Home Page Tools.

Making the source code free and available to all who were interested, PHP rapidly developed into a robust Web development language. Today organizations such as NASA, Mitsubishi, and Capital One Services use PHP. According to a Netcraft survey, more than five million domains use PHP technology today.

Java Server Pages

Java Server Pages (JSP) is considered an extension of the Java Servlets and was developed by Sun Microsystems to compete with Microsoft's Active Server Pages (ASP) technology. The major difference between JSP and ASP is that JSP is considered platform independent.

Java Servlets

Run on a Web server, Java Servlets are programs that provide an interface for requests coming from another source. They were developed to do the following tasks:

- Read data sent by a user

- Read any embedded information in a request

- Generate results

- Format results

- Set HTTP response parameters

- Return documents to a client

In general, Java Servlets are considered to be more efficient than CGI or other CGI-like technologies.

VBScript

Microsoft Visual Basic Scripting Edition (VBScript), the newest member of the Visual Basic (VB) family of programming languages, brings active scripting to a wide variety of environments, including Web client scripting in Microsoft Internet Explorer and Web server scripting in Microsoft Internet Information Server.

VBScript is very similar to VB or Visual Basic for Applications; developers who already know VB can quickly learn VBScript (and vice versa). VB is considered the complete Microsoft programming language; it is a superset of both VB for Applications and VBScript. Complete applications can be written and compiled in VB. VB for Applications is a user interface language that is used within Microsoft Office for macro development. VBScript is the most limited of the three. It can be used to develop ASP pages on the server, or in place of JavaScript within Microsoft Internet Explorer.

Python

Python is a free, open source, object-oriented programming language developed by Guido van Rossum. In 1989 van Rossum was a researcher based in the Netherlands with considerable experience as a computer programming language developer. From Python's first public distribution release in 1991, the language grew in popularity due to its clear syntax, power, and ease of use.

As with the C++, Java, and Perl programming languages, Python can also be used for server-side CGI programming applications. The Python programming language is available on a broad range of computing platforms and operating systems.

IBM, NASA, Bellco Credit Union, and Disney are just a few of the major organizations using the Python programming language for application development.

ADO

ActiveX Data Objects (ADO) is a Microsoft solution that interfaces Web applications with almost any kind of data. It will work with single-tier to n-tier client/server and Web-based environments. The ADO model strives to expose everything that the underlying data provider can do, while still adding value by providing shortcuts for common operations. It is an easy-to-learn application level interface. Using Object Linking and Embedding Database (OLE DB), it provides access to all types of data, including text and graphics, e-mail, and databases.

C/C++

C (or its object-oriented version, C++) is a classic programming language. Its major drawback is its compiled nature. CGI programs tend to be fairly small, targeted applications; thus, many CGI programmers use an interpreted language to avoid the extra step of compilation. However, compiled programs do run faster than interpreted code. Depending on the specific application, processing speed may or may not be a significant factor.

C is also a more demanding language to learn and use. It provides the programmer a great deal of control; however, it requires more skill to use.

Thus, the choice of a language often comes down to the trade-off of coding ease versus execution speed. If you already know C, you can certainly use it for CGI programming. If you do not, and if processing speed is not a factor, C is probably not the best choice for your first scripting projects.

Web Services

Web services is a strategy and accompanying set of technologies that enable Internet-based applications to seamlessly and easily integrate into a broad range of disparate business system platforms. Web-based software applications can be developed as services, which are reusable components. Web service components can then be individually used and linked together at the enterprise level, making use of XML as a common data exchange medium and the Internet as the service-delivery network.

A goal of the Web services strategy is to enable organizations to sell software as a subscription-based Web service, as an alternative to providing shrink-wrapped, boxed software through conventional retail distribution channels. This approach reduces the cost of software development and maintenance, while reducing or eliminating the need for users to install and maintain software packages on their personal computers. Web services advocates claim subscribers will soon have increased access to a variety of applications and services, delivered by means of a desktop computer, cell phone, or other Internet-enabled handheld device.

In February 2002, IBM, Microsoft, BEA Systems, and Intel announced the launch of a new industry consortium—the Web Services Interoperability Organization (WSIO)—to educate businesses on the development and use of Web services. WSIO is leading the development of Web services standards and protocols, such as Simple Object Access Protocol (SOAP), Web Services Description Language (WSDL), Universal Description, Discovery, and Integration (UDDI) as they continue to rapidly evolve.

Presently, companies such as General Motors, Nordstrom, and Dollar Rent-A-Car use Web services to provide real-time data feeds and meet business challenges. Based on recent industry surveys, many more organizations are expected to implement Web services technologies through 2003.

Activities

1. Match the following technical goals with the most suitable Web programming method.

   Avoid client browser capability issues _____

   Minimize the load on the Web server _____

   Determine the client browser version and type _____

   Implement "onMouseOver( )" functionality _____

   Implement CGI scripts _____

   Insert environment variables before serving a page _____

   a. Server-side programming

   b. Client-side programming

2. What interpreted language limitation do server-side programming techniques overcome?

   ____

   ____

   ____

3. Your site needs the sort of database-driven functionality that ASP delivers. However, your site is hosted on a Linux server running Apache. What technology should you consider?

   ____

Extended Activities

1. What is the main issue challenging the adoption of a Web services approach to delivering Internet-based service applications?

   ____

   ____

   ____

2. Find a frequently asked questions (FAQ) list, tutorial, or presentation for each of the following scripting languages:

    ActiveX, a Microsoft product

    (http://www.microsoft.com/com/tech/activex.asp)

    Java, a Sun Microsystems product

    (http://java.sun.com/)

    JavaScript, a Netscape (now AOL) product

    (http://developer.netscape.com/tech/javascript/index.html)

    Jscript, a Microsoft product

    (http://msdn.microsoft.com/scripting/jscript/default.htm)

    VBScript

    (http://msdn.microsoft.com/scripting/vbscript/default.htm)

Lesson 4—Structured Content

As Web sites become more dynamic and database-driven, they rely more heavily on flexible page designs that handle appearance and content separately. This lesson introduces the main concepts behind structured content, and explains why structured formats, such as XML, give Web developers the flexibility they need to deliver content to diverse output devices.

Objectives

At the end of this lesson you will be able to:

- Explain the relationship of SGML, HTML, and XML

- Describe the difference between an XML file and a DTD

- Explain the relationship of XML and XSL

Key Point

XML is a well-supported, platform-independent technology based on open standards.

The Need to Separate Content From Appearance

HTML was designed to display documents on a very wide range of simple text monitors. The Web's architects created HTML to describe the internal structure of a document, such as its major headings and subheads, lists, quotations, and other markup appropriate for academic documents. Using this structural markups, each viewing system could then use different display techniques for each type of structure. For example, emphasized words could be bold or italic, headings could be large, or block quotes could be indented. The Web's designers assumed that each receiving system would decide how best to display each tagged element.

The first graphical browsers for personal computers gave graphic designers an amazing new toy. They quickly discovered that HTML was never meant to create visually pleasing layouts, but that did not stop them from making it work somehow. Soon they were using tables to create columns, margins, and layouts that wrapped text around graphics. They used invisible GIF images as spacers and props to force other elements into position. To override each browser's default text display settings, they made heavy use of the `<font>` tag to control the font, size, and color of text.

Today, a Web designer's toolbox is stuffed with workarounds, tricks, and proprietary elements, most of which are designed to make HTML do things it was not designed for. The resulting code is dense, difficult to read, and hard to maintain. Although the Web has become a much more interesting place, from an information systems perspective, it is a mess.

Cascading Style Sheets

Cascading Style Sheets (CSS) offer a compromise that allows HTML to get back to doing its rightful job. The key to CSS is the principle of separating a document's content from its appearance, which is what HTML's designers had in mind from the start. However, instead of a document's appearance being controlled by the browser's default display settings, CSS allows Web designers to create their own settings. These settings are then stored in a separate file, or style sheet, which is downloaded with an HTML page.

For example, a Web page's body copy can be tagged with the `<body>` element alone, with no formatting attributes. The separate style sheet then specifies what font, color, or size will be applied to all `<body>` text. This approach not only makes the body copy easier to read, but it also makes it possible to change all of a Web site's body copy with a single change to the style sheet specification for the `<body>` element.

When CSS is used to define individual page elements, a Web author can use a scripting language to control those elements. This combination of CSS and scripting can give each element a level of behavior and feedback that is not possible with simple HTML. For example, layers can move independently of each other, or some elements can display differently depending on the condition of others. Some of these Dynamic HTML DHTML (DHTML) effects, such as mouse rollovers, have already been adopted as standard practice by many Web developers.

Structured Data

The concept of structured data goes beyond separation of content and appearance, by assuming that a document's content should be organized in some sort of logical system. Databases and spreadsheets are the most common examples of structured data. In a database, fields act like containers that store different items of information, such as names or addresses. Furthermore, the database fields provide information about the data that they contain.

For example, you can check the field name to determine whether "Scott" is someone's first name or last name.

Of course, it wouldn't make sense to use a database to store something like a book chapter or a personal letter. But those documents do have their own sort of logical structure. Chapters have titles, subheads, and paragraphs. Letters have addresses, salutations, body text, and signatures. If we mark each part of a document according to what it is, rather than how it looks, we can handle documents in a more intelligent way. For example, your e-mail program can sort your messages by date, sender, or subject, because all e-mail messages identify those structural elements.

SGML

The first major system that applied this principle to documents was the Standard Generalized Markup Language (SGML), which identifies document elements according to their logical and structural function. SGML has been a standard for decades, though it is used mainly by large corporations and the U.S. military establishment.

XML

Objective 2.2
Understand and be able to describe differences between popular client-side and server-side programming languages ... XML

Extensible Markup Language (XML) and HTML are both descendants of SGML. XML is a vendor-neutral, open standard that allows data to be maintained in highly structured text files. XML has only been a W3C standard since February, 1998. But since XML is built on the conceptual foundation of SGML, it is really not new.

According the World Wide Web Consortium (W3C), which created and maintains both the HTML and XML standards, XML is "the universal format for structured documents and data on the Web."

Structured Data Means Independence

XML is powerful because it completely separates a document's content from its presentation. Therefore, XML documents are:

- **Output independent** A single XML file can be processed to create Web; pages, synthesized speech for the blind, or printed books.

- **Platform independent** XML files are written in plain text, and can be processed by any application that supports the XML standard.

- **Vendor independent** XML is based on an open standard, not proprietary technology.

The XML Architecture

The XML architecture is comprised of three interrelated pieces that each perform a specific function: elements, attributes, and Document Type Definition (DTD).

Elements

An XML element is an author-specified chunk of information that consists of an element name and element content. For example, an XML element can be as simple as:

```
<booktitle>Structured Content</booktitle>
```

As you can see, simple XML elements are very similar to HTML elements, because they were both derived from SGML. Like HTML, each XML element can contain:

- data

- other elements

- nothing (for example, an empty element like the HTML <hr>)

Attributes

Attributes add additional information to element tags. Each attribute has a name and a value, and several attribute name/value pairs can be associated with a single element. Again, this procedure of assigning attributes to elements is similar to that used in HTML.

The primary difference between HTML and XML is that an XML author can define new XML tags, and attributes for those tags. In contrast, both tags and attributes in HTML are rigidly defined in the standard.

DTD

Objective 2.2
Understand and be able to describe differences between popular client-side and server-side programming languages.
… Document Type Definitions-DTD

In structured data terms, a Document Type Definition (DTD) contains the "metadata" for a category of XML documents. Metadata is any information that describes other information. Therefore, a DTD is a document that defines the correct content and structure of an XML document. Each DTD describes a general type of XML document, lists the elements that are allowed in that document, and formally describes the document structure.

Each type of XML document is described by a different DTD. An organization that uses XML has separate DTDs to define business letters, memos, engineering specifications, technical manuals, and any other type of document that an organization produces. For example, the office memo DTD might list allowed elements such as <sender>, <recipient>, <subject>, <date>, and <body>. It can specify required elements, and define the

631

relationship between other elements. For example, a memo DTD could specify that `<sender>` must appear before `<recipient>`.

XML authoring applications use DTDs to enforce the structure of each type of document. For example, the application can warn a writer of structural inconsistencies, and may even prevent certain changes that violate the rules of the DTD. XML output applications, such as publishing programs, use the structural information in the DTD to determine how to format the document for each output medium.

Applications of XML

The uses of XML are vast and varied. Because XML allows data to be represented in a way that can be universally understood, any computer system that must exchange structured data can potentially benefit from the use of XML.

XML is especially useful to commercial applications that exchange large amounts of data. E-commerce applications can use DTDs and XML parsers to verify the contents of XML documents independent of languages or locales. Some possible e-commerce applications for XML include: Web-based shopping malls, direct merchandising, business-to-business applications, supply chain and distribution applications, and customer support and self-service applications.

Complementary Standards

To enhance and complement XML, several other standards have been created or are in the process of being created. Each of these specialized standards extends the usefulness of XML in one direction.

XSL

Objective 2.2
Understand and be able to describe differences between popular client-side and server-side programming languages.
... XSL

The most important of the various XML complimentary standards is Extensible Style Sheets (XSL). An XSL stylesheet uses XML syntax to provide the presentation information that does not appear in an XML document. Applications that display XML documents, such as Web browsers, can use an XSL stylesheet to apply formatting information, similar to the way CSS stylesheets are used to format HTML documents. XSL is a very robust standard that brings a new level of presentation services to this medium.

XLink

(XLink) XML Linking Language, is a specification that allows cross-linking within XML documents. XLink is far more robust in its linking ability than HTML, and supports more than simple one-directional links.

XHTML

The World Wide Web Consortium (W3C) describes Extensible Hypertext Markup Language (XHTML) as "… a reformulation of HTML 4.0 as an application of the Extensible Markup Language (XML)." Thus, HTML has been redesigned to allow it to support some features of XML. The result is XHTML, an application of XML for displaying Web pages.

WML

Objective 2.6
Identify the common formats used to deliver content to wireless devices.

Wireless Markup Language (WML), based on HTML and XML, is used to tag text to be displayed on the very small screens of cell phones and wireless personal digital assistants (PDA). WML is part of a proposed standard called the Wireless Application Protocol (WAP), that aims to standardize the transmission of data among mobile handheld devices.

Dynamic Site Technologies

Activities

1. What is the key difference between XML and HTML?

   ____

   ____

   ____

2. In a Web site that uses XML, text formatting is defined in:

   ____

3. The correct structure of an XML document is specified in:

   ____

4. Name the three components of the XML architecture.

   ____

   ____

   ____

5. WML is intended to eventually replace XML and HTML. True or False?

Extended Activities

1. On the Web, learn more about WML, and whether it offers any practical benefits. Go to **www.webmonkey.com** and perform a search on WML. Summarize your findings and experiences in a short report.

2. The World Wide Web Consortium (W3C) manages all technical standards that relate to the World Wide Web. Visit **www.w3c.org** to learn more about any of the standards introduced in this lesson.

Summary

This unit explored several technologies that developers can use to create dynamic Web sites. Since many dynamic sites rely on some sort of database access, Lesson 1 introduced the basic concepts that underlie most databases, and briefly introduced SQL and ODBC.

Lesson 2 introduced the Common Gateway Interface (CGI), which is not a program, but only an interface that defines the interaction between a program on a Web server and another program on a browser. CGI programs can do many different tasks, but are commonly used to look up records in a database or process HTML form input. Server-side CGI scripts usually return output to a browser by creating an HTML page that contains the data.

Web developers can use a variety of programming languages to create pairs of client-side and server-side scripts that conform to CGI, and we introduced the most important of these in Lesson 3. Client-side functionality can be created using scripting languages such as JavaScript, VBScript or JScript. Downloadable client-side programs are often created as Java Applets. Perl is often the tool of choice for server-side processing of form data, because of its strong text-handling features. When HTML pages must include variable content stored in a database, Windows-based Web sites typically use Microsoft's proprietary ASP, while sites on Linux platforms often use the open-source PHP. Another proprietary solution for dynamic sites, ColdFusion, is available for many different platforms.

Lesson 4 introduced the basic concepts of structured content, which uses structural tagging to permit extremely flexible text handling. The most important technology for using structured content on the Web is Extensible Markup Language (XML). This open-standards technology offers the exciting possibility of creating documents that can be flexibly displayed across a wide variety of platforms. By completely separating content from presentation, XML documents can be freely exchanged between different organizations, applications, and output media.

Unit 8 Quiz

1. The `post` method, when used with a `<form>` tag:

   a. Retrieves data from the server

   b. Sends form data to a program on the server

   c. Requests only header information from the server

   d. None of the above.

2. The HTML tag `<input type=submit value="OK">` displays:

   a. A button with the caption **OK**

   b. A button with the caption **Submit**

   c. Input submitted by the user

   d. None of the above

3. Which of the following is NOT used to dynamically display database information in Web pages?

   a. Cold Fusion

   b. ADO

   c. ASP

   d. Java Servlets

4. Which of the following is not a valid HTTP method?

   a. `Get`

   b. `Post`

   c. `Head`

   d. `Update`

5. What is one reason to consider running a Web application on a client?

   a. The program needs direct access to server data.

   b. The program will download quickly.

   c. This will allow the server to control the program's execution.

   d. The program needs a good deal of processing power.

6. What type of programming can help determine whether a client is running the most recent version of a browser?

    a. Server side script

    b. Client side script

    c. Server side include

    d. Web services

7. What technology uses the HTTP GET and POST methods to exchange information between Web clients and servers.

    a. Java

    b. ActiveX

    c. CGI

    d. VBScript

8. Which of the following is a programming language designed to allow application portability across platforms?

    a. ActiveX

    b. JScript

    c. VBScript

    d. Java

9. Netscape browsers do not support:

    a. ActiveX

    b. CGI

    c. JavaScript

    d. Java

10. PHP is primarily used on what platform?

    a. Windows NT

    b. Linux

    c. Sun

    d. Mac OS X

11. PHP is primarily used for:

    a. Downloadable client applications

    b. Emulating Microsoft's IIS on a UNIX machine

    c. Embedded client-side scripts

    d. Database-driven sites on Linux platforms

12. Object Linking and Embedding (OLE) is a high-level interface for exchanging data objects. True or False?

13. The XML standard was derived from:

    a. WML

    b. HTTP

    c. SGML

    d. DTD

14. XML tags describe a document's:

    a. Meaning

    b. Structure

    c. Appearance

    d. Importance

15. An XML-compliant Web page might require all of the following components EXCEPT:

    a. DTD

    b. XSL style sheet

    c. XML page code

    d. DHTML page code

Unit 9
Troubleshooting

The truth of the computer business is that you spend most of your valuable time either troubleshooting a problem or preparing to troubleshoot a problem. Although computer systems have become easier to use, they have also had more mission-critical demands placed upon them and the staff that runs them. When a company stakes its claim on the World Wide Web, a malfunctioning e-commerce site may jeopardize the survival of the business. Thus, it is more important than ever to be able to quickly diagnose and correct network problems.

This unit explains the basic methods of testing Web sites and servers, and introduces the most common software and hardware tools used to troubleshoot network problems. But while software and hardware are important, the most important troubleshooting tool sits between the administrator's ears. All the tools in the world will not find a solution unless you think through each problem in a consistent, disciplined manner. Many network professionals recommend following these eight steps when analyzing a problem:

1. Establish the symptoms

2. Identify the affected area

3. Establish what has changed

4. Select the most probable cause

5. Implement a solution

6. Test the result

7. Recognize the potential effects of the solution

8. Document the solution

Thus, good troubleshooting requires both technological tools and mental tools. To illustrate this combination, we present a series of real-world problems that show how an Internet administrator can use various combinations of tools, and a disciplined approach, to identify and correct many common problems.

Lessons

1. Testing a Web Site and Web Server

2. Common Network Testing Tools

3. Troubleshooting an Unreachable FTP Site

4. Troubleshooting an Unreachable Web Site

5. Troubleshooting a Firewall Problem

6. Troubleshooting a Home Office DSL Problem

Terms

Address Resolution Protocol (ARP)—ARP is a TCP/IP protocol used to associate an IP address with a MAC address. The ARP utility allows a user to inspect or change a computer's ARP cache.

Domain Name System (DNS)—DNS is the online distributed database system used to map human-readable computer names into IP addresses. DNS servers throughout the connected Internet implement a hierarchical namespace that allows sites freedom in assigning computer names and addresses. In addition, DNS supports separate mappings between mail destinations and IP addresses.

fat ping—A fat ping is a ping issued with the -l option, specifying a large packet size. This can be used to test for intermittent network component or link failures between end nodes. A useful packet size is 512 bytes, although sizes up to the network segment's MTU can also be used. This term also refers to a TCP/IP denial of service attack, where the sender floods the receiver's network with oversized packets.

hexadecimal—Hexadecimal is the base 16 numbering system used to represent binary information in a condensed format. Hexadecimal numbers consist of 15 symbols: 0 through 9, plus A through F. In a hexadecimal number, each position is 16 times greater than the position to its right.

IFconfig—IFconfig displays TCP/IP addressing information on UNIX computers, and configures TCP/IP settings for network adapters.

Internet Control Message Protocol (ICMP)—ICMP is a Network Layer protocol that handles error and control messages about IP communication. Gateways and hosts use ICMP to report problems about packets back to their source. ICMP also includes an echo request/reply used to test whether a destination is reachable and responding.

IPconfig—IPconfig displays TCP/IP addressing information on Windows NT and 2000 computers.

Netstat—Netstat shows the current status of all connections on a computer. The Netstat utility shows remote connected computer IP addresses and port numbers and the corresponding computer name; the local computer IP address, port, and name; and the protocol the connection uses.

NSlookup—NSlookup is a utility that allows a user to query a DNS server to resolve a hostname to an IP address.

Packet Internet Groper (Ping)—Ping is used to verify that a computer's IP software is running properly and to verify the connectivity between computers.

promiscuous mode—Promiscuous mode is a setting that forces a NIC to process every frame it receives. For example, the NIC in a network analyzer is set to promiscuous mode.

Systems Development Life Cycle (SDLC)—SDLC is the process of creating a new system, or changing an existing system, from concept to completion.

Tracert—Tracert is a utility that traces the route between two computers and sends information about each router hop along the way.

utilization—Utilization refers to the amount of bandwidth being used at a given point in time or over a period of time. For example, if a 10-Mbps Ethernet LAN is running at 40-percent utilization, it is using 4 of the 10-Mbps bandwidth available.

Winipcfg—Winipcfg is a utility that displays TCP/IP addressing information on Windows 95/98 and Windows ME computers.

Lesson 1—Testing a Web Site and Web Server

As you have learned in this course, a Web site consists of many components, such as HTML pages, the server platform, scripts and applications, and Internet connections. If the site's users are to have a productive, enjoyable experience, all of these components must function both individually and in combination with each other. Thus, every Web site must be thoroughly tested before it "goes live" to the public. This lesson outlines some of the main testing principles that are common to most Web sites.

Objectives

At the end of this lesson you will be able to:

- Describe what a systems development life cycle is

- Explain why components must be tested both individually and in combinations

- Explain the difference between a prototype and a beta test

- Explain the difference between functionality testing and stress testing

 **Key Point**

Every component of a Web site must be thoroughly tested before the site is released to its audience.

Overview of Systems Development Life Cycles

The process of creating a new system, or changing an existing system, is referred to as a life cycle. Although no single life cycle perfectly describes all development projects, software engineers have identified several general life cycle patterns. One or more of these life cycles describes every Web site to some extent. In some cases, different parts of the Web site may follow different life cycles. Since every life cycle includes a testing phase, different parts of a site may be tested at different times in the development project.

The two most common SDLCs are the waterfall cycle and spiral cycle. Many modern processes follow one of these two models, or a variation of one or both.

Troubleshooting

Waterfall Cycle

The waterfall life cycle is defined by distinct stages. Different waterfall-based processes have different names for the stages; however, they all tend to follow these five general steps:

1. Analyze
2. Design
3. Build
4. Test
5. Deploy

This life cycle is called a waterfall, because work "flows down" from one stage into the next, as shown on the Waterfall Cycle Diagram. After the system is deployed, the life cycle begins again for the next update.

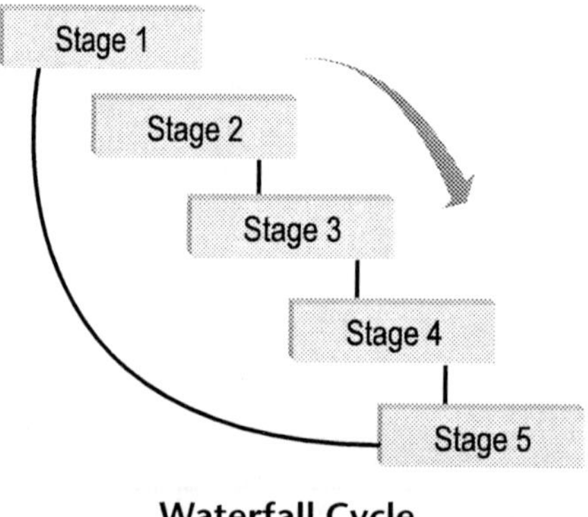

Waterfall Cycle

When a development process follows the waterfall model, each stage must be completed before the next stage can begin. Returning to a previous stage is often not permissible. In this case, changes that are not possible during the current development cycle are scheduled to be part of the next. When returning to an earlier stage is permissible, there are usually repercussions. The release date for new features is often extended as a result, and significant budget overruns are common.

The major advantage of the waterfall cycle is that all planning is done in the early stages. All system stakeholders know exactly what is expected and the current stage of the process. Release dates can be determined at an early stage, and coordination is simplified.

Although the rigidity of the waterfall appeals to many developers (because they can use it as a shield against users who suggest late-project changes), it can be cumbersome for any but the smallest projects. In addition, because the requirements of a project often change before the project has been completed, the rigidity of the waterfall cycle can lead to development setbacks.

Spiral Cycle

The spiral cycle, or whirlpool cycle, is a variation of the waterfall cycle. It is a more recent approach, meant to overcome some of the limitations of the waterfall cycle.

The guiding principle behind the spiral cycle is change management. Unlike the waterfall cycle, the spiral cycle can adapt quickly to new requirements. This is accomplished by looping through all stages several times, producing a limited version of the product each time, as shown on the Spiral Cycle Diagram.

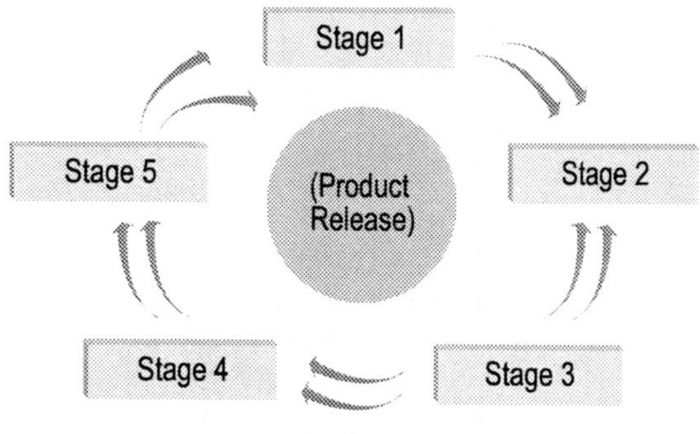

Spiral Cycle

By building only a small subset of the eventual features in each iteration, users get an opportunity to provide feedback on the product before it is finished. Their feedback is then incorporated in the next iteration of the spiral. With each iteration, new features are added and tested, and prior problems are fixed. Eventually, all of the required features are implemented, and the project is released.

Although the spiral life cycle handles changing requirements much better than the waterfall cycle, it also has significant limitations. Because there is no way to guess what new features may be requested, it is difficult to estimate the eventual cost and release date. Also, major features that require longer development times and a stable system are difficult to implement. Users accustomed to seeing continual updates may not want to wait long periods for new functionality. Additionally, and most importantly, when following a spiral development life cycle it is very easy to fall into a never-ending project. At some point the project must be deployed, and that "one more change" must wait until later.

Web Cycle?

The waterfall and spiral cycles do not perfectly describe all Web development projects, and a single project may change from one cycle to another. For example, a waterfall model may describe the process of designing and launching a new site, while a spiral model might better describe its ongoing updates and maintenance.

Furthermore, a Web site moves through either of these processes much faster than any software development project. "Web time" usually means getting things done yesterday, thus a single feature change may spin through several iterations in a single day.

The concept of SDLCs, like other software engineering concepts, is gradually being adapted to describe the shorter, faster life cycles of Web projects. However, regardless of the process employed by the Web development team, each Web site still experiences some kind of cyclical growth. Even when no formal process is used, a cycle still exists. As a Web developer, your challenge is to create a managed, orderly process that fits the life cycle of your site.

Typical Levels of Testing

A systems development life cycle applies to a Web site as a whole, but each subsystem or component of a site may also have its own life cycle. A new Web site development project may consist of several subprojects, each at a different stage of their respective life cycles. Thus, testing is not an activity that is saved for the end of the overall project, but is an ongoing process that ensures the quality of individual components and complex systems.

The type of testing often varies according to the phase that a component or project is in. Many Web development projects conduct some or all of the following types of tests:

- **Individual component testing**—Test each functional element (script, applet, etc.) individually, to ensure that it does the job it was designed for. If an element is changed later in the development process, it must be individually tested again.

- **Site prototype**—Early in the design process, the development team creates a prototype site that demonstrates how the overall system will behave. A prototype typically looks nothing like a real site, because it concentrates on the underlying functions instead of appearance. Often, individual components have not been created when the prototype is built, and simple "placeholder" elements may represent real features. But though it lacks real functionality, a good prototype may point out issues that must be considered when building real components.

- **Alpha test**—Alpha testing is done on the first version of a site that contains the most important functionality and content of the finished site. An alpha site is work in progress, and is usually incomplete, so alpha testing is generally done by the development team. However, a development team may also demonstrate an alpha site to key decision-makers, to make sure the development process is on track.

- **Beta test**—When a site is nearly ready for public release, and its developers seem to have fixed all of its problems, it's ready for private testing by a selected group of real users. A beta test is a valuable opportunity to refine the user interface, and will often reveal problems that the development team never thought to test for. To get the most value from a beta test, make it as close to real conditions as possible. For example, have beta testers connect to the site from remote locations, instead of testing in the development offices. When appropriate, give the users specific tasks to perform, such as searching for content, placing an order, or making changes to a shopping cart. Encourage beta testers to be free with their opinions, and keep an open mind to their suggestions.

Testing Principles

Objective 2.8
Test pre-production Web and e-commerce servers.

Testing cannot be done from a standard checklist, because each site is different. However, the following general goals can help you develop a testing plan that is right for your project.

Follow the User

To determine what components you need to test, trace the user's path of activity through your site. For example, your user "enters" your site over an Internet connection from your ISP. That traffic may cross a firewall before reaching your Web server. The server may then connect to a back-end database or credit-card processing system. Thus, each link of this chain must be tested to ensure that it functions properly with enough throughput to avoid becoming a bottleneck.

Testing Basic Site Functionality

Even if a site has no interaction with outside systems or databases, there are many features that must be carefully, consistently tested before a site is released to the public. Some of the most important of these are:

- **Site content**—While testers tend to focus on problems in the technical functions, do not forget to do traditional proofreading to correct flaws in a site's facts, grammar, or diagrams.

647

- **Appearance**—Check the site on different browsers and versions, different computers and monitors, and different screen resolutions. Watch for inconsistencies in color, text fonts, and other formatting details. Look for pages that download too slowly because of excessive graphics or other overhead.

- **Link tracing**—Test every hyperlink in the site, to detect dead links (to nonexistent pages) or bad links (to the wrong pages). This can be the most tedious part of site testing, but it is essential.

- **Client-side features**—Check all dynamic client-side elements, such as mouseover effects, animations, or calculators.

- **Server-side features**—Test to ensure that form data is correctly processed, or that dynamic pages are correctly retrieving and presenting database information.

- **Back-end features**—Test the site's interaction with other servers, such as credit processing, databases, or ordering applications.

- **Security**—Test your security defenses by attempting to penetrate them. If possible, have this job done by a security consultant who did not design your defenses. An objective tester will be more likely to find problems that the security designer did not consider.

Stress Testing

When testing individual components or a site's basic functionality, your goal is to prove that each feature works. The goal of stress testing is to determine *how well* each feature works under heavy traffic conditions. A good stress test should reveal potential performance bottlenecks in your Web site, such as:

- ISP connection bandwidth

- Server processing speed and throughput

- Firewall throughput

- Database access speed, and the number of simultaneous queries that the database can process

- Credit processing speed, and the number of simultaneous transactions the credit system can handle

Web teams often work with software developers to create custom applications that simulate the activity of many simultaneous users. As you tell a programmer what you need in a stress testing application, remember to test for the anticipated average traffic load, as well as an overload. For example, a good test scenario would assume that a positive news article suddenly sends thousands of new users to your site. Of course, it may not be cost effective to maintain enough capacity to handle huge spikes in user traffic. But the results of your stress testing can help your upper management decide how much volume the organization can reasonably plan to handle.

A Few Testing Guidelines

Testing, like troubleshooting, is often closer to art than science. Some people have a natural knack for creating just the right tests to reveal critical problems; if possible, you should get these people to work on your project. For the rest of us, the following principles can improve testing:

- **Be organized.** Use your test plan to create a checklist before you start testing, and document the results of each test. As you think of new things to test, add them to the checklist. This disciplined approach is essential when you must perform the same tests on dozens or hundreds of HTML pages. When testing finds problems, your written documentation will help you identify the cause more quickly.

- **Consider your intended audience.** Site performance that satisfies a 65-year-old gardener may be painfully slow to a 16-year-old video game expert. Thus, beta testers should represent the audience your site wants to serve.

- **Look for "boundary" conditions.** Computer applications determine what actions to take by testing for measurable conditions, such as the date, time of day, or a customer's credit limit. Program bugs are often created when a condition is not well defined. For example, a program may test to see if the current time is before midnight or after midnight. But if the programmer has not allowed for the possibility that the time is *exactly* midnight, the application may create errors. Good testers use these boundary conditions to look for potential problems.

- **Use unbiased testers.** To be most effective, a tester should have no preconceived ideas about a feature. Thus, it's usually best for a feature to be tested by someone other than its creator. This approach is also good because most people have a hard time finding their own mistakes.

- **Actively try to break the system.** The best testers analyze a design to identify a system's most likely weaknesses, then aggressively test those features. As a result, one measure of the success of a testing program is the number of problems it finds. To encourage this attitude, some development projects treat testing as a game, with praise or prizes for the tester who finds the most bugs. This can be unsettling to upper management, so take care to maintain good communication during any major site testing.

- **Testing is never finished.** While new sites require the greatest volume of testing, every change to an existing site, no matter how minor, must also be tested before it "goes live." The time pressure of the Web often tempt developers to skip testing of simple changes and new features. However, the small additional time spent testing is an investment that will pay off in increased customer trust.

Activities

1. Observing how a site handles a high traffic load is called __________.

2. Match the concepts below with the most appropriate SDLC, either the waterfall cycle or the spiral cycle.

   a. Limited, distinct stages

      ____

   b. Never-ending projects

      ____

   c. Handles change easily

      ____

   d. Similar to building a house

      ____

   e. Easy cost and schedule estimation

      ____

Extended Activity

Search the Web for information regarding one specific systems development process. One such process is the Unified Software Development Process created by Rational Software Corp (**http://www.rational.com**) and another is the Microsoft Solutions Framework (MSF) (**http://www.microsoft.com/MSF/**). Is the process a waterfall cycle, spiral cycle, variation of one, or combination of the two? Explain your answer. What are the strengths and weaknesses of the process? Compare and contrast the process you researched with those your classmates researched.

Troubleshooting

Lesson 2—Common Network Testing Tools

The network administrator's toolkit consists of hardware tools, software utilities, and some combinations of both. Hardware tools typically isolate problems at the Physical Layer, such as damaged wiring or improperly-installed connectors. Most software tools have been traditionally included in implementations of TCP/IP, and are essential for any LAN that uses those protocols. A few tools run software utilities on specialized hardware. This lesson introduces the essential tools for LAN troubleshooting, and describes the purpose of each one.

Objectives

At the end of this lesson you will be able to:

- Use Winipcfg, IPconfig, or IFconfig to inspect a computer's TCP/IP configuration

- Use ping to verify TCP/IP connectivity

- Use Tracert to count the hops between a source and destination node

- Use Netstat to observe active TCP connections

- Use ARP to resolve IP addresses to NIC addresses

- Explain when to use a media tester, or a tone generator and probe

Key Point

An administrator uses a different combination of specialized tools to identify and solve each type of problem.

Winipcfg, IPconfig, and IFconfig

Objective 3.6
Identify when to use various diagnostic tools for resolving Internet problems
... Winipcfg
... Ipconfig
... Ifconfig

Winipcfg and IPconfig are Microsoft Windows utilities that display a computer's IP addressing and connectivity settings. IFconfig (interface config) is a UNIX utility used to assign an IP address to a physical interface, or report the configuration status of that interface. All of these utilities are frequently used as a starting point for problem isolation on their respective systems:

- Winipcfg is a graphical utility for Windows 95/98/Me

- IPconfig is a command-line utility for Windows NT and Windows 2000

- IFconfig is a command-line utility for UNIX

These utilities only affect the local workstation. In other words, an administrator cannot use these to troubleshoot a networked computer from a different workstation.

Winipcfg Operation

Winipcfg can be run from a DOS prompt or the Windows 95/98 Start menu:

1. From the Start menu in Windows 95/98/Me, select **Run**.

2. In the Run dialog box, type **winipcfg** and click **OK**.

   The following screen appears, as shown on the IP Configuration Screen Capture.

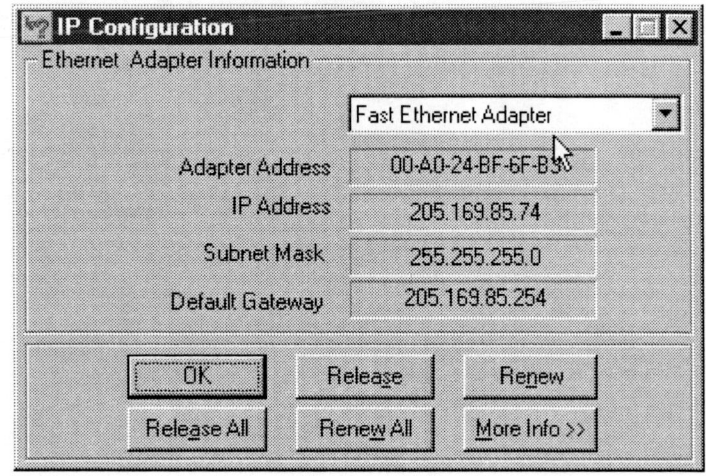

IP Configuration

Winipcfg displays the computer's current TCP/IP network configuration values. These values include the host name, Domain Name System (DNS) server name, and other pertinent information.

3. To see more detailed information, click the **More Info** button.

    The additional details appear as shown on the Expanded IP Configuration Screen Capture.

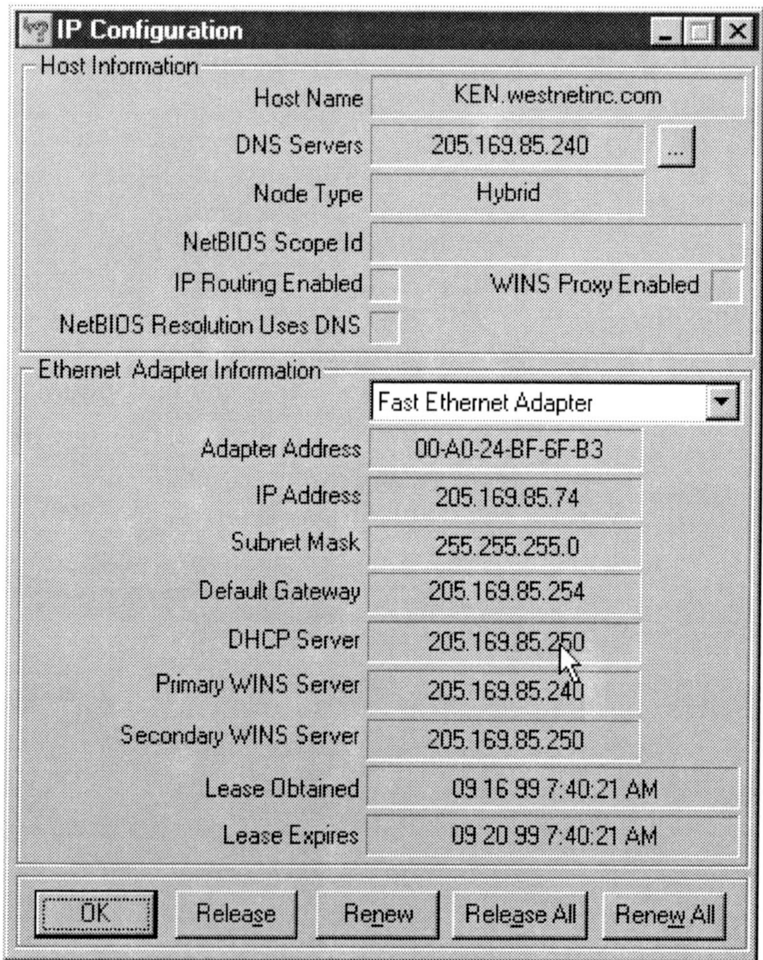

Expanded IP Configuration

This screen tells us a lot about the computer. It tells us the host name, KEN. It also gives us quite a bit of addressing information, including the address of the first DNS server that will be used for name resolution. It also tells us the Fast Ethernet network interface card (NIC) address, referred to on this screen as the adapter address. It includes the IP address and subnet mask associated with this IP address. And finally, it includes the address of the router (default gateway) used for connectivity to the Internet.

Additional information is available as well. Clicking the button next to the DNS Servers entry will cause it to cycle through additional DNS server addresses, if so configured. Clicking the down arrow next to the Fast Ethernet Adapter entry selects additional adapters and shows their configuration information.

The buttons along the Windows' bottom control the local computer's Dynamic Host Configuration Protocol (DHCP) information. The Release button releases the currently selected adapter's address lease and related information. The Renew button updates the current adapter's lease information. The Release All button releases configuration information for all adapters, and the Renew All button renews all adapter information.

IPconfig Operation

To run IPconfig:

1. From the Windows NT or 2000 Start Menu, select Programs, then Accessories, then Command Prompt.

2. In the DOS window, type **ipconfig**, then press **Enter or Return**.

    Basic configuration is displayed, as shown in the Basic IPconfig Results Diagram.

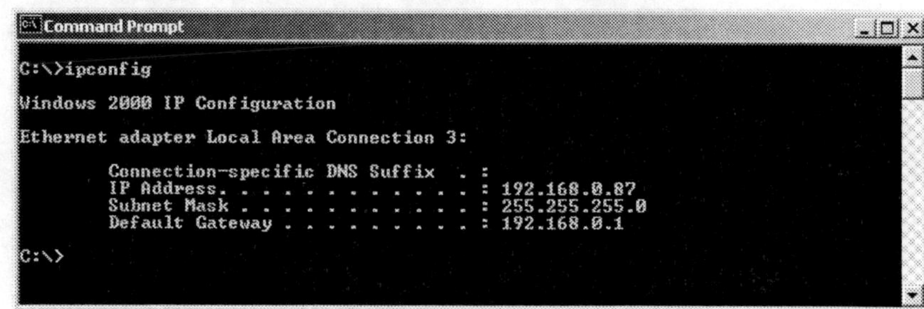

Basic IPconfig Results

The IPconfig utility is often used to verify IP addresses and default gateway assignments. However, by adding command-line switches, an administrator can also use it to change IP addresses

655

through DHCP, or view DNS mappings. The IPconfig Command-Line Switches Table lists these switches.

IPconfig Command-Line Switches

Switch	Effect
/?	Displays all command-line switches.
/all	Displays complete configuration details.
/release /renew	Releases or renews the IP address lease for a specified NIC. If no adapter is specified, the leases of all NICs bound to TCP/IP are released or renewed.
/flushdns	Purges the DNS resolver cache.
/registerdns	Refreshes all DHCP leases and reregisters DNS names.
/displaydns	Displays the contents of the DNS resolver cache.
/showclassid	Displays all DHCP class IDs allowed for a specified NIC.
/setclassid	Modifies the DHCP class ID.

For example, use the command **ipconfig/all** to see all TCP/IP configuration information for a computer, as shown in the IPconfig/all Diagram.

IPconfig/all

IFconfig Operation

IFconfig is a UNIX command-line utility that displays a computer's current TCP/IP configuration. It can also to used to set or change that configuration. Depending on the command-line switches used, if any, IFconfig can report all details, or only those specific to one interface or protocol family. See the IPconfig Command-Line Switches Table.

IFconfig Command-Line Switches

Switch	Effect
-a	Display details for all interfaces
-d	Report only on interfaces that are down
-u	Report only on interfaces that are up
-l	List all interfaces, without details (May be combined with -d or -u only)
-m	List the media supported by each interface

Ping

Objective 3.6
Identify when to use various diagnostic tools for resolving Internet problems.
… Ping

The quickest and easiest way to evaluate whether a computer is up and running and attached to a TCP/IP network is to use the command-line utility called ping. Ping tests to see whether a host on a TCP/IP network is reachable by sending an IP packet to that computer and requesting a reply.

Ping sends an Internet Control Message Protocol (ICMP) Echo Request message to a destination computer. The receiving computer responds by sending back an ICMP Echo Reply message. If the destination computer does not reply, that could mean any of these things:

- The destination computer is down

- Something is wrong with the network path (links, routers, etc.) between source and destination

- For security reasons, the destination is configured to not respond to ping

When using ping, you can specify the destination host by its IP address or its hostname. For example, typing **ping www. cudenver.edu** might give the results shown on the Ping Command www.cudenver.edu Screen Capture.

Ping Command www.cudenver.edu

There are several things that can be noted from the successful result of this Ping. First, the host computer's Web server IP process is up and running, because it returned a reply. We also know the IP address of this host (132.194.10.4). Ping also reports the round-trip time of each pair of request-reply packets.

ICMP messages are encapsulated within IP packets, so a successful ping confirms that two computers have good communication from the Network Layer down. Since ping messages can travel wherever IP packets can be routed, ping can detect connectivity problems in remote locations. Ping also works with any combination of TCP/IP hosts, so a Windows machine can ping a UNIX host, or vice versa.

Because ping can work with both hostnames and IP addresses, it is valuable for detecting problems with a network's Domain Name System (DNS). For example, if you can ping a remote host by IP address, but not by name, then you know that connectivity is working but DNS name resolution is not.

Command-Line Switches

By adding various command-line switches, you can use ping to report different types of information. These switches are listed in the Ping Command-Line Switches Table; you can also see them by simply typing **ping** from a command line.

Ping Command-Line Switches

Switch (n = number)	Effect
-t	Ping the destination until stopped (To stop, press Ctrl+C. To see statistics and continue, press Ctrl+Break)
-a	Resolves destination IP address to hostname
-n [n]	Specifies number of request messages to send
-l [n]	Specifies size of Echo Request message in bytes
-f	Sets the IP Don't Fragment flag to true
-i [TTL value]	Specifies the IP TTL value
-v [TOS value]	Specifies the IP Type of Service (TOS) value
-r [n]	Records router IP addresses for this number of hops
-s [n]	Records router time stamps for this number of hops
-j [host list]	Packets must use these routers, but may use others
-k [host list]	Packets must only use these routers
-w [n]	Specifies number of milliseconds that system should wait for each reply

If you use command-line switches, they must come after the ping command, and before the destination address or hostname. You may also combine more than one switch with a single ping command, as long as you separate them with spaces. For example, consider the following ping command:

```
ping -l 512 www.westnetinc.com
```

The -l switch allows us to specify the packet buffer size. By setting this to a large value, such as 512 bytes, we now have what is known as a "Fat Ping." This "Fat Ping" exercises the various network components between the end devices, testing for intermittent component or link failures.

If we want a better sample, we could add the -n switch to specify that 10 packets be sent:

```
ping -l 512 -n 10 www.westnetinc.com
```

Tracert or Traceroute

Objective 3.6
Identify when to use various diagnostic tools for resolving Internet problems.
... TraceRT

This command-line utility is called Tracert on Windows systems, and Traceroute on UNIX. By either name, it identifies each router that an IP packet goes through from source to destination across a TCP/IP network.

However, because IP routing is dynamic, the results of one trace may differ from a trace run a few minutes later. This effect depends on the extent of the trace and the size of the network. On a small network, perhaps with only one router, there may be only one possible path. But several traces across the Internet may reveal very different routing patterns.

Tracert measures a packet's round trip time by sending ICMP echo messages to a destination host. The sender sends packets in sets of three.

Each time a sender sends a packet set to a destination, the sending host increments the packet's Time-to-Live (TTL) field by one. For example, the sending host sets the first three packets' TTL field to 1. The first router "kills" the packets by decrementing their TTLs to 0 and sending back to the sender an ICMP response Message Type 11, indicating the packets' TTL has been exceeded.

The sender sets the next set's TTL to 2. The first router decrements each packet's TTL by one and forwards them on to the next hop router. The second router kills the packets (sets the TTLs to 0), and sends a response saying the TTLs have been exceeded. This procedure continues until the sending host contacts the final router, or the maximum hop count is reached. This allows the Tracert program to track which routers a packet goes through from source to destination.

If we simply type **tracert** with a host name, the program logs each hop along the way toward the final destination. For example, if we type **tracert www.cudenver.edu**, we will get the results shown on the Tracert Command **www.cudenver.edu** Screen Capture.

```
MS-DOS Prompt

Usage: tracert [-d] [-h maximum_hops] [-j host-list] [-w timeout] target_name

Options:
    -d                      Do not resolve addresses to hostnames.
    -h maximum_hops         Maximum number of hops to search for target.
    -j host-list            Loose source route along host-list.
    -w timeout              Wait timeout milliseconds for each reply.

C:\WINDOWS>tracert www.cudenver.edu

Tracing route to carbon.cudenver.edu [132.194.10.4]
over a maximum of 30 hops:

  1     2 ms     2 ms     2 ms  gateway.westnetinc.com [205.169.85.254]
  2     8 ms     7 ms     9 ms  den-edge-14.inet.qwest.net [205.169.243.9]
  3     8 ms     8 ms     8 ms  cnb7505.sni.net [205.169.234.254]
  4    10 ms    10 ms     9 ms  cuatm.inet.qwest.net [205.169.250.50]
  5    23 ms    25 ms    24 ms  denatm.inet.qwest.net [204.131.62.30]
  6    22 ms    37 ms    12 ms  chief100.cudenver.edu [132.194.100.1]
  7    43 ms    21 ms    22 ms  carbon.cudenver.edu [132.194.10.4]

Trace complete.

C:\WINDOWS>
```

Tracert Command www.cudenver.edu

This screen first shows the value of the TTL field in the IP datagram, beginning with 1, then 2, and so forth. It then shows the time it takes to get to a specific router. Every packet is sent three times to each router. In the example above, the first packet sent took 2 milliseconds (ms) to get from the client to the first router in the network. In general, the time increases with each hop because it is farther and farther toward the final destination. However, because of congestion and other variables, times do not always increase with the number of hops. The sixth router in the example above has a time of 12 ms, shorter than the previous packet's, using a TTL of 5. The last part of each line is the router IP address and name, if available.

The roundtrip times are calculated by the Tracert program on the sending computer. They are the total roundtrip times from the Tracert program to the router. If we are interested in the link time between routers, we have to subtract the time for TTL n from the value printed for TTL n + 1.

For example, if we wish to measure the roundtrip time between router 1 and 2, we would subtract the roundtrip time between the sending host and router 1 (n) from the roundtrip time from the sending host and router 2 (n + 1). The time from router 1 to router 2 is 9 ms – 2 ms = 7 ms. This calculation does not always work, however, as network conditions can vary widely over a matter of milliseconds.

Like ping, Tracert can reach as far as IP packets can be routed. It is often used to analyze network traffic patterns.

Command-Line Switches

Tracert has only a few command-line switches, which you can see by entering **tracert** from the command line. The command-line switches are listed in the Tracert Command-Line Switches Table.

Tracert Command-Line Switches

Switch	Effect
[none]	Displays all command-line switches
-d	Do not resolve IP addresses to hostnames
-h [n]	Specifies maximum number of hops to search for destination
-j [host list]	Packets must use these routers, but may use others
-w [n]	Specifies number of milliseconds that system should wait for each reply

Netstat

Netstat is a command-line utility that displays the active connections for the local computer. (You must run it on the computer to be analyzed.) To see a basic list of active connections, type **netstat** at the command line. The Netstat Command Screen Capture shows an example of this display.

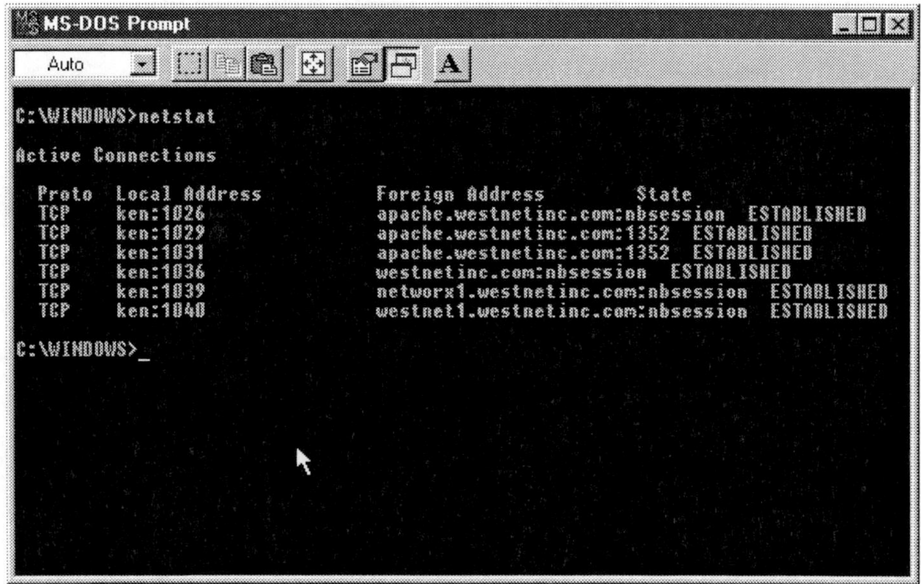

Netstat Command

This screen shows that TCP is the protocol being used. It also shows the port numbers that are active for each session. For example, there are current active sessions with the Web server (Apache server software running on a Linux box). Local port numbers 1026, 1029, and 1031 are being used, and the server is using port number 1352. HTTP sessions often open multiple TCP connections, and this is the case here.

**Command-Line
Switches**

By adding command-line switches, Netstat can analyze a wide range of network problems and conditions, such as traffic volumes, hung connections, IP routing, and bad packets. See the Netstat Command-Line Switches Table.

Netstat Command-Line Switches

Switch	Effect
/?	Displays all command-line switches
-a	Displays both TCP and UDP connections
-e	Displays Ethernet NIC statistics, including numbers of incoming and outgoing frames, discarded frames, and unknown protocols received
-r	Displays the current route table and default gateway
-s	Displays traffic statistics by protocol
-n	Combine with other switches to display IP addresses instead of hostnames
-p	Combine with other switches to specify one protocol (Example: netstat -s -p UDP)

**Repeating a
Netstat
Command**

You can tell Netstat to automatically repeat by adding a time value to the end of the command. For example, the following command runs Netstat every 30 seconds until you press Ctrl+Break:

```
Netstat -a 30
```

ARP

Objective 3.6
*Identify when to use various diagnostic tools for resolving Internet problems.
... ARP*

If two hosts on the same network wish to communicate, they must know more than each other's IP address. They must also know each other's physical address so they can use Data Link Layer protocols to transmit datagrams on the local media. Address Resolution Protocol (ARP) maps IP addresses to Data Link Layer addresses, such as Ethernet NIC addresses.

How ARP Works

Assume that Host A needs to transmit data to Host B, but does not have Host B's physical address. To learn Host B's physical address, Host A broadcasts an ARP request packet that contains Host B's IP address. The ARP request asks that the host with the specified IP address respond with its NIC address.

All hosts on the network receive the broadcast request, including those connected by bridges or switches. However, only Host B recognizes its IP address, and transmits an ARP reply that contains its NIC address. Host A now has the physical address it needs to send packets to Host B over the local network. Host A then stores this address in its ARP cache. When Host A next needs to communicate with Host B, it will first check its ARP cache for the NIC address.

ARP for Troubleshooting

You can use the ARP command to inspect a local computer's ARP cache, change the contents of the cache, or return the NIC address of a computer with a known IP address.

ARP is useful for detecting IP address resolution problems, such as two computers that have received the same IP address (either from an administrator, or from two different DHCP servers). Once you detect a duplicate address, you can also use ARP to remove the bad address from a computer's ARP cache.

Command-Line Switches

The ARP command requires at least one command-line switch. Enter **arp** at the command line to display a list of these switches, which are described in the ARP Command-Line Switches Table.

ARP Command-Line Switches

Switch	Effect
-a or -g	Displays the ARP cache
-d [IP address]	Deletes an IP address from the ARP cache
-s [IP address] [NIC address]	Maps an IP address to a NIC address, and adds that mapping to the ARP cache

Troubleshooting

Type **ARP -a** to display the contents of an ARP cache. The result of this command is shown in the ARP - a Command Screen Capture.

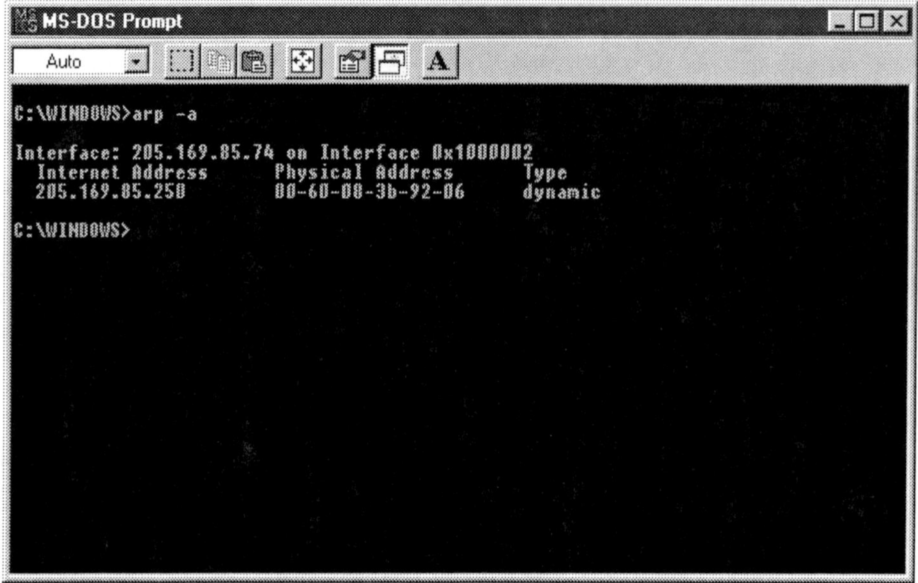

ARP -a Command

This screen indicates there is one entry in the ARP cache, the IP address of a computer on the network. We can use the Nbtstat command to discover the NetBIOS name of the computer that is assigned this IP address, or we can ping the IP address.

Changing the ARP Cache

The -d and -s switches allow us to delete or add entries to the ARP cache. For example, to delete the entry from this ARP cache, the command is:

```
arp -d 205.169.85.250
```

If no address conflicts exist, you can also change the contents of the ARP cache by sending information to another computer. To do this artificially, we might use the ping command. For example, if we ping the www.cudenver.edu host and then display the ARP cache, we get the results shown on the Ping www.cudenver.edu Display ARP Cache Screen Capture.

```
MS-DOS Prompt

 205.169.85.250        00-60-08-3b-92-06       dynamic

C:\WINDOWS>ping www.cudenver.edu

Pinging carbon.cudenver.edu [132.194.10.4] with 32 bytes of data:

Reply from 132.194.10.4: bytes=32 time=43ms TTL=58
Reply from 132.194.10.4: bytes=32 time=22ms TTL=58
Reply from 132.194.10.4: bytes=32 time=16ms TTL=58
Reply from 132.194.10.4: bytes=32 time=21ms TTL=58

Ping statistics for 132.194.10.4:
    Packets: Sent = 4, Received = 4, Lost = 0 (0% loss),
Approximate round trip times in milli-seconds:
    Minimum = 16ms, Maximum =  43ms, Average =  25ms

C:\WINDOWS>arp -a

Interface: 205.169.85.74 on Interface 0x1000002
  Internet Address      Physical Address      Type
  205.169.85.240        00-60-97-9d-32-06     dynamic
  205.169.85.250        00-60-08-3b-92-06     dynamic
  205.169.85.254        00-c0-7b-6e-12-35     dynamic

C:\WINDOWS>
```

Ping www.cudenver.edu Display ARP Cache

The last entry in the ARP cache shows the IP and NIC addresses of the destination computer. In this case, it is the router of the internal network that provides connectivity to the Internet. ARP only caches addresses on the local network segment; if a destination host is on another subnet, then ARP cannot obtain the destination host MAC address. Because we pinged an external Web server (**http://www.cudenver.edu**), we had to go to the router first (205.169.85.254). The router was then responsible for getting the Hypertext Transfer Protocol (HTTP) request from the internal network to the Internet, where it was sent on to the final destination.

NSlookup

Objective 3.3
Understand and be able to describe the use of Internet domain names and DNS.
... NSlookup

The NSlookup utility is used to troubleshoot DNS servers, because it reports the mapping of IP addresses to DNS hostnames. NSlookup is available for UNIX, Windows NT, and Windows 2000, but not Windows 95/98.

To use NSlookup, you must know the hostname or IP address of a DNS server, or your computer must be configured with the address of a default DNS server. Once you have this information, there are two ways to use the utility:

- **Interactive mode**—To start interactive mode with your default DNS server, type **nslookup** at the command line. To contact a specific DNS server, add that server's name or address. For example:

```
nslookup nameserver1
```

  The NSlookup program provides a command prompt (>). At that prompt, enter a hostname or IP address to resolve. If you enter a hostname, the DNS server provides the corresponding IP address. If you enter an IP address, it provides the hostname. To exit the program, type Ctrl+C.

- **Noninteractive mode**—At the command line, type **nslookup**, followed by either the IP address or hostname that you want to resolve, plus the address or hostname of the server. For example:

```
nslookup mysteryhost nameserver1
```

To see a list of NSlookup commands, type **help** at the interactive command prompt, or use the noninteractive command **nslookup/help**.

Protocol Analyzers (Sniffers)

Objective 3.6
Identify when to use various diagnostic tools for resolving Internet problems … Network analyzer

Because computer protocols were designed to be understood by machines, it is a lot faster and easier to let machines, called protocol analyzers, work with them. Protocol analyzers detect patterns of network operation by capturing and reading frames. For example, a protocol analyzer can identify a device that is sending out too many broadcast frames, or one that is consistently transmitting damaged frames. These tools fall into two main categories:

- WAN analyzers capture data on external links, such as Point-to-Point Protocol (PPP), Frame Relay, ATM, and others. It uses special interface cards to read frames off a WAN connection. Additionally, WAN analyzers are typically connected to the wide area line with a "Y" connector. This allows the monitor to capture traffic as it flows normally across the link.

- LAN analyzers capture and display frames from LAN protocols such as Ethernet, Token Ring, and FDDI. These analyzers are connected to the LAN segment by means of a hub or a switch, just like any other node. However, when a protocol analyzer is connected to a switch port, it will only capture information directed to the switch port it is connected to. For that reason, certain switches allow us to designate a monitor port and an analyzer port. In that case, all traffic appearing on the port that is being monitored will be copied to the analyzer port.

Components of a LAN Protocol Analyzer

A LAN protocol analyzer has two components:

- Hardware may be a dedicated portable computer temporarily connected to the LAN, or a computer that is permanently part of the LAN. The key hardware element is a NIC that is set to operate in "promiscuous mode." That simply means that the NIC eavesdrops on all traffic on its segment. It copies and processes all frames, not just those addressed to it.

- Proprietary software interprets frames and packets, and detects useful trends and patterns.

Popular protocol analysers include Network Associates' Sniffer, Hewlett-Packard's LAN Advisor, Novell's LANalyzer, NetXray's Sniffer Basic, Shomiti Systems' Surveyor, and the freeware Ethereal protocol analyzer (distributed under the GNU General Public License). Sniffer originally dominated the analyzer market, thus many network professionals use the word "sniffer" to refer to any protocol analyzer.

Note: Get permission from your network administrator before you install or run a protocol analyzer. If you don't, your experiment may be misinterpreted as a security attack.

**Protocol
Analyzer Traces**

One of the simplest services of a protocol analyzer is to translate data streams into a neatly formatted report, called a trace, that is easier for humans to understand. An example trace is shown here:

```
DLC:  ----- DLC Header -----
DLC:
DLC:  Frame 1 arrived at 23:33:39.6638; frame size is 60 (003C hex) bytes.
DLC:  Destination = BROADCAST FFFFFFFFFFFF, Broadcast
DLC:  Source      = Station WstDig488C11
DLC:  Ethertype  = 0806 (ARP)
DLC:
ARP:  ----- ARP/RARP frame -----
ARP:
ARP:  Hardware type = 1 (10Mb Ethernet)
ARP:  Protocol type = 0800 (IP)
ARP:  Length of hardware address = 6 bytes
ARP:  Length of protocol address = 4 bytes
ARP:  Opcode 1 (ARP request)
ARP:  Sender's hardware address = WstDig488C11
ARP:  Sender's protocol address = [128.1.0.2]
ARP:  Target hardware address = 000000000000
ARP:  Target protocol address = [128.1.0.1]

ADDR  HEX
ASCII
0000  FF FF FF FF FF FF 00 00  C0 48 8C 11 08 06 00 01   .........H......
0010  08 00 06 04 00 01 00 00  C0 48 8C 11 80 01 00 02   .........H......
0020  00 00 00 00 00 00 80 01  00 01 00 00 00 00 00 00   ................
0030  00 00 00 00 00 00 00 00  00 00 00 00               ............
```

As you can see, the protocol analyzer has helpfully identified both the frame header (Data Link Control [DLC] header) and the encapsulated ARP request. It also includes the data in hexadecimal format. The numbers at the beginning of the hexadecimal lines simply identify each line of that part of the trace. To the right of each line of hexadecimal is the ASCII representation of the hexadecimal. When the application data is in ASCII format (such as word processor text or e-mail), this display makes it easy to read.

Protocol analysis tools offer many other sophisticated services, beyond simple trace generation. Many display network statistics in a user-friendly "dashboard" format that shows overall network health at a glance. Network administrators can configure some analysis packages to monitor the network, and sound an alarm if key statistics exceed a defined threshold. The most sophisticated analyzers even include expert systems that detect broader trends and suggest likely problems.

Troubleshooting

Activities

1. Refer to the Winipcfg screen shot used earlier in this lesson to answer the following questions:

    a. What is the class of IP address in this network?

    ____

    b. How many subnets are used in this network?

    ____

    c. What part of the IP number is associated with KEN, and what part of the IP number is the network portion?

    ____

    d. What is the speed of the portion of the network where this device is connected?

    ____

2. Name the ping command that will accomplish each of the following:

    a. Send two pings to 10.100.0.36, and repeat every two minutes.

    ____

    b. Ping 10.100.0.36, and record the addresses of the first six routers.

    ____

    c. Continuously ping 10.100.0.36.

    ____

3. From your office in Newark, NJ, you use Tracert to list the Internet routers between you and Microsoft, in Redmond, WA. When you do this again ten minutes later, why do you see several different routers listed?

    ____

    ____

    ____

4. What command would you use for each of the following tasks?

    a. Force a workstation to renew its IP address lease

    b. Delete the ARP cache entry for the IP address 192.168.35.1

    c. See what protocol generates most of a computer's traffic

5. What is a protocol analyzer used for?

6. Using the hexadecimal detail located in the lesson, identify the following key portions of the ARP request:

    a. Sender's IP address

    b. Sender's MAC address

    c. Destination IP address

Extended Activities

1. If you have a Windows-based computer, use Winipcfg or Ipconfig to inspect your TCP/IP configuration. List your findings.

2. Ping a computer on another network, then repeat that ping. Notice that if two ping commands are issued one after the other, the second is much quicker. This is because the first ping most likely requires an ARP request to resolve the destination IP address to the destination MAC address. The second ping is faster because it uses the information in the ARP cache. Sample sites to ping are:

   a. westnetinc.com (Arvada, CO)

   b. beijing.gov.cn (Beijing, China)

   c. dartmouth.edu (Hanover, NH)

   d. cudenver.edu (Denver, CO)

   e. shakespeare-globe.org (United Kingdom)

   f. microsoft.com

3. Test each of the ping switches to see how each can be used when troubleshooting a network.

4. Trace the route to the sites listed in Activity 2. Use various command-line switches and record your results.

Lesson 3—Troubleshooting an Unreachable FTP Site

As network administrator, you are responsible for all servers and user workstations on the company LAN. Your employer is a well-known Business-to-Business marketing consulting firm. The company president has been toying with the idea of hosting web sites for their clients, and using these sites to gather potential sales lead information.

She offers this service to a new customer, who promptly signs up and states they want their site up in one month. A third-party site development firm will create the web site, but the web server configuration and connectivity issues are your job.

You take an older file server out of storage, load the latest version of Linux, and configure the Apache web server. The site developers have established a location on their FTP server from which you can download the latest site updates. From your Windows 2000 administrative workstation you download the original client site files and copy them to a CD. You then copy the files from the CD to the appropriate web server directory.

But the developers change the site contents weekly. Rather than copy each update to a CD, and then copy from the CD to the web server, you want to use FTP to download updates to your workstation, then use FTP to copy the files from your workstation to your web server. You have used this method many times before.

Objectives

At the end of this lesson you will be able to:

- Explain how a computer's role as a server is determined by the applications it runs and the protocols it supports

- Identify the main security problem with FTP, and describe the minimum security safeguards necessary for an FTP server

 **Key Point**

FTP has both client and server components.

Troubleshooting

The Problem

When you try to set up an FTP connection between your workstation and web server, the transfer attempt fails. You need to resolve this communications problem, so the web server will accept FTP uploads from your workstation.

Establish the Symptoms

When the FTP transfer attempt fails, the results are shown in the FTP Attempt Diagram.

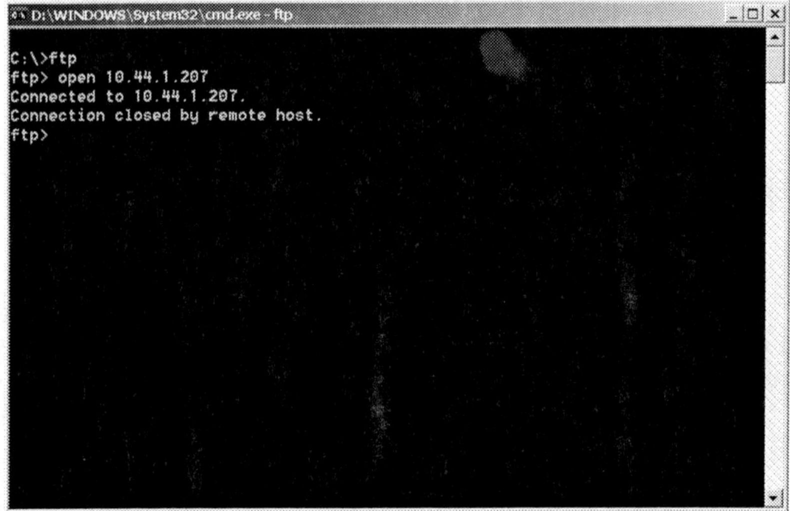

FTP Attempt

Identify the Affected Area

You can browse the hosted web sites from both the local network and from remote networks. This tells you that both the web server and TCP/IP are working properly.

Establish What Has Changed

You have successfully used FTP to transfer files to and from your workstation. The most recent change was the setup of the new Linux computer.

Select the Most Probable Cause

Objective 3.2
*Identify problems with Internet connectivity from source to destination for various types of servers
… FTP server*

Objective 3.5
*Understand how various protocols or services apply to the function of their corresponding server
… FTP*

Upon installation, Linux allows you to choose which application and service packages you wish to run on the server. Because HTTP and FTP are separate protocols that provide different application layer functions, Linux loads them individually. This leads you to suspect that the problem lies with the FTP protocol.

You open the server's package manager application, and look at the loaded applications list. You notice that upon server configuration you only loaded the FTP client, not the server. With the FTP client, a computer can connect to an FTP server, but it cannot accept FTP connection requests from other clients. So the most likely cause of this problem is that the Linux computer is functioning as a Web server, but not as an FTP server.

Implement a Solution

You locate the FTP server application and tell the package manager to install it. The package manager asks for the root password (if you are not currently logged in as root), and installs the application.

Test the Result

You then locate the FTP daemon, start it, and attempt again to connect from your workstation to the server. The FTP Server Connection Diagram illustrates the results.

FTP Server Connection

Recognize the Potential Effects of the Solution

Your problem is solved, because you can now use FTP to connect to the Web server computer and upload the site updates. However, FTP uploads may create a serious security hole for this Web server if crackers are able to use FTP to upload malicious applications or replace Web pages with vandalized content. Therefore, before the Web server is placed in public service, you must tighten security on the FTP service. At the minimum, you must disable anonymous logins, and create a strong administrative password.

Document the Solution

Objective 3.2
Identify problems with Internet connectivity from source to destination for various types of servers.
... FTP server

This troubleshooting process has revealed two important things to remember:

- When setting up a new Linux-based Web server, remember to install the FTP server

- Create security safeguards to protect the server from attacks uploaded via FTP

Since your company intends to sell more Web site hosting services, you'll need this information again soon. If business is good, you may also need to train new staff. Therefore, capture these two points as part of a complete manual that describes how to set up a new Web server.

Activities

1. For security reasons, your Chief Technology Officer refuses to allow you to install an FTP server on any Web server. He does not object to an FTP client, however. Can you still use FTP to transfer new Web site files to the Web server computer? If so, how?

____

____

____

____

____

2. The client loves the new web site, but also wants to use the server computer as a mail server. Based on what you've learned in this problem, what should you check?

____

____

____

____

____

Extended Activity

FTP has several well-known security problems. Summarize these problems, and the most common solutions, in a short report.

Lesson 4—Troubleshooting an Unreachable Web Site

In this lesson, you will use various tools to troubleshoot an Internet access problem. Several of your network's users have been unable to connect to a company Web site that is hosted at an off-site location.

Objectives

At the end of this lesson you will be able to:

* Identify the steps required to troubleshoot IP connectivity problems

* Use IP troubleshooting tools to locate and isolate the problem

* Choose the correct course of action to resolve the problem

 **Key Point**

Internet connectivity depends on many different factors.

The Problem

Users on your network complain that they intermittently receive browser messages stating the company's Internet site is unreachable. You are to isolate and correct the problem.

Establish the Symptoms

When users attempt to access the company site, **http://www.big dotcom.com**, the browser window shows an "HTTP 404 Not Found" message. If they refresh the page, sometimes the home page loads and the error goes away, but at other times it does not.

You are able to re-create the problem from any browser on the company LAN. You use only one vendor's browser.

Identify the Affected Area

The problem is widespread across all internal network users, but it exists only inside the LAN. You verify, by contacting external customers and professional acquaintances, that external users experience no problems connecting to the site.

Establish What Has Changed

When the problem occurred, users were performing routine tasks. You look in the network maintenance logs and talk to your coworkers. The only recent network change is a new router installed to replace a failed router on your Internet connection.

Select the Most Probable Cause

Objective 3.2
Identify problems with Internet connectivity from source to destination for various types of servers.
... Web server
... DNS server

Because the Web server is located offsite, the new router is a possible cause. If it is misconfigured or malfunctioning, it could prevent the LAN from reaching the Web site. However, there are other potential causes:

- Internal client TCP/IP settings are incorrect

- Internal browsers are misconfigured

- An internal network component is faulty (switch, bridge, or hub)

- There is a problem at your Internet service provider (ISP)

- There is a problem at your Web site hosting firm

This is a fairly long list of potential problems, so you must eliminate as many of these as you can. If possible, you can gradually narrow the list down to the one problem source.

Note: It is not uncommon for the solution to include more than one option on the potential problem list. Often, a problem is caused by a combination of individual issues, so fixing one problem will not correct the failure. The only way to be sure of your solution is to test thoroughly after implementing it.

Because potential causes are located both on the local network and at remote locations, you must systematically test each point on the LAN and work outward, eliminating each potential cause along the way. Although you could have just as easily chosen to work from the outside in, general troubleshooting techniques work from the inside out, eliminating those areas for which you are responsible. This also provides reinforcing documentation in case you run into resistance from the network support personnel of the ISP or the hosting firm. With good troubleshooting documentation, you stand a better chance of obtaining their cooperation in resolving the problem.

The IP Troubleshooting Diagram illustrates the various points on the network where you will test.

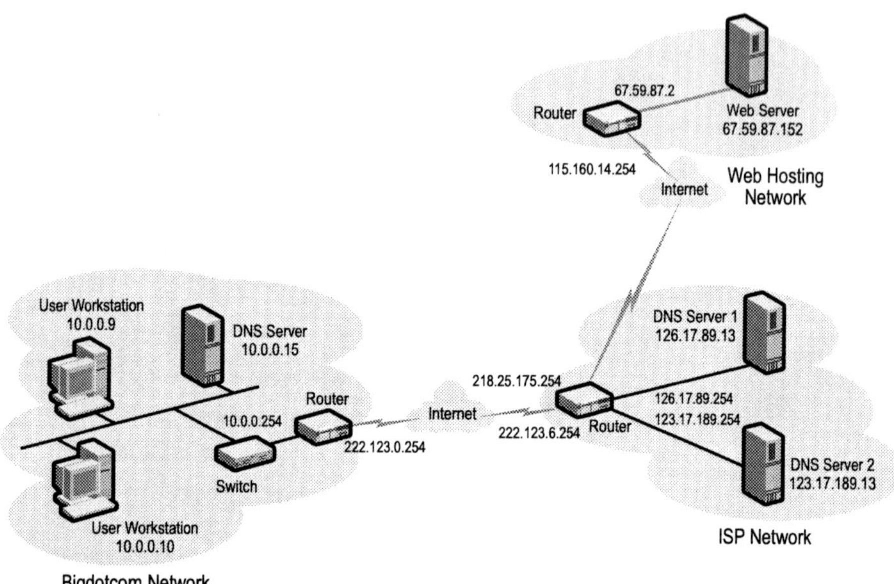

IP Troubleshooting

The various network devices are assigned the following IP addresses:

- The Bigdotcom network uses the following addresses:
    - 10.0.0.0/8 IP address range
    - The router's internal address is 10.0.0.254/8
- The local DNS Server address is 10.0.0.15/8
    - The router's external address is 222.123.0.254/24
- The ISP router uses the following addresses:
    - External to Bigdotcom, 222.123.6.254/24
    - External to the Web hosting firm, 218.25.175.254/24
    - Internal to DNS Server 1, 126.17.89.254/24
    - Internal to DNS Server 2, 123.17.189.254/24

- The ISP provides two DNS servers:
    - DNS Server 1 with address 126.17.89.13/24
    - DNS Server 2 with address 123.17.189.13/24
- The Web hosting firm's router addresses are:
    - External to Internet, 115.160.14.254/16
    - Internal, 67.59.87.2/8
- The Web server address is 67.59.87.152/8

You will test in phases, starting with the local network, then moving on to test communications with your ISP and the Web hosting firm.

Testing Internal Communications

Objective 3.6
Identify when to use various diagnostic tools for resolving Internet problems.
… Ping
… ARP

You choose host 10.0.0.9 as your internal test host and verify that this host has the same symptoms as the others. You then begin testing:

1. First, you successfully ping the local loopback address, 127.0.0.1, to test that TCP/IP is working on the test host.

2. Next, you successfully ping the test host's address, 10.0.0.9. This verifies that TCP/IP works to the NIC port.

3. You successfully ping another network host, host 10.0.0.10. This successfully verifies communications on the network.

4. You successfully ping the local DNS server, 10.0.0.15. This verifies communications with the local DNS server.

5. You then successfully ping host 10.0.0.10 by its fully qualified domain name (FQDN), host10.bigdotcom.com. This verifies that the local DNS server resolves the name host10.bigdotcom.com to the correct IP address, 10.0.0.10.

6. Next, you successfully ping the local router's internal port address, 10.0.0.254. This verifies that you can communicate with the router.

7. You successfully ping the router's external address, 222.123.0.254. This verifies that the router can route packets to the outside network.

Note: This step may fail if the router uses access control lists (ACL) or packet filters to block Internet Control Message Protocol (ICMP) replies. Many networks use these filters to protect the internal network from denial of service attacks. If this is the case, then you will have to modify the filters or ACLs, or try some other testing method, such as Telneting to the external router port.

8. You can, if you wish, examine the test host's ARP cache contents for the IP-to-MAC address mappings for all contacted hosts. You should at least see entries for those devices you have pinged in the last two minutes. Remember that a router does not pass ARP broadcasts; thus, instead of an entry for the router's external port MAC address, you will see the internal port MAC address.

Testing ISP Communications

Your next step is to test communications with your ISP. You will probably need to coordinate your efforts with the ISP support staff, because it's likely that they also block ICMP replies. Your documentation of your troubleshooting efforts to this point will be helpful here. To test your ISP communications:

1. First, you successfully ping the ISP's external router port address, 222.123.6.254. This verifies communications across the link that connects your network router to the ISP router.

2. You then successfully ping the ISP router's internal ports, 123.17.189.254 and 126.17.89.254. This verifies the ISP router routes and switches packets correctly.

3. You ping DNS Server 1, 126.17.89.13, by name and address. The ping by address succeeds, but the ping by name fails intermittently. You note this in your troubleshooting logs.

4. You ping DNS Server 2, 123.17.189.13, by name and address. Because you were sometimes unable to ping DNS Server 1 by name, you ping both name and address several times. All pings succeed.

5. You successfully ping the ISP router's external interface to the Web hosting firm's network, address 218.25.175.254. This verifies that the router can switch and route packets to our Web server host's network.

Now you know that pings by name to the ISP's DNS Server 1 fail intermittently. However, rather than prematurely identify the ISP's DNS server as the most likely cause, you choose to continue testing to verify that all is well with the Web host's network.

Testing Web Host Firm Communications

As with the ISP's network, this round of testing will probably require the cooperation of the Web host's network support group:

1. First, you successfully ping the hosting firm's external router address, 115.160.14.254. This verifies that you can contact the Web hosting firm's network.

2. Next, you successfully ping the firm's inside router port, 67.59.87.2. This verifies that the hosting firm's router can route and switch packets.

3. You successfully ping your Web server by address, 67.59.87.152, several times. This verifies that you can communicate with your Web server.

4. You ping the Web server by name, **http://www.bigdot com.com**, several times. This ping fails intermittently. You first see the ping succeed to address 67.59.87.152. Later, you see it fail and present a message stating "Bad IP address www.bigdotcom.com."

Tallying the Test Results

The first round of tests showed that your internal network is functioning correctly. However, external testing revealed the following symptoms:

- Pings by IP address always succeed

- Pings by name to DNS Server 1 intermittently fail

- Pings by name to your Web server intermittently fail

Based on these symptoms, you conclude that you have an intermittent name resolution problem.

Isolating the Cause

Objective 1.4
Understand and be able to describe the infrastructure needed to support an Internet client ... DHCP

Objective 3.2
Identify problems with Internet connectivity from source to destination for various types of servers
... Web server
... DNS server

Objective 3.6
Identify when to use various diagnostic tools for resolving Internet problems
... WinIPcfg

Since name resolution failures occur only for external hosts, it is likely that your internal DNS server is functioning properly. However, you must also verify that your clients are configured to use the correct DNS servers to resolve names. You look at a client TCP/IP configuration using the Winipcfg utility, and find that the clients are configured to use DNS servers 10.0.0.15, 126.17.89.13, and 123.17.189.13. These addresses match those of the three DNS servers you use to resolve names internally and externally. Thus, you determine that your clients are configured correctly.

By now, the most probable cause of the problem is one of the ISP's DNS servers. The next step then is to isolate the servers, to determine which one is failing. Because your clients download their TCP/IP configurations from a local DHCP server, including their DNS server information, you decide to manually configure your local test host, to exclude one of the external DNS servers from its list. Because DNS Server 1 failed, you remove its entry from the test host's DNS configuration first, as shown on the Test Host DNS Configuration Screen Capture. This will force the client to use DSN Server 2 for external name resolution, and your local DNS server for internal resolution.

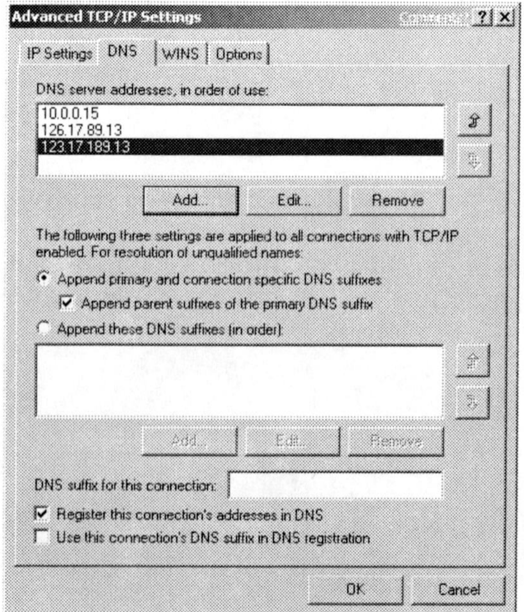

Test Host DNS Configuration

You attempt several pings by name to DNS Server 1, and they succeed each time. You then attempt several pings by name to **http://www.bigdotcom.com**, and again they succeed each time.

You then reconfigure your local test host to use only the local DNS and DNS Server 1, removing the address for DNS Server 2. This time, both pings fail by name, but still succeed by address.

Therefore, the most likely cause of the problem is a malfunction of the ISP's DNS Server 1.

Implement a Solution

Objective 1.4
Understand and be able to describe the infrastructure needed to support an Internet client ... DHCP

You contact your ISP and suggest that there might be a malfunction on DNS Server 1. They troubleshoot, and find there is a problem with the DNS server software. They suggest you reconfigure your clients to use an alternate DNS server, DNS Server 3, using IP address 126.17.89.14, leaving the DNS Server 2 entries intact.

Because you use DHCP to download client TCP/IP configuration information, including IP addresses, the subnet mask, the default gateway address, and DNS server information, you easily set up your DHCP scopes with the new DNS information. To force your test host to renew its DHCP lease and receive the new settings, you open Winipcfg and select the Renew button.

Test the Result

You then ping by name both of the ISP DNS servers and the Web server; all three pings succeed. You use the test host's browser to contact our Web site, and find that the site comes up each time.

You report the solution to your help desk. The support technicians contact each user who called about this problem, and ask them to renew their DHCP leases and contact the Web server again. In a short time, the help desk reports back that those users can now connect to the company site.

Recognize the Potential Effects of the Solution

Objective 1.4
Understand and be able to describe the infrastructure needed to support an Internet client
... DHCP
... Client software configuration

So far, the problem is solved only on those hosts that have manually renewed their DHCP leases and DNS settings. It will require a great deal of time and effort to manually renew the leases of all network hosts. Furthermore, most company employees don't check the company Web site very often, and don't notice the problem.

You explain to the help desk manager that the remaining internal clients will renew their leases in a maximum of three days. Together, you agree to wait for each client to download the new DNS information on the next lease renewal cycle. If users call the help desk with access problems, the support staff will instruct them to run Winipcfg and select the Renew button to manually update the DNS server information.

Document the Solution

Your help desk uses a problem tracking database to record all computer and network problems. When users first called with complaints, the support technicians recorded the problems. When you reported the problem and the resolution, that information was added to those problem records. So, by working closely with your company help desk, your documentation is already done.

Activities

1. How do you verify that TCP/IP is working on the local host?

   a. Ping the default gateway

   b. Ping the subnet mask

   c. Ping the wire address

   d. Ping the local loopback address

2. How can you verify that name resolution is working correctly?

   a. Ping the local loopback address on the DNS server

   b. Ping one or more network hosts by both name and address

   c. Ping the DNS server by IP address to verify it is operational

   d. Ping the local host by name and IP

3. Which ping tests would indicate that TCP/IP is working correctly on a network segment? (Choose three.)

   a. Ping the local IP address

   b. Ping other local segment hosts by IP address

   c. Ping the local network segment router port

   d. Ping the local loopback address

4. Which TCP/IP client/server service would allow an administrator to quickly reconfigure host configuration information?

   a. DNS

   b. DHCP

   c. ARP

   d. RARP

5. When troubleshooting a problem that crosses network responsibilities, most network professionals agree that is it best to start with the local network and work out. Which one of the following is NOT a reason for this approach?

   a. It allows us to eliminate and resolve any internal problems first.

   b. It provides information we can use to support our case, if the problem proves to be external to our network.

   c. It eliminates the need for cooperation from outside sources, if troubleshooting moves outside the local network.

   d. It breaks up the troubleshooting effort to specific areas of responsibility.

Extended Activity

Ask one of your local ISPs how its technical support staff would have handled the scenario presented in this lesson. How much troubleshooting would you have been required (or allowed) to do from a private LAN? How much troubleshooting would the ISP have done for you?

Lesson 5—Troubleshooting a Firewall Problem

You provide remote network support to several small companies. You use a remote control program to access your customers' servers and workstations over Virtual Private Network (VPN) connections.

Today is a typical day. Before you can begin to troubleshoot one problem, you must solve another.

Objectives

At the end of this lesson you will be able to:

- Explain how router port mappings affect VPN operation

- Identify technical practices that could have prevented this problem

Key Point

Router configuration is a major element of a firewall solution.

The Environment

Objective 3.7
Create a logic diagram of Internet components from the client to the server.

Your customers have high-speed Internet access over ISDN or ADSL connections. Each customer's router runs Network Address Translation (NAT) and a firewall. The firewall provides inbound port and IP address filtering capabilities and VPN services. A typical network looks as shown in the Customer's Network Diagram.

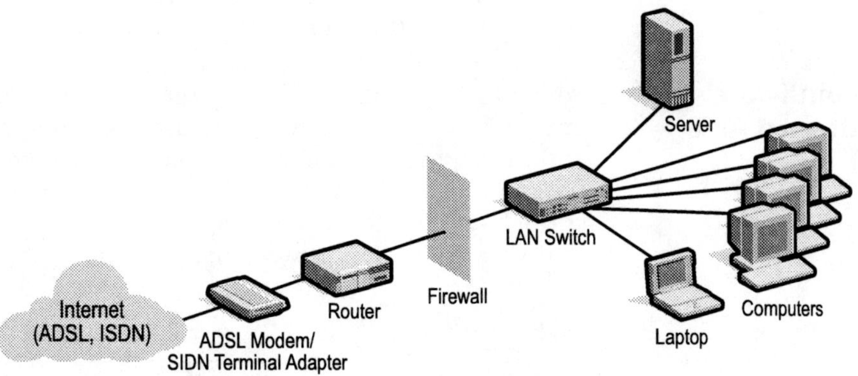

Customer's Network

Troubleshooting

Objective 3.2
*Identify problems with Internet connectivity from source to destination for various types of servers
… Connecting through a firewall*

Objective 4.7
Describe how firewalls are used to protect private networks … Port filtering

The router's NAT software maps each inbound connection to an internal server, depending on the destination application's TCP or UDP port number. Your VPN client requests a Point-to-Point Tunneling Protocol (PPTP) connection on TCP port 1723 on the router's outside port IP address. The router in turn maps this inbound connection request to the firewall's outside port IP address and TCP port 1723. The firewall either allows or disallows the connection, based on the credentials your client passes to the VPN server. Once the tunnel is established and you obtain an IP address from the VPN server, you can connect to the target server's remote control service.

The Problem

One of your customers, a small heating and plumbing company located in Colorado, recently took a lightning hit on its ISDN line. The CO's equipment was unharmed, but your customer's ISDN Terminal Adapter (TA) and router were irreparably damaged. Your customer hired a local network integrator to install and configure a new TA and router.

Establish the Symptoms

About a week after the integrator replaced the TA and router, your customer calls to report reduced file server performance. To troubleshoot the file server problem, you must log on to the server remotely, so you sit down at your management workstation and open your VPN client. You request a connection to the customer's VPN server via the router's outside port IP address, but the VPN connection to the router fails.

Identify the Affected Area

Your VPN client has worked all morning, connecting to other clients' VPNs. This makes you doubt that the problem is at your end. You ping the client's outside router port address, and the ping succeeds. Thus, you are now sure that you have Internet connectivity up to the customer's router, and you are mostly sure that your VPN client is working.

Establish What Has Changed

This client site has recently replaced two important elements: the ISDN Terminal Adapter and the router. However, you know that the ISDN TA is functioning because you can ping the router.

Select the Most Probable Cause

So far, most clues point to the new router as the most probable cause. To confirm this, you must inspect the router's settings. You bring up a Telnet session with the router, and attempt to log in using your administrative username and password. This login attempt fails, and the router returns a message that the username and password are unknown. This tells you that your authentication settings were not transferred to the new router.

Objective 4.1
Understand and be able to describe various Internet security concepts ... Access control

At first, it seems as if you won't be able to log in and check the router's settings. But then you remember that many router installers neglect to change the default username and password for Telnet sessions. You use the defaults, and successfully log in.

Pause to Administer First Aid

Before continuing to troubleshoot the original VPN problem, you decide to repair this gaping hole in the router's security. You change the administrator's default username and password to a new set, only known to you. You log out, then Telnet back in with your new username and password.

Continue to Isolate the Problem

Now you can get back to checking the router's configuration. You find that the network integrator also failed to re-create the router's inbound to outbound PPTP port mappings. Without these mappings, the router cannot route inbound traffic to the firewall. You have now identified the most probable cause of this problem.

Implement a Solution

You add a rule that maps the inbound connection port to the firewall's outside port IP address and the PPTP well-known TCP port number. The Port Mapping Diagram illustrates the mapped entries.

Port Mapping

As shown on the diagram, the first rule maps any undefined ports to a specific internal IP address. In this example, undefined ports map to address 0.0.0.0. The second rule makes your VPN connection possible. It maps any inbound connections for TCP port 1723 to the internal network device 10.1.30.200:1723. This mapping says that the router will forward inbound service requests for TCP port 1723 to the internal network server with the IP address 10.1.30.200 listening on port 1723. Rule 12 is reserved by the router operation system.

Test the Result

You save your port mapping changes and close the Telnet session. To test your solution, you open your VPN client, and again attempt to connect to the VPN server. This time the connection succeeds. Now, you can finally open the remote control software on your management workstation, request a connection to the customer's file server, and use the various server diagnostic tools to locate and resolve the original server performance problem.

Recognize the Potential Effects of the Solution

As part of your VPN solution, you made two configuration changes to your client's new router:

- Reset the default Telnet username and password to a new set known only to you.

- Added a port mapping rule to enable inbound VPN connections.

These changes should merely return the client's network to its original configuration.

Document the Solution

To be certain, however, you should tell your customer about the problems you discovered and the solution you applied. This information has important implications for your customer's network security. And, with any luck, this knowledge will remind your customer to be more selective when hiring installation technicians in the future.

Activities

1. In this scenario, several immediate or potential problems were caused by the integration technician who installed the new router. How could the installer have prevented some or all of these problems?

____

____

____

____

2. What would happen if you had mistakenly entered port 1724 in the router's port mapping rule instead of 1723?

____

____

3. How would the customer's VPN be changed by replacing the ISDN line with an FT1 line?

____

____

Extended Activity

Use a search engine to locate product descriptions of VPN software. Summarize and compare the features of several applications.

Lesson 6—Troubleshooting a Home Office DSL Problem

You run a small web site development company, working with clients all over the country. Your DSL connection is an essential business tool that makes it possible for you to work from home and minimize operating expenses. This lesson shows how an orderly approach to troubleshooting can keep this lifeline intact.

Objectives

At the end of this lesson you will be able to:

- Recognize the meaning of indicator lights on an ADSL access device

- Explain how Internet connectivity works in this home office network

Key Point

Documentation is important when we don't find a problem's cause.

The Environment

Objective 1.4
Understand and be able to describe the infrastructure needed to support an Internet client.

Objective 3.7
Create a logic diagram of Internet components from the client to the server.

You connect to the Internet over a 640-Kbps (downstream) ADSL connection. Your home network appears as shown in the Home Network Diagram.

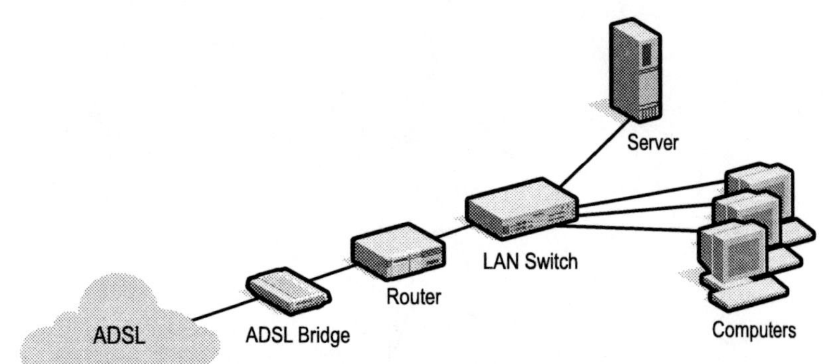

Home Network

The ADSL access device works in bridging mode; that is, it merely passes Layer 3 and above traffic directly between your internal Ethernet network and your carrier's ADSL line. The router runs NAT, acting as a rudimentary firewall by hiding your internal network addresses from the public Internet. Your ISP's DHCP server provides you with one dynamically assigned IP address, and the router acts as a DHCP client. The ISP's DHCP server times out the address lease every 24 hours, requiring your router to renew its address every night at midnight.

Your router acts as a DHCP server for the internal network hosts, with the exception of the web server. Your internal clients' lease times are set to renew every six days. You use a scope of private IP addresses on your internal network.

The Problem

You work odd hours, sometimes working late, or starting early. You start early one morning, and bring up your development workstation and web server. You are able to connect to your own web server, but when you try to access a customer's site located on an Internet hosting service, the connection fails.

Establish the Symptoms

The following error message appears in your browser window, as shown in the Browser Error Diagram.

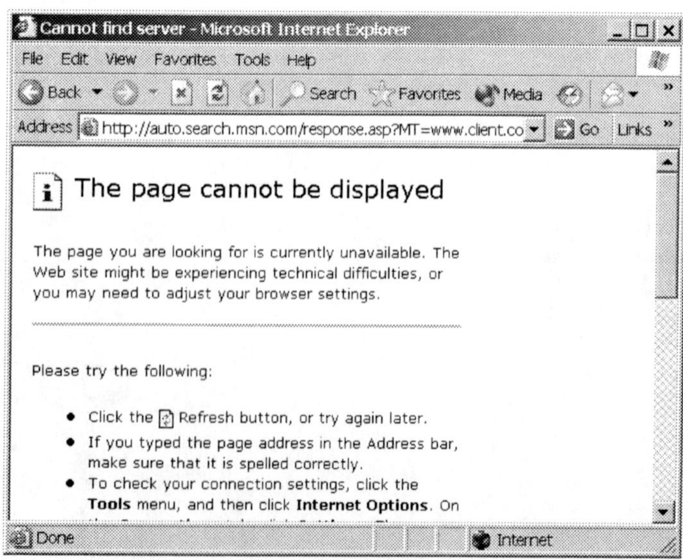

Browser Error

Identify the Affected Area

__Objective 3.6__
Identify when to use various diagnostic tools for resolving Internet problems ... Ping

There are many reasons why a browser will receive this "file not found" message. To determine whether the problem lies with the client's Web server, you try to access several other sites. These attempts also fail.

Since you can browse locally, but not over the Internet, you deduce that the problem is likely your Internet connectivity. You confirm this when you are unable to ping your ISP's router. However, your Internet connection is established over several different devices, any one of which might be the source of the problem. To isolate the affected area, you decide to work outward, from your workstation toward the ISP.

Since you can communicate across the local network, you conclude that your LAN switch is working. The router is next in line, but you decide to first look at your ADSL bridge to verify the line is up, because it has simple indicator lights that display the status of your connection. The number and arrangement of these status indicators vary, depending on the manufacturer and model, but the typical indicators are shown on the ADSL Bridge Indicators Diagram.

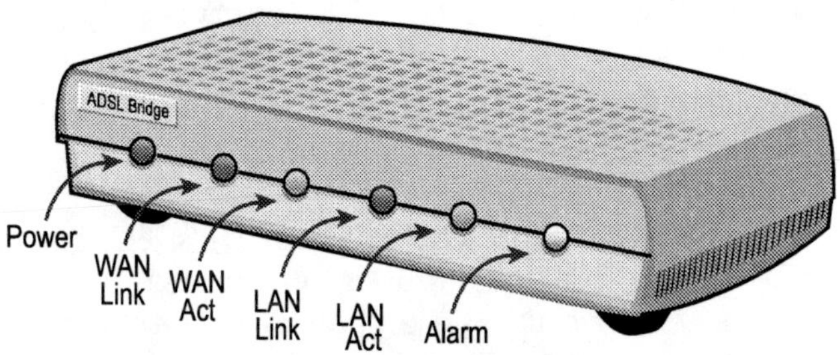

ADSL Bridge Indicators

The WAN and LAN link indicator are both green, which indicates a good ADSL line connection, as well as a good Ethernet link. The WAN and LAN activity lights blink occasionally, indicating that some traffic is traversing the ADSL line. The Alarm indicator is dark.

You manage the ADSL bridge over a serial link, and through this link you observe that the line is connected to the central office (CO). You also see that the bridge has been "trained," or optimized for current line conditions, by exchanging test signals with the DSLAM at the CO.

The bridge indicators show that the Physical and Data Link Layer protocols are functioning properly. Since the bridge passes Layer 3 and above traffic directly between your router and your ISP's network, you conclude that something is amiss at the Network Layer. Now it's time to look at your router.

Establish What Has Changed

You Telnet into your router, and bring up the screen that illustrates the LAN and WAN interface status. You have assigned the LAN interface a permanent IP address from the internal network; however, the WAN interface (which obtains its address dynamically from your ISP) shows no IP address assigned.

So the factor that has changed is that your router has lost its external IP address. Based on the flickering of the DSL bridge's WAN activity light, you assume that the traffic across the bridge's WAN interface is the router requesting a new address. But the router routinely gets a new address every midnight, so the question now is why the router is not receiving its new address.

Select the Most Probable Cause

By now, you've isolated the problem to three potential areas:

- Your router may not be communicating its address request properly

- The ISP's DHCP server may not be responding to the address request

- Your ADSL bridge may not be properly transmitting the router's request or the DHCP server's response

Before you call your ISP's tech support, you must finish checking all possibilities on your end. So, for now, your most probable cause is a problem with either the router or the bridge. You have already inspected both of their settings, so now it's time to try the time-honored computer cure: reboot.

Implement a Solution

You manually initiate an IP address request from your router, and the request fails. You try both a soft (reboot) and hard (power off/on) reset on the router, each time attempting to request an address; again each request fails. You then turn your attention to the bridge.

You try a hard reset on the bridge, and watch as the bridge cycles through its self-test. You then tell the router to request an address, and the request succeeds.

Test the Result

You ping your ISP's router, and the ping succeeds. You then open your browser, and are able to connect to your client's web site.

Recognize the Potential Effects of the Solution

For now, you've fixed your Internet connection. However, you still don't know the root cause of the problem. Today's bridge problem may never occur again, or it may be the first occurrence of a string of intermittent problems that will signal the gradual failure of the ADSL bridge.

Document the Solution

If the bridge is starting to fail, you'll need documentation to support a warranty claim. Because your ADSL connection is essential to your business, you'll also want to replace the bridge before it fails completely. Therefore, you must record as many details as you can about this problem. With those notes, you can recognize the problem if it ever happens again, and notice if its frequency begins to increase.

Activities

1. In this scenario, your home network includes a Web server. Based on what you know about this environment, is this server used for internal testing, or to host a public Web site? What single clue justifies your answer?

   ____

   ____

   ____

   ____

2. How would this network's configuration change if the ADSL bridge were replaced with an ADSL router?

   ____

   ____

   ____

   ____

Extended Activity

Use a search engine to locate product descriptions of DSL access devices. Summarize and compare the features of several devices.

Summary

This unit discussed the methods and tools used to test Internet sites before they go live, and troubleshoot them when they fail.

The goal of Web site testing is to ensure that each site component—such as server platform, site content, scripts, or databases—functions properly by itself and in combination with other components. Since the failure of any single component can shut down or degrade site performance, each piece of a site must be tested using a consistent, disciplined method.

To troubleshoot an Internet problem, a technician must understand the role and function of each component, and how it relates to other links in the chain between user and Web site. To give you a feel for this approach, this unit presented several Internet troubleshooting scenarios that concentrated on the software tools commonly found with implementations of TCP/IP.

To inspect the configuration of client computers, you can use Winipcfg, Ipconfig, or Netstat. To understand the connectivity of a network, use ping or Tracert. To explore possible name resolution problems, use ARP or NSlookup. Protocol analyzers, or "sniffers," analyze all traffic on a segment, and summarize their findings in statistical displays.

Using these tools effectively requires careful study. But it's important to recognize that studying alone will not make you a great troubleshooter. Problem solving, like most skills, improves with practice and experience. Some people have an inherent talent for troubleshooting, just as others are talented at music or sports. However, even naturally-talented problem solvers still rely on a combination of study, practical experience, careful observation, and disciplined methods. Your problem solving will improve quickly if you follow their example.

Troubleshooting

Unit 9 Quiz

1. Which SDLC makes it easier to predict the time needed to complete a project?

    ____

2. You are part of a team developing a new Web site that makes medical research information available to the public free of charge. Which of the following should you include in your stress testing plan?

    a. Database

    b. Internet connection

    c. Credit card processing

    d. Search engine

3. Which of the following statements correctly describes a waterfall life cycle?

    a. It creates never-ending projects.

    b. It handles project changes easily.

    c. It makes cost and time estimates difficult.

    d. It is defined by distinct stages.

4. Which of the following statements correctly describes a spiral life cycle?

    a. It slowly adapts to new requirements.

    b. It does not allow developers to incorporate feedback into their product.

    c. It allows developers to loop through all stages of the project several times.

    d. It makes cost and time estimates easy.

5. Which of the following shows the IP address assigned to a PC running Windows 95/98?

    a. IFconfig

    b. Winipcfg

    c. IPconfig

    d. PCconfig

6. Which of the following commands shows the path between source and destination in a TCP/IP network?

    a. Ping

    b. Winipcfg

    c. Tracert

    d. Nbtstat

7. Which of the following confirms connectivity between hosts?

    a. Ping

    b. Winipcfg

    c. Netstat

    d. Nbtstat

8. What should you use to inspect the IP address of a Windows 2000 PC?

    a. Ping

    b. Winipcfg

    c. IPconfig

    d. IFconfig

9. Which of the following troubleshooting tools tells you the distance, in hops, to the destination computer?

    a. Ping

    b. Winipcfg

    c. Tracert

    d. Nbtstat

10. Tracert uses which of the following commands and IP fields to carry out its operation?

    a. Ping and header

    b. Nbtstat and trailer

    c. Ping and TTL

    d. Ping and type

Troubleshooting

11. Which two TCP/IP tools can you use to force a workstation to renew its DHCP lease? (Choose two.)

    a. Netstat

    b. Nbtstat

    c. Winipcfg

    d. Ipconfig

12. Which TCP/IP tool is the fastest and easiest method to evaluate whether a host is available across a TCP/IP network?

    a. Winipcfg

    b. Telnet

    c. Nbtstat

    d. Ping

13. You are troubleshooting a communication error on a TCP/IP network. Your users complain that whenever they try to connect to your new Internet Web site, **http://www.newserver. com**, the connection fails.

    You attempt a connection to the site from your workstation, and that too fails. However, you try to connect to the Web server by IP address, and it succeeds. You suspect that your ISP entered the Web server in their DNS incorrectly.

    The server is configured as follows:

    IP address–125.38.79.124

    FQDN–www.newserver.com

    Which command can you issue to verify that name resolution is the cause of the problem?

    a. Ipconfig 125.38.79.124

    b. Ping 125.38.79.124

    c. Ping www.newserver.com

    d. Ipconfig/all

14. Which key combination will terminate a continuous ping?

    a. Ctrl+S

    b. Ctrl+C

    c. Ctrl+Esc

    d. Ctrl+T

15. To determine the path your IP packets take to reach a remote office router, you issue the Tracert command from a local network host, targeted at the remote office routers outside interface. Previous tracert replies showed the router nine hops away, so you set the Tracert command's maximum hops option to 10.

    You ping the remote router interface, 191.67.17.2, and it succeeds. You issue the command Tracert -h 10 191.67.17.2, but the tracert result does not list the router interface's IP address. Which might be a reason why this occurred?

    a. You did not include the subnet mask in the Tracert command.

    b. DNS is not correctly resolving the name Tracert to an IP address.

    c. Your ISP has added routers between your local and remote network.

    d. You should have issued the Tracert command by name, not by IP address.

16. Your customer called and stated that they have installed a new border router in their subnetted network. This router supports CIDR, and they are excited that they can now advertise a single network route to the Internet, instead of the six they had advertised before.

    They own the Class C address range 220.68.0.0/18, and use the following class C network addresses on their internal network segments:

    220.68.7.0

    220.68.11.0

    220.68.17.0

    220.68.21.0

    220.68.23.0

    220.68.24.0

They state that some of the networks can no longer connect to Internet services. You Telnet into their border router and look at the routing table entries. You see that their router administrator configured their router to advertise the following internal network:

220.68.0.0/21

Which of the following might be the problem's cause?

a. The router is not passing route information to the ISP router.

b. They do not own all the addresses specified in the advertised network.

c. The CIDR prefix is incorrect for this range of addresses.

d. The internal routers must also support CIDR.

17. Which ARP command option shows the contents of the local ARP cache?

a. ARP -a

b. ARP -c

c. ARP -N

d. ARP -s

18. Which two of the following might cause a ping across network boundaries to fail? (Choose two.)

a. Pinging by name instead of IP address

b. Access Control Lists on the router ports

c. ICMP filters on the router ports

d. Pinging a host on an indirectly connected network

Unit 10
Security

A company's Web site is often called its "electronic storefront," because the Internet now serves as just another "place" for businesses to sell products, communicate, exchange funds, and advertise. Although the Internet has provided an environment for the growth of new kinds of legitimate business operations, it has also become a new turf for criminal activity.

Every business protects its physical storefront from known threats by including protective measures, such as strong door locks, burglar alarms, and security guards. Any crime that threatens the brick-and-mortar world has an equivalent form on the Web, such as online vandalism, theft, embezzlement, fraud, espionage, and terrorism. Despite this fact, many businesses have not invested the same level of effort to protect their online activities.

This unit introduces some of the most basic concepts and techniques in computer security. However, security is a broad and complex field that changes constantly as motivated criminals learn new tricks. Thus, consider this unit to be a starting point for your continued study of this important topic.

Lessons

1. A Layered Approach to Security
2. Security Management
3. Internet Firewalls

Terms

ActiveX Control—ActiveX control is a broad category of software components that can be downloaded and run by a Web browser to add extra functionality to a Web page. ActiveX, developed by Microsoft, is an outgrowth of two technologies: Object Linking and Embedding (OLE) and Component Object Model (COM).

asymmetric encryption—See public-key encryption.

brute-force attack—A security attack that tries to break a code by simply testing each possibility until it finds the right one is referred to as a brute-force attack.

certificate authority (CA)—A CA is an organization that creates digital certificates for individuals and servers, after verifying the identity of those persons or sites. A CA signs each digital certificate with its own digital signature; thus, vouching for the identity and trustworthiness of the owners of the certificates.

clipper chip—This microprocessor chip contains an 80-bit single-key encryption algorithm. It uses a key-escrow system in which two decryption keys are separately held in escrow by the U.S. Treasury Department and the National Institute of Standards and Technology (NIST). A law enforcement agency could gain access to the keys through a court order.

common carrier—A company that must offer its services to all customers at the prices and conditions outlined in a public record is referred to as a common carrier.

Common Gateway Interface (CGI)—CGI is a standard specification for creating Web server programs that accept data from Web clients, process the data, and return a result. For example, each HTML form needs a corresponding CGI program to process form data sent to its Web site. CGI programs can be written in a variety of languages, including C, Perl, Visual Basic, and Java.

Common Internet File System (CIFS)—CIFS allows clients to use the Internet to access and share files on remote servers. The CIFS protocol runs over TCP/IP, and is an enhanced version of the Server Message Block (SMB) protocol used by Windows operating systems.

Data Encryption Standard (DES)—DES is a popular single-key encryption system that uses a 56-bit key. Triple-DES uses the DES algorithm to encrypt a message three times, using three 56-bit keys. Because hardware is faster than software, it is considered a hardware solution to encryption because of the time necessary to encrypt and decrypt a message.

default gateway—A gateway or router where TCP/IP sends packets addressed to remote networks is referred to as a default gateway.

digital certificate—A digital certificate is a unique electronic file used to authenticate a user, program, provider, service, or transaction. Usually, the certificate consists of a file containing a copy of the user's or service's public encryption key, along with the signature of a trusted person verifying that the key does, indeed, belong to the user or service claimed. A CA creates a certificate, and the certificate is encrypted in a way that makes it impossible to forge.

digital signature—A digital signature is a digital code that can be embedded into a document to prove its authenticity. Digital signatures are an application of public-key encryption technology. The sender of a document uses a private encryption key to encrypt a text string or the digest of the message. Document recipients use the sender's public encryption key to decrypt the signature and authenticate the sender.

Domain Name System (DNS)—DNS is a distributed database that maps IP addresses to host names in a TCP/IP network.

Dynamic Host Configuration Protocol (DHCP)—DHCP provides configuration parameters to Internet hosts. DHCP consists of two components: a protocol for delivering host-specific configuration parameters from a DHCP server to a host and a mechanism for allocation of network addresses to hosts. DHCP is built on a client/server model, where designated DHCP server hosts allocate network addresses and deliver configuration parameters to dynamically configured hosts.

ECMA Script—ECMA Script is a standard object-oriented scripting language derived largely from Netscape's Java Script. The European Computer Manufacturers Association (ECMA) supervised the development of ECMA Script to provide a Standard, Cross-browser language for Web scripting. However, like Java Script, ECMA Script may also be used to create non-Web applications.

event—An event is any significant occurrence in a system or application that requires users to be notified or an entry to be added to a log file.

frame relay—A frame relay is a packet-forwarding WAN protocol that normally operates at speeds of 56 Kbps to 1.5 Mbps.

Security

hash algorithm—A hash algorithm is a mathematical formula used to generate a number from a variable-length text string. Commonly used in security applications, a hash creates an encrypted number sent along with a message that the recipient decrypts to verify the message's integrity.

Hypertext Transfer Protocol (HTTP)—HTTP is the Application Layer protocol used to request and transmit HTML documents. HTTP is the underlying protocol of the Web.

Integrated Services Digital Network (ISDN)—ISDN is a WAN technology used to move voice and data over the telecommunication network. ISDN operates at speeds of 144 Kbps to 1.5 Mbps.

International Data Encryption Algorithm (IDEA)—IDEA is a block encryption algorithm that was first published in 1990.

Internet Protocol (IP)—IP is a Network Layer protocol responsible for routing a packet (datagram) through a network. It is the "IP" in "TCP/IP."

Internet Protocol Security (IPSec)—IPSec consists of a set of IETF protocols, under development, to support secure IP packet communication. When completed, IPSec is intended to implement VPNs.

Internet service provider (ISP)—Companies that provide Internet access to individuals and businesses are referred to as ISPs. ISPs typically provide a range of services necessary to provide corporate networks and other users with dedicated or dial-up access to the Internet.

Internetwork Packet Exchange (IPX)—IPX is Novell NetWare's proprietary Network Layer protocol.

intranet—An intranet is a network that uses Internet applications, but is designed for use only by the personnel of a company or organization; that is, it is a "private internet."

Java—Java is an interpreted, platform-independent, high-level programming language developed by Sun Microsystems. Java is a powerful language with many features that make it attractive for the Web.

JavaScript—JavaScript is an interpreted, client-side scripting language developed by Netscape. All major browsers offer built-in support for JavaScript, and can interpret blocks of JavaScript code embedded in an HTML page. An international open standard called ECMAScript is based on JavaScript.

Kerberos—Kerberos is a UNIX-based user authentication system for client/server networks.

local loop—A local loop is the pair of copper wires that connects a customer's telephone to the LEC's CO switching system.

message digest 5 (MD5)—MD5 is a one-way hash algorithm that converts a message into a fixed string of digits called a message digest. It is used to create digital signatures.

modem—Modem is a contraction for modulator/demodulator. Modems are used to convert binary data into analog signals suitable for transmission across a telephone network.

Network Address Translator (NAT)—NAT is a system that allows an administrator to use one set of IP addresses within a LAN, and another set for external traffic. NAT can shield internal addresses from public networks, and make more efficient use of a few globally unique IP addresses.

permission—A rule associated with an object (usually a directory, file, or printer) that regulates which users can have access to the object and in what manner is referred to as a permission.

Practical Extraction and Report Language (Perl)—Perl is an interpreted programming language designed for processing text. Because of its strong text-handling features, Perl has become one of the most popular languages for writing server-side CGI scripts.

Pretty Good Privacy (PGP)—PGP is the most commonly used asymmetric encryption (public-key method) application for protecting messages across the Internet.

public-key (asymmetric) encryption—Public-key encryption is a cryptographic system that uses two mathematically related keys: one key is used to encrypt a message, and the other to decrypt it. People who need to receive encrypted messages distribute their public keys, but keep their private keys secret.

remote access service (RAS)—A RAS is normally used in the context of Windows NT and the ability to access NT and LAN services from a remote location.

RSA—The acronym RSA stands for Rivest, Shamir, and Adelman, the inventors of a widely used public-key encryption algorithm. The RSA encryption algorithm has become the de facto standard for industrial-strength encryption across the Internet.

Secure Hash Algorithm-1 (SHA-1)—SHA-1 produces a 160-bit message digest from a message shorter than 264 bits. It is slightly slower than MD5, but more secure. A revision to SHA-1 is specified in SHA.

Secure Sockets Layer (SSL)—SSL is an application of both public-key and single-key encryption that secures an Internet connection between browser and server. Web-page URLs that use SSL begin with "https://."

security policies—Policies governing security, including Account, User Rights, Audit, and Trust Relationship policies, are referred to as security policies.

Serial Line Internet Protocol (SLIP)—SLIP is not an official Internet standard, but a de facto standard included in many implementations of TCP/IP. It was originally developed for use over dedicated circuits or leased lines, and therefore does not include provisions for establishing a connection over the telephone network.

Simple Mail Transfer Protocol (SMTP)—SMTP is an Internet protocol for transferring e-mail.

smart card—A plastic card that contains embedded IC microprocessors and a standard magnetic strip is referred to as a smart card. A user inserts a smart card into a chip-reading terminal, which reads the information stored on the card. Smart cards can eliminate the need for users to remember passwords and other authentication information.

tunneling—The process of encapsulating one network protocol within the packets of another is referred to as tunneling. For example, tunneling can be used to encapsulate various network protocols within IP packets for transmission across the Internet. The encapsulated data is encrypted, creating a secure VPN.

virus—A virus is a self-replicating malicious program that spreads by attaching itself to a shared or copied file. Viruses create effects that range from mildly irritating to highly destructive.

worm—Like viruses, worms are malicious programs. However, worms do not attach themselves to other files. They actively copy themselves to different computers, often by using e-mail.

Lesson 1—A Layered Approach to Security

Providing an effective network security strategy is a balancing act. To protect the network from threats, both external and internal, an administrator must erect as many barriers and defenses as possible. This multiple-layered approach greatly reduces the chances of a site being breached because, generally speaking, most intruders are not patient. They do not want to spend time battling several different types of obstacles when attempting to access a computing environment.

However, multiple layers of safeguards are potentially frustrating for a network's users, and can interfere with their ability to perform productive work. Therefore, a network designer must balance the need for safety against users' need for convenience.

This need for balance means no system can provide 100 percent security and still be usable. However, several key security technologies present real barriers to criminals while remaining fairly transparent to users. In this lesson, we will consider the technologies and architectures that can safeguard both your organization's network and its productivity.

Objectives

At the end of this lesson you will be able to:

- Name and briefly describe some of the key layers of an overall security solution

- Explain the challenges inherent in user authentication

- Describe the difference between single-key (symmetric) and public-key (asymmetric) cryptography

 **Key Point**

If a security system becomes a barrier to productivity, users will likely find a way around it.

Security Threats

Threats to network security come in several forms. A great deal of attention is paid to deliberate threats originating from viruses and criminals; however, accidental damage can be just as devastating. Whether intentional or not, information losses generally fall into three categories:

- Modification

- Destruction

- Disclosure

Intentional Attacks

A person who wants to cause one of these types of damage can attack a computer networking system in a number of ways:

- Criminal hackers (crackers)—Insiders or outsiders motivated by the thrill of breaching a secure system without detection. Crackers tend to be more concerned about developing subtle techniques for penetrating systems and are not necessarily interested in stealing data. In contrast, the term "hacker" generally refers to a highly skilled and clever programmer.

- Script kiddies—Unskilled intruders, often teenagers, who use readily-available programs or methods to exploit known weaknesses in Internet hosts. Unlike hackers, script kiddies have little understanding of the systems they penetrate, and are more interested in getting attention.

- Viruses and worms—Self-replicating, destructive programs that damage executable programs and network data in a variety of ways.

- Trojan horses—Covert programs hidden in system or application software that wait to suddenly destroy information using predetermined parameters. Once inside a system, some Trojan horses can also use e-mail messages to transmit confidential data out of an organization. Unlike viruses and worms, Trojans do not self-replicate.

- Denial of service—This type of attack leads to disruption of system availability by crashing or overloading a critical device such as a server, router, or firewall.

- Theft of information—The attacker, often an insider, acquires proprietary information such as trade secrets or business plans. This can be done by eavesdropping on network transmissions, masquerading as an authorized entity, or a brute-force attack such as the use of a computer program that guesses passwords.

- Corruption of data—The attacker either destroys or corrupts data stored on disk or corrupts data as it is transmitted across a network.

Network Vulnerabilities

Threats to the availability, ownership, and integrity of information assets can arise at any of the locations shown on the Security Threats Diagram.

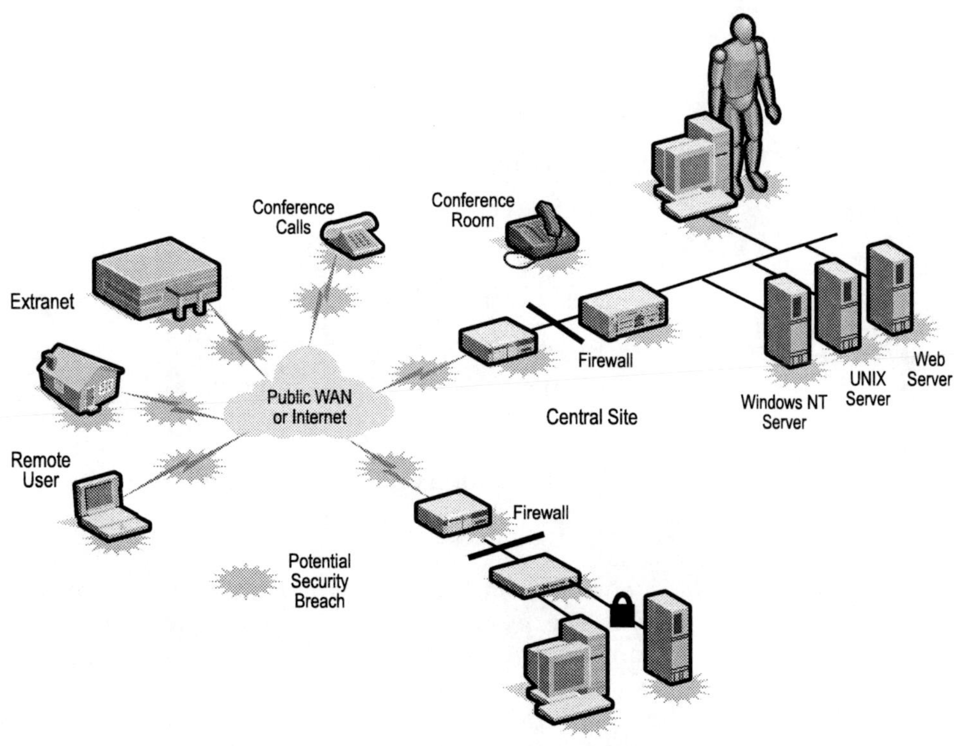

Security Threats

Potential security threats include:

- Careless users who reveal passwords or lose access cards

- Internal network connections such as routers and switches

- Interconnection points such as gateways between corporate intranets and the Internet

- Third-party network carriers such as long distance carriers and Internet service providers (ISPs)

- Application-level imposters, eavesdroppers, and attackers

Layers of Security

Objective 4.1
Understand and be able to describe various Internet security concepts
… Access control
… Authentication
… Encryption-PKI
… Secure socket layers (SSL)
… Access security tools
… Auditing
… Secure Electronic Transactions (SET)

Because a network has many layers of vulnerability, security requires a layered management approach that protects data from both unintentional and malicious damage. Depending on the security needs of an organization, these protective layers should include some or all of the following:

- Security policy

- User awareness training

- Physical security

- Encryption

- Access control

- User authentication

- Firewalls

- Internet Protocol Security (IPSec)

- Virus prevention and detection

- Security management

An enterprise may employ any or all of these elements in a comprehensive security solution. Establishing impenetrable security at one point of attack, while leaving other points uncovered, is like posting a guard at the front desk and leaving the company's doors and windows wide open. An attacker will try every avenue of entry, particularly if the value of the information is great and access is relatively easy.

Security Policy

An overall corporate security policy identifies the systems and data that must be protected, and describes the amount of protection appropriate to each system. A security policy also forms the basis of user training and an end-user acceptable use policy, that helps protect an organization from simple mistakes or malicious actions by its own employees.

User Awareness Training

One of the most important features of an overall security policy is an end-user training program. User training is vital, because the best network security measures will not protect an organization against an employee who shares sensitive data, gives away a password, or installs shareware infected with a virus.

A good user education program should clearly describe the company's security measures, procedures, and policies, and explain the reasons for the policies.

Acceptable Use Agreement

After completing this training, each employee should sign a formal agreement that clearly states the acceptable use of corporate network and Internet resources, including specific guidelines for:

- Password use and secrecy

- Information that may be transmitted over e-mail, including definitions of sensitive and confidential information

- External access policies that define what type of internal resources and information may be accessed by external users, and what actions may be performed (add, change, read, delete, and/or download) on data accessed by external users

- Rules for downloads and virus protection

- Acceptable World Wide Web (Web) site access for business use, or personal use of business equipment

- Rules protecting intellectual property, copyrights, patents, or software licensing

- Ethical, moral, and social issues related to the corporate culture, such as the appropriate content of e-mail messages

- Company monitoring of employees' online activities

Monitoring

To ensure the security policies and acceptable use guidelines are being followed, it is often necessary to establish some sort of automated monitoring. Various technologies and applications, implemented at the access points to computing resources, can collect data about user access and traffic patterns. Firewalls can create log files listing access requests from users and potential security crackers.

Some monitoring technology goes beyond passive data collecting, to actively controlling user access to certain categories of Web sites. For example, if a corporate policy forbids the use of company resources for shopping or sports, a blocking application can prevent it.

Enforcement

An important component of a user education program is a formal Human Resource policy that outlines possible disciplinary actions that can be taken by the company if an employee violates the agreement. To make this policy effective, senior management must demonstrate a firm commitment to Human Resource actions that enforce the security policies.

Although this level of commitment may seem heavy-handed, it is important to remember that not all threats are external. The Federal Bureau of Investigations (FBI) Computer Crime Unit reports that more than 80 percent of all network security breaches are inside jobs committed by disgruntled or dishonest employees. Your company's user-level security policy may constitute its first, best line of defense.

Physical Security

Physical security risks most often involve access to machines or people. A number of strategies can be used to enhance physical security:

- Provide a secure physical environment for the server (at a minimum, lock the door) that safeguards its console, keyboard, and monitor. Physical access to a computer is a common opening to an intruder. Depending on the level of physical security needed, organizations may use receptionists, security guards, physical keys, combination or electronic door locks, or other access controls.

- Destroy sensitive documents, including disks, when no longer used. Sophisticated tools can reconstruct files supposedly erased from a disk. Only destroying the disk itself guarantees the destruction of the data it once contained.

- Store digital encryption keys on smart cards, not on disks. Disks can be duplicated; smart cards are more difficult to copy.

- Keep passwords and personal identification numbers (PINs) secure. Remind users to avoid writing passwords down, sending them through e-mail, or placing them in messages that are archived or incorporated in group discussion systems.

Explain that writing a PIN on an ID card is as obvious as hiding the front door key under the door mat.

- Lock down portable equipment. As the U.S. State Department now knows all too well, a laptop computer represents one of the greatest physical threats to a security system, because it contains a great deal of information and can so easily be carried off. The same is true of other portable devices such as external disk drives, tape backup systems, and the like. These devices must be locked away or bolted to the desk to guard against theft. BIOS-level passwords can help safeguard laptops in the field; however, the best protection is user awareness.

Encryption

Objective 1.1
Identify the issues that affect Internet site functionality ...Security, including Data encryption

*Objective **3.10***
Given a scenario, predict the impact of a particular security implementation on network functionality

*Objective **4.6***
Be able to describe the uses and proper instances to use various client security add-ons ... Encryption software

*Objective **4.9***
Understand and be able to describe various authentication/encryption technologies.

Even if both access control and authentication security systems are completely effective, an enterprise can still be at risk when data communications travel over a third-party network such as the Internet. Indeed, the low cost and ease of connecting to the Internet have made it an extremely attractive medium for communication within and between enterprises.

Encryption prevents eavesdropping by making data unreadable to all except those who have the key needed to decrypt the data. It does not matter whether a third party intercepts packets over the Internet; the data still cannot be read. This approach can be used throughout the enterprise network, including within the enterprise (intranet), between enterprises (extranet), or over the public Internet to carry private data in a virtual private network (VPN).

Encryption is the process of scrambling data by changing it in a series of logical steps, called an encryption algorithm. To increase security, an encryption algorithm uses a numerical pattern, or "key," to guide the scrambling process. This means different algorithms and keys will each produce data scrambled, or encrypted, in different patterns. There are two main methods of encryption:

- **Single-key, or symmetric, encryption** uses the same key to both encrypt and decrypt the message. Therefore, both the sender and recipient must have the same key before they can exchange coded messages. Symmetric encryption systems include Data Encryption Standard (DES), 3DES, RC5, International Data Encryption Algorithm (IDEA), and other algorithms that are extremely fast. Their strength lies in the length of the key and the difficulty of analyzing the encrypted data.

- **Public-key, or asymmetric, encryption** uses a pair of encryption keys for each party that needs to receive encrypted information. Each key in the pair acts as a one-way channel. One key (either one) is used to encrypt data; the other is used to decrypt the data. Data encrypted with one key cannot be decrypted with the same key, only with its corresponding "partner" key. To use public-key encryption, a person or organization freely distributes its public encryption key and safeguards the corresponding private key. Anyone may use the public key to encrypt messages to a recipient, who uses the private key to decrypt them. Public-key encryption is very CPU-intensive, so it can reduce network performance. It is typically used for small amounts of data where strong security is required.

Some encryption systems use both single-key and public-key algorithms. For example, in a secure key exchange session, both parties first authenticate themselves (often using digital certificates, described later in this lesson) during a session-specific encryption key distribution process. This is illustrated on the Secure Key Exchange Diagram. A single-session key is created based on data generated by both parties at the time of communication. This symmetric encryption key can then be used to encrypt and decrypt all other communications in the session.

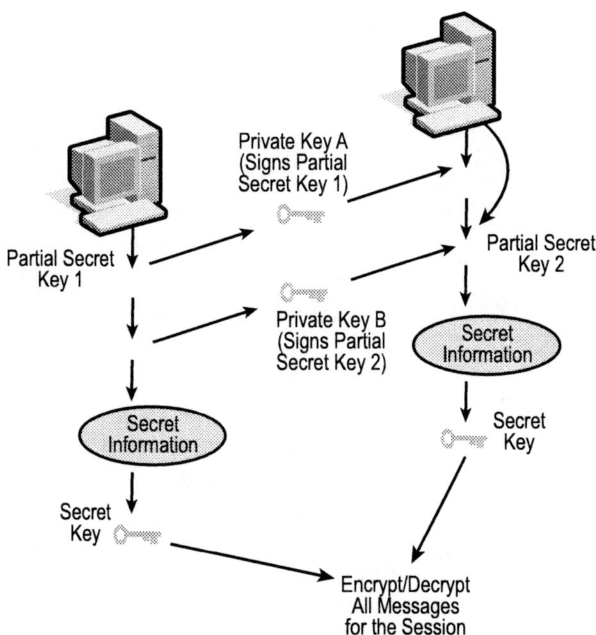

Secure Key Exchange

Directory servers from Novell, Netscape, and others can store a digital certificate that contains a user's public key. This system can also be combined with data exchanged at the time of communication to arrive at a shared, session-specific secret key. The public key/private key system can also be used to create a digital signature, which is a digest of a plain message encrypted using a key and appended to the plain message. This digest makes it possible to authenticate the sender of the message and verify that the message has not been altered since being sent by the author.

Key Size and Encryption Strength

A brute-force attack tries to break a code by simply testing each key possibility until it finds the right one. Therefore, the degree of protection afforded by encryption is closely related to the size of its keys; longer keys are more secure because they take longer to guess.

Legal Issues in Cryptography

The same encryption system that keeps love letters private can also hide messages about drug deals, terrorist attacks, or political opposition. Therefore, most government agencies resist the spread of stronger encryption technology that would make it difficult or impossible to break an encrypted message.

Each national government has regulations that govern the type of encryption algorithms its citizens may use or export, and the length of the numerical keys each algorithm may use (longer keys are more secure because they are harder to guess). Currently, the United States permits 128-bit encryption keys; however, most other governments allow only 56-bit encryption keys, and France allows only a 40-bit key. The U.S. government considers some encryption software to be munitions-level technology, and prohibits the export of those programs.

Commonly Used Encryption Systems

All encryption systems place an additional load on a network, because one or more round trips are needed to authenticate the parties. The machines involved in the communication must also perform large mathematical operations to encrypt and decrypt data, and this can amount to a noticeable increase of CPU cycles on systems that pass many packets. To free the CPU from this task, the conventional burden of encryption systems can be moved to firmware or hardware, such as a coprocessor on the NIC or elsewhere in an embedded system. The following are some commonly used encryption systems:

- **Data Encryption Standard (DES)**—DES, originally used in military and intelligence environments, is a single-key cryptography system. It involves a 16-stage encryption process in which each stage expands and contracts the data using a 56-bit key. (A Triple Data Encryption Standard system [3DES] uses either 112-bit or 168-bit keys.) The process at each stage is similar; however, different expansions and elements of the key are employed. The cryptography system performs "block mode" encryption; a block of input is transformed into a block of output that is independent of any other blocks. This mode is suitable for most communications applications only when feedback is used to protect transmission of repetitive plaintext; thus, removing repetitive ciphertext and further protecting the transmission.

The DES cryptography system has been subjected to more scrutiny than any other algorithm in history. No significant weaknesses have been found, and it is used for unclassified data protection in the United States and many foreign countries. It has been adopted as an ISO standard.

- **Clipper Chip**—An alternative to DES is the Clipper Chip, an 80-bit single-key encryption algorithm contained on a single chip. It also contains the Digital Signature standard, the Secure Hash Algorithm (SHA), a method for key exchange, and a randomizer. A public-key version is known as Capstone, which uses the same Skipjack encryption algorithm used for the Clipper Chip.

  The Clipper Chip uses a key-escrow system that addresses the concerns of U.S. law enforcement agencies. Under this system, two decryption keys are held separately by the U.S. Treasury Department and the National Institute of Standards and Technology (NIST). If necessary, a law enforcement agency could seek a court order to get access to the keys; both keys are necessary to decrypt a message encrypted with a Clipper Chip.

- **Kerberos**—Kerberos validates user access requests to applications and databases. Kerberos uses three different components to accomplish secure access: a database, an authentication server, and a ticket-granting server all residing on a single, physically secure system. The database contains all network resources, user IDs, passwords, and an encryption key. The database is the only location where passwords are stored; it controls every network service.

  The authentication server validates access requests, ensuring the identity of every user, using only the user's name and the name of the requested service. Passwords are not transmitted over a network. The authentication server compares each request with its database, and determines whether the user has the access rights to the service. If successful, the server then issues a ticket for the ticket-granting server. This ticket contains the user's name, name of the server, time and a time window, user's network address, and a temporary private session key. All of these are DES encrypted, using a key known only to the authentication and ticket-granting servers.

  The workstation-to-authentication server transmission is then encrypted a second time using a mutually known key. At this point, the workstation requests access to specific hosts and applications from the ticket-granting server. After decrypting the request and verifying the session key, the ticket-granting server then allows access to the requested host or application. It also compares the current time against the authenticator to verify the transmissions.

- **Secure Sockets Layer (SSL)**—SSL has become the dominant technology for ensuring secure electronic commerce. It is considered a standard Web server feature but, thus far, is not generally used for internal network encryption. SSL is a general-purpose protocol for sending encrypted information over a Hypertext Transfer Protocol (HTTP) network. It uses public-key encryption to encrypt HTTP data packets as they travel between two computers; however, it does not safeguard the computers on each end of the channel. Furthermore, SSL only works on HTTP packets; it does not protect data transferred by means of FTP, SMTP, Telnet, or other TCP/IP services. The basic version of SSL uses 40-bit keys; a 128-bit version is also available.

- **Secure Electronic Transaction (SET)**—Visa International and MasterCard developed the SET protocols to protect online e-commerce payment transactions. The SET protocol authenticates customers, merchants, and the merchant bank using digital certificates. Information that is passed over the Internet is secured by public-key encryption. This protocol has not become overwhelmingly popular due to higher processing costs associated with it. SSL is still by far the more widely used technology.

- **Pretty Good Privacy (PGP)**—PGP (**http://www.pgp.com**) is public-key encryption software for individual users, and is popular for sending secure e-mail with digital signatures. PGP also compresses the data before encrypting it, using the ZIP algorithm. PGP generates a random 128-bit session key for each connection from browser to server, or for each message to be encrypted.

Access Control

Only authorized personnel or systems should be able to access, modify, or delete confidential information. Any network management system must include a set of rules to determine whether a given person may access a specific managed element (device or resource). In addition, the OS's security mechanisms must be in place and monitored. For example, the number of user accounts should be minimized and the directory permissions should be scrutinized. Default accounts and user names that ship with the system and are enabled by default should always be disabled.

Remote access control governs an external user's ability to connect to a network, computer, or application, or to a specific kind of data traffic. Remote access control systems are generally implemented using firewalls, which provide a centralized point from which to permit or deny access.

User Authentication

It is fairly simple to define each user's network rights and permissions; however, it can be difficult to positively identify an individual user. Proof of identity is the only way to differentiate authorized users from intruders. The greater the need for security, the more stringent the identification system must be.

In addition to proving identity, authentication systems are used to determine what information a requestor can access (for example, a human resources database or corporate financial database). Authentication is also necessary to confirm the identity of a message's sender. Authentication generally relies on one or more of the following elements:

- Something the user knows (password)

- Something the user possesses (smart card or digital certificate)

- A physical attribute or biometric information (fingerprint or retinal scan)

Authentication is most often achieved through challenge and response, digital certificates, or message digests and digital signatures.

Passwords

A password is the simplest kind of user identification. However, it is one of the least secure methods, because users normally choose bad passwords, or they lose, forget, or accidentally reveal a password. Stricter password techniques, such as time-based passwords or one-time passwords, can reduce some of these common problems. However, human memory remains the biggest problem. In some organizations, 30 to 40 percent of help desk calls involve lost or forgotten passwords.

Attackers can also use password-guessing programs to gain unauthorized network access. These programs use fairly simple techniques, such as repeatedly trying words from a dictionary, or trying various combinations of letters. Thus, security awareness training must teach users the following guidelines for creating strong passwords:

- Make passwords 12 characters or longer. The shorter the password, the faster it can be guessed.

- Do not use words that appear in the dictionary.

- Do not use the names of family members, pets, hobbies, or other words that can be inferred from conversation or from items in the work area.

- Use a combination of upper and lower case letters, numbers, and special characters. Whenever possible, use random combinations instead of recognizable words.

- Pick a password that can be remembered without writing it down. If it is absolutely necessary to record a password, keep it in a secure location, and not in the work area.

- Change passwords regularly, at least once per month.

Smart Cards

Smart cards are plastic cards that contain embedded integrated circuit (IC) microprocessors and a standard magnetic strip. A user inserts a smart card into a chip-reading terminal, which reads the information stored on it. Smart cards can eliminate the need for users to remember (and frequently change) passwords and other authentication information. Of course, with great convenience comes great risk; users who are careless with passwords are also likely to lose smart cards.

Digital Certificates

A digital certificate is the electronic equivalent of an ID card or passport. Issued by a trusted Certificate Authority (CA), it contains information that uniquely identifies the person who holds it. Digital certificates are one of several applications of public-key encryption. The certificate sits securely in the consumer's browser or e-mail software, and can be used to digitally sign or encrypt e-mail messages. Digital certificates can eliminate the need for passwords in some cases, or can serve as an employee's ID when remotely accessing a network. However, they are not perfect, especially if an impostor can gain access to a computer that contains an employee's digital certificate.

One of the earliest uses of digital certificate technology was Privacy-Enhanced Mail (PEM), the predecessor to Secure/Multipurpose Internet Mail Extension (S/MIME), and a widely used specification that brought a higher level of security to e-mail through encryption and digital, signature-based authentication. Since their introduction, the use of digital certificates has continued to grow steadily.

Biometric Authentication

Biometric techniques identify users by some physical feature, such as a fingerprint or handprint, the pattern of blood vessels in the retina of the eye, or voice characteristics. As with most security techniques, increased reliability comes at increased cost. For example, retinal scanning techniques are highly accurate, but the cost of the special cameras makes this technique impractical for all but the most security-conscious organizations.

Currently, fingerprint authentication is the simplest, least intrusive, and most economical technique for identifying PC users. With scanner/software packages starting at U.S. $100, this method is practical for even remote employees.

The main drawback to fingerprint scanning is that some users consider any biometric authentication to be a violation of personal privacy. In addition, fingerprints have long been associated with law enforcement; some users feel insulted to be asked to provide them, or worry that their fingerprints will be added to some governmental database.

Thus far, these concerns are unfounded. No government has moved to collect fingerprint identification data from private organizations. And, unlike the high-quality fingerprints required by law enforcement, computer fingerprint scanners record only the intersections of lines in the finger or thumbprint. However, any company that implements biometric authentication must address these concerns in its user training.

**Message Digests
and Digital
Signatures**

Message digests and digital signatures are different methods that are commonly used together. Both are applications of public-key cryptography. Message digests ensure message integrity, by showing that a message has not been altered in transit. Digital signatures authenticate the identity of the sender of a message. When used together, they can help prevent message forgery or tampering.

A message digest is created by applying a one-way hash function such as Message Digest 5 (MD5) or SHA-1 to a message. "One-way" means that the original message cannot be re-created from the digest. A digital signature uses the private key of an individual to encrypt the message digest, as shown on the Authenticating a Digital Signature Diagram. At the receiving end, the digest is re-created from the message text, the sender's public key is used to decrypt the digest from the digital signature, and the two message digests are compared. If they match, the messages are in all probability the same. Comparison of the message digests provides both a means of authenticating the signature and a check of message integrity.

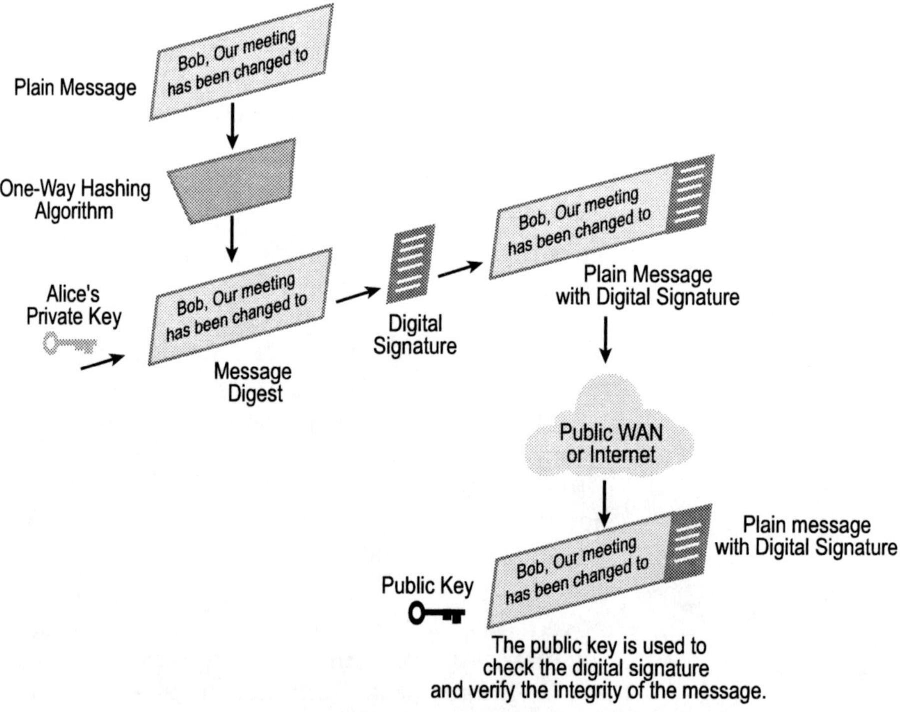

Authenticating a Digital Signature

Firewalls

According to the International Computer Security Association (ICSA), a firewall is "a system or combination of systems that enforces a boundary between two or more networks." The primary application for firewalls in most networks today is as a secure layer between a private network and the Internet. An Internet firewall is a controlled gateway that protects the internal network from outside intrusion. However, it cannot stop attacks from malicious insiders, nor can it take the place of education and security policies and procedures.

A firewall is normally composed of both software and hardware products. These physical devices or software agents filter packets heading into or out of an organization based on a set of policy rules. They can allow access to an enterprise network by username/ password, type of service requested (FTP, HTTP, or Telnet), location of destination (network or computer), or location of requestor (network address). A firewall can request authentication before allowing any traffic to pass at all, and in so doing can take advantage of the various authentication schemes described earlier.

We continue discussing firewalls, in more detail, in Lesson 3 of this unit.

IPSec

Objective 2.13
Identify the following security protocols and describe their purpose and function.
… IPSec

In addition to firewalls, an enterprise may implement a network-level security protocol, such as IPSec, to protect information as it moves through a network. The Internet Engineering Task Force (IETF) developed IPSec, which offers standards-based, consistent security for IP networks.

IPSec works at the packet level. Every packet is protected to provide authentication, integrity, and (optionally) confidentiality. Any of the firewall devices described above, as well as each of the individual computers or servers on a network, can implement IPSec.

In an IPSec communication, the two communicating entities (individual hosts or intervening devices such as routers or firewalls) first establish a Security Association (SA). During negotiation of the SA, the two entities agree on what kind of security will be employed. The Internet Security Architecture document (Request for Comment [RFC] 2401) specifies two major traffic security protocols:

- **Authentication Header (AH)**—The AH contains a Message Authentication Code (MAC), which authenticates the sender of the packet and ensures that its contents have not been altered.

731

- **Encapsulating Security Payload (ESP)**—In the ESP method, the actual payload data of a packet is encrypted using a session key. This key is often derived for the session itself using a public-key encryption system.

In addition to encrypting the data portion of the message, ESP can also be used to provide authentication and integrity, features provided by the AH. However, ESP security is less comprehensive than that provided by AH. The AH header protects entire messages, whereas ESP only covers the portion of the message after the ESP header.

IPSec offers a complete and integrated system for securing data networks. IPSec can be used within the organization or on the Internet because it is based on a set of open specifications, including the entire TCP/IP protocol suite. Also, like TCP/IP (and unlike proprietary schemes), IPSec is designed for interoperability between enterprise systems.

Network system designers can integrate IPSec into an existing system in three ways:

- Integrating IPSec processing into the TCP/IP network stack of the host or other device. This requires the host CPU to perform security processing.

- Performing IPSec processing in software before the data packets are processed by the existing TCP/IP networking stack (known as a "bump in the stack" [BITS]). This approach also requires the host CPU to perform security processing.

- Performing IPSec processing before the data packets are processed by the host computer (known as a "bump in the wire" [BITW]). This system offloads security processing to a processor on a network component, such as a NIC with an on-board encryption chip, and leaves the CPU free. The use of an additional processor to handle IPSec security tasks promises the greatest throughput while still delivering the full benefit of a comprehensive security system.

Virus Prevention and Detection

Objective 4.5
Be able to describe the uses and proper instances to use anti-virus software.

Viruses and worms are both destructive and self-replicating applications that work in similar ways:

- A virus is designed to spread from file to file within a single computer. The virus attaches itself to a legitimate "host" application. When the host application is launched, the virus copies itself to other files, then performs the job it was designed to do. Some viruses only display a political message. Others erase entire hard drives. Viruses spread passively when an infected application is copied from one computer to another, via floppy disks, e-mail attachments, or a LAN.

- A worm is designed to actively spread itself to other computers on a network. It is usually packaged within an innocent-looking file, but it does not infect other host files. Instead of waiting for a user to copy it to another machine, a worm seeks out paths to other computers, such as network connections or an e-mail application. For example, a worm can mail copies of itself to every entry in a user's e-mail address book. Some of the newest e-mail attachment worms can take effect when a user views the message that contains the bad attachment; the user does not need to specifically launch the worm attachment.

A single virus or worm can infect an entire network within minutes, thus virus prevention software is essential for every node on a network. When a new virus is discovered anywhere in the world, the developers of virus control software quickly create a software plug-in, or "signature" file, that allows their application to recognize and eradicate the new threat. While virus prevention programs are blind to new viruses that use new and unknown techniques, many new viruses use the same well-known methods.

By using the following recommendations, an administrator can protect a network from a destructive virus outbreak:

- Install virus detection software on both network servers and user desktops.

- Keep virus protection software up to date. Immediately after installing a virus control application, download and install the latest signature files. Set up automatic nightly processes to download and install new signature files (automatic update features are built in to many applications), then "push" those updates to all user desktops. Some applications can be configured to check for new signatures whenever a user accesses the Internet; these applications are simple and effective for small networks or home offices.

- Once your software is installed, use it. It takes a little extra time to scan all incoming floppy disks; however, it is time well spent.

- Teach users to be wary of e-mail attachments. Many of the most famous viruses and worms of the past few years have been spread through e-mail systems. Thus, if you receive an e-mail with an attached executable file, even from a friend, do not launch that program until you verify what it is. If you are not totally sure of an attachment, simply delete the entire message.

- Consider configuring the e-mail server to reject or quarantine all executable e-mail attachments. Most of these are not work-related.

- Be wary of downloadable software. Reputable Web sites that provide free downloadable applications do everything they can to ensure that their content is virus-free. However, for all the reasons we have discussed, it is impossible to be totally sure. Some users who enjoy downloading programs and games set up a non-networked computer as a quarantine area. All new programs are tested on that platform before being used on the "real" system.

Security Management

A security system should allow for oversight and control by a human authority. Any system that uses authentication requires some central authority to verify the identities, whether it be the / etc./password file on a UNIX host, a Windows NT domain controller, or an NDS server. The ability to see histories, such as repeated failed attempts to breach a firewall, can provide invaluable information to those charged with protecting information assets. Some of the more recent security specifications, such as IPSec, require the presence of a database containing policy rules. All these elements must be managed for the system to work correctly.

However, management consoles or functions themselves represent another potential point of failure of a security system. It is therefore important to ensure that these systems are physically secured and that authentication is in place for any logon to a management console.

A comprehensive design process should specify security services and implementations. Security-related information is conceptually stored in the management information base (MIB) of a network management system. This ensures that every collection of managed network systems has a single, common security policy. The security policy may be null (if the administrator never enables security), or it may contain an extensive set of rules controlling the communication conditions of all managed elements in the network.

We discuss security management, and typical precautions, in the next lesson.

Activities

1. When using a digital certificate containing a user's private key, a digital signature is created as part of a message digest to enable sender authentication. True or False?

2. A digital signature guards against a message being altered in transit. True or False?

3. Match the term with the description below.

   Denial of service __________

   Corruption of data __________

   Crackers __________

   Theft of information __________

   Viruses __________

   Trojan horses __________

   a. People motivated by the challenge breaking into a secure system

   b. Programs hidden within other programs to gather or destroy information

   c. Self-replicating destructive programs that damage data

   d. Overloading a server to affect availability

   e. Acquiring trade secrets or business plans

   f. Destroys data transmitted across networks

4. Which of the passwords below is stronger than the others? Why?

   ____

   ____

   a. &D#i

   b. give*me#chocolate!

   c. 12/15/1963

   d. aS*td3Qr&MA1J

5. Compare single-key encryption and public-key encryption.

    ____

    ____

    ____

6. Describe how key size relates to encryption strength.

    ____

    ____

7. Contrast the challenges of ensuring reliable and secure user authentication with ease of use.

    ____

    ____

    ____

    ____

8. As a network system designer, list three ways available for integrating IPSec, and describe which method allows for the highest throughput.

    ____

    ____

    ____

Extended Activity

Symantec Corporation has created a free application that simulates the spread of three types of worms (this is only a simulator, not a virus protection program). Download VBSIM.EXE from **http://www. symantec.com/avcenter/vbsim.exe** and perform a simulation.

Lesson 2—Security Management

Web site security management is another broad topic that fills whole books. This lesson introduces the most important technical precautions and practices in any Web administrator's security strategy.

As you read this lesson, it is easy to feel that the Web, by its very nature, is so full of security holes that real site security is impossible. However, you can plug many of these holes by taking the simple precautions outlined in this lesson, just as you can stop most car thieves by simply locking the door and taking your keys. This is because most Web criminals, like street criminals, are not very expert at what they do. If you can avoid being an easy target, many crackers will pass you by.

Objectives

At the end of this lesson you will be able to:

- Describe the types of threats and attacks that any security plan must prevent

- List the most common security problems with e-mail, FTP, Practical Extraction and Report Language (Perl), and ActiveX controls

- Describe briefly a proper response to a security incident

- List some of the most important security precautions at the OS level

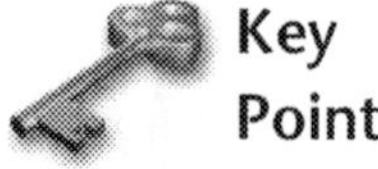

Key Point

Most Internet applications were not designed with security in mind.

Types of Attacks

Objective 4.2
Identify suspicious network activities.

The ways your Web site can be attacked are endless. The following are the most prevalent types of attacks against Web sites and Internet servers.

Multiple Login Failures

The best way to stop a brute force attack on client passwords is to place a lock on the account after it exceeds a set number of tries. Multiple log in failure is achieved when a person has tried to log in with the wrong information more times than is allowed by a system. The set number of tries is usually between three and five; after the number of tries has been exceeded, the account must be reset.

Denial of Service Attacks

A denial of service (DoS) attacker tries to slow down a service so much that a legitimate user cannot access that service. DoS attacks try to overwhelm a computer's resources by sending it an extraordinary number of requests. Most computers will at least slow down, and in some cases the computer will stop functioning and will need to be restarted.

Ping Flood Attacks

A ping utility is used to see if a host is available on a TCP/IP network. The utility sends an Internet Control Message Protocol (ICMP) request to a host and waits for a response from the designated host. If alive, the host will respond; if not, the request will time out. A ping uses a very small percent of the available amount of the processing power, but when a host is flooded with ping transactions in a very short amount of time, it can use a large percent of processing power. This can create a denial of service situation by bringing down the host or overloading its incoming communication lines.

Mail Flooding

During mail flooding, an attacker sends a bombardment of mail to an e-mail account to make the account inaccessible. One way of doing this is to subscribe an e-mail account to hundreds of mailing lists. Another way of mail flooding is to send a large message to the targeted account, full of bogus characters.

Syn Floods

On a TCP/IP network, a host has a buffer set at a certain size to facilitate connections while they are being made. An attacker fills a buffer by overwhelming the host with half-open connections. When the buffer is full, the host cannot make any connections with any other host, and the connection to the network is rendered useless.

IP Spoofing

IP spoofing is used to gain access to a restricted network, or trick a host into thinking that a request is coming from a trusted network. An attacker uses IP spoofing to gain unauthorized access to a network or computer. The attacker must first find an IP that is accepted by the host. The attacker then must change the packet header to make it appear that the packet is coming from a trusted host. When this is achieved, the host is tricked into accepting the packet.

A famous use of IP spoofing is the "man-in-the-middle" or "bucket brigade" attack, which attempts to intercept message traffic between a client and server. To avoid detection, the attacker spoofs addresses so that the attacker appears to the client to be the server, or to the server to be the client.

General Web Security Precautions

Web security management is an eclectic and constantly changing discipline because the Web includes many and varied technologies, and one technology may introduce or interact with another technology to introduce a security hole.

Private Web Site Design

Objective 4.1
*Understand and be able to describe various Internet security concepts
… Access control*

*Objective **4.4***
Identify appropriate access-control security features for an Internet server.

Most Web sites are designed for public access. However, the following mechanisms enable intranets and extranets to limit access to their select audiences:

- Hidden Uniform Resource Locators (URLs) are Web page locations that have no visible links from a main Web site. They can give authorized users direct access to private site resources. However, this technique is vulnerable to simple user carelessness; therefore, highly secure data should not rely on it.

- A challenge/response process is a more secure approach to access an entire Web server or select pages on the server. Mechanisms to activate a browser challenge/response architecture are typically implemented at both the Web server administration level and OS level. We will discuss server-level access control in a moment.

- A Web site can be configured to demand a client-side digital certificate.

HTTP Server Access Control

Objective 1.7
Assist in the administration of Internet/ intranet sites.

In the HTTP/1.0 specification, user access to Web content can be controlled by placing an access control file in each restricted directory. This text file, usually named *#haccess.ctl*, lists the usernames of authorized users. A separate file in the directory associates each username with a password.

When a user clicks a link to a page stored within a restricted directory, the Web server reads the access control file and prompts the user for a username and password. If the user's reply matches the username and password stored in the access control files for that directory, the server then transmits the requested page.

Once a user has access to a directory, that user may view any page within that directory. The user may also view pages within any subdirectories, provided that the subdirectories do not have separate access control files of their own. If necessary, each restricted directory may use a different access control file; in that case, a user may need to provide different usernames and passwords to access content in different directories.

On small, lightly used, Web sites, Web server administrators can create access control lists and assign new username/password pairs to new users. Larger sites provide automated systems that allow users to define their own usernames and passwords.

RFC 2617 specifies two types of directory-based access control for HTTP. Both of these methods work as just described, but differ in the way they handle user passwords:

- **Basic Access Authentication**—Basic Access Authentication transmits username/password pairs as unencrypted text, similar to the insecure approach used by FTP and Telnet. If users create their own passwords, Web professionals recommend against using this method, even if the restricted content is not particularly sensitive. That's because most users tend to use the same password to access multiple sites and their personal workstations. Thus, a cleartext password captured from a small club's site might be used to compromise other sites or steal a user's confidential data.

- **Digest Access Authentication**—Digest Access Authentication does not transmit a user's password to a server. Instead, the server transmits a one-time random number to the client computer. The client and the server then both apply the same encryption algorithm to both the random number and the user's password. The client transmits the result of the calculation (called a digest) to the server. If the client's digest matches the server's digest, that proves that the client's password matches the password stored on the server.

  Thus, Digest Access Authentication authenticates users without revealing passwords. The encryption algorithm works as a one way process, so that a password cannot be extracted by anyone who captures a digest. Furthermore, the server uses a different random number each time it authenticates a user. So a captured digest cannot be used to authenticate an eavesdropper.

Though Digest Access Authentication is more secure than Basic Access Authentication, it is vulnerable to many other common security attacks. Even its designers recommend using Digest Access Authentication only when security requirements are low. Sites that must protect sensitive data should use stronger methods of authentication and encryption.

JavaScript

JavaScript cannot access a client computer's file system or open connections to other computers on the network. The primary threat to the current implementation of JavaScript is related to privacy violations, because JavaScript applications can be written to track a user's URL destinations.

Earlier versions of JavaScript had the ability to open a Web browser window of any size. An application could be opened within a 1x1 pixel window, practically invisible to the user. The "hidden" application could then review the browser's URL history table. This problem has been fixed in the current version of JavaScript.

Java Applets (Active Content)

Bytecodes intercept Java applets. This feature makes Java browser- and platform-independent. However, it also provides the following mechanisms to help protect a client from possible malicious acts using Java bytecode, as illustrated on the Java Security Features Diagram:

- The Class Loader checks Java bytecode classes as they are downloaded, looking for instructions that may disable the Security Manager.

- The ByteCode Verifier verifies that the Java bytecode does not violate access restrictions, and prevents Java code from jumping to an arbitrary memory location.

- The Sandbox is a restricted workspace where the Java code actually runs. It includes restrictions against accessing computer hardware or making direct calls to the OS.

- The Security Manager class determines whether each requested operation, such as disk access or device input/output (I/O), is appropriate.

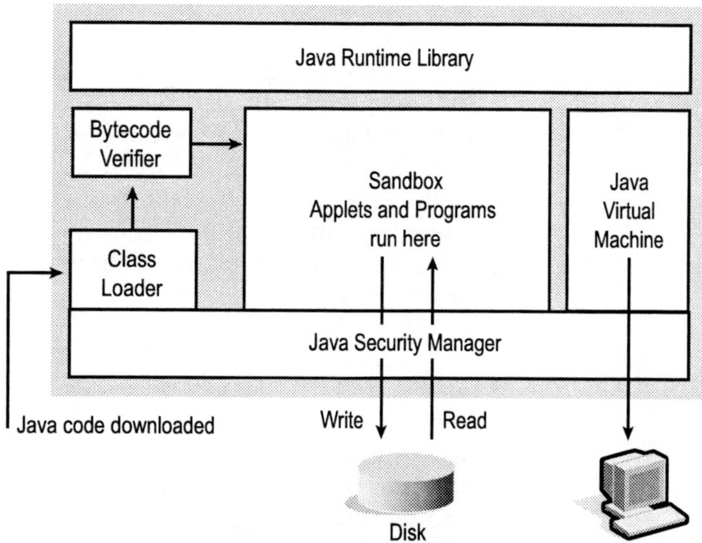

Java Security Features

Stand-Alone Java Applications

Java was designed from the ground up to be as secure as possible, provided the Java code is compiled as an applet. However, if Java code is complied as a stand-alone application, security can easily be compromised. Stand-alone Java applications can have almost as much power as C/C++ to change, modify, or otherwise compromise a computer system.

Perl

One of the main security problems with HTTP servers is the ability to execute Common Gateway Interface (CGI) scripts. Some scripting engines, such as Perl, generally interpret these scripts. When configuring scripting engines on their HTTP servers, Web server administrators must be extremely cautious to prevent crackers from using these interpreters maliciously.

The main form of attack comes when a scripting language's interpreter is available for direct public access. When Perl was first released for the Windows NT platform, some unsuspecting souls conveniently placed the Perl interpreter in the common gateway interface (CGI)-bin directory on their servers. Unfortunately, Perl has a command line switch (-e) that allows you to pass commands directly to Perl. With this command line switch, a cracker could make Perl do just about anything. The simple way to counteract this vulnerability is to move Perl out of the CGI-bin executable directory to a location where the Web server application can call it, but external users cannot.

Operating System Precautions

Effective Web server security begins with the underlying operating system (OS), and when a server administrator follows the best practices of system management and administration. Examples of OS precautions are as follows:

- Apply patches in a timely manner.

- Activate Activity Logging to monitor any unauthorized changes or failed access attempts, and review the resulting logs often. Many system administrators make the simple mistake of turning on Activity Logging, but never checking the logs.

- Develop policies that clearly define who has access to the system, what processes are allowed to run on the system, and how the organization should react to security incidents.

- Provide a secure physical environment for the server (at a minimum, lock the door). Approximately 80 percent of all break-ins are committed by local intruders; therefore, after you lock the server door, hide the key or combination.

- Implement a security tool that can run on the server to help you analyze and identify security holes in the system configuration.

- Ensure that the OS's security mechanisms are in place and monitored. For example, minimize the number of user accounts, do not run the Web server process as a privileged user, and scrutinize directory permissions. In addition, always disable the default accounts and user names that ship with the system and are enabled by default.

Internet Services Precautions

The variety of TCP/IP applications that makes the Internet so useful also provides a wide variety of opportunities for crackers.

E-Mail (SMTP Sendmail)

All Internet e-mail is based on SMTP, which was not originally designed with security in mind. The sendmail process runs with privileged access on the system. With more than 11,000 lines of code to work with, and many years to try, crackers have found many bugs and back doors to exploit. As a result, e-mail is one of the least secure processes on the Internet for several reasons, including the following:

- **Lack of confidentiality**—Because messages are forwarded through intermediate systems, all e-mail is subject to simple eavesdropping attacks. Anyone with the right equipment can simply copy an e-mail message as it goes by, without the sender or receiver being aware of it. Furthermore, e-mail messages sit in message queues for days and remain on backup media for years. Therefore, users should assume that all e-mail messages are indefinitely viewable by anyone, on or off the Internet. For example, as part of a child pornography investigation, America Online provided information to the FBI based on two years of e-mail and chat data. This eventually led to 120 search warrants and dozens of arrests.

- **Lack of authenticity**—Standard SMTP provides no mechanism to authenticate the sender of a message. For example, the typical e-mail client software allows you to enter any e-mail address for the sender, without making any attempt to verify it. Other software, called anonymous mailers, sends e-mail after removing all information about the sender and source environment. This technology originally developed in response to repressive Eastern European government control over private speech. Individuals and political groups used anonymous mailers to freely discuss politics without fear of government persecution. (Some remailing services have since closed, in the face of allegations that they unintentionally contribute to the distribution of child pornography.)

- **Lack of integrity**—Standard SMTP provides no mechanism to ensure that the message you receive is the same message that was originally sent to you. Someone snooping the Internet could intercept and pull off an e-mail message, change it, and then send the new message to the recipient.

- **Multipurpose Internet Mail Extensions (MIME)**—
  MIME is an extension to the SMTP standard. It allows standard SMTP processes to process binary attachments, such as application files, PostScript and word processor files, graphics, and other nontext formats. The MIME interpreter translates the binary files to and from a text representation, which can be sent and received over SMTP. The original Internet infrastructure was based around a seven-bit American Standard Code for Information Interchange (ASCII) character set; MIME files typically need to use the extended 8-bit ASCII character set. If malicious MIME attachments are automatically opened from within the e-mail client software, they can erase hard drive information, transfer additional files to your system, or do other serious damage.

As you can imagine, vendors and experts are working to address these problems. The Internet Engineering Task Force (IETF) has developed the MIME Object Security Services (MOSS) proposal for providing secure MIME. In the meantime, RSA Data Security has developed Secure/Multipurpose Internet Mail Extensions (S/MIME), an enhanced MIME that provides a security component to the standard insecure MIME. Many of the major e-mail vendors now support S/MIME in their SMTP implementations.

Third-party encryption applications are also available to users who require confidentiality, authenticity, and integrity in e-mail, such as Privacy Enhanced Mail (PEM), and the most popular and more secure, Pretty Good Privacy (PGP).

HTTP Server (Web Server)

Take the following precautions to secure the Web server application itself:

- Allow "Directory Browsing" (Automatic Directory Listing) only where necessary. This will limit the exposure/viewing of files and the internal structure of the Web server, which could help a cracker navigate the system inappropriately. In addition, place a file called index.html in each directory you do not wish surfers to get a file listing for.

- Turn on features to log Web activity, and monitor the logs.

- Minimize the number of other Internet services (FTP, SMTP, Domain Name System [DNS], etc.) you run on your Web server.

- Ensure that remote contributors use secure methods to transfer content to the site. FTP sends cleartext (unencrypted) passwords over the Internet. Therefore, site updates should be made using Web posting tools, such as FrontPage Server Extensions and Microsoft Web Poster, which do not send cleartext passwords.

TCP/IP Utilities

The following precautions can help prevent attacks via standard TC/IP utilities:

- Only offer FTP or Telnet on systems that truly require it. Both of these applications are inherently insecure, because they transmit cleartext user names and passwords insecurely over the network.

- Wherever possible, do not allow anonymous FTP sessions. If anonymous FTP is necessary for user downloads, do not allow it for uploads.

- Configure your firewall to block ICMP Echo (ping) packets.

User Browser Setup: ActiveX Controls

ActiveX is a collection of protocols and application programming interfaces (APIs), developed by Microsoft, that allow programmers to create executable components that can be downloaded by a browser. This executable code is permanently stored on the client's computer system; thus, it can be used as needed during subsequent visits to a Web site. In this way, ActiveX is very similar to Netscape Plug-Ins.

Its creator can digitally sign an ActiveX control. This signature identifies the programmer in the event of a problem with the ActiveX control's behavior.

There is virtually no limit to what an ActiveX control can do on a client's system. Therefore, browsers should be configured to not accept unsigned controls. The browser can be configured to prompt the user to decide whether to allow the downloading of an ActiveX control. A browser can also notify the user if a digital signature is registered with an unknown certificate authority.

Key Point

Set browser Active Content Security rating to Medium.

Security

Cookies

Cookies do not pose a real security risk. However, many users have gotten the idea that cookies exist to violate their privacy.

In reality, cookies are a form of CallerID, which a Web server uses to identify a browser session as it traverses the various Web pages of a site. For example, online stores use cookies to keep track of items in a customer's online shopping cart. Many sites also store each user's preferences (colors, interests, passwords, etc.), so the application can re-create the preferred settings each time a user visits a site.

Cookies do not gather information about the user. They simply store information that the user transmits to a Web server by means of a Web page. A Web server, not a user, controls all cookies, and cookies are only available to the sites that created them.

Cookies are ASCII text files. It is remotely possible that viruses (active content) or malicious software applications can be stored in a cookie. However, this is highly unlikely, because there are easier and better ways of doing this without using cookies.

In practice, cookies are safe. If users are worried about them, they can set their browsers to turn them off.

Responding to a Security Incident

No one likes to think of the possibility of a security breach. However, breaches can happen despite the best precautions. Therefore, your organization's security policy should include a set of incident response guidelines that spell out how to respond to a security incident. Your guidelines should include the factor presented in the following sections.

Detection

Objective 4.3
Identify various methods for performing intrusion detection.

Short-lived incidents have become more the rule than the exception. With this in mind, it is more important than ever to have automated detection mechanisms that can immediately notify an administrator of a problem by means of e-mail or a pager. The two main types of detectors are as follows:

- **Statistical tools** measure the deviation from what is considered a normal user's behavior. These applications build statistical norms over time, by collecting and analyzing a site's routine use patterns. A trigger is fired when the application detects a substantial deviation from the statistical norm, such as a very high level of ICMP packets that could reveal a ping flood attack. SRI International's Next Generation Intrusion Detection Expert System is an example of this type of product.

- **Signature-based tools** monitor the execution of certain commands that a typical nonprivileged user should not use.

Documentation

In one way, a security incident is like any other technical problem: solving it requires a clear, logical look at the facts. Therefore, it is important to document the facts in the following way:

- Describe the problem with as much detail as you can. The smallest bit of seemingly trivial evidence can make it possible to see a pattern in various cracker activities and help you correct the problem.

- Maintain a chronological, time-stamped activity log of all known behaviors and actions.

- Record any known technical actions taken by the crackers: how they accessed the system, the processes they used, and the files they accessed.

Communication

Generally, information about a security breach should only be communicated on a need-to-know basis. Report the incident to upper management (system owners) as outlined in your Guidelines. Otherwise, restrict communication of the incident to authorized individuals who can help solve the problem. Make sure to contact the vendors who provide your security technology. They can help evaluate your activity logs and may be able to offer other help based on their broader security experience.

Activities

1. __________ runs an interpreter on servers that can allow a cracker remote control of the system.

   a. Perl

   b. MIME

   c. FTP

   d. HTTP

2. To secure an HTTP server, a Web administrator should _______________.

   a. Turn off logging

   b. Allow users to browse all directories

   c. Remove all index.html files

   d. Minimize the number of running services

3. What is one way to protect against destructive Active X controls?

   a. Set browser Active Content Security to minimum

   b. Allow only signed controls

   c. Allow only unsigned controls

   d. Require no user action when a control is loaded

4. In the case of a security incident, the administrator should notify all users of the breach. True or False?

5. Documentation is an important part of determining the cause of a security incident. True or False?

6. How does Java protect a client from malicious acts?

   ____

   ____

   ____

7. Name and describe the vulnerabilities of e-mail.

   ____

   ____

   ____

Extended Activities

1. A popular method of introducing malicious code to networked computers is through e-mail attachments. The attachments appear innocuous; however, once opened they exploit vulnerabilities of the e-mail client, damaging or destroying user data and automatically replicating themselves to other users and e-mail servers.

   Visit **http://www.sarc.com** and research some of the precautions users and administrators can take to protect their systems from these malicious attacks. Should users run attachments directly from an e-mail? Are products available that can scan attachments at the server, protecting users from their bad habits? Are they worth the time and expense to implement?

2. Popular network operating systems (NOSs), including WindowsNT, Windows 2000, and Linux, have hidden security vulnerabilities that crackers eventually find and exploit. Research security fixes for these NOSs. How many are available for each, and how frequently are they released?

Lesson 3—Internet Firewalls

Objective 3.8
Describe various hardware and software connection devices and when to use them ... Firewall

An Internet firewall is a security solution that includes both hardware and software components. Depending on the specific needs of an organization, a firewall may include multiple layers of hardware and software.

A firewall can be thought of as a pair of functions: one function blocks traffic from entering a private network, and the other permits traffic to exit a private network. Some firewalls place a greater emphasis on blocking traffic, while others emphasize permitting traffic.

Internet firewalls are also important because they can provide a focal point where security and auditing can be provided. Firewalls provide an important logging and auditing function. They often provide summaries to an administrator about what kinds and amount of traffic passed through it, how many attempts there were to break into it, and so forth.

This lesson presents the main issues that a network administrator must address when designing an Internet firewall:

- Type of firewall

- Stance of the firewall

- Overall security policy of the organization

- Financial cost of the firewall

- Components or building blocks of the firewall system

Objectives

At the end of this lesson you will be able to:

- Name and describe the main categories of firewalls

- Describe briefly the components of a typical firewall

- Describe, in general, how a proxy server operates

Key Point

A firewall can protect an organization from specific types of external threats. It cannot guard against internal attacks.

Types of Firewalls

Objective 3.8
Describe various hardware and software connection devices and when to use them ... Firewall

The difference between firewall types is primarily related to how they handle external traffic. There are many types of firewalls and applications for firewall usage, but firewalls can be grouped into these categories:

- Network Layer firewalls

- Transport Layer firewalls

- Application firewalls

- Hybrid firewalls

Network Layer Firewalls

Objective 4.7
Describe how firewalls are used to protect private networks.
... Packet filtering

Network Layer firewalls use the IP packet header for determining firewall decisions. They look at the source and destination IP addresses, and either allow or disallow the passage of a packet based on access lists stored in the router. They can permit or deny access based on the protocol, source or destination port, and source and destination of IP addresses. One type of Network Layer firewall is the screened host firewall, illustrated on the Screened Host Firewall Diagram.

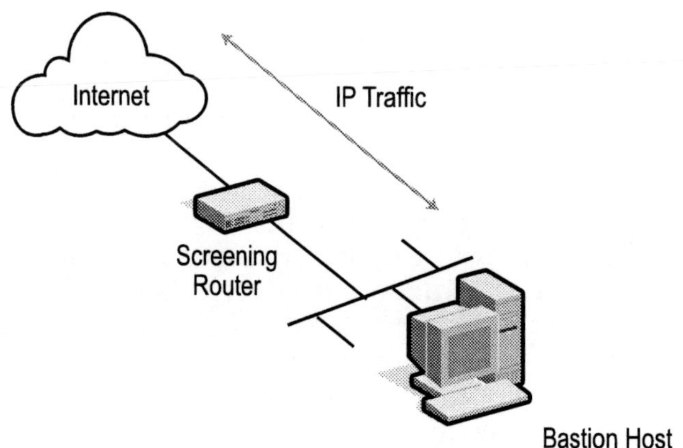

Screened Host Firewall

A screened host firewall uses a router to screen the source and destination addresses, based on rules configured by an administrator, before sending a packet on to a specific host in the internal network. This type of firewall is also referred to as a filtering firewall, filtering gateway, or screening router. These firewalls are fast and inexpensive. However, they are inflexible because they only use one protocol layer to make decisions. Furthermore, these firewalls typically do not employ any kind of user authentication, because the environments in which they are usually deployed handle levels of traffic that are too high to allow for it.

Transport Layer Firewalls

Objective 4.7
Describe how firewalls are used to protect private networks.
... Port filtering

A Transport Layer firewall, or port filtering firewall, evaluates traffic according to its TCP or UDP port number. Port filtering is more flexible than simple packet filtering, because it filters certain types of traffic, not just source and destination addresses.

For example, assume that a company wants to provide public access to its Web server, but it also wants to protect that server from unauthorized intrusion via Telnet or FTP. The company could accomplish this by placing the Web server behind a firewall that is configured to pass only traffic on TCP port 80—HTTP requests and replies.

Application Firewalls

Objective 4.7
Describe how firewalls are used to protect private networks.
... Application filtering

Application firewalls use a router that acts as a proxy server for the end user in the internal network. IP traffic from the external network essentially stops at the router. The proxy server serves as a middleman that does not permit direct packet communication between external nodes and the internal network. For example, if an external node requests data from the internal network, the proxy server intercepts the message. If it decides to allow the request, based on administrator-configured rules, the proxy server obtains the data from the internal network and passes it out to the external node.

Software applications running on the proxy server are also called "dual-homed gateways," because they take external application data and communicate with the internal host. A dual-homed gateway, illustrated on the Application Firewall Diagram, is a highly secure host.

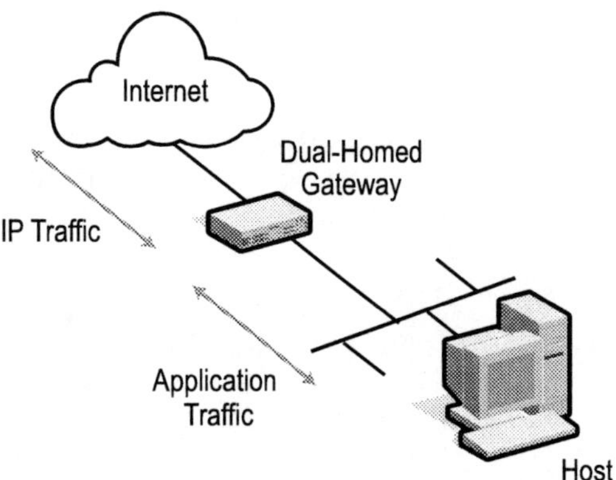

Application Firewall

Application/proxy firewalls typically support local caching of Web content and address translation, thereby hiding internal IP addresses from Internet surfers. Proxy firewalls can allow access based on source address, destination address, or an identity (authentication).

Because application firewalls base decisions on more than just the Network Layer of the protocol stack, they are also used for logging and auditing information that passes to and from the external network. Application firewalls are slower than Network Layer firewalls; however, they provide more functionality and security.

Hybrid Firewalls

A hybrid firewall contains features of both the Network Layer firewall and the application firewall. These firewalls are sometimes referred to as "dynamic packet filtering firewalls." A hybrid firewall allows communication between internal and external hosts, but only if the internal host initiates the session. When an internal host begins communicating with an external host, the hybrid firewall records the identity of the external host, and allows data from that host to enter the internal network for the duration of the session.

Stance of a Firewall

The stance of a firewall system describes the fundamental security philosophy of the organization. An Internet firewall may take one of two diametrically opposed stances.

Everything is Denied Unless Specifically Permitted	This stance assumes a firewall should block all traffic, and each desired service or application should be implemented on a case-by-case basis. This is the recommended approach. It creates a very secure environment, because only carefully selected services are supported. The disadvantage is that it places security ahead of ease of use, limiting the number of options available to the user community.
Everything is Permitted Unless Specifically Denied	This stance assumes a firewall should forward all traffic, and each potentially harmful service should be shut off on a case-by-case basis. This approach creates a more flexible environment, with more services available to the user community. The disadvantage is that it puts ease of use ahead of security, putting the network administrator in a reactive mode and making it increasingly difficult to provide security as the size of the protected network grows.

Cost of a Firewall

How much security can the organization afford? A simple packet-filtering firewall is available at a minimal cost because the organization needs a router to connect to the Internet, and packet filtering is part of the standard router feature set. A commercial firewall system provides increased security, but may cost from US $4,000 to $30,000, depending on its complexity and the number of systems protected. If an organization has the in-house expertise, a home-brewed firewall can be constructed from public domain software, but there are still costs in terms of the time to develop and deploy the firewall system. Finally, all firewalls require continuing support for administration, general maintenance, software updates, security patches, and incident handling.

Components of a Firewall System

After making decisions about firewall stance, security policy, and budget issues, an organization can determine the specific components of its firewall system. A typical firewall is composed of one or more of the following building blocks:

- Packet-filtering router

- Application-level gateway (or proxy server)

- Circuit-level gateway

Building Block: Packet-Filtering Router

A packet-filtering router, shown on the Packet Filtering Diagram, examines each datagram to determine whether it matches one of its packet-filtering rules. Based on those rules, the router makes a permit/deny decision for each packet it receives.

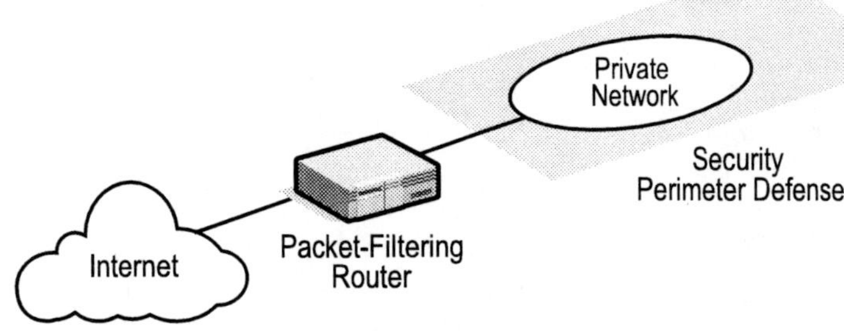

Packet Filtering

Objective 4.7
Describe how firewalls are used to protect private networks.
... Packet filtering

The filtering rules are based on the IP packet header information. This information consists of the following:

- IP source address

- IP destination address

- Encapsulated protocol (TCP, UDP, Internet Control Message Protocol [ICMP], or IP tunneling protocols)

- TCP/UDP source port

- TCP/UDP destination port

- ICMP message type

- Incoming interface of the packet

- Outgoing interface of the packet

If the router finds a rule that permits the packet, it forwards the packet according to the information in the routing table. If the router finds a rule that denies the packet, the router discards the packet. If there is no rule that applies to the packet, a user-configurable default parameter determines whether the packet is forwarded or discarded.

Service-Dependent (Port) Filtering

Objective 4.4
Identify appropriate access-control security features for an Internet server.

*Objective **4.7**
Describe how firewalls are used to protect private networks.
... Port filtering*

The packet-filtering rules allow a router to permit or deny traffic based on a specific service, because most service listeners reside on well-known TCP/UDP ports. For example, a Telnet server listens for remote connections on Port 23, and an SMTP server listens for incoming connections on Port 25. To block all incoming Telnet connections, the router simply discards all packets that contain a destination port value equal to 23. While this approach blocks Telnet-based attacks, it also blocks user access to Telnet services.

If some users require Telnet, the firewall can be configured to restrict incoming Telnet connections to a limited number of internal hosts. For example, the router must deny all packets that contain a destination port value equal to 23 and do not contain the destination IP address of one of the permitted hosts. Some typical filtering rules include:

- Permit incoming Telnet sessions only to a specific list of internal hosts.

- Permit incoming FTP sessions only to specific internal hosts.

- Permit all outbound Telnet sessions.

- Permit all outbound FTP sessions.

- Deny all incoming traffic from specific external networks.

Service-Independent Filtering

There are certain types of attacks that are difficult to identify using basic packet header information because the attacks are service independent. For example, in a data-driven attack, seemingly harmless data is forwarded by the router to an internal host. The data contains hidden instructions that cause the host to modify access control and security-related files, making it easier for the intruder to gain access to the system.

Routers can be configured to protect against these types of attacks. However, the rules are more difficult to specify because the filtering rules require additional information that can be learned only by examining the routing table, inspecting for specific IP options, checking for a special fragment offset, and so on. Examples of these types of attacks are described here:

- **Source IP Address Spoofing Attacks**—For this type of attack, an intruder transmits packets from the outside that falsely contain the source IP address of an inside system. The attacker hopes that the use of a spoofed source IP address will allow penetration of systems that simply accept packets from specific trusted internal hosts and discard packets from other hosts. Source spoofing attacks can be defeated by discarding each packet with an inside source IP address if the packet arrives on one of the router's outside interfaces.

- **Source Routing Attacks**—In a source routing attack, the source station uses the Source Route Option feature of IP to specify a specific list of IP addresses a packet must follow as it crosses the Internet. This type of attack is designed to bypass security measures and cause the packet to follow an unexpected path to its destination. A source routing attack can be defeated by simply discarding all packets that contain a specific routing path in the Options field.

- **Tiny Fragment Attacks**—For this type of attack, an intruder uses the IP fragmentation feature to create extremely small fragments and force the TCP header information into a separate packet fragment. Tiny fragment attacks are designed to circumvent user-defined filtering rules; the hacker hopes that a filtering router will examine only the first fragment and allow all other fragments to pass. A tiny fragment attack can be defeated by discarding all packets with a protocol type of TCP and an IP FragmentOffset equal to 1.

Benefits of Packet-Filtering Routers

The majority of Internet firewall systems are deployed using only a packet-filtering router. Other than the time spent planning the filters and configuring the router, there is little or no cost to implement packet filtering because the feature is included as part of standard router software releases. Because Internet access is generally provided over a WAN interface, there is little impact on router performance if traffic loads are moderate and few filters are defined. Finally, a packet-filtering router is generally transparent to users and applications; thus, it does not require specialized user training or specific software on each host.

Limitations of Packet-Filtering Routers

Defining packet filters can be a complex task because network administrators must have a detailed understanding of the various Internet services, packet header formats, and specific values they expect to find in each field. This low-level detail is necessary because any packet that passes directly through a router could potentially be used to launch a data-driven attack, in which seemingly harmless data contains hidden instructions. Unfortunately, there are few testing facilities to verify the correctness of the filtering rules after they are configured on the router. This can potentially leave a site open to untested vulnerabilities.

If complex filtering requirements must be supported, the filtering rule set can become very long and complicated, making it difficult to manage and comprehend. Also, the packet throughput of a router decreases as the number of filters increases. Routers are optimized to extract the destination IP address from each packet, make a relatively simple routing table lookup, and then forward the packet to the proper interface for transmission. If filtering is enabled, the router must not only make a forwarding decision for each packet, but also apply all of the filter rules to each packet. This can consume CPU cycles and degrade system performance.

IP packet filters may not be able to provide enough control over traffic. A packet-filtering router can permit or deny a particular service; however, it is not capable of understanding the context/ data of a particular service. For example, a network administrator may need to filter traffic at the Application Layer to limit access to a subset of the available FTP or Telnet commands, or block the import of mail or newsgroups concerning specific topics. This type of control is best performed at a higher layer by proxy services and application-level gateways.

Example 1: Packet-Filtering Router

The most common Internet firewall system, shown on the Packet-Filtering Router Diagram, consists of nothing more than a packet-filtering router deployed between a private network and the Internet. A packet-filtering router performs the typical routing functions of forwarding traffic between networks, as well as using packet-filtering rules to permit or deny traffic. Typically, the filter rules are defined so that hosts on the private network have direct access to the Internet, while hosts on the Internet have limited access to systems on the private network. The external stance of this type of firewall system is usually that everything is denied unless specifically permitted.

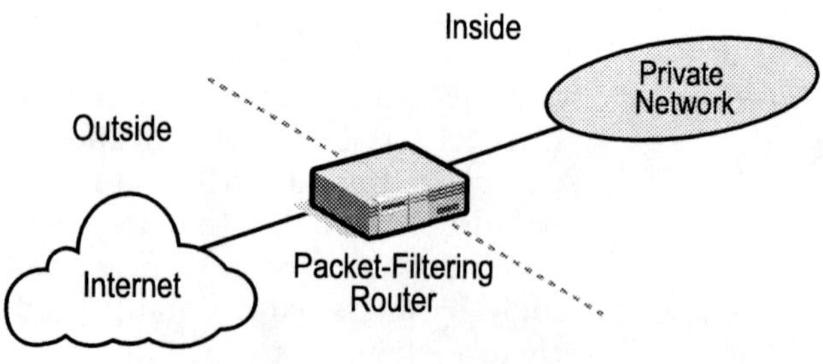

Packet-Filtering Router

Although this firewall system has the benefit of being inexpensive and transparent to users, it possesses all of the limitations of a packet-filtering router, such as exposure to attacks from improperly configured filters, and attacks that are tunneled within permitted services. Because direct exchange of packets is permitted between outside and inside systems, the potential extent of an attack is determined by the total number of hosts and services to which the packet-filtering router permits access. This means that each host directly accessible from the Internet must support sophisticated user authentication, and be regularly examined by the network administrator for signs of an attack. In addition, if the single packet-filtering router is penetrated, every system on the private network may be compromised.

Building Block: Application-Level Gateway (Proxy Server)

Objective 3.8
Describe various hardware and software connection devices and when to use them … Proxy server

An application-level gateway allows a network administrator to implement a much stricter security policy than with a packet-filtering router. Rather than relying on a generic packet-filtering tool to manage the flow of Internet services through a firewall, special-purpose code (proxy service) is installed on the gateway for each desired Internet service.

A proxy service acts as a "middleman" between a source and destination system. Instead of communicating directly with each other, the two systems establish a connection with the proxy server, which then exchanges messages between them.

If the network administrator does not install the proxy code for a particular application, the service is not supported and cannot be forwarded across the firewall. Also, the proxy code can be configured to support only those specific features of a service that the network administrator considers acceptable, while denying all other features.

This enhanced security comes with an increased cost. The gateway hardware and proxy service applications are expensive, additional time and knowledge is required to configure the gateway, and increased security means a decrease in service and transparency to users. As always, the network administrator must balance the organization's need for security with the user community's demand for ease of use.

It is important to note that users are permitted access to the proxy services, but they are never permitted to log in to the application-level gateway itself. If users are permitted to log in to the firewall system, an intruder could potentially compromise the effectiveness of the firewall. For example, after gaining root access, an intruder could install Trojan horses to collect passwords, or modify the security configuration files of the firewall to create additional access holes.

Bastion Host

Unlike packet-filtering routers, which allow the direct flow of packets between inside and outside systems, application-level gateways allow information to flow between systems but do not allow the direct exchange of packets. The chief risk of allowing packets to be exchanged between inside and outside systems is that the host applications residing on the protected network's systems must be secured against any threat posed by the incoming packets.

An application-level gateway is often called a "bastion host," because it is a guardian system specifically armored and protected against attacks. Several design features are used to provide security for a bastion host:

- The bastion host hardware platform executes a "secure" version of its OS. For example, if the bastion host is a UNIX platform, it executes a secure version of the UNIX OS specifically designed to protect against OS vulnerabilities and ensure firewall integrity.

- Only services the network administrator considers essential are installed on the bastion host. The reasoning is that if a service is not installed, it cannot be attacked. Generally, a limited set of proxy applications, such as Telnet, DNS, FTP, SMTP, and user authentication, are installed on a bastion host.

- The bastion host may require additional authentication before a user is allowed access to the proxy services. For example, the bastion host is the ideal location for installing strong authentication using a one-time password technology, in which a smart card cryptographic authenticator generates a unique one-time access code. In addition, each proxy service may require its own authentication before granting user access.

- Each proxy is configured to support only a subset of the standard application's command set. If a standard command is not supported by the proxy application, it is simply not available to the authenticated user.

- Each proxy is configured to allow access only to specific host systems. This means that the limited command/feature set may be applied only to a subset of systems on the protected network.

- Each proxy maintains detailed audit information by logging all traffic, each connection, and the duration of each connection. The audit log is an essential tool for discovering and terminating intruder attacks.

- Each proxy is a small and uncomplicated program specifically designed for network security. This allows the source code of the proxy application to be reviewed and checked for potential bugs and security holes. For example, a typical UNIX mail application may contain over 20,000 lines of code, while a mail proxy may contain fewer than 1,000.

- Each proxy is independent of all other proxies on the bastion host. If there is a problem with the operation of any proxy, or if a vulnerability is discovered, one proxy can be uninstalled without affecting the operation of the other proxy applications. Also, if the user population requires support for a new service, the network administrator can easily install the required proxy on the bastion host.

- A proxy generally performs no disk access other than to read its initial configuration file. This makes it difficult for an intruder to install Trojan horse password sniffers or other dangerous files on the bastion host.

- Each proxy runs as a nonprivileged user in a private and secured directory on the bastion host.

Example 2: Telnet Proxy

The Telnet Proxy Diagram illustrates the operation of a Telnet proxy on a bastion host. For this example, the outside client wants to Telnet to an inside server that is protected by the application-level gateway.

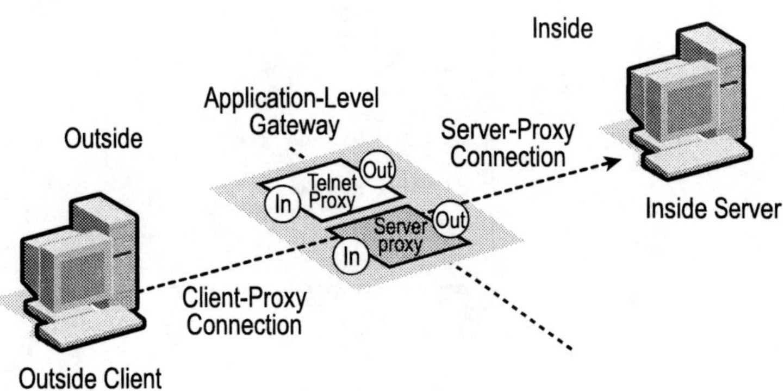

Telnet Proxy

The Telnet proxy never allows the remote user to log in or have direct access to the internal server. The outside client uses Telnet to connect to the bastion host, which authenticates the user by using one-time password technology. After user authentication, the outside client gains access to the user interface of the Telnet proxy. The Telnet proxy permits only a subset of the Telnet command set, and determines which inside hosts are available for Telnet access. When the outside user specifies the destination host, the Telnet proxy makes its own connection to the inside server and forwards commands to the inside server on behalf of the outside client. The outside client believes that the Telnet proxy is the real inside server, while the inside server believes that the Telnet proxy is the outside client.

The Telnet Proxy Authentication Diagram shows the output to the outside client's terminal screen as the connection to the inside server is established. Note that the client is not performing a logon to the bastion host; the user is being authenticated by the bastion host and a challenge is issued before the user is permitted to communicate with the Telnet proxy. After passing the challenge, the proxy server limits the set of commands and destinations available to the outside client.

```
Outside-Client > telnet bastion_host
Username: John Smith
Challenge Number "237936"
Challenge Response: 723456
Trying 200.43.67.17 ...

HostOS UNIX (bastion_host)

bh-telent-proxy> help
Valid commands are:

connect hostname
help/?
quit/exit

bh-telent-proxy> connect inside_server

HostOS UNIX (inside_server)

login: John Smith
Password: #####
Last login: Wednesday April 15 11:17:15
```

Telnet Proxy Authentication

User authentication can be based on something the user knows (password) or something the user physically possesses (smart card). Both techniques are subject to theft; however, using a combination of both methods increases the likelihood of correct user authentication. In the Telnet example, the proxy transmits a challenge and the user, with the aid of a smart card, responds to the challenge. Typically, a user unlocks the smart card by entering a personal identification number (PIN). The card, using a shared secret encryption key and its own internal clock, returns an encrypted value for the user to enter as a response to the challenge.

Advantages of Proxy Servers

By using this indirect communication method and by focusing on application-specific traffic, proxy servers provide more flexible protection than simply blocking IP addresses or well-known ports:

- Proxy servers inspect the contents of packets. Thus, a proxy can be configured to support only those features of a service that the network administrator considers acceptable, while it denies all other features.

- Internal network details, such as addressing, are hidden from outside view. All outgoing packets contain the source address of the proxy server, not the addresses of all internal users.

- Proxy servers can authenticate the identity of users before allowing communication through the firewall.

- Before passing data in either direction, a proxy can check the request against company security policies.

- Proxy servers can gather statistics on Web application usage and traffic patterns. If these logs show that a stock brokerage's most-accessed Web sites are ESPN and Victoria's Secret, then management may decide to block access to those sites so the company's Internet bandwidth can be used more productively.

Disadvantages of Proxy Servers

The greatest limitation of an application-level gateway is its reduced transparency. To access the Web, users may need to provide a password before the proxy will complete a connection.

Also, each client computer must be set up to work with the proxy server, so that outgoing packets are routed to that device for forwarding to the Internet. The Windows 2000 Proxy Server Setup Screen Capture shows how a user can specify a different proxy server for each protocol, if necessary.

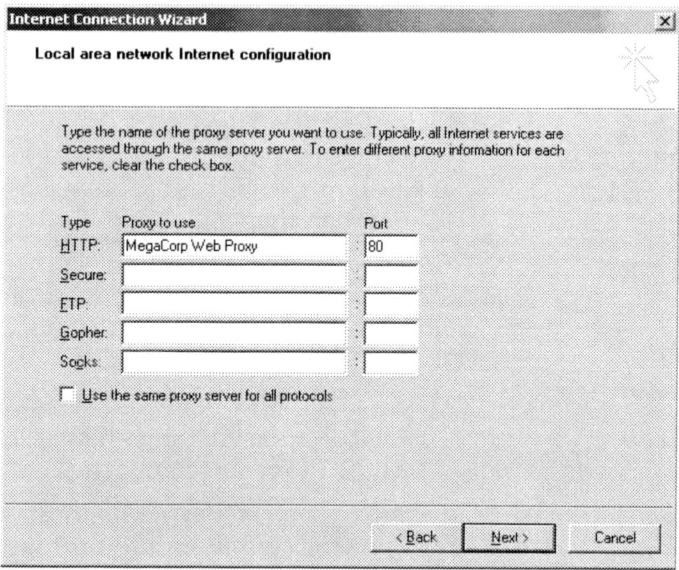

Windows 2000 Proxy Server Setup

Building Block: Circuit-Level Gateway

A circuit-level gateway is a specialized function that can be performed by an application-level gateway. A circuit-level gateway simply relays TCP connections without performing any additional packet processing or filtering.

Circuit-level gateways are often used for outgoing connections when a system administrator trusts the internal users. Their chief advantage is that a bastion host can be configured as a hybrid gateway, supporting application-level or proxy services for inbound connections, and circuit-level functions for outbound connections. This makes the firewall system easier to use for internal users who want direct access to Internet services, while still providing the firewall functions needed to protect the organization from external attack.

The Circuit-Level Gateway Diagram illustrates the operation of a typical Telnet connection through a circuit-level gateway. The circuit-level gateway simply relays the Telnet connection through the firewall; it does no additional examination, filtering, or management of the Telnet protocol. The circuit-level gateway acts like a wire, copying bytes back and forth between the inside and outside connections. However, because the connection appears to originate from the firewall system, it conceals information about the protected network.

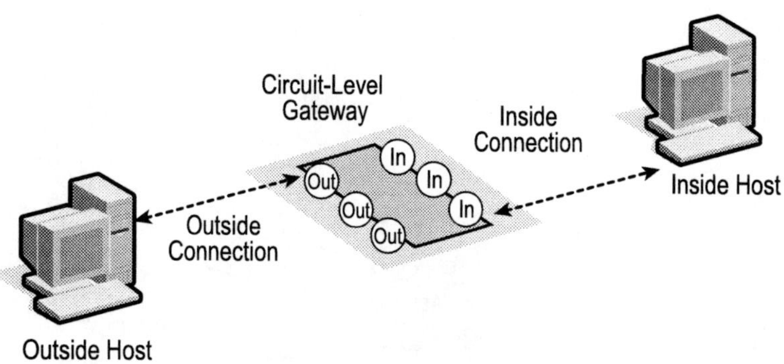

Circuit-Level Gateway

SOCKS

Many proxy server applications support a standard circuit-level proxy protocol called SOCKS. Since SOCKS sets up outbound TCP connections, it supports any application. This allows users to take advantage of new Internet technologies without having to wait for the firewall to be reconfigured to allow them.

SOCKS provides all of the security features we've discussed in this lesson. In requiring internal users to provide a password or other form of identification, it also authenticates these users before completing an outbound connection. By authenticating internal users, SOCKS guards against security attacks that originate from within a network, such as intruders or Trojan Horse programs that capture confidential information and transmit it to an outside criminal.

Web Caching

Objective 1.2
Understand and be able to describe the concept of caching and its implications.

In addition to enhancing security, many proxy servers increase Web response speed by caching frequently accessed Web pages and other files. See the Proxy Serving Page Not in Cache Diagram, below.

When a user requests a Web page for the first time, the proxy server retrieves that page from the remote Web server. It then places a copy of that data in the cache on its local hard drive.

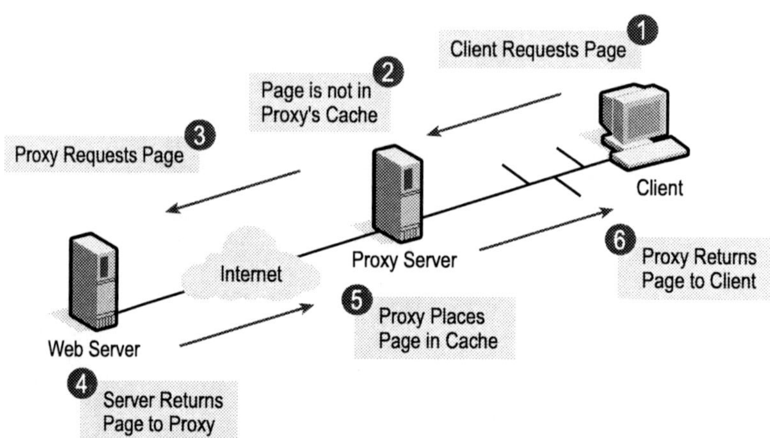

Proxy Serving Page Not in Cache

If another user later requests the same page, the proxy server retrieves the page from the cache. This local file transfer is faster than retrieving the page from the distant Web server, so users notice much faster Web response times. See the Proxy Serving Page From Cache Diagram, below.

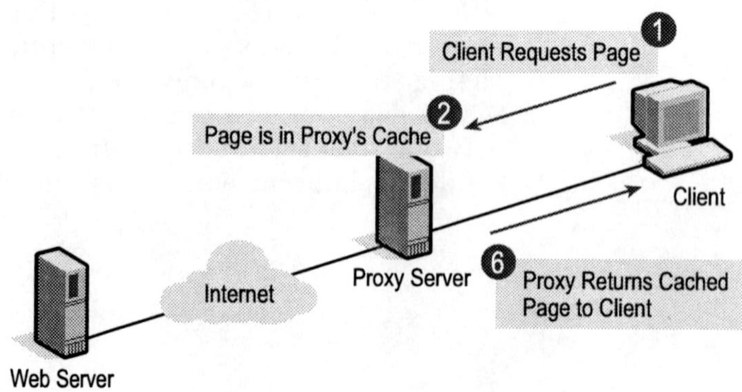

Proxy Serving Page From Cache

Caching also occurs on browsers and at major ISPs. Each time you request a Web page, the actual data may not be served from the remote Web site. Instead, the page may come from the cache on your browser, your LAN's proxy server, or a regional ISP.

Caching can cut costs by significantly reducing a company's Web traffic. However, a proxy server needs large amounts of disk space to support Web caching. Individual users can reclaim significant disk space by occasionally emptying their browser caches.

"Faster" or "Fresher"

Some information ages gracefully. It doesn't matter whether a recipe has been stored in some cache for weeks. But if you're keeping up with fast-breaking news, you want to be sure that you're seeing the most current version of a Web page.

When a proxy server gets a request for a Web page that is in its cache, it must decide whether to provide the fastest response by serving the cached page, or provide the freshest data by getting the most recent version from the remote Web server. The major proxy server products base this decision on several factors:

- The age of the page (date the page was last modified). Newer pages are refreshed more often than old content.

- An expiration date built into the page by the content author.

- Specific instructions to retrieve fresh data from important sites. For example, if a group of stockbrokers frequently checks a few sites for financial information, then the proxy can be configured to always pull fresh data from those sites, or to frequently refresh the cache during periods of low activity.

Proxy servers and browsers also ensure fresh content by using an HTTP method called a "conditional GET." A typical GET tells the Web server to transmit a page. But a conditional GET includes the date and time of the page currently in the cache of the requesting device (proxy server or client browser). If the Web server contains a more recent version of that page, the server sends it. If the page has not been updated, the server returns the HTTP response message 304: "not modified." This tells the client to use the cached page. A conditional GET is not as fast as going straight to the cache, but it is faster than unnecessarily downloading a page.

**Example 3:
Screened Host
Firewall**

A screened host firewall employs both a packet-filtering router and bastion host, as shown on the Screened Host Diagram. This firewall system provides a higher level of security than the previous example because it implements both Network Layer security (packet-filtering) and Application Layer security (proxy services). Also, an intruder must penetrate two separate systems before the security of the private network can be compromised.

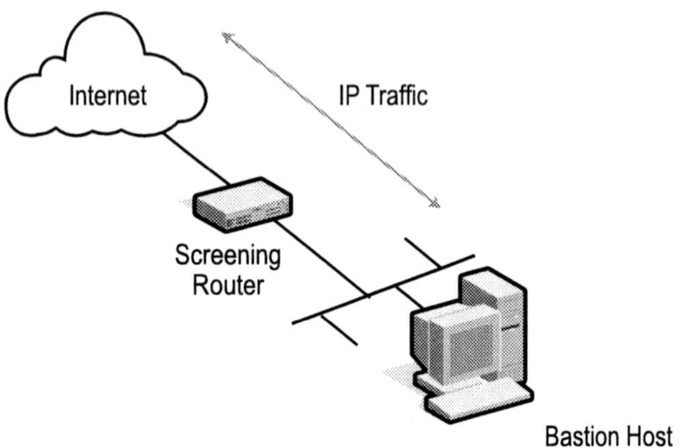

Screened Host

In this firewall system, the bastion host is configured on the private network, with a packet-filtering router between the Internet and bastion host. The filtering rules on the packet-filtering router are configured so that outside systems can access only the bastion host; traffic addressed to all other internal systems is blocked.

Because the inside hosts reside on the same network as the bastion host, the security policy of the organization determines whether inside systems are permitted direct access to the Internet, or they are required to use the proxy services on the bastion host. Inside users can be forced to use the proxy services by configuring the router's filter rules to accept only internal traffic that originates from the bastion host.

One of the benefits of this firewall system is that a public information server providing Web and FTP services can be placed on the segment shared by the packet-filtering router and bastion host. If the strongest security is required, the bastion host can run proxy services that require both internal and external users to access the bastion host before communicating with the information server. If a lower level of security is adequate, the router may be configured to allow outside users direct access to the public information server.

Example 4: Dual-Homed Bastion Host

An even more secure firewall system is illustrated on the Dual-Homed Bastion Host Diagram. A dual-homed bastion host has two network interfaces —one for the packet-filtering router and one for the internal network. However, the host cannot directly forward traffic between the two interfaces, all traffic must pass through the proxy services. This physical topology forces all traffic destined for the private network through the bastion host, and provides additional security if outside users are granted direct access to an information server.

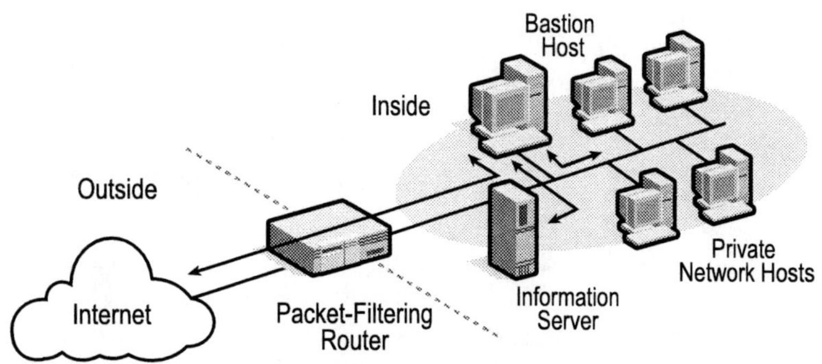

Dual-Homed Bastion Host

Because a bastion host is the only internal system that can be directly accessed from the Internet, the potential set of systems open to attack is limited to the bastion host. However, if users are allowed to log on to the bastion host itself, the entire private network is threatened because an intruder could log on as well. It is critical that the bastion host be hardened and protected from penetration, and that users never be allowed to log on to the bastion host.

Example 5: "Demilitarized Zone" or Screened-Subnet Firewall

The final firewall example employs two packet-filtering routers and a bastion host, as shown on the Screened-Subnet Firewall Diagram. This firewall system is the most secure, because it supports both Network and Application Layer security while defining a "demilitarized zone" (DMZ) network. Because traffic must flow through both routers in sequence, the screened-subnet configuration is also called a "back-to-back" firewall.

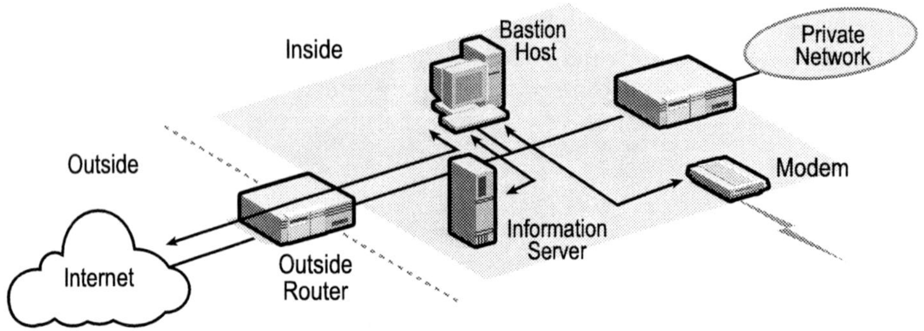

Screened-Subnet Firewall

Objective *4.4*
Identify appropriate access-control security features for an Internet server.

Objective 4.8
Identify when to use various DMZ configurations.

The network administrator places the bastion host, information (Web, FTP) servers, modem pools, and other public servers on the DMZ network. The DMZ network functions as a small, isolated network positioned between the Internet and private network. Typically, the DMZ is configured so that systems on the Internet and systems on the private network can access only a limited number of systems on the DMZ network; however, direct transmission of traffic across the DMZ network is prohibited.

The outside router protects against standard attacks from incoming traffic (source IP address spoofing, source routing attacks, etc.) and manages Internet access to the DMZ network. It permits external systems to access only the bastion host (and possibly the information server). The inside router provides a second line of defense, managing DMZ access to the private network by accepting only traffic that originates from the bastion host.

For Internet-bound traffic, the inside router manages private network access to the DMZ network. It permits internal systems to access only the bastion host (and possibly the information server). The filtering rules on the outside router require use of the proxy services, by accepting Internet-bound traffic only from the bastion host.

A variation of this configuration further isolates the DMZ by using three network interfaces on the bastion host: one for the outside router, one for the DMZ information server(s), and one for the inside router. In that case, the bastion host is called a "three-homed router" or "three-homed firewall."

There are several key benefits to the deployment of a screened-subnet firewall system:

- An intruder must crack three separate devices (without detection) to infiltrate the private network: outside router, bastion host, and inside router.

- Because the outside router advertises only the DMZ network to the Internet, systems on the Internet do not have routes to the protected private network. This allows the network manager to ensure that the private network is "invisible" from the outside, and only select systems on the DMZ are known to the Internet by means of routing table and DNS information exchanges.

- Because the inside router advertises only the DMZ network to the private network, systems on the private network do not have routes to the Internet. This means that the Internet is invisible to the private network.

- Because packet-filtering routers direct traffic to specific systems on the DMZ network, there is no need for the bastion host to be dual-homed.

- The inside router supports greater packet throughput than a dual-homed bastion host, when it functions as the final firewall system between the private network and Internet.

- Because the DMZ network is a different network than the private network, a Network Address Translator (NAT) can be installed on the bastion host to eliminate the need to renumber or resubnet the private network.

Living With a Firewall

Security can be inconvenient for users. In order to put barriers in the way of "the bad guys," a firewall designer often must hinder "the good guys" to some extent. Therefore, there probably isn't a single firewall in the world that everyone likes. Users want the firewall loosened, so they can enjoy some of the Web's flashier features. LAN administrators—especially those who have suffered security attacks—usually wish they could make the firewall even more restrictive.

There can never be one perfect firewall, because each firewall must satisfy a unique combination of security needs, user demands, and administrator preferences. Thus, firewalls are as different as the companies that use them. Some firewall designers take a liberal stance: everything is permitted unless specifically prohibited. Others are more conservative: everything is prohibited unless specifically permitted. In either case, a corporate user's experience of the Internet is limited to what the firewall will allow.

Activities

1. Describe a firewall stance. Give examples.

2. Name the three building blocks of a firewall system.

3. An access router connects 15 nodes on an Ethernet LAN to the Internet. One of the nodes is an intranet server, as well as a file and print server; the rest are workstations. The workstations access the server through browsers as well as standard office applications, such as word processing and spreadsheets. The server also handles internal mail, Telnet, and file transfer operations. The corporate security policy requires protecting server assets from outside intruders. Describe the service-dependent filtering you would implement in the router.

4. How would you protect against IP address spoofing attacks?

5. How would you protect against source routing attacks?

6. How would you protect against tiny fragment attacks?

7. Describe some limitations of packet-filtering routers.

8. As a network designer, why would you recommend a proxy server instead of a packet-filtering router?

9. Describe the operation and benefits of a bastion host.

10. Describe the relationship of a Telnet proxy to an actual Telnet server and how the authentication procedure works.

11. What type of application-level gateway function would you recommend to protect against external attacks, yet allow trusted internal users easy access?

12. What is a DMZ firewall and why is it considered a very secure system?

Extended Activity

Using your favorite Internet search engine, find information on ZoneAlarm, BlackICE, and Checkpoint firewall products. List some of the technical specifications of these products as they relate to the lesson.

Summary

You have seen in this unit that no single technique, technology, or design can create a network of Web sites that is totally secure. The nature of Web communications and TCP/IP applications offers crackers a wide variety of opportunities to exploit.

As a Web professional, you must close these security holes with a combination of OS settings, monitoring systems, firewalls, and simple user training. Your challenge is to balance security against utility. You must create a series of protective layers that will frustrate a would-be intruder, while keeping the network and Web site usable for a company's employees and customers.

Creating this sort of secure, usable site requires a commitment to continually learn the latest techniques and best practices. It may not be possible to get ahead of the crackers, but you must at least keep up. This unit presented the philosophy of network security and described several example security setups.

Unit 10 Quiz

1. Firewalls are routers used to provide what type of functionality?

    a. Security

    b. Performance enhancements

    c. Remote access

    d. E-mail services

2. An example of a Network Layer security protocol is:

    a. IPSec

    b. IPX

    c. SPX

    d. X.25

3. Which of the following is NOT used by firewalls to filter Internet traffic?

    a. IP addresses

    b. TCP or UDP ports

    c. Frame addresses

    d. Application-specific commands

4. A circuit-level gateway is typically used for:

    a. Outbound connections

    b. Inbound connections

    c. SSL connections

    d. Stateless connections

5. What does a browser cache consist of?

    a. IP addresses of Web sites

    b. RAM reserved for the browser's use

    c. Names and e-mail addresses

    d. Copies of previously-viewed Web pages

6. What would you most likely find in a DMZ?

    a. An HTTP server

    b. A workgroup file server

    c. An SMTP server

    d. A user's workstation

    e. A or C

    f. B or D

7. Why would someone call a computer a "dual-homed host"?

    a. It hosts two different Web sites.

    b. It belongs to two different organizations.

    c. It serves files to both on-site and remote users.

    d. It contains two NICs, each with a different network number.

8. Of the following, which portion of a corporate network security policy is the most vital to ensure all users understand the policy rules?

    a. Acceptable use agreement

    b. User awareness training

    c. Risk analysis

    d. Monitoring

9. The _______________ portion of a corporate network security policy verifies compliance with the policy rules.

    a. Monitoring

    b. Acceptable use agreement

    c. User awareness training

    d. Risk analysis

10. To ensure that a recipient can trust a source, a _______________ may be transmitted with a network document.

    a. Digital signature

    b. Password

    c. Digital certificate

    d. Class 1 ID

11. Defining the rules for Internet access from corporate resources in a formal document is part of the ___________________ portion of a corporate network security policy.

    a. Monitoring

    b. Acceptable use agreement

    c. User awareness training

    d. Risk analysis

12. _______________ runs code in a "sandbox," providing built-in client protection mechanisms that restrict code access to a client's hardware and OS.

    a. JavaScript

    b. Java

    c. Perl

    d. ActiveX

13. Which of the following actions will secure a Web server application?

    a. Only run those Internet services necessary for the site's operation

    b. Turn off all logging

    c. Allow site content posts by means of anonymous FTP

    d. Allow directory browsing on the Web server

14. Traffic coming in to your Web site has slowed to nearly zero. Your firewall logs show that the router has blocked very high volumes of ICMP packets. What is probably happening?

    a. A man-in-the-middle attack

    b. A mail flood

    c. A ping flood

    d. A SYN flood

15. Most attacks against a corporation's network security come from:

    a. Political terrorists

    b. The corporation's own employees

    c. Independent crackers

    d. Industrial spies

16. Confidential data moving between users and e-commerce Web sites is typically protected by:

    a. SSL

    b. SET

    c. PGP

    d. IPSec

Course Quiz

1. What is frame relay used for?

   a. To move frames across a switch

   b. To transmit frames from one LAN node to another

   c. To link the floors of a building

   d. To connect LANs over a metropolitan or wide area

2. You're searching for Web pages with information about laser-guided missiles. Which of the following search strings is most likely to find the best information?

   a. laser technology

   b. laser OR missiles

   c. "laser missile"

   d. +laser +missile –printer

3. Which of the following HTML tags does a search site's spider program usually NOT read?

   a. <title>

   b. <meta>

   c. <body>

   d. <alt>

4. A welfare recipient uses a government-issued smart card to pay for groceries. This is an example of:

    a. B2C

    b. EBT

    c. ATM

    d. EFT

5. Which of the following would you expect to find on a C2B site?

    a. Requests for goods or services

    b. Goods or services offered for sale

    c. A company's intranet

    d. Auctions

6. When you surf the Web from home, on a dial-up connection, what protocols are you most likely to use?

    a. HTTP, PPP, IP

    b. SMTP, IP, SLIP

    c. Ethernet, TCP, IP

    d. ATM, POTS, ISP

7. What unit of information does a router operate on?

    a. Bit

    b. Byte

    c. Frame

    d. Packet

    e. Socket

8. Name the layers of the OSI model from top to bottom.

    ____

    ____

    ____

    ____

    ____

    ____

9. Where should you look for a daemon?

   a. On a malfunctioning router

   b. On a UNIX host that provides a server process

   c. On a workstation with faulty virus control

   d. In a hackers' chat room

10. What is the main difference between a standard switch and a bridge?

   a. Switches do not forward broadcast frames.

   b. Bridges are faster than switches.

   c. Switches effectively multiply the network's bandwidth.

   d. Bridges operate at Layer 3.

11. Which type of address is unique anywhere in the world?

   a. Port address

   b. IP address

   c. Subnet mask

   d. NIC address

12. The biggest obstacle to high-speed Internet access is which of the following?

   a. Government regulations

   b. T1 multiplexing

   c. Competing telecom companies

   d. Analog local loops

13. When a router forwards data from a frame relay network to an Ethernet network, what happens?

   a. It repeats the frame without changes onto the Ethernet network.

   b. It removes the frame relay header and trailer, and transmits the packet onto the Ethernet network.

   c. It removes the frame relay header and trailer, inspects the packet header, builds a new Ethernet frame around the packet, and transmits the frame onto the Ethernet network.

   d. It builds an Ethernet frame around the frame relay frame and transmits the frame onto the Ethernet network.

14. In a client/server arrangement, where are requests normally generated?

    a. Client

    b. Server

    c. Either client or server

    d. NIC

15. How are frames and packets different?

    a. Frames travel from NIC to NIC, packets travel from end to end.

    b. Frames have both headers and trailers, but packets have only headers.

    c. Packets are carried within frames.

    d. All of the above.

16. From your home office, you need to inspect the configuration of a router in another city. What would you most likely use to do this?

    a. FTP

    b. SMTP

    c. RIP

    d. Telnet

17. You want to see the names of the files in a remote directory, without details such as file size or date/time. What FTP command should you use?

    a. DIR

    b. LIST

    c. LS

    d. FILES

18. What is the main drawback to FTP?

    a. Security

    b. Speed

    c. Reliability

    d. Cost

19. How would you specify the color green in a Web page?

    a. #00FF00

    b. 0.255.0

    c. #green

    d. "R=0,G=100,B=0"

20. Which of the following HTML tag pairs creates a table cell?

    a. <tr> </tr>

    b. <tc> </tc>

    c. <td> </td>

    d. <cell> </cell>

21. Which of the following best describes an e-mail message's communication flow through the TCP/IP model layers?

    a. The Internetwork Layer breaks the message into pieces, the Network Access Layer forwards the datagram to its final destination, and the Transport Layer places the packets into frames.

    b. The Network Access Layer passes the data stream to the Transport Layer, which breaks the data into pieces. The Transport Layer passes the pieces to the Internetwork Layer, which build frames to carry the datagrams to the next node on the physical network.

    c. The Transport Layer breaks the data stream into pieces, which it passes to the Network Access Layer. The Network Access Layer adds the source and destination IP addresses, and forwards the packets to the Internetwork Layer. The Internetwork Layer builds frames and converts them to bits for transport across the physical network.

    d. The Transport Layer breaks the data stream into pieces, which it passes to the Internetwork Layer. The Internetwork Layer adds the source and destination IP addresses and forwards the packets to the Network Access Layer. The Network Access Layer builds frames, and converts them to bits for transport across the physical network.

22. On your LAN, one server computer provides DHCP service to all nodes. You are about to add a router to the network, which also runs DHCP by default. What two approaches would work? (Choose two.)

    a. Disable DHCP on the router

    b. Configure the router with the same address scope as the server, but designate the router as the backup DHCP server

    c. Configure the server to manage half of the IP address pool, and the router to manage the other half

    d. Do not change the default router settings, and let the router and the server synchronize their DHCP databases

23. Which two of the following are Class C addresses? (Choose two.)

    a. 10.1.23.46

    b. 199.17.89.253

    c. 192.168.40.15

    d. 172.16.45.134

24. Bridges and switches filter traffic in which way?

    a. By building routing tables and making forwarding decisions based on packet addresses

    b. By building physical address to port mappings and making forwarding decisions based on these mappings

    c. By looking at the source MAC address and forwarding frames only to the same segment on which the source resides

    d. By looking at the destination IP address and forwarding all unknown packets to all ports

25. Which network device can isolate broadcast traffic to the local network segment?

    a. Router

    b. Hub

    c. Bridge

    d. Switch

26. Which statement best describes IMAP?

    a. IMAP uses POP3 for client/server e-mail communications.

    b. IMAP allows users to search e-mail messages for keywords directly on the e-mail client.

    c. IMAP allows users to manage mail messages on the e-mail server, without downloading them.

    d. IMAP is a protocol for transferring e-mail messages between servers.

27. Which two of the following are reasons why an organization would choose to subnet their network? (Choose two.)

    a. To control collisions across multiple sites

    b. To build a more scalable network

    c. To support a single site from one address range

    d. To conserve network addresses

28. Which best describes a DHCP scope?

    a. A list of DHCP servers from which the client can choose to obtain its configuration

    b. A list of clients the server is allowed to answer

    c. A range of addresses from which the server chooses a client address assignment

    d. A range of addresses from which a server can choose a client address assignment, limited to a single subnet

29. How does network address translation enhance network security?

    a. It assigns each host the same address, making each internal connection easily traceable.

    b. It only maps internal hosts to external addresses for the duration of the connection.

    c. It blocks external attacks while the internal host is online.

    d. It disconnects any externally initiated connections while the internal host is online.

30. In order to communicate with a host on a remote network, the source IP device must forward its packets to which of the following?

    a. The remote host's default gateway

    b. The remote host's nearest exit router

    c. The source host's default gateway

    d. The source host's nearest internal router

31. You wish to measure the round-trip time your IP packets experience between your local router, RouterA, and a directly connected router, RouterB. You issue a Tracert command to measure the round trip time between the routers. The routers are configured as follows:

Local router:

* Router name—RouterA

* Internal network port IP address—10.0.12.1

* External network port IP address—10.0.14.1

Remote router:

* Router name—RouterB

* Directly connected port IP address—10.0.14.2

Next hop port IP address—171.68.123.250

The tracert command results are as follows:

Tracing route to routerb.bigdotcom.com [10.0.14.2] over a maximum of 30 hops

1. 2 ms   2 ms   2 ms   routera.bigdotcom.com [10.0.12.1]

2. 5 ms   7 ms   6 ms   routerb.bigdotcom.com [10.0.14.2]

Trace complete

The Tracert command results are as follows:

You calculate the round-trip time based on each hop's third ICMP packet set. Based on your calculations, which of the following choices represents the round-trip time your packets experience traveling between RouterA and RouterB?

a. 2 ms

b. 4 ms

c. 6 ms

d. 7 ms

32. You are troubleshooting a name resolution problem on your local network. You run two internal DNS servers, and they resolve all local hostnames. Where would you look to verify that your Windows 98 clients are configured to use the correct DNS servers?

    a. The local ARP cache

    b. The Netstat window

    c. The Winipcfg window

    d. The DNS server hosts file

33. Which of the following are kept in a computer's ARP cache?

    a. IP address and port number

    b. IP address and MAC address

    c. MAC address and LAN ID

    d. TCP address and IP address

34. The number of routers a packet must go through to get to the final destination is referred to as:

    a. Aspect ratio

    b. Interleaf ratio

    c. Multicast number

    d. Hop count

35. Latency is a measurement associated with which one of the following?

    a.   Delay through an individual network component

    b.   Delay through a router

    c.   Delay across a wide area link

    d.   Delay across a LAN link

36. As CPU utilization of a network component increases, normally response time:

    a.   Remains flat

    b.   Increases

    c.   Decreases

    d.   None of the above

37. Which of the following technologies provides the most bandwidth?

    a.   Dial-up using modems

    b.   ISDN basic rate

    c.   FT1

    d.   T3

38. Which of the following applications requires the most bandwidth?

    a.   PC communications

    b.   Digital audio

    c.   Compressed video

    d.   Full-motion video

39. Which measurement refers to the amount of user data being transferred across a network?

    a.   Protocol efficiency

    b.   Throughput

    c.   Capacity

    d.   Bandwidth

40. WAN service options fall into what two categories? (Choose two.)

    a. Point-to-point/point-to-multipoint

    b. T1 and E1

    c. Dial-up

    d. Switched

    e. Leased

41. What topology best describes a group of cable modem users on the same street?

    a. Bus

    b. Star

    c. Mesh

    d. Cloud

42. You travel a lot for business, and must check your e-mail from many different computers. You should choose an e-mail provider that uses:

    a. POP3

    b. SMTP

    c. IMAP4

    d. Uuencode

43. Joe pays $15 to a certificate authority, and gets a key pair for asymmetric encryption. He puts the public key in his corporate directory entry, which is available to the public. He keeps his private key secure on his computer. Which of the following is now true?

    a. Anyone in the world can send encrypted messages to Joe.

    b. Joe can send encrypted messages to anyone in the world.

    c. Joe can send encrypted messages to anyone, so long as he sends that person his private key first.

    d. Joe has made a serious security mistake. He should have put the private key in the directory, and kept the public key secret.

44. The SMTP receiver accepts incoming e-mail on which well-known port?

    a. TCP Port 23

    b. TCP Port 25

    c. UDP Port 23

    d. UDP Port 25

45. What type of e-mail protocol is IMAP4?

    a. Store-and-forward

    b. Direct delivery

    c. Stateless

    d. Packet switched

46. What does DHCP provide that BOOTP cannot?

    a. DHCP allows hosts to request configuration information from a server.

    b. DHCP only assigns manually mapped addresses.

    c. DHCP assigns reusable addresses to any requesting host.

    d. DHCP uses relay agents.

47. How does a NAT use static mapping to convert internal addresses to external addresses?

    a. It changes the subnet mask, concealing the network on which the packets' source host resides.

    b. It converts the host portion of the internal address to a different, preconfigured host address.

    c. It changes the internal address to a randomly-chosen address.

    d. It converts the network portion of the packet address from the internal network address to the external network address.

48. A DNS client is called a:

    a. Resolver

    b. Redirector

    c. Requestor

    d. Resource Record

49. The maximum length of a domain name is:

    a.   64 bytes

    b.   255 bytes

    c.   128 bytes

    d.   16 bytes

50. Which of the following is authoritative for the entire DNS namespace of a corporation?

    a.   Primary Name Server

    b.   Top Level Name Server

    c.   Resource Record Repository

    d.   Root Server

51. Domain names are expressed as:

    a.   Hexadecimal numbers

    b.   Dotted decimal notation

    c.   Strings of letters and numbers, separated by dots

    d.   None of the above

52. When an e-mail server transmits a POP3 message, that message is going to:

    a.   A user

    b.   The destination mail server

    c.   The mail system administrator

    d.   A network management application

53. Your security-conscious CEO wants each of the company's 5,000 employees to get a key pair so they can encrypt internal e-mail messages to each other. Your cost-conscious controller is shocked that each user's key pair will cost $15 per year. You should suggest:

    a.   Abandon e-mail encryption as too expensive

    b.   Use a single-key encryption system

    c.   Require all confidential messages to stay within the company LAN

    d.   Set up a company certificate server

54. Why do many Web administrators prefer to install each server application on a separate dedicated computer?

    a. Each server process needs its own Internet connection.

    b. It's easier to maintain and secure a server application that's alone on a platform.

    c. Load balancing. If the FTP server is idle, the Web server can use its processor.

    d. All server applications need a great deal of disk space and memory.

55. Which of the following is not a valid HTTP method?

    a. GET

    b. POST

    c. HEAD

    d. UPDATE

56. The two most common types of graphics used in Web pages are:

    a. BMP and JPEG

    b. JPEG and GIF

    c. GIF and PNG

    d. JPEG and VRML

57. Which of the following HTML tags will display the word "HELLO" in red?

    a. `<font color=#red>HELLO</font>`

    b. `<color=#FF0000>HELLO</color>`

    c. `<font color=#0000FF>HELLO</font>`

    d. `<font color=#FF0000>HELLO</font>`

58. Which of the following is NOT needed to view a QuickTime movie?

    a. An Internet connection and modem

    b. A QuickTime plug-in

    c. A QTVR codec

    d. A Web browser

59. Which of the following is a streaming format?

    a. GIF89a

    b. Flash

    c. PNG

    d. JPG

60. You want your Web page to include a cartoon drawing of a hand that continually waves a flag. Which of the following is the simplest format that can do this?

    a. GIF87a

    b. Shockwave

    c. GIF89a

    d. Flash

61. A frame relay network can operate at OC-48 speeds.
    True or False?

62. You need to share a DSL connection among three computers in your home office. What device can do this, and provide the highest level of security?

    a. DSLAM

    b. Router

    c. Hub

    d. DSL Modem

63. When you order your bridged DSL Internet connection, your ISP says that you must install a particular software application to allow multiple users at your site to use the connection at the same time. What protocol does this application probably implement?

    a. ATM

    b. PPPoE

    c. PPTP

    d. PPP over DSL

64. In what way is a proxy server like NAT?

    a.   It changes the destination addresses of outgoing packets.

    b.   It changes the source address of incoming packets.

    c.   It changes the source address of outgoing packets.

    d.   It changes the port numbers of outgoing packets.

65. A company's DMZ uses one outside router and one inside router. A Web server is installed inside the DMZ. Which of the following must have a unique public IP address?

    a.   Inside router

    b.   Outside router

    c.   Web server

    d.   All of the above

    e.   B and C

66. When a Web site retrieves variable data from a database, its request is typically processed by:

    a.   DBMS

    b.   XML

    c.   ASP

    d.   PHP

67. What database standard is typically used by dynamic Web sites on Microsoft platforms?

    a.   PHP

    b.   ODBC

    c.   SGML

    d.   XML

68. CGI-compliant Web applications use what protocol to exchange data?

    a.   HTML

    b.   TELNET

    c.   ODBC

    d.   HTTP

69. When using CGI to pass form data to a server-side script, what method is best for longer items of information?

    a. POST

    b. SUBMIT

    c. GET

    d. FORM

70. The POST method passes data to a CGI program via the program's:

    a. Environment space

    b. URI

    c. STDOUT

    d. STDIN

71. Your Web page must perform a simple calculation using data supplied by the user. What should you create to perform this task?

    a. Server-side script

    b. Server-side include

    c. Client-side script

    d. Browser plug-in

72. Which of the following tasks should NOT be performed on a Web server?

    a. User authentication for Web site access

    b. Interface with outside systems

    c. Searching

    d. Mouseover effects

73. Which of the following is used for different tasks than the others?

    a. ASP

    b. Perl

    c. PHP

    d. ColdFusion

74. In an XML-based Web site, where is text formatting information stored?

    a. In the `<font>` tag

    b. In the `<head>` section

    c. In a style sheet

    d. In a database

75. Why is XML called "extensible"?

    a. Site designers may create new tags

    b. Sites may include an unlimited number of pages

    c. Sites may be hosted on multiple servers

    d. All of the above

76. Which of the following would you use to create content to display on cell phones?

    a. XML

    b. XLink

    c. WML

    d. XSL

77. Which of the following allow a user to make Internet purchases with a fairly high degree of anonymity?

    a. Electronic Funds Transfer

    b. Credit cards

    c. Electronic cash

    d. Electronic Benefits Transfer

78. Which of the following development options is best for a company that can afford to build a high-quality custom Web site, but does not want to hire the staff necessary to maintain it?

    a. Application Service Provider

    b. Template-based development package

    c. Turn-key development package

    d. Custom application toolkit

79. What type of law protects the intellectual property of a sculptor?

    a. Trademark

    b. Copyright

    c. Patent

    d. Artistic license

80. The HTML code of a Web site is typically protected by a patent. True or false?

81. What does the ® symbol tell you about a corporate logo?

    a. The logo has been legally registered as a trademark

    b. The logo represents a patented product

    c. The logo is copyrighted

    d. The corporation intends to register the logo as a trademark, but has not completed the registration process yet

82. What term describes the process of translating a site into the language of its intended audience, and tailoring content to meet the needs of that audience?

    a. Customization

    b. Localization

    c. Mirroring

    d. Fragmentation

83. Your e-commerce Web site is hosted in New York, and serves customers in Africa, South America, Indonesia, and the Middle East. When should you perform routine maintenance and backups on your server?

    a. Midnight in New York

    b. Midnight Greenwich Mean Time

    c. Never

    d. Whenever traffic is lowest

84. What is the main factor that makes it difficult to create laws protecting children from inappropriate content on the Web?

    a. Congress does not understand Internet technology

    b. Public apathy

    c. Conflicts with the free-speech rights of adults

    d. High-profile lobbying by porn site operators

85. A(n) ______________ firewall forwards traffic without authentication.

    a. Dual-homed host

    b. VPN

    c. Extranet

    d. Screening router

86. A __________________ acts on behalf of the source and destination system, requiring these systems to run a pair of communications applications configured with a specific server address.

    a. Proxy server

    b. Packet filter

    c. Screening router

    d. Dual-homed host

87. A(n) __________________ controls access to an internal or external network using rules to allow or deny traffic to and from specific addressees and ports.

    a. Proxy server

    b. Extranet

    c. Packet filter

    d. VPN

88. ______________ tools allow an administrator to automatically monitor Web systems for suspicious activity.

    a. Documentation

    b. Restriction

    c. Communication

    d. Detection

89. Of the following, which does not present a real security threat?

    a. ActiveX controls

    b. Java

    c. E-mail

    d. Cookies

90. If a security breach occurs, whom should you NOT notify? (Choose two.)

    a. Upper management

    b. Internal users

    c. Customers

    d. Authorized staff or consultants who can help

    e. Your firewall vendor

91. Your Web site's graphic designers have just finished the new visual layout for the next version of the site. What should you do now?

    a. Upload the new files to the live site immediately

    b. Test the new graphics on as many browsers and platforms as possible

    c. Stress test the graphics

    d. Do nothing until all of the other new elements have been finished

92. Which of the following approaches is best for developing an effective Web site?

    a. Rush it to production in "Web time"

    b. Build it first, because it's impossible to estimate software projects

    c. Apply software engineering processes

    d. Ignore the lessons of the past

93. The process of creating a new system, or changing an existing system, is known as a ________________.

    a. Life cycle

    b. Web cycle

    c. Methodology

    d. Procedure

94. What are the two most common SDLCs?

    a. Downhill and descending

    b. Waterfall and spiral

    c. Spiral and downhill

    d. Staircase and landing

For additional terms and definitions, visit WestNet's IT Multimedia Glossary—complete with animations and graphics—at **http://glossary.westnetinc.com**.

active loop—An active loop consists of two or more paths between a pair of devices on a bridged network. This type of loop is formed when one node is inadvertently connected to more than one bridge. See spanning tree algorithm (STA).

Active Server Pages (ASP)—ASP is a Microsoft technology for dynamic Web pages. ASP contains blocks of VBScript or Jscript, which a Web server interprets to create a unique HTML page for each browser request.

ActiveX Control—ActiveX control is a broad category of software components that can be downloaded and run by a Web browser to add extra functionality to a Web page. ActiveX, developed by Microsoft, is an outgrowth of two technologies: Object Linking and Embedding (OLE) and Component Object Model (COM).

ActiveX Data Objects (ADO)—ADO is Microsoft's interface for data objects. ADO is designed to replace Data Access Objects (DAO) and Remote Data Objects (RDO). Unlike RDO and DAO, which are designed only for accessing relational databases, ADO is more general and can be used to access all sorts of different types of data, such as spreadsheets and Web sites.

Address Resolution Protocol (ARP)—ARP is a TCP/IP protocol used to match an IP address with a related physical address, such as an Ethernet address. A host wishing to obtain a physical address broadcasts an ARP request onto the TCP/IP network. The host on the network that has the IP address in the request then replies with its physical hardware address.

address translation table—An address translation table is the internal-to-external IP and/or port address mappings maintained by a NAT device. The table's contents will vary depending on the NAT type used.

Advanced Research Projects Agency Network (ARPANET)—ARPANET is a long-haul network funded by the ARPA (later DARPA) and built by Bolt, Beranek, and Newman, Inc. From 1969 through 1990, ARPANET served as the basis for early networking research, as well as a central backbone during development of the Internet.

American Standard Code for Information Interchange (ASCII)—ASCII is one of the most widely used codes for representing text in computers. ASCII codes represent letters, numerals, punctuation, and keyboard characters as numbers. For example, when the character "A" is pressed on the keyboard, the ASCII binary representation of that character is 100 0001 (hexadecimal 41). The basic ASCII character set uses 7 bits to represent the 128 text and keyboard elements. Most files available for FTP are ASCII files.

application programming interface (API)—API is a software interface that formats requests from an application to a network operating system.

application specific integrated circuit (ASIC)—ASIC is an electronics technology that hard-wires a device to switch a specific Layer 2 protocol, such as Ethernet, or a Layer 3 protocol, such as IP. Switches that use ASIC hardware are much faster than switches that rely on slower software.

asymmetric encryption—See public-key encryption.

Asynchronous Transfer Mode (ATM)—ATM is a connection-oriented cell relay technology based on small (53-byte) cells. An ATM network consists of ATM switches that form multiple virtual circuits to carry groups of cells from source to destination. ATM can provide high-speed transport services for audio, data, and video.

backbone—A backbone is the portion of a network that carries the most significant traffic. It is also the part of the network that connects many smaller networks to form a larger network.

bandwidth—Bandwidth is a measure of the information-carrying capacity of a channel. In analog networks, bandwidth is the difference between the highest and lowest frequencies that can be transmitted across a communication link. Analog networks measure bandwidth in cycles per second (Hz). Digital networks measure bandwidth in Kbps (bites per second), Mbps, and Gbps.

Base64—Base64 is a standard algorithm for encoding and decoding non-ASCII data for attachment to an e-mail message; it is the foundation for MIME. Base64 uses a 65-character subset of ASCII to represent non-ASCII data in e-mail attachments.

binary—Binary refers to the base 2 numbering system used by computers to represent information. Binary numbers consist of only two values: 1 and 0. In a binary number, each position is two times greater than the position to its right.

bit—A bit, also referred to as a binary digit, is a single value that makes up a binary number. A bit can be either 1 or 0. See binary.

bits per second (bps)—The number of binary bits transmitted per second is measured in bps. For example, common modem speeds are 28,800 bps and 56,000 bps. Another way of writing 28,800 bps is 28.8 Kbps, because "kilo" means 1,000.

Bootstrap Protocol (BOOTP)—BOOTP is an Internet protocol for enabling a diskless workstation to boot and determine its configuration information, such as its IP address, from information available on a BOOTP server.

bridge—A bridge is a device that operates at the Data Link Layer of the OSI model. A bridge can connect several LANs or LAN segments. It can connect LANs of the same media access type, such as two Token Ring segments, or different LANs, such as Ethernet and Token Ring.

broadcast domain—A broadcast domain is the area of a network through which broadcast packets are forwarded. Routers, Layer 3 switches, and VLANs create network segments that are separate broadcast domains, because they do not forward broadcast packets from one segment to another.

broadcast storm—Due to differences between nodes and bridges in different parts of the network, a broadcast frame can sometimes be misinterpreted. This leads to another broadcast frame by the bridge which misinterprets it. The second broadcast frame is again misinterpreted, and so on. The result is a "storm" of broadcast frames that can severely impact network performance. Sometimes storms can persist and eventually bring down the entire network.

brouter—A brouter is an internetworking device that combines the functions of both a bridge and a router.

browser (Web browser)—A Web browser is an Internet client application used to locate and display Web pages. The two most popular browsers are Netscape Navigator and Microsoft Internet Explorer.

brute-force attack—A security attack that tries to break a code by simply testing each possibility until it finds the right one is referred to as a brute-force attack.

business to business (B2B)—A B2B is a business that sells to other businesses, not to consumers.

business to consumer (B2C)—A B2C is a retail business that sells directly to consumers.

business to employee (B2E)—A B2E is a company intranet that provides employees access to company information, forms, and so forth.

business to government (B2G)—A B2G is a business that conducts commerce with the U.S. and foreign governments.

cache memory—Disk cache memory is a portion of random access memory (RAM) that holds a copy of most-commonly requested data. Using disk cache speeds up computer operations because accessing data stored in RAM is much faster than accessing data stored on a hard drive.

cache server (proxy server)—A cache server is a hardware device that holds copies of frequently requested Web pages. It reduces traffic on a Web server by intercepting and responding to HTTP requests for pages held in cache.

Carrier Sense Multiple Access with Collision Detection (CSMA/CD)—CSMA/CD is the technique Ethernet uses for controlling access to the shared transmission medium (the bus). In CSMA/CD, a node may not transmit unless the medium is idle. If the transmitting node detects that another station has begun to transmit at the same time, both nodes stop, then wait a random time interval before attempting to retransmit.

cc:Mail—cc:Mail is a Lotus Development Corporation proprietary mail system. cc:Mail does not provide Internet mail access, and thus must use an e-mail gateway to send and receive SMTP mail.

cell—A cell is a unit of data similar to a frame. It is very small (53 bytes for ATM) and fixed in length. Cells are typically associated with ATM technology.

central office (CO)—A CO is a telephone company facility where local loops are terminated. The function of a CO is to connect individual telephones through a series of switches. COs are tied together in a hierarchy for efficiency in switching. Other terms for a CO are "local exchange," "wiring center," and "end office."

certificate authority (CA)—A CA is an organization that creates digital certificates for individuals and servers, after verifying the identity of those persons or sites. A CA signs each digital certificate with its own digital signature; thus, vouching for the identity and trustworthiness of the owners of the certificates.

channel—A portion of the total bandwidth of a physical transmission path, used to carry a single signal is referred to as a channel. Channels are also called links, lines, circuits, or paths. A physical connection, such as a cable, may support more than one channel.

channel service unit (CSU)—A CSU is a device that connects to the end of a T1 or T3 line, between the line and a DSU. The CSU maintains an electrical connection on the line and functions as a repeater, regenerating and amplifying both incoming and outgoing signals. A CSU is usually combined with a DSU in a device called a "CSU/DSU."

checksum—A checksum is a simple error detection strategy that computes a running total based on a packet's transmitted byte values and then applies a simple operation to compute the checksum value. The receiver compares the checksums computed by the sender and the receiver, and, if they match, assumes error-free transmission.

Child Online Protection Act (COPA)—COPA is a federal law passed in response to the Supreme Court's rejection of a portion of the CDA. COPA restricts material that is "harmful to minors," and applies to communications that are made for commercial purposes and that might be accessed by minors.

Child Pornography Prevention Act (CPPA)—A federal law that, among other things, prohibits images that depict or appear to depict minors engaged in sexually explicit conduct. Unlike previous child pornography laws, CPPA restricted images created without the involvement of any actual children. In 2002 the Supreme Court ruled that the CPPA was unconstitutional.

Children's Internet Protection Act (CIPA)—CIPA is a law that makes federal funding for Internet access at public libraries dependent upon the implementation of policies and technologies for blocking obscenity, child pornography, and material deemed harmful to minors.

Children's Online Privacy Protection Act (COPPA)—COPPA is a federal law regulating the collection and use of personal information from children less than 13 years of age.

Classless Interdomain Routing (CIDR)—CIDR replaces the older IP network addressing system based on classes A, B, and C. With CIDR, a single IP address can be used to designate many unique IP addresses. A CIDR IP address looks like a normal IP address except that it ends with a slash followed by a number, called the IP prefix. The IP prefix specifies how many addresses are covered by the CIDR address, with lower prefix values covering more addresses. For example, an IP prefix of /16, can be used to address 256 former Class C addresses.

client—A client is any program that requests a service or resource from another program, either on the same computer or a different one. This term is often used to refer to the computer that hosts the client program; however, a client program may also run on a computer that normally functions as a server. See server.

client/server—Client/server (or client server) is a model in computer networking where individual PCs can access data or services from a common high-performance computer. For example, when a PC needs data from a common database located on a computer on a LAN, the PC is the client and the network computer is the server.

client-side script—A client-side script is a program that runs on the client side of a client/server process. For example, client-side scripts in Web pages run on Web clients (browsers).

clipper chip—This microprocessor chip contains an 80-bit single-key encryption algorithm. It uses a key-escrow system in which two decryption keys are separately held in escrow by the U.S. Treasury Department and the National Institute of Standards and Technology (NIST). A law enforcement agency could gain access to the keys through a court order.

coaxial—Coaxial cable is a type of copper wiring typically used for cable television transmission and high-speed Internet connectivity. Coaxial cable typically consists of a central copper or copper-coated conductor surrounded by flexible insulation, a shield of wire mesh, and an outer plastic jacket. Older installations of Ethernet LANs also used coax cable.

coder/decoder (codec)—A codec is a hardware/software device that takes an analog video signal and converts (codes) it to digital format for compression and transmission. On the receiving end, the digital signal is put back (decoded) into the original analog signal.

collision—A collision occurs in an Ethernet network when two frames are put onto the physical medium at the same time and overlap fully or partially. When a collision occurs, the data on the physical segment is no longer valid.

collision domain—A collision domain is the portion of a network where all nodes receive every frame transmitted. It is a part of a network in which nodes compete for access to the same physical medium.

common carrier—A company that must offer its services to all customers at the prices and conditions outlined in a public record is referred to as a common carrier.

Common Gateway Interface (CGI)—CGI is a standard specification for creating Web server programs that accept data from Web clients, process the data, and return a result. For example, each HTML form needs a corresponding CGI program to process form data sent to its Web site. CGI programs can be written in a variety of languages, including C, Perl, Visual Basic, or Java.

Common Internet File System (CIFS)—CIFS allows clients to use the Internet to access and share files on remote servers. The CIFS protocol runs over TCP/IP, and is an enhanced version of the Server Message Block (SMB) protocol used by Windows operating systems.

Communications Decency Act (CDA)—CDA is part of the Telecommunications Act of 1996, which, among other things, prohibited the posting of "indecent" or "patently offensive" materials on publicly accessible Web sites and other Internet forums that might be accessed by minors. The U.S. Supreme Court ruled the CDA portion of the Telecommunications Act of 1996 unconstitutional.

compiler—A compiler is a software program that takes source code from a programming language such as C++, and converts it into machine-readable, executable code to be run on a computer.

Computer Crime and Intellectual Property Section (CCIPS)—The CCIPS was created by the Criminal Division of the United States Department of Justice to focus on criminal activity related to computers, the Internet, and intellectual property.

Computer Fraud and Abuse Act—The Computer Fraud and Abuse Act is a federal law that addresses crimes such as unauthorized computer access, damage or threats relating to computers, and trafficking in illicit computer passwords.

connectionless—Connectionless service is a characteristic of the packet delivery service offered by most hardware and the IP. Connectionless service treats each packet or datagram as a separate entity that contains the source and destination addresses. Connectionless services can drop or deliver packets out of sequence.

connection-oriented—A connection-oriented data communication mode is one in which the sending and receiving computers stay in contact for the duration of a session, while packets or frames are being sent back and forth.

consumer to consumer (C2C)—Also called marketplace, a C2C is an environment where multiple sellers transact with multiple buyers.

cookies—A cookie is a small file that a Web site places on your computer. The cookie stores information about your preferences or about what you viewed on the site previously. The next time you visit that site, the cookie gets sent back to the site. Cookies can be used to rotate the banner ads that a site sends. They can also be used to customize pages for you based on information you have provided to the Web site. Settings in your browser allow you to control how it handles cookies.

copyright—Copyright is the legal protection of original human expression, such as writings, musical compositions, video productions, and software programs. United States copyright law is specifically authorized by the Constitution, and is implemented through federal laws and regulations. The Library of Congress administers registration of copyrights in the United States.

country code top level domain (ccTLD)—Each country in the world is assigned an Internet country code, a two-character code designating the country in which a domain resides. This country code is appended to the end of the FQDN.

cut—A DNS cut divides DNS zone responsibilities between the root domain name server and subdomain nameservers, and in turn between subdomains and further subordinate domains. For example, in the domain westnetinc.com, a subdomain contracts.westnetinc.com could exist. When the DNS administrator cuts the westnetinc.com domain, he or she delegates responsibility for the subdomain contracts.westnetinc.com to the subdomain nameserver.

cyclic redundancy check (CRC)—CRC is the mathematical process used to check the accuracy of the data being transmitted across a network. Before transmitting a block of data, the sending station performs a calculation on the data block and appends the resulting value to the end of the block. The receiving station takes the data and the CRC value, and performs the same calculation to check the accuracy of the data.

daemon—A daemon (pronounced "deemon") is a UNIX process that runs in the background and performs an operation at a specified time or in response to a certain event. A Microsoft Windows equivalent to a daemon is a service or system agent.

Data Encryption Standard (DES)—DES is a popular single-key encryption system that uses a 56-bit key. Triple-DES uses the DES algorithm to encrypt a message three times, using three 56-bit keys. Because hardware is faster than software, it is considered a hardware solution to encryption because of the time necessary to encrypt and decrypt a message.

database management system (DBMS)—A database management system is a suite of applications for creating, maintaining, and querying database files.

data service unit (DSU)—A DSU is a device that converts a binary signal from the format used on a LAN to that used by a T1 line. It resolves differences in the way each system represents binary numbers. It sits between a CSU and a T1 MUX, and is usually combined with a CSU in a device called a "CSU/DSU."

datagram—A datagram is another name for a packet. See packet.

deep linking—Deep linking is the practice of linking to another site not through its home page, but to a page—or smaller element, such as an image or sound file—located elsewhere within the site.

default gateway—A default gateway is a router that provides access to all hosts on remote networks. Typically, the network administrator configures a default gateway for each host on the network.

delay—Delay is the amount of time needed for a device, such as a switch or router, to process information (such as a frame or packet). It is the duration from the time a device reads the first byte of a frame or packet, until the time it forwards that byte. In this sense, delay is another word for latency. Delay is also associated with the length of time it takes to get information across a physical link.

DHCP lease—A DHCP lease is the IP address the DHCP server dynamically issues to DHCP clients. The server maintains the lease for a specific period of time, and as the lease expiration time approaches, the client must renew the lease.

DHCPv6—Short for DHCP version 6, DHCPv6 assigns host IPv6 addresses dynamically. DHCPv6 is specified in Internet Draft form, and adds additional message types and larger Address fields, commensurate with IPv6 addressing, over DHCPv4. DHCPv6 uses UDP Port 546 for the client, and 547 for the server.

digital access cross-connect switch (DACS)—A DACS is a connection system that establishes semipermanent (not switched) paths for voice or data signals. All physical wires are attached to the DACS once, and then electronic connections between them are made by entering instructions.

digital certificate—A digital certificate is a unique electronic file used to authenticate a user, program, provider, service, or transaction. Usually, the certificate consists of a file containing a copy of the user's or service's public encryption key, along with the signature of a trusted person verifying that the key does, indeed, belong to the user or service claimed. A CA creates a certificate, and the certificate is encrypted in a way that makes it impossible to forge.

Digital Millennium Copyright Act (DMCA)—The DMCA is a controversial federal law concerning the protection of copyrighted material in digital formats. Among other things, the DMCA includes provisions to protect ISPs from liability for copyright infringement by users. It also restricts the creation, distribution, and use of devices for circumventing copy protection and access control technologies.

digital signature—A digital signature is a digital code that can be embedded into a document to prove its authenticity. Digital signatures are an application of public-key encryption technology. The sender of a document uses a private encryption key to encrypt a text string or the digest of the message. Document recipients use the sender's public encryption key to decrypt the signature and authenticate the sender.

Digital Subscriber Line (DSL)—DSL is a modem technology that converts existing twisted pair telephone lines into high-speed data lines that can also carry separate telephone communications. Variants of DSL include ADSL, RADSL, ADSL Lite, IDSL, and VDSL.

disk operating system (DOS)—DOS is the low-level software that resides on many PCs and controls the operation of a computer and its peripheral devices. MS-DOS is the operating system that preceded Microsoft Windows and still exists as an extension of the Windows OS.

distance vector algorithm (DVA)—DVA is a routing protocol used to express the route a packet will take as it moves between computer networks. DVA expresses this route in "hops." The entity that is hopped over is any other network which must be traversed on the way to the target network. The hop count is actually the number of routers a packet encounters on the way to its destination. DV routers use hop counts to choose the shortest route for each packet. The Routing Information Protocol (RIP) is an example of a DVA protocol.

Document Type Definition (DTD)—A DTD is a specification that accompanies an XML document and defines the codes that are used to format a document, such as a code that has been defined to separate paragraphs or identify topic headings and so forth, and how each is to be processed.

domain name—A human-friendly name that identifies a Web site.

Domain Name System (DNS)—DNS is the online distributed database system used to map human-readable computer names into IP addresses. DNS servers throughout the connected Internet implement a hierarchical namespace that allows sites freedom in assigning computer names and addresses. In addition, DNS supports separate mappings between mail destinations and IP addresses.

Domain Name System (DNS) zone—The part of the DNS namespace for which a DNS server has complete information is organized into units called zones; zones are the main units of replication in DNS. A zone contains one or more resource records (RRs) for one or more related DNS domains. Each DNS server contains the resource records (RR) relating to those portions of the DNS namespace for which it is authoritative (for which it can answer queries sent by a host). When a DNS server is authoritative for a portion of the DNS name space, those systems' administrators are responsible for ensuring that the information about that DNS name space portion is correct. To increase efficiency, a given DNS server can cache the RRs relating to a domain in any part of the domain tree.

dotted decimal notation—Dotted decimal notation is the syntactic representation for a 32-bit integer that consists of four 8-bit numbers with periods (dots) separating them. Many TCP/IP application programs accept dotted decimal notation in place of destination computer names (for example, 205.169.85.200).

Dynamic Host Configuration Protocol (DHCP)—DHCP is a server process that simplifies IP network management by dynamically or statically assigning IP addresses to logical end stations for fixed periods of time. See digital access cross-connect switch (DACS). DHCP is built on a client/server model, where designated DHCP server hosts allocate network addresses and deliver configuration parameters to dynamically configured hosts.

ECMA Script—ECMA Script is a standard object-oriented scripting language derived largely from Netscape's Java Script. The European Computer Manufacturers Association (ECMA) supervised the development of ECMA Script to provide a standard, cross-browser language for Web scripting. However, like Java Script, ECMA Script may also be used to create non-Web applications.

Electronic Benefit Transfer (EBT)—The EBT system is intended to replace food stamps and public assistance checks with a debit type credit card.

Electronic Funds Transfer (EFT)—EFT is the process of transferring funds between accounts, banks, even countries.

encryption—Encryption is the process of scrambling data by changing it in a series of logical steps, called an encryption algorithm. To increase security, an encryption algorithm uses a numerical pattern, or "key," to guide the scrambling process. Different algorithms and keys each produce data scrambled, or encrypted, in different patterns. Encryption is the process of scrambling data so it cannot be read by anyone except the intended recipient.

Ethernet—The Ethernet protocol, originally developed in the 1970s by Xerox Corporation, in conjunction with Intel and DEC, is now the primary protocol for local area networking. The original Ethernet provides 10-Mbps throughput. Fast Ethernet (100 Mbps) and Gigabit Ethernet (1,000 Mbps) use the same basic technology, but at higher speeds.

event—An event is any significant occurrence in a system or application that requires users to be notified or an entry to be added to a log file.

Extended Binary Coded Decimal Interchange Code (EBCDIC)—EBCDIC is a character encoding scheme developed by IBM. A character encoding scheme is a way to represent alphanumeric characters on a computer system in binary format.

Extensible Hypertext Markup Language (XHTML)—XHTML is defined by the World Wide Web Consortium (W3C) as "a reformulation of HTML 4.0 as an application of XML." In XHTML, all HTML 4 markup elements and attributes are supported. Unlike HTML, XHTML can be extended by anyone that uses it. Programmers can define and add new elements and attributes to those that already exist.

Extensible Markup Language (XML)—XML is a simplified version of Standard Generalized Markup Language (SGML) that allows Web designers to add functionality beyond HTML by creating their own formatting tags. W3C created the official XML recommendation for XML 1.0.

facilities—The term "facilities" refers to the physical media that are necessary to provide a telecommunication service. For example, twisted pairs of copper wire, or fiber optic cables, are facilities. Private facilities are owned and used by a private organization. Public facilities are leased from a telecommunication carrier, such as a local telephone company or long-distance service provider.

fair use—Fair use is the right to reproduce a portion of a copyrighted work for certain kinds of purposes, without needing the permission of the copyright owner. This effectively carves out a small limitation from the copyright holder's rights for the benefit of educators, critics, and others.

fat ping—A fat ping is a ping issued with the -l option, specifying a large packet size. This can be used to test for intermittent network component or link failures between end nodes. A useful packet size is 512 bytes, although sizes up to the network segment's MTU can also be used. This term also refers to a TCP/IP denial of service attack, where the sender floods the receiver's network with oversized packets.

Fiber Distributed Data Interface (FDDI)—FDDI is a token-passing network architecture that uses two ring channels. FDDI provides 100 Mbps over optical fiber.

File Transfer Protocol (FTP)—FTP is a TCP/IP Application Layer protocol used to transfer files between two computers.

firewall—A firewall is, according to the National Computer Security Association, "a system or combination of systems that enforces a boundary between two or more networks." It is a controlled gateway between one network and another, typically between a private network and the Internet, which blocks messages that do not meet specified security criteria.

flow control—Flow control refers to control of the rate at which hosts or gateways inject packets into a network or internet. Flow control is used to avoid congestion and can be implemented at various protocol levels. Simplistic schemes, like ICMP source quench, instruct the sender to cease transmission until congestion ends. More complex schemes vary the transmission rate continuously.

form—A form is a Web page designed to collect information or input from a user and send it to a Web server for processing. Forms can contain data-entry fields, checkboxes, drop-down lists, buttons, and other interactive controls.

fractional T1 (FT1)—FT1 is a telephone company service that provides data rates from 64 Kbps to 1.544 Mbps, by allowing a user to purchase one or more channels of a T1 link. If the customer needs less bandwidth than 1.544 Mbps, FT1 is a low-cost alternative to purchasing a full T1.

fragmentation—Fragmentation is the IP process of dividing a datagram into smaller pieces that will better suit the transporting network's MTU.

frame—A frame is a unit of information transmitted across a data link. Ethernet frames, for example, are frames generated by an Ethernet NIC. Frames typically carry packets across a single physical link. In a LAN, the address found in a frame designates the NIC card that the frame is intended for.

frames—Frames are HTML documents displayed in separate areas of the browser display. Each frame contains its own set of headers, footers, and body of text.

frame relay—A frame relay is a packet-forwarding WAN protocol that normally operates at speeds of 56 Kbps to 1.5 Mbps.

framing—Similar to deep linking, framing is the practice of presenting material from another Web site on your own site, surrounded by your own material. This can lead to confusion among users about where "framed" material originates, and who is responsible for it.

FrontPage extensions—Extensions are optional Web server software components that support additional functionality on Web sites created with Microsoft's FrontPage authoring application. For example, if a Web server supports the FrontPage extensions, a site author can use FrontPage to easily add features such as searching and forms support.

fully qualified domain name (FQDN)—The FQDN is the complete Internet system name. The FQDN includes the hostname and the domain name. An example of a FQDN is ken.westnetinc.com.

Gbps (Gigabits per second)—A term that identifies the rate at which information travels down a physical medium or through space (wireless). Gbps is equivalent to 1 billion bits per second; 2.488 Gbps is equivalent to 2,488,000,000 bits per second.

globalization—Globalization refers to the process of making a Web site accessible and useful to users in a variety of countries and regions around the world.

graphical user interface (GUI)—A GUI provides easy access to computer programs and often hides details of a program from the user.

graphics interchange format (GIF)—GIF is one of two graphic image formats used in HTML (JPEG is the other type). GIF files, the more popular format for small or simple images, are limited to 256 colors, have a lower resolution than JPEG files, offer lossless compression, and can be made transparent for a popular type of borderless effect.

hash algorithm—A hash algorithm is a mathematical formula used to generate a number from a variable-length text string. Commonly used in security applications, a hash creates an encrypted number sent along with a message that the recipient decrypts to verify the message's integrity.

heading—A heading in HTML is text that is tagged to appear larger or bolder than plain text. HTML offers six levels of headline size: from largest (`<h1>`) to smallest (`<h6>`). The specific type style and size of each heading depends on each user's browser settings.

hertz (Hz)—Radio signals are measured in cycles per second, or Hz. One Hz is 1 cycle of an electromagnetic wave in one second; 1,000 cycles per second is 1 kHz; one million cycles per second is 1 MHz and one billion cycles per second is 1 GHz.

hexadecimal—Hexadecimal is the base 16 numbering system used to represent binary information in a condensed format. Hexadecimal numbers consist of 15 symbols: 0 through 9, plus A through F. In a hexadecimal number, each position is 16 times greater than the position to its right.

hit—Each request for a file on a Web server is recorded as one "hit" in the server's log. One hit is recorded for each HTML page, graphic image, or other file that a server transmits to a client. Thus, several hits may be generated for each page that a client views.

hop count—Hop count is the number of intermediate routers that a packet must traverse to travel from source to destination in a multirouter environment.

hub—Also called a wiring concentrator, a simple hub is a repeater with multiple ports. A signal coming into one port is repeated out the other ports.

hyperlink—A hyperlink is a connection to another Web page or location within the current page. When a user clicks the text or graphic that contains the hyperlink, the browser displays the Web page targeted by the link. Hyperlinks are created with the HTML "anchor" (`<a> ...</a>`) container tags, plus the `href` attribute and a Uniform Resource Locator (URL).

Hypertext Markup Language (HTML)—HTML is a text-based formatting language used to generically format text for Web pages. It is a simplified derivative of Standard Generalized Markup Language (SGML) that tags different parts of a document more in terms of their function than their appearance. A Web browser reads an HTML document and displays it as indicated by the HTML formatting tags and the browser's settings.

Hypertext Transfer Protocol (HTTP)—HTTP is the Application Layer protocol used to request and transmit HTML documents. HTTP is the underlying protocol of the Web.

IFconfig—IFconfig displays TCP/IP addressing information on UNIX computers, and configures TCP/IP settings for network adapters.

Integrated Services Digital Network (ISDN)—ISDN is a WAN technology used to move voice and data over the telecommunication network. ISDN operates at speeds of 144 Kbps to 1.5 Mbps.

intellectual property—Intellectual property is property whose value lies not in any physical object, but in its creative or expressive content. Examples include literature, music, computer software, and the ideas behind practical inventions. Intellectual property is also used to refer to the body of law, including copyright, patent, and trademark law, which governs the protection and use of such property.

interexchange carrier (IXC)—An IXC is a long-distance company that provides telephone and data services between LATAs.

International Data Encryption Algorithm (IDEA)—IDEA is a block encryption algorithm that was first published in 1990.

Internet Control Message Protocol (ICMP)—ICMP is a Network Layer protocol that handles error and control messages about IP communication. Gateways and hosts use ICMP to report problems about packets back to their source. ICMP also includes an echo request/reply used to test whether a destination is reachable and responding.

Internet Corporation of Assigned Names and Numbers (ICANN)—ICANN is a private, nonprofit organization responsible for overseeing the domain name registration process, assigning IP addresses, assigning protocol parameters, and managing the DNS root servers. Learn more about ICANN at **http://www. icann.org**.

Internet Gateway Routing Protocol (IGRP)— IGRP is a DVA protocol developed by Cisco Systems for use in large, heterogeneous networks. It uses metrics, such as bandwidth, delay, MTU, and hop count, to compute the best path to a destination network.

Internet Group Management Protocol (IGMP)—IGMP is the Internet standard by which hosts can communicate their multicast group membership status to multicast routers. This protocol is used to keep up-to-date information on which host is in which multicast group.

Internet Message Access Protocol (IMAP)— IMAP is a protocol used for retrieving e-mail messages from a mail server. IMAP4 is a version of IMAP similar to POP3, but it supports additional features such as allowing keyword searches in e-mail messages while the messages remain on the mail server.

Internet Protocol (IP)—IP is a Network Layer protocol responsible for getting a packet (datagram) through a network from source to destination. It is the "IP" in "TCP/IP." IP provides connectionless, best-effort packet delivery service.

Internet Protocol Security (IPSec)—IPSec consists of a set of IETF protocols, under development, to support secure IP packet communication. When completed, IPSec is intended to implement VPNs.

Internet service provider (ISP)—ISPs are companies that provide Internet access to individuals and businesses. ISPs typically supply a range of services necessary to provide corporate networks and other users with dedicated or dial-up access to the Internet.

Internetwork Packet Exchange (IPX)—IPX is Novell NetWare's proprietary Network Layer protocol.

interpreter—An interpreter is a program that reads and executes programming script written in a high-level language. The interpreter reads a script line by line, and then executes it line by line. See parser.

intranet—An intranet is a network that uses Internet applications, but is designed for use only by the personnel of a company or organization; that is, it is a "private internet."

IPconfig—IPconfig displays TCP/IP addressing information on Windows NT and 2000 computers.

IP Version 6 (IPv6)—IPv6, also known as IP next generation, is a new version of the IP currently being reviewed in the IETF standards committees. IPv6 adds features over the current IPv4, including longer addresses (128 bits) and better QoS support.

Java—Java is an interpreted, platform-independent, high-level programming language developed by Sun Microsystems. Java is a powerful language with many features that make it attractive for the Web.

Java Database Connectivity (JDBC)—JDBC is the Java API for accessing relational databases.

JavaScript—JavaScript is an interpreted, client-side scripting language developed by Netscape. All major browsers offer built-in support for JavaScript, and can interpret blocks of JavaScript code embedded in an HTML page. An international open standard called ECMAScript is based on JavaScript.

Joint Photographic Experts Group (JPEG)— JPEG is an open standard that defines a method of compressing still images. See JPEG File Interchange Format.

JPEG File Interchange Format (JFIF)—JFIF is a public domain graphic compression format that conforms to the JPEG standard for image compression. It is one of two popular graphic image formats used in HTML pages (GIF is the other). JPEG/JFIF files offer higher resolution, with up to 16.7 million colors, and are generally used in continuous-tone images such as photographs. However, JPEG/JFIF compression is lossy (some image information is lost), even at the highest quality setting.

JScript—As Microsoft's implementation of ECMAScript, JScript is the international standard based on Netscape's JavaScript. JScript is natively supported by Microsoft ASP, and is preferred for writing ASP client-side script blocks.

Kbps (Kilobits per second)—A term that identifies the rate at which information travels down a physical medium or through space (wireless). Kbps is equivalent to 1,000 bits per second. 56 Kbps is equivalent to 56,000 bits per second.

Kerberos—Kerberos is a UNIX-based user authentication system for client/server networks.

latency—Latency is the transmission delay created as a device processes a frame or packet. It is the duration from the time a device reads the first byte of a frame or packet, until the time it forwards that byte.

Lightweight Directory Access Protocol (LDAP)—LDAP is an Internet standard for organizing information in a hierarchical tree structure that conforms to the X.500 directory standard.

line break—A line break in HTML is a tag that commands the browser to display text on a new line. The <br> tag creates a line break. A line break does not insert extra vertical space between lines.

load balancer—A load balancer is a device that intercepts incoming HTTP requests and evenly distributes them to multiple identical Web servers. Load balancing improves overall site performance, and it provides fault tolerance by automatically routing traffic around a malfunctioning server.

local access and transport area (LATA)— LATAs are the geographic calling areas within which an RBOC may provide local and long-distance services. LATA boundaries, for the most part, fall within states and do not cross state lines, although, one state may have several LATAs.

local exchange carrier (LEC)—A LEC is a company that makes telephone connections to subscribers' homes and businesses, provides telephone services, and collects fees for those services. The terms LEC, ILEC, and RBOC are equivalent.

local loop—A local loop is the pair of copper wires that connects a customer's telephone to the LEC's CO switching system.

localization—Localization is the process of adapting a Web site or other software for use in a specific country or region. Usually the Web site or software is adapted to a place other than that for which it was originally developed. Localization requirements can include translation of text into another language, changes to region-specific formats for addresses and telephone numbers, and even the creation of entirely new content for a foreign audience.

management information base (MIB)—A MIB is an SNMP database that lists information objects relevant to each managed object. A managed element's MIB includes its own information objects. The management application's MIB is a compilation of all the individual managed element's MIBs.

marketplace—Also called C2C, marketplace is an application/network infrastructure that brings multiple buyers and multiple sellers together to transact business.

Maximum Transmission Unit (MTU)—MTU is the maximum amount of information that can be carried by a datagram or frame. For example, the MTU of Ethernet is 1,500 bytes of information.

Mbps (Megabits per second)—A term that identifies the rate at which information travels down a physical medium or through space (wireless). Mbps is equivalent to 1,000,000 bits per second; 1.544 Mbps is equivalent to 1,544,000 bits per second.

message digest 5 (MD5)—MD5 is a one-way hash algorithm that converts a message into a fixed string of digits called a message digest. It is used to create digital signatures.

method—Methods are active capabilities of an object. They often represent verbs. For example, one method of an object representing a database command may be Execute.

modem—The term "modem" is a contraction for modulator/demodulator. Modems are used to convert binary data into analog signals suitable for transmission across a telephone network.

modulation—Modulation is the process of modifying the form of a carrier wave (electrical signal) so that it can carry intelligent information on a communications medium.

Motion Picture Experts Group (MPEG)—MPEG is a standard for compressing video to fewer bits for storage and transmission.

MPEG, Audio Layer 3 (MP3)—MP3 is an audio coding technique to reduce the number of bits required to represent audio signals by removing redundant and irrelevant sounds. MP3 files offer high quality sound with compression ratios of approximately 1:12.

multiplexer (MUX)—A MUX is a device that transmits multiple signals over the same physical medium. Multiple signals are fed into a MUX and combined to form one output stream.

multiplexing—Multiplexing is a technology that allows multiple signals to travel over the same physical medium. Multiple signals are fed into a multiplexer and combined to form one output stream.

Multipurpose Internet Mail Extension (MIME)—MIME is an extension of SMTP that supports the exchange of a wide variety of document files by means of an e-mail system.

multistation access unit (MAU)—A MAU is a device used in Token Ring networks to provide connectivity between individual workstations. It is also called a Token Ring hub.

Netstat—Netstat shows the current status of all connections on a computer. The Netstat utility shows remote connected computer IP addresses and port numbers and the corresponding computer name; the local computer IP address, port, and name; and the protocol the connection uses.

Network Address Port Translation (NAPT)— NAPT is also known as "masquerading" because it is a NAT technique that hides all internal devices behind a single public IP address (usually the NAT's outside port IP address). The NAT assigns each internal device connection this address and a new TCP or UDP port number taken from the registered port number range. This IP address/registered port number combination identifies a specific internal host on the Internet.

Network Address Translator (NAT)—NAT is a system that allows an administrator to use one set of IP addresses within a LAN, and another set for external traffic. NAT can shield internal addresses from public networks, and make more efficient use of a few globally unique IP addresses.

Network Basic Input/Output System (NetBIOS)—IBM and Sytek developed NetBIOS to link a NOS to specific hardware, augmenting DOS to provide LAN functions to the operating system. NetBIOS uses SMBs as the message format for sharing Windows files, directories, and devices.

Network File System (NFS)—A file management system used with TCP/IP and UNIX systems originally developed by SUN Microsystems. NFS can be found on various systems and platforms, especially PC-based platforms that utilize the TCP/IP protocol.

network interface card (NIC)—A NIC is an expansion board inserted into a computer to enable the computer to be connected to a network.

Network Management System (NMS)— NMS is a comprehensive equipment system used to monitor, control, and manage a data communications network.

Network News Transfer Protocol (NNTP)— NNTP is the TCP/IP protocol used to distribute news article collections, or news feeds, over the Internet.

network operating system (NOS)—NOS is the software that manages server operations and provides services to clients. The NOS manages the interface between the network's underlying transport capabilities and the applications resident on the server.

NSlookup—NSlookup is a utility that allows a user to query a DNS server to resolve a hostname to an IP address.

Open Database Connectivity (ODBC)— ODBC is an API that mediates SQL communication between multiple applications and databases.

Open Shortest Path First (OSPF)—OSPF is an intraautonomous system routing protocol. OSPF is based on link-state technology and scales well with large networks. Its features include least-cost routing, multipath routing, and load balancing. OSPF provides more advantages than the older RIP.

operating system (OS)—An OS is the basic system software of a computer that provides low-level services to applications.

ordered list—An ordered list in HTML is a list of numbered items. To create an ordered list, use the container tags `<ol>` and `</ol>`.

packet—A packet is a unit of information processed by the Network Layer of the OSI reference model. The packet header contains the logical (network) address of the destination node. Intermediate nodes forward a packet until it reaches its destination. A packet can contain an entire message generated by higher OSI layers, or a segment of a much larger message. IP packets are also referred to as datagrams.

Packet Internet Groper (Ping)—Ping is used to verify that a computer's IP software is running properly and to verify the connectivity between computers.

paragraph break—A paragraph in HTML is a tag that commands the browser to display text on a new line and add extra empty vertical space between the old and new lines. To create a paragraph break, use the `<p>` and `</p>` tags.

parser—A parser is a program that reads and executes programming scripts written in a high-level language.

patch—Patches, also called service packs, apply relatively small changes to a portion of an application's code. Patches are distributed free of charge to correct bugs or security vulnerabilities that cannot wait for the next upgrade release.

patent—Patent law is the field of intellectual property that protects and encourages original inventions. The holder of a patent has a legally enforceable right to exclusive use of his or her invention for a limited amount of time. In exchange, the patent process requires the inventor to make public the workings of the invention, so that after the patent expires, anyone knowledgeable in the same field will be able to make use of the invention. In the United States, patent law is specifically authorized by the Constitution, and is administered by the United States Patent and Trademark Office. See United States Patent and Trademark Office.

Peripheral Component Interconnect (PCI) bus—PCI bus is a newer 64-bit local bus technology for PCs. A bus connects the central processor of a PC with the video controller, disk controller, hard drives, and memory.

permission—A rule associated with an object (usually a directory, file, or printer) that regulates which users can have access to the object and in what manner is referred to as a permission.

Personal Home Page (PHP)—PHP is a popular open source, server-side scripting language that is especially suited for creating Web sites featuring dynamic content and complex Web applications.

personal jurisdiction—Personal jurisdiction refers to the power of a court to hear a case and issue a judgment or order that is binding on a particular person (or a corporation). In the United States, a state court generally has personal jurisdiction over persons within the state's borders. A state court can also assume jurisdiction over a person outside the state who has established sufficient contacts within the state (for example, by actively selling or marketing products to residents in the state).

plug-in—A plug-in is a software module that adds a specific feature to a browser. For example, plug-ins for the Netscape Navigator browser enable it to play sound files and animations.

port—There are two primary ways the term "port" is used in networking. Port can refer to a physical connection point in a device, such as a port on a switch or multiplexer. Port can also refer to a number that identifies a software process within a computer. "Well-known" ports in TCP architecture are examples of the second type of port.

Portable Network Graphics (PNG)—PNG is a file format for image compression that may replace the GIF file format. The PNG format was developed by an Internet committee to be patent-free.

portal—A portal is a Web site that pulls needed information from many different sites.

Post Office Protocol (POP3)—POP is an e-mail service implemented on TCP Port 110 that provides clients access to a mail drop or post office in which their messages are stored. POP3 is the latest iteration of the protocol.

Practical Extraction and Report Language (Perl)—Perl is an interpreted programming language designed for processing text. Because of its strong text-handling features, Perl has become one of the most popular languages for writing server-side CGI scripts.

Pretty Good Privacy (PGP)—PGP is the most commonly used asymmetric encryption (public-key method) application for protecting messages across the Internet.

programmable read-only memory (PROM)—A PROM is a memory chip on which you can store a program. After the PROM has been programmed, you cannot wipe it clean and reprogram it.

promiscuous mode—Promiscuous mode is a setting that forces a NIC to process every frame it receives. For example, the NIC in a network analyzer is set to promiscuous mode.

protocol—A protocol is a defined method of communication between computers or computer applications.

protocol data unit (PDU)—The concept of a PDU is used in the OSI reference model. From the perspective of a protocol layer, a PDU consists of information from the layer above plus the protocol information appended to the data by that layer. For example, a frame is a PDU of the Data Link Layer, and a packet is a PDU of the Network Layer.

proxy—See cache server.

Proxy ARP—Proxy ARP is a variation of the ARP protocol, where an intermediate device, such as a router, sends an ARP response to the requesting host on behalf of the end node.

public-key (asymmetric) encryption—Public-key encryption is a cryptographic system that uses two mathematically related keys: one key is used to encrypt a message, and the other to decrypt it. People who need to receive encrypted messages distribute their public keys, but keep their private keys secret.

push technology—Push technology is the process by which customized Web content is automatically sent to a subscriber, according to predetermined user preferences.

Python—Python is an interpreted, object-oriented programming language. Python interpreters are available for most operating systems.

quality of service (QoS)—QoS defines the type of service a communications link can provide. QoS often specifies factors such as delay, throughput, and error rate.

random access memory (RAM)—A computer's main working memory is referred to as its RAM. Applications use RAM to hold instructions and data during processing. This type of memory is both changeable and volatile. Applications can repeatedly write new data to the same RAM; however, all data is erased from RAM when a computer loses power or shuts down.

read-only memory (ROM)—Unlike RAM, ROM cannot be written to after it is initially programmed. However, the data contained in ROM is nonvolatile; data is not lost if the power is turned off. Computers almost always contain a small amount of ROM that holds instructions for starting up the computer.

RealAudio, RealVideo—RealAudio and RealVideo are popular formats for playing streaming audio and video files.

registration—Copyrights and trademarks may be registered with the federal government, through the Library of Congress and the USPTO, respectively. Registration is not required for protection of copyrights or trademarks, but it brings definite advantages for the legal enforcement of an owner's rights.

remote access service (RAS)—A RAS is normally used in the context of Windows NT and the ability to access NT and LAN services from a remote location.

repeater—A device that regenerates and boosts electrical or radio signals is referred to as a repeater. It can be used to lengthen a wire or a wireless transmission path.

Request for Comment (RFC)—RFCs are the working documents of the Internet research and development community. A document in this series may be on any topic related to computer communication and may be anything from a meeting report to the specification of a standard.

resolver—The DNS resolver is a DNS system component that performs DNS queries against a DNS server (or servers). The resolver is a part of the DNS client and is usually installed when TCP/IP is installed.

resource record (RR)—An RR is a DNS database record containing information relating to a domain that a DNS client can retrieve and use. For example, the host RR for a specific domain holds the IP address of that domain (host); a DNS client uses this RR to obtain the IP address for the domain.

Reverse Address Resolution Protocol (RARP)—RARP is the protocol a diskless computer uses at startup to find its IP address. The computer broadcasts a request that contains its physical hardware address, and a server responds by sending the computer its IP address. RARP takes its name and message format from the IP ARP.

Rich Music Format (RMF)—RMF is an audio file format that includes features such as embedded copyright information and custom "mixing" of tracks.

router—A router is a Layer 3 device with several ports that can each connect to a network or another router. The router examines the logical network address of each packet, then uses its internal routing table to forward the packet to the routing port associated with the best path to the packet's destination. If the packet is addressed to a network not connected to the router, the router will forward the packet to another router closer to the final destination. Each router, in turn, evaluates each packet, and then either delivers the packet or forwards it to another router.

Routing Information Protocol (RIP)—RIP is a distance-vector routing protocol supported by TCP/IP and Novell networks, designed for use within small autonomous systems.

RS-232—RS-232 cables are used for connecting a computer to a modem. The RS-232 specification details the electrical and mechanical interface between the computer and modem.

RSA—The acronym RSA stands for Rivest, Shamir, and Adelman, the inventors of a widely used public-key encryption algorithm. The RSA encryption algorithm has become the de facto standard for industrial-strength encryption across the Internet.

scripts—Scripts are interpreted programs that are both human readable and executable, in contrast to compiled programs, which are converted into machine-readable code that humans cannot understand. Common interpreted scripting languages include Perl, UNIX Shells, JavaScript, and VBScript.

Secure Hash Algorithm-1 (SHA-1)—SHA-1 produces a 160-bit message digest from a message shorter than 264 bits. It is slightly slower than MD5, but more secure. A revision to SHA-1 is specified in SHA.

Secure Sockets Layer (SSL)—SSL is an application of both public-key and single-key encryption, which secures an Internet connection between browser and server. Web pages that use SSL carry the URL "https://."

Secure/MIME (S/MIME)—S/MIME is a MIME version that supports message encryption using public-key encryption technology. This ensures that e-mail is sent and received in a manner that is secure from interception or tampering.

security policies—Policies governing security, including Account, User Rights, Audit, and Trust Relationship policies, are referred to as security policies.

Sendmail—Sendmail is a UNIX application that handles electronic mail. Sendmail supports backend message routing and handling for SMTP-based e-mail systems.

Serial Line Internet Protocol (SLIP)—SLIP is not an official Internet standard, but a de facto standard included in many implementations of TCP/IP. It was originally developed for use over dedicated circuits or leased lines, and therefore does not include provisions for establishing a connection over the telephone network.

server—A server is any program that provides a service to a client program. This term is often used to refer to the computer that hosts the server program; however, a server program may also run on a computer that normally functions as a client. See client.

Server Message Block (SMB)—SMB is the IBM PC LAN protocol used to communicate with devices located on a LAN. It uses NetBIOS at the Session Layer to communicate across a LAN. Functions requiring LAN support, such as retrieving files from a file server, are translated into SMB commands before they are sent to a remote device.

server-side includes—Server-side includes are a type of HTML embedded command that allow Web developers to create customized Web pages, depending on time of day or other factors. These documents usually have an SHTML extension.

server-side script—A server-side script is a program that runs on the server side of a client/server process. For example, server-side Web programs (such as CGI programs and server-side scripts embedded in Web pages) run on Web servers.

shell—A shell is another term for a user interface. OSs sometimes provide an alternative shell to make program interaction easier. For example, the shell may provide a menu-driven system that translates user menu choices to OS commands.

signal reflection—Signal reflection refers to the situation where part, or all, of an electrical signal bounces back from an improperly made cable connection. This effect creates signal noise that can be misinterpreted as frame collisions.

Simple Mail Transfer Protocol (SMTP)—SMTP is an Application Layer protocol used to send e-mail from a client to a mail server, and transfer e-mail between mail servers, across a TCP/IP network.

Simple Network Management Protocol (SNMP)—SNMP is a TCP/IP Application Layer protocol used to send and receive information about the status of network resources on a TCP/IP network. Network management, by means of SNMP, consists of several elements that work together, including the managed elements and manager, and means by which they communicate.

single-key (symmetric) encryption—Single-key encryption is a cryptographic system that uses the same key to both encrypt and decrypt a message. Single-key encryption systems require both the sender and receiver of a message to share the same key before using it to communicate.

slashdot effect—Named for the popular technology news site, **www.slashdot.org**, the slashdot effect is what happens when a large and popular site links to a much smaller site, bringing an overload of traffic and possibly overwhelming the smaller site's server and bandwidth capabilities.

smart card—A plastic card that contains embedded IC microprocessors and a standard magnetic strip is referred to as a smart card. A user inserts a smart card into a chip-reading terminal, which reads the information stored on the card. Smart cards can eliminate the need for users to remember passwords and other authentication information.

socket—A socket is a software object that connects an application to a network protocol. In UNIX, for example, a program can send and receive TCP/IP messages by opening a socket and reading and writing data to and from the socket. A TCP process creates a socket from the host's IP address combined with a port number, and each TCP connection includes two sockets, one for each connected host.

source quench—Source quench is a congestion control technique in which a congested computer sends a message back to the source causing the congestion, requesting that the source stop transmitting. In a TCP/IP internet, gateways use ICMP source quench to stop or reduce the transmission of IP datagrams.

spanning tree algorithm (STA)—STA is a bridging algorithm that avoids active loops (multiple paths between nodes that could create infinite loop transmission patterns). If multiple paths exist between a bridge and a destination, the algorithm requires the bridge to use only one path. If the best path fails, the algorithm finds the next best route. See active loop.

Standard Generalized Markup Language (SGML)—SGML was developed by the International Organization for Standards (ISO) in 1986. SGML does not specify any particular formatting; rather, it specifies the rules for tagging different parts of a document in terms of their function rather than appearance.

store-and-forward—In a messaging system, a store-and-forward application accepts messages on their way to their final destination and stores them until the destination host requests them. When the destination host requests the messages, the store-and-forward system forwards them on to the requesting host. POP3 is a store-and-forward application protocol.

streaming—Streaming is the ability to begin playing a downloaded audio or video file as it arrives at the user's computer, without waiting for the entire file to be received first.

Structured Query Language (SQL)—SQL is a standardized language used to retrieve data from a database.

subnet address—Subnet address is an extension of the IP addressing scheme that allows a site to use a single IP network address for multiple physical networks. Gateways and hosts using subnet addressing interpret the local portion of the address by dividing it into a physical network portion and host portion.

subnetwork—A subnetwork is a smaller network created by borrowing host bits (subnetting) from a larger Class A, B, or C network.

switch—A switch is a device that operates at the Data Link Layer of the OSI reference model. A switch can connect LANs or segments of the same media access type. A switch dedicates its entire bandwidth to each frame it switches. Switches are also found in Wide Area Networks (WANs), as devices such as Frame Relay switches and ATM switches are used to move information from one network to another.

Synchronous Optical Network (SONET)—SONET is an optical transmission standard that defines a signal hierarchy. The basic building block is the STS-1 51.84-Mbps signal, chosen to accommodate a T3 signal. The STS designation refers to the interface for electrical signals. The optical signal standards are correspondingly designated OC-1, OC-2, and so on.

Systems Development Life Cycle (SDLC)—SDLC is the process of creating a new system, or changing an existing system, from concept to completion.

T1—T1 is one of the T-carrier telecommunication standards for multiplexing digitized voice signals. A T1 channel operates at 1.544 Mbps. Each T1 channel (64 Kbps) was designed to carry a digitized representation of an analog signal (a telephone call) that has a bandwidth of 4,000 Hz. Originally, 64 Kbps was required to digi-

tize a 4,000-Hz voice signal. Current technology has reduced that requirement to 32 Kbps or less; however, a T-carrier channel is still 64 Kbps.

T1 multiplexer (MUX)—A T1 MUX is a device that breaks an outgoing bit stream into T1 time slices, and reassembles incoming time slices into a continuous bit stream. It sits between a LAN and a DSU (or DSU side of a CSU/DSU).

table—A table is a section of an HTML document that arranges information in rows and columns. Table cells can display numerical or text data, or they can be used to provide an invisible layout framework to control the placement of text and graphics on a Web page.

tag—A tag is an HTML command inserted in a document that specifies how the document or a portion of the document should be formatted by a Web browser.

Telnet—Telnet is a TCP/IP Application Layer protocol that provides remote login capability to another computer on a network.

terminal emulation—A terminal emulation program allows a local computer to connect to a remote computer and appear to be logged on to the remote computer locally. Terminal emulation programs are often used to access mainframe computers.

terminator—A terminator is an electrical resistor that absorbs an electrical pulse when it reaches the end of a coaxial bus cable segment. If a terminator is not installed, a signal will reflect back down the bus cable, increasing the number of signal collisions.

Thinnet—Thinnet is another name for RG58A coaxial cable, specified in the 10Base2 standard for Ethernet bus networks. Because it is thinner and less expensive than the "Thicknet" used in 10Base5 Ethernets, Thinnet is also known as "Cheapernet."

throughput—Throughput describes the overall capacity of a network to perform useful work. While bandwidth measurements focus on the raw number of bits a network can carry, throughput measurements express the actual or effective data rates of a network. Throughput is most often used to describe the overall performance of a network. It is measured in PPS or bps.

Time to Live (TTL)—TTL is a technique used in best-effort delivery systems to avoid packet loops. Each IP datagram is assigned an integer TTL when it is created. IP gateways decrement the TTL field when they process a datagram and discard it if the TTL value reaches zero.

time-division multiplexing (TDM)—TDM is a technology that allows multiple signals to travel over the same physical medium by guaranteeing each signal a fixed amount of bandwidth on a rotating basis.

Token Ring—Token Ring is a LAN protocol for ring topologies that operates at 4 and 16 Mbps.

top level domain (TLD)—TLDs are the groupings of lower level domain types. A TCP/IP network can be segmented into a hierarchy of domains or groupings; the Internet is an example of this segmentation type. For example, the .com TLD groups commercial domains, while the .edu TLD groups educational institutions.

Tracert—Tracert is a utility that traces the route between two computers and sends information about each router hop along the way.

trade dress—Trade dress is a concept related to trademarks. It refers to the distinctive overall appearance of a product or a service provider in the marketplace.

trade secret—A trade secret is a proprietary business process or method that is kept secret. Although it is generally an owner's responsibility to keep trade secrets secret, the law offers some protection if a competitor obtains a trade secret through improper means despite the owner's best efforts.

trademark—A trademark is a name, word, image, or other device with which a business identifies itself and its products in the marketplace. The term can also refer to the field of intellectual property law that provides legal protection for such marks. Ownership of trademark rights to a name, term, or image includes the right to prevent others from using that mark or confusingly similar marks. In the United States, federal and state laws govern trademarks. The United States Patent and Trademark Office administers Federal trademarks.

trespass—Trespass is entering onto or remaining on someone else's property without permission. It is possible that the law of trespass could be used against someone who accesses computers on the Internet without authorization.

Trivial File Transfer Protocol (TFTP)—TFTP is the TCP/IP protocol for file transfer with minimal capability and overhead. TFTP depends on the unreliable, connectionless, datagram delivery service UDP. TFTP is designed for use on diskless workstations that keep such software in ROM.

tunneling—The process of encapsulating one network protocol within the packets of another is referred to as tunneling. For example, tunneling can be used to encapsulate various network protocols within IP packets for transmission across the Internet. The encapsulated data is encrypted, creating a secure VPN.

twisted pair—Twisted pair is a type of copper wiring typically used for telephone and computer network transmission. A twisted pair consists of two thin copper wires, twisted around each other to cancel EMI and RFI.

Uniform Resource Locator (URL)—A URL is an Internet address used to locate resources from within a Web browser. It can lead you to an Internet-connected computer anywhere in the world.

United States Patent and Trademark Office (USPTO)—The USPTO is the office of the federal government responsible for administering patents and Federal trademark registrations.

Universal Serial Bus (USB)—USB is an external bus that can transfer up to 12 Mbps. Up to 127 peripheral devices can be connected to a single USB port.

UNIX to UNIX Copy Program (UUCP)—UUCP is a standard UNIX utility that copies files between UNIX systems. It can be used for e-mail transfer.

unordered list—An anchored list in HTML is an unnumbered list of items, usually displayed as a bullet list. To create an unordered list, use the container tags <ul> and </ul>.

unroutable protocol—An unroutable protocol is a network protocol that does not support routing at OSI Layer 3, such as NetBIOS or DEC-LAT. This type of proto-col does not create packets; thus, Layer 3 devices, such as routers, cannot be used.

unshielded twisted pair (UTP)—UTP is the most common type of network cabling, and is used extensively in telephone networks and many data communication applications. UTP can carry a 100-Mbps digital signal 100 meters using twisted pairs of cable without requiring that the signal be repeated.

upgrade—Upgrades are new versions of an application, that implement new features. An upgrade may be installed by replacing an old application with a new one, or by installing a partial code change.

Usenet—Usenet is a global news distribution service that relies on the Internet for much of its news traffic. News servers agree to share and distribute newsfeeds, which are collections of related news articles. Users post news messages in newsfeeds using a news reader client.

User Datagram Protocol (UDP)—UDP is a Transport Layer protocol that provides a simple, connectionless datagram delivery service, without error checking, for certain specialized application services that do not require the full services of TCP.

utilization—Utilization refers to the amount of bandwidth being used at a given point in time or over a period of time. For example, if a 10-Mbps Ethernet LAN is running at 40-percent utilization, it is using 4 of the 10-Mbps bandwidth available.

Uuencode—Uuencode is a set of algorithms for converting e-mail attachments into a series of 7-bit ASCII characters for transmission over the Internet. Uuencode originally stood for UNIX-to-UNIX encode, but is now considered a universal protocol used to transfer file attachments between different operating system platforms. Nearly all e-mail applications support uuencoding.

virtual circuit—A virtual circuit is a communication path that appears to be a single circuit to the sending and receiving devices, even though the data may take varying routes between the source and destination nodes.

virtual private network (VPN)—VPNs use end-to-end network encryption to establish a secure connection from machine to machine. Each VPN is an encrypted data stream that travels over a public network, such as the Internet.

Virtual Reality Modeling Language (VRML)—VRML is a specification for displaying three-dimensional images on the Web.

virus—A virus is a self-replicating malicious program that spreads by attaching itself to a shared or copied file. Viruses create effects that range from mildly irritating to highly destructive.

Visual Basic Scripting Edition (VBScript)—Microsoft's VBScript is similar to its Visual Basic, but is simpler to use. VBScript is natively supported by Microsoft ASP, and is preferred for writing ASP server-side script blocks. Microsoft Internet Explorer supports client-side VBScripts, but the lack of VBScript support in Netscape Navigator limits this practice. Many ASP developers follow the mantra "JScript on the client, VBScript on the server."

Waveform Audio File (WAV)—WAV is one of several formats for storing sound in files developed jointly by Microsoft and IBM. Support for WAV files is built-in to Windows 95, making it the de facto standard for sound on PCs. WAV sound files end with a .WAV extension and can be played by nearly all Windows applications that support sound.

Web services—Web services is a strategy and set of technologies that enable Internet-based applications to be seamlessly and easily integrated into a broad range of disparate business system platforms. Web-based software applications can be developed as reusable components, called services. Web service components can then be individually used and linked together at the enterprise level, making use of XML as a common data exchange medium and the Internet as the service-delivery network.

well-known port—Any preassigned port number for a specific use by a Transport Layer protocol, such as TCP or UDP, is referred to as a well-known port. Examples of well-known ports include ports assigned to remote login (Telnet) servers and FTP servers.

Windows Internet Naming Service (WINS)—WINS is a Microsoft client/server application that resolves network computer host names to IP addresses. WINS works in conjunction with DHCP, where the WINS server maintains a dynamic database of hostname-to-address mappings. Because DHCP clients may not maintain the same address over time, WINS works well for this application. Standard DNS supports only hosts with statically assigned IP addresses.

Windows service—A Windows service is the equivalent of a UNIX daemon. Windows services provide specific functions, such as enabling file sharing or automatic virus protection, and can start automatically on system startup, manually as directed by the user, or when scheduled to run at a particular time of the day.

Winipcfg—Winipcfg is a utility that displays TCP/IP addressing information on Windows 95/98 and Windows ME computers.

Wireless Markup Language (WML)—A subset of XML that is optimized to display small items of information on handheld wireless devices such as cellular phones.

worm—Like viruses, worms are malicious programs. However, worms do not attach themselves to other files. They actively copy themselves to different computers, often by using e-mail.

X.25—X.25 is a connection-oriented packet-switching network, public or private, typically built upon leased lines from public telephone networks. In the United States, X.25 is offered by most carriers. The X.25 interface lies at OSI Layer 3, rather than Layer 1. X.25 defines its own three-layer protocol stack and provides data rates only up to 56 Kbps.

zone of authority—A DNS zone of authority is the DNS zone namespace for which a DNS nameserver is responsible. When a DNS domain is created, the new domain's root becomes the domain and its subdomains' zone of authority. A DNS server can maintain responsibility for more than one zone of authority.

A

F

Facilities 170
Fair use 90, 138
Fat ping 640
FDDI 4
Fiber
    Distributed Data Interface (FDDI) 4
    optic cable 52
File Transfer Protocol (See FTP)
Filtering 758
Firewall
    application 754
    components 756
    cost 756
    definition 427
    host 767
    hybrid 755
    logical design 731
    network layer 753
    screened-subnet 772
    stance 755
    troubleshooting 691
Flash 578
Flow control 252
Font 437, 444, 532
Form 496, 551 to ??
Format
    table 540
    text 531, 533
Fractional T1 (FT1) 170
Fragmentation 252
Frame
    attributes 546
    creating 544
    definition 496
    relay 53, 211
    tag 546
    target names 547
Framing 90, 155
FrontPage extensions 427
FT1 190

FTP
    anonymous 364, 365
    browser 369
    clients 365
    commands 366, 368
    definition 363
    protocol 259
    servers 486
    server software 364
    troubleshooting 675 to 678
    uses 363
Fully qualified domain name
    (FQDN) 334

G

Gateway 73 to 74, 766
Geography and crime 152
GET 613
GIF 334, 497, 565, 577
Globalization 90, 103 to 112
Graphic
    adding 516, 518
    background 522
    color values 524
    GIF 497, 565
    hyperlink 528
    JPEG 497, 566
    MPEG 497
    multimedia 565
    scalable vector 568
Graphical user interface (GUI) 334
Graphics interchange format (See GIF)
GUI 334

H

Hash algorithm 712
HDLC 53
Heading
    levels 506
    tags 497, 505

Overall Course Evaluation Survey

Congratulations on completing this course! We hope you enjoyed your learning journey.

This survey will help us identify where we can focus our strengths and improve our weaknesses. As a token of our appreciation for your time in completing this, we will send you a Certificate of Appreciation (if you tell us who you are!).

i-Net+ Certification Study Guide

Course # (see book cover): _______________________

Location of course: _____________________________

Instructor-led ☐   Self-paced ☐

Did you use the CD?   Yes ☐   No ☐   Comments: ____

Did you access the online course?   Yes ☐   No ☐   Comments: ____________________________

Did you use the Web board for support?   Yes ☐   No ☐   Comments: ____________________________

Did you visit the student Web site?   Yes ☐   No ☐   Comments: ____________________________

What are this course's strengths? ____

What did you like best? ____

What are this course's weaknesses? ____

What did you like least? ____

Would you be interested in other titles from this publisher? _____________________________________

If so, what specific topics would you like to see addressed? ____________________________________

Optional (must provide this information if you would like a Certificate of Appreciation):

Name: ____

Occupation/Title: ____

Company: ____

Address: ____

City/State/ZIP: ____

Country (if outside USA): ____

E-mail address: ____

Gender: Male ☐   Female ☐

Age: Under 25 ☐   26-40 ☐   41-60 ☐   61+ ☐

Please return this survey to: WestNet Learning Technologies, Attn: Executive Vice President, 5420 Ward Rd., Suite 150, Arvada, CO 80002 USA

Or fax to: 303-432-2565

BUSINESS REPLY MAIL
BULK RATE MAIL   PERMIT NO. 83   ARVADA CO

POSTAGE WILL BE PAID BY ADDRESSEE

5420 WARD ROAD STE 150
ARVADA CO 80002-9929